# THE PRENTICE HALL READER

## GEORGE MILLER
*University of Delaware*

**Prentice Hall**
Upper Saddle River   London   Singapore
Toronto   Tokyo   Sydney   Hong Kong   Mexico City

# For Evan, Adam, and Nathan, their book

**VP/Editorial Director:** Leah Jewell
**Editor-in-Chief:** Craig Campanella
**Senior Acquisitions Editor:**
Brad Potthoff
**Editorial Assistant:** Gina Aloe
**Director of Marketing:**
Tim Stookesberry
**Executive Marketing Manager:**
Megan Galvin-Fak
**Marketing Manager:** Sandra McGuire
**Marketing Assistant:**
Jean-Pierre Dufresne
**Text Permission Specialist:**
Kathleen Karcher
**Senior Operations Supervisor:**
Sherry Lewis
**Assistant Managing Editor:**
Melissa Feimer
**Project Manager:** Maureen Benicasa
**Interior Design:** Aptara Corp

**Creative Director:** Jayne Conte
**Cover Art Designer:** Margaret Kenselaar
**Cover Image:** Vlaming Head Light-
house, Exmouth Peninsula, Western
Australia © Doug Pearson / CORBIS
All Rights Reserved
**Manager, Cover Visual Research and
Permissions:** Karen Sanatar
**Manager, Rights and Permissions:**
Zina Arabia
**Manager, Visual Research:**
Beth Brenzel
**Image Permissions Coordinator:**
Nancy Seise
**Full-Service Production and
Composition:** Aptara Corp
**Full-Service Project Management:**
Peggy Kellar
**Printer/Binder:** RR Donnelley & Sons
**Cover Printer:** RR Donnelley & Sons

Credits and acknowledgments borrowed from other sources and reproduced, with permission,
in this textbook appear on appropriate page within text (or on page 639).

**Library of Congress Cataloging-in-Publication Data**

The Prentice Hall reader / [compiled by] George Miller.—9th ed.
    p. cm.
    Includes bibliographical references and index.
    ISBN-13: 978-0-205-66452-8
    ISBN-10: 0-205-66452-0
    1. College readers. 2. English language—Rhetoric—Problems,
exercises, etc. I. Miller, George, 1943–
PE1417.P74 2009
808'.0427—dc 22                                        2008051998

**Prentice Hall**
is an imprint of

10 9 8 7 6 5 4 3 2
ISBN 13: 978-0-205-66452-8
ISBN 10: 0-205-66452-0

www.pearsonhighered.com

# TABLE OF CONTENTS

# CHAPTER 2

## NARRATION   112

# CHAPTER 7

# CHAPTER 8

# CHAPTER 9

## ARGUMENT AND PERSUASION    475

# THEMATIC CONTENTS

# PREFACE

*The Prentice Hall Reader* is predicated on two premises: that reading plays a vital role in learning how to write and that writing and reading can best be organized around the traditional division of discourse into a number of structural patterns. Such a division is not the only way that the forms of writing can be classified, but it does have several advantages.

First, practice in these structural patterns encourages students to organize knowledge and to see the ways in which information can be conveyed. How else does the mind know except by classifying, comparing, defining, or seeking cause-and-effect relationships? Second, the most common use of these patterns occurs in writing done in academic courses. There students are asked to narrate a chain of events, to describe an artistic style, to classify plant forms, to compare two political systems, to tell how a laboratory experiment was performed, to analyze why famine occurs in Africa, to define a philosophical concept, or to argue for or against building a space station. Learning how to structure papers using these patterns is an exercise that has immediate application in students' other academic work. Finally, because the readings use these patterns as structural devices, they offer an excellent way in which to integrate reading into a writing course. Students can see the patterns at work and learn how to use them to become more effective writers and better, more efficient readers.

## WHAT IS NEW IN THE NINTH EDITION?

The ninth edition of *The Prentice Hall Reader* features sixty essays, fifteen of which are new, twelve papers written by student writers, and nine poems or short, short stories that show the organizational strategies at work. As in the previous editions, the readings are chosen on the basis of several criteria: how well they demonstrate a particular pattern of organization, appeal to an audience of first-year students, and promote interesting and appropriate discussion and writing activities.

The ninth edition of *The Prentice Hall Reader* includes a number of new features:

- Fifteen new essays on timely topics such as Wikipedia, Facebook, and Iraq
- Greatly expanded coverage of the research paper in a chapter that includes two new student papers, which are followed from idea through revision to final draft. The chapter treats finding, evaluating, using, and documenting sources, with special emphasis on Web searching, avoiding plagiarism, and cautions about using sources such as Wikipedia.
- New design for each chapter which allows students to find answers quickly to their questions about finding a topic, writing, and revising a paper
- New, extensive links between the advice in each chapter introduction and the essays it includes in special sections marked "In the essays, look for"
- Expanded chapter on argument and persuasion, with three sets of paired essays
- New and expanded section on writing suggestions at the end of each chapter
- New and expanded suggestions for writing about images

## WHAT IS DISTINCTIVE ABOUT *THE PRENTICE HALL READER*?

The ninth edition retains and improves on some of the popular student features from earlier editions:

- **Selections arranged by difficulty.** *The Prentice Hall Reader* offers flexibility in choosing readings. No chapter has fewer than five selections, most have six or more. The readings are scaled in terms of length and sophistication—moving from a student example in the chapter's introduction to examples written by professional writers arranged in increasing length, difficulty, and sophistication.
- **Clear introductions to each chapter.** Each chapter's introductory material is organized around key questions about writing.
- **Links between chapter introductions and readings.** Sections labeled "In the readings, look for" connect introductory material with the chapter's readings.
- **Detailed and extensive writing suggestions.** Each reading is followed by four writing suggestions: the first asks students to write in a journal or blog; the second calls for a paragraph-length response; the third, an essay; and the fourth, an essay involving research. Each suggestion is related to the content of the reading, and each calls for a response in the particular pattern being studied.

In addition, each chapter contains an extensive new list of writing suggestions related to the chapter's organizational strategy. In all, the *Reader* has nearly five hundred writing suggestions.

- **Links between grammar and writing and between reading and writing.** In addition to the three opening units on reading, writing, and revising, each reading has a Focusing on Grammar and Writing activity.

- **Glossary and Ready Reference.** This tool at the end of the book explains and illustrates common problems with grammar and writing, tying these explanations back to activities in the text. The links help build bridges between the content of the essays and the writing skills they reveal.

- **Literary examples of each organizational strategy.** A poem or short story is included in most of the chapters. These creative examples show how the strategies can be used to structure not just essays but poetry and fiction as well. Each selection has discussion questions and writing suggestions.

- **Emphasis on critical reading skills.** In addition to the unit How to Read an Essay, which appears at the beginning of the text, each chapter has an example of how critical reading skills can be applied to reading each strategy. Each essay is preceded by two questions that invite students to connect the reading to their own experience and to focus their attention on a close reading of the essay. Each reading has a Criticial Reading Activity (in the *Annotated Instructor's Edition*).

- **Extensive Web activities.** Throughout the text, students are directed to the Web. To enhance student use of the Web, advice is given on Web searching and evaluating Web resources.

- **Writing about images.** Chapters include a section with a visual image and suggestions on writing about such images.

- **Greatly expanded chapter on writing the research paper.** The research paper is traced from idea to finished draft. Detailed advice indicates how to locate and evaluate print and online sources. Two new student research papers are presented, one with annotations that highlight important conventions of research writing.

## WHAT ADDITIONAL RESOURCES ARE AVAILABLE TO THE INSTRUCTOR?

### Annotated Instructor's Edition

An annotated edition of *The Prentice Hall Reader* is available to instructors. Each of the selections in the text is annotated in several ways:

- A Teaching Strategy that suggests ways in which to teach the reading and to keep attention focused on how the selection works as a piece of writing

- Appropriate background information that explains allusions or historical contexts

- Specific critical reading activities that can be used with the reading

- Possible responses to all of the discussion questions included in the text

- An additional writing suggestion

**Instructor's Quiz Booklet**   A separate *Instructor's Quiz Booklet* for *The Prentice Hall Reader* is available from your Prentice Hall representative. The booklet contains two quizzes for each selection in the *Reader*, one on content and the other on vocabulary. Each quiz has five multiple-choice questions. The quizzes are intended to be administered and graded quickly. They provide the instructor with a brief and efficient means of testing the students' ability to extract significant ideas from the readings and of demonstrating their understanding of certain vocabulary words as they are used in the essays. Keys to both content and vocabulary quizzes are included at the back of the *Quiz Booklet*.

**Teaching Writing with *The Prentice Hall Reader***   A separate manual on planning the writing and the reading in a composition course is available from your Prentice Hall representative. Primarily addressed to the new graduate teaching assistant or the adjunct instructor, the manual includes sections on teaching the writing process, including how to use prewriting activities, to conference, to design and implement collaborative learning activities, and to grade. In addition, it provides advice on how to plan a class discussion of a reading and how to avoid pointless discussions. An appendix contains an index to all of the activities and questions in *The Prentice Hall Reader* that involve grammatical, mechanical, sentence- or paragraph-level subjects, three additional sample syllabi, and a variety of sample course materials including self-assessment sheets, peer editing worksheets, and directions for small-group activities.

**The NEW MyCompLab Web Site**   The new MyCompLab integrates the market-leading instruction, multimedia tutorials, and exercises for writing, grammar and research that users have come to identify with the program with a new online composing space and new assessment tools.  The result is a revolutionary application that offers a seamless and flexible teaching and learning environment built specifically for writers.  Created after years of extensive research and in partnership with composition faculty and students across the country, the new MyCompLab provides help for writers in the context of their writing, with instructor and peer commenting functionality, proven tutorials and exercises for writing, grammar and research, an e-portfolio, an assignment-builder, a bibliography tool, tutoring services, and a gradebook and course management organization created specifically for writing classes. Visit www.mycomplab.com for more information.

## ACKNOWLEDGMENTS

Although writing is a solitary activity, no one can publish without the assistance of others. This text, as always, owes much to many people. To the staff at Prentice Hall who over the years have continued to play a role in shaping and developing this text: Brad Potthoff, Senior Editor; Craig Campanela, Editor-in-Chief; Sandy McGuire, Marketing Manager; Tim Stookesberry, Director of Marketing; and Gina Aloe, Editorial Assistant.

To my reviewers who wrote extensive critiques of the previous edition and made many helpful suggestions: Patrick White, University of Delaware; Jay Gordon, Youngstown State University; Robin Nealy, Wharton County Junior College; Minati Roychoudhuri, Three Rivers Community College; Richard Carr, University of Alaska at Fairbanks; Karen Lescure, Wharton County Junior College; Nancy Schneider, University of Maine at Augusta; Robert Kellerman, University of Maine at Augusta; Carmela B. Arnoldt, Glendale Community College; Marsha Anderson, Wharton County Junior College; Mary Lang, Wharton County Junior College; and April Dolata, Northwestern CT Community College.

To the writing program staff at the University of Delaware, especially to John Jebb and Daniel Lees. To my former students, both graduate and undergraduate, who tested materials, offered suggestions, and contributed essays to the introductions. To Kristen LaPorte and Bailey Kung, whose comments on their writing process and research papers are reproduced (exactly as they were written) in Chapter 11. To Susan Brynteson, the May Morris Director of Libraries at the University of Delaware, and her staff, who are always accommodating and helpful. Most especially to Thomas Melvin of the Reference Department and Charles Robinson of the English Department who reviewed Chapter 11 for me.

To my wife Vicki, who is always there to encourage. And to my children, Lisa, Jon, Craig, Valerie, Eric, Evan, Adam, and Nathan, and my stepchildren Alicia and Eric, who have learned over the years to live with a father who writes.

George Miller
University of Delaware

# How to Read
# an Essay

## Exploring the Links Between
## Reading and Writing

---

### 🔑 ❓ KEY QUESTIONS

Why do you read essays in a writing course?

How does reading an essay help you write an essay?

How does writing help you become a better reader?

What is the difference between an active reader and a passive reader?

What steps do you follow to become an active reader?

  *Prereading*
  *Reading*
  *Rereading*

**Practicing Active Reading: A Model**

  *Lewis Thomas, "On Cloning a Human Being"*

**Some Things to Remember About Active Reading**

---

## Why Do You Read Essays in a Writing Course?

Why should you "read" in a writing course? After all, your grade in most writing courses is determined by the papers you write rather than by exams based on the essays you have read. How do the activities of reading and writing fit together?

You read in a writing course for three purposes:

1. Essays *provide information* that can be used in your writing, and they suggest ways in which to research topics more fully.

2. Essays *offer a perspective* on a particular subject, one with which you might agree or disagree. In this sense they serve as catalysts to spark your writing.
3. Essays *offer models for writing*. They show how another writer dealt with a particular subject or writing problem.

## How Does Reading an Essay Help You Write an Essay?

The first two purposes of readings—as a source of information and as a stimulus to writing—seem fairly obvious, but the third purpose might be confusing. Exactly how do you, as a student writer, use an essay written by a professional writer as a model? Are you to sound like Maya Angelou or Scott Russell Sanders or Richard Rodriguez? Are you to imitate their styles or adopt the structures they use in their essays?

To *model*, in the sense that the word is used here, does not mean to produce an imitation. You are not expected to use another writer's organizational structure or to imitate someone else's style, tone, or approach. Rather, from these writers you can learn how to select information; how to address a particular audience; how to structure the body of an essay; how to begin, make transitions, and end; and how to construct effective paragraphs and achieve sentence variety. In short, readings represent an album of performances, examples that you can use to study writing techniques.

Models, or examples, are important to you as a writer because you learn to write effectively in the same way that you learn any other activity. You study the rules or advice on how the activity is done; you practice, especially under the watchful eye of an instructor or coach; and you study how others have mastered similar problems and techniques. A young musician learns how to read music and play an instrument, practices daily, studies with a teacher, and listens to and watches how other musicians play. A baseball player learns the proper offensive and defensive techniques, practices daily, heeds a coach's advice, and watches other team members play the game.

To improve your writing, remember these steps:

- Follow the advice of your instructor and textbooks.
- Practice by writing frequently.
- Share your work with peers and listen to their comments.
- Study carefully what other writers do.

## How Does Writing Help You Become a Better Reader?

Reading and writing work together: being a good reader will help you become a more effective writer, and being a good writer will help you become a more effective reader. As a writer, you learn how to plan an argument and how to make an effective transition from one point to another. You learn how to write beginnings, middles, and ends, and most important, you learn how to organize an essay. As a reader, you learn that comparison and contrast essays can be organized in either the subject-by-subject or the point-by-point pattern, that narratives are structured chronologically, and that cause-and-effect analyses are linear and sequential. So devices such as structure and pattern are not only creative tools used in writing, but also analytical tools that can be used in reading. By revealing an underlying organization, such devices help you understand what the essay says. To become an efficient reader, however, you need to exercise the same care and attention that you do when you write. In other words, become an active reader rather than a passive reader.

## What Is the Difference Between an Active Reader and a Passive Reader?

As a reader your first concern is usually plot or subject matter: What happens? What is the subject? Is the subject new and interesting? Generally that first reading is done quickly, even superficially. You are a spectator waiting passively to be entertained or informed; you might even skim or hurry through the text. Then, if it is important for you to use that piece of writing in some way or to understand it in detail or in depth, active reading begins. You ask questions, seek answers, look for organizational strategies, and concentrate on themes and images or on the thesis and the quality of the evidence presented. Careful reading requires active participation. Writing and reading are social acts of communication; as such, they involve an implied contract between writer and audience. A writer's job is to communicate clearly and effectively; a reader's job is to read attentively and critically.

As a reader you are an active participant in the process of communication. Therefore, always read any piece of writing that you are using in a course or on your job more than once. Rereading an essay or a textbook involves the same types of critical activities involved in rereading a poem, a novel, or a set of directions. You must examine how the writer embodies meaning, purpose, or direction in the prose. You must seek answers to a variety of questions: How does the author structure the text? How does the author select, organize, and present information? To whom is the author writing? How does that audience influence the essay?

You can increase your effectiveness as an active and critical reader by following a three-step model.

## What Steps Do You Follow to Become an Active Reader?

As you read here about the three steps of prereading, reading, and rereading, look briefly at the format of the first essay in this book, "On Cloning a Human Being."

When you prepare to write a paper, you engage in preliminary activities such as finding a topic, narrowing that into a thesis, and gathering information. Similarly, you start the active reading process with preliminaries: Get an overview of the text you are about to read. Size it up; get a sense of what it is about and how it seems to work. Active reading involves a process that starts before you actually begin to read the essay itself.

**PREREADING ----------> READING ----------> REREADING**

*Prereading Selected Essays*

1. Look closely at the title of the essay. What expectations does it set up?
2. Read the biographical note about the author.
3. Check where the text was first published. What does that tell you?
4. Think about the two Before Reading questions.
5. Check for obvious subdivisions (for example, subheadings, extra white space between paragraphs). What do they suggest about structure?
6. Read the first sentence of each paragraph.
7. Look at the questions that follow the essay. What do they want you to watch for when reading the essay?
8. Get a marker, pencil, or pen to annotate the text and ask questions.
9. Have a dictionary to look up unfamiliar words.

After you have finished prereading, you are ready to read the essay. When you begin to read a selection in this book, you already have an important piece of information about its structure. Each essay was chosen to demonstrate a particular type of writing (narration, description, exposition, or argumentation) and a particular pattern of organization (chronological, spatial, division, classification, comparison, contrast, process, cause and effect, definition, induction or deduction). As you read, think about why the essay was placed into that category.

PREREADING ----------> **READING** ----------> REREADING

*Reading Selected Essays*

1. What is the essay's subject?
2. What particular point is the author trying to make about this subject?
3. How is the essay organized?
4. Why might the author have begun the essay with that introduction?
5. How does the author bring the essay to a conclusion?
6. What examples or evidence does the author use? Where did they come from? Are they appropriate and convincing?
7. How readable is the essay? What makes it either easy or difficult to read?
8. To whom does the author seem to be writing? How do you sense that?
9. What purpose does the author seem to have for writing this essay?

Remember that an essay typically expresses a particular idea or assertion (*thesis*) about a *subject* to an *audience* for a particular reason (*purpose*). One reading of an essay will probably be enough to answer questions about its subject, but you may have to reread the essay several times to identify the author's thesis and purpose. Keep these elements separate and clear in your mind; it will help to answer the following questions as you read and reread:

**Subject:** What is this essay about?
**Thesis:** What particular point is the author trying to make about this subject?

**Audience:** To whom does the author seem to be writing? How does this intended audience help shape the essay and influence its language and style?

**Purpose:** Why might the author have written this essay? Is the intention to entertain? To inform? To persuade?

Rereading, like rewriting, is not always a discrete stage in a linear process. When writing, you might pause after several sentences and go back and make immediate changes. As a reader, you might stop at the end of a paragraph then go back and reread what you have just read. Depending on the difficulty of the essay, it might take several rereadings for you to be able to answer the questions posed about the writer's thesis and purpose. Even if you feel certain about your understanding of the essay, a final rereading is important. A rereading is also the time to focus on the essay as an example of the writer's craft. Strive not only for a detailed understanding of what is happening in the essay, but also for what you (a practicing writer) can learn about the craft of writing.

PREREADING -----------> READING -----------> **REREADING**

*Rereading Selected Essays*

1. Use the questions at the end of each selection as a way to gauge your understanding of the essay.
2. Outline the essay to reveal its structure—a simple one will do.
3. Look carefully at how the essay is paragraphed. Paragraphs can represent shifts in thought or content, or they might be required because of the format in which an essay was originally published.
4. Pay attention to the author's sentence structures. How do these sentences differ from those you typically write?
5. Is there anything unusual about word choice? Do you use a similar range of vocabulary when you write?
6. How has the author kept the intended audience in mind?
7. How effective are the details and examples? Could any have been better?
8. Is the introduction effective? Do you want to keep reading? Does the conclusion seem like the right place at which to stop?
9. Jot down a few things that you have learned about writing from reading and studying this essay.

## PRACTICING ACTIVE READING: A MODEL

Before you begin reading in the ninth edition of *The Prentice Hall Reader*, you can see how one student used the techniques of prereading, reading, and rereading on the following essay. The student's annotations required several rereadings of the essay. Following the essay are the student's prereading, reading, and rereading notes. Remember, one reading of any essay is never enough.

# On Cloning a Human Being

Lewis Thomas

*Lewis Thomas (1913–1993) was born in Flushing, New York, and received his M.D. from Harvard University. He served on the medical faculty at Johns Hopkins, Tulane, Cornell, and Yale before assuming the position of chancellor of the Memorial Sloan-Kettering Cancer Center in New York. Thomas published widely in his research specialty, pathology, the study of diseases and their causes.*

*In 1971 he began contributing a 1,200-word monthly column, focusing on current topics related to medicine and biological science, to the* New England Journal of Medicine. *Titled "Notes of a Biology Watcher," the column proved highly popular with professionals who subscribed to the journal as well as nonspecialists. Several collections of these essays have been published, including* The Lives of a Cell: Notes of a Biology Watcher *(1974),* The Medusa and the Snail *(1979),* Late Night Thoughts on Listening to Mahler's Ninth Symphony *(1983), and* Fragile Species *(1992).*

*In "On Cloning a Human Being," originally published in the* New England Journal of Medicine, *Thomas sets out to analyze the effect that an experiment to clone a human being would have on the rest of the world.*

## Before Reading

**Connecting:** What do you know about cloning, both in fact and from science fiction? Do you find cloning a positive technological development or a frightening one?

**Anticipating:** What seems to be Thomas's attitude toward cloning? As a scientist, does he express the opinion you expect?

1

Definition of
cloning

It is now theoretically possible to recreate an identical creature from any animal or plant, from the DNA contained in the nucleus of any somatic cell. A single plant root-tip cell can be teased and seduced into conceiving a perfect copy of the whole plant; a frog's intestinal epithelial cell possesses the complete instructions needed for a new, same frog. If the technology were further advanced, you could do this with a human being, and there are now startling predictions all over the place that this will in fact be done, someday, in order to provide a version of immortality for carefully selected, especially valuable people.

The cloning of humans is on most of the lists of things to worry about from Science, along with behavior control, genetic engineering, <u>transplanted heads</u>, <u>computer poetry</u>, and the <u>unrestrained growth of plastic flowers</u>.

**2**

*Joking here.*

Cloning is the most dismaying of prospects, mandating as it does the elimination of sex with only a metaphoric elimination of death as compensation. It is almost no comfort to know that one's cloned, identical surrogate lives on, especially when the living will very likely involve edging one's real, now aging self off to the side, sooner or later. It is hard to imagine anything like filial affection or respect for a single, unmated nucleus; harder still to think of one's new, self-generated self as anything but an absolute, desolate orphan. Not to mention the complex interpersonal relationship involved in raising one's self from infancy, teaching the language, enforcing discipline, instilling good manners, and the like. How would you feel if you became an incorrigible juvenile delinquent by (proxy) at the age of fifty-five?

**3**

*Two versions of the same person living at once—the original and the clone. Wild idea.*

*proxy: person acting for another person*

The public questions are obvious. Who is to be selected, and on what qualifications? How to handle the risks of misused technology, such as self-determined cloning by the rich and powerful but socially objectionable, or the cloning by governments of dumb, docile masses for the world's work? What will be the effect on all the uncloned rest of us of human sameness? After all, we've accustomed ourselves through hundreds of millennia to the continual exhilaration of uniqueness; each of us is totally different, in a fundamental sense, from all the other four billion. Selfness is an essential fact of life. The thought of human nonselfness, precise sameness, is terrifying, when you think about it.

**4** *paragraph introduction sets up negatives about cloning*

Well, don't think about it, because it isn't a probable possibility, not even as a long shot for the distant future, in my opinion. I agree that you might clone some people who would look amazingly like their parental cell donors, but the odds are that they'd be almost as different as you or me, and certainly more different than any of today's identical twins.

**5** *Thesis: Cloning human beings is not really possible.*

The time required for the experiment is only one of the problems, but a formidable one. Suppose you wanted to clone a <u>prominent, spectacularly successful diplomat, to look after the Middle East problems of the distant future</u>. You'd have to catch him and persuade him, probably not very hard to do, and extirpate a cell. But then you'd have to wait for him to grow up through embryonic life and then for at least forty years more, and you'd have to be sure all observers remained patient and unmeddlesome through his unpromising, ambiguous childhood and adolescence.

**6** *Reason 1: Time involved*

*"valuable person"*

7   Reason 2: Environment would have to be created.

Moreover, you'd have to be sure of recreating his environment, perhaps down to the last detail. "Environment" is a word which really means people, so you'd have to do a lot more cloning than just the diplomat himself.

8
To be the same, the clone would have to have the same environment.

This is a very important part of the cloning problem, largely overlooked in our excitement about the cloned individual himself. You don't have to agree all the way with B. F. Skinner to acknowledge that the environment does make a difference, and when you examine what we really mean by the word "environment" it comes down to other human beings. We use euphemisms and jargon for this, like "social forces," "cultural influences," even Skinner's "verbal community," but what is meant is the dense crowd of nearby people who talk to, listen to, smile or frown at, give to, withhold from, nudge, push, caress, or flail out at the individual.

genome: genetic organism

No matter what the genome says, these people have a lot to do with shaping a character. Indeed, if all you had was the genome, and no people around, you'd grow a sort of vertebrate plant, nothing more.

9
Causal chain: clone parents, grandparents, family, people outside the family who came in contact with the individual, the whole world.

So, to start with, you will undoubtedly need to clone the parents. No question about this. This means the diplomat is out, even in theory, since you couldn't have gotten cells from both his parents at the time when he was himself just recognizable as an early social treasure. You'd have to limit the list of clones to people already certified as sufficiently valuable for the effort, with both parents still alive. The parents would need cloning and, for consistency, their parents as well. I suppose you'd also need the usual informed-consent forms, filled out and signed, not easy to get if I know parents, even harder for grandparents.

10

But this is only the beginning. It is the whole family that really influences the way a person turns out, not just the parents, according to current psychiatric thinking. Clone the family.

11

Then what? The way each member of the family develops has already been determined by the environment set around him, and this environment is more people, people outside the family, schoolmates, acquaintances, lovers, enemies, carpool partners, even, in special circumstances, peculiar strangers across the aisle on the subway. Find them, and clone them.

12
Isn't this an exaggeration?

But there is no end to the protocol. Each of the outer contacts has his own surrounding family, and his and their outer contacts. Clone them all.

13

To do the thing properly, with any hope of ending up with a genuine duplicate of a single person, you really have no choice. You must clone the world, no less.

We are not ready for an experiment of this size, nor, I should think, are we willing. For one thing, it would mean replacing today's world by an entirely identical world to follow immediately, and this means no new, natural, spontaneous, random, chancy children. No children at all, except for the manufactured doubles of those now on the scene. Plus all those identical adults, including all of today's politicians, all seen double. It is too much to contemplate.

14

*He's really joking here.*

Moreover, when the whole experiment is finally finished, fifty years or so from now, how could you get a responsible scientific reading on the outcome? Somewhere in there would be the original clonee, probably lost and overworked, now well into middle age, but everyone around him would be precise duplicates of today's everyone. It would be today's same world, filled to overflowing with duplicates of today's people and their same, duplicated problems, probably all resentful at having had to go through our whole thing all over, sore enough at the clone to make endless trouble for him, if they found him.

15

*With the world cloned, everything would be the same, leading to dissatisfaction.*

And obviously, if the whole thing were done precisely right, they would still be casting about for ways to solve the problem of universal dissatisfaction, and sooner or later they'd surely begin to look around at each other, wondering who should be cloned for his special value to society, to get us out of all this. And so it would go, in regular cycles, perhaps forever.

16

I once lived through a period when I wondered what Hell could be like, and I stretched my imagination to try to think of a perpetual sort of damnation. I have to confess, I never thought of anything like this.

17

I have an alternative suggestion, if you're looking for a way out. Set cloning aside, and don't try it. Instead, go in the other direction. Look for ways to get mutations more quickly, new variety, different songs. Fiddle around, if you must fiddle, but never with ways to keep things the same, no matter who, not even yourself. Heaven, somewhere ahead, has got to be a change.

18

*The author's real purpose comes out here; ties to paragraph 4.*

## Prereading Notes

The headnote indicates that the author, Lewis Thomas, was a physician and medical researcher and that most of his essays—including this one—were written for the New England Journal of Medicine. These facts and the title "On Cloning a Human Being" initially suggest that this will be a pretty serious, probably dry essay and that it may be full of a lot of technical information. However, scanning the essay by looking at the first sentence in each paragraph shows the tone to be fairly informal: paragraph 5, for example, begins, "Well, don't think about it...." It is also clear from a quick scan of the essay that it is really on <u>not</u> cloning a human being. Thomas is focusing on the problems involved in cloning human beings and seems to say that it will never happen.

### Reading Notes

Outline:

par. 1 Introduction to cloning and predictions that "especially valuable people" will be cloned

pars. 2–4 Worries about cloning

par. 5 Thomas says cloning "isn't a probable possibility"

par. 6 Reason 1: Too much time involved in any experiment with human cloning

pars. 7–15 Reason 2: Since individuals are shaped by their environments, to clone a person would require cloning his or her parents, grandparents, the whole family, "the world, no less." People are not ready to replace today's world with "an entirely identical world to follow immediately," so everyone would hate the original clonee for causing all the trouble.

par. 16 The cloning cycle would have to start again to duplicate someone who could "solve the problem of universal dissatisfaction" with the original cloning experiment.

par. 17 To Thomas, this would be worse than Hell.

par. 18 Instead of cloning, it would be better to experiment with "ways to get mutations more quickly, new variety, different songs."

After an initial reading, it is clear that Thomas's subject is cloning and predictions that "valuable people" will be cloned experimentally in the future. He states his thesis explicitly in paragraph 5: cloning "isn't a probable possibility, not even as a long shot for the distant future...." Even though the essay was written for the <u>New England Journal of Medicine,</u> it would seem that Thomas intended to reach a general educated audience; for example, he includes very little specialized terminology and doesn't assume any particular medical or scientific expertise. His purpose seems to be basically to inform, to explain to his audience why cloning of human beings isn't likely to happen in the future.

But in explaining why human beings aren't likely to be cloned, Thomas gives reasons that seem exaggerated. Could it really be necessary to clone the whole world, as he says? Why would he want to suggest that the effects of cloning a single human being would be so drastic?

## Rereading Notes

Rereading the essay reveals that Thomas is deliberately pushing the idea of cloning a human being to the point of absurdity. His tone is humorous from the beginning: in paragraph 2, for example, he lists as some of our worries about science—"transplanted heads, computer poetry, and the unrestrained growth of plastic flowers." When he describes the effects of an experiment in cloning an important diplomat and what would really be required to clone a human being (pars. 10–13), he builds each paragraph up to its logical—and increasingly absurd—conclusion: "Clone the family." "Find them, and clone them." "Clone them all." "You must clone the world, no less." In paragraph 14 he pushes the absurdity one step further, imagining a world where there are no longer unique children who grow up to be unique adults but only identical doubles of those who already exist— "including all of today's politicians.... It is too much to contemplate." The next two paragraphs continue in this vein, ending with the most absurd idea of all: that another cloning would have to take place of the person who could get everyone out of this mess. "And so it would go," Thomas says, "in regular cycles, perhaps forever."

Thomas is saying that it is absurd to imagine that an exact replica of another human being could ever be cloned; given the fact that the clone would necessarily grow up under different influences, the two might look alike, but "they'd be almost as different as you and me, and certainly more different than any of today's identical twins" (par. 5). Moreover, an even more substantial point emerges on rereading: there can be no benefit from cloning human beings to begin with. "Precise sameness," Thomas says, "is terrifying" (par. 4), an idea that he returns to in his conclusion, where he suggests that it is better for humans to experiment with "mutations," "variety," and "change" than with clones.

Thomas's purpose, therefore, seems to be more than simply informing readers about the impossibility of creating a human clone; at the core, he is arguing for a view of human nature that recognizes the value of "variety" over some standard of "perfection," and his method is to do so in an entertainingly humorous way.

Each of the essays in the ninth edition of *The Prentice Hall Reader* will repay you for the time and effort you put into reading it carefully and critically. Each essay shows an artful craftsperson at work, solving the problems inherent in communicating experiences, feelings, ideas, and opinions to an audience. Each writer is someone from whom you, as a reader and as a thinker, can learn. So when your instructor assigns a selection from the text, remember that as a reader you must assume an active role. Don't assume that reading an essay once—to see what it is "about"—will mean that you are prepared to write about it or that you have learned all that you can learn from the essay. Ask questions, seek answers to those questions, analyze, and reread.

## SOME THINGS TO REMEMBER ABOUT ACTIVE READING

1. Read the headnote to the selection. How does this information help you understand the author and the context in which the selection was written?

2. Look at the questions that precede and follow each reading. They will help focus your attention on the important aspects of the selection. After you read, write out answers to each question.

3. Read through the selection first to see what happens and to satisfy your curiosity.

4. Reread the selection several times, taking notes or underlining as you go.

5. Write or locate in the essay a thesis statement. Remember that the thesis is the particular point that the writer is trying to make about the subject.

6. Define a purpose for the essay. Why is the author writing? Does the author make that purpose explicit?

7. Imagine the audience for such an essay. Who is the likely reader? What does that reader already know about the subject? Is the reader likely to have any preconceptions or prejudices about the subject?

8. Isolate a structure in the selection. How is it put together? Into how many parts can it be divided? How do those parts work together? Outline the essay.

9. Be sure that you understand every sentence. How does the writer vary sentence structures?

10. Look up every word that you cannot define with some degree of certainty. Remember, you might misinterpret what the author is saying if you simply skip over unfamiliar words.

11. Reread the essay one final time, reassembling its parts into the artful whole it was intended to be.

# HOW TO
# WRITE AN ESSAY

## Drafting the Essay

While watching a performance, whether it is athletic or artistic, our attention is focused on the achievement displayed in that moment. Many times we forget the long hours of practice that lie behind that achievement. Writing is no different. Mystery novelist Walter Mosley, in "For Authors, Fragile Ideas Need Loving Every Day" (Chapter 6), observes, "If you want to be a writer, you have to write every day." That is not the kind of advice that most of us want to hear. Typically, we procrastinate when it comes to writing. We put off the process until the last minute. After all, it is not easy to put words on paper or on a screen: there is so much to worry about. However, it is even harder to write an essay for a college course in a few hours. You need to allow time to think about what type of paper you have to write; to gather the information you will need; to write a coherent draft that has a beginning, middle, and end; and to get the right words in complete and correct sentences. Ironically, the more time you can give to writing a paper, the easier the task can become.

## CHOOSING A SUBJECT ----------> HAVING A PURPOSE ----------> DEFINING AN AUDIENCE

The first step in writing is to determine a subject, that is, what your paper will be about. Sometimes subjects are suggested by your instructor; sometimes you must find your own subject. In either situation, often the subject needs to be narrowed or focused. The length of the paper, for example, dictates in part how detailed or focused you have to be. Once you have a subject, you must restrict, focus, or narrow that subject into a workable topic. Although the words *subject* and *topic* are sometimes used interchangeably, think of subject as the broader, more general word. You move from a subject to a topic by limiting or restructuring what you will include or cover. The shift from subject to topic is a gradual one that is not marked by a clearly definable line. Just remember that a topic is a more restricted version of a larger subject.

## CHOOSING A SUBJECT ----------> **HAVING A PURPOSE** ----------> DEFINING AN AUDIENCE

A writer has three fundamental purposes: *to entertain*, *to inform*, and *to persuade*. These purposes are not necessarily separate. For example, an interesting, maybe even humorous, essay that documents the health hazards caused by smoking can, at the same time, attempt to persuade the reader to give up smoking. In this case the main purpose is persuasion; entertainment and information play subordinate roles in catching the reader's interest and in providing appropriate evidence for the argument being advanced.

These three purposes are generally associated with the traditional division of writing into four forms: *narration*, *description*, *exposition* (including classification, comparison and contrast, process, cause and effect, definition), and *argumentation*. Narrative and descriptive essays typically tell a story or describe a person, object, or place in order to entertain a reader and to re-create or lend insight into the significance of the experience. Expository essays primarily provide information for a reader. Argumentative, or persuasive, essays seek to move a reader, to gain support, or to advocate a particular course of action.

CHOOSING A SUBJECT ----------->  HAVING A PURPOSE ----------->
**DEFINING AN AUDIENCE**

Audience is a key factor in every writing situation. Writing is a form of communication and as such it implies an audience. In many writing situations, audience is a controlling factor that affects both the content of the paper and the
style in which it is written. An effective writer learns to adjust to an audience
and to write for that audience, because a writer, like a performer, needs and
wants an audience.

Writers adjust their style and tone on a spectrum ranging from informal to formal. Articles that appear in popular, wide-circulation magazines often are written in the first person, use contractions, favor popular and
colloquial words, and contain relatively short sentences and paragraphs. Articles in scholarly journals exhibit a formal style that involves an objective and
serious tone, a more advanced vocabulary, and longer and more complicated
sentence and paragraph constructions. In the informal style, the writer injects
his or her personality into the prose; in the formal style, the writer remains
detached and impersonal. A writer adopts whatever style seems appropriate
for a particular audience or context. An effective writer does not have one
style or voice but many.

## GETTING READY TO WRITE

### Where Do You Start When You Have an Assigned Topic?

In most college courses, you will be writing papers in response to a specific assignment. That assignment will contain a set of clues or instructions about
what you are to do in the paper. Before you begin to write, before you even
begin to gather information, spend time analyzing the assignment and the directions you have been given. Look at five areas in the assigned topic to see
what clues they give you about the paper you are going to write.

                                   1. Length
                                   2. Purpose

Use as clues       3. Structure

                                   4. Audience
                                   5. Sources

**Using Length as a Clue**   How long is the paper to be? If your instructor
specifies length (a certain number of pages or an approximate number of
words), you have an idea of how detailed your paper must be. If the subject
seems fairly large and the length modest, then clearly you must focus your paper on the key or significant issues. If your instructor wants a longer paper or
a research paper, then you must respond to the assignment with extensive
detail or evidence. The specified length is a key to how much detail you need
to respond adequately to the assignment.

**Using Purpose as a Clue**   Do not confuse the reason why your instructor assigned a paper (for example, to have something to grade!) with the purpose of the paper as it is stated in the assignment. To establish that, look for verbs or descriptive phrases in the assignment. For example, does it ask you to *narrate*, *argue for*, *evaluate*, *analyze*, *summarize*, *recommend*, *explain*? As you begin work on the paper, keep that purpose verb in mind.

**Using Structure as a Clue**   Purpose and structure are often closely related. Look at the accompanying table which connects assignment verbs with both purposes and structures. If you are told to *analyze*, you are dividing something into its component parts or assessing strengths and weaknesses. If you are to *argue for*, you will use an inductive or a deductive order.

**Using Audience as a Clue**   Audience can be more complicated than it sounds. The answer to "who?" is not simply "I'm writing to my instructor." You need to think about how much your audience (typically peers as well as instructor) knows about the subject. Are you going to be using words or concepts that might not be familiar to those readers? Will you have to find analogies that will help your audience understand? Will you have to define technical words and phrases? Is your audience likely to know everything that you are writing about? If so, then why would the audience be interested in reading your paper? If you are arguing for something, how deeply does your audience feel about the topic? Does the topic, for example, challenge your audience's deeply held beliefs?

**Using Possible Sources as a Clue**   What does the assignment suggest about where to find the information you need? Are you expected to draw from the readings that might be part of the assignment? From class lectures or discussions? Are you to use your own personal experiences? Are you to do some research? Interview people? Search the Web? Locate books and articles on the topic?

| Looking for Key Words | Usually Means | Likely Organizational Pattern |
|---|---|---|
| **Narrate** **Tell** | to tell a story; to describe how something works | chronological; flashbacks can be used; first step to last |
| **Summarize** | to rehearse the key points | structure according to what is being summarized |
| **Describe** | to tell how something was perceived by the senses | spatial patterns: top to bottom, side to side, front to back, prominent to background |
| **Classify** | to place similar items into categories or groups | largest to smallest; most important to least |
| **Divide** | to separate a whole into its parts | largest to smallest; most important to least |

| Analyze | to show component parts; to assess correctness | how something works; component parts; strengths and weaknesses |
|---|---|---|
| Compare | to show similarities between two or more items | subject-by-subject (A, B), point-by-point (A1/B1, A2/B2) |
| Contrast | to show differences between two or more items | subject-by-subject (A, B), point-by-point (A1/B1, A2/B2) |
| Explain | to clarify an idea, a process; to make clear | step-by-step |
| Identify Causes and Effects | to identify causes of a certain event; to identify effects that arise from a certain event | forward or backward; causes to event; event and its effects |
| Define | to provide an explanation for a word, concept, or event | placement in a class and addition of distinguishing features; definition followed by examples |
| Argue or Persuade | to get a reader to agree with your position | inductive; deductive; logical (argument); emotional (persuasion) |

## PRACTICING WITH CLUES

Let's look at two sample writing assignments from this text. The first follows "The Inheritance of Tools" by Scott Russell Sanders (Chapter 3). In the essay Sanders is building an interior wall in his house when he learns that his father has died. He has inherited from his father both the physical tools he is using and the knowledge of how to use them. In the essay, he reflects on that "inheritance" and what it means to him. Here is one of the writing assignments that follows that essay:

> **For an essay:** Think about a skill, talent, attitude, or habit that you have learned from or share with a family member. What does that inheritance mean to you? How does it affect our life? In an essay, describe the inheritance and identify its effects on you.
>
> **Using clues as a way of preparing to write:**
> **Length:** An essay, typically defined as three to four pages
> **Purpose:** "Describe the inheritance and identify its effect on you." You are asked to do two things. First, you are to select a "skill, talent, attitude, or habit" that you have inherited from or share with a family member and describe it. Second, you are to identify the effects that inheritance has had on you.
> **Structure:** The key phrases "describe" and "identify the effects" suggest that the essay will have two main parts. The first part of the

essay will involve description, focusing on something and explaining or describing what it is. The second part of the essay will trace the effects that inheritance has had on you. The complete essay will be a description followed by an analysis of effects.

**Audience:** Not specified, but typically imagined as an audience of peers

**Sources of information:** Personal experience and reflection

The second example follows Peter Singer's "The Singer Solution to World Poverty" (Chapter 10).

**For an essay:** Singer notes (citing the research of someone else) that a donation of two hundred dollars would "help a sickly two-year-old transform into a healthy six-year-old." That works out to about fifty-five cents per day yearly. Could you and your friends, even as college students, find a way to trim fifty-five cents a day (or less than four dollars a week) out of what you already spend? In an essay aimed at undergraduates at your school, argue for a schoolwide campaign to get everyone to contribute to such a cause.

**Using clues as a way of preparing to write:**

**Length:** An essay, typically defined as three to four pages

**Purpose:** "Argue for a schoolwide campaign"

**Structure:** Establish the problem and define a solution, which would involve showing how such a small sum of money could be saved no matter how tight the students' budgets

**Audience:** "Undergraduates at your school" (who would have relatively little extra money)

**Sources of information:** Some research on the problem (probably drawn from Singer's essay) and some research on the cost of the items consumed daily (such as cup of coffee, can of soda, candy)

## Where Do You Start When You Have to Choose Your Own Topic?

Writing from an assigned topic can seem frustrating and confining. At some point probably every writer has resented being told what to write and has felt confined to a topic about which she or he has little or no interest. Devising your own topic may be more rewarding but also more difficult. You might be excited or terrified about a completely open-ended assignment that simply says, "Write a paper on a topic of your choice." Your response might be a series of questions that we have referred to as clues: "How long should this paper be?" "What is it supposed to do?"

Whether the topic is given to you or you choose it, the key is to define the set of parameters within which you will write. Before you start to write, answer each of the following questions:

**Length:** How long will my paper be? Is it a one-page response paper, a three-to-four page essay, a research paper with documentation? What level of detail will I need?

**Purpose:** What do I want my paper to do? Am I narrating or describing what happened? Am I conveying information? Am I arguing for something? What are the key words that I will use?

**Structure:** What do my key words suggest about the structure of my paper? How does that structure work within the page limit I have chosen?

**Audience:** Who is my audience? What do they know about this subject? What might need to be explained to them?

**Sources:** What type of information will I need for this paper and where can I find it?

## How Do You Gather Information?

What makes writing entertaining, informative, or persuasive is information—specific, relevant detail. If you try to write without gathering information, you end up skimming the surface of your subject, even if you already know something about it.

How you go about gathering information for your paper depends on your subject and your purpose for writing. Some topics, such as those involving a personal experience, require a memory search; other assignments, such as describing a particular place, require careful observation. Essays that convey information or argue particular positions often require gathering information through research. Some possible strategies for gathering information about your subject are listed here. Before you start this step in your prewriting, remember three things:

1. *Different tactics work for different subjects and for different writers.* You might find that freewriting is great for some assignments but not for others. As a writer, explore your options. Do not rule out any strategy until you have tried it.

2. *Prewriting activities sometimes produce information and sometimes just produce questions that you will need to answer.* In other words, prewriting often involves learning what you don't know and need to find out. Learning to ask the right questions is just as important as knowing the right answers.

3. *Prewriting activities are an excellent way to find a focus, to narrow a subject, or to suggest a working plan for your essay.* As you begin to explore a subject, the possibilities spread out before you. Try not to be wedded to a particular topic or thesis until you have explored a subject through prewriting activities.

**Exploring Personal Experience and Observation**    Even your most unforgettable experience has probably been forgotten in part. If you are going to re-create it for a reader, you will have to do some active searching among your memories. By focusing your attention, you can slowly recall more details. Ask yourself a series of questions about the chronology of the experience. For example, start with a particular detail and try to stimulate your memory: What happened just before? Just after? Who was there? Where did the experience take place? Why did it happen? When did it happen? How did it happen?

Sense impressions, like factual details, fade from memory. In the height of summer, it is not easy to recall a crisp fall day. Furthermore, sensory details are not always noticed at the time or mentally recorded. How many times have you passed by a particular location without really seeing it?

Descriptions, like every other form of writing, demand specific information, and the easiest way to gather details is to observe. Before you try to describe a person, place, or object, take some time to list specific details on a piece of paper. At first, record everything you notice. Do not worry about having too much, you can always edit later. At this stage, it is better to have too much than too little.

The next step is to decide what to include in your description and what to exclude. As a general principle, an effective written description does not try to record everything. The selection of detail should be governed by your purpose in the description. Ask yourself what you are trying to show or reveal. For what reason? What is particularly important about this person, place, or object? A description is not the verbal equivalent of a photograph or a tape recording.

**Freewriting to Get Words Down**    Putting words down on a page or a computer screen can be intimidating. Your editing instincts immediately want to take over: Are the words spelled correctly? Are the sentences complete? Do they contain mechanical or grammatical errors? Not only must you express your ideas in words, but suddenly those words must be the correct words.

If you translate thoughts into written words and at the same time edit those words, writing can seem impossibly difficult. Instead of allowing ideas to take shape through the words or allowing the writing to stimulate your thinking, you become fearful of committing anything to paper or a screen.

Writing can, however, stimulate thought. Every writer has experienced a time when an idea became clear only as it was written down. If your editing instincts can be turned off, you can use writing as a way of generating ideas.

Freewriting is an effective way to deal with this dilemma. Write without stopping for a fixed period of time; write for a period as short as ten minutes or as long as an hour. Do not stop; do not edit; do not worry about mistakes. If you find yourself stuck for something to write, repeat the last word or phrase you wrote until a new thought comes to mind. You are looking for a focus point—an idea or a subject for a paper. You are trying to externalize your thinking into writing. What will emerge is a free association of ideas. Some will be relevant and some will be worthless. After you have ideas on paper, you can decide what is worth saving, developing, or simply throwing away.

You can also do freewriting on a computer. One technique many writers find effective is using the contrast control. Darken the screen so that you cannot read what you have typed. Then as you write, you will not be distracted by errors and will not be tempted to stop and read what you have written. Freewriting in this way provides an opportunity to free-associate, almost as you might when you are speaking.

**Writing Daily in Journals and Blogs**   A daily journal or blog can be an effective seedbed for writing projects. Such a journal is not a daily log of your activities (got up, went to class, had lunch) but rather a place where you record ideas, observations, memories, and feelings. Set aside a specific notebook or a particular file on your computer in which to keep your journal. Try to write for at least ten minutes every day. Over a period of time, such as a semester, you will be surprised at how many ideas for papers or projects you will accumulate. When you are working on a paper, you might want to confine part of your daily journal entries to that particular subject. If your class uses blogs or posts responses online, pay attention to what your classmates suggest about your ideas.

**Brainstorming and Mapping**   Brainstorming is oral freewriting among a group of people jointly trying to solve a problem by spontaneously contributing ideas. Whatever comes to mind, no matter how obvious or unusual, gets said. The hope is that out of the jumble of ideas that surface, some possible solutions to the problem will be found.

Although brainstorming is by definition a group activity, it can be done by an individual writer. In the center of a blank sheet of paper, write down a key word or phrase that refers to your subject. Then in the space around that word, quickly jot down any ideas that come to mind. Do not write in sentences, just key words and phrases. Because you are not filling consecutive lines with words and because you have space in which the ideas can be arranged, this form of brainstorming often suggests structural relationships. You can increase the usefulness of such an idea generator by adding graphic devices such as circles, arrows, or connecting lines to indicate possible relationships among ideas. These devices can be added to your brainstorming sheet later, and they become a framework for the points you might want to cover in your essay.

**Asking Formal Questions**   One particularly effective way to gather information on any topic is to ask yourself questions about it. This allows you to explore the subject from a variety of angles. The secret to finding answers always lies in knowing the right questions to ask. A good place to start is with the list of questions presented here. Remember, though, not every question is appropriate for every topic.

*Illustration*

1. What examples of _____ can be found?
2. In what ways are these things examples of _____?
3. What details about _____ seem the most important?

*Comparison and Contrast*

1. To what is _____ similar? List the points of similarity.
2. From what is _____ different? List the points of difference.

3. Which points of similarity or difference seem most important?
4. What does the comparison or contrast tell the reader about
   _____?

### Division and Classification

1. Into how many parts can _____ be divided?
2. How many parts is _____ composed of?
3. What other category of things is _____ most like?
4. How does _____ work?
5. What are _____'s component parts?

### Process

1. How many steps or stages are involved in _____?
2. In what order do those steps or stages occur?

### Cause and Effect

1. What precedes _____?
2. Is that a cause of _____?
3. What follows _____?
4. Is that an effect of _____?
5. How many causes of _____ can you find?
6. How many effects of _____ can you find?
7. Why does _____ happen?

### Definition

1. How is _____ defined in a dictionary?
2. Does everyone agree about the meaning of _____?
3. Does _____ have any connotations? What are they?
4. Has the meaning of _____ changed over time?
5. What words are synonymous with _____?

### Argument and Persuasion

1. How do your readers feel about _____?
2. How do you feel about _____?
3. What are the arguments in favor of _____? List those
   arguments in order of strength.
4. What are the arguments against _____? List those
   arguments in order of strength.

**Finding Print and Online Sources**   Chapter 11 offers detailed advice about how to go about gathering information for a paper using print and online sources. Be sure to read that chapter before you start a search for materials.

Not long ago, locating information meant going to your school's library, looking up a subject in the card catalog and checking the bound volumes of indexes to material published in periodicals or newspapers. Now nearly everything—from library catalogs to indexes of articles published in journals, magazines, and newspapers—is available through computer databases. Most everyone looking for "quick" information simply goes to a computer to search an appropriate term or phrase. More often than not, Wikipedia turns up high on the list of retrieved sources. There is nothing wrong with such a strategy as long as you keep these cautions in mind:

1. Many instructors do not want you to use Wikipedia as a source for a paper. See Brock Read's "Can Wikipedia Ever Make the Grade?" (Chapter 1) for some reasons why.
2. Anyone can produce an impressive Website that looks authoritative and reliable. Unless there is some scholarly, professional, or educational editorial oversight, you can never be sure that the information posted on a Website is accurate.
3. Google (or any other search engine) turns up the "best" *matches* to your choice of key words and phrases, not necessarily the best sources. What are the best choices for words or phrases to search?
4. Your school's library has an online catalog of its holdings. But it probably also has a variety of online databases that allow access to articles in more scholarly journals, popular magazines, newspapers, and even government documents.

**Interviewing**   Print or electronic sources are not always available for a topic. In such a case, people often are a great source of information for a writer. Of course the people should have special credentials or knowledge about the writer's subject.

Interviewing requires special skills and tact. When you first contact someone to request an interview, always explain who you are, what you want to know, and how you will use the information. Remember that specific questions will produce more useful information than general ones. Take notes that you can expand later, or use a tape recorder or digital recorder. Keep attention focused on the information that you need, and do not be afraid to ask questions to keep your informant on the subject. If you plan to use direct quotations, make sure that the wording is accurate. If possible, check quotations with your source one final time.

## How Do You Write a Thesis Statement?

**Defining a Thesis Statement**   The information-gathering stage of the writing process is the time in which to sharpen your general subject into a narrower topic. Your subject is a broad, general idea, for example, violence on television. That subject is simply too large for an essay. Consider a few possible approaches that the subject suggests:

- History of violence on television
- Vivid description of a violent act depicted on television
- Classification of the types of violence found on television
- Comparison of the role of violence in European television and American television
- Step-by-step guide to what parents can do to monitor violence shown on television
- Analysis of why violence is so prevalent on television
- Definition of televised violence with examples
- Argument for or against the censorship of televised violence

You need to narrow the *subject* into a *topic*, that is, a more focused, more detailed, more limiting statement. A topic limits a subject by narrowing its scope, by suggesting a specific approach to the subject, and by defining a particular purpose for the essay. A topic is the first step in making a subject more manageable.

**Subject:**   Violence on television
**Topic:**   Impact that televised violence has on young children

The final step in the process is to move from a topic to a *thesis*. The word *thesis* is derived from a Greek word that means "placing," "position," or "proposition." When you formulate a thesis, you are defining your position on the subject. A thesis lets your reader know exactly where you stand. Because it represents your "final" position, a thesis is typically something that you develop and refine as you move through the stages of gathering information and testing ideas. Don't try to start with a final thesis; instead, begin with a tentative thesis (also called a *hypothesis*, from the Greek for "supposition"). Allow your final position to emerge based on what you discover as you gather information and refine your writing plan.

Before you write a thesis statement, consider the facts that will control or influence the form that your thesis will take. For example, a thesis is a reflection of your purpose in writing. If you are working with an assigned topic, look for a verb in the assignment that suggests what your purpose is supposed to be. If you are defining your own topic, make sure that you have determined a purpose verb for your paper. If your purpose is to persuade your audience, your thesis will urge your reader to accept your position. If your purpose is to convey information to your readers, your thesis will forecast your main points and indicate how your paper will be organized.

Your thesis will also be shaped by the scope and length of your paper. Your topic and your thesis must be manageable within the space that you have available; otherwise, you will end up skimming the surface. A short paper requires a more precise, limited focus than a longer one. When you move from subject to topic to thesis, make such that each step is more specific and has an increasingly sharper focus.

---

✔ **CHECKLIST FOR THE FOCUSING PROCESS**

Ask yourself the following questions:
1.   What is my general subject?
2.   What is my specific topic within that general subject?
3.   What do I intend to do in my paper? What is my purpose?
4.   What is my position on that specific topic?

---

**Writing a Thesis Statement**    When you have answered the questions about your purpose, when you have sharpened your general subject into a topic, and when you have defined your position on that topic, you are ready to write a *thesis statement*. The process is simple. You write a thesis statement by linking together your topic and your position on that topic:

**Subject:**    Violence on television

**Topic:**    Impact that televised violence has on young children

**Thesis:**    Televised violence makes young children numb to violence in the real world, distorts their perceptions of how people behave, and teaches them to be violent.

Notice that this thesis not only limits the scope of the paper and defines a precise position and purpose, but it also signals the structure that the body of the essay will have. That structure could be outlined as follows:

Introduction
Body (three assertions)

1.   Makes children numb to violence in the real world
2.   Distorts their perceptions of how people behave
3.   Teaches them to be violent

Conclusion

---

✔ **CHECKLIST FOR AN EFFECTIVE THESIS**

A thesis has these characteristics:
1.   Clearly signals the purpose of the paper
2.   States or takes a definite position, stating specifically what the paper will be doing
3.   Expresses that definite purpose and position in precise, familiar terms
4.   Is appropriate in scope for the paper's length
5.   Signals the structure that will follow in the paper

## PRACTICING NARROWING AND WRITING A THESIS STATEMENT

Review the following list of subjects. Narrow each subject first into a topic and then into a tentative thesis.

| Subject | Topic | Tentative Thesis |
|---|---|---|
| Cell phones | | |
| Texting | | |
| College majors | | |
| Performance-enhancing drugs | | |
| State lotteries | | |
| Cigarettes | | |
| Credit cards | | |

## Writing a Draft

Now it is time to write, because you have answered your key questions about the assignment or your proposed topic, you have thought about what the essay should do, you have gathered the information you will use in the paper, and you have a tentative thesis. Do not expect that this initial draft of the essay will be the final, ready-to-be-handed-in paper. Rather, consider this draft a work in progress—a first version of what will become the final, polished essay.

### How Do You Structure Your Paper?

**How Do You Organize the Middle?**   No matter what their length, papers consist of three parts: an introduction, a body or middle, and a conclusion. The introduction generally ranges from one to two, or at most, three paragraphs. Conclusions are rarely longer than one paragraph. The body of the essay is thus the longest section of any paper. It is difficult, even impossible, to write an introduction or a conclusion until you know what it is that you are introducing or ending. Therefore, the place to begin with most essays is the middle. Always keep in mind your working thesis to ensure that you have a controlling idea. This idea will help you decide how to structure the body of your paper and what information is relevant.

The following organizational strategies suggest ways in which the middle of your paper might be arranged.

| Strategy | Typical Body Arrangement |
|---|---|
| Narration | To tell a story or narrate an event or action |
| | • Chronological, from first to last |
| | • Flashbacks to rearrange time |
| Description | To record sense impressions |
| | • Visual, from side to side, front to back |
| | • Most obvious or important to least |

| | |
|---|---|
| **Division** | To break a whole into its component parts |
| | • Largest to smallest |
| | • Most important to least |
| **Classification** | To place similar items in categories or groups |
| | • Largest to smallest |
| | • Most important to least |
| **Comparison** | To find similarities between two or more items |
| | • Compare subject-by-subject (all of A to all of B) |
| | • Compare point-by-point (A point 1 to B point 1) |
| **Contrast** | To find difference between two or more items |
| | • Contrast subject-by-subject (all of A to all of B) |
| | • Contrast point-by-point (A point 1 to B point 1) |
| **Process** | To tell how to do something |
| | • First step, next step |
| | • Chronological order |
| **Cause and Effect** | To explain what caused something or what the effects of that something are |
| | • Forward and backward, lineal order |
| | • Causes or effects arranged in order of time or importance |
| **Definition** | To offer an explanation of a word, concept, or event |
| | • Item placed in a class and added distinguishing features |
| | • Extended examples, explanation of how item works, comparison to something familiar |
| **Argumentation** | To offer logical reasons for a particular course of action or conclusion |
| | • Inductive |
| | • Deductive |
| **Persuasion** | To offer emotional reasons for a particular course of action or conclusion |
| | • Strongest to weakest |
| | • Weakest to strongest |

**How Do You Write an Introduction?**   Do you always finish everything you start to read? Every newspaper or magazine article? Every piece of mail? Every book? The truth is readers are far more likely to stop reading than they are to continue. You stop because you get distracted; you stop because you are bored by the subject or already know the information; you stop because you completely disagree with what the author is saying. Only in school, where you must read what is assigned to prepare for examinations, do you force yourself to keep going. Only in school do you have a reader who will read every word that you write—a teacher.

As a writer, remember that your readers are more likely to quit reading than to continue. No one thing is the key to keeping a reader interested. All the elements of good writing contribute: an interesting subject, valuable and accurate information, insightful analyses, clear organization, grammatically correct and varied sentences, careful proofreading. Beginnings of essays are, however, especially important. Every paper needs a strong, effective introduction that will catch readers' attention and pull them in. Introductions are typically divided into two categories, reflecting the two goals that every introduction should have:

**Hook**—intended to "hook" readers and "pull" them into the body of the paper
**Thesis**—intended to state clearly and concisely the thesis or controlling idea of the paper

Introductions vary in length depending on the length of the paper that follows. They can be a single paragraph long or several paragraphs long. An effective introduction can consist of a hook and a thesis. Perhaps the first sentence, or even paragraph, is a hook; the later sentences or the last paragraph in the introduction might be the thesis. Note the fundamental differences between the two types in these examples from student essays.

The *hook introduction* is from an essay that contrasts two different search strategies to be used in a library's online catalog (Chapter 5). It appeals to the reader's self-interest and arouses curiosity: most of us probably never realized that more than one approach is necessary to locate books on any particular subject.

**Hook**    The Cecil College Library has twenty books dealing with the death penalty, but unless you pay attention to the next couple of pages, you will never find all of them. Why? Because no single search strategy will lead you to all twenty books.

The *thesis introduction* is from an essay on the American "hobo" (Chapter 4), which explains where the term came from and what the factors were in American society that led to the creation of this huge group of people. The paragraph does not start with a vivid example or a startling statistic; instead, it gets right to the thesis.

**Thesis**    Although homelessness and vagrancy might seem to be a distinctively modern phenomenon, the problem is probably less acute today (in terms of percentage of our total population) than it was at the turn of the twentieth century. At that time, a series of factors combined to create a large migratory population comprised almost exclusively of young males.

Your introduction is an extremely important part of your paper. Spend time in planning and polishing it. For specific suggestions on types of introductions, check the Glossary and Ready Reference at the back of this text.

**How Do You Write a Conclusion?**    Generally the conclusion is the last thing you write in a paper. Because it comes last and your time may be running short, a conclusion often gets the least amount of attention. You might revise your introduction a couple of times, trying to get it to reflect what is happening in the middle of your paper, but you may only have time to write one draft of your conclusion. (That happens to professional writers as well—see Nora Ephron's "Revision and Life" in Chapter 6.) Worse yet, sometimes the paper comes to an abrupt stop instead of achieving a sense of an ending, a closure.

The introduction is the first impression that a reader gets of your paper, and the conclusion is the last impression. Every paper should have a planned conclusion. Do not just stop.

Conclusions can employ a variety of strategies depending on the length and nature of the paper. Typically conclusions use one of three general strategies:

| Purpose | Types of conclusions |
| --- | --- |
| Entertain | End with the climatic moment or realization: the "end" of the story, the reason for telling the story or for describing something |
| Inform | End with a summary of the key points |
| Argue/Persuade | End with a call to action or for agreement on an issue |

Langston Hughes in the narrative "Salvation" (Chapter 2) recounts an experience he had at a church revival meeting when he was twelve. The narrative ends at a climatic moment, the "last moment" in the story. Hughes concludes by reflecting on the significance of that experience on the rest of his life:

> That night, for the last time in my life but one—I was a big boy twelve years old—I cried, I cried, in bed alone, and couldn't stop. I buried my head under the quilts, but my aunt heard me. She woke up and told my uncle I was crying because the Holy Ghost had come into my life, and because I had seen Jesus. But I was really crying because I couldn't bear to tell her that I had lied, that I had deceived everybody in the church, that I hadn't seen Jesus, and that now I didn't believe there was a Jesus any more, since he didn't come to help me.

David Bodanis in "What's in Your Toothpaste" (Chapter 4), a humorous, informational essay that identifies the ingredients in a typical tube of toothpaste, ends with a summary of the ingredients:

> So it's chalk, water, paint, seaweed, antifreeze, paraffin oil, detergent, peppermint, formaldehyde, and fluoride (which can go some way towards preserving children's teeth)—that's the usual mixture raised to the mouth on the toothbrush for a fresh morning's clean. If it sounds too unfortunate, take heart. Studies show that thoroughly brushing with just plain water will often do as good a job.

Joshua Ortega in "Water Wars" (Chapter 9) argues that access to water is the most important issue many people will face in their lifetimes. It is an issue, however, that we probably do not think much about as we buy bottles of water on the way to class or work. Since the essay is long, Ortega's conclusion is actually three paragraphs. Notice how he suggests what we might change in our own habits to make a difference and what courses of public action we might take, and then how he closes with an emotional appeal to our patriotism:

> Thankfully, there are solutions to the problem. The simplest way to start making a difference is to choose tap water over bottled. If the taste of your local water is unappealing, buy a filter for your tap, or invest the money you would spend on bottled water into public infrastructure or watershed protection. Nothing speaks louder than where you spend your dollar. Bottled water will only be produced if there is a demand for it.

If you want to do more than that, then tell your representatives that you will not accept the selling of American water to foreign, multinational or corporate interests. Support public-sector projects and programs that encourage and create long-term, sustainable water solutions. Get involved with groups such as The Blue Planet Project (www.blueplanetproject.net), which is actively finding ways to solve the world's looming water crisis.

And above all else, remember that it is not too late. Clean, affordable water is still a reality in this country. It is our patriotic duty as Americans to ensure that it stays that way.

Plan a conclusion to your essay; try out different strategies. For additional advice on writing conclusions, consult the Glossary and Ready Reference at the back of this text.

## How Do You Check the Structure of Your Paper?

The body of your essay needs to be organized coherently and logically. Organize in units that are phrased in parallel form and in a hierarchical structure in which paragraphs and sentences are related either coordinately or subordinately. To be coordinate means to be on the same level of hierarchy and to be phrased in parallel form. To be subordinate means to stem from the idea or point immediately above.

The logical structure of your essay can be checked in several ways, but one of the easiest is to construct an outline. An outline is a visual display in which paragraphs and sentences are arranged on levels that reveal the relationships among them. The basic idea is to display the coordinate (equal) and the subordinate (unequal) structures. An abbreviated model looks something like this:

**A.** Topic sentence for Paragraph 1 (which is coordinate and equal to B)
  **1.** Support/detail (subordinate to A but coordinate to 2 and 3)
  **2.** Support/detail
  **3.** Support/detail
**B.** Topic sentence for Paragraph 2

The full form of an outline consists of coordinate and subordinate items that are labeled using Roman numerals (I, II, II), alphabet letters (A, a), and Arabic numbers (1, 2). Word processing software can automatically create outlines for you.

  **I.**
     **A.**
        **1.**
           **a.**
              **(1).**
                 **(a).**

Sometimes teachers and textbooks tell you to outline your paper before you begin drafting. It is a rare writer who can do so. Nevertheless, it is helpful if, as you draft your paper, you jot down each new idea and paragraph in a rough outline form to see if it fits in the evolving structure of the paper. An outline will reveal problems with the structure of both the paper as a whole and with individual paragraphs.

## SOME THINGS TO REMEMBER ABOUT WRITING A DRAFT

1.  Do not start writing before you have spent some time studying the assigned topic or defining a topic of your choice.

2.  Think about the number of pages you are to write. Is this a three- to four-page essay or a fifteen-page research paper? Can you write about this subject in that amount of space? You might need either to narrow your subject or make it larger.

3.  Plan a timeline for writing the paper. Allow sufficient time to move through the prewriting and writing stages. Try to avoid starting a paper the night before it is due. Ideally, try to have it finished at least a day early so that you will have time to revise it.

4.  Locate or create key words in the topic. What is it that you are to do? Key words are verbs such as *narrate, describe, explain, compare, contrast, analyze, argue.*

5.  Consider what those key words imply about the structure of your essay. How will the body of your essay be structured?

6.  Define a thesis or key idea for your paper. Write it out in a sentence and keep it before you as you begin to draft.

7.  Define your audience. How much do they already know about the subject? What will be the appropriate level of detail or explanation that you will need to provide?

8.  Gather information before you start to write. Once you begin writing, you may need to gather more, but do not start writing without having a sense of what will go into your paper.

9.  Plan a structure for the body of your essay. Try to outline it as you write to make sure that it is logically structured and developed.

10. Write an introduction for your essay. If you start by writing an introduction before you write the body of the paper, go back once you have a complete draft and see if the introduction needs to be sharpened or focused.

11. Allow time to write an effective conclusion for your paper. Do not just stop. Find a way to signal to your reader that the paper has closure.

12. Make sure that your essay has a real title. No paper should ever be titled "Essay 1" or "Persuasive Essay."

# HOW TO

# REVISE AN ESSAY

## Revising the Essay

### 🔑 ❓ KEY QUESTIONS

What does revising mean?

What are the steps in revising?

*Begin with the larger issues*
*Focus on paragraphing*
*Re-see sentences and word choices*

What is a revision log, and why is it important?

Why should you get help from your peers?

*Peer editing*
*Group editing*

What can you expect from a writing center or writing tutor?

How should you prepare for a conference with your instructor?

Why is proofreading important?

Is an error-free paper an "A" paper?

**Some Things to Remember About Revising**

The idea of revising an essay may not sound appealing at all. By the time you have finished a draft, often the last thing you want to do is revise it. Nevertheless, revising is a crucial step in the writing process, one you cannot afford to skip. Not even the best professional writers produce only perfect sentences and paragraphs. Effective writing almost always results from rewriting and revising.

## What Does Revising Mean?

The word *revision* literally means "to see again." You do not revise a paper just by proofreading it for mechanical and grammatical errors, although that is the expected final step in the writing process. A revision is a reseeing of what you have written. In its broadest sense, reseeing is a complete rethinking of a paper from idea through execution.

Revision takes place after a draft of the whole paper or a part of it has been completed. Ideally, you revise after a period of time has elapsed and you have had a chance to get advice or criticism on what you wrote. Revision is quite different from proofreading. When you proofread, you are mostly looking for small things such as misspellings or typographical errors, incorrect punctuation, awkwardly constructed sentences, undeveloped paragraphs. In a revision, on the other hand, you look at everything: from the larger issues (subject, thesis, purpose, audience), to the structure of paragraphs and sentences, and to smaller issues such as word choices and the paper's title. Everything in a paper should be scrutinized actively and carefully.

Revising does not occur only after a complete draft. In fact, many writers revise as they draft. They might write a sentence, then stop to change its structure, even erase it and start over; they might shift the order of sentences and paragraphs or even delete them altogether. In their search for the right words, the graceful sentence, and the clear paragraph, writers revise constantly. The revising that writers do while composing usually focuses on the sentence or paragraph being composed.

When you are struggling to find the right word or the right sentence structure, you are probably not thinking much about the larger whole. Consequently, allowing time to elapse between drafts of your paper is important. You need to put the completed draft aside for a while so that you gain perspective on what you have written and read your paper objectively. Try to finish a complete draft at least one day before you hand in the paper. If circumstances prevent you from finishing a paper until an hour or two before class, you will not have a chance to revise. You will only be able to proofread.

## What Are the Steps in Revising?

**Begin with the Larger Issues**   The key to improving your writing is self-awareness. You have to look carefully and critically at what you have written, focus on areas that caused you the most problems, and work to correct the problem areas. Most writers can identify the key problems they faced in a particular paper or in writing in general, even though they might not know how to solve those problems. Knowing what causes your problems is the essential first step toward solving them.

When you analyze the first draft of an essay, begin by asking a series of specific questions. Start with the larger issues and work toward the smaller ones. Ideally, you should write out your answers because doing so forces you to have a specific response.

| | |
|---|---|
| **Length** | **Is your paper long enough?** The specified length of a paper suggests the amount of space that you will need to develop and illustrate your thesis sufficiently. If your papers are consistently short, you have probably not included enough examples or illustrating details. |

**Is your paper too long?** If your papers consistently exceed your instructor's guidelines, you have probably not sufficiently narrowed your subject or you have included too many details and examples. Of the material available to support, develop, and illustrate a thesis, some is more significant and relevant than the rest. Never try to include everything; rather, select the best, the most appropriate, and the most convincing.

**Purpose**    **Did you do what the assignment asked?** Look again at the assignment and circle the key words, verbs such as *analyze, argue, classify, compare, criticize, define, evaluate, narrate, describe, summarize,* and *recommend.* Such words tell you what your purpose should have been. Is that purpose clear in your paper?

**Thesis**    **What is the thesis of your paper?** Can you find a single sentence in your paper that states the position you have taken on your subject? If so, underline it. If not, write a one-sentence thesis statement. If you are unsure about what a thesis is, review the material in the Glossary and Ready Reference at the back of this text.

**Structure**    **Does your paper have a clear structure that is visible in how you paragraphed your paper?** Your paper must have a beginning (introduction), a middle (a series of body paragraphs), and an ending (conclusion). The introduction states the subject and thesis of the paper and tries to catch the reader's interest. The middle, or body, of the paper needs to have a coherent, logical structure that is revealed by how this section is paragraphed. The conclusion must bring a sense of an ending to the reader. Endings typically summarize, reinforce the thesis, or appeal to the reader to do something. A paper should never just stop.

**Audience**    **To whom are you writing?** In one sense, your answer is always your instructor. If class members share papers electronically or swap and critique papers in class, your peer readers are an important source of feedback. Did the assigned topic define an audience for the paper: peers, people who need this information, people trying to make some decisions? What does your audience already know about this subject? How much previous knowledge or experience do you assume your audience will have?

**Sources**    **What types of information were you to use in the paper?** Personal experiences or observations? Your own opinions? Factual information that you found in online or printed sources? Did you gather what you needed?

Always start by reseeing the larger issues. If your essay has serious problems with these larger issues, you will need to rethink what you have written. Cleaning up grammatical and writing errors will not "save" a paper that does not fulfill the assignment, lacks a thesis, has an unclear purpose, or ignores its audience.

**Focus on Paragraphing**   You can check the structure of your essay by first looking at how you have paragraphed it. Remember, paragraphs reveal the structure of a paper and provide readers with places at which to rest. If you have only several paragraphs in a three-page essay, you have not clearly indicated the structure of your essay to your reader, or you have not developed a clear, logical organization. Likewise, a paper full of very short paragraphs probably is poorly developed. You might be shifting ideas too quickly, failing to provide supporting evidence and details. A good paragraph is meaty; a good essay is not a string of undeveloped ideas and bare generalizations.

A useful analytical tool for checking structure is outlining the body of the paper. An outline reveals main points and relationships among those points. Ideas, as an outline reveals, are either coordinate (equal) or subordinate (unequal). Outlining was discussed earlier in How to Write an Essay.

| | |
|---|---|
| **Paragraph structure** | **Is each paragraph structured around a single idea?** Is there an explicit statement of that idea— often called a *topic sentence*? If so, underline it. If not, jot down in the margin the key word or words in that paragraph. Consider adding a sentence that states what that paragraph is about. Typically, such a sentence appears early in the paragraph as either the first sentence or the second sentence if the first sentence serves as a transition from the material in the previous paragraph. |
| **Paragraph development** | **Are the paragraphs in the body of the paper well developed with a series of details, support, and examples?** Outline each paragraph to reveal the coordinate and subordinate pattern. Does the outline reveal anything that is out of place? |
| **Introduction** | **Does the introduction indicate both the subject and thesis of the paper? Does it attempt to catch its reader's interest?** Remember that an introduction can be more than one paragraph, especially in a longer essay. The first paragraph might "hook" the reader; the second might contain the thesis statement. Check to see if your introduction is proportional to the rest of the paper; for example, a three-page paper should not have a one-page introduction. For suggestions, consult How to Write an Essay and the Glossary and Ready Reference at the back of this text. |
| **Conclusion** | **Does the paper really have a conclusion or did you just stop?** Conclusions are sometimes difficult to write because they are written last when time is often short. For suggestions, consult How to Write an Essay and the Glossary and Ready Reference at the back of this text. |
| **Transitions** | **Does the paper help the reader see transitions between ideas, sentences, and paragraphs?** If a |

paper is logically structured, it will have coherence. Nevertheless, the use of transitional expressions and transitional sentences will help your reader by providing signposts that direct the reader from one point to another. Such devices promote unity and coherence between paragraphs. For suggestions, consult the Glossary and Ready Reference at the back of this text.

**Title**

**Does the paper have a "real" title?** Every essay needs a title, not a descriptive phrase like "Essay 1" or "Argument Paper." An interesting, descriptive title is part of the attraction for readers. After all, no company ever sold its product with no name on the box or with a title like "Cereal" or "Automobile." Brainstorm some ideas; check them out with potential readers and ask for suggestions. For help with titles, consult the Glossary and Ready Reference at the back of this text.

**Re-See Sentences and Word Choices**    Only after you have asked and answered questions about the larger elements of your essay should you consider questions dealing with style, grammar, and mechanics.

**Sentence or fragment**

**Is everything that you punctuated as a sentence— that is, with a beginning capital letter and an end mark such as a period—really a complete sentence?** Are any just fragments? If you are not sure of the difference, check the Glossary and Ready Reference at the back of this text. Fragments are acceptable in certain writing situations; if you are intentionally using a fragment for effect, check with your instructor first.

**Sentence variety**

**Have you used a variety of sentence types and lengths?** Check the Glossary and Ready Reference for an explanation. Ideally, your paper should have a mix of sentence types and a variety of lengths. Be particularly careful that you do not write strings of very short, simple sentences. They will make you sound either like a young, immature writer or like a writer addressing an elementary school audience.

**Punctuation**

**Is every mark of punctuation used correctly?** Check each mark. Is it the right choice for this place in the sentence? Every mark of punctuation has certain conditions under which it is used. A quick review of the major uses of each punctuation mark can be found in the Glossary and Ready Reference.

**Misspellings**

**Is every word spelled correctly?** Pronunciations and spellings do not always agree. Word processing software will not pick up every misspelling. If you are uncertain about any word, or if you know that you have trouble with spelling, check the words about which you are uncertain in a dictionary.

| | |
|---|---|
| **Wrong words** | **Are you certain what each word means?** Do you know the difference between *then* and *than*, *effect* and *affect*, *there*, *their*, *they're*? |
| **Diction** | **Are there any words or expressions that might be too informal or too colloquial?** These are words you might use in conversation with friends but not in academic writing. If you are using technical words, can you assume that your reader will know what they mean? The Glossary and Ready Reference provides some guidelines for problems with diction. |

## What Is a Revision Log, and Why Is It Important?

Keeping a log of writing problems you most often encounter is an excellent way of promoting self-awareness. Your log should include a wide range of writing problems, not just grammatical and mechanical errors. The log will help you keep track of the areas with which you know you have trouble and those that your instructor, peer readers, or writing tutors point out as needing improvement. Do you have a tendency to overparagraph? To stop rather than conclude? Do you have trouble with subject-verb agreement or with parallel structures? Do you keep misusing *then* and *than*? Each time you discover a problem or one is pointed out to you, list it in your log. Then, as you revise a paper, look back through your log to remind yourself of frequent problems and look closely for them in your current draft.

If a revision log seems like a lot of trouble, remember, only you can improve your writing. Improvement in writing, like improvement in any skill area, comes with recognizing problems that need attention and working to correct them.

## Why Should You Get Help from Your Peers?

Most of the writing you do in college is aimed toward only one reader—your instructor. Writing just for an instructor has both advantages and disadvantages. A teacher is a critical reader who evaluates your paper by a set of standards, but a teacher is also a sympathetic reader, one who understands the difficulties of writing and is patient with problems writers have. Classmates, colleagues, and supervisors can be as critical as teachers, but less sympathetic.

Only in school do you have someone who will read everything you write and offer constructive criticism. After you graduate, your letters and reports will be read by many different readers, but you will no longer have a teacher to offer advice or a tutor to meet in conference with you. Instead, you will have to rely on your own analysis of your writing and on the advice of fellow workers. For these reasons, learning to use a peer reader as a resource in your revising process is extremely important. At first you might feel uncomfortable asking someone other than your instructor to read your papers, but after some experience, you will likely feel more relaxed about sharing. Remember, every reader is potentially a valuable resource for suggestions.

Often it is difficult to accept criticism, but if you want to improve your writing skills, you need someone to say, "Why not do this?" After all, you expect an athletic coach or a music teacher to offer criticism. Your writing instructor and other readers play the same role. The advice and criticism they offer is meant to make your writing more effective; it is not intended as personal criticism of you or your abilities.

**Peer Editing**   Many college writing courses include peer editing as a regular classroom activity. On a peer editing day, students swap papers and critique one another's work, typically using a list of peer editing guidelines. You don't have to do peer editing in class to get the benefits of such an activity. If your instructor approves, arrange to swap papers with a classmate outside of class, or ask a roommate or a friend to do a peer reading for you. If your class posts drafts and papers online, you have easy access to what others have written.

Regardless of how peer editings are arranged, several ground rules are important. First, remember that when you ask a peer to edit your paper, you are asking for advice and criticism. You cannot expect that your reader will love everything you have written. Second, peer editing is not proofreading. You should not ask your reader to look for misspelled words and missing commas. Rather, encourage your reader to react to the whole paper; keep your reader's attention focused on significant issues. Give your reader a checklist—a set of questions that reflect the criteria appropriate for evaluating this kind of paper. Third, you want a peer reader to offer specific and constructive criticism. To get that type of response, you need to ask questions that invite, or even require, a reader to comment in more than yes and no answers. For example, do not ask your reader, "Is the thesis clear?"; instead ask, "What is the thesis of this paper?" If your reader has trouble answering that question, or if the answer differs from your own, you know that this aspect of your paper needs more work.

---

 **CHECKLIST OF WHAT TO ASK FOR IN PEER EDITING**

1. Does the paper meet the requirements of the assignment?
2. Does it have a clearly stated thesis?
3. Does it have a clear organization reflected in how it is paragraphed?
4. Is the content interesting? Clear? Informative? Persuasive?
5. Does it have an effective introduction? A conclusion?
6. How effective is the title of the paper?

---

**Group Editing**   Sharing your writing in a small group is another way to seek reader reaction. Such an editing activity can take place either inside or outside of the classroom. In either case, you can prepare for a group editing session in the same way. Plan to form a group of four or five students, and make a copy of your paper for each group member. If possible, distribute the copies or e-mail them before the group editing session so that each member has a chance to read and prepare comments for the discussion. Then follow these guidelines:

*Before the group editing session*

1. Read each paper carefully, marking or underlining the writer's main idea and key supporting points. Make any other notes about the paper that seem appropriate.
2. On a separate sheet, comment specifically on one or two aspects of the paper that most need improvement.

*At the group editing session*

1. When it is your turn, read your paper aloud to the group. You might become aware of problems as you read, so keep a pen or pencil handy to jot down notes.
2. When you are finished, tell the group members what you would like them to comment on.
3. Listen to their remarks and make notes. Feel free to ask members to explain or expand on their observations. Remember, you want as much advice as you can get.
4. Collect the copies of your paper and the sheets on which group members commented on specific areas that need improvement.

*After the group editing session*

1. Carefully consider both the oral and written comments of your group. You may not agree with everything that was said, but you need to weigh each comment. If the group members agree in a criticism, they are right, whether you agree with them or not.
2. Revise your paper. Remember that you are responsible for your own work. No one else—not your instructor, your peer editors, or your group readers—can or should tell you everything that you need to change.

---

✓ **CHECKLIST OF WHAT TO EXPECT IN GROUP EDITING**

1. Make sure everyone has a copy of your paper in advance.
2. Ask specific questions of the group.
3. Listen to what people say about your paper and take notes.
4. Collect the written comments of other group members.
5. Carefully consider every suggestion.
6. Remember that you have obligations to help others in the same way.

---

## What Can You Expect from a Writing Center or Writing Tutor?

Most colleges operate writing centers, writing labs, or writing tutor programs. Their purpose is to provide individual assistance to any student who has a question about a paper. They are staffed by trained tutors who want to help. In part, such services are intended to supplement the instruction that students receive in a writing class. Most writing teachers have too many students to be able to offer extensive help outside of class to everyone. These services also exist to provide advice to students who are writing papers for courses in disciplines where writing might be required but not discussed.

If you are having trouble with grammar or mechanics, if you consistently have problems with beginnings or middles or ends of papers, if you are baffled by a particular assignment, do not be afraid to ask for help. Every writer can benefit from constructive advice or additional explanations, and writing centers and tutors exist to provide that help. Remember, though, that a writing tutor's job is to explain and to instruct. You do not drop your paper off at a writing center like you drop your automobile off at a garage. Your tutor will suggest ways that you can improve your paper or follow a particular convention. A tutor will not do the work for you.

Come to your appointment with a specific set of questions or problems. Why are you there? What do you want help with? What are the problem areas in your paper? What don't you understand about your instructor's comments? When you have a medical problem, you make an appointment with a medical professional to discuss a particular set of symptoms. A conference with a tutor should work in the same way.

Finally, keep some form of written record of your conference. Jot down what the tutor suggested or explained. Those notes will serve as a valuable reminder of what to do when you are revising a paper.

---

✓  **CHECKLIST OF HOW TO PREPARE FOR AND USE HELP FROM A TUTOR**

1.  Have a list of specific questions or problems.
2.  Ask for explanations of grammatical or mechanical problems.
3.  Take notes on what is said.
4.  Do not expect the tutor to "correct" your paper for you.

---

## How Should You Prepare for a Conference with Your Instructor?

Your instructor in a writing class is always willing to talk with you about your writing. You can, of course, visit your instructor during scheduled office hours. In addition, many instructors, if their teaching schedules permit it, schedule a set of regular conference times spaced throughout the term or semester. Whatever the arrangement, a conference is an opportunity for you to ask questions about your writing in general or about a particular paper or problem.

Whether you have asked for the conference or the instructor has scheduled it as part of class requirements, several ground rules apply. As with a tutoring session, you should always come to a conference with a definite agenda and a specific set of questions. Writing these questions out is an excellent way to prepare for a conference. Generally, conferences are dialogues, so your active participation is expected. Do not be surprised, for example, if your instructor begins by asking you what you want to talk about. As time is always limited (remember your instructor might have to see dozens of students), you will not be able to ask about everything. Try to concentrate on the issues that trouble you the most.

Instructors consider conferences opportunities to discuss the larger issues of a paper: Is the thesis well defined? Is the structure as clear as it might be? Are there adequate transitions? Although your instructor may politely explain a troublesome grammatical or mechanical problem, do not expect the instructor to find and fix every mistake in your paper. A conference is not a proofreading session.

A conference is also not an oral grading of your paper. Grading a paper is a complicated task, one that frequently involves evaluating your essay in the context of the other papers from the class. As a result, your instructor cannot make a quick judgment. Do not ask about a grade.

As the conference proceeds, take notes about what is said. Do not rely on your memory. Those notes will constitute a plan for revising your paper.

---

✔ **CHECKLIST OF HOW TO PREPARE FOR AND USE A CONFERENCE WITH YOUR INSTRUCTOR**

1. Be prepared to identify what *you* want to talk about.
2. Make a list of questions to ask.
3. Take specific notes on what you need to do.
4. Do not expect your teacher to identify every problem.
5. Do not ask for a grade on the paper.

---

## Why Is Proofreading Important?

Everyone has had the comment "proofread!" written on a paper. The process of proofreading comes from printing terminology: a printer reads and corrects "proofs"—trial impressions made of pages of set type—before printing the job. You probably stared in dismay at obvious slips that somehow managed to escape your eye. Did you wonder why you were penalized for what were obviously just careless mistakes? Think about this question: Why do businesses and industries spend so much money making sure that their final written products are as free from errors as possible?

The answer focuses on audience perception of the writer (or the business). If a paper, letter, report, or advertisement contains even minor mistakes, these errors act as a form of "static" that interferes with the communication process. The reader's attention shifts away from the message to fundamental questions about the writer. A reader might wonder why you, the writer, did not have enough pride in your work to check it before handing it in. Even worse, a reader might question your basic competence as a writer and researcher. As the number of errors in proportion to the number of words rises, the reader's distraction grows. In college, such static can have serious consequences. Studies in New York city colleges, for example, revealed that readers would tolerate on average only five to six basic errors in a three-hundred-word passage before assigning a student to a remedial writing course. Careless mistakes are rhetorically damaging to you as a writer; they undermine your voice and authority.

After you have revised your paper thoroughly, you are ready for a final proofreading. The secret of proofreading is to read each word as you have written it. If you read too quickly, your mind corrects or skips over problems. Force yourself to read each word by moving a ruler or a piece of paper slowly down the page. Read aloud. When you combine looking at the page slowly with listening to the words, you increase your chances of catching mistakes that are visual (such as misspellings) and those that are aural (such as awkward constructions).

Misspellings are so common that they need special attention. Everyone misspells some words; even the most experienced writer, teacher, or editor has to check a dictionary for correct spelling of certain words. English is a particularly tricky language, for words are not always spelled the way in which they are pronounced. English has silent *e*'s as in *live*; *ph*'s and *gh*'s that sound like *f*'s as in *phone* and *tough*; silent *ough*'s and *gh*'s as in *through* and *bright*. It is easy to get confused about when to double consonants before adding *-ed* to the end of a word or when to drop the final *e* before adding *-able*. All of these difficulties are common. No one expects you to remember how to spell every word in your speaking vocabulary, but people do expect that you will check your writing for misspelled words.

Most misspellings can be eliminated if you do two things. First, recognize the kinds of words that you are likely to misspell. Do not assume that you know how to spell words that sound alike, such as *there* and *their* and *its* and *it's*. Second, once you have finished your paper, go back and check your spelling. Do not rely on your computer to catch everything: it will not tell you that you used *there* instead of *their*. Keep a dictionary handy and use it. If you know that you have a tendency to misspell words, look up every word that might be a problem.

---

✓ **CHECKLIST OF WHAT TO LOOK FOR WHEN PROOFREADING**

1.  Read each word of your paper aloud.
2.  Listen for awkward phrasing or passages that are difficult to read aloud.
3.  Check the spelling and meaning of words about which you are uncertain in a dictionary.
4.  Scrutinize each mark of punctuation. Is it used correctly?
5.  Watch for typographical errors where a letter is deleted or letters are transposed.
6.  Make sure your paper has a real title.

---

## Is an Error-Free Paper an "A" Paper?

Although good, effective writing is mechanically and grammatically correct, you cannot reverse the equation. It is certainly possible to write a paper that has no "errors" but is still a poor paper. An effective paper fulfills the requirements of the assignment, has something interesting or meaningful to say, and provides specific evidence and examples rather than vague generalizations. Effective writing is a combination of many factors: appropriate content, focused purpose, clear organization, and fluent expression.

Although perfect grammar and mechanics do not make a perfect paper, such things are important. Minor errors are like static in your writing. Too many of them distract your reader and focus the reader's attention on your apparent carelessness instead of on your message. Minor errors can undermine your reader's confidence in you as a qualified authority. If you made errors in spelling or punctuation, for example, your reader might assume that you made similar errors in reporting information. So while revision is not just proofreading, proofreading should be a part of the revision process.

## SOME THINGS TO REMEMBER ABOUT REVISING

1. Put your paper aside for a period of time before you attempt to revise it.

2. Seek the advice of your instructor or a writing center tutor or the help of classmates.

3. Reconsider your choice of topic. Were you able to treat it adequately in the space you had available?

4. State your thesis in a sentence as a way of checking your content. Is everything in the paper relevant to that thesis?

5. Check to make sure you have given enough examples to clarify your topic, to support your argument, or to make your thesis clear. Relevant specifics convince and interest a reader.

6. Look through the advice given in each of the introductions to this text. (How to Read an Essay, How to Write an Essay, How to Revise an Essay.) Have you organized your paper carefully? Is its structure clear?

7. Define your audience. To whom are you writing? What assumptions have you made about your audience? What changes are necessary to make your paper clear and interesting to that audience?

8. Check the guidelines your instructor provided. Have you done what was asked? Is your paper too short or too long?

9. Examine each sentence to make sure that it is complete and grammatically correct. Try for a variety of sentence structures and lengths.

10. Look carefully at each paragraph. Does it obey the rules for effective paragraph construction? Do your paragraphs clearly indicate the structure of your essay?

11. Check your word choice. Have you avoided slang, jargon, and clichés? Have you used specific words? Have you used appropriate words for your intended audience?

12. Proofread one final time.

# WRITERS AT WORK

When you have the time in which to plan, draft, and then revise an essay, the result will be considerably better than when you start and finish a paper the night before it is due. The key is time—you need to begin planning and gathering information before you put words on paper or screen; you need to allow some time between your first draft and the final; you need to ask other writers to respond to your drafts. This process of prewriting, writing a draft, and then revising can be seen in the work of the two writers reproduced here. Tina Burton is a student writer producing a paper for a course; Gordon Grice is a professional writer who worked on his essay intermittently for over two years. Despite those differences, both essays show how the writing process ideally works.

# A STUDENT WRITER: TINA BURTON'S "THE WATERMELON WOOER"

## Prewriting: Finding a Topic and Gathering Information

Tina's essay was written in response to a totally open assignment: she was asked to write an essay using examples. The paper was due in three weeks. The openness of the assignment proved initially frustrating to Tina. When she first began work on the essay, she started with a completely different topic than the one she eventually decided on.

On the weekend after she received the assignment, she went home to visit her parents. Her grandfather had died a few months before, and the family was sorting through some photographs and reminiscing about him. Suddenly she had the idea she wanted. She would write about her grandfather and

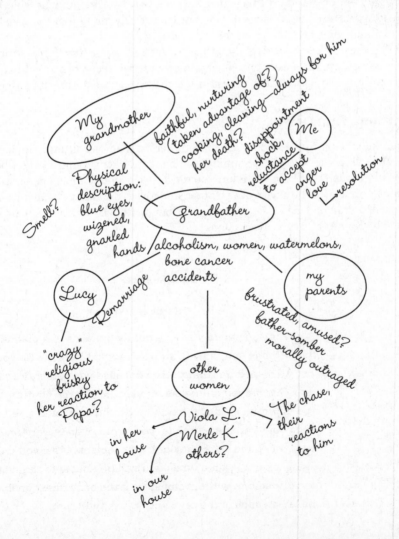

her ambivalent feelings toward him. Once she had settled on this specific topic, she also determined her purpose (to inform readers about her grandfather and her mixed feelings, as well as to entertain through a vivid description of this unusual old man) and her audience (her instructor and peers). When Tina filled out answers to the questions her instructor had posed, she noted:

> **Subject:** My grandfather, a character sketch
>
> **Topic:** My ambivalent feelings about my grandfather—love and embarrassment
>
> **Purpose:** To inform my reader and to entertain
>
> **Audience:** My peers—we all have grandparents, and we often have ambivalent feelings toward them

Tina's first written work on the assignment was a list of about thirty things that she remembered about her grandfather. "The list had to be cut," Tina said, "so I marked off things that were too bawdy or too unbelievable. I wanted to portray him as sympathetic, but I was really afraid that the whole piece would come off as too sentimental or drippy."

At the next class meeting, the instructor set aside some time for prewriting activities. Students were encouraged to try either a freewriting or a brainstorming exercise. Tina did the brainstorming that appears on the previous page.

## Drafting: First Draft

From here, Tina wrote a complete draft of her essay in one sitting. She had the most difficulty with the beginning of the essay. "I kept trying to describe him, but I found that I was including too much," she commented. "The breakthrough came with the advice of two other students in the class. The first page of the first draft of Tina's essay follows. The handwritten comments were provided by Kathrine Varnes, a classmate.

EARLIER DRAFT

The Watermelon Wooer

When someone you love dearly behaves in a manner that offends you, do you stop loving that person? Do you lose all respect for that person because you cannot forget the act (that you judged as repulsive?) (On the contrary), *repulsive [?]* *Eventually?* you might (eventually) fondly recall the once offensive behavior. (Perhaps,) In time, you might even understand why you found the behavior loathesome. Maybe, you will *so?* reach a point in time when you will be unable to think of your loved one without thinking of the once questionable behavior. Such is the case with my grandfather.

*\*I have a personal dislike for this 3-word transition*

*some way to condense?*

Before I tell the story of how my grandfather behaved in ways that I could neither understand nor tolerate, I must first (give some *introduce?* background information on) him. A wizened little man with dancing blue eyes and hands gnarled from years of carpentry work, "Papa" was a notorious womanizer and an alcoholic. Born and raised in Halifax County, Virginia, he spent most of his life building houses, distilling and selling corn liquor, and chasing women. After he and my grandmother had been married for thirty years or so, he decided to <u>curtail some of his wild behavior and treat her with more respect.</u> Actually, he remained faithful to her only after he discovered that she was ill and probably wouldn't be around to feed and nurture him for much longer. ~~So, as you can see,~~ <u>m</u> y grandfather (~~does~~ not) *didn't* have a <u>spotless</u>, or even a remotely commendable (record *reputation* of personal achievements.)

*both of these things? or respect by curtailing?*

*Use alternative diction to soften tone?*

## Revising: Second Draft

"Kathrine wanted me to condense and to find a way in which to jump right into the story," Tina noted. "She also said, 'You're trying to tell too much. Let the story tell itself. Try to think of one thing that might capture something essential or important about him.'" In a second peer edit, Tina sought the advice of Stephen Palley, another classmate. Stephen offered these comments on the first page of Tina's second draft.

### The Watermelon Wooer

*my grandfather never really (settled down)*
Let me tell you a story about my grandfather ~~and, I guess, me see. I don't pretend to know whether my story will shock, offend, amuse, or bore.~~ I only know that I feel the need to tell ~~the story~~ *it*.
*For a time he*                                                    *but eventually*
~~Before I tell the story of how my grandfather~~ behaved in ways that I could neither understand nor tolerate, I must *(I see him now)*          *Let me introduce*
first introduce him. A wizened little man with ~~dancing blue eyes~~ and hands ~~gnarled from years of carpentry work.~~
*smell?*
"Papa" was a notorious womanizer and an alcoholic. Born and raised in Halifax County, Virginia, he spent most of his life building houses, distilling and selling corn liquor, and chasing women. After he and my grandmother had been married for thirty years or so, he decided to show her some

*characterize an essential part of his eccentricity intro?*

*It's funny but when I think of my grandfather I think lst of the way he smelled*

*Miller, ponies, fertilizer*

respect by curtailing his wild behavior. Actually, he
remained faithful to her only after he discovered that she
was ill and probably wouldn't be around to feed and nurture
him for much longer. Papa didn't have a spotless reputation.

"Stephen offered me quite a few helpful suggestions," Tina recalled, "but he also suggested something that I just didn't quite feel comfortable with." As you can see in the revised draft. Tina had queried Stephen about including her memories of scent. In a conversation, Stephen urged Tina to substitute memories of smells for memories of sights. In the end, though, Tina observed, "I just couldn't do what Stephen suggested."

## Revising: Final Draft

Before the three weeks were over, Tina actually wrote five separate drafts of her essay. "Everything here is true," she said, "but I worried so much about what was included because I didn't want to embarrass anyone in my family."

"Throughout the process," she added, "I was also worried about my tone. I wanted it to be funny; I wanted my readers to like my grandfather and his watermelon adventures." As she moved toward her final draft, Tina was also able to write a thesis statement for her essay. Even though the essay is a humorous character sketch using narration and description, it still has a clearly stated thesis. Notice, however, that the thesis is placed not at the beginning of the essay but at the very end.

**Thesis:**   The acts that troubled me eventually allowed me to glimpse the frail side
of my grandfather, to see him as a human being possessed of fears and
flaws rather than a cardboard ideal.

Reproduced here is Tina's final draft of her essay.

The Watermelon Wooer

Tina M. Burton

I see him now, sprawled on our couch, clutching a frayed afghan, one
brown toenail escaping his sock. His darting eyes are betraying his withered
body.

Born and raised in backwoods Virginia, my grandfather spent most of
his life building houses, distilling and selling corn liquor, and chasing
women. After he and my grandmother had been married for thirty years or
so, he decided to show her some respect by curtailing his wild behavior.

Actually, he remained faithful to her only after he discovered that she was ill and probably wouldn't be around to feed and nurture him much longer. Papa didn't have a spotless reputation.

Because he'd been on the wagon for several years and hadn't had any affairs for the last ten years, my family thought that Papa would continue to behave in a "respectable" manner even after my grandmother died. I guess we were hoping for some sort of miracle. After my grandmother died in 1983, Papa became a rogue again: he insisted on reveling in wild abandon. When my father found out that Papa was drinking heavily again and crashing his car into mailboxes, houses, and other large obstacles, he asked Papa to move into our house. The fact that three of Papa's female neighbors had complained to the police about Papa's exposing himself probably had something to do with my father's decision.

The year that Papa lived with us rivaled the agony of Hell.

I was always Papa's favorite grandchild, his "gal," and I worshipped him from the time that I was old enough to spend summers with him on his farm. Until I saw him every day, witnessed for myself his sometimes lewd behavior and his odd personality quirks, I never really believed the stories about him that I had heard from my mother and father. Every morning, he baited my mother with comments like "the gravy's too thick," "my room's too cold," "your kids are too loud," and "the phone rings too often." Against my mother's wishes, he smoked in the house. In mixed company, he gleefully explained how to have sex in an inner tube in the ocean without getting caught and gave detailed physical descriptions of the women he'd had sex with. It surprised me how much my opinion of Papa changed in one year.

During this one year, Papa did many things that I thought were embarrassing and inexcusable. I came face-to-face with the "dark" side of his personality. One week after moving into my parents' home, Papa began to sneak the orange juice from the refrigerator and doctor it with Smirnoff's vodka. I knew he'd been pickling his brain with alcohol for years and that this was part of the disease, but he'd said that he'd gone dry. Besides, he was violating my father's most important rule: no alcohol in the house. I didn't know that his drinking was only the first of a long line of incredible acts.

The behaviors that ultimately endeared Papa to me, that made me forgive him his shortcomings, are also those which I recall with a great deal of sadness. These are the memories of him that I treasure, the stories that I will tell to my grandchildren when they are old enough to deal with graphic material. A year ago, I never would have believed that I could fondly remember, much less write about, these episodes.

For about a year, Papa engaged in what I refer to as the "watermelon affairs." Perhaps because he had lived on a vegetable farm for the majority of his life Papa had a special affinity for a wide variety of fruits and vegetables. Especially dear to him were watermelons. So, he assumed that other elderly people, particularly women, shared his proclivity for produce. One week after he moved into my parent's house, he embarked upon his mission—to woo with watermelons as many women as he could.

A shrewd man, possessed of a generous supply of common sense and watermelons, Papa decided to seduce a woman who lived very close to him. This woman happened to be my maternal grandmother who also lived in our house. Unaware of his lascivious intentions and bent on helping him assuage his grief over the loss of his wife, Grandmother Merle prepared special meals for Papa and spent long hours conversing with him about farming, grandchildren, and life in the "Old South." Merle assumed that the watermelons Papa brought to her were nothing more than a token of his appreciation for her kindness. When Papa grabbed a part of Merle that she preferred to remain untouched, these conversations came to an abrupt halt. Of course, we were mortified by his inappropriate behavior, but I suspect that my parents secretly were amused. While Papa's indiscretion with Merle was upsetting, at least no one other than members of my immediate family knew about the incident. His next romantic adventure earned him immediate notoriety in the neighborhood. One afternoon, huge watermelon in hand, he trotted over to visit Viola Lampson, a decrepit and cranky elderly woman with whom my family had been friendly for twenty years. Twenty minutes after Papa entered her house, the police came. Poor Viola was in a state of disrepair because my grandfather had been chasing her around her kitchen table demanding kisses. Fortunately, the policeman who arrived at the scene of the crime was quite understanding and polite; he advised my father to keep a careful watch on Papa at all times. My somber father was very embarrassed. Finally, we were all beginning to see the relationship between watermelons and women. He'd disappear with a watermelon and return with the police.

I was mortified by Papa's lecherous desire for other women. After all, wasn't he supposed to be grieving over the death of my grandmother, his wife of fifty years? I resigned myself to the fact that I never would love him or respect him in the manner that I once had. For a while, I avoided his company and refused to answer his frequent questions about why I was avoiding him. I didn't think about why he was behaving the way he was; I simply cast judgment on his behavior and shut myself off from him. Not until Papa remarried did I even try to understand his needs or his behavior.

Approximately one year after his wife died, Papa remarried. Finally, he found a woman who not only loved watermelon but also loved him and his frisky behavior. Lucy, often referred to as "crazy Lucy" by her neighbors who had heard her speak of miracle healings and visions of Christ, wed Papa and took him into her already jam-packed home. Amazingly, she convinced him to stop drinking and to refrain from molesting other women. She could not, however, convince Papa to "get the religion" as she called it. My family was nonplussed both by Papa's decision to remarry at age 77 and to stop drinking after all these years. We all were annoyed by the fact that Lucy convinced him to do in several months what we had been trying to get him to do for many years.

Not until I learned that Papa was dying of bone cancer did I try to understand why he needed to remarry and why I found that fact unbearable. Until this time, I harbored the feeling that Papa somehow was degrading the memory of my grandmother by remarrying. His attempted seductions of women disturbed me, but his decision to marry Lucy saddened me. Only after I spent many afternoons with Papa and Lucy did I realize that they truly loved each other. More importantly, I realized that Papa, devastated by his wife's death, was afraid to be alone in his old age. Perhaps sensing his illness, even though he knew nothing of its development at this time, he wanted to recapture some of his stamina, some of his youth. He really wasn't searching for someone to replace my grandmother: he simply wanted to have a companion to comfort him, to distract him from his grief.

Fortunately, I accepted Papa's actions and resolved my conflict with him before he died. Once again, I was his "gal" in spirit, and I even came to love and respect Lucy. Now, I find that I cannot conjure images of Papa without thinking of watermelons and his romantic escapades. The acts that once troubled me eventually allowed me to glimpse the frail side of my grandfather, to see him as a human being possessed of fears and flaws rather than a cardboard ideal.

## A PROFESSIONAL WRITER: GORDON GRICE'S "CAUGHT IN THE WIDOW'S WEB"

### Prewriting: Finding a Topic and Gathering Information

Gordon Grice began work on the essay "Caught in the Widow's Web" in a journal. He wrote a series of consecutive entries over a two-month period. This is not his usual way of working. He commented, "I rarely use this technique. I don't use it when I have a good idea of where I am going. Keeping a journal helps me when I don't really have a good subject in mind." He continued, "I kept this one while I was taking a nonfiction writing workshop, because I had to turn in pieces on deadline and didn't really know how to start."

Reproduced here are some of the original journal entries for the essay. Grice printed his entries in ink in a spiral-bound notebook. His revisions of those entries—made while he was keeping the journal—are preserved here. Crossed-out words are indicated by a line running through the word. Additions placed above or to the side of the cross-outs are reproduced here in brackets. As the entries show, writers often revise even as they first begin work on an essay.

## Entry 1

1/16/93

1 Idea for essay: What people have nightmares about. Paul dreamed of people vomiting up human flesh, knew he was in hell.

1/16/93

2 The black widow has the ugliest web of any spider. The orb weavers ~~have~~ make those seemingly delicate nets that poets have ~~turned~~ traditionally used as symbols of imagination (~~Dickinson~~), order (~~Shakespeare~~), [and] perfection. The sheet-web weavers make spiders weave crisp linens for the lawn [~~on the lawn~~] ~~some of these have impressive looking underlayers and tunnels~~. But the widow makes messy-looking tangles in the corners and bends of things and under logs and debris. Often the web ~~has~~ is littered with leaves. Beneath ~~the web~~ it lie the ~~corpses~~ husks of insect prey, [their antenna stiff as gargoyle horns], cut loose and dropped; on them and the surrounding ground are splashes of the spider's white ~~dung~~ [urine], which looks like bird ~~urine~~ [guano] and smells of ammonia even at a distance of several feet. ~~If these spiders this ground is bioleg~~. This fetid material draws scavengers—ants, sow bugs, crickets, roaches, and so on—which ~~walk into~~ become tangled in vertical strands of ~~web~~ [silk] reaching from the ground up into the web. The widow comes down and, with a bicycling ~~motion~~ of the hind [pair of] legs, throws [gummy] ~~liquid~~ silk onto this new prey.

*Point of Comparison: Compare this entry with paragraphs 2 and 3 in "Caught in the Widow's Web."*

## Entry 2

1/20/93

3 When the prey is seriously tangled but still struggling, the widow cautiously descends and bites the creature, usually on a leg joint. This is ~~the~~ a killing

bite. ~~She will~~, it pumps neurotoxin into the victim. She will deliver a series of bites as the creature dies: these later bites inject substances that liquify the organs. And finally she will settle down to suck the liquified innards out of the prey, changing her ~~position~~ [place] two or three times to get [it] all.

> *Point of Comparison: Compare this entry with paragraph 3 in "Caught in the Widow's Web."*

## Entry 3

4    The [architectural] complexity[ities] of the widow-web ~~are beyond us. As a home~~ do not particularly impress the widow. ~~She~~ They move around in these webs ~~essentially~~ [almost] blind, yet they never snare themselves, misstep, or ~~lose their we~~ get lost. In fact, a widow forcibly removed from her web and put back at a different point does not seem confused: she will quickly return to her habitual resting place. ~~All this~~

> *Point of Comparison: This material does not appear in "Caught in the Widow's Web."*

## Entry 4

2/3/93

5    The first thing people ask when they [hear] about my fascination with the widow is why I'~~m~~ [am] not afraid. The truth is that my fascination is rooted in fear.

6        I know a man who ~~as~~ a child was frightened by ~~the~~ his preacher's ~~claim that~~ invitation to eat the flesh of Jesus. The man's [worst] nightmares are about ~~cannibals. His hobby~~ vomiting up human meat. The thing he likes best to watch [horror] ~~movies~~ [films] about cannibals.

> *Point of Comparison: Compare this entry with paragraph 6 in "Caught in the Widow's Web."*

## Entry 5

2/4/93

7    There is, of course, one pragmatic reason for fearing the widow.

8        These markings include a pair of triangles on the ventral side of the abdomen—the infamous "hourglass."

9        The widow's venom is, of course, a soundly pragmatic reason for fear. The venom contains a neurotoxin that produces chills, [sweats], vomiting, ~~and~~ fiery pain, ~~sometimes~~ [and] convulsions and death. ~~Death It is [And]~~ Occasionally ~~a person~~ [people] dies from ~~the~~ widow bites ~~but less than the~~ Some researchers ~~have theorized~~ [hypothesized] that the virulence of the

venom was necessary for killing ~~scarab~~ beetles of the scarab family. This family contains thousands of ~~beetles~~ [species], including the june bug and the famous ~~Egyptian~~ dung beetle the Egyptians thought immortal. All the scarabs have thick, strong bodies and [unusually] tough exoskeletons, and ~~these~~ many of them are common prey for the widow.

*Point of Comparison: Compare this entry with paragraphs 11 and 12 in "Caught in the Widow's Web."*

## Entry 6

2/9/93

10 The widow, it was proposed, needs a strong venom to kill such thick-hided creatures. But this idea is yet another that owes more to ~~the widow's~~ dark romance ~~than~~ with the widow than to hard evidence. The venom is thousands of times too virulent ~~for this than~~ [for] this purpose. ~~We see~~ An emblem of immortality ~~trapped~~, killed by a creature ~~thing~~ whose most distinctive [blood-colored] markings people invariably describe as an hourglass: scientists, being human, want to see a deep causality.

11 But no one has ever offered a sufficient explanation for the widow's [dangerous] venom. It ~~has no~~ provides no evolutionary advantages: all of ~~its~~ [the widow's] prey items ~~are~~ would find lesser toxins fatal, and there is no particular ~~advantage to~~ benefit in harming or killing larger animals. A widow biting a human or other large animal is almost certain to be killed. Evolution does occasionally produce such flowers of [natural] evil—traits that are not functional, but vestiges of lost functions, but ~~pure~~ utterly pointless. ~~This~~ Such ~~things~~ [traits] come about because natural selection merely ~~works against~~ [favors] the inheritance of useful ~~traits~~ [characteristics] that arise from random mutation and extinguishes disadvantageous characteristics. All other characteristics, the ones that neither help nor hinder survival, are preserved [or not] (almost) randomly; when mutation links a useless but harmless trait to a useful one, both are preserved. Many people—even many scientists—assume that every animal is elegantly engineered for its ecological niche, that every bit of an animal's anatomy and behavior ~~can be~~ has a functional explanation. This assumption is false. Nothing in evolutionary theory sanctions it; fact refutes it. ~~It is in fact a lapse into magical thinking. But we want to order and explain things. But We all want order and order in the world and in the room of order In the ordered rooms~~

12 We want the world to be an ordered room, but in a corner of that room there hangs an untidy web ~~that says~~. Here the analytic mind finds an irreducible mystery, a motiveless evil in nature; [and] the scientist's vision

of evil comes to match the vision of a religious woman with a ten-foot pole. No picture of the cosmos as elegant design accounts for the widow. No picture of a benevolent God explains the widow. She hangs in her haphazard web (that marvel of design) defying teleology.

> *Point of Comparison: Compare the entry with paragraphs 12–15 of "Caught in the Widow's Web."*

## Questions for Discussion

1. What thought or idea appears to trigger Grice's essay? Does he ever return to that idea in the sections of the journal reproduced here?
2. How does the black widow's web differ from those of most spiders?
3. What is puzzling about the widow's venom?
4. What associations do we have with the hourglass (paragraph 10)?
5. In what sense does the widow's web "defy teleology" (paragraph 12)? What is teleology?
6. What are the most common types of revisions that Grice makes in these journal entries?
7. Be prepared to define the following words: *gargoyle* (paragraph 2), *scavengers* (2), *neurotoxin* (3), *innards* (3), *habitual* (4), *pragmatic* (9), *exoskeletons* (9), *causality* (10), *vestiges* (11), *benevolent* (12).

## Drafting: Next Drafts

Grice moved from his journal entries to a first draft of the essay. In a conversation, Grice commented extensively on how the essay was revised.

> When I started revising the black widow piece, I went to a junkyard with an empty mayonnaise jar and caught a widow. I kept her on my desk as I wrote. I kept observing interesting things I had never thought of putting in the piece before. If I'm writing about something I can't catch in a jar, I find some other way to research it. I hit the library or interview people. This helps me find interesting details that will fire up a boring draft.
>
> I try to figure out what's working in a draft and what's not. I put it away for a while so I can get some distance on it. I get other people to criticize it. I don't trust anybody who likes everything I write or anybody who hates everything I write.
>
> I analyze a draft like this: I want something interesting in the first sentence. Usually my first draft begins badly, so my job on revision is to decapitate the essay. I cut until I hit something interesting. Or I may find an interesting part somewhere else in the draft and move it to the beginning. I move things around a lot. If I get frustrated trying to keep it all straight on the computer, I print it out and sit on the floor with scissors rearranging things.
>
> I look for long sections of exposition or summary and try to break these up with vivid examples or details. If some part is boring, I try to think of ways to make it into a story.

I fiddle with the sentences as I go. I try to cut all the passive voice verbs and all the *be* verbs. I strike filler words like *very*. If it doesn't sound right without the filler, I take that as a clue that something's wrong with the ideas themselves. I aim for the prose to sound simple, even if the ideas are complex.

Grice tried to get the revised draft published but with no success. He reflected: "I wasn't having any luck. I theorized that the opening wasn't catchy enough. I also thought that the piece didn't fit any magazine I could think of—it was too arty for a science magazine, and most of the essays I saw in literary journals had more personal material than I used."

A considerable amount of time elapsed: "I carried the piece around with me until I got the chance to work on it. I was substitute teaching a middle school shop class when I scribbled down a new opening." In the new opening, Grice describes having young widow spiders crawl all over his arms: "I thought the danger made it interesting." Grice sent off the essay—with its new opening—and it was immediately published in the *High Plains Literary Review* under the title "The Black Widow."

## Revising: Final Draft

Grice's essay actually has three "final" forms. After the essay appeared in *High Plains Literary Review*, it was rewritten and reprinted in the large-circulation monthly magazine *Harper's*. Ironically, the new, more personal opening that Grice had written was cut and some other minor changes were made. Revision did not stop there, though, for the essay was later included in a collection of Grice's essays titled *The Red Hourglass: Inner Lives of the Predators* (1998). Commenting on that revision, he said, "It's five or six times longer, so I covered a lot of new material. For example, I developed the section about the widow's venom with some case studies. I added details and changed the overall shape of the essay. I changed word choices and sentence structures as well."

The draft reproduced here is the one that originally appeared in *Harper's* magazine.

# Caught in the Widow's Web

Gordon Grice

*Gordon Grice earned his B.A. at Oklahoma State University and his M.F.A. at the University of Arkansas. Grice has published essays and poems in a wide range of literary magazines. His first collection of essays was* The Red Hourglass: Lives of the Predators *(1998). The following essay, originally titled "The Black Widow," first appeared in the* High Plains Literary Review. *Grice reworked it for its appearance in* Harper's *magazine and then again for* The Red Hourglass. *The version reproduced here appeared in* Harper's.

**On Writing:** *Widely praised for his precise and detailed attention to the "microworld," Grice has said, "Personal observation and experience are part of my approach to writing as a whole. I like to delve into the details and give my readers the feeling of being there and having their own hands in it."*

## Before Reading

**Connecting:** How do you feel about spiders? To what do you attribute your reaction?

**Anticipating:** As you read, think about what the black widow symbolizes for Grice.

1  I hunt black widows. When I find one, I capture it. I have found them in discarded wheels and tires and under railroad ties. I have found them in house foundations and cellars, in automotive shops and toolsheds, in water meters and rock gardens, against fences and in cinder-block walls.

2  Black widows have the ugliest webs of any spider, messy looking tangles in the corners and bends of things and under logs and debris. Often the widow's web is littered with leaves. Beneath it lie the husks of consumed insects, their antennae stiff as gargoyle horns; on them and the surrounding ground are splashes of the spider's white urine, which looks like bird guano and smells of ammonia even at a distance of several feet.

3  This fetid material draws scavengers—ants, sow bugs, crickets, roaches, and so on—which become tangled in vertical strands of silk reaching from the ground up into the web. The widow climbs down and throws gummy silk onto this new prey. When the insect is seriously tangled but still struggling, the widow cautiously descends and bites it, usually on a leg joint. This is a killing bite; it pumps poison into the victim. As the creature dies, the widow delivers still more bites, injecting substances that liquefy the organs. Finally it settles

down to suck the liquefied innards out of the prey, changing position two or three times to get it all.

4      Widows reportedly eat mice, toads, tarantulas—anything that wanders into that remarkable web. I have never witnessed a widow performing a gustatory act of that magnitude, but I have seen them eat scarab beetles heavy as pecans, carabid beetles strong enough to prey on wolf spiders, cockroaches more than an inch long, and hundreds of other arthropods of various sizes.

5      Many widows will eat as much as opportunity allows. One aggressive female I raised had an abdomen a little bigger than a pea. She snared a huge cockroach and spent several hours subduing it, then three days consuming it. Her abdomen swelled to the size of a largish marble, its glossy black stretching to a tight red-brown. With a different widow, I decided to see whether that appetite really was insatiable. I collected dozens of large crickets and grasshoppers and began to drop them into her web at a rate of one every three or four hours. After catching and devouring her tenth victim, this bloated widow fell from her web, landing on her back. She remained in this position for hours, making only feeble attempts to move. Then she died.

6      The first thing people ask when they hear about my fascination with the widow is why I am not afraid. The truth is that my fascination is rooted in fear.

7      I have childhood memories that partly account for this. When I was six my mother took my sister and me into the cellar of our farmhouse and told us to watch as she killed a widow. With great ceremony she produced a long stick (I am tempted to say a ten-foot pole) and, narrating her technique in exactly the hushed voice she used for discussing religion or sex, went to work. Her flashlight beam found a point halfway up the cement wall where two marbles hung together—one a crisp white, the other a shiny black. My mother ran her stick through the dirty silver web around them. As it tore it sounded like the crackling of paper in fire. The black marble rose on thin legs to fight off the intruder. My mother smashed the widow onto the stick and carried it up into the light. It was still kicking its remaining legs. Mom scraped it against the floor, grinding it into a paste. Then she returned for the white marble—the widow's egg sac. This, too, came to an abrasive end.

8      My mother's stated purpose was to teach us how to recognize and deal with a dangerous creature that we would probably encounter on the farm. But, of course, we also took away the understanding that widows were actively malevolent, that they waited in dark places to ambush us, that they were worthy of ritual disposition, like an enemy whose death is not sufficient but must be followed by the murder of his children and the salting of his land and whose unclean remains must not touch our hands.

9      The odd thing is that so *many* people, some of whom presumably did not first encounter the widow in such an atmosphere of mystic reverence, hold the widow in awe. Various friends have told me that the widow's bite is always fatal to humans—in fact, it almost never is. I have heard told for truth that goods imported from the Orient are likely to be infested with widows and that women with bouffant hairdos have died of widow infestation. Any contradiction of such tales is received as if it were a proclamation of atheism.

10      We project our archetypal terrors onto the widow. It is black; it avoids the light; it is a voracious carnivore. Its red markings suggest blood. The female's habit of eating her lovers invites a strangely sexual discomfort; the widow becomes an emblem for a man's fear of extending himself into the blood and darkness of a woman, something like the legendary Eskimo vampire that takes the form of a fanged vagina.

11      The widow's venom is, of course, a sound reason for fear. The venom contains a neurotoxin that can produce sweats, vomiting, swelling, convulsions, and dozens of other symptoms. The variation in symptoms from one person to the next is remarkable. The constant is pain. A useful question for a doctor trying to diagnose an uncertain case: "Is this the worst pain you've ever felt?" A "yes" suggests a diagnosis of a black widow bite. Occasionally people die from widow bites. The very young and the very old are especially vulnerable. Some people seem to die not from the venom but from the infection that may follow: because of its habitat, the widow carries dangerous microbes.

12      Researchers once hypothesized that the virulence of the venom was necessary for killing beetles of the scarabaeidae family. This family contains thousands of species, including the June beetle and the famous dung beetle that the Egyptians thought immortal. All the scarabs have thick, strong bodies and unusually tough exoskeletons, and many of them are common prey for the widow. The tough hide was supposed to require a particularly nasty venom. As it turns out, the venom is thousands of times more virulent than necessary for this purpose.

13      No one has ever offered a sufficient explanation for the dangerous venom. It provides no evolutionary advantages: all of the widow's prey would find lesser toxins fatal, and there is no particular benefit in killing or harming larger animals. A widow that bites a human being or other large animal is likely to be killed.

14      Natural selection favors the inheritance of useful characteristics that arise from random mutation and tends to extinguish disadvantageous traits. All other characteristics, the ones that neither help nor hinder survival, are preserved or extinguished at random as mutation links them with useful or harmful traits. Many people—even many scientists—assume that every animal is elegantly engineered for its ecological niche, that every bit of an animal's anatomy and behavior has a functional explanation. This assumption is false. Evolution sometimes produces flowers of natural evil—traits that are neither functional nor vestigial but utterly pointless.

15      We want the world to be an ordered room, but in a corner of that room there hangs an untidy web. Here the analytical mind finds an irreducible mystery, a motiveless evil in nature; here the scientist's vision of evil comes to match the vision of a God-fearing country woman with a ten-foot pole. No idea of the cosmos as elegant design accounts for the widow. No idea of a benevolent God is comfortable in a world with the widow. She hangs in her web, that marvel of design, and defies reason.

## Questions on Subject and Purpose

1. Why is Grice so fascinated by black widow spiders? To what does he trace his fascination?
2. What particular aspects of the black widow spider does Grice focus on?
3. What does the spider symbolize to Grice?

## Questions on Strategy and Audience

1. Explain why Grice begins with the simple sentence "I hunt black widows." What is the effect of that sentence?
2. Grice divides his essay into three sections through the use of additional white space (after paragraphs 5 and 10). How does that division reflect the structure of the essay?
3. What assumptions could Grice make about his audience and their attitudes toward spiders?

## Questions on Vocabulary and Style

1. In describing how his mother killed the spider, Grice writes, "With great ceremony she produced a long stick (I am tempted to say a ten-foot pole)" (paragraph 7). Why does he add the material in the parentheses?
2. What is the effect of labeling the spider a "voracious carnivore"? To what extent is that an accurate phrase?
3. Be prepared to define the following words: *fetid* (paragraph 3), *gustatory* (4), *malevolent* (8), *bouffant* (9), *voracious* (10), *carnivore* (10), *virulence* (12), *niche* (14), *vestigial* (14).

## Writing Suggestions

1. **For Your Journal or Blog.** We tend to ignore the natural details that surround us. Try looking closely, even minutely, at the things around you. For example, take a magnifying glass and carefully examine an insect or a plant leaf. Take a walk and sit down with your journal or laptop. Study the landscape around you. Make entries in your journal or blog, about what you are suddenly able to see.
2. **For a Paragraph.** Select one of your journal or blog entries and expand the entry into a descriptive paragraph. Try to make your reader see with you.
3. **For an Essay.** Nature can be seen and interpreted in many ways. Look back over your entries, look around you, select some natural thing—a living creature, a plant or leaf, an event, or even a landscape. In an essay, describe it to your reader in such a way as to reveal a significance. You are not writing an encyclopedia article or a guide book for tourists; you are seeing a meaning.
4. **For Research.** Grice does not attempt to tell the "full" story of the black widow. Research the black widow (or any other poisonous insect or reptile) using traditional library resources. You could also explore resources on the Web and other online information sources. Your object is not to present an informational report—"here is everything about the subject." Rather, try to

formulate a thesis about your subject. For example, you might explore the myths and symbols that have attached themselves to your subject or the role of the creature in our environment or the "lethalness" of its venom.

## For Further Study

**Focusing on Grammar and Writing.** Look closely at the first five paragraphs in Grice's essay. How does he create vivid images? To what extent does he use precise nouns, vivid verbs, and arresting details? What can writers learn from Grice's descriptive techniques?

**Working Together.** Divide into small groups. Check the Glossary and Ready Reference for the definitions of *simile* and *metaphor*. Each group should then take a block of paragraphs and locate all the similes and metaphors that Grice uses. Report your findings to the class.

**Seeing Other Modes at Work.** The essay makes extensive use of narration and of process narrative in its description of how the black widow kills its prey and how Grice's mother went black widow hunting.

**Finding Connections.** For a discussion of how each writer sees nature, Grice's essay can be paired with N. Scott Momaday's "The Way to Rainy Mountain" (Chapter 3).

**Exploring the Web.** Want to know more about the black widow spider and how its name came to represent a murderous woman? Check the Web.

# 1

# GATHERING AND USING EXAMPLES

# GETTING READY TO WRITE

## How Important are Examples in Your Writing?

Settling into your seat, you look at the midterm essay questions that your professor has just handed out in your Introduction to Sociology course:

> PART II. Essay (25%). Identify the advantages and disadvantages of a "voucher" or "choice" system in providing education from public funds. Be sure to provide specific examples drawn from the assigned readings.

The success of your answer depends on gathering and organizing appropriate examples from the course readings. Good answers have specifics, not just generalizations and personal opinions. Effective writing in any form depends on details and examples. Relevant details and examples make writing interesting, informative, and persuasive. If you try to write without gathering these essential specifics, you will be forced to skim the surface of your subject, relying on generalizations, incomplete and sometimes inaccurate details, and unsubstantiated opinions. Without specifics, even a paper with a strong, clearly stated thesis becomes superficial. For example, how convinced would you be by the following argument?

> In their quest for big-time football programs, American universities have lost sight of their educational responsibilities. Eager for the revenues and alumni support that come with winning teams, universities exploit their football players. They do not care if the players get an education. They care only that they remain academically eligible to play for four seasons. At many schools only a small percentage of these athletes graduate. Throughout their college careers they are encouraged to take easy courses and to put athletics first. It does not matter how they perform in the classroom as long as they distinguish themselves every Saturday afternoon. This exploitation should not be allowed to continue. Universities have the responsibility to educate their students, not to use them to gain publicity and to raise money.

Even if you agree with the writer's thesis, the paragraph does not go beyond the obvious. The writer generalizes—and probably distorts as a result. What the reader gets is an opinion unsupported by any evidence. For example, you might reasonably ask questions about the statement, "At many schools only a small percentage of these athletes graduate."

How many schools?
How small a percentage?
How does this percentage compare with that of nonathletes? After all, not everyone who starts college graduates.

To persuade your reader—even to interest your reader—you need specific information, details, and examples that illustrate the points you are trying to make.

## Where Can You Find Your Examples?

You gather details and examples either from your own experiences and observations or from research. Your sources may vary depending on what you are writing about. For example, *Life* magazine once asked writer Malcolm Cowley for an essay on what is was like to turn eighty. Cowley was already eighty years old, so he had a wealth of firsthand experiences from which to draw. Cowley decided to show his readers, most of whom were younger than eighty, what it was like to be old by listing occasions on which his body reminds him that he is old:

- When it becomes an achievement to do thoughtfully, step-by-step, what he once did instinctively
- When his bones ache
- When there are more and more little bottles in the medicine cabinet, with instructions for taking four times a day
- When he fumbles and drops his toothbrush (butterfingers)
- When his face has bumps and wrinkles, so that he cuts himself while shaving (blood on the towel)
- When year by year his feet seem farther from his hands
- When he can't stand on one leg and has trouble pulling on his pants
- When he hesitates on the landing before walking down a flight of stairs
- When he spends more time looking for things misplaced than he spends using them after he (or more often his wife) has found them
- When he falls asleep in the afternoon
- When it becomes harder to bear in mind two things at once
- When a pretty girl passes him in the street and he doesn't turn his head

Much of what you might be writing about, however, lies outside of your own experiences and observations. David Guterson, for example, set out to write a magazine article for *Harper's* about the Mall of America in Minneapolis. He chose to begin his essay with a series of facts:

> Last April, on a visit to the new Mall of America near Minneapolis, I carried with me the public-relations press kit provided for the benefit of reporters. It included an assortment of "fun facts" about the mall: 140,000 hot dogs sold each week, 10,000 permanent jobs, 44 escalators and 17 elevators, 12,750 parking places, 13,300 short tons of steel, $1 million in cash disbursed weekly from 8 automatic-teller machines. Opened in the summer of 1992, the mall was built on a 78-acre site of the former Metropolitan Stadium, a five-minute drive from the Minneapolis–St. Paul International Airport. With 4.2 million square feet of floor space—including twenty-two times the retail footage of the average American shopping center—the Mall of America was "the largest fully enclosed combination retail and family entertainment center in the United States."

Listing facts from the press kit is a way of catching the reader's attention. In a nation impressed by size, what better to "capture" the country's largest mall than by heaping up facts and statistics.

As the examples in this chapter show, writers sometimes draw exclusively on their own experiences, as do Anna Quindlen in "The Name Is Mine" and Edwidge Danticat in "Westbury Court." Bob Greene in "Cut" uses both his own experiences and those of other men he interviewed. Oscar Casares in "Ready for Some Fótbol?" writes as a reporter covering a state soccer championship game in Texas; he includes his own experiences, his observations and interviews, and some research. For his article "Can Wikipedia Ever Make the Grade?", Brock Read conducted extensive interviews with scholars and authorities to assess the accuracy of the widely used online reference source.

Regardless of where you find them, specific, relevant examples are important in everything you write. They add life and interest to your writing, and they illustrate or support the points you are trying to make.

## How Do You Gather Examples from Your Experiences?

Where do you start when you want to narrate an experience that happened to you or describe something that you saw? You will spend some time remembering the event, sorting out the details of the experience, and deciding which example best supports the point you are trying to make. The best way to begin your memory and observation search is to consider the advice offered earlier in How to Write an Essay and to consider the resources available to you. Exploring a personal experience can involve a number of different activities:

| **Within Yourself** | **Outside** |
| --- | --- |
| Probing memory | Seeing old photographs |
| Reexperiencing sense impressions | Talking with people |
| Revisiting places | Looking for material evidence |

Many of the essays in this (and later chapters) begin with the writer's memories, experiences, and observations.

---

 **IN THE READINGS, LOOK FOR**

| | Source of examples |
| --- | --- |
| Anna Quindlen, "Name is Mine" | Experiences as a wife and mother |
| Edwidge Danticat, "Westbury Court" | Childhood memory |
| Bob Greene, "Cut" | Childhood memory |

Even when writers add information from sources outside their own experiences, personal observation and experience might still play a significant role in shaping the essay.

## How Do You Gather Examples from Outside Sources?

When you think about researching a subject, you might think only of going to the Web to search for appropriate sites or of going to a library to look for printed books and articles. As varied as these search methods are, you can also find information in many other ways:

| Using Outside Sources | Interviewing people, conducting polls |
| --- | --- |
| | Locating books and articles |
| | Searching for Internet sites |
| | Exploring media resources (such as film and music) |
| | Performing an experiment or test |

The experiences of other people can be excellent sources of information. Bob Greene, for example, recounts the experiences of four other men who were also cut from athletic teams when they were young. Many of the articles that appear in magazines and newspapers make extensive use of interviews rather than printed sources. In "Can Wikipedia Ever Make the Grade?" Brock Read gathers his information about the reliability of Wikipedia from scholars and executives from the Website.

When you use information gathered from outside sources—whether those sources are printed or e-texts, Websites, or interviews—it is important that you document those sources. Even though articles in newspapers and magazines do not provide the type of documentation that you find in a paper written for a college course, you are a student not a reporter. Be sure to ask your instructor how you are to document quotations and paraphrases: Is it all right just to mention the sources in the text, or do you need to provide formal, parenthetical documentation and a list of works cited? Additional advice and samples can be found in Chapter 11: The Research Paper. Be sure to read that material before you hand in a paper that uses outside sources.

 **IN THE READINGS, LOOK FOR**

|  | Source of examples |
| --- | --- |
| Bob Greene, "Cut" | Interviews with other men |
| Oscar Casares, "Fútbol?" | Interviews, observation, research |
| Brock Read, "Wikipedia" | Interviews, research |

## PREWRITING TIPS FOR GATHERING EXAMPLES

1.  Do not rush the example-gathering stage of your prewriting. Good writing depends on good examples, and quality is more important than quantity. Before sitting down to write, try to spend some hours locating examples.

2.  Remember that examples can be gathered from personal experience, from interviews with people, and from information in printed or online sources. Think about where you might find the best examples for your topic, and remember that finding them often requires research.

3.  Choose examples for a reason: to support a point or a thesis. On a separate sheet of paper, list each example and explain why that example supports the larger point you are trying to make.

4.  Think about ways to order the examples in your essay. If you are narrating an event, will you use a chronological order or a flashback? If you are using examples to support an argument, will you start with the strongest example or end with it? Decide on an organizational strategy for the paper.

5.  Plan an opening strategy for your essay. Maybe you will start with a vivid example, maybe with a statement of your thesis. Your opening paragraph is crucial, because that is where you will either catch your reader's attention or lose it.

## WRITING

### How Many Examples Do You Need?

Every writer's job would be much easier if there were a simple answer to the question of how many examples to use. Instead, the answer is "enough to interest or convince your reader." Sometimes one fully developed example might be enough. Advertisements for organizations such as Save the Children or the Christian Children's Fund often tell the story of a specific child who needs food and shelter. The single example, accompanied by a photograph, is enough to persuade many people to sponsor a child.

Readers are not going to respond to a statement like "millions of people are starving throughout the world." Most of us would throw up our hands in frustration. What can I do about millions? On the other hand, I can help one child on a monthly basis. Anna Quindlen in "The Name Is Mine" focuses on a single example drawn from her own experience. She uses that example as a way to make her point about the significance and consequences of keeping your own name when you marry.

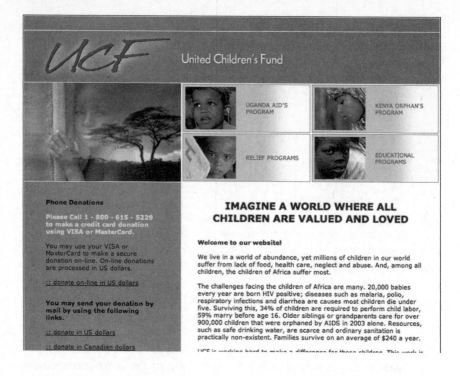

At other times you might need to use many examples—appropriate, accurate, and convincing examples. Many college instructors tell their students not to use Wikipedia as a source in writing a research paper because anyone can contribute an article to the Website, not just "experts." In an essay, simply saying that Wikipedia is not a reliable scholarly source is not convincing. Specific examples of inaccuracy or inadequacy are needed. Brock Read in "Can Wikipedia Ever Make the Grade?" documents problems by quoting users and citing specific examples of weaknesses.

When you write from personal experience, your readers might not demand a great level of detail and accuracy in your examples. In "Cut," Bob Greene writes about how being cut from a junior high basketball team changed his life. To support his thesis and extend it beyond his own personal experience, Greene includes the stories of four other men who had similar experiences. But why give five examples? Why not three or seven? There is nothing magical about the number five. Green might have used five because he had that much column space in the magazine; nevertheless, the five lend credibility to Greene's thesis, or at least they create the illusion of credibility. Proving the validity of Green's thesis would require a proper statistical sample. Only then could it be said with some certainty that the experience of being cut makes men superachievers later in life. In most writing situations, however, such thoroughness is not needed. If the details and examples are well chosen and relevant, the reader is likely to accept your assertions.

## How Do You Place Examples in Your Essay?

Whether you use one example or many, examples alone do not make an essay. There is no such thing as an "exemplification essay." Examples are always subordinated to a thesis, an assertion, a story, an argument. Examples fill out the framework of an essay; they are the supporting evidence and the details that justify that thesis, assertion, story, or argument. Every essay, whether structured using narration, description, comparison and contrast, or any other rhetorical strategies used to organize information, uses examples. Without examples, an essay is just a bare framework of statements, opinions, and generalizations.

That initial framework is derived from one of the organizational strategies or patterns that you are using. In a narrative, details and examples are inserted into a chronological timeline; in a description, details and examples are added to a spatial pattern as the eye and ear move over the person, place, or landscape being described. The same procedure applies to each of the other organizational structures. A classification scheme is fleshed out with examples; a comparison demands that specific shared or differing examples and details be cited. Finally, in argument and persuasion, examples show that your position is the right and logical one to take.

Examples may be part of the beginning, middle, or end of an essay. An essay might begin with a particularly arresting example that is intended to catch readers' attention and draw them into the essay. If you are using an example as a "hook" for your introduction, begin with the example and place the essay's thesis or assertion either at the end of the opening paragraph or at the beginning of the next paragraph.

Examples make up a substantial part of the body of most essays. An extended example might occupy a whole body paragraph; smaller, shorter examples might be grouped into a single paragraph. Remember, though, that there is no reward for providing the greatest number of examples. The guiding principle is always quality and relevance not quantity. The purpose of your essay is a deciding factor in how to order your examples. Rank examples on the basis of their prominence or importance. Generally arrange your examples in that order, either beginning or ending with the strongest and best example.

Sometimes you might end an essay with a relevant or emotional example. At the end of an essay, readers encounter the last of your message. A well-chosen example can be quite powerful.

 **IN THE READINGS, LOOK FOR**

| | |
|---|---|
| Anna Quindlen, "Name Is Mine" | Use of the opening example |
| Bob Greene, "Cut" | Structure of five examples |
| Edwidge Danticat, "Westbury Court" | Example recalled from memory |
| Oscar Casares, "Fútbol?" | Closing example of the telephone call |
| Brock Read, "Wikipedia" | Extended opening example |

**DRAFTING TIPS FOR USING EXAMPLES**

1. Look carefully at each example you plan to use. It is completely relevant? Does it really prove the point that you want to make or support? Is it accurate and fair, or is it distorted? In college writing, you are not trying to be a propagandist.

2. Do you have enough examples? Too many? A single example is rarely enough to convince a reader of anything. On the other hand, a long list of examples can overwhelm your reader with unnecessary detail.

3. Are your examples specific? Or are they really just generalizations or unsubstantiated opinions? Do you provide facts? Statistics? Quotations? Or do you just assume that your readers will agree with you? Go through your draft and color-code or label each example.

4. Are your examples subordinated to the larger point you are trying to make? Giving examples is not a goal in itself rather, the examples are there to support or justify a larger goal. Examples must be proportional to the essay. Check to see if any of your examples are too long or too detailed. Do they obscure the real reason for their use?

5. Have you provided clear transitional statements or markers as you move from one example to another? Your examples need to be connected in ways that make your essay flow smoothly.

## REVISING

### Are Your Examples Good Choices?

The examples you selected should meet specific criteria for the type of essay you are writing. In informational or persuasive writing, your examples must be accurate and unbiased. We are bombarded, for instance, by misleading, inaccurate examples in advertisements and in political rhetoric, but such techniques are not appropriate for college writing. Look carefully at your examples. Are they fair? Accurate? Examples must also be relevant or important. Do they really support or clarify your assertion or thesis? Look at the examples you are using and number them in terms of their importance. Forget about those that are weak; use only your strongest examples. The number of examples you need depends on the length of your paper. A short paper, several pages in length, typically will not require as many examples as a many-paged research paper. Did you choose examples that are interesting or attention-gettings? This is particularly important if you are starting or ending your essay with an example.

## How Did You Order or Arrange Your Examples?

If you numbered or graded your examples in terms of their relevance and importance, now look at how you arranged them in your paper. Remember, you are only using the best examples. You should then have arranged them in either descending order (the best comes first) or ascending order (the best comes last). That choice is yours: one order is not better or more correct than the other. The greatest danger in arranging examples in an essay comes when you start with a thesis or assertion and follow with a series of short examples that trail off into insignificance.

In some essays, because each example is different, you may be tempted to put each example into its own paragraph. The result may be a string of short, thin, poorly developed paragraphs. Look carefully at your essay. Count the number of paragraphs you have written. A three-page paper that has twenty short paragraphs needs to be revised: some examples can be deleted and other examples might be expanded. Do not assume that each example must be set off in a separate paragraph. Long, developed examples must be set off, but shorter, related examples can often be grouped under a topic sentence.

## Did You Make Transitions as You Moved from Example to Example?

Check your essay to see if you have provided clear transition markers as you move from example to example. Transitional markers include words and phrases such as *for example, first, next, finally, also, on the other hand, in addition*. The Glossary and Ready Reference at the back of this text provides a fuller explanation and a more complete listing of such devices. Transitional devices, however, are no substitute for logical order and a clear sense of organization and purpose. Still, you need to help your reader see how all of these examples fit into the essay. A logical arrangement and transitional markers are like highway signs; they indicate to the reader what is coming and how it connects with what has already been covered in the essay.

## IN THE READINGS, LOOK FOR

| | |
|---|---|
| Anna Quindlen, "Name is Mine" | Choice of the opening example and the return to it at end |
| Bob Greene, "Cut" | Order of the examples |
| Edwidge Danticat, "Westbury Court" | Transitions into other examples of violence |
| Oscar Casares, "Fútbol?" | Use of "Speedy Gonzales" example |
| Brock Read, "Wikipedia" | Effectiveness of the examples of inadequacies or inaccuracies |

## REVISING TIPS WHEN USING EXAMPLES

1. If you are writing about yourself, it is especially important to keep your readers interested. They need to feel how significant this experience was. They need to become involved in the situation—to sympathize or empathize with what happened. Do not just tell them: show them. One way to do this is to dramatize the experience, to tell it as if it were happening at that moment.

2. Print a copy of your paper, cut it apart, and try different arrangements of the examples, sentences, and even paragraphs. Which order seems to work best? Consider other alternatives. Do not just assume that your essay can be assembled in only one way.

3. How effective is your conclusion? Do you stop abruptly? Do you just repeat in slightly altered words what you said in your introduction? Remember the end of your essay—especially if you are arguing for something—is what will stay with your readers.

4. If you interviewed people in your research or used information from printed or online sources, make sure you punctuated your quotations properly and documented those sources.

5. Find someone to read your essay: a friend, roommate, classmate, or tutor in a writing center. Ask your reader for some constructive criticism and listen to what you hear.

## STUDENT ESSAY

### First Draft

Frank Smite, recently divorced and recently returned to college, chose to work on an essay about the difficulties that older single or newly single people have in meeting people they can date. "Young college kids have it easy," Frank complained. "You are constantly surrounded by eligible people your own age. Try meeting someone when you're thirty-five, slightly balding, just divorced, and working all day." His first draft of the opening of his essay appears here:

My Search for Love

My wife and I separated and then quickly divorced a year ago. I figured that I would be able to forget some of the pain by returning to dating. At first, I was excited about the prospect of meeting new people.

It made me feel young again. Besides, this time I'd be able to avoid the problems that led to my divorce. While I'm not exactly a male movie star—I'm thirty-five, a little overweight, kind of thin on the top, and have one daughter who I desperately miss seeing every day—I figured that romance was just around the corner.

It wasn't until I started to look for people to ask out that I realized how far away that corner was. Frankly, in my immediate world, there seemed to be no one who was roughly my age and unmarried. That's when I began to look at the various ways that people in my situation can meet people. I attended several meetings of the local Parents Without Partners group, but that didn't seem promising; I joined a computerized dating service; and, believe it or not, I started reading the "personals" in the newspaper.

## Comments

When Frank came to revise his essay, he had his instructor's comments and the reactions of several classmates. Everyone agreed that he had an excellent subject and some good detail, but several readers were a little troubled by Frank's overuse of "I." One reader asked Frank if he could make his essay focus a little less on his own immediate experience and a little more on what anyone in his position might do. His instructor suggested that with the right type of revision, Frank might be able to publish his essay in the local newspaper—after all, she noted, many people are in the same situation. His instructor also suggested that Frank might eliminate the reference to his daughter and how much he misses her. Although those feelings are important, that is not where Frank wanted to center the essay. Frank liked the idea of sharing his experiences with a wider audience. His revised introduction—complete with a new title—follows.

## Revised Draft

### Looking for Love

Ask any single or divorced adult about the problems of meeting "prospective partners" and you are likely to get a litany of complaints and horrifying experiences. No longer can people rely on introductions from well-meaning friends. After all, most of those friends are also looking for love. Matchmaking has become big business—even, in fact, a franchised business.

Today the search for love takes many forms, from bar hopping, to organizations such as Parents Without Partners, to computerized and videotaped "search services," to singles groups organized around a shared concern (for example, those who are concerned about the environment or who love books). A little more desperate (and risky and certainly tacky) is the newspaper classified. Titled "Getting Personal" in my local newspaper, advertisements typically read like this one running today: "Single white female, pretty, petite blond, 40's ISO [in search of] WM [white male] for a perfect relationship (it does exist!)."

## SOME THINGS TO REMEMBER ABOUT USING EXAMPLES

1. Use details and examples—effective writing depends on them.

2. For some subjects you can find the illustrations you need from your own experiences and observations. You will, however, probably need to work at remembering and gathering specifics.

3. For some subjects you will need to do some type of research such as interviewing people, looking up material in your school's library, using the Internet and the Web to locate relevant documents and sites. Remember as well that you are always connecting your observations with knowledge that you have acquired in other courses and other experiences.

4. Choose examples that are relevant and accurate. Quality is more important than quantity. Make sure your examples support your argument or illustrate the points you are trying to make. If you use an outside authority—an interview, a printed text, an electronic source—make sure that the source is knowledgeable and accurate. Remember also to document those sources.

5. The number of details and examples you need necessarily varies. Sometimes one will do; sometimes you will need many. If you want your readers to do or to believe something, you must supply some evidence to gain their support or confidence.

## SEEING EXAMPLES IN OTHER CONTEXTS

### As a Literary Strategy

We could find examples in any literary work, but Bret Lott's very short story "Night" uses a single example to capture a continuing painful reality. A father wakes up to hear what he thinks is his child breathing. It seems at first like an ordinary experience, but we quickly discover what that single example reveals.

# Night

Bret Lott

He woke up. He thought he could hear their child's breathing in the next room, the near-silent, smooth sound of air in and out.

He touched his wife. The room was too dark to let him see her, but he felt her movement, the shift of blanket and sheet.

"Listen," he whispered.

"Yesterday," she mumbled. "Why not yesterday," and she moved back into sleep.

He listened harder, though he could hear his wife's breath, thick and heavy next to him, there was beneath this the thin frost of his child's breathing.

The hardwood floor was cold beneath his feet. He held out a hand in front of him, and when he touched the doorjamb, he paused, listened again, heard the life of his child.

His fingertips led him along the hall and to the next room. Then he was in the doorway of a room as dark, as hollow as his own. He cut on the light.

The room, of course, was empty. They had left the bed just as their child had made it, the spread merely thrown over bunched and wrinkled sheets, the pillow crooked at the head. The small blue desk was littered with colored pencils and scraps of construction paper, a bottle of white glue.

He turned off the light and listened. He heard nothing, then backed out of the room and moved down the hall, back to his room, his hands at his sides, his fingertips helpless.

This happened each night, like a dream, but not.

## Discussion Questions

1. What does this experience reveal to the reader? Is the single example sufficient to capture the emotion that the father feels? Would more examples, more experiences, be necessary?
2. Who narrates the experience? How does that point of view contribute to the story? What would the story be like if it were told by the father?
3. At what point in the story do you realize what is happening? Why might the author not reveal what has happened earlier?
4. Which of the descriptive details in the story seem most effective? Why?
5. What effect does the final sentence have?

## Writing Suggestions

Lott does not tell us how the parents felt; he allows the single example to reveal the loss that the father feels. It is simple and sparse, but extremely effective. Think about an emotion that you have had and try to capture and convey that feeling in a single example. You might think about the following as possible starting points for your essay:

    **a.** A life-changing event—something that has forever changed your life or your expectations

    **b.** A loss—of a person, a pet, a personal possession

    **c.** A discovery or a realization—a moment of insight into life, your identity, your future

## AS A CRITICAL READING STRATEGY

Examples are essential to all types of writing: writers explain, entertain, analyze, persuade by citing specific, relevant examples. Examples make writing vivid and interesting. Without examples, there is just a framework, a skeletal outline of an essay. When we read, we should notice certain things about the examples and about the role they play in effective writing. The paragraph below is taken from Steven Pinker's *The Language Instinct: How the Mind Creates Language.* As you read, remember what you have learned about how to write with examples—that knowledge can help you as a reader.

- Examples do not provide a structure for an essay. They are inserted into essays to fill out a predetermined rhetorical strategy or organizational pattern. Consequently, if you outlined the essay or the paragraph in which they occur, you would find that the examples support the assertions. They are subordinated to the frame of the essay and to the structure of the paragraph.

- Examples are organized; that is, the writer has planned the arrangement of the examples in the essay or the paragraph. In an argument essay, for example, the strongest and best example might be placed first.

- Examples are taken from personal experience or observation, from research such as interviews with people, from printed sources such as articles or books, and from online research.

- Examples must be accurate, relevant, and interesting. Each example should be judged by those tests.

    Topic sentence—the frame into which the examples will fit

For centuries people have been terrified that their programmed creations might outsmart them, overpower them, or put them out of work. The fear has been played out in fiction, from the medieval Jewish legend of the Golem, a clay automaton animated by an inscription of the name of God placed in its mouth, to HAL, the mutinous computer of *2001: A Space Odyssey.*

Two examples—Golem and HAL support the initial assertion "for centuries"

Examples of what computers can do supporting the fears people have. Number tasks are understandable; thinking tasks scary to people.

Examples arranged chronologically (growth of problem solving)

Familiar examples from popular films. Example of what experts thought might be possible

Topic sentence—frame

Example—what a four-year-old can do that a computer cannot

Example—seemingly smart robots are dumb

Examples—questions that computers cannot answer (and a four-year-old probably could)

Examples—jobs that might be done by computers and jobs that cannot; ties back to the topic sentence of the previous paragraph

But when the branch of engineering called "artificial intelligence" (AI) was born in the 1950s, it looked as though fiction was about to turn into frightening fact. It is easy to accept a computer calculating pi to a million decimal places or keeping track of a company's payroll, but suddenly computers were also proving theorems in logic and playing respectable chess. In the years following there came computers that could beat anyone but a grand master and programs that outperformed most experts at recommending treatments for bacterial infections and investing pension funds. With computers solving such brainy tasks, it seemed like only a matter of time before a C3P0 or a Terminator would be available from the mail-order catalogues; only the easy tasks remained to be programmed. According to legend, in the 1970s, Marvin Minsky, one of the founders of AI, assigned "vision" to a graduate student as a seminar project.

But household robots are still confined to science fiction. The main lesson of thirty-five years of AI research is that the hard problems are easy and the easy problems are hard. The mental abilities of a four-year-old that we take for granted—recognizing a face, lifting a pencil, walking across a room, answering a question—in fact solve some of the hardest engineering problems ever conceived. Do not be fooled by the assembly-line robots in the automobile commercials; all they do is weld and spray paint, tasks that do not require these clumsy Mr. Magoos to see or hold or place anything. And if you want to stump an artificial intelligence system, ask it questions like, Which is bigger, Chicago or a breadbox? Do zebras wear underwear? Is the floor likely to rise up and bite you? If Susan goes to the store, does her head go with her? Most fears of automation are misplaced. As the new generation of intelligent devices appears, it will be the stock analysts and petrochemical engineers and parole board members who are in danger of being replaced by machines. The gardeners, receptionists, and cooks are secure in their jobs for decades to come.

## AS A VISUAL STRATEGY

Visuals—tables, photographs, charts, diagrams—are also forms of examples. Information can often be displayed more efficiently and effectively through visuals than through words. Many of your textbooks, for example, make extensive use of visual elements to help you understand complex information. Advertisements use photographs to catch your attention. If you are planning a vacation or renting a hotel room, you want to see photographs before you make your reservations.

During your junior and senior years of high school, when you were trying to make a decision about which college to attend, you probably received many catalogs and admission folders that were full of color photographs of the campus, the students, and the college's facilities. Those visual examples might have been influential in your final decision. Following are four photographs that appear in one college's admission materials. Study each photograph. What "thesis" or purpose might have been behind choosing these photographs? How do these examples support that thesis? What do they suggest about the school? In what ways might these photographs persuade a student to apply?

## WRITING ABOUT IMAGES

1. Given your college experiences so far, think about a group of photographs that you might include in an "insider's guide to college life at ———."
   Using photographs, write an essay that describes and pictures what you think is most accurate and revealing about life at your school.

2. Choose a page from Facebook or MySpace. What does the selection of images and other elements suggest or imply about that person? What is the image that the person appears to be projecting? Analyze what you find.

3. Select a product that is widely advertised in print or electronic media. It can be a generic product (for example, an automobile or a cell phone) or a specific brand. Locate examples of the images that are used to "sell" the product. Analyze how the advertising seeks to create a desirable or even irresistible image for the product and its user.

## ADDITIONAL WRITING SUGGESTIONS USING EXAMPLES

Examples are typically used in papers to explain a concept or an assertion, to make a point vivid or interesting, or to support a thesis or argument. Remember, examples can come from your own personal experiences or the experiences of others; from authorities or experts you interview; from newspaper, magazine, or online articles; from books or Websites. Using a range of examples, write an essay in which you use examples to achieve one of the following purposes. Remember that you will have to narrow the topics and define a stance or thesis for your paper.

### Explain a concept or assertion

1. The "language" of text messaging
2. Patriotism
3. Courage
4. Success
5. Function or purpose of a college education
6. "Going green"
7. Organic or natural
8. Fame
9. Best friend (or BFF—in text messaging)
10. Love

### Make a point vivid or interesting

1. Dormitory life
2. Commuting
3. Campus parking
4. Parenthood

5. The date from hell
6. Highlight of my life
7. Being an only or youngest or oldest child
8. An embarrassing moment
9. Part-time job
10. An achievement

## SUPPORT A THESIS OR ARGUMENT

1. Ban on cigarette smoking in public places
2. Use of a cell phone while driving
3. Popularity of Facebook or MySpace
4. Changes in the driving age
5. Performance-enhancing drugs for athletes
6. Importance of high grades in college
7. Distribution requirements for college students
8. Popularity of reality-based TV shows
9. Popularity of "texting"
10. Value of studying abroad

# The Name Is Mine

Anna Quindlen

*Born in 1953, Anna Quindlen attended Barnard College in New York City. She enjoyed a successful career at* The New York Times, *where she wrote three different weekly columns, including her syndicated column, "Public and Private," for which she won the 1992 Pulitzer Prize for commentary. A regular columnist for* Newsweek, *Quindlen's most recent book is* Good Dog, Stay *(2007).*

*This essay first appeared in "Life in the 30's," a weekly column that Quindlen wrote for the* Times *from 1986 to 1988. Based on her own experiences as a mother, a wife, and a journalist, the column attracted millions of readers and was syndicated in some sixty other newspapers. She ended the column because of its personal nature: "It wasn't just that I was in the spotlight; it was like I was in the spotlight naked. . . . I became public property."*

**On Writing:** *Quindlen writes on a laptop computer and observes, "I listen to all those authors who say they write longhand in diaries they buy in London, and I say, 'Get a life.'" A perfectionist who "wants every sentence to be the best it can be," Quindlen notes, "I don't want anything to be loose or sloppy."*

## Before Reading

**Connecting:** Can you remember times when your "identity" was defined not by yourself but by your association with someone else, when you were the child *of*, the sibling *of*, the spouse *of*, the parent *of*, the employee *of*? How did these occasions make you feel?

**Anticipating:** Every decision we make has consequences—some of which we are immediately aware of and some of which only emerge later. What are the consequences of Quindlen's decision not to take her husband's name?

1   I am on the telephone to the emergency room of the local hospital. My elder son is getting stitches in his palm, and I have called to make myself feel better, because I am at home, waiting, and my husband is there, holding him. I am 34 years old, and I am crying like a child, making a slippery mess of my face. "Mrs. Krovatin?" says the nurse, and for the first time in my life I answer "Yes."

2   This is a story about a name. The name is mine. I was given it at birth, and I have never changed it, although I married. I could come up with lots of

reasons why. It was a political decision, a simple statement that I was some-body and not an adjunct of anybody, especially a husband. As a friend of mine told her horrified mother, "He didn't adopt me, he married me."

3      It was a professional and a personal decision, too. I grew up with an ugly dog of a name, one I came to love because I thought it was weird and unlov-able. Amid the Debbies and Kathys of my childhood, I had a first name only my grandmothers had and a last name that began with a strange letter. "Sorry, the letters, I, O, Q, U, V, X, Y and Z are not available," the catalogues said about monogrammed key rings and cocktail napkins. Seeing my name in black on white at the top of a good story, suddenly it wasn't an ugly dog anymore.

4      But neither of these are honest reasons, because they assume rational consideration, and it so happens that when it came to changing my name, there was no consideration, rational or otherwise. It was mine. It belonged to me. I don't even share a checking account with my husband. Damned if I was going to be hidden beneath the umbrella of his identity.

5      It seemed like a simple decision. But nowadays I think the only simple decisions are whether to have grilled cheese or tuna fish for lunch. Last week, my older child wanted an explanation of why he, his dad and his brother have one name, and I have another.

6      My answer was long, philosophical and rambling—that is to say, unsat-isfactory. What's in a name? I could have said disingenuously. But I was talk-ing to a person who had just spent three torturous, exhilarating years learning names for things, and I wanted to communicate to him that mine meant some-thing quite special to me, had seemed as form-fitting as my skin, and as painful to remove. Personal identity and independence, however, were not what he was looking for; he just wanted to make sure I was one of them. And I am—and then again, I am not. When I made this decision, I was part of a couple. Now, there are two me's, the me who is the individual and the me who is part of a family of four, a family of four in which, in a small way, I am left out.

7      A wise friend who finds herself in the same fix says she never wants to change her name, only to have a slightly different identity as a family member, an identity for pediatricians' offices and parent-teacher conferences. She also says that the entire situation reminds her of the women's movement as a whole. We did these things as individuals, made these decisions about ourselves and what we wanted to be and do. And they were good decisions, the right decisions. But we based them on individual choice, not on group dynamics. We thought in terms of our sense of ourselves, not our relationships with others.

8      Some people found alternative solutions: hyphenated names, merged names, matriarchal names for the girls and patriarchal ones for the boys, one name at work and another at home. I did not like those choices; I thought they were middle grounds, and I didn't live much in the middle ground at the time. I was once slightly disdainful of women who went all the way and changed their names. But I now know too many smart, independent, terrific women who have the same last names as their husbands to be disdainful anymore. (Besides, if I made this decision as part of a feminist world view, it seems dis-honest to turn around and trash other women for deciding as they did.)

9    I made my choice. I haven't changed my mind. I've just changed my life. Sometimes I feel like one of those worms I used to hear about in biology, the ones that, chopped in half, walked off in different directions. My name works fine for one half, not quite as well for the other. I would never give it up. Except for that one morning when I talked to the nurse at the hospital, I always answer the question "Mrs. Krovatin?" with "No, this is Mr. Krovatin's wife." It's just that I understand the down side now.

10   When I decided not to disappear beneath my husband's umbrella, it did not occur to me that I would be the only one left outside. It did not occur to me that I would ever care—not enough to change, just enough to think about the things we do on our own and what they mean when we aren't on our own anymore.

## Questions on Subject and Purpose

1.  Why did Quindlen not change her last name when she married?
2.  How does she feel about her decision now?
3.  Since Quindlen does not plan to change her name, what purpose might she have in writing the essay?

## Questions on Strategy and Audience

1.  The essay could begin at the second paragraph. Why might Quindlen have chosen to begin the essay with the telephone call experience?
2.  In paragraph 9, Quindlen returns to the incident at the hospital. How does this device help hold the essay together?
3.  The essay appeared in a column headed "Life in the 30's." How might that affect the nature of the audience who might read the essay?

## Questions on Vocabulary and Style

1.  At the beginning of paragraphs 2 and 9, Quindlen uses three very short simple sentences in a row. Why?
2.  Twice in the essay (paragraphs 4 and 10), Quindlen refers to coming under her husband's "umbrella." What is the effect of such an image?
3.  Be able to define the following words: *disingenuously* (paragraph 6) and *disdainful* (8).

## Writing Suggestions

1.  **For Your Journal or Blog.** Do you have any desire to change your name? If so, why? If not, why not? In your journal or blog, explore what changing or not changing your name might mean. Would "you" be any different?
2.  **For a Paragraph.** In a paragraph, explore the meaning that you find in your last name. How does that name define you?

3. **For an Essay.** In paragraph 6, Quindlen remarks, "There are two me's, the me who is the individual and the me who is part of a family of four." Everyone experiences such moments of awareness. Think about those times when you have been "two," and in an essay, explore the dilemma posed by being an individual and, at the same time, a part of a larger whole.

4. **For Research.** How widespread and recent is the phenomenon of a woman not taking her husbands' name? Research the phenomenon through the various databases your library has. A crucial problem will be identifying the subject headings and keywords to use in your search. If you have problems, ask a reference librarian for guidance. Remember as well that people make excellent sources of information. Then, using that research, write one of the following essays:

   a. An article intended for a male audience

   b. An article intended for an audience of unmarried women who might be considering such a decision

   c. A traditional research paper for a college course

## For Further Study

**Focusing on Grammar and Writing.** Quindlen uses a number of words and phrases that are colloquial and perhaps too informal. Make a list of these. Why might she mix levels of diction in the essay? What does that suggest about your own writing?

**Working Together.** Divide into small groups. Each group should choose a detail or example that Quindlen uses in the essay (for instance, the opening example in the emergency room, the catalog of monogrammed goods, her name at the top of a new story, the umbrella image, the older child's questions about her different name). How effective is each example or detail?

**Seeing Other Modes at Work.** Quindlen makes use of cause and effect in explaining how she decided to keep her own name and what the effects of that decision proved to be.

**Finding Connections.** On the basis of their essays, how might Judy Brady ("I Want a Wife") and Margaret Atwood ("The Female Body"), both in Chapter 8, feel about Quindlen's decision?

**Exploring the Web.** What percentage of women in the United States choose not to take their husband's last name? What factors—for example, socioeconomic, age, education—influence that decision? Explore the Web for answers to these questions.

# Cut

Bob Greene

*Bob Greene was born in Columbus, Ohio, in 1947 and received a B.J.
from Northwestern University in 1969. A columnist and essayist,
Greene's most recent books are* And You Know You Should Be Glad
(2006) *and* When We Get to Surf City (2008).

> **On Writing:** *Greene is, in many ways, a reporter of everyday
> events. He rarely tries to be profound but concentrates instead on human
> interest stories, the experiences that we all share. "Beyond entertaining or
> informing [my readers]," he has said, "the only responsibility I feel is . . .
> to make sure that they get to the last period of the last sentence of the last
> paragraph of the story . . . I feel I have a responsibility to make the story
> interesting enough for them to read all the way through." In this essay
> from* Esquire, *a magazine aimed at a male audience, Greene relates the
> stories of five successful men who shared the experience of being "cut from
> the team." Does being cut, Greene wonders, make you a superachiever
> later in life?*

## Before Reading

**Connecting:** Was there ever a time when you realized that you
were not going to be allowed to participate in something that you
wanted very much? Did someone tell you, "You're not good
enough," or did you realize it yourself?

**Anticipating:** Writers recount personal experiences for some reason, and that reason is never just "here is what happened to me";
instead, writers focus on the significance of the experience. What
significance does Greene see in these narratives?

1   I remember vividly the last time I cried. I was twelve years old, in the seventh
grade, and I had tried out for the junior high school basketball team. I walked
into the gymnasium; there was a piece of paper tacked to the bulletin board.

2   It was a cut list. The seventh-grade coach had put it up on the board.
The boys whose names were on the list were still on the team; they were welcome to keep coming to practices. The boys whose names were not on the
list had been cut; their presence was no longer desired. My name was not on
the list.

3   I had not known the cut was coming that day. I stood and stared at the
list. The coach had not composed it with a great deal of subtlety; the names

of the very best athletes were at the top of the sheet of paper, and the other members of the squad were listed in what appeared to be a descending order of talent. I kept looking at the bottom of the list, hoping against hope that my name would miraculously appear there if I looked hard enough.

4       I held myself together as I walked out of the gym and out of the school, but when I got home I began to sob. I couldn't stop. For the first time in my life, I had been told officially that I wasn't good enough. Athletics meant everything to boys that age; if you were on the team, even a substitute, it put you in the desirable group. If you weren't on the team, you might as well not be alive.

5       I had tried desperately in practice, but the coach never seemed to notice. It didn't matter how hard I was willing to work; he didn't want me there. I knew that when I went to school the next morning I would have to face the boys who had not been cut—the boys whose names were on the list, who were still on the team, who had been judged worthy while I had been judged unworthy.

6       All these years later, I remember it as if I were still standing right there in the gym. And a curious thing has happened: in traveling around the country, I have found that an inordinately large proportion of successful men share that same memory—the memory of being cut from a sports team as a boy.

7       I don't know how the mind works in matters like this; I don't know what went on in my head following that day when I was cut. But I know that my ambition has been enormous ever since then; I know that for all of my life since that day, I have done more work than I had to be doing, taken more assignments than I had to be taking, put in more hours than I had to be spending. I don't know if all of that came from a determination never to allow myself to be cut again—never to allow someone to tell me that I'm not good enough again—but I know it's there. And apparently it's there in a lot of other men, too.

8  Bob Graham, thirty-six, is a partner with the Jenner & Block law firm in Chicago. "When I was sixteen, baseball was my whole life," he said. "I had gone to a relatively small high school, and I had been on the team. But then my family moved, and I was going to a much bigger high school. All during the winter months I told everyone that I was a ballplayer. When spring came, of course I went out for the team.

9       "The cut list went up. I did not make the team. Reading that cut list is one of the clearest things I have in my memory. I wanted not to believe it, but there it was.

10       "I went home and told my father about it. He suggested that maybe I should talk to the coach. So I did. I pleaded to be put back on the team. He said there was nothing he could do; he said he didn't have enough room.

11       "I know for a fact that it altered my perception of myself. My view of myself was knocked down; my self-esteem was lowered. I felt so embarrassed; my whole life up to that point had revolved around sports, and particularly around playing baseball. That was the group I wanted to be in—the guys on the baseball team. And I was told that I wasn't good enough to be one of them.

12      "I know now that it changed me. I found out, even though I couldn't articulate it at the time, that there would be times in my life when certain people would be in a position to say 'You're not good enough' to me. I did not want that to happen ever again.

13      "It seems obvious to me now that being cut was what started me in determining that my success would always be based on my own abilities, and not on someone else's perceptions. Since then I've always been something of an overachiever; when I came to the law firm I was very aggressive in trying to run my own cases right away, to be the lead lawyer in the cases with which I was involved. I made partner at thirty-one; I never wanted to be left behind.

14      "Looking back, maybe it shouldn't have been that important. It was only baseball. You pass that by. Here I am. That coach is probably still there, still a high school baseball coach, still cutting boys off the baseball team every year. I wonder how many hundreds of boys he's cut in his life?"

15  Maurice McGrath is senior vice-president of Genstar Mortgage Corporation, a mortgage banking firm in Glendale, California. "I'm forty-seven years old, and I was fourteen when it happened to me, and I still feel something when I think about it," he said.

16      "I was in the eighth grade. I went to St. Philip's School in Pasadena. I went out for the baseball team, and one day at practice the coach came over to me. He was an Occidental College student who had been hired as the eighth-grade coach.

17      "He said, 'You're no good.' Those were his words. I asked him why he was saying that. He said, 'You can't hit the ball. I don't want you here.' I didn't know what to do, so I went over and sat off to the side, watching the others practice. The coach said I should leave the practice field. He said that I wasn't on the team, and that I didn't belong there anymore.

18      "I was outwardly stoic about it. I didn't want anyone to see how I felt. I didn't want to show that it hurt. But oh, did it hurt. All my friends played baseball after school every day. My best friend was the pitcher on the team. After I got whittled down by the coach, I would hear the other boys talking in class about what they were going to do at practice after school. I knew that I'd just have to go home.

19      "I guess you make your mind up never to allow yourself to be hurt like that again. In some way I must have been saying to myself, 'I'll play the game better.' Not the sports game, but anything I tried. I must have been saying, 'If I have to, I'll sit on the bench, but I'll be part of the team.'

20      "I try to make my own kids believe that, too. I try to tell them that they should show that they're a little bit better than the rest. I tell them to think of themselves as better. Who cares what anyone else thinks? You know, I can almost hear that coach saying the words. 'You're no good.' "

21  Author Malcolm MacPherson *(The Blood of His Servants)*, forty, lives in New York. "It happened to me in the ninth grade, at the Yalesville School in Yalesville, Connecticut," he said. "Both of my parents had just been killed in a car crash, and as you can imagine, it was a very difficult time in my life. I went out for the baseball team, and I did pretty well in practice.

22    "But in the first game I clutched. I was playing second base; the batter hit a pop-up, and I moved back to catch it. I can see it now. I felt dizzy as I looked up at the ball. It was like I was moving in slow motion, but the ball was going at regular speed. I couldn't get out of the way of my own feet. The ball dropped to the ground. I didn't catch it.

23    "The next day at practice, the coach read off the lineup. I wasn't on it. I was off the squad.

24    "I remember what I did: I walked. It was a cold spring afternoon, and the ground was wet, and I just walked. I was living with an aunt and uncle, and I didn't want to go home. I just wanted to walk forever.

25    "It drove my opinion of myself right into a tunnel. Right into a cave. And when I came out of the cave, something inside of me wanted to make sure in one manner or another that I would never again be told I wasn't good enough.

26    "I will confess that my ambition, to this day, is out of control. It's like a fire. I think the fire would have pretty much stayed in control if I hadn't been cut from that team. But that got it going. You don't slice ambition two ways; it's either there or it isn't. Those of us who went through something like that always know that we have to catch the ball. We'd rather die than have the ball fall at our feet.

27    "Once that fire is started in us, it never gets extinguished, until we die or have heart attacks or something. Sometimes I wonder about the home-run hitters; the guys who never even had to worry about being cut. They may have gotten the applause and the attention back then, but I wonder if they ever got the fire. I doubt it. I think maybe you have to get kicked in the teeth to get the fire started.

28    "You can tell the effect of something like that by examining the trail you've left in your life, and tracing it backward. It's almost like being a junkie with a need for success. You get attention and applause and you like it, but you never quite trust it. Because you know that back then you were good enough if only they would have given you a chance. You don't trust what you achieve, because you're afraid that someone will take it away from you. You know that it can happen; it already did.

29    "So you try to show people how good you are. Maybe you don't go out and become Dan Rather; maybe you just end up owning the Pontiac dealership in your town. But it's your dealership, and you're the top man, and every day you're showing people that you're good enough."

30  Dan Rather, fifty-two, is anchor of the CBS *Evening News*. "When I was thirteen, I had rheumatic fever," he said. "I became extremely skinny and extremely weak, but I still went out for the seventh-grade baseball team at Alexander Hamilton Junior High School in Houston.

31    "The school was small enough that there was no cut as such; you were supposed to figure out that you weren't good enough, and quit. Game after game I sat at the end of the bench, hoping that maybe this was the time I would get in. The coach never even looked at me; I might as well have been invisible.

32    "I told my mother about it. Her advice was not to quit. So I went to practice every day, and I tried to do well so that the coach would be impressed. He

never even knew I was there. At home in my room I would fantasize that there was a big game, and the three guys in front of me would all get hurt, and the coach would turn to me and put me in, and I would make the winning hit. But then there'd be another game, and the late innings would come, and if we were way ahead I'd keep hoping that this was the game when the coach would put me in. He never did.

33    "When you're that age, you're looking for someone to tell you you're okay. Your sense of self-esteem is just being formed. And what that experience that baseball season did was make me think that perhaps I wasn't okay.

34    "In the last game of the season something terrible happened. It was the last of the ninth inning, there were two outs, and there were two strikes on the batter. And the coach turned to me and told me to go out to right field.

35    "It was a totally humiliating thing for him to do. For him to put me in for one pitch, the last pitch of the season, in front of all the other boys on the team . . . I stood out there for that one pitch, and I just wanted to sink into the ground and disappear. Looking back on it, it was an extremely unkind thing for him to have done. That was nearly forty years ago, and I don't know why the memory should be so vivid now; I've never known if the coach was purposely making fun of me—and if he was, why a grown man would do that to a thirteen-year-old boy.

36    "I'm not a psychologist. I don't know if a man can point to one event in his life and say that that's the thing that made him the way he is. But when you're that age, and you're searching for your own identity, and all you want is to be told that you're all right . . . I wish I understood it better, but I know the feeling is still there."

## Questions on Subject and Purpose

1.  Greene's "cuts" all refer to not making an athletic team. What other kinds of "cuts" can you experience?
2.  It is always risky to speculate on an author's purpose, but why would Greene write about this? Why reveal to everyone something that hurt so much?
3.  How might Greene have gone about gathering examples of other men's similar experiences? Why would they be willing to contribute? Would everyone who has been cut be so candid?
4.  What can be said in the coaches' defense? Should everyone who tries out be automatically guaranteed a place on the team?

## Questions on Strategy and Audience

1.  Greene structures his essay in an unusual way. How can the essay be divided? Why give a series of examples of other men who were "cut"?
2.  How many examples are enough? What if Greene had used two examples? Eight examples? How would either extreme have influenced your reaction as a reader?

3. Greene does not provide a final concluding paragraph. Why?

4. Are you skeptical after you have finished the essay? Does everyone react to being cut in the same way? What would it take to convince you that these reactions are typical?

## Questions on Vocabulary and Style

1. How would you characterize the tone of Greene's essay? How is it achieved? Through language? Sentence structure? Paragraphing?

2. Why does Greene allow each man to tell his own story? Why not just summarize their experiences? Each story is enclosed in quotation marks. Do you think that these were the exact words of each man? Why?

3. What do *inordinately* (paragraph 6) and *stoic* (18) mean?

## Writing Suggestions

1. **For Your Journal or Blog.** Greene attributes enormous significance to a single experience; he feels that it literally changed his entire life. Try to remember some occasions when a disappointment seemed to change your life by changing your expectations for yourself. In your journal or blog, list some possible instances, and then explore one.

2. **For a Paragraph.** As children, we imagine ourselves doing or being anything we want. As we grow older, however, we discover that our choices become increasingly limited; in fact, each choice we make seems to cut off whole paths of alternative choices. We cannot be or do everything that we once thought we could. Choose a time in your life when you realized that a particular expectation or dream would never come true. In a paragraph, narrate that experience. Be sure to make the significance of your realization clear to your reader.

3. **For an Essay.** Describe an experience similar to the one that Greene narrates. It might have happened in an academic course during your school years, in a school or community activity, in athletics, or on the job: we can be "cut," "released," or "fired" from almost anything. Remember to make your narrative vivid through the use of detail and to make the significance of your narrative clear to the reader.

4. **For Research.** Check the validity of Greene's argument. Is there any evidence from research studies about the psychological effects of such vivid rejections? Using print and online sources (if they are available), see what you can find. A reference librarian can help you start your search for information. Use that research in an essay about the positive or negative effects of such experiences. Remember to document all sources. You might write your paper in one of the following forms (each has a slightly different audience):

   a. A conventional research paper for a college course

   b. An article for a popular magazine (for example, *Esquire, Working Woman, Parents*)

   c. A feature article for your school's newspaper

## For Further Study

**Focusing on Grammar and Writing.** Greene uses *ands* and *buts* to connect many sentences in his essay. We use both words more frequently in oral than in written speech. Why might Greene use them in his essay? What cautions might be offered in using such words to link sentences together?

**Working Together.** Working in small groups, discuss what evidence Greene would need in order to "prove" his assertion that being cut makes you an overachiever in life. What is the strength and the weakness of the type of example that Green uses as evidence?

**Seeing Other Modes at Work.** Each example is a narrative. How does Greene tell each story? To what extent are the narratives similar in structure? To what extent different?

**Finding Connections.** For a discussion of how a personal experience can be the springboard for a more general comment on human experience, read Scott Russell Sanders, "The Inheritance of Tools" (Chapter 3).

**Exploring the Web.** Greene's essay originally appeared in *Esquire*, not a sports magazine such as *Sports Illustrated* or *Sporting News*. Why? You can compare the magazines electronically to see how their target audiences shape their content.

# Westbury Court

Edwidge Danticat

*Edwidge Danticat (1969–) was born in Port-au-Prince, Haiti. At the age of twelve she came to New York City to join her parents who had emigrated some years earlier. She earned a degree in French literature from Barnard College and an M.F.A. from Brown University. At twenty-six she was a finalist for a National Book Award for her collection of short stories* Krik? Krak! *Her other books include* The Farming of Bones *(1998),* Behind the Mountains *(2002),* The Dew Breaker *(2004), and* Brother, I'm Dying *(2007).*

**On Writing:** *Danticat's native languages were Haitian Creole and French. She comments, "My writing in English is a consequence of my migration, in the same way that immigrant children speaking to each other in English is a consequence of their migration." She continues, "When I first started writing, I wasn't thinking about publishing it. I was working at writing. . . . Writing in any language is difficult. . . . I like to walk and think things out. . . . I prefer silence when writing. That was hard to come by when growing up with three [brothers]."*

## Before Reading

**Connecting:** Danticat writes of a tragic experience that occurred when she was fourteen and living in Brooklyn. Do you have a particular sad or joyful experience that you connect with a place that you lived?

**Anticipating:** The core experience about which Danticat writes in the essay occurred almost twenty years ago. Why does she remember it now? What significance does it still have for her?

1      When I was fourteen years old, we lived in a six-story brick building in a cul-de-sac off of Flatbush Avenue, in Brooklyn, called Westbury Court. Beneath the building ran a subway station through which rattled the D, M, and Q trains every fifteen minutes or so. Though there was graffiti on most of the walls of Westbury Court, and hills of trash piled up outside, and though the elevator wasn't always there when we opened the door to step inside and the heat and hot water weren't always on, I never dreamed of leaving Westbury Court until the year of the fire.

2      I was watching television one afternoon when the fire began. I loved television then, especially the afternoon soap operas, my favorite of which was

*General Hospital.* I would bolt out of my last high school class every day, pick up my youngest brother, Karl, from day care, and watch *General Hospital* with him on my lap while doing my homework during the commercials. My other two brothers, André and Kelly, would later join us in the apartment, but they preferred to watch cartoons in the back bedroom.

3        One afternoon while *General Hospital* and afternoon cartoons were on, a fire started in apartment 6E, across the hall. There in that apartment lived our new neighbors, an African-American mother and her two boys. We didn't know the name of the mother, or the names and ages of her boys, but I venture to guess that they were around five and ten years old.

4        I didn't know a fire had started until two masked, burly firemen came knocking on our door. My brothers and I rushed out into the hallway filled with smoke and were quickly escorted down to the first floor by some other firemen already on our floor. While we ran by, the door to apartment 6E had already been knocked over by the fire squad and inside was filled with bright flames and murky smoke.

5        All of the tenants of the building who were home at that time were crowded on the sidewalk outside. My brothers and I, it seemed, were the last to be evacuated. Clutching my brothers' hands, I wondered if I had remembered to lock our apartment door. Was there anything valuable we could have taken?

6        An ambulance screeched to a stop in front of the building, and the two firemen who had knocked on our door came out carrying the pliant and lifeless bodies of the two children from across the hall. Their mother jumped out of the crowd and ran toward them, screaming, "My babies—not my babies," as the children were lowered into the back of the ambulance and transferred into the arms of the emergency medical personnel. The fire was started by the two boys, after their mother had stepped out to pick up some groceries at the supermarket down the street. They had been playing with matches.

7        (Later my mother would tell us, "See, this is what happens to children who play with matches. Sometimes it is too late to say, 'I shouldn't have.' " My brother Kelly, who was fascinated with fire and liked to hold up a match to the middle of his palm until the light fizzled out, gave up this party trick after the fire.)

8        We were quiet that afternoon when both our parents came home. We were the closest to the fire in the building, and the most religious of our parents' friends saw it as a miracle that we had escaped safe and sound. When my mother asked how come I, the oldest one, hadn't heard the children scream or hadn't smelled the smoke coming from across the hall, I confessed that I had been watching *General Hospital* and was too consumed in the intricate plot.

9        (After the fire, my mother had us stay with a family on the second floor for a few months, after school. I felt better not having to be wholly responsible for myself and my brothers, in case something like that fire should ever happen again.)

10        The apartment across the hall stayed empty for a long time, and whenever I walked past it, a piece of its inner skeleton would squeak, and occasionally burnt wood that might have been hanging by a fragile singed thread would

crash down and cause a domino effect of further ruptures, unleashed like those children's last cries, which I had not heard because I had been so wrapped up in the made-up drama of a world where, even though the adults' lives were often in turmoil, the children came home to the welcoming arms of waiting mommies and nannies who served them freshly baked cookies on porcelain plates and helped them to remove their mud-soaked boots, if it was raining, lest they soil the lily-white carpets. But should their boots accidentally sully the carpet, or should their bright yellow raincoats inadvertently drip on the sparkling linoleum, there would be a remedy for that as well. And if their house should ever catch fire, a smart dog or a good neighbor would rescue them just in time, and the fire trucks would come right quick because some attentive neighbor would call them.

11    Through the trail of voices that came up to comfort us, I heard that the children's mother would be prosecuted for negligence and child abandonment. I couldn't help but wonder, would our parents have suffered the same fate had it been my brothers and me who were killed in the fire?

12    When they began to repair the apartment across the hall, I would occasionally sneak out to watch the workmen. They were shelling the inside of the apartment and replacing everything from the bedroom closets to the kitchen floors. I never saw the mother of the dead boys again and never heard anything of her fate.

13    A year later, after the apartment was well polished and painted, two blind Haitian brothers and their sister moved in. They were all musicians and were part of a group called les Frères Parent, the Parent Brothers. Once my parents allowed my brothers and me to come home from school to our apartment, I would always listen carefully for our new tenants, so I'd be the first to know if anything went awry.

14    What I heard coming from the apartment soon after they moved in was music, "engagé" music, which the brothers were composing to protest against the dictatorship in Haiti, from which they had fled. The Parent Brothers and their sister, Lydie, did nothing but rehearse a cappella most days when they were not receiving religious and political leaders from Haiti and from the Haitian community in New York.

15    The same year after the fire, a cabdriver who lived down the hall in 6J was killed on a night shift in Manhattan; a good friend of my father's, a man who gave great Sunday afternoon parties in 6F, died of cirrhosis of the liver. One day while my brothers and I were at school and my parents were at work, someone came into our apartment through our fire escape and stole my father's expensive camera. That same year a Nigerian immigrant was shot and killed in front of the building across the street. To appease us, my mother said, "Nothing like that ever happens out of the blue. He was in a fight with someone." It was too troublesome for her to acknowledge that people could die randomly, senselessly, at Westbury Court or anywhere else.

16    Every day on my way back from school, I hurried past the flowers and candles piled in front of the spot where the Nigerian, whose name I didn't know, had been murdered. Still I never thought I was living in a violent place.

It was an elevated castle above a clattering train tunnel, a blind alley where children from our building and the building across the street had erected a common basketball court for hot summer afternoon games, an urban yellow brick road where hopscotch squares dotted the sidewalk next to burned-out, abandoned cars. It was home.

17    My family and I moved out of Westbury Court three years after the fire. Every once in a while, though, the place came up in conversation, linked to either a joyous or a painful memory. One of the girls who had scalded her legs while boiling a pot of water for her bath during one of those no-heat days got married last year. After the burglar had broken into the house and taken my father's camera, my father—an amateur photography buff—never took another picture.

18    My family and I often reminisce about the Parent Brothers when we see them in Haitian newspapers or on television; we brag that we knew them when, before one of the brothers became a senator in Haiti and the sister, Lydie, became mayor of one of the better-off Haitian suburbs, Pétion-Ville. We never talk about the lost children.

19    Even now, I question what I remember about the children. Did they really die? Or did their mother simply move away with them after the fire? Maybe they were not even boys at all. Maybe they were two girls. Or one boy and one girl. Or maybe I am struggling to phase them out of my memory altogether. Not just them, but the fear that their destiny could have so easily been mine and my brothers'.

20    A few months ago, I asked my mother, "Do you remember the children and the fire at Westbury Court?"

21    Without missing a flutter of my breath, my mother replied, "Oh those children, those poor children, their poor mother. Sometimes it is too late to say, 'I shouldn't have.' "

## Questions on Subject and Purpose

1.  How long ago did the fire take place? What details in the story allow you to arrive at an approximate answer?

2.  How many examples of life at Westbury Court does Danticat include?

3.  Why might the essay be titled "Westbury Court"? What does that suggest about the essay? How appropriate would a title such as "Sometimes It Is Too Late" have been?

## Questions on Strategy and Audience

1.  In paragraphs 7 and 21, Danticat repeats her mother's observation: "Sometimes it is too late to say, 'I shouldn't have.' " Why?

2.  Danticat encloses paragraphs 7 and 9 within parentheses. Why?

3.  What is it about the essay and the experiences that it relates that might appeal to a reader?

## Questions on Vocabulary and Style

1. What is the effect of the typical televised depiction of children returning home in paragraph 10?

2. In paragraph 16, Danticat describes Westbury Court as an "elevated castle," "a blind alley," "an urban yellow brick road." What are these figures of speech called?

3. Be prepared to define the following words: *pliant* (paragraph 6), *sully* (10), *appease* (15).

## Writing Suggestions

1. **For Your Journal or Blog.** Everyone has had scary experiences, but sometimes an experience will forever change the way we think or act. In your journal or blog brainstorm about some past experiences that altered your later life. Jot down both a short account of what happened and a sentence or two about the significance of that single experience.

2. **For a Paragraph.** Expand your journal or blog entry into a paragraph. Concentrate on a single event, focusing especially on its significance.

3. **For an Essay.** "Sometimes it is too late to say, 'I shouldn't have.' " Use the mother's observation for the basis of an essay in which you explore an example or series of related examples or experiences that taught you the truth (or the falseness) of such a claim.

4. **For Research.** When children suddenly and unexpectedly die, schools (elementary, secondary, colleges, and universities) often have grief counselors available for their peers. What do we know about the impact that the sudden death of a friend or a classmate might have on a peer? Research the topic—or an aspect of the topic—and present your findings in a longer essay. If you recall a similar experience from your life, you might use that as a departure point for your paper.

## For Further Study

**Focusing on Grammar and Writing.** Select one or more of Danticat's paragraphs (1–3, 7–8, or 1–14 would be good choices) and explain why she uses each comma. A grammar handbook will give you a list of rules for comma usage. Remember that we use marks of punctuation to help our readers see the structures of our sentences.

**Working Together.** Divide into small groups. Each group should choose a group of paragraphs (there are twenty-one in all) and list the details or examples that Danticat uses. How effective is each example or detail?

**Seeing Other Modes at Work.** Where can you see both narration and description at work in the essay?

**Finding Connections.** Bob Greene's "Cut" offers another example of how a personal experience changes our perceptions, as does Terry Tempest Williams' "The Village Watchman" (Chapter 3).

**Exploring the Web.** What do we know about the impact that a sudden death of a friend or classmate might have on a peer? Use the Web to gather information and examples.

# Ready for Some Fútbol?

Oscar Casares

*Oscar Casares graduated from the University of Texas and worked in advertising before earning his M.F.A. from the University of Iowa's Writers' workshop. A native of Brownsville, Texas, the town from which the Potter Cowboys in the essay come, Casares writes short stories drawing on his years of growing up in the Rio Grande Valley.* Brownsville, *a collection of short stories, appeared in 2003.*

*"Ready for Some Fútbol?" was first published in* Texas Monthly *in November 2006. It was included in* The Best American Sports Writing, 2007.

**On Writing:** *Talking about his choice of subjects for stories, Casares said: "I sort of feel my form of activism is that by showing Mexican-Americans involved in ordinary things as I have always seen them, by normalizing them, what I'm doing is sort of showing the humanity of the group."*

## Before Reading

**Connecting:** Do you remember anytime in high school sports in which your school made banners or floats that made fun of the rival team? Was that any different than what happens at this game?

**Anticipating:** The event described in this essay was a high school state soccer championship game. What expectations might you have about a story that reports on a championship game?

1 **S**peedy Gonzales, the famous cartoon star of the fifties and sixties, has been in the news again lately. It seems the image of the "fastest mouse in all Mexico" was evoked recently at the boys' 5A state soccer championship, pitting the nationally ranked Coppell Cowboys, from North Texas, against the Porter Cowboys, from Brownsville, the southernmost city on the U.S.-Mexico border. In an effort to belittle their opponents, the Coppell fans held up a poster showing Speedy Gonzales about to be squashed by a large shoe. The sign read STOMP ON BROWNVILLE! (and no, that's not a typo). When officials forced Coppell to remove the sign, the Porter fans continued cheering for their underdog team with the chant "*¡Sí se puede!*" ("Yes, we can!"), a call to action recovered from the era of Cesar Chavez's marches with the United Farm Workers of America. The Coppell fans answered this with their own chant of "USA! USA!" implying that the Porter players and their fans were not citizens

of the United States. And when that didn't work, one of the fans called out, "You suck, you beaner!" In the end, though, their taunts were as effective as Sylvester the Cat's were on Speedy Gonzales, Porter won 2-1 in overtime.

2    Interestingly enough, this was all happening while Congress debated an immigration reform bill, including the possibility of a seven-hundred-mile wall along our southern border (one end of which would pass about a mile from Gladys Porter High School, my alma mater), and while hundreds of thousands of undocumented immigrants and their supporters marched in cities across the United States, also chanting "¡Sí se puede!" Soon several thousand National Guard troops would be deployed to assist the Border Patrol in certain areas, including South Texas.

3    What the Coppell fans and the players on the charged soccer field probably didn't realize was that their reaction toward a group they assumed was not American could hardly be counted as new. One of the most concentrated efforts to rid the country of illegal immigrants occurred in 1954, when the U.S. government officially passed Operation Wetback, a mandate to expel all illegal workers, particularly those from Mexico (as the name may have clued you in to). Led by the Immigration and Naturalization Service and aided by the municipal, county, state, and federal authorities, as well as the military, the operation resulted in a massive sweep of Mexican-American neighborhoods and random stops of "Mexican-looking" people.

4    A year earlier, when these bitter feelings were already escalating, Warner Bros. introduced a new cartoon character named Speedy Gonzales. The original Speedy debuted in a cartoon titled "Cat-Tails for Two," where his character looked more like a rat, mean and sleazy and with a gold tooth the animator must have thought would add a touch of realism. Speedy Gonzales then disappeared for a time, only to make a comeback in 1955 in what could be described as a more user-friendly version of the original drawing. Warner Bros. had fixed his teeth, worked on his English, expanded his wardrobe—from an old T-shirt, barely covering his privates, to white campesino pants and shirt, both finely pressed, and a red bandanna he kept neatly wound into what looked like a bow tie—and then added a bit of panache with the sombrero, worn slightly askew, that would soon become his trademark. Later that same year, Warner Bros. won the Academy Award for Best Short Subject with the cartoon *Speedy Gonzales.*

5    How strange then that the Coppell fans would choose to taunt their opponents with a poster of a mouse known for running circles around his enemies. What started out as mockery quickly turned into a self-fulfilling prophecy, as the little guy used his speed to even things out against a bigger, more physical competitor. Along the way, the Porter team would prove that the game amounted to more than just some name-calling. Because for all questions of nationality, this actually turns out to be the classic American story: underdog sports team from a small, remote town defies the odds and earns a bid to play in the championship game, where these players must now face a formidable opponent in a match that forces them to look inward if they hope to win.

6    Gladys Porter High School is located on International Boulevard, about two miles from the Gateway International Bridge, which crosses into Matamoros.

The school is also a block from Southmost, historically one of the poorest areas of town, where at one time it was said that even the cops wouldn't go after dark. Locally, Porter was known as the school that couldn't win, in the classroom or on the playing field; it seemed the only people who believed in Porter were from Porter. The school has changed dramatically since I left some twenty years ago—it is now the district's magnet school for engineering and technology, and in 2003 the football team came close to capturing the district title—and it has gathered an almost cultlike following of fans, collectively known as the Porter Nation.

7    A few days before the big game, the Porter soccer players loaded their equipment onto the school bus that would take them the 370 miles from the border to Round Rock, just north of Austin, the site of the state championship. Now they just had to wait for the drug-detection dog to inspect the vehicle. The Brownsville Independent School District has a policy of bringing dogs to check any bus that is scheduled to leave the region; according to James Kizer, Porter's athletic coordinator, the searches are done to prevent any "surprises" later. The argument could be made that the inspections are in the best interest of the team and the school, as a preventive measure, should there be a player who decides to smuggle illegal drugs and run the risk of serious charges. But in a way, the searches are not so different from the ones the players would be subjected to if they were down the street at the bridge, trying to enter the United States from Mexico.

8    Once the team passed the inspection, it was clear to leave the area. That is, until the next inspection some ninety miles later, near the King Ranch. By law the bus driver was required to stop at the Border Patrol's Sarita checkpoint so federal agents and their drug-detection dogs could search the vehicle. To facilitate the process, the players wore special tags that identified them as student athletes en route to a competition. (These tags prevent the sort of incident that occurred earlier this year when another team made it through the checkpoint only for it to be discovered later that some of the passengers were not actually with the team and had slipped away from the bus during a stop, supposedly to make their way into Texas illegally.) The Porter players were used to stopping at the checkpoint on their way to tournaments, including the semifinal match that had led to the championship game. Still, there is something disconcerting about being in your own country and having to identify yourself to a federal agent.

9    This time around, the Border Patrol agent happened to be female. As she boarded the bus, another agent led a dog around the perimeter of the vehicle. The players knew the drill: sit up in your seat and give the agent your full attention.

10    "Everybody U.S. citizens?" she asked, stepping into the aisle.

11    The coaches and players all nodded and said yes.

12    "Where are you coming from?" she asked.

13    "Brownsville," one of the nearby players answered.

14    "Which high school in Brownsville?"

15    "Porter."

16    "Hey," she said, "I went to Porter!"

17    After so many such inspections during the season, the players were more than happy to meet another member of the Porter Nation and hear her wish them luck. These warm feelings lasted only until the following afternoon, when they walked onto the field and fully realized the level of competition they were up against. The Coppell team was ranked second in the nation, with three of its players having already been recruited to play at the collegiate level. This was also Coppell's third straight year to compete in the state championship, including 2004, when it won the title. As if this weren't enough to contend with, there was also that Speedy Gonzales poster waving in the stands.

18    If Coppell fans noticed anything less than American about the Porter team, it might have been its style of play. Spectators in this country are used to watching the type of soccer showcased during the recent World Cup, which tends to be more physical (even when the players aren't giving each other head butts in the sternum). But Porter plays a faster-paced soccer that focuses on shorter passes, in what some people might describe as more of a Mexican style. It certainly isn't the kind of soccer most kids across suburbia grow up with. The quicker technique makes sense because of the smaller size of the players in the Rio Grande Valley. Porter's approach to the game is actually quite common in this region of Texas, as well as on the other side of the river, because until recently, crossing over to Matamoros was the only way for boys to play on leagues year-round.

19    These contrasting styles just added to what was already happening in the stands. As the game wore on and the tension grew, Porter coach Luis Zarate, who himself had grown up playing on both sides of the river before becoming a place kicker for the University of Houston, called a time-out to center his team and deal with the slurs. "Focus on your game. At the end of the day, people are going to be talking about who won the game, not about these other things," he said, probably in Spanish, since his players are bilingual and this is the common language of soccer along the border.

20    What Coach Zarate wanted more than anything was to impress upon his players that they had fought hard all season to make it to this final game and had earned every right to be on the field. "You're here. You belong here!"

21    He repeated this until it began to sink in. "You're here. You belong here!" Here at the state championship, here in Texas, here in the United States. They had traveled all the way from Gladys Porter High School, in the shadows of a proposed anti-immigration wall, to the 5A state championship, and they were exactly where they should be. "You're here. You belong here!" His words held an immediacy, but they also managed to convey a message his players could carry with them off the soccer field.

22    Jorge Briones, described as "a scoring machine" by his coach, went on to make the two goals that won the game, and the Porter Cowboys became the first Rio Grande Valley team to win a 5A division title in any sport. The team returned to Brownsville to a hero's welcome. Everyone, from alumni dating back thirty years to local politicians, lined up to publicly offer his congratulations. What no one could offer the players, though, was a way to afford the $300 championship rings. The University Interscholastic League, the governing

body for most high school athletics programs in the state, sets limits on what gifts a team can receive from its school or school district. Eventually, businesses came together to offer the players jobs at various car dealerships in town. Briones spent a couple weeks washing cars at Marroquin Auto Sales, a used-car dealership along the freeway, so he could earn the money for his state MVP ring.

23      When I called Coach Zarate on his cell phone, he and his team happened to be the guests of honor, along with a few Dallas Cowboys Cheerleaders, at the grand opening of the new Wal-Mart Supercenter in Brownsville. The store manager had just donated $1,000 to go toward the team's funds for next season. I spoke to Coach Zarate a few minutes before he asked if I wanted to talk to Briones. Then he turned to his star player and in Spanish told him there was a guy from a magazine who wanted to ask him some questions.

24      "Can 1 talk to him in Spanish?" I heard Briones ask.

25      "Sure," the coach said. "He's from down here."

26      Then Briones came on the line and I congratulated him, until it got so loud at the grand opening that he could hardly hear me. It sounded as if there were a pep rally going on.

27      "Can you wait a minute, sir?" he asked.

28      And then we both stayed on the line, listening to "The Star-Spangled Banner" playing in the background.

## Questions on Subject and Purpose

1.  What is the subject of the essay? How might this essay differ from a newspaper account of the championship game?

2.  Paragraphs 7 through 16 deal with the bus ride and the two inspection stops that the Porter team must make. Why include these details?

3.  What might Casares want to show or reveal in the essay?

## Questions on Strategy and Audience

1.  Casares acknowledges that Porter is his "alma mater" (paragraph 2). What is the effect of that disclosure?

2.  Why might Casares have chosen to end the essay with the telephone conversation?

3.  Presumably the essay was seen by many readers, the majority of whom are not Mexican-American. How do you think that the audience might have reacted to the essay? What about the supporters of the Coppell team?

## Questions on Vocabulary and Style

1.  What is ironic about displaying Speedy Gonzales, "the fastest mouse in all Mexico"?

2.  Why might Casares choose to record the conversation between the Border Patrol agent and the team (paragraphs 9–16)?

3.  Be prepared to define the following words: *deployed* (paragraph 2), *panache* (4), *askew* (4).

## Writing Suggestions

1. **For Your Journal or Blog**. Have you ever drawn criticism or taunts from others based, for example, on your appearance, ethnic or racial identity, religious preference, abilities or interests, sexual orientation, socioeconomic status? Maybe as a younger child? Did you ever tease or make fun of anyone for one of these reasons? Explore a memory.

2. **For a Paragraph**. Expand your journal or blog in a paragraph. Try to focus on a single moment—not a series of moments—in which you were either the object of ridicule or when you engaged in such behavior. Do not tell the reader how it made you feel, allow the story to show the reader.

3. **For an Essay.** Gather a series of examples from different categories of taunts. Look especially for those that are not blatantly racial or ethnic. Your goal in the essay is to use the examples to alert your audience to the often unthinking remarks people make all the time that reveal prejudice, disapproval, even disdain.

4. **For Research.** Children tease and bully one another; people make fun of those who are different, regardless of what that difference is. Why? What is it about human nature or human interaction that occasions such behavior? Research the topic in your library and online and see what explanations have been offered. Present your findings in a documented essay.

## For Further Study

**Focusing on Grammar and Writing.** Casares inserts material into the middle of sentences using a variety of punctuation: commas, parentheses, and dashes. Locate examples of each type in the essay and offer an explanation for why he choose that particular way to punctuate the inserted information.

**Working Together.** Working in small groups, gather examples of taunting behavior that you have encountered or observed at school. Compile a list and then speculate on what it was that lead people to engage in such behavior. When was it intentionally malicious? When thoughtless? When meant to be funny (whether it was or not)?

**Seeing Other Modes at Work.** The overall structure of the essay is a narrative, following the Porter Cowboys from the point when the team leaves for the game until the point at which the town is celebrating the team's victory. To what extent might the essay also have a persuasive intention?

**Finding Connections.** Interesting pairings can be made with Judith Ortiz Cofer's "The Myth of the Latin Woman" (Chapter 4), Brent Staples's "Black Men and Public Space" (Chapter 7), and Diane Ravitch's "You Can't Say That" (Chapter 8).

**Exploring the Web.** How should you respond if someone taunts you or if you see someone being taunted? What reactions might be appropriate? Explore the Web to locate sites that offer advice on how to respond to (or ignore) slurs and similar verbal cruelties.

# Can Wikipedia Ever Make the Grade?

Brock Read

*Brock Read is a regular contributor to* The Chronicle of Higher
Education *where this article first appeared in October 2006. The*
Chronicle *is a weekly newspaper for college and university administrators, staff, and faculty. Wikipedia explains that its name is a combination of two words:* "wiki *(a type of collaborative Website) and
encyclopedia."*

## Before Reading

**Connecting:** How often have you looked up something on
Wikipedia? Did you ever question its accuracy?

**Anticipating:** At the time of this writing, Wikipedia has nearly
2.5 million articles in English (probably the number is considerably higher as you read this). What kind of evidence would it take
to persuade you that Wikipedia might not be a good source for a
research paper?

1   **A**lexander M.C. Halavais, an assistant professor of communications at
Quinnipiac College, has spent hours and hours wading through Wikipedia,
which has become the Internet's hottest information source. Like thousands
of his colleagues, he has turned to the open-source encyclopedia for timely information and trivia; unlike most of his peers, he has, from time to time, contributed his own expertise to the site.

2   But to Wikipedia's legions of ardent amateur editors, Mr. Halavais may
be best remembered as a troll.

3   Two years ago, when he was teaching at the State University of New
York at Buffalo, the professor hatched a plan designed to undermine the site's
veracity—which, at that time, had gone largely unchallenged by scholars.
Adopting the pseudonym "Dr. al-Halawi" and billing himself as a "visiting lec-
turer in law, Jesus College, Oxford University," Mr. Halavais snuck onto
Wikipedia and slipped 13 errors into its various articles. He knew that no
one would check his persona's credentials: Anyone can add material to the
encyclopedia's entries without having to show any proof of expertise.

4   Some of the errata he inserted—like a claim that Frederick Douglass,
the abolitionist, had made Syracuse, N.Y., his home for four years—seemed

entirely credible. Some—like an Oscar for film editing that Mr. Halavais awarded to *The Rescuers Down Under*, an animated Disney film—were more obviously false, and easier to fact-check. And others were downright odd: In an obscure article on a short-lived political party in New Brunswick, Canada, the professor wrote of a politician felled by "a very public scandal relating to an official Party event at which cocaine and prostitutes were made available."

5    Mr. Halavais expected some of his fabrications to languish online for some time. Like many academics, he was skeptical about a mob-edited publication that called itself an authoritative encyclopedia. But less than three hours after he posted them, all of his false facts had been deleted, thanks to the vigilance of Wikipedia editors who regularly check a page on the Website that displays recently updated entries. On Dr. al-Halawi's "user talk" page, one Wikipedian pleaded with him to "refrain from writing nonsense articles and falsifying information."

6    Mr. Halavais realized that the jig was up.

7    Writing about the experiment on his blog (http://alex.halavais.net), Mr. Halavais argued that a more determined "troll"—in Web-forum parlence, a poster who contributes only inflammatory or disruptive content—could have done a better job of slipping mistakes into the encyclopedia. But he said he was "impressed" by Wikipedia participants' ability to root out his fabrications. Since then several other high-profile studies have confirmed that the site does a fairly good job at getting its facts straight—particularly in articles on science, an area where Wikipedia excels.

8    Among academics, however, Wikipedia continues to receive mixed—and often failing—grades. Wikipedia's supporters often portray the site as a brave new world in which scholars can rub elbows with the general public. But doubters of the approach—and in academe, there are many—say Wikipedia devalues the notion of expertise itself.

9    Those skeptics include Michael Gorman, the immediate past president of the American Library Association. "The problem with an online encyclopedia created by anybody is that you have no idea whether you are reading an established person in the field or someone with an ax to grind," said Mr. Gorman, dean of library services at California State University at Fresno, in an interview with the *San Francisco Chronicle*.

10    Perhaps because of the site's refusal to give professors or other experts priority—and because of an editing process that can resemble a free-for-all—a clear preponderance of Wikipedia's contents has been written by people outside academe. In fact, the dearth of scholarly contributions to the site has prompted one prominent former Wikipedian—Larry Sanger, one of the site's co-founders—to start an alternative online encyclopedia, vetted by experts.

11    But as the encyclopedia's popularly continues to grow, some professors are calling on scholars to contribute articles to Wikipedia, or at least to hone less-than-inspiring entries in the site's vast and growing collection. Those scholars' take is simple: If you can't beat the Wikipedians, join 'em.

12      Proponents of that strategy showed up in force at Wikimania, the annual meeting for Wikipedia contributors, a three-day event held in August at Harvard University. Leaders of Wikipedia said there that they had turned their attention to increasing the accuracy of information on the Website, announcing several policies intended to prevent editorial vandalism and to improve or erase Wikipedia's least-trusted entries. "We can no longer feel satisfied and happy when we see these numbers going up." said Jimmy Wales, Wikipedia's other co-founder, referring to the site's ever-expanding base of articles. "We should continue to turn our attention away from growth and towards quality."

13      Still, not all of Wikipedia's most-active contributors want academics in their club. They argue that an army of hobbyists, teenagers, and even the occasional troll can create a more comprehensive, more useful, and possibly even more accurate resource than can be found in the ivied halls.

14      "The university needs Wikipedia more than Wikipedia needs the university," said Elijah Meeks at Wikimania. He has studied the site as he pursues a master's degree at the University of California at Merced. The encyclopedia, he contended, will keep on humming—and will improve—whether scholars sign on or not.

## 'Scurrilous' Content

15  The openness that makes Wikipedia so alluring to its contributors is precisely what discomfits scholars. Because anyone can post, the site is in a constant state of flux—which creates plenty of opportunity for abuse. The common scholarly perception that the site is error-prone is true, if momentary lapses in accuracy are counted. Mr. Halavais's fabrications may have stayed online for only a couple of hours, but any visitors who happened upon the article on Syracuse during that time would have absorbed some bad information.

16      Then there are the mistakes that linger—most famously, perhaps, in the case of John Seigenthaler Sr.

17      Last November, Mr. Seigenthaler, a longtime journalist, noticed that a Wikipedia entry claimed that he was "thought to have been directly involved in the Kennedy assassinations of both John and his brother, Bobby." The comment—which Mr. Seigenthaler called "malicious" and "scurrilous" in a widely published newspaper article—had sat, uncorrected, for more than four months.

18      In that time the misinformation had reached other popular Websites, like Reference.com and Answers.com, which regularly cull material from Wikipedia. Arguing that his reputation had been tarnished, Mr. Seigenthaler called Wikipedia "a flawed and irresponsible research tool."

19      The site's administrators responded by requiring users to register before they post articles. (The new rule would not have stopped the vandal who changed Mr. Seigenthaler's article, since he edited the text rather than created it.) But the incident was nevertheless damaging to Wikipedia's reputation.

20      Relatively obscure articles like the one on Mr. Seigenthaler—and among Wikipedia's almost 1.5 million entries, there's plenty of esoterica—are especially

vulnerable to vandalism, says Mr. Halavais: "The high-traffic areas are going to be the cleanest."

21    But errors on Wikipedia are not confined to its margins. C. Earl Edmondson, a professor of history at Davidson College, recalls visiting Wikipedia's article on the Mayerling Incident, a 19th century scandal in which Rudolf, crown prince of Austria, died along with his mistress under mysterious circumstances. European historians consider the incident important. But Wikipedia's treatment of it, says Mr. Edmondson, is troubling.

22    "Much of the article seems to be valid, even if not comprehensive," he says, but its concluding comments—including a passage that cites the incident as "the end of the ancient house of Habsburg"—are "atrociously erroneous." (In fact, the Habsburgs were deposed in 1918. And Wikipedia's article on the royal house makes no mention of the Mayerling Incident.)

## Signs of Success

23  Perhaps the biggest and most well-known attempt to grade the quality of Wikipedia was done last year by the journal *Nature*, which published a study comparing the accuracy of scientific articles in Wikipedia and the *Encyclopaedia Britannica*. Staff members at the journal chose articles from each reference work and sent them to a panel of experts in the respective fields, who reviewed the texts for factual accuracy, misleading statements, and key omissions. The reviewers found, somewhat surprisingly, that Wikipedia was playing in *Britannica's* ballpark: An average *Britannica* article had about three errors, while a typical Wikipedia post on the same subject had about four.

24  *Britannica* editors were quick to assail the study: The test, they argued in a lengthy rebuttal on the encyclopedia's Website, "was so poorly carried out and its findings so error-laden that it was completely without merit." Still, the report caused some scholars to rethink their skepticism about Wikipedia, says Mr. Halavais.

25    In an article for the June issue of *The Journal of American History*, Roy Rosenzweig, a history professor at George Mason University and director of its Center for History and New Media, gave a passing—if conflicted—grade to Wikipedia's coverage of history. Like the *Nature* editors, he found that Wikipedia was almost as factually accurate as a commercial encyclopedia (in this case, Microsoft's online *Encarta*).

26    "Are Wikipedians good historians?" he asked. "As in the old tale of the blind men and the elephant, your assessment of Wikipedia as history depends a great deal on what part you touch."

27    Wikipedia, Mr. Rosenzweig found, had produced thorough, fairly well-written essays on such topics as Red Faber, a Hall of Fame pitcher for the Chicago White Sox, and "Postage Stamps and Postal History of the United States." But a number of issues that most historians would deem far more important received "incomplete, almost capricious, coverage." An article on

American history from 1918 to 1945 made no mention of "dozens of standard topics—the Red Scare, the Ku Klux Klan, the Harlem Renaissance, woman suffrage, the rise of radio," he said. And an article on women's rights in the United States, he wrote "leaves out the 19th Amendment but devotes a paragraph to splits in the National Organization for Women over the defense of Valerie Solanas [who shot Andy Warhol]."

28     Mr. Rosenzweig notes, amusedly, that several Wikipedians appear to have since read his critiques and edited a number of articles in response to his concerns.

29     It's no surprise that Mr. Rosenzweig is more ambivalent about Wikipedia than are the editors of *Nature*. Mr. Wales, Wikipedia's co-founder, says science is the Web publication's strongest suit. The encyclopedia's contributors—a group that, at Wikimania, included plenty of people wearing shirts emblazoned with the logos of open-source-software projects—tend to be tech-savvy and scientific-minded, he says.

30     "A computer scientist is quite comfortable banging out Wikipedia articles, but a poetry expert is less likely to do it," he says. "That's a barrier that's really unfortunate."

31     The gap between Wikipedia's coverage of science and its coverage of the humanities may not be a matter of simple demographics, though. Mr. Meeks, the Merced student, who is an occasional Wikipedia poster himself, points out that the science articles benefit from a reliance on concrete facts.

32     "In the academy, it's the science professors who give Wikipedia the most credence because it's easier for them to confirm or deny articles," he says. "It's much easier to tell if someone is writing a good article on selenium than on Soviet folk art."

33     What's more, says Mr. Rosenzweig, scientists are experienced in the type of collaborative scholarship that Wikipedia thrives on. But many of the areas that Mr. Wales says are Wikipedia's weakest—art and law, for example—demand contextual analysis and interpretive finesse, areas that are typically the domain of individual scholars.

34     It is in those areas, Mr. Rosenzweig says, that "professors should go in and participate in the process."

35     Mr. Wales says he would welcome more professors to the site, as long as they are willing to work with other contributors without talking down to them. "Putting out the message that we're eager to have more academic participation is quite important," he says.

36     Encouraging that participation may be easier said than done. Professors have, for the most part, stayed away. The site now has more than 40,000 active, registered contributors, members of an online community who bond over shared interests even as they spar over changes in articles. About 1,100 of those contributors have identified themselves as graduate students, says Mr. Meeks. Far fewer have identified themselves as professors.

37     Among the reasons that so few professors have joined is the site's mission—which, depending on whom you ask, is either nobly anti-elitist or distressingly anti-intellectual.

38    Mr. Sanger left Wikipedia in 2002 because he felt the site exuded a distaste for expertise that drove talented scholars away. Wikipedia's worst feature, the co-founder says, is the notion, held by some contributors, "that nonexperts should be able to treat with disdain anything an expert says."

39    Shortly after Mr. Halavais's career as a troll ended, the professor—this time posting anonymously—contributed another article to Wikipedia, a piece on theories of communication, his area of expertise.

40    "It got shut down pretty quick, and I think there's just a small piece of it left online," he says. "Some other professors I talked to said the same thing happened to them: They were experts in their fields, they wrote something well in their areas of expertise, and it got cut up."

41    The site values concision—some lengthy articles are even marked as entries that should be tightened—so detailed scholarly papers are not looked upon fondly. Peer review may be hard on a professor's ego, but Wikipedia, it seems, is even less forgiving.

42    And even minor editing changes can lead to frustrating debates. Mr. Rosenzweig once edited a Wikipedia article on the financier Haym Solomon, removing a false but widely held claim that the 18th-century broker had lent money to the infant U.S. government during the Revolutionary War. Almost immediately after he removed the passage, another contributor reinserted it, citing its appearance in a number of books, which Mr. Rosenzweig says have been debunked. Only a seasoned historian would be likely to know that the claim was false, he says.

43    Academic historians are more likely to spend their time working on projects that can earn them scholarly respect and career advancement than writing or editing Wikipedia entries. Because of its transitory nature and its ban on original research, Wikipedia "doesn't have a lot of credibility within the academy," says Mr. Halavais.

44    "Generally, it's a time commitment that doesn't pay off reputationally," he says. "You certainly couldn't throw it on a CV." Writing for *Britannica* might not put professors on the tenure track, either, but it confers a certain amount of credibility, says Mr. Halavais.

45    Besides, say some critics of Wikipedia, it's not clear why an expert in a given field would want to see his work diluted by laymen. In an online essay called "Digital Maoism," Jaron Lanier, a computer scientist, has argued that Wikipedia is at the forefront of a disturbing Web trend—a tendency to value anonymous communal thought over individual intellect.

46    "A desirable text is more than a collection of accurate references," wrote Mr. Lanier, who spent time as chief scientist for the engineering office at Internet2, the high-speed-networking group. "It is also an expression of personality."

47    Mr. Wales says most Wikipedia articles are actually written by two or three people, not an anonymous collective. But otherwise, he says, Mr. Lanier's criticism isn't so much wrong as it is immaterial, "One aspect of Jaron Lanier's criticism had to do with the passionate, unique, individual voice he prefers, rather than this sort of bland, royal-we voice of Wikipedia," Mr. Wales says. "To that, I'd say 'yes, we plead guilty quite happily.' We're an encyclopedia."

48    But some critics say that Wikipedia's acceptance of anonymity—many of its posters never register on the site—causes more serious problems than personality-free prose. The site's open-door policy has emboldened trolls and vandals, whose efforts many academics would rather not suffer, says Mr. Sanger. "To many professors, it seems to be a waste of time to negotiate with people who in any other context would be taking a class from them."

49    Mr. Wales acknowledges that the site has, at times, seemed unappealing to scholars.

50    "There have definitely been cases where there were academics who came to the site, made good contributions, and the rough-and-tumble of the process really turned them off," he says.

## Attitude Adjustment

51  But fans of Wikipedia, like Mr. Meeks, argue that scholars must adapt to the aggressive, transparent approach to scholarship favored on the Web.

52    "Professors who get worked up about Wikipedia, and say it can never be anything but a poor source of knowledge, don't realize that these sort of hard-scrabble open-source projects have been incredibly competitive—for example, in the software industry," he says.

53    Of course, there is no consensus on whether Wikipedia's debates—what Mr. Meeks calls "living disagreements"—amount to real scholarship.

54    According to some of its supporters, Wikipedia's editing process constantly pushes its articles toward a Platonic ideal by adding details, clarifying arguments, and tightening prose.

55    But to critics like Mr. Sanger, the site is all too often just spinning its wheels. "Certain articles on Wikipedia"—many of its entries on philosophy, for example—"have been there for, like, six years, and they've been worked on endlessly," he says. "But in many cases, they seem to have come to a point that is less than optimal from any expert's point of view."

56    With a newly announced project called Citizendium, Mr. Sanger aims to create an alternate version of Wikipedia that lets an editorial panel of experts put articles through a form of peer review before certifying them as worthy of public view. Citizendium will stick with Wikipedia's policy against original research but will give its expert editors the final say over how articles appear. "There are large numbers of people who are upset with the state of things on Wikipedia, and they're just sort of looking for something to do," he says.

57    For users like Mr. Halavais, the kind of hierarchy Mr. Sanger proposes would eliminate Wikipedia's efficiency—and, quite possibly, its raison d'etre.

58    Still, Mr. Halavais is keenly interested in the idea of forming a body that could certify particularly well-written Wikipedia posts. The professor recently started to assemble an editorial board of recognized experts in Internet studies who "would go through the process of finding appropriate peer reviewers and certifying particular versions of Wikipedia articles as being peer reviewed."

59     So far, he says, that response has been mixed. "A bunch of people have already told me, 'You'll ruin this pure thing that is Wikipedia.'"

60     Mr. Wales is not one of those people. "I'm all for certification projects like that," he says, but he phrases his support as a plea for help: "I'd prefer it, though, if instead of certifying what's good, they'd point out all the bad stuff that we need to fix."

## Questions on Subject and Purpose

1. What reasons does Brock cite for why Wikipedia's articles on science are so reliable?

2. Wikipedia clearly states in its editorial policy that it does not publish "original research"? What does that phrase mean to you? How does that justify the assertion that anyone can contribute to Wikipedia and not just "experts" or "academics"?

3. Does Read ever take a personal stand on the use of Wikipedia? Does he ever argue for its use or disuse? What do you think he might be trying to do in the essay and why?

## Questions on Strategy and Audience

1. Why might Read begin the essay with the example of Alexander Halavais's "troll" experience on Wikipedia?

2. At three points in the essay, Read introduces subheadings (after paragraphs 14, 22, and 50). Such devices are common in magazine and newspaper articles. What role do they have?

3. Why might a publication such as *The Chronicle of Higher Education* (see the headnote) have published an article such as this?

## Questions on Vocabulary and Style

1. In paragraph 5, Read uses the phrase "mob-edited publication" to refer to Wikipedia. He does not quote the phrase from Halavais, but he may be implying that the phrase characterizes the premise with which Halavais starts. What does the phrase suggest to you?

2. The essay is composed of many small paragraphs. Why? What does the place of publication have to do with the physical appearance of the text?

3. Be prepared to define the following words: *ardent* (paragraph 2), *veracity* (3), *errata* (4), *languish* (5), *parlance* (7), *dearth* (10), *vetted* (10), *hone* (11), *scurrilous* (17), *esoterica* (20), *assail* (24), *capricious* (27), *finesse* (33), *debunked* (42), *hardscrabble* (52), *raison d'etre* (57).

## Writing Suggestions

1. **For Your Journal or Blog.** Think about what is happening around you at this very moment—an event, a trend, a new invention, a celebrity or important person who has just emerged, a new musical group, a new sports star, a new

discovery. What might be a good choice for an entry in Wikipedia? Remember, Wikipedia can instantly respond to whatever is happening, but you must be able to document from other sources the entry you contribute. What contribution to Wikipedia might you make? Brainstorm some possibilities.

2. **For a Paragraph.** After using your journal or blog to brainstorm for a possible contribution to Wikipedia, select one item. Check Wikipedia to see if an entry already exists. If not, in a paragraph plan your contribution. What will you write? What existing sources will you use?

3. **For an Essay.** Write an entry for Wikipedia, but hand it to your instructor instead of submitting it to Wikipedia! Use existing Wikipedia articles on similar types of subjects as a model. Be sure to include the documentation necessary to establish that you are writing from existing knowledge and not depending on unsubstantiated information. For example, it would not be appropriate for you to write about a band you are in unless information about it is available in printed or online sources.

4. **For Research.** The controversial comparison between *Encyclopedia Britannica* and Wikipedia cited in paragraph 23 of Read's essay can be studied by looking at the first article published in *Nature*, *Britannica's* reply, and *Nature's* response. All of the articles can be found at *Nature's* Website (www.nature.com) where you can search the archives. Read the articles. Who do you think "wins" the argument? In a researched essay using these articles, evaluate the two positions.

## For Further Study

**Focusing on Grammar and Writing.** What is a cliché? Why do we use them in writing? Can you find examples of clichés in Read's essay? Check the Glossary and Ready Reference at the back of this text for a definition and examples.

**Working Together.** Consider only the information Read provides. Do you think that the ban on using Wikipedia in papers written for school is justified? Divide into groups and after a careful analysis of the evidence Read provides, have a debate about the conclusion: yes, no, or justified only for certain subjects.

**Seeing Other Modes at Work.** Read's long opening example (paragraphs 1–6) is basically a narrative. How does this example work in the essay? Is it effective? If so, why? If not, why not?

**Finding Connections.** Before you start your research paper, be sure to read this article again. What cautions does it offer about sources, even about information that is found in a variety of print sources? Look at paragraph 42.

**Exploring the Web.** What can you find in Wikipedia that you cannot find in a print encyclopedia or even in another online encyclopedia? Explore some topics. One hint: On its Website, Wikipedia notes that it is "continually update, with the creation or updating of articles on topical events within seconds, minutes or hours, rather than months or years with printed encyclopedias." Look for specific examples.

# 2

# NARRATION

## GETTING READY TO WRITE

### What Is Narration and What are its Elements?

> Once upon a time . . .
> Did you hear the one about . . . ?
> What did you two do last night?
> Well, officer, it was like this . . .
> What happened at the Battle of Gettysburg?

What follows each of those lines is a story or a narrative. All stories, whether they are personal experiences, jokes, novels, histories, films, or television serials, have the same essential ingredients: a series of events arranged in a chosen order and told by a narrator for some particular purpose.

On the simplest level, all stories are composed of three elements:

| | |
|---|---|
| **Plot** | Beginning (the initiating action) |
| | Middle |
| | End (concluding action) |

As these terms suggest, stories are told in time: the fundamental arrangement of those events is chronological. Stories, though, do not always begin at the beginning. The time order of events can be rearranged by using flashbacks. Stories can begin with the last event in the chronological sequence or with any event that occurs in the middle.

Stories also involve tellers, or narrators, who relate the story. The narrators of stories almost always tell the story themselves (using "I"—a first-person point of view) or tell the story as an observer ("she"/"he"/"it"—a third-person point of view).

| | |
|---|---|
| **Point of View** | **First person** ("I was saved from sin when I was going on thirteen."—Langston Hughes', "Salvation") |
| | **Third person** ("One of the captains of the high school football team had something big he wanted to tell the other players."—Bob Greene, "Cut") |

Finally, stories have a purpose, a reason for being told, and that purpose controls the narrative and its selection of details. As you start to write a narrative, always ask yourself what point you are trying to make. Force yourself to finish the following statement:

**Purpose**   "I am telling this story because _____."

Any type of writing can use narration; it is not something found only in personal experience essays or in fiction. Narration can also be used as examples to support a thesis, as Bob Greene does in "Cut" (Chapter 1) by providing five personal narratives to support his assertion that being cut from an athletic team can make a person a superachiever later in life. Narration can also be found with description as in William Least Heat Moon's "Nameless, Tennessee" (Chapter 3) or underlying a persuasive argument as in Richard Rodriguez's "None of This Is Fair" (Chapter 9). In fact, you can find examples of narration in readings throughout this text.

## What Are the Common Forms of Narrative Writing?

In writing courses, the narratives you tend to produce come in several forms. Most common are personal experience narratives: you recount an experience that happened to you. You are the narrator; the event is more or less true (that is, you might add a few minor details or rearrange some elements to make the story more interesting or more artful). Typically, you recount the experience to share with your reader an insight. It might be funny or serious, but either way, it must connect with your readers' experiences: it should be about something that is universal—a realization, a sudden understanding, an awareness the experience brought to you. Most of the essays in this chapter are personal experience narratives.

The second, less common, form of narrative in freshman writing courses is the "here-is-what-happened" narrative. Stories in newspapers and histories are good examples of this type of narrative. Writing such a narrative generally requires that you do some research. A newspaper reporter cannot write any news story without first gathering the facts. Factual or historical narratives are typically told by an omniscient narrator who is not part of the story; the stories are intended to inform a reader, to provide information. This type of narrative also occurs in process writing (see Chapter 6) when you are describing how something happens or works.

The third common form for narratives in writing courses is the story designed to entertain: a short story, a joke, or a tall tale. The story might be intended to scare us, to puzzle us, or to get us to think about a situation or a course of action. Typically, such narratives are fictionalized; that is, the author invents the characters and the plot.

## What Do You Write About if Nothing Ever Happened to You?

Writing a personal narrative can pose some specific prewriting problems. It is easy to assume that the only things worth writing about are once-in-a-lifetime experiences—an heroic or death-defying act, a personal tragedy, an Olympic medal-winning performance. Few readers have been in a lockdown in prison (Evans Hopkins, "Lockdown"), and probably even fewer have visited famine-torn Africa (Tom Haines, "Facing Famine"). However, there is nothing extraordinary, for example, about the events Langston Hughes relates in "Salvation," even though Hughes's experience was a turning point in his life. Bob Greene in "Cut" (Chapter 1) narrates the kind of story—about being cut from a team—that is all too familiar to most readers; in one way or another, probably everyone has experienced a similar rejection and subsequent disappointment.

The secret to writing an effective personal narrative is two-fold. First, you must tell your story in an organized manner, following the advice just outlined. Simply relating what happened, however, is not enough. Second, and equally important, you must reveal a purpose in your story. Purposes can be many. You might offer insight into human behavior or motivation; you might mark a significant moment in your life; you might reveal an awareness of what it is to be young and to have dreams; you might reflect on the precariousness of life and the inevitability of change and decay; you might even use your experience to argue, as Evans Hopkins does, for a change in social attitudes toward crime and punishment. However you use your narrative, make sure your story has a point, a reason for being, and make that reason clear to your reader.

 **IN THE READINGS, LOOK FOR**

|  | **Likely purpose** |
|---|---|
| Maya Angelou, "Sister Monroe" | Entertain |
| Tom Haines, "Facing Famine" | Evoke sympathy for and an understanding of famine |
| Allison Perkins, "Mission Iraq" | Explain the impact of Iraq war experiences |
| Evans Hopkins, "Lockdown" | Persuade audience of the impact of changes in prison sentencing and rehabilitation |

## What Do You Include in a Narrative?

Just tell me what happened!
Get to the punch line!

No one, probably not even your mother, wants to hear everything you did today. Readers, like listeners, want you to be selective, for some things are more important or more interesting than others. Historians review a mass of data and select what they will include and emphasize; they choose a place to begin and a place to end. Even in relating personal experiences, you must select and condense. Generally, you need to pare away, to cut out the unnecessary and the uninteresting. What you include depends, of course, on what happened and, more importantly, on the purpose or meaning you are trying to convey.

Maya Angelou's story, "Sister Monroe," actually blends two experiences, widely separated in time, into a single story. The story opens on a Sunday morning in church, but Sister Monroe's comic performance does not occur on that morning. Once the initial story is underway, Angelou shifts to an earlier point in time, on a morning when Sister Monroe seized Reverend Taylor ("once she [Sister Monroe] hadn't been to church for a few months . . . she got the spirit and started shouting"). Angelou focuses our attention on the significant action—she does not relate every event that occurred.

## PREWRITING TIPS FOR WRITING NARRATIVE

1.  Before you start writing, set aside some time to brainstorm about your paper. If you are writing about a personal experience, you will discover that with time you will remember more and more details. Do you need to do research? Talk to people who were there? Gather information and take notes before you start to write.

2.  Complete the following sentence: "I am narrating this story because . . . ." As you gather information, use your purpose statement to decide what to include and what to exclude.

3.  Choose a point of view from which to tell the story. Personal narratives tend to be told in the first person ("I"); historical narratives and journalistic stories in the third person ("they," "he," "she").

4.  Remember, your narrative must have a beginning, a middle, and an end, but stories do not have to be told in chronological order. You can flash back or forward in your narrative.

5.  Look at the narratives in this chapter. Think about how each is organized. Do you see any strategies that might work in your essay?

## WRITING

### How Do You Structure a Narrative?

Time structures all narratives, although events need not always be arranged in chronological order. A narrative can begin at one point in time and then flash back to an earlier action or event. Langston Hughes's "Salvation" begins with a narrator looking back at an experience that occurred when he was thirteen, although the story itself is told in the order in which it happened. The most typical inversion is to begin at the end of the narrative and move backward in time to explain how that end was reached. More complex narratives may shift several times back and forth between incidents in the past or between the past and the present. Two cautions may be helpful: first, do not switch time too frequently, especially in short papers; second, make sure that any switches you make are clearly marked for your readers.

Remember as well that you control where your narrative begins and ends. For example, Evans Hopkins begins "Lockdown" with a predawn visit from two prison guards in armored vests and riot helmets; he does not begin with an account of the events that led to the lockdown or with the events that led to his imprisonment. Those details Hopkins fills in later, for they are not as dramatic or central to the points he is trying to make.

Writers frequently change or modify a personal experience in order to tell the story more effectively, heighten the tension, or make their purpose clearer. In her essay "On Keeping a Notebook," essayist and novelist Joan Didion remarks:

> I tell what some would call lies. "That's simply not true," the members of my family frequently tell me when they come up against my memory of a shared event. "The party was not for you, the spider was not a black widow, it wasn't that way at all." Very likely they are right, for not only have I always had trouble distinguishing between what happened and what merely might have happened, but I remain unconvinced that the distinction, for my purposes, matters.

Whenever you recall an experience, even if it happened last week, you do not necessarily remember it exactly as it occurred. The value of a personal narrative does not rest on relating the original experience with absolute accuracy. It does not matter, for example, whether the scene with Sister Monroe in the Christian Methodist Episcopal Church occurred exactly as Maya Angelou describes it years later. What does matter is that it could have happened as she describes it and that it is faithful to Angelou's purpose.

## How Do You End a Narrative?

This question might seem to have a really simple answer: your narrative stops at the end of the moment or incident you are narrating. An ending, though, should reflect the reason or purpose for narrating a story. If you are telling a joke, for example, you end with the punch line in order to elicit laughter. In a story that focuses on the significance of the event in your life, you might want to lead up to the climactic moment of insight. Langston Hughes ("Salvation") does that in his final concluding paragraph where he explains the impact this experience had on the rest of his life. If you are using a narrative for a persuasive purpose, end by explaining what you want your reader to take away from the story. Evans Hopkins ("Lockdown") recounts his personal experience of a prison lockdown not just to share his feelings and experiences, but to trace the recent evolution in American attitudes toward prisons and prisoners and to suggest the consequences such attitudes have on the "young lives being thrown away." If you are using narrative to recount an historical event, end with a summary statement of the significance of that event. The short historical narrative—"Blue Hen's Chicks"—at the end of this introduction tells a story about an event during the American Revolution and concludes with a sentence that uses the narrative to explain why Delaware is today known as "The Blue Hen State." Your conclusion should reflect your purpose for telling this story.

## IN THE READINGS, LOOK FOR

| | Conclusions |
| --- | --- |
| Langston Hughes, "Salvation" | Significance of the event in his life |
| Tom Haines, "Facing Famine" | His emotional reaction to the event |
| Allison Perkins, "Mission Iraq" | Her realization of the reason for the question "Are you OK?" |
| Evans Hopkins, "Lockdown" | His concluding paragraph as persuasion |

*"It's plotted out. I just have to write it."*

Keep your plots simple. Do not approach your construction of plot like this writer.

© *The New Yorker Collection 1996 Charles Barsotti from* **cartoonbank.com.** *All Rights Reserved.*

## How Do You Tell a Narrative?

Two things are especially important in relating your narrative. First, you must choose a *point of view* from which to tell the story. Personal experience narratives, such as those by Hughes, Angelou, and Hopkins, are generally told in the first person: the narrator is an actor in the story. Historical narratives and narratives used as illustrations in a larger piece of writing are generally told in the third person. The historian or the reporter, for example, stands outside the narrative and provides an objective view of the actions described. Point of view can vary in one other way. The narrator can reveal only his or her thoughts (using what is known as a limited point of view), or the narrator can reveal what anyone else in the narrative thinks or feels (using the omniscient, or all-knowing) point of view.

Second, you need to decide whether you are going to *show* or *tell* or mix the two. Showing in a narrative involves dramatizing a scene and creating dialogue. Hughes re-creates his experience for the reader by showing what happened and by recording some of the conversation that took place the night he was "saved from sin." Telling, by contrast, means summarizing what happened. Showing makes a narrative more vivid, for it allows the reader to experience the scene directly. Telling allows you to include a greater number of events and details. Either way, selectivity is essential. Even when the experience being narrated took place over a short period of time, such as Hughes's experiences one evening at church, a writer cannot dramatize everything that happened. When an experience lasts four and a half months, as does the lockdown Hopkins describes, a writer could never summarize events on a day-to-day basis. Each writer selects the moments that best give shape and significance to the experience.

## IN THE READINGS, LOOK FOR

|  |  |
|---|---|
|  | **Point of view** |
| Peggy McNally, "Waiting" | Third person ("she'll teach back-to-back classes") |
| Maya Angelou, "Sister Monroe" | First person ("I saw Sister Monroe") |
|  | **Examples of the omission of time** |
| Langston Hughes, "Salvation" | "Finally" (paragraph 6) |
|  | "Now it was really getting late" (11) |
| Tom Haines, "Facing Famine" | Extra white space after paragraphs (21 and 50) |
| Allison Perkins, "Mission Iraq" | "Today, we're both home" (34) |

## How Do You Write Dialogue?

Dialogue creates the illusion of speech, of verbal interaction among the characters in the narrative. It is an illusion because real conversation is longer, slower, and much more boring than written dialogue. You use dialogue when you create scenes in which your characters talk to one another. Dialogue is a way of dramatizing. It reveals characters; your readers can "hear" the characters and get a sense of their personalities from how they react and what they say. Creating small scenes with dialogue in your narrative increases its vividness. Instead of just telling the reader what happened, dialogue allows you to "show" what happened.

Writing effective dialogue in a narrative means recognizing when it can play an important role in your story. Use dialogue sparingly. Dialogue slows down the action of a story, and too much dialogue can bring a narrative to a crawl. The purpose of dialogue is to reveal character or to generate tension, not to have characters summarize the events that are happening in the plot. In "Salvation," Hughes creates tension in his narrative by including four tiny scenes with dialogue—two are the appeals that the minister makes to him, one is his aunt's appeal, and one voices Westley's decision to fake being "saved." Hughes might have written, "My aunt begged me to be saved," a simple summary statement. Instead, he generates tension and makes the scene more vivid by having his aunt say, "Langston, why don't you come? Why don't you come and be saved? Oh, Lamb of God! Why don't you come?"

Short exchanges of dialogue are typically set off as if they were separate paragraphs and are "tagged" with something like "he said" or "she replied." Do not get too clever in the verbs used in the tags; they are only likely to distract the reader. The assumption behind dialogue is that speakers take turns. In an exchange of dialogue, you can omit the tags and even the quotation marks that typically are used to mark speech. Toward the end of his essay "Facing Famine," Haines records a conversation in which he tries to find the right English words to convey the feelings that the famine generates in those who suffer through it:

> Misery?
> Yes, Berhanu said calmly, that is a part of it.
> Emptiness? Yes, he said, that too.
> Anguish? Despair?
> His eyes sparkled at the connection.
> Anger? Yes.
> Frustration? Yes.
> Fear? No.
> Fear, Berhanu said, like sorry, was too light a word.
> Terror?
> Yes, Berhanu said, "terror" is a good word.

## 🔍 IN THE READINGS, LOOK FOR

**Use of showing and telling**

| | |
|---|---|
| Langston Hughes, "Salvation" | Sparse use of dialogue |
| Maya Angelou, "Sister Monroe" | Essentially no dialogue |
| Tom Haines, "Facing Famine" | Mixture that reveals the despair of the people |
| Allison Perkins, "Mission Iraq" | Only the repetition of the question asked, "Are you OK?" |
| Evans Hopkins, "Lockdown" | Mixture in scene in paragraphs 17 to 27 |

**DRAFTING TIPS FOR WRITING NARRATIVE**

1. Outline your narrative. Is the plot clear? Are there any places where your readers might have difficulty following the sequence of events?

2. Look carefully at any moment that you have dramatized. Does it add to the tension of your story? Does it reveal something about the characters and their reactions or feelings? Write a one-line justification for any scene you have included.

3. Check your use of point of view. Are you consistent throughout the essay or do you switch from first person to third?

4. Have you signaled the structure of your narrative to your reader? Do you need to introduce some type of typographical device (such as extra white space between blocks of paragraphs) to indicate that the story comes in sections?

5. Recruit readers for your draft, ask them questions, then follow their advice.

## REVISING

### How Do You Revise a Narrative?

Once you have a complete draft of your essay—not just a series of notes—always get feedback: from peer readers, from your instructor, from a writing center tutor. Listen carefully to what your readers say. If several readers see the same problem in your essay, they are right, even if you do not agree. Reconsider each choice that you have made; do not limit your revising to correcting obvious errors and changing an occasional word. Typically, your revision should be directed at three concerns:

- Pruning out unnecessary detail
- Making the structure clear
- Looking again at the difference between showing and telling

**Pruning Out Unnecessary Detail**   Remember that your narrative has a purpose; you have a reason for telling this story. Your purpose might be to entertain, to inform, to persuade, or a mixture of all three. On a separate sheet of paper write down your purpose statement and use that statement to test every detail you have included in your narrative. Think about how frustrated you become when someone tries to tell a joke and obscures the punch line. Think about how often you get impatient when people are relating what happened and include lots of unnecessary details. Prune away details in your narrative that do not support or illustrate your purpose.

**Making the Structure Clear**   Narratives are told in time. They can be organized in a straightforward, chronological order, or they can manipulate time by flashing back or even forward. Remember that time changes can be puzzling to your reader unless you clearly signal them. Sometimes changing verb tenses—moving from past tense to present or present to future—is enough of a marker for your reader. More often, writers use a variety of typographical devices to mark such shifts: setting off a section that occurs at a different time by using extra white space before and after; numbering or lettering sections of the essay; or italicizing a section set in a different time. When you are getting advice from your readers, make sure to ask them if they were ever confused by the sequence of events in the story. A good test, for example, is to ask them to construct a chronological timeline for what happens. If they have problems or make mistakes, you know that you must revise the time changes in your essay.

**Looking Again at the Difference Between Showing and Telling**   Most narratives benefit from having a mixture of showing (dramatizing) and telling (summarizing). Dramatizing a scene involves having the characters verbally interact through dialogue. Remember, though, to keep these scenes short and to choose only appropriate moments. Such scenes can add tension to a story, reveal a conflict among the characters, or show how characters interact. Ask yourself if there are moments in your narrative in which dramatization might be particularly effective. Do not have your characters speak in dialogue unless there is a clear and important reason for including that scene. Do not try to summarize what is happening in the story by having one character narrate events to another: "And so, Maria, remember that I told you yesterday that John took me out for dinner last night and we went to the restaurant where we saw his former girlfriend who dumped him three years ago."

## REVISING TIPS WHEN WRITING NARRATIVES

1. Look again at your essay's title. An informative, even catchy, title is a tremendous asset to an essay. If your title seems a little boring, brainstorm some other possibilities. Never title your paper "Narrative Essay," or "Essay," or "Essay #1"!

2. Remember to catch your reader's attention in the opening paragraphs. Look closely at your introduction. Ask a friend or classmate to read it. Does your reader want to continue or to quit?

3. Ask a reader to construct a timeline for what happened in your story. Is the plot clear and unambiguous? Do you ever shift time in the story? If so, is the shift clearly marked or signaled?

4.   Look carefully at the dialogue. Does it sound plausible that characters might speak like this? Is it too long? Too wordy? Too formal? Remember, you are creating the illusion of speech rather than transcribing actual speech.

5.   Look at your conclusion. How did you end? Did you lead up to a climatic moment or did you just end with a flat conclusion ("And so you can see why this experience was important to me.")? Compare how writers in this chapter end their narratives. You might be able to use similar strategies.

## STUDENT ESSAY

### First Draft

Hope Zucker decided to write about a powerful childhood memory—a pair of red shoes that became her "ruby slippers" and the key to the Land of Oz.

### My New Shoes

When you are four years old anything longer than five minutes feels like eternity, so when the clerk told me and my mom that it would take three to four weeks for my new shoes to arrive, I was almost in tears. Since seeing *The Wizard of Oz,* I had thought of little else other than owning a pair of ruby slippers. My dreams were full of spinning houses, little munchkins, flying monkeys, and talking lions. All I wanted was to be Dorothy, and the shoe store had made a promise to find me a pair of red mary-janes which would hopefully take me to Munchkin Land and Oz.

For the next three weeks I made all the preparations I could think of in order to become Dorothy. It did not matter how convincing Judy Garland was because I knew in my heart that I was the true Dorothy. I sang "Somewhere Over the Rainbow" day and night, and I played dress up with an old light blue checked dress of my mother's. I even went as far as to carry my dog in a basket, but that did not work out too well. I had my mom braid my long brown hair, and after I insisted, she tied a light blue ribbon around each braid. I skipped wherever I went, and I even went as far as coloring part of our driveway with chalk to create my very own yellow brick road.

The only thing missing to my new persona was my ruby slippers. After my mother explained to me that three weeks really was not that far off in the future, I decided to help the store in their search for my red mary-janes. For a month I called the store everyday when I got home from preschool. Mr. Rogers and Big Bird could wait because there was nothing in the whole wide world that was more important than my red patent leather shoes. By the end of the month, the nice little old ladies at the store knew me by name and thought that I was the cutest child. Lucky for them, they did not have to put up with me.

Finally, after what seemed like years, the lady on the other side of the phone said that yes, my shiny red shoes had arrived. Now I had only to plead with my mother to get her to make a special trip into the city. After a few days of delay and a great deal of futile temper tantrums, my mom took me to the store. I could hardly contain my excitement. During the ride, I practiced the one and only line that only the real Dorothy could say, "There's no place like home." And of course, I clicked my beat up boondockers three times each time I recited my part. It was all practice for the real thing.

As we pulled into the parking lot, all the little old ladies inside the store waved to me as if they had been expecting me for days. I finally got to see my shoes, and they were as perfect as I knew they'd be. I was practically jumping out of my seat when she began to remove the stiff tissue paper surrounding my shoes, so rather than wait for her to fit my little feet into my slippers, I grabbed them from her and did it myself. They were the prettiest pair of shoes any girl could have!

For the next few weeks I was Dorothy and I'd stop everyone I'd see in order to prove it by tapping my heels together and saying, "There's no place like home." But soon my feet grew too big for my ruby slippers, and as I graduated into the next larger size, I no longer wanted to be Dorothy. As I grew up, so did my dreams. Cinderella, now she was someone to be! Yet, once again that phase, like the phases I am going through now, passed fairly quickly.

## Comments

Hope made enough copies of her essay so that the whole class could read and then discuss it. After reading her essay to the class, Hope asked her classmates for their reactions. Several students suggested that she tighten her narrative, eliminating details that were not essential to the story. Most of their suggestions were centered in paragraphs 3 and 4. "Why mention Mr. Rogers and Big Bird?" someone asked. "I didn't want you to have to wait several days to pick them up, and I didn't want to be reminded of your temper," commented another. When Hope came to revise her draft, she used this advice. She also eliminated a number of clichés and made a significant change in the ending of the paper. Notice how much more effective the final version is as the result of these minor revisions.

## Final Draft

The Ruby Slippers

To a four-year old, anything longer than five minutes feels like eternity, so when the clerk told me and my mom that it would take three to four weeks for my new shoes to arrive, I was almost in tears. Since seeing *The Wizard of Oz*, I had thought of little else other than owning a pair of ruby slippers. My dreams were full of spinning houses, little munchkins, flying monkeys, and talking lions. All I wanted was to be Dorothy, and the shoe store had made a promise to find me a pair of red mary-janes which would hopefully take me to Munchkin Land and Oz.

For the next three weeks I made all the preparations I could think of in order to become Dorothy. It did not matter how convincing Judy Garland was because I knew in my heart that I was the true Dorothy. I sang "Somewhere Over the Rainbow" day and night, and I played dress up with an old light blue checked dress of my mother's. I even went as far as to carry my dog in a basket. My mom braided my long brown hair, and after I insisted, she tied a light blue ribbon around each braid. I skipped everywhere I went and colored part of our driveway with chalk to create my very own yellow brick road.

The only thing missing was my ruby slippers. After my mother explained that three weeks really was not that far off, I decided to help the store in their search for my red mary-janes. For a month I called the store everyday when I got home from preschool. By the end of the month, the ladies at the store knew me by name.

Finally, the woman on the other end of the phone said that yes, my shiny red shoes had arrived. I could hardly contain my excitement. During the ride, I practiced the one line that only the real Dorothy could say, "There's no place like home." And of course, I clicked my beat up loafers three times each time I recited that line. It was all practice for the real thing.

As we pulled into the parking lot, all the ladies inside the store waved to me as if they had been expecting me. I finally got to see my shoes, and they were as perfect as I had imagined. I was practically jumping out of my seat when she began to remove the stiff tissue paper surrounding my shoes, so rather than wait for her to fit my little feet into my slippers, I grabbed them from her and did it myself. They were the prettiest pair of shoes any girl could have!

For the next few weeks I was Dorothy and I'd stop everyone I'd see in order to prove it by tapping my heels together and saying, "There's no place like home." But soon my feet grew too big for my ruby slippers, and as I graduated into the next larger size, I no longer wanted to be Dorothy. As I grew up, so did my dreams.

## SOME THINGS TO REMEMBER ABOUT WRITING NARRATION

1. Decide first why you are telling the reader *this* story. You must have a purpose clearly in mind.
2. Choose an illustration, event, or experience that can be covered adequately within the space limitations you face. Do not try to narrate the history of your life in an essay!
3. Decide on which point of view you will use. Do you want to be a part of the narrative or an objective observer? Which is more appropriate for your purpose?
4. Keeping your purpose in mind, select the details or events that seem the most important or the most revealing.
5. Arrange those details in an order—either a strict chronological one or one that uses a flashback. Keep your verb tenses consistent and signal any switches in time.
6. Remember the differences between showing and telling. Which method will be better for your narrative?

## SEEING NARRATION IN OTHER CONTEXTS

### As a Literary Strategy

All stories—whether they are personal essays, imaginative fictions, journalistic reports, or histories—contain the same essential ingredients: a series of events arranged in an order structured through time recounted by a "narrator" for some particular purpose. Narratives can range from hundreds, even thousands, of pages to only a single paragraph. Peggy McNally's short story "Waiting" is an example of what is called "microfiction," a genre that is limited to a maximum of 250 words.

# *Waiting*

Peggy McNally

Five days a week the lowest-paid substitute teacher in the district drives her father's used Mercury to Hough and 79th, where she eases it, mud flaps and all, down the ramp into the garage of Patrick Henry Junior High, a school where she'll teach back-to-back classes without so much as a coffee break and all of this depressing her until she remembers her date last night, and hopes it might lead to bigger things, maybe love, so she quickens her pace towards the main office to pick up her class lists with the names of students she'll never know as well as she has come to know the specials in the cafeteria, where she hopes the coffee will be perking and someone will have brought in those donuts she has come to love so much, loves more than the idea of teaching seventh-graders the meaning of a poem, because after all she's a sub who'll finish her day, head south to her father's house, and at dinner, he'll ask her how her job is going, and she'll say okay, and he'll remind her that it might lead to a full-position with benefits but she knows what teaching in that school is like, and her date from last night calls to ask if she's busy and she says yes because she's promised her father she'd wash his car and promises to her father are sacred since her mother died, besides it is the least she can do now that he lets her drive his car five days a week towards the big lake, to the NE corner of Hough and 79th and you know the rest.

## Discussion Questions

1. McNally composes her story as a single sentence. Why might she have chosen to do this? How does the story's form (as a single sentence) relate to what is occurring in the story?
2. The story contains a number of details, yet the woman is never named. Why is she nameless?
3. Who narrates the story? Why might this point of view be used? What would happen if the point of view were changed?
4. Stories have beginnings, middles, and ends. Is there an end to McNally's story? What shape does the story seem to take and why? How is that shape appropriate to what happens in the story?
5. What central impression does the story leave in your mind?

## Writing Suggestions

Often we find ourselves locked into repetitive patterns, small daily or weekly cycles that define us. Think about a pattern that you see in your own life. In a short personal essay, narrate that cycle for your readers. You don't need to use McNally's story as a structural model; you can narrate the story from the first person, and you can include dialogue if you wish. Remember, though, to have a purpose for your narrative. What does the pattern reveal about you? As a possible starting point, you might consider the following:

**a.** A bad (or good) habit or behavior

**b.** Situations in which you know how you will always react

**c.** An endless quarrel or disagreement

## AS A CRITICAL READING STRATEGY

Every state has a nickname, and the origins of those nicknames are frequently related in a folktale, a short narrative that explains how the state or the people from the state acquired that name. Delaware has an unusual name—the Blue Hen State—and here S. E. Schlosser recounts the folktale that explains how that name came about.

As you read this short narrative, remember what you have learned about how to write a narrative, because that knowledge can help you as a reader.

- Narratives (stories) are told for a reason or purpose: they might be purely informational (here is what happened or how it happened); they might be entertaining (jokes, for example, are mini-narratives); they might be persuasive (a vivid story of what happened to someone can move you to action or empathy). As you read a narrative, ask yourself why the writer is telling this story. Is there a thesis or obvious reason for the story?

- Narratives are structured in time. They might open with the first event in the chronological sequence or they might use flashbacks. You can always construct a timeline for a narrative.

- Narratives are always told by someone. The teller might be an objective, omniscient narrator (as in a history text or a newspaper story) or the teller might be a person involved in the story. A guide to types of narration can be found in the Glossary and Ready Reference. Always ask yourself as you read a narrative, who is telling this story and why might the writer be using this type of narration?

- Narratives are economical, that is, they do not tell everything. As you read, ask yourself: What has the writer not told me in this narrative? What is left out is just as revealing as what is included.

- Narratives frequently dramatize scenes within the story by using dialogue. Although dialogue can make the characters come alive for the reader, dialogue also slows down the pace of the story. Does the narrative you are reading use dialogue? Why might the writer choose to render part of a scene in dialogue rather than just describe or summarize what happens?

Blue Hen's Chicks

Opening sentence places
the story in time and place

<u>A Delaware man went to war during the
American Revolution</u>. For entertainment, he
brought with him two fighting cocks. When asked
about these chickens, the soldier said slyly, "They

Character introduced, single
sentence of dialogue—an
exaggeration; they are only
the "babies" of the hen at
home

are the chicks of a blue hen that I have at home."

Well, those cocks could fight. They were so
fierce, they caused quite a stir among the men.
It did not take long for the Delaware troops to
begin boasting among the troops from the other
states that they could outfight anyone, just like

Story told chronologically
Application of story to the
men
Final explanation of the
nickname

those famous fighting cocks. <u>"We're the Blue
Hen's Chickens. We will fight to the end!"</u> became
the theme of the Delaware troops. The other
troops took to calling the men from Delaware
"The Blue Hen's Chicks," and to this day,
Delaware is known as the Blue Hen State.

## AS A VISUAL STRATEGY

Every photograph is a part of a story—something was happening before it was
taken; something happened afterwards. A photograph is a frozen moment in
time. Looking through a family photograph album, you can relive events from

your life. The photographs become single frames in a movie that your memory re-creates. Because they trigger memories, people take photographs of the good and memorable, times not the sad or depressing times. Look at the two photographs of people crying on p. 129: one of a young woman and one of a young man.

## WRITING ABOUT IMAGES

1. Write a narrative essay that could accompany one of the photographs. The photograph could be either the end point of the story (narrate the events that led up to this moment) or the beginning point (tell what happened after the photograph was taken). As you begin to think about your response, consider how gender differences might influence your story. Can the same scenarios make both the young woman and the young man cry? Or do you expect that the circumstances that triggered this crying were different?

2. Select a group of images—from magazines, from the Web, from photographs—that represent your life until this moment or what you imagine your life to be in the next ten to twenty years. Make photocopies and arrange them in a collage or poster. Then in an essay, construct a narrative that explains how you became who you are or who you see yourself becoming in the next phase of your life. Consider sharing your narrative (and pictures) with a classmate of the opposite gender.

3. Test the truth of the cliché "a picture is worth a thousand words." Select a famous photograph and write an essay in which you narrate a plausible situation behind the photograph (it should not be the "real" situation). Which is more vivid or creates the stronger impact? Think about the article "Facing Famine" by Tom Haines. Would a photograph have been more effective than the essay?

## ADDITIONAL WRITING SUGGESTIONS FOR NARRATION

Narration is storytelling and is used for a variety of purposes. Stories make us laugh and cry; understand and sympathize with situations that we have never experienced; interpret the impact our experiences have had on us; move us to do or believe something. Use narration to respond to these different types of purposes. Remember, some cases you will need to do some research and you will need to narrow and shape the experience. Remember also that your readers must find your narrative interesting, important, and universal.

## TELL A STORY

1. Write a joke of at least a couple of paragraphs long that ends with a punch line.
2. Offer an explanation for the nickname of your home state.
3. Offer an explanation (real or imagined) for a local place name—on campus, in your community, at home.
4. Narrate and explain the historical significance of a local event.
5. Trace the events leading up to (or following from) a particular occasion.
6. Tell a story about a campus legend, ghost, or famous or infamous graduate.
7. Create a biography of a campus personality.
8. Select a current event and trace the actions that lead up to it.

## FIND MEANING IN A PERSONAL EXPERIENCE

1. A moment of terror (or heartbreak, joy, triumph, embarrassment)
2. Hardest (best, worst, stupidest) decision I ever made
3. My greatest regret
4. I will never forget when . . .
5. I knew I was growing up when . . .
6. Overcoming obstacles
7. Loss of a relative or friend
8. Disappointment

## TELL A STORY TO MOVE YOUR AUDIENCE TO A PARTICULAR ACTION OR BELIEF

1. Environmental awareness
2. An encounter with sexual, racial, or ethnic discrimination
3. Support or oppose sale of firearms
4. Support or oppose sale of tobacco products
5. Support or oppose state-run gambling lotteries or casinos
6. Advocate or criticize a particular style of dress
7. Argue for or against the censorship of violent videos on YouTube or violent or aggressive song lyrics
8. Ban on certain types of advertisements

# *Salvation*

Langston Hughes

*Born in Joplin, Missouri, Langston Hughes (1902–1967) was an important figure in the Harlem Renaissance. He is best known for his jazz- and blues-inspired poetry, though he was also a talented prose writer and playwright. Among his writings are* Simple Speaks His Mind *(1950), the first of four volumes of some of his best-loved stories, and* Ask Your Mama: 12 Moods for Jazz *(1961), one of his later, angry collections of poetry fueled by emotions surrounding the civil rights movements.*

*The* Big Sea: An Autobiography *(1940), published when Hughes was thirty-eight years old, is a memoir of his early years, consisting of a series of short narratives focusing on events and people. After the death of his grandmother, Hughes was raised by Auntie Reed, one of his grandmother's friends. Uncle Reed, Auntie's husband, was, as Hughes notes in* The Big Sea, *"a sinner and never went to church as long as he lived . . . but both of them were very good and kind. . . . And no doubt from them I learned to like both Christians and sinners equally well."*

**On Writing:** *Hughes once noted that, to him, the prime function of creative writing is "to affirm life, to yeah-say the excitement of living in relation to the vast rhythms of the universe of which we are a part, to untie the riddles of the gutter in order to closer tie the knot between man and God."*

## Before Reading

**Connecting:** Was there a time in your teenage years when you were disappointed by someone or something?

**Anticipating:** No narrative recounts every minute of an experience. Writers must leave out far more than they include. What events connected with this experience does Hughes leave out of his narrative? Why?

1   I was saved from sin when I was going on thirteen. But not really saved. It happened like this. There was a big revival at my Auntie Reed's church. Every night for weeks there had been much preaching, singing, praying, and shouting, and some very hardened sinners had been brought to Christ, and the membership of the church had grown by leaps and bounds. Then just before the revival ended, they held a special meeting for children, "to bring the young lambs to the fold." My aunt spoke of it for days ahead. That night I was escorted

to the front row and placed on the mourners' bench with all the other young sinners, who had not yet been brought to Jesus.

2    My aunt told me that when you were saved you saw a light, and something happened to you inside! And Jesus came into your life! And God was with you from then on! She said you could see and hear and feel Jesus in your soul. I believed her. I had heard a great many old people say the same thing and it seemed to me they ought to know. So I sat there calmly in the hot, crowded church, waiting for Jesus to come to me.

3    The preacher preached a wonderful rhythmical sermon, all moans and shouts and lonely cries and dire pictures of hell, and then he sang a song about the ninety and nine safe in the fold, but one little lamb was left out in the cold. Then he said: "Won't you come? Won't you come to Jesus? Young lambs, won't you come?" And he held out his arms to all us young sinners there on the mourners' bench. And the little girls cried. And some of them jumped up and went to Jesus right away. But most of us just sat there.

4    A great many old people came and knelt around us and prayed, old women with jet-black faces and braided hair, old men with work-gnarled hands. And the church sang a song about the lower lights are burning, some poor sinners to be saved. And the whole building rocked with prayer and song.

5    Still I kept waiting to *see* Jesus.

6    Finally all the young people had gone to the altar and were saved, but one boy and me. He was a rounder's son named Westley. Westley and I were surrounded by sisters and deacons praying. It was very hot in the church, and getting late now. Finally Westley said to me in a whisper: "God damn! I'm tired o' sitting here. Let's get up and be saved." So he got up and was saved.

7    Then I was left all alone on the mourners' bench. My aunt came and knelt at my knees and cried, while prayers and song swirled all around me in the little church. The whole congregation prayed for me alone, in a mighty wail of moans and voices. And I kept waiting serenely for Jesus, waiting, waiting—but he didn't come. I wanted to see him, but nothing happened to me. Nothing! I wanted something to happen to me, but nothing happened.

8    I heard the songs and the minister saying: "Why don't you come? My dear child, why don't you come to Jesus? Jesus is waiting for you. He wants you. Why don't you come? Sister Reed, what is this child's name?"

9    "Langston," my aunt sobbed.

10    "Langston, why don't you come? Why don't you come and be saved? Oh, Lamb of God! Why don't you come?"

11    Now it was really getting late. I began to be ashamed of myself, holding everything up so long. I began to wonder what God thought about Westley, who certainly hadn't seen Jesus either, but who was now sitting proudly on the platform, swinging his knickerbockered legs and grinning down at me, surrounded by deacons and old women on their knees praying. God had not struck Westley dead for taking his name in vain or for lying in the temple. So I decided that maybe to save further trouble, I'd better lie, too, and say that Jesus had come, and get up and be saved.

12    So I got up.

13      Suddenly the whole room broke into a sea of shouting, as they saw me rise. Waves of rejoicing swept the place. Women leaped in the air. My aunt threw her arms around me. The minister took me by the hand and led me to the platform.

14      When things quieted down, in a hushed silence, punctuated by a few ecstatic "Amens," all the new young lambs were blessed in the name of God. Then joyous singing filled the room.

15      That night, for the last time in my life but one—for I was a big boy twelve years old—I cried. I cried, in bed alone, and couldn't stop. I buried my head under the quilts, but my aunt heard me. She woke up and told my uncle I was crying because the Holy Ghost had come into my life, and because I had seen Jesus. But I was really crying because I couldn't bear to tell her that I had lied, that I had deceived everybody in the church, that I hadn't seen Jesus, and that now I didn't believe there was a Jesus any more, since he didn't come to help me.

## Questions on Subject and Purpose

1. Who narrates the story? From what point in time is it told?
2. What does the narrator expect to happen when he is to be saved? What does happen?
3. Why does the narrator cry at the end of the story?
4. What was Hughes's attitude toward his experience when it first happened? At the time he originally wrote this selection? How does the opening sentence reflect that change in attitude?

## Questions on Strategy and Audience

1. Why did Hughes not tell the story in the present tense? How would doing so change the story?
2. How much dialogue is used in the narration? Why does Hughes not use more?
3. Why does Hughes blend telling with showing in the story?
4. How much time is represented by the events in the story? Where does Hughes compress the time in his narrative? Why does he do so?

## Questions on Vocabulary and Style

1. What is the effect of the short paragraphs (5, 9, and 12)? How does Hughes use paragraphing to help shape his story?
2. How much description does Hughes include in his narrative? What types of details does he single out?
3. What is the effect of the exclamation marks used in paragraph 2?
4. Try to identify or explain the following phrases: *the ninety and nine safe in the fold* (paragraph 3), *the lower lights are burning* (4), *a rounder's son* (6), *knickerbockered legs* (11).

## Writing Suggestions

1. **For Your Journal or Blog.** What can you remember from your early teenage years? In your journal or blog, first make a list of significant moments—both high and low points—and then re-create one moment in prose.

2. **For a Paragraph.** We have all been disappointed by someone or something. Single out a particular moment from your past. After spending some time remembering what happened and how you felt, narrate that experience for a general reader in a paragraph. Remember, your paragraph must reveal what the experience meant to you. Try using some dialogue.

3. **For an Essay.** Have you ever experienced anything that changed your life? It does not need to be a dramatic change—perhaps just a conviction that you will never do that again or that you will *always* be sure to do that again. In an essay, narrate that experience. Remember that your narrative should illustrate or prove the experience's significance to you.

4. **For Research.** Does Hughes seem to be serious about his experience? Did he "lose" his faith as a result of what happened? Find other examples of Hughes's writing (check your college's library catalog for books by Hughes and perhaps some of the online databases). Then, in an essay, analyze the significance (or insignificance) of this event in Hughes's writing. Be sure to formulate an explicit thesis about the importance of the event in Hughes's work. Be sure to document any direct quotations or information taken from other sources.

## For Further Study

**Focusing on Grammar and Writing.** First, be sure that you can identify adjectives and adverbs (see the Glossary and Ready Reference). Then go through Hughes's narrative and make a list of all the adjectives and adverbs. Are there as many as you expected? Sometimes we assume that vividness in writing comes from using many adjectives and adverbs. Is that true here? What parts of speech make Hughes's narrative vivid? What does that suggest about writing narration and description?

**Working Together.** Divide into small groups. Focus your collaboration on how Hughes creates tension in his narrative. What devices does he use to keep the reader in suspense, wondering what the outcome can possibly be? How does the ending fit with the tension Hughes has generated throughout the narrative? Once your group has finished its analysis, choose someone to report to the class.

**Seeing Other Modes at Work.** Hughes uses description to create a vivid sense of the place in which the experience occurs.

**Finding Connections.** For a similar handling of point of view, try Maya Angelou's "Sister Monroe" also in this chapter.

**Exploring the Web.** Do you think that the episode Hughes narrates in the essay actually happened? Do you think it really did become a memory he never forgot? Use the Web to check the biographical background for the essay.

# Sister Monroe

Maya Angelou

*Maya Angelou was born Marguerita Johnson in St. Louis, Missouri, in 1928. A talented performing artist as well as a poet and autobiographer, Angelou has used much of her writing to explore the American black female identity. Her most significant writings have been her six volumes of autobiography (1970–2002).*

*The following selection is from the first of Angelou's memoirs,* I Know Why the Caged Bird Sings *(1970), a work that describes her early years in Stamps, Arkansas. One critic called that work a "revealing portrait of the customs and harsh circumstances of black life in the segregated South." Here in a brilliantly comic moment, Angelou recalls how Sister Monroe "got the spirit" one Sunday morning at church.*

**On Writing:** *In an interview about her goals as a writer, Angelou observed: "When I'm writing, I am trying to find out who I am, who we are, what we're capable of, how we feel, how we lose and stand up. . . . But I'm also trying for the language. I'm trying to see how it can really sound. I really love language. I love it for what it does for us, how it allows us to explain the pain and the glory, the nuances and delicacies of our existence. And then it allows us to laugh. . . . We need language."*

## Before Reading

**Connecting:** As a spectator, when do you find a physical mishap, such as a fight or fall, comic? What is necessary for us to laugh at slapstick comedy and not be concerned about the welfare of the people involved?

**Anticipating:** How does Angelou create humor in this narrative? What makes it funny?

1   In the Christian Methodist Episcopal Church the children's section was on the right, cater-cornered from the pew that held those ominous women called the Mothers of the Church. In the young people's section the benches were placed close together, and when a child's legs no longer comfortably fitted in the narrow space, it was an indication to the elders that that person could now move into the intermediate area (center church). Bailey and I were allowed to sit with the other children only when there were informal meetings, church socials or the like. But on the Sundays when Reverend Thomas preached, it was ordained that we occupy the first row, called the mourners' bench. I

thought we were placed in front because Momma was proud of us, but Bailey assured me that she just wanted to keep her grandchildren under her thumb and eye.

2      Reverend Thomas took his text from Deuteronomy. And I was stretched between loathing his voice and wanting to listen to the sermon. Deuteronomy was my favorite book in the Bible. The laws were so absolute, so clearly set down, that I knew if a person truly wanted to avoid hell and brimstone, and being roasted forever in the devil's fire, all she had to do was memorize Deuteronomy and follow its teaching, word for word. I also liked the way the word rolled off the tongue.

3      Bailey and I sat alone on the front bench, the wooden slats pressing hard on our behinds and the backs of our thighs. I would have wriggled just a bit, but each time I looked over at Momma, she seemed to threaten, "Move and I'll tear you up," so, obedient to the unvoiced command, I sat still. The church ladies were warming up behind me with a few hallelujahs and praise the Lords and Amens, and the preacher hadn't really moved into the meat of the sermon.

4      It was going to be a hot service.

5      On my way into church, I saw Sister Monroe, her open-faced gold crown glinting when she opened her mouth to return a neighborly greeting. She lived in the country and couldn't get to church every Sunday, so she made up for her absences by shouting so hard when she did make it that she shook the whole church. As soon as she took her seat, all the ushers would move to her side of the church because it took three women and sometimes a man or two to hold her.

6      Once she hadn't been to church for a few months (she had taken off to have a child), she got the spirit and started shouting, throwing her arms around and jerking her body, so that the ushers went over to hold her down, but she tore herself away from them and ran up to the pulpit. She stood in front of the altar, shaking like a freshly caught trout. She screamed at Reverend Taylor. "Preach it. I say, preach it." Naturally he kept on preaching as if she wasn't standing there telling him what to do. Then she screamed an extremely fierce "I said, preach it" and stepped up on the altar. The Reverend kept on throwing out phrases like home-run balls and Sister Monroe made a quick break and grasped for him. For just a second, everything and everyone in the church except Reverend Taylor and Sister Monroe hung loose like stockings on a washline. Then she caught the minister by the sleeve of his jacket and his coattail, then she rocked him from side to side.

7      I have to say this for our minister, he never stopped giving us the lesson. The usher board made its way to the pulpit, going up both aisles with a little more haste than is customarily seen in church. Truth to tell, they fairly ran to the minister's aid. Then two of the deacons, in their shiny Sunday suits, joined the ladies in white on the pulpit, and each time they pried Sister Monroe loose from the preacher he took another deep breath and kept on preaching, and Sister Monroe grabbed him in another place, and more firmly. Reverend Taylor was helping his rescuers as much as possible by jumping around when he got a chance. His voice at one point got so low it sounded like a roll of thunder, then

Sister Monroe's "Preach it" cut through the roar, and we all wondered (I did, in any case) if it would ever end. Would they go on forever, or get tired out at last like a game of blindman's bluff that lasted too long, with nobody caring who was "it"?

8      I'll never know what might have happened, because magically the pandemonium spread. The spirit infused Deacon Jackson and Sister Willson, the chairman of the usher board, at the same time. Deacon Jackson, a tall, thin, quiet man, who was also a part-time Sunday school teacher, gave a scream like a falling tree, leaned back on thin air and punched Reverend Taylor on the arm. It must have hurt as much as it caught the Reverend unawares. There was a moment's break in the rolling sounds and Reverend Taylor jerked around surprised, and hauled off and punched Deacon Jackson. In the same second Sister Willson caught his tie, looped it over her fist a few times, and pressed down on him. There wasn't time to laugh or cry before all three of them were down on the floor behind the altar. Their legs spiked out like kindling wood.

9      Sister Monroe, who had been the cause of all the excitement, walked off the dais, cool and spent, and raised her flinty voice in the hymn, "I came to Jesus, as I was, worried, wounded, and sad, I found in Him a resting place and He has made me glad."

10     The minister took advantage of already being on the floor and asked in a choky little voice if the church would kneel with him to offer a prayer of thanksgiving. He said we had been visited with a mighty spirit, and let the whole church say Amen.

11     On the next Sunday, he took his text from the eighteenth chapter of the Gospel according to St. Luke, and talked quietly but seriously about the Pharisees, who prayed in the streets so that the public would be impressed with their religious devotion. I doubt that anyone got the message—certainly not those to whom it was directed. The deacon board, however, did appropriate funds for him to buy a new suit. The other was a total loss.

## Questions on Subject and Purpose

1. Who is the narrator? How old does she seem to be? How do you know?
2. Why does Sister Monroe behave as she does?
3. How does the section on the narrator and Bailey act as a preface to the story of Sister Monroe? Is it relevant, for example, that the narrator's favorite book of the Bible is Deuteronomy?

## Questions on Strategy and Audience

1. Part of the art of narration is knowing what events to select. Look carefully at Angelou's story of Sister Monroe (paragraphs 5–9). What events does she choose to include in her narrative?

2. How is Sister Monroe described? Make a list of all of the physical particulars we are given about her. How, other than direct description, is Sister Monroe revealed to the reader?

3. What shift occurs between paragraphs 5 and 6? Did you notice it the first time you read the selection?

## Questions on Vocabulary and Style

1. Other than a few words uttered by Sister Monroe, Angelou uses no other dialogue in the selection. How, then, is the story told? What advantage does this method have?

2. Writing humor is never easy. Having a funny situation is essential, but in addition, the story must be told in the right way. (Remember how people can ruin a good joke?) How does Angelou's language and style contribute to the humor in the selection?

3. How effective are the following images:
   a. "She stood in front of the altar, shaking like a freshly caught trout" (paragraph 6).
   b. "The Reverend kept on throwing out phrases like home-run balls" (6).
   c. "Everyone in the church . . . hung loose like stockings on a washline" (6).
   d. "Their legs spiked out like kindling wood" (8).

## Writing Suggestions

1. **For Your Journal or Blog.** Observe people for a day. In your journal or blog, make a list of the funny or comic moments that you notice. Select one of those moments, describe the situation you witnessed, then analyze why it seemed funny to you.

2. **For a Paragraph.** Everyone has experienced a funny, embarrassing moment, perhaps it happened to you or maybe you just witnessed it. In a paragraph, narrate that incident for your reader. Remember to keep the narrative focused.

3. **For an Essay.** Select a "first" from your experience—your first day in junior high school, your first date, your first time driving a car, your first day on a job or at college. Re-create that first for your reader. Remember to shape your narrative, and select only important contributing details. Focus your narrative around a significant aspect of that first experience, whether it was funny or serious.

4. **For Research.** What is an autobiography? Is it always a factual account of events in the writer's life? Is it ever fictional? Is it ever propagandistic? What purposes do autobiographies have? Select an autobiography written by someone who interests you; check your college's library catalog for possibilities. Analyze that work as an autobiography. Do not summarize. Instead, formulate a thesis about what you see as the writer's sense of purpose in the book. Support your argument with evidence from the text, and be sure to document your quotations.

## For Further Study

**Focusing on Grammar and Writing.** First, be sure that you can identify figurative language, especially simile and metaphor (see the Glossary and Ready Reference). Then go through Angelou's narrative and make a list of all the similes and metaphors. What effect do these devices have on the narrative? Why does she use them? Have you tried creating similes and metaphors in your own narrative writing? What cautions should you be aware of when you use these devices?

**Working Together.** Working in small groups, look closely at how Angelou manipulates time in the narrative. Does the story take place on one day? If there are time shifts, where do they come and how does Angelou make sure that readers are not confused? Once your group has finished work, choose someone to report your findings to the class.

**Seeing Other Modes at Work.** Angelou is equally skillful in her use of description to create a sense of both place and character.

**Finding Connections.** For a good comparison of both context and narrative technique, read Langston Hughes's "Salvation," also in this chapter.

**Exploring the Web.** The Web has many sites with extensive information about Maya Angelou, including interviews and audio and video clips.

# Facing Famine

Tom Haines

*Tom Haines grew up in the suburbs of Pittsburgh, Pennsylvania, and worked as a computer programmer in a bank after college. He took three months off to travel and never returned to his old job. He went to Berkeley for a journalism degree and spent the next ten years as a news reporter. After a period as a freelance writer, he accepted a position as staff travel writer at the* Boston Globe. *Haines has accumulated a number of awards for his travel writing, including Travel Journalist of the Year by the Society of Travel Writers. "Facing Famine" originally appeared in the* Boston Globe *in 2003.*

**On Writing:** *Commenting on the role of the writer as a narrator in an essay such as this, Haines remarked: "If you have something to say compelling about yourself, fine, but it better be pretty compelling. . . . I think that the standard has to be pretty high when you introduce yourself into the story—not necessarily if you're doing this as a part of the narrative, such as 'I went there . . . ; we went there . . .' in order to move the plot along, but more if you are making a point about your perceptions."*

## Before Reading

**Connecting:** American media regularly carry stories about famine in Africa. Famine, of course, is something that Americans have never experienced. Does Haines's essay make the famine "more real" to you as a reader than what you have seen or read elsewhere? If so, why? If not, why?

**Anticipating:** As you read, think about why Haines might be telling this story in this way. What might he want his readers to feel or to do after reading the essay? Can you find any evidence in the essay to support your conclusion?

1    **B**URTUKAN Abe braces against the hard mud wall as Osman, her two-year-old son, wails and wobbles on stick legs.

2    Are there others? I ask.

3    Yes, one, she says. A boy, one month old. He is inside.

4    There is no turning back. Through the low, narrow doorway, in the darkness that guards cool by day, heat by night, lies little Nurhusein.

5    May I see him?

6    This journey began weeks earlier, when yet another report described widespread drought and the threat of famine across much of Africa.

7    What can that life be like?

8    Travel often approaches boundaries of wealth and health. But what does it feel like to cross those boundaries and enter a place that is, everywhere, collapsing? What comes from knowing people who, with an empty grain basket or a thinning goat, edge closer to death?

9    The route led first to Addis Ababa, a highland capital, then east and south, down into rolling stretches of the Great Rift Valley. In the tattered town of Ogolcho, Berhanu Muse, a local irrigation specialist, agreed to serve as translator and guide.

10    A narrow road of rock headed south, through one village, then another, for one hour, then two.

11    In late afternoon, before evening wind lifted dirt from north to south, east to west, we stopped and parked near a hilltop. A man and woman collected grain from a tall stick bin on the corner of their rectangular plot of land.

12    Gebi Egato offered his hand from his perch inside the bin. Halima, his wife, smiled warmly, then carried a half-filled sack toward the family's low, round hut. Abdo, a three-year-old with determined eyes, barreled out the door.

13    I asked if we could stay.

14    "Welcome," Gebi said.

15    For four nights, a photographer and I would sleep here, beneath open sky, then wake to wander this village of one thousand people. We would step into a schoolhouse, a clinic, and other thatch-roofed huts, including the one that held Nurhusein.

16    But that first afternoon, the village came to us. They were mostly old, all men, a group of perhaps two dozen. Many held walking sticks, one a long spear. One man said he would like to show us something: a hole, not too far, that used to hold water. The hole was shallow and wide, perhaps the size of a Boston backyard. It was empty, nothing but hard earth.

17    The men calmly debated how many months it had been since water filled the hole. Flies buzzed and jumped from eyelids to lips.

18    A young schoolteacher, a specialist in math and science, sat at my side, his legs crossed, hands in his lap.

19    "Thirst is thirst, hunger is hunger," he said.

20    Hours later, I awoke to a setting moon and could imagine this land as it long had been: Beneath my cot, wheat, barley, and teff shot from the ground. Birds swarmed tree branches, trading throaty, bubbling calls. Water pooled in ditches and holes. Thick green hedges framed the farmyard.

21    Gebi would describe to me what this can feel like. The land offers so much bounty, so much comfort, he said, that even when the sun is high and hot, you want to lie down on the earth, close your eyes, and sleep.

22    In the hut's outer room there is a low wooden bench, but little else. The food, furniture, even a grandmother and three uncles have gone.

23    Now five people remain: Burtukan, the mother, age nineteen; Abdurkedir Beriso, her husband, twenty-seven; Abduraman Beriso, his brother, sixteen. And the children, Osman and Nurhusein.

24    They have no animals, no money. Neighbors share hard bread and flour.

25    "I have nowhere to go," Abdurkedir told me. "I will die here."

26    From behind a curtain, in the hut's back room, I hear the rustle of blankets, a whimper, a soothing voice: sounds of a mother gathering a baby in her arms.

***

27    On our first morning, as nighttime hilltop sounds—a howling hyena, a barking dog, a farting donkey—gave way to those of dawn, we were outsiders, in the cool air, listening.

28    Beneath Gebi and Halima's thatch roof, Abdo squealed and pouted. Bontu, barely a year old, cried for breakfast.

29    Soon, with the fire made, the children fed, Halima strapped plastic canisters on the back of the family donkey and began to walk. Gebi followed with the ox.

30    Halima sauntered gracefully, as though out for a stroll. She crossed a parched soccer field to a footpath lined with huts. She greeted a woman walking toward her. They held hands and talked.

31    Farther along, in an empty cradle of land set back from the trail, a stack of branches and twigs covered a hole roughly twelve inches in diameter. Three times, the government had tried to dig a well in this village, which sits far from any river. The last time, a powerful machine made the narrow hole and bore in search of water. Villagers gathered and watched as earth spit upward. Then the drill bit broke, 820 feet underground. It was there still.

32    Halima walked on for more than an hour, then stopped in a spot of shade. She untied the canisters and knelt by a wide pond of muddy water. The pond teemed with salmonella, the root of typhoid fever, and parasites that thrive in intestines, infecting 70 percent of Adere Lepho's children.

33    Another young woman leaned at the pond's edge and filled every last ounce of space in her canister. She stuffed the spout with a plug of withered grass.

34    Hundreds of people came each day to this pond, the only water source for Adere Lepho and two neighboring villages, and carted home water to quench the thirst of thousands.

35    A month earlier, this pond, too, had been nearly empty. Then two days of heavy February rain filled it. How long would it last? Even village elders, men and women forty, forty-five, and fifty years old, had never seen this kind of drought.

36    Two years earlier, and two years before that, meager rains had fallen. Families had to sell animals, eat thinner harvests, and spend precious savings just to survive. But this was worse: the February downpour was the first time it had rained in nearly a year.

37    Late the next afternoon, rain fell. As the drops landed thick and heavy, men, women, and children took shelter in the low, open building that houses the village's grain mill. After three, maybe four minutes, the rain stopped.

39    Women heaved sacks of grain, some of them holding well-rationed harvests from years past, others gifts from farmland half a world away, onto a scale. Across the room, the mill owner sat alongside a conveyor belt spun by a

howling generator, the only power in the village. The owner opened sacks into the mouth of a grinder that turned kernel to flour. Dust filled the air, sticking to hair and eyelashes.

39      Outside, dozens of men gathered beneath the branches of a wide tree.

40      Gebi Tola, elected leader of a local farmers' group, explained that the government had offered land for ten volunteers to move to another region. The government owns all land in Ethiopia. This resettlement program provided a rare chance.

41      The men, sitting on the ground in orderly rows, faced Tola. He explained that some plots of land were north, in a neighboring district. Most would be farther, three hundred miles to the west.

42      Voices rose. How can we know this land is good? one man asked. How can we trust that life will be better there?

43      Kedir Husein, a young father who had stood to ask many questions, stepped away from the group. He told me he had decided not to volunteer to leave.

44      "I am afraid," he said.


45      Nurhusein emerges, his head resting in the crook of his mother's left elbow.

46      A soft cotton blanket opens to shocks of slick, curly hair. Tiny fingers spread in the air. I touch Nurhusein's forehead, cool and smooth.

47      "He is beautiful," I say.

48      Nurhusein bleats softly. His lips often latch on to a dry breast. He has a small stomachache, Burtukan tells me.

49      The bleating rises then falls, just beyond the blanket's edge.

50      Nurhusein is already too wise. It is as if he knows.


51      Morning inside Gebi Egato's hut. Glowing coals. Boisterous children. Hearty porridge. A calf, head low, softly chewed its cud.

52      Shilla, the oldest at five, licked her fingers and pondered her favorite foods as Abdo crammed both hands full of porridge.

53      "Milk," she said. She raised her head and smiled. "And sugar."

54      Finished, Shilla and Abdo scrambled to waiting friends. Gebi and Halima took turns digging a wooden scoop deep into a jug decorated with shells.

55      Each bite brought more peril.

56      Gebi's tired cow and thirsty goats were giving little milk. The porridge was made from wheat that had been meant as seed for planting if the spring rains came. Neighbors with less were already selling cows and goats, driving prices down.

57      As the coals darkened, I asked how long the family could last.

58      Gebi told me that in two weeks the family's wheat would be gone. He would then sell his goats, then the cow. Then the ox and, finally, the donkey. He paused.

59      "Five months," he said.

60      Gebi, like most villagers a Muslim, said he was confident rain would come. Then he could partner his ox with that of a neighbor and together they could churn the dark, moist earth.

61     "We have seen so much hardship already, God will not add more," Gebi said. "I hope."

62     After breakfast, Gebi took the donkey and walked beneath the high sun for three hours. He crested three low ridges and crossed three shallow valleys. The first was carpeted in six inches of dust. The second traced the steep gorge of a dry creek. The third, staggered with acacia trees, opened widely toward the village of Cheffe Jilla.

63     A group of men, women, children, and donkeys swayed in the village's main square. White sacks of grain sat in lopsided piles. Gebi joined the hopeful and registered his name in a government office.

64     I saw Gebi Tola, the leader of Adere Lepho's farmers' association, standing beneath a tree. He told me families from his village would take home five hundred sacks of grain. But they could use a thousand. How do you judge the needy when a whole village is staggering?

65     He spoke quickly. A crowd of dozens, young, old, pressed in around us.

66     I asked Gebi how he felt.

67     "I feel sorry," he said.

68     I had grown used to stoicism. But sorry? I stepped aside with Berhanu, our translator. "Sorry" does not feel like the right word, I said.

69     In English, I explained, "sorry" often has a light sense. Sorry I stepped on your toe. Sorry I'm late for dinner. It is not something felt by someone watching his friends and neighbors beginning to starve.

70     Berhanu is a compassionate, intimate man. He raised his hand to his chin.

71     He told me that, in that case, "sorry" was not the word he meant.

72     The crowd moved in again and curious eyes followed our exchange.

73     I asked Berhanu to choose another English word that more closely matched the Oromigna word Tola had used.

74     He could not find an exact translation. I asked him to describe the feeling.

75     "Well," Berhanu said, "it is the feeling you have when something bad happens. Say, for example, when you lose your lovely brother. Is there a word in English for that?"

76     Misery?

77     Yes, Berhanu said calmly, that is part of it.

78     Emptiness? Yes, he said, that too.

79     Anguish, despair?

80     His eyes sparked at the connection.

81     Anger? Yes.

82     Frustration? Yes.

83     Fear? No.

84     Fear, Berhanu said, like sorry, was too light a word.

85     Terror?

86     Yes, Berhanu said, "terror" is a good word.

87     I stand before Nurhusein and start to cry.

88     Is it empathy? I have a ten-month-old son, a spirited boy with muscles across his back and a quick laugh.

89    Or am I crying from fear?

90    In the hot sun, looking from hut to hut, from face to face, the problem was always too vast.

91    I stare at Nurhusein. I cannot look again into his mother's eyes.

## Questions on Subject and Purpose

1. Haines is a travel writer and the story appeared in the travel section of a newspaper. Is this the type of essay that you would expect to find in this section of a newspaper? Why or why not?

2. Where is this story taking place? In what part of the world?

3. Based on your reading experience, what purpose might Haines have had in writing the essay?

## Questions on Strategy and Audience

1. Look carefully at the essay. In five places in the essay, Haines uses extra white space to mark divisions within the text. Locate those places.

2. Why is Haines so moved by the sight of the infant Nurhusein?

3. Who is Haines's audience? How does that audience influence the essay?

## Questions on Vocabulary and Style

1. How does its place of original publication (a newspaper) influence the paragraphing of the essay?

2. What is the effect of the passage in which Haines tries to find English words to describe the emotions that Gebi Tola felt (paragraphs 66–86)?

3. Be prepared to define the following words: *sauntered* (paragraph 30), *teemed* (32), *stoicism* (68), *empathy* (88).

## Writing Suggestions

1. **For Your Journal or Blog.** How do you react to the story that Haines narrates? Do you have any emotional reaction? Do you feel indifferent or that it is not your problem? Is the problem simply too large or too distant for you to worry about? Do you want to do something but do not know what? In your journal or blog, explore your reaction to Haines's essay.

2. **For a Paragraph.** Assume that you have been hired as a writer for an international agency that tries to find sponsors for children in need. Using the material from the essay, write a paragraph in which you attempt to get donors to support the infant Nurhusein.

3. **For an Essay.** A single narrative (story) can be extremely effective in helping people to understand a situation or in persuading people to do something about it. The single example makes it easier to empathize—it puts a human face on the situation that can never be achieved with just facts and statistics. Pick a painful social issue—for example, poverty, homelessness, chronic illness,

disability, hate crimes, drug addiction, sexual abuse—and put a human face on the problem. You might want to interview a victim or create a fictional victim, then look for stories that victims have told, explore stories on the Web, and talk with professionals who counsel such victims. Using your research, construct a narrative in which you use this one story to create empathy and understanding in your readers.

4. **For Research.** What are things like in Ethiopia today? Is there still a famine? Has anything improved? Using print and online sources, gather information about living conditions there. You might want to use a mix of data—photographs, statistics, examples—to make your essay more vivid and informative.

## For Further Study

**Focusing on Grammar and Writing.** In the essay, Haines uses a number of sentence fragments. See how many you can locate. Check the Glossary and Ready Reference if you need a definition of a fragment. Why might Haines have used the fragments that he does? What effect is he trying to achieve? Would it make any difference if the fragments were rewritten as complete sentences?

**Working Together.** Haines's essay originally appeared in the narrow columns of a newspaper. That is why it contains so many paragraphs. How easily could the essay be reparagraphed to reduce the total number of paragraphs? Divide into small groups. Each group should take one of the six sections of the essay and discuss how small, often one-sentence paragraphs might be combined into larger units. What changes, if any, would need to be made?

**Seeing Other Modes at Work.** The essay includes description, cause and effect, and even elements of definition (how a famine makes you feel) and persuasion.

**Finding Connections.** An interesting pairing would be Peter Singer's "The Singer Solution to World Poverty" (Chapter 10).

**Exploring the Web.** You can read other travel articles by Haines at the *Boston Globe* Website. You might also look for additional information about and maps of Ethiopia and the famine in parts of Africa. The CIA Fact Book has maps and background information that are helpful.

# Mission Iraq

Allison Perkins

*Allison Perkins, a 1998 graduate of Northeastern University, has spent much of her career covering the military, both in the United States and abroad. As a bureau chief in South Korea for* Stars and Stripes, *she covered U.S. troop exercises throughout Asia. Later, at the* News & Record *in North Carolina, Allison was a feature writer for the "Life" section. In 2005, she traveled for that newspaper with local Marines to Iraq. Currently, she freelances for several publications, including* Our State Magazine, *in North Carolina, and CinCHouse (www.cinchouse.com), a Website for military families.*

**On Writing:** *"I never intended to be a writer, but I guess this is what happens to students who fail trigonometry. Truthfully, I never enjoyed writing, never enjoyed English class. I loathed my freshman grammar class. But journalism, that was something completely different. Following the story. Tracking down sources. Learning how to really listen to people and create the most honest, informative, interesting, even entertaining, piece of work I could, all by five o'clock—now that is fun. I love the fact that you don't have to write for the biggest newspaper or write the top story of the day to make a difference in a life. All that community news that everyone likes to stick in the weeklies? That's where neighborhoods happen and where people live their lives. I like to be there. I like to find those interesting stories happening in every town, every day, that most people are too busy to notice. There's a whole world full of amazing, astonishing, even horrifying things, to write about. I really appreciate the fact that journalism has let me roam and do just that. And, it's turned out to be a lot less stressful than trig."*

## Before Reading

**Connecting:** How easy or how difficult is it to talk to a close relative or significant other during a period of separation? What role can separation play in a relationship?

**Anticipating:** What is the issue that originally troubles Perkins and how does her own experience in Iraq provide an answer to that problem?

1  **H**e didn't tell me it was dark. He didn't tell me it was quiet.

2  When my husband returned from his first tour in Iraq, he told me (in this order) that it was hot, that he missed eating real scrambled eggs and that sand was everywhere.

3       On his second tour, he split his time between Iraq and Kuwait. When he returned home, his account of his 12 months away was even shorter.

4       Simply put, "It was good to be home," he said.

5       His letters and phone calls in those two years were polite, light conversation about nothing in particular. The war and his part in it were never discussed.

6       In those same two years, I e-mailed weekly pictures of our kids with the Easter bunny, at the Fourth of July parade, carving pumpkins and visiting Santa. I wrote detailed letters of their first steps, first solid foods and of one-liner jokes from television shows I thought were hysterical. My letters dripped with emotion as I tried to tell him how much I missed him and cheerfully outline the plans I had for our future.

7       I wanted to know where he slept, what he heard, what the Iraqi people he met said to him, what the night sky looked like.

8       Last summer, I had the chance to find out.

9       I traveled to the war zone for the North Carolina paper for which I am a staff writer.

10      It was 10 days of little sleep, drinking water the temperature of bath water and nerve-racking helicopter flights.

11      At one point, I spent the night on the wooden floor in a makeshift airport hangar. I bathed, kind of, in a dirty sink. I scratched at the sand glued to my scalp by a constant, thick coat of sweat.

12      I put my feet up and sipped a raspberry smoothie in the most surreal coffee shop on earth, which by the way, had the best customer service I've ever encountered.

13      I laughed and joked with guys on guard duty who caught massive, hairy camel spiders and battled them against each other like great boxing champions.

14      I watched a Marine blink away tears as he told me about working in a hospital, watching young guys come in, shot to hell and dying.

15      I saw a world my husband never would, and probably never will, talk about.

16      And I finally understand why.

17      When I left Iraq and sat down to write my reports, the news and facts came easy. Explaining what I had seen and felt was impossible. I felt lost between reality and this strange place that somehow seemed like it couldn't really exist. It was a world where danger waited at every turn, where strangers became family in an instant and where laughter, jokes and fun could thrive despite the circumstances.

18      Where I was could be deafening for a second and then silent for a week. My legs ached as I marched from place to place and managed to keep up with the guys in front of me, though it felt like I was moving under no power of my own.

19      There was no color, just brown—on the ground, covering the sky, in my bunk and on my clothes. At night, there were no stars, no lights from nearby towns—just darkness.

20      I called home once from Baghdad and couldn't think of a thing to say.

21      I remembered all the times I envied other wives who received long, lovey-dovey letters from their husbands, detailing every aspect of what was seen and how they felt.

22      My husband made small talk—the weather, how his beloved University of Alabama football team was faring, what type of gas I should use in the lawn-mower.

23      And now, here I was, ho-humming my way through a conversation that, if I soon found myself in the wrong place at the wrong time, could be our last. He never pressed me for details and never asked me what I ate that day or where I slept.

24      "Are you OK?" was all he asked. That's all he needed to ask. He knew better.

25      He knew I was hungry, that I was tired, that I fell asleep dreaming of an ice-cold glass of water. He knew my legs were covered in bruises and that if I didn't say much, it wasn't because I didn't love him and wish I could bury myself in his chest and stay there until I was ready to leave.

26      It was because I was lost in this chaotic world I had jumped in to, and saying anything would mean trying to make sense of it. I just couldn't manage that in a seven-minute phone call.

27      Only once throughout my journey did he talk about the "what if"—the chance that I wouldn't come home. It was the same topic that I hated but somehow seemed to have spent ridiculous amounts of time talking and worrying about.

28      He pulled aside a public affairs officer as I boarded a bus to the airfield. I pestered my husband until he told me what was said.

29      "I wanted to make sure he would call me if something happened. I want to make sure that I come get you. That I take you home—the whole way. The things that might happen to your body," he stopped.

30      He didn't say anything else. He didn't have to.

31      When I finally arrived home, he hugged me and asked, again, only one question. "Are you OK?"

32      Yeah. I was.

33      We never talked about Iraq again.

34      Today, we're both home. We discuss summer vacation plans and look forward to spending holidays together as a family.

35      I know that my time at war is done. The cost and risk of sending a reporter into war is too great. My husband knows that he will likely return to Iraq. It's an inevitable duty we're both bracing for. But this time, when the letters and phone calls are cordial, rather than emotional, I won't nag and worry and question.

36      I'll just ask him, "Are you OK?" And, he'll know I understand.

## Questions on Subject and Purpose

1. The essay carried a subtitle in its original publication, "A wife's trip to Iraq changes her need to know." What does the trip change?

2. Perkins writes, "When I left Iraq and sat down to write my reports, the news and the facts came easy. Explaining what I had seen and felt was impossible." What is the difference?

3. If you had the chance to ask Perkins why she wrote the essay and what she wanted her readers to take away from it, what do you think she might say?

## Question on Strategy and Audience

1. Why might Perkins have chosen to structure her essay as a narrative? Why not simply offer advice to her readers on what to expect and why?

2. What might Perkins mean when she comments after her own experience that she "finally understands why" her husband probably never will talk about his experiences?

3. The essay was originally published in the magazine *Military Spouse*. What does the title of the magazine and the content of Perkins's essay suggest about the audience for such a magazine? Why might that audience be interested in this article?

## Questions on Vocabulary and Style

1. Perkins's essay is easy to read and her points are quite clear. What aspects of writing style promote that clarity for the reader?

2. Perkins uses direct quotations only a few times in the essay. What do those times have in common?

3. Be prepared to define the following word: *surreal* (paragraph 12).

## Writing Suggestions

1. **For Your Journal or Blog.** Have you ever been separated from someone you love or care about for a long time? How did you stay in touch? Did it seem difficult? Did you worry that the person had changed? When you are not in regular, daily contact with someone to whom you are usually close, what seems to happen? Explore those thoughts and feelings in a journal entry or blog.

2. **For a Paragraph.** Have you ever been frustrated in a relationship because you felt the other person simply could not talk to you in the way you needed or wanted? Or have you ever felt that someone wanted something from you in terms of communication that you simply were not able to give? Explore in a paragraph a story or narrative that reveals such tension and frustration. *Show* your reader.

3. **For an Essay.** Expand your paragraph into an essay. Use either a series of moments or a single moment developed at length. Avoid simply summarizing the problem for your reader; instead, use a story or stories to make your point. Your essay will be much more vivid that way.

4. **For Research.** The divorce rate among military personnel returning from active combat duty is high. Explore the facts behind that phenomenon. What role does separation because of combat play in military divorces? What role does communication play?

## For Further Study

**Focusing on Grammar and Writing.** What role does parallelism play in the essay—from phrases and clauses, through sentence and paragraph structures? Locate as many examples as you can and speculate on why there is so much. Check the Glossary and Ready Reference for a definition of parallelism and examples.

**Working Together.** Perkins's essay contains a large number of short paragraphs. Working in small groups, see how many of those little paragraphs might be combined into larger paragraphs. Does anything need to be added to do so—is it just a question of changing the spacing? What does this exercise suggest about the nature of paragraphs?

**Seeing Other Modes at Work.** Comparison and contrast is also at work in the essay. Perkins compares how she reacts to being Iraq with the way in which her spouse reacts. The comparison allows her to understand the situation.

**Finding Connections.** Deborah Tannen's "But What Do You Mean?" (Chapter 4) makes an interesting pairing.

**Exploring the Web.** You can find literally hundreds of military (and spouse) blogs on the Web, many of which have daily entries. Search for *military blogs* or go to www.blogged.com, a helpful starting place.

# *Lockdown*

Evans D. Hopkins

*A former inmate at Nottoway Correctional Center in Virginia and writer for the Black Panther Party, Evans Hopkins was paroled in 1997 after serving sixteen years for armed robbery. He has published essays in the* Washington Post, Nerve, *and* The New Yorker, *where this essay first appeared. His memoir,* Life After Life: A Story of Rage and Redemption, *was published in 2005.*

## Before Reading

**Connecting:** What associations do you have with the words *prison* and *prisoner?*

**Anticipating:** Before you start to read, write down in a sentence or two how you feel about people sentenced to prison. For example, how should they be treated while they are in jail? Then read the essay.

1   I know something serious has happened when I wake up well before dawn to discover two guards wearing armored vests and riot helmets taking a head count. I'd gone to bed early this August evening, so that I might write in the early morning, as is my custom, before the prison clamor begins. So when I wake up I have no idea what was going down while I slept. But it's apparent that the prison is on "full lockdown status." At the minimum, we will be locked in our cells twenty-four hours a day for the next several days.

2   While lockdowns at Nottoway Correctional Center in Virginia are never announced in advance, I'm not altogether surprised by this one. The buzz among the eleven-hundred-man prison population was that a lockdown was imminent. The experienced prisoner knows to be prepared for a few weeks of complete isolation.

3   But I'm hardly prepared for the news I receive later in the day from a local TV station: two corrections officers and two nurses were taken hostage by three prisoners, following what authorities are calling "a terribly botched escape attempt" that included a fourth man. The incident was ended around 5:30 A.M. by a Department of Corrections strike-force team, with the hostages unharmed. However, according to authorities, eight of the rescuers, including the warden, were slightly wounded when a shotgun was discharged accidentally.

4        Oh, God, I think. Forget a few weeks. No telling how long we'll be on
lock *now*. I try to take heart by telling myself, "It's nothing you haven't seen
before, might as well take the opportunity to get the old typewriter pumpin',
maybe even finish your book."

5        The idea that most people have of prison life consists of images from
worst-case-scenario movies, or from news footage of local jails. Visitors to
prison often comment on how surprised they are to see men moving around,
without apparent restraint, having believed that prisoners are kept in their
cells most of the time. In modern prisons, however, there is usually lots of orderly movement, as inmates go about the activities of normal life: working,
eating, education, recreation, etc.

6        In a well-run institution, long lockdowns—where all inmate movement
stops—are aberrations. Yet major institutions lock down regularly, for short
periods, so that the prison can be searched for weapons and other contraband.
Lockdowns are also called for emergencies, as this one has been at Nottoway,
or, in fact, for any reason deemed necessary for security.

7        By the second week of the lockdown, one of our hot meals has been replaced with a bag lunch—four slices of bread, two slices of either cheese or a
luncheon meat, and a small piece of plain cake or, more rarely, fruit. Since
counsellors or administrative personnel must do most of the cooking, the lockdown menu usually consists of meals that require minimal culinary skills. Today we have chili-mac (an ungodly concoction of macaroni and ground beef),
along with three tablespoons of anemic mixed vegetables and a piece of plain
cake—all served on a disposable aluminum tray the size of a hard-cover book.

8        We have not yet been allowed out to shower, so I lay newspaper on the
concrete floor and bathe at the sink. There is a hot water tap, in contrast to
the cells at the now demolished State Penitentiary, in Richmond, where I
served the first several years of my life sentence for armed robbery, and where
I went through many very long lockdowns.

9        I have endured lockdowns in buildings with little or no heat; lockdowns
during which authorities cut off the plumbing completely, so contraband
couldn't be flushed away; and lockdowns where we weren't allowed out to
shower for more than a month. I have been in prison since 1981, and my attitude has had to be "I can do time on the moon," if that is what's called for. So
I'm not about to let this lockdown faze me. (Besides, I am in what is known as
the "honor building," where conditions are marginally better.)

10       Around one o'clock in the morning, the three guards of the "shower
squad" finally get around to our building. They have full riot gear on, and a
Rottweiler in tow. One by one, we are handcuffed and escorted to the shower
stalls at the center of the dayroom area. As I walk past the huge dog, I turn my
head to keep an eye on it. The beast suddenly lunges against the handler's
leash and barks at me with such ferocity that I actually feel the force of air on
my face. I walk to the shower with feigned insouciance, but my heart is pumping furiously. I can forget sleeping for a while.

11      Back in the cell, I contemplate what's happening to this place. Information about the hostage incident has been trickling in. While the show of force seems absurd to those of us here in the honor building, I have heard reports of assaults on guards in the cell houses of the main compound, where the treatment of the inmates is said to have been more severe. On the night of the original incident, some men in a section of one building refused to return to their cells, and in at least one section there was open rebellion—destruction and burning.

12      Today a memorandum from the warden is passed out, and the warden himself appears on a video broadcast on the prison's TV system. He announces that there will be no visitation until some time in October—about two months from now.

13      Other restrictions are to be imposed, he says, including immediate implementation of a new Department of Corrections guideline, stripping all prisoners of most personal property: televisions with screens larger than five and a half inches; any tape player other than a Walkman; nearly all personal clothing (jeans, nongray sweatsuits, colored underwear, etc.); and—most devastating for me—*all typewriters.*

14      I find this news disquieting, to say the least, and I decide to lie down, to try to get some sleep. This is difficult, as men are yelling back and forth from their cells, upset about this latest development. Many of them have done ten or fifteen years, like me, obeying all the rules and saving the meagre pay from prison jobs to buy a few personal items—items that we must now surrender.

15      I awaken in the night, sweating and feverish in the humid summer air. Sitting on the edge of my bed while considering my plight, I look at photographs of my family. My eyes rest on the school portrait of my son, taken shortly before he died from heart disease ten years ago, at age twelve. Sorrow overwhelms me, and I find myself giving in to grief, then to great, mournful sobs.

16      The tears stop as suddenly as they began. It has been years since I've wept so, and I realize that the grief has been only a trigger—that I am, by and large, really feeling sorry for myself. This is no good, if I'm to survive with my mind and spirit intact. I can't afford to succumb to self-pity.

17      This new day begins shortly after 8 A.M., when three guards come to my cell door. One of them says, "We're here to escort you to Personal Property. You have to pack up everything in your cell, and they will sort out what you have to send out, and what you can keep, over there."

18      He looks through the long, narrow vertical slot in the steel door and—seeing all the books, magazines, journal notebooks, and piles of papers I have stacked around the cell—shakes his head in disbelief. "Looks like you're gonna need a lot of boxes," he says. I have the accumulated papers, magazines, and books of a practicing freelance writer. The only problem is that my "office" is about as big as your average bathroom—complete with toilet and sink, but with a steel cot where your bathtub would be.

19    Now the new rules say twelve books, twelve magazines, twelve audio-tapes. Period. And "a reasonable number of personal and legal papers." I wonder how much of all this stuff they will say is reasonable, when sometimes even I question the sanity of holding on to so much. But who knows *when* I'll be able to get to any files, manuscripts, books, and notes that I send home? I finish packing after three hours, ending up with twelve full boxes. I sit and smoke a cigarette while waiting for the guards to return, and contemplate the stacked boxes filling the eight feet between the cot and the door. *Where are all the books, plays, and film scripts I dreamed of producing?*

20    As I walk to the property building, on the far side of the compound, the sun is bright, the sky is cloudless, and the air of the Virginia countryside is refreshing. I look away from the fortress-gray concrete buildings of the prison, and out through the twin perimeter fences and the gleaming rolls of razor wire, to note that the leaves of a distant maple have gone to orange. I realize that the season has changed since I was last out of the building.

21    I am accompanied by three guards. Two push a cart laden with my boxes, grumbling; the third, an older man I know, walks beside me, making small talk.

22    "Man, things are really changing here," this guard says. Lowering his voice so that the other two cannot hear him, he tells me that he considered transferring to work at another institution, but that the entire system is now going through similar changes.

23    Back in my cell, I don't have the energy to unpack the four boxes I've returned with. I am glad to have at least salvaged the part of the manuscripts I've worked on over the years.

24    I lie upon the bed like a mummy, feet crossed at the ankle and hands folded over my chest, and try to meditate. However, with my tape player gone (along with my television), I have no music to drown out the sounds coming from the cell house. A wave of defeat settles over me.

25    I think of what I've often told people who ask about my crime—that I got life for a robbery in which no one was hurt. I'll have to rephrase that from now on. If robbery can be said to be theft by force, I can't help but feel like I've just been robbed. And I've most certainly been *hurt*. Maybe that's the whole idea, I think—to injure us, eye for an eye.

26    Perhaps I should acknowledge that the lockdown—and, indeed, all these years—have damaged me more than I want to believe. But self-pity is anathema to the prisoner, and self-doubt is deadly to the writer.

27    I get up quickly, pull out a yellow pad and ballpoint from one of the boxes, and stuff spongy plugs in my ears to block out the noise. I know that if I don't go back to work immediately—on *something*—the loss of my typewriter may throw up a block that I'll never overcome.

28    Just before Christmas, the lockdown officially ends. The four and a half months have taken their toll on everyone. There have been reports of two or three suicides. Some inmates have become unhinged, and can be seen shuffling around, on Thorazine or something.

29    Things are far from being back to "normal operations." There is now the strictest control of *all* movement; attack dogs are everywhere and officers escort you wherever you go. The gym is closed, and recreation and visitation privileges have been drastically curtailed. At least the educational programs, which were once touted as among the best in the state's prison system, are to resume again in the new year.

30    On Christmas Eve, the first baked "real chicken on the bone" since summer is served. But the cafeteria-style serving line has been replaced with a wall of concrete blocks. Now the prisoner gets a standard tray served through a small slot at the end of the wall.

31    As I hasten to finish my food in the allotted fifteen minutes, I look at the men from another building in the serving line. There is a drab sameness to the men, all dressed in the required ill-fitting uniform of denim jeans, blue work shirts, and prison jackets.

32    I spot a friend of more than fifteen years, whom I haven't seen in months. I can only wave and call out a greeting, for as we are seated separately, "mingling" with men from another building is nearly impossible in the chow hall. "I'm a grandfather now," he shouts to me, beaming. "I've got some pictures to show you, when we get a chance." Then he remembers the strict segregation by building now, and his smile fades. He knows that I may never get a chance to see them.

33    I notice a large number of new faces among the men in line. Most of them are black. Many are quite young, with a few appearing to be still in their teens.

34    Such young men are a primary reason for the new lockdown policies, which are calculated largely to contain the "eighty-five-per-centers"—those now entering Virginia's growing prison system, who must serve eighty-five percent of their sentences, under new, no-parole laws.

35    Virginia, like most states and the federal government, has passed punitive sentencing laws in recent years. This has led to an unprecedented United States prison/jail population of more than a million six hundred thousand—about three times what it was when I entered prison, sixteen years ago. In the resulting expansion of the nation's prison systems, authorities have tended to dispense with much of the rehabilitative programming once prevalent in America's penal institutions.

36    When I was sent to the State Penitentiary, in 1981, I was twenty-six—the quintessential angry young black male. However, there was a very different attitude toward rehabilitation at that time, particularly as regards education. I was able to take college courses for a number of years on a Pell grant. Vocational training was available, and literacy (or at least enrollment in school) was encouraged and increased one's chances for making parole.

37    In the late seventies, there was a growing recognition that rehabilitation programs paid off in lower rates of recidivism. But things began to change a few years later. First, the highly publicized violence of the crack epidemic encouraged mandatory minimum sentencing. The throw-away-the-key fever really took off in 1988, when George Bush's Presidential campaign hit the Willie Horton hot button, and sparked the tough-on-crime political climate that continues to this day. The transformation was nearly complete when President Clinton endorsed

the concept of "three strikes you're out" in his 1994 State of the Union address. And when Congress outlawed Pell grants for prisoners later that year the message became clear: We really don't give a damn if you change or not.

38      Although the men are glad, after more than four months, to be out of their cells, there is little holiday spirit; it's just another day. Several watch whatever banality is on the dayroom TV screen. Most sit on the stainless-steel tables and listlessly play cards to kill time, while others wait for a place at the table. Some wait to use one of two telephones, while others, standing around in bathrobes or towels, wait for a shower stall to become available.

39      Most of the men in this section of the building are in their forties or fifties, with a few elderly. It strikes me that for most of them prison has become a life of waiting: waiting in line to eat, for a phone call, the mail, or a visit. Or just waiting for tomorrow—for parole and freedom. For the older ones, with no hope of release, I suppose that they wait for the deliverance of death.

40      As I record the day in my notebook, I find myself thinking about my aunt's grandnephew—her adopted son. He was rumored to have been dealing drugs, and he was shot dead in the doorway of her home on Thanksgiving Day, just over a month ago; my father, who is seventy-five, was called to comfort her. With violence affecting so many lives, one can understand the desire—driven by fear—to lock away young male offenders. But considering their impoverished, danger-filled lives, I wonder whether the threat of being locked up for decades can really deter them from crime.

41      I understand the philosophy behind the increased use of long sentences and harsh incarceration. The idea is to make prison a secular hell on earth—a place where the young potential felon will fear to go, where the ex-con will fear to return. But an underlying theme is that "these people" are irredeemable "predators" (i.e., "animals"), who are without worth. Why, then, provide them with the opportunity to rehabilitate—or give them any hope?

42      Still, what really bothers me is knowing that many thousands of the young men entering prison now may *never* get the "last chance to change," which I was able to put to good use—in an era that, I'm afraid, is now in the past. And more disturbing, to my mind, are the long "no hope" sentences given to so many young men now—they can be given even to people as young as thirteen and fourteen. Although I personally remain eligible for parole—and in all likelihood will be released eventually—I can't help thinking of all the young lives that are now being thrown away. I know that if I had been born in another time I might very well have suffered the same fate.

## Questions on Subject and Purpose

1. How long does the lockdown last? How many specific days during that period does Hopkins write about?
2. At what point in the essay does Hopkins move away from his narrative account of the lockdown? What does Hopkins then do in the essay?
3. What objectives might Hopkins have in writing his essay?

## Questions on Strategy and Audience

1. At times, Hopkins seems to talk to himself—even using quotation marks around his words, as in paragraph 4. Why? What is the effect of this strategy?
2. Hopkins uses white space to separate sections of the essay. How many divisions are there?
3. Who might Hopkins imagine as his readers? To whom is he writing? How do you know?

## Questions on Vocabulary and Style

1. When the Rottweiler lunges at him, Hopkins writes, "I walk to the shower with feigned insouciance" (paragraph 10). What is the effect of his word choice?
2. Hopkins chooses to quote a few remarks that the guards make when he is asked to pack up his possessions (paragraphs 17, 18, and 22). Why?
3. Be prepared to define the following words: *clamor* (paragraph 1), *aberrations* (6), *insouciance* (10), *anathema* (26), *punitive* (35), *quintessential* (36), *recidivism* (37), *banality* (38).

## Writing Suggestions

1. **For Your Journal or Blog.** Spend some time thinking about how a personal experience that you had might be used to argue for a change in society's attitudes. For example, were you ever discriminated against for any reason? Were you ever needlessly embarrassed or ridiculed for something? Make a list of some possible experiences.
2. **For a Paragraph.** Look at the list of personal experiences that you made for your journal or in your blog. Select one of those experiences and in a paragraph narrate what happened; then reflect on the significance of that experience. Try to make your reader see the injustice that was done.
3. **For an Essay.** If you have written the paragraph in suggestion 2, treat that as a draft for a longer, fuller narrative. Write an essay in which you narrate a personal experience for a specific purpose. If you are having trouble finding a suitable experience from your own life, narrate the experience of someone else.
4. **For Research.** What evidence is there to support or to refute the idea that prison can be a place for rehabilitation, can offer a "last chance to change"? Research the problem using your library's resources. Some online or CD-ROM databases would also be good places to start. You might want to talk to a reference librarian for search strategy suggestions. Use your findings to argue for or against providing educational or vocational opportunities to people in prison.

## For Further Study

**Focusing on Grammar and Writing.** What is the mark of punctuation called the *dash*? How do you use it in your writing? How does a dash differ from parentheses or a comma? When might you use one and not the others?

Hopkins uses dashes throughout his essay. Could you write a rule for the use of the dash using Hopkins's sentences as examples?

**Working Together.** Working in small groups, choose one substantial paragraph from the essay. What does Hopkins focus on in that paragraph? How does that one paragraph fit into the whole? Some good examples would be the lockdown meals (paragraph 7), the walk to the shower (10), the walk to the property building (20), the encounter with a friend (32), the waiting (39), and the death of his aunt's grandnephew (40).

**Seeing Other Modes at Work.** In the latter third of the essay, Hopkins abandons narration for reflection and then persuasion, trying to make his audience realize the implications of denying prisoners opportunities for rehabilitation.

**Finding Connections.** Interesting pairings can be made with Brent Staples's "Black Men and Public Space" (Chapter 7) and Richard Rodriguez's "None of This is Fair" (Chapter 9).

**Exploring the Web.** Additional essays by Hopkins can be found online, as can a number of sources that debate the value and appropriateness of educational programs in prison.

# 3

# DESCRIPTION

# GETTING READY TO WRITE

## What Is Description?

Description, like narration, is an everyday activity. You describe to a friend what cooked snails really taste like, how your favorite perfume smells, how your body feels when you have a fever, how a local band sounded last night, what you are wearing to the Halloween party. Description records and re-creates sense impressions by translating them into words.

Consider, for example, Darcy Frey's description of the playground on which Russell Thomas, a star basketball player at a Brooklyn, New York, high school, practices on an August evening:

> At this hour Russell usually has the court to himself; most of the other players won't come out until after dark, when the thick humid air begins to stir with night breezes and the court lights come on. But this evening is turning out to be a fine one—cool and foggy. The low, slanting sun sheds a feeble pink light over the silvery Atlantic a block away, and milky sheets of fog roll off the ocean and drift in tatters along the project walkways. The air smells of sewage and saltwater. At the far end of the court, where someone has torn a hole in the chicken wire fence, other players climb through and begin warming up.

Frey uses descriptive words and phrases to record sense impressions—sights and smells. Sensory details make it easy for the reader to create mentally a feeling and a visual impression for what it must have been like that evening on the basketball court at the project.

Translating sense impressions into words is not easy. When you have a firsthand experience, all of your senses are working at the same time: you see, taste, small, feel, hear; you experience feelings and have thoughts about the experience. When you convey that experience to a reader or a listener, you can record only one sense impression at a time. Furthermore, sometimes it is difficult to find an adequate translation for a particular sense impression—how do you describe the smell of musk perfume or the taste of freshly squeezed orange juice?

Descriptions occur in all forms of writing. When you write a narrative, you include passages of description; when you compare and contrast two things, you describe both as part of that process; when you try to persuade an audience that strip mining destroys the landscape, you describe the abandoned mine site. Scientists write descriptions; writers create descriptions. Sometimes descriptions are a sentence long, sometimes a paragraph; sometimes an entire essay is composed of description.

## Why Record Sense Impressions in Words?

Many types of sense impressions—smells, tastes, textures—cannot really be captured in any way except in words or in a physical re-creation of the original experiences. Sights and sounds, on the other hand, can be recorded in photographs and audio and video recordings. Indeed, at times a photograph or a video works much better than a verbal description. We cannot deny the power of the visual. Look, for example at the following photograph of a sod house, probably taken in the midwest in the 1880s. If we wanted to know what a settler's life was like on the Great Plains, if we wanted to experience the physical reality of that life, what better way than to study a group of photographs?

Nebraska State Historical Society Photograph

At the same time, though, words can do something that photographs never can. Photographs are static—a visual but unchanging moment captured in time. But what were the people in the photograph thinking? What were they feeling? What impression did the landscape leave on their minds and lives? What was it like to go to bed and wake up each morning in a sod house? How cold did it get in the winter? How wet and damp in the spring? What did it smell like? Descriptions in words attempt to argument such question; they do not try to capture a photographic reality. Images are filtered through the mind of the writer—the writer evokes our feelings, our senses, our memories and emotions. The writer makes us feel that we are there. The writer of description records what she or he saw as important in the scene. For example, three of the writers in this chapter write about people important in their lives. Would their descriptions have been more effective—or even unnecessary—if they had included a photograph of the person about whom they were writing? Of course not. In each case, what is important about the person is not that static external appearance, Rather, the importance lies in what the person meant to the writer and how that person is revealed in action and in speech.

Translating sense impressions into words offers two distinct advantages. First, ideally, it isolates the most important aspects of the experience, ruling out anything else that might distract a reader's attention. Many things can be noticed in a scene, but what are the important ones on which the reader is to focus? Second, translating into words makes experiences more permanent. Sensory impressions decay in seconds, but written descriptions survive indefinitely and can reaccessed each time they are reread.

## How Do Objective and Subjective Description Differ?

Traditionally, descriptions are divided into two categories: objective and subjective. In objective description, you record details without making any personal evaluation or reaction. For example, Roger Angell offers this purely objective description of a baseball, recording weight, dimensions, colors, and materials:

> It weighs just five ounces and measures between 2.86 and 2.94 inches in diameter. It is made of a composition-cork nucleus encased in two thin layers of rubber, one black and one red, surrounded by 121 yards of tightly wrapped blue-gray wool yarn, 45 yards of white wool yarn, 53 more yards of blue-gray wool yarn, 150 yards of fine cotton yarn, a coat of rubber cement, and a cowhide (formerly horsehide) exterior, which is held together with 216 slightly raised red cotton stitches.

Few descriptions outside of science writing, however, are completely objective. Instead of trying to include every detail, writers choose a few details carefully. That process of selection is determined by the writer's purpose and by the impression that the writer wants to create. Consider this example from writer Eric Liu. Visiting his elderly grandmother, he goes to wash his hands in the bathroom. As he looks around the bathroom, he records a small selection of details:

> In the small bath were the accessories of her everyday life: a frayed toothbrush in a plastic Star Wars mug I'd given her in 1979, stiff washrags and aged pantyhose hanging from a clothesline, medicine bottles and hair dye cluttered the sinktop.

Liu captures a loneliness and sadness through these few details. Nothing else in the bathroom is described. Liu is not interested in visually describing the bathroom, in capturing it photographically in words; he is creating an emotion, an impression.

In subjective description, you are free to interpret details for your reader; your choice of words and images can be suggestive, emotional, and value-loaded. Subjective descriptions frequently make use of figurative language—similes and metaphors that forge connections in the reader's mind. When Gordon Grice, in "Caught in the Widow's Web" (a descriptive essay found in Writers at Work), sees the debris that litters the ground under the spider's web, he uses a *simile* (a comparison that uses *like* or *as*) when he writes, "the husks of consumed insects, their antennae stiff as gargoyle horns." When Scott Russell Sanders, in "The Inheritance of Tools" (in this chapter), looks at his smashed thumbnail, he creates a *metaphor* (an analogy that directly identifies one thing with another) when he describes the wound as a "crescent moon" that "month by month. . . . rose across the pink sky of my thumbnail."

## What Do You Include or Exclude from a Description?

Writing a description, like writing a narrative, involves selection. If your mother asks you what happened today, she does not expect you to report the events minute by minute. Much as she might be interested in you, she still wants the high points, the significant moments of your day. When you write a narrative, you have a purpose, a shaping focus, for the story. You strip away the unnecessary details and focus on the points or details that relate to your focus. The same principle holds true for writing a description. You cannot record every detail about a person, object, place, or landscape. How could you capture every aspect of anything? How could you include all that could be seen, or smelled, or heard, or felt? Like your mother, your reader wants to know the main points and is distracted by unnecessary details. As you write description, stay focused on your purpose and be selective about the details you include.

Descriptions can serve a variety of purposes, but in every case it is important to make that purpose clear to your reader. Some description is done solely to record the facts, as in Angell's description of a baseball, or to evoke an atmosphere, as in Frey's description of an August evening at a basketball court in Brooklyn. More often, description is used to support subjective purposes. Gordon Grice, in describing the black widow spider, is not trying to describe the spider as a scientist might. He uses description to emphasize the evil or malevolence that he sees embodied in the "flower of natural evil." The spider is more than just a physical thing; it becomes a symbol.

Ask yourself, "What am I trying to describe and why?" Write a purpose statement for your descriptive essay or even for a passage of description. Then use that purpose statement as a tool to measure the relevance or irrelevance of every detail that you are thinking about including.

## IN THE READINGS, LOOK FOR

| | **Focus of the description** |
|---|---|
| Debra Anne Davis, "A Pen" | What descriptive details are important about her father? |
| N. Scott Momaday, "Rainy Mountain" | Momaday comes to visit his grandmother's grave, but what is the focus of his essay? |
| William Least Heat Moon, "Nameless" | How much description can you find in the essay and what is described? |
| Terry Tempest Williams, "The Village" | Why might Williams have chosen to write about Alan? What might be her purpose? |
| Scott Russell Sanders, "Inheritance" | Why does Sanders never describe his father? What does he do instead? |

**PREWRITING TIPS FOR WRITING DESCRIPTION**

1.  Decide what you are going to describe in your essay—a person, a place, an object. Decide as well about length. Will this be a paragraph? A full-length essay?

2.  Make a list of the details that best describe your subject. Consider all of the senses. Which of the details are objective and which are subjective? Do you want to be as precise as possible or to create an atmosphere or emotion?

3.  If possible, reexperience the place, person, or subject of your paper. Go and visit. Take notes. Listen. Look. Jot down details.

4.  Once you have gathered details, write a purpose statement for your description. What are you trying to do? Create an emotion? Set a mood? Verbally photograph or record an event? Use that purpose statement to test each detail that you plan to include. Do all of your details contribute to that purpose?

5.  Remember that extended descriptions are static and may bore a reader. Be careful not if record too much detail. You are not describing everything about your subject; you are being selective.

## WRITING

### How Do You Describe an Object or a Place?

The first task in writing a description is to decide what you want to describe. As in every other writing task, if you make a good choice, the act of writing will be easier and probably more successful. Before you begin, keep two things in mind. First, there is rarely any point in describing a common object or place—something every reader has seen—unless you do it in a fresh and perceptive way. Roger Angell describes a baseball, but he does so by dissecting it, giving a series of facts about its composition. Probably most of Darcy Frey's readers had at least seen pictures of a project playground, but after reading his description, they come away with a sense of vividness—the passage evokes a mental picture of what it was like on the playground that evening.

Second, remember that your description must create a focused impression. Select details that contribute to your purpose; this will give you a way of deciding which details of the many available are relevant. Details in a description must be carefully chosen and arranged; otherwise, your reader will be overwhelmed or bored by an accumulation of irrelevancies.

**IN THE READINGS, LOOK FOR**

**How a place is described**

N. Scott Momaday, "Rainy Mountain"    How is place described
                                      and why?

William Least Heat Moon, "Nameless"   What does the author focus on
                                      in his description of the
                                      Wattses' store?

Scott Russell Sanders, "Inheritance"  What role does "building"
                                      things play in the essay?

## How Do You Describe a Person?

Before you begin to describe a person, remember an experience that every-one has had. You have read a novel and then seen a film or a made-for-television version, and the two experiences did not mesh. The characters, you are convinced, just did not look like the actors and actresses who played the roles: "She was—taller and had red hair" or "He was all wrong—not big enough, not rugged enough." Any time you read a narrative that contains a character, either real or fictional, you form a mental picture of the person, and that picture is generally not based on any physical description that the author has provided. In fact, in many narratives, authors provide only min-imal description of the people involved. For example, if you look closely at the Thurmond Watts family in William Least Heat Moon's "Nameless, Tennessee," you will find almost no physical description of the people. Thurmond, we are told, is "tall" and "thin"—those are the only adjectives used to describe him. The rest of the family—his wife, Miss Ginny; his sister-in-law, Marilyn; and his daughter, Hilda—are not physically de-scribed at all. Nevertheless, we get a vivid sense of all four as people.

Why might that be so? Fictional characters or real people are created or revealed primarily through ways other than direct physical description. What a person does or says, for example, also reveals personality. The reader "sees" Alan in Terry Tempest Williams's "The Village Watchman" in part through what he says. The Wattses, in Least Heat Moon's essay, are revealed by how they react, what they say, how their speech sounds, and what they consider to be important. These are the key factors in re-creating Least Heat Moon's ex-perience for the reader.

In fact, descriptions of people should not try to be verbal portraits recording physical attributes in photographic detail. Words are never as efficient in doing that as photographs. If the reason for describing a person is not photographic accuracy, what then is it? What is it about the person that is worth describing? In all likelihood the answer will be something other than physical attributes. Once you know what that something is, you can then choose the details that best reveal or display the person.

---

## 🔍 IN THE READINGS, LOOK FOR

| | **How a person is described** |
| --- | --- |
| Debra Anne Davis, "A Pen" | What aspects of her father does Davis describe? What does she not mention? |
| N. Scott Momaday, "Rainy Mountain" | In paragraph 10, Momaday offers the only physical description of his grandmother. What does he focus on? |
| William Least Heat Moon, "Nameless" | What role does dialogue have in creating character? |
| Terry Tempest Williams, "The Village" | How does Alan's behavior help create a sense of his character? What is the role of dialogue in revealing character? |

---

## How Do You Organize a Description?

You have a subject; you have studied it—either firsthand or in memory; you have decided on a reason for describing this particular subject; you have selected details that contribute to that reason or purpose. Now you need to organize your paragraph or essay. Descriptions, like narratives, have principles of order, although the principles vary depending on what sensory impressions are involved. When the primary descriptive emphasis is on seeing, the most obvious organization is spatial: from front to back, side to side, outside to inside, topic to bottom, general to specific. The description moves as a camera would. Roger Angell's description of a baseball moves outward from the cork nucleus through the layers of rubber, wool yarn, and rubber cement to the cowhide exterior.

Other sensory experiences might be arranged in order of importance, from the most obvious to the least—the loudest noise at the concert, the most pervasive odor in the restaurant—or even in chronological order.

## IN THE READINGS, LOOK FOR

|  | **Organization of the description** |
|---|---|
| Debra Anne Davis, "A Pen" | What is the role of memory in organizing the description and story? |
| William Least Heat Moon, "Nameless" | How is the description of the interior of the store organized? |
| N. Scott Momaday, "Rainy Mountain" | How is the description of the landscape organized? What role does it have in the essay? |
| Terry Tempest Williams, "The Village" | Why does the writer begin with the totem poles in Sitka and end with the same reference? What is the function of this frame? |
| Scott Russell Sanders, "Inheritance" | What is the principle organizing device in the essay? |

## DRAFTING TIPS FOR WRITING DESCRIPTION

1.  Plan a structure for your essay. Does your description move spatially? From the most obvious to the least obvious? Does time underlie the structure of your description? Remember, you need an organizational structure to control the details of your description.

2.  Look again at your purpose statement. Go through your essay and check each detail against that purpose. Do the details in your description match with your intended purpose?

3.  Have you included too many details? Do parts of the paper seem too long, too crowded, too detailed? Because description is static (with minimal action), it tends to blend with narration. Relatively few essays contain only description.

4.  Plan an opening for your paper. Think of at least three possible ways in which to begin. Write sample beginnings and ask friends to rate them.

5.  Plan an ending for your essay. Think of several different ways to end. How do you know when you are finished? How does your reader know? Do you end with a summary? What will signal a conclusion to your reader?

# REVISING

## How Do You Revise a Description?

Always try to finish a complete draft of your essay days before its due date. That will allow time to put the paper aside for awhile. When you come back to it, you will have a fresh perspective on what you have written. After you look again at the paper, you may be pleased with how good it seems, or you may realize that more work needs to be done. Try to get feedback from other readers. Ask for constructive advice; do not settle for empty responses such as "it's OK" or "I liked it." In writing descriptive passages or essays, problems tend to cluster around several key areas.

**Overusing Adjectives and Adverbs**    You can create an image without providing a mountain of adjectives and adverbs—just as you can imagine what a character looks like without being told. When Terry Tempest Williams describes Alan's behavior at the bowling alley, the scene and Alan come alive for the reader: "When it was Alan's turn, it was an event. Nothing subtle. His style was Herculean. Big man. Big ball. Big roll. Big bang. Whether it was a strike or a gutter ball, he clapped his hands, spun around on the floor, clapped his thighs, and cried, 'Goddamn! Did you see that one? Send me another ball, sweet Jesus!'" One of the greatest dangers in writing a description is attempting to describe too much, trying to qualify every noun with at least one adjective and every verb with an adverb. Precise, vivid nouns and verbs will do most of the work for you.

**Overusing Figurative Language**    Similes and metaphors can be powerful descriptive tools, but such figurative devices can present problems. Similes and metaphors add freshness and vividness to writing, and they help readers understand the unfamiliar by linking it to the familiar, Nevertheless, similes and metaphors are artificial language constructs that tend to call attention to themselves. The point to a description should not be to display your cleverness as a writer. You are describing something for a reason, a purpose, not to show off your verbal skills. Do not try to be too clever: on the other hand, do not use similes and metaphors that are nothing more than clichés. If a character in your essay does things in an unconventional way, do not write that she "marches to a different drummer"; if someone has no hair, do not write, he "was as bald as a billiard ball." Finally, do not write strings of similes and metaphors; use them sparingly. For definitions and advice about figurative language, go to the Glossary and Ready Reference at the back of this text.

**Keeping Focused**    An effective description is focused and tight. Never try to describe everything about a person, a scene, or an object; never feel compelled to include every possible sense impression. Descriptions can sprawl out of control, and because they are static, readers can easily get bored by the accumulation of descriptive detail. If you are describing a person, for example, do not give your reader several paragraphs of description—what the person looks like, what the person is wearing, what the person is thinking or feeling. Instead, put that person in motion: have the person do something, interact with someone, say lines of dialogue. Intermix descriptive details with action.

## REVISING TIPS FOR WRITING DESCRIPTION

1.  Check to see if have used vivid nouns and verbs to carry most of the descriptive burden.

2.  Consider whether you have you been too heavy-handed in emphasizing the significance or importance that you see in the object of your description. Remember, you are trying to reveal significance; you are not lecturing on the "meaning" of your description.

3.  Go through your essay and underline every descriptive detail. Are there too many? Are you trying to make the reader experience too much? Compare your descriptive technique with those of writers in this chapter.

4.  Find readers for your draft—a roommate, a classmate, a writing lab tutor. Ask your readers for honest advice. What did they like about your paper? What did they find tedious? What did they identify as your purpose was in writing this paper? Are they right?

5.  Look at your title again. Does it arouse interest? Will it attract a reader or scare one away? Remember that "Descriptive Essay" is not an acceptable title.

## STUDENT ESSAY

Nadine Resnick chose to describe her favorite childhood toy, a stuffed doll named Natalie.

### First Draft

Pretty in Pink

Standing in the middle of the aisle, staring up at the world as most children in nursery school do, something pink caught my eye. Just like Rapunzel in her high tower, there was a girl inside a cardboard and plastic prison atop a high shelf that smiled down at me. I pointed to the doll and brought her home with me that same day. Somehow I knew that she was special.

She was named Natalie. I do not know why, but the name just seemed perfect, like the rest of her. Natalie was less than twelve inches tall and wore a pink outfit. Her hands and grimacing face were made of plastic while the rest of her body was stuffed with love. She had brown eyes and brown hair, just like me, which peeked through her burgundy and pink-flowered bonnet. Perhaps the most unusual feature about her was that my mom had tattooed my name on her large bottom so that if Natalie ever strayed from me at nursery school or at the supermarket, she would be able to find me.

There was some kind of magic about Natalie's face. I think it was her grin from ear to ear. Even if I had played with her until she was so dirty that most of her facial features were hidden, Natalie's never-ending smile usually shone through. When I neglected her for days to play with some new toy and then later returned, her friendly smirk was still there. When I was left home alone for a few hours, her smile assured me that I need not be afraid. Natalie's bright smile also cheered me up when I was sick or had a bad day. And she always had enough hugs for me.

As I was growing up, Natalie and her beaming face could usually be found somewhere in my room—on my bed, in her carriage, hiding under a pile of junk, and later piled in my closet with the rest of my other dolls and stuffed animals. When I got older, I foolishly decided that I no longer needed such childish toys. So I put Natalie and the rest of my stuffed animals in a large black plastic bag in a dark corner of the basement. I now realize that the basement really is not an honorable place for someone who has meant so much to me. But, I will bet that she is still smiling anyway.

## Comments

Nadine had a chance to read her essay to a small group of classmates during a collaborative editing session. Everyone liked the essay and most of their suggested changes were fairly minor. For example, several people objected to her choice of the words *grimaced* and *smirk*, feeling that such words were not appropriate choices for a lovable doll. Another student, however, suggested a revision in the final paragraph. "It seems like you put her farther and farther away from you as you got older. Why don't you emphasize that distancing by having it occur in stages?" he commented. When Nadine rewrote her essay, she made a number of minor changes in the first three paragraphs and then followed her classmate's idea in the fourth paragraph.

## Revised Draft

Natalie

Standing in the store's aisle, staring up at the world as most pre-school children do, something pink caught my eye. Just like Rapunzel in her high tower, a girl trapped inside a cardboard and plastic prison atop a high shelf smiled down at me. I pointed to the doll and brought her home with me that same day. Somehow I knew that she was special.

She was named Natalie. I do not know why, but the name just seemed perfect, like the rest of her. Natalie was less than twelve inches tall and wore a pink outfit. Her hands and smiling face were made of plastic while the rest of her body was plumply stuffed. Just like me, she had brown eyes and brown hair which peeked through her burgundy and pink-flowered bonnet. Perhaps her most unusual feature was my name tattooed on her bottom so that if Natalie ever strayed from me at nursery school or at the supermarket, she would be able to find me.

Natalie's face had a certain glow, some kind of magic. I think it was her grin from ear to ear. After I had played with her, no matter how dirty her face was, Natalie's never-ending smile still beamed through. When I neglected her for days to play with some new toy and then later returned, her friendly grin was still there. Years later, when I was old enough to be left home alone for a few hours, her smile assured me that I need not be afraid. Natalie's bright smile also cheered me up when I was sick or had a bad day. And she always had enough hugs for me.

As I was growing up, Natalie and her beaming face could usually be found somewhere in my room. However, she seemed to move further away from me as I got older. Natalie no longer slept with me; she slept in her own carriage. Then she rested on a high shelf across my room. Later she made her way into my closet with the rest of the dolls and stuffed animals that I had outgrown. Eventually, I decided that I no longer needed such childish toys, so I put Natalie and my other stuffed animals in a large black plastic bag in a dark cellar corner. Even though I abandoned her, I am sure that Natalie is still smiling at me today.

## SOME THINGS TO REMEMBER
## ABOUT WRITING DESCRIPTION

1. Choose your subject carefully, make sure you have a specific reason or purpose in mind for whatever you describe.

2. Study or observe your subject—try to see it or experience it in a fresh way. Gather details; make a list; use all your senses.

3. Use your purpose as a way of deciding which details ought to be included and which excluded.

4. Choose a pattern of organization to focus your reader's attention.

5. Use precise, vivid nouns and verbs, as well as adjectives and adverbs, to create your descriptions.

## SEEING DESCRIPTION IN OTHER CONTEXTS

### As a Literary Strategy

Description is often intertwined with narration as it is in "Traveling to Town," a poem by Duane BigEagle that recalls a recurring experience during his childhood near the Osage Reservation in Oklahoma. As he explains in a note to the poem, "Monkey Ward" was the name many people used to refer to catalog merchandiser Montgomery Ward (once a competitor of Sears). As you read the poem, think about how sparse, but effective, the use of description is here.

# Traveling to Town

Duane BigEagle

*When I was very young,*
*we always went to town*
*in the flatbed wagon.*
*We'd leave as soon as the day's first heat*
*had stopped the mare's breath*
*from forming a cloud*
*in the air.*
*Kids sprawled in the back*
*among the dusty bushels*
*of corn and beans.*
*As we rode down main street,*
*the town revealed itself*
*backwards*
*for my sister and me to see.*
*We loved the brick and sandstone buildings*
*and the farmer's market*
*with its sawdust floor.*
*Best of all*
*was Monkey Ward*
*with its large wood paneled center room*
*and little wires*
*with paper messages*
*that flew back and forth*
*like trained birds.*
*We finally got to Safeway*
*where Grandma did the shopping*
*and Grandpa sat outside*
*on the brick steps in the sunlight*
*watching all the grandkids.*
*From a shady coolness*
*on the other side of the street*
*the ice cream store*
*would call to us*
*with its banging screen door.*
*Grandpa always had money for ice cream*
*and we'd ride home down main street*
*licking ice cream*
*watching the town reveal itself*
*backwards again*
*in afternoon sun.*

## Discussion Questions

1. Probably few readers have ridden to town in a horse-drawn wagon. Despite the lack of similar experiences, can you visualize the scene that BigEagle is describing? Why or why not?

2. The trip presumably takes an entire day. Out of the whole experience, what does BigEagle describe? Why these things?

3. Description doesn't always mean surrounding nouns with clusters of adjectives and verbs with adverbs. Focus on a detail or two in the poem that adds to the description. What does BigEagle do to make the detail seem vivid? What does that suggest about writing effective descriptions?

4. What is the overall impression that BigEagle seems to be trying to convey to his readers? How do the individual details contribute to that impression?

5. How is the description organized in the poem?

## Writing Suggestions

Describe an experience from your childhood or adolescence. Notice that description often works best when it is sparsely done. Some possible places to start

a. An experience you had with your grandparents or parents

b. A place that you (or you and your family) regularly visited

c. A trip—a ride, for example, in a car, train, bus, subway, or airplane

# AS A CRITICAL READING STRATEGY

One of the most famous examples of subjective description comes from the opening paragraphs of Charles Dickens's *Bleak House* (1853). The novel is set in London, a city with muddy streets and polluted air from the coal-burning stoves, a city enveloped in fog. Dickens is not just describing a place, however; he is creating a symbolic landscape. The mud, mire, and suffocating fog of the city reflect the London legal system and the eternally unsettled litigation of the Jarndyce estate case, which is as murky and miserable as the weather Dickens describes in these paragraphs.

As you read these paragraphs, remember what you have learned about how to write a description—and see how that knowledge can help you as a reader.

- Descriptions are written with a purpose in mind, and the details are chosen to reinforce that purpose. What the author includes and excludes are both important, and both choices are made with an eye to purpose.

- Descriptions can be either objective or subjective. A scientist attempting to describe something precisely produces an objective description. A writer trying to evoke an emotion in you through the description (or a real estate agent trying to sell you a property) relies on subjective description.

- Descriptions are organized so that the reader can sense an order to the material. Sometimes that order follows a chronological pattern; sometimes it moves from the most obvious to the least obvious. Whatever the pattern, the organizational scheme allows the reader to orient within the description.
- Descriptions frequently use figurative language, especially simile and metaphor, and capture a range of sense impressions.

| | |
|---|---|
| Opening sentence places the scene in the legal district; season is winter | <u>London, Michaelmas Term lately over, and the Lord Chancellor sitting in Lincoln's Inn Hall</u>. Implacable November weather. As much mud in the streets, <u>as if the waters</u> had but newly retired from the face of the earth, and it would not be wonderful to meet Megalosaurus, forty |
| Extended similes | feet long or so, waddling <u>like an elephantine lizard</u> up Holborn Hill. Smoke lowering down from chimney pots, making a soft black drizzle, |
| Metaphor | with flakes of soot in it <u>as big as full-grown</u> snow-flakes—<u>gone into mourning</u>, one might imagine, for the death of the sun. Dogs, undistinguishable in mire. Horses, scarcely better, splashed to their very blinkers. Foot passengers, jostling one another's umbrellas, in a general infection of ill-temper, and losing their foothold at street-corners, where tens of thousands of other foot passengers have been slipping and sliding since the day broke (if this day ever broke), adding new deposits to the crust upon crust of mud, sticking at these points tenaciously in the pavement, and |
| Metaphor | <u>accumulating at compound interest</u>. |

## AS A VISUAL STRATEGY

Photographs can transport us backward in time. We can see ourselves as children and relive what our childhood home was like and where we went to elementary school. We can see our parents as children, our grandparents as young men and women. We can experience a world that was very different from what we see around us now. The following photograph is of Mulberry Street in New York City, taken about 1900. The passage from Dickens's *Bleak House* is a subjective, symbolic description; the photograph is an objective, visual record of exactly what this street looked like on the day when the photograph was taken.

## WRITING ABOUT IMAGES

1. Using this photograph as a departure point, write one of two possible essays. Try to render the scene in the photograph as an objective description. Suppose the photograph could not be reproduced, but you want to describe for your reader what urban street life was like at the turn of the twentieth century. Do so in descriptive prose. An alternate possibility is to write a subjective description in which you evoke in your reader an emotional reaction to the scene shown. Either way, make sure that you use a variety of sense impressions in your description.

2. Can you imagine yourself living in an earlier time in America? What might it have been like to live in a sod house on the northern Great Plains in the 1800s? To be a suffragette campaigning for women's right to vote at the turn of the twentieth century? To live in Chicago or Manhattan between 1902 and 1930? American Memory at the Library of Congress in (Washington, D.C.), has spectacular online collections of photographs and exhibitions covering a broad range of topics, time frames, and geographical regions of the United States. Visit the Website, select a collection that interests you, and based on one or more of the digitized images, write a descriptive essay that puts the reader back into that time and place.

3. Most colleges and universities have at least some postcards that picture campus buildings and locations. Check to see what is available. What do the images suggest about the school? Are they

accurate visual depictions? Write a descriptive essay about your campus using the postcards as illustrations. If no cards exist, take photographs and write a descriptive essay to represent the campus accurately to parents and prospective donors. Or use your photographs and write an essay to represent the campus accurately to potential students.

## ADDITIONAL WRITING SUGGESTIONS FOR DESCRIPTION

Descriptions always have a purpose—*why* are you describing this person, place, or object? That purpose is never simply to capture objectively the word equivalent of a photograph. A visual image (a photograph or a video clip) will always be much more effective than a collection of words. Descriptions are evocative. They reveal characters, and bring them to life for a reader. Descriptions capture a sense of place and what it means to you, the emotions and associations that you have attached to it. Descriptions allow readers to see objects in a new, fresh way, thereby provoking thought and emotion. Keeping a purpose in mind, try one of the following topics:

## DESCRIBE A PERSON

1. A relative or friend who has made a difference in your life
2. A great/horrible teacher or coach
3. A celebrity
4. A "personal hero"
5. A child in great need—perhaps in another part of the world
6. You at an earlier age
7. Someone you fear or love
8. The "you" no one else knows

## DESCRIBE A PLACE

1. A polluted landscape
2. A favorite or popular campus or community location
3. A scary place (evoke powerful emotions)
4. Your room or apartment (capture either the reality or the fantasy)
5. A sacred or holy place
6. A remembered childhood location
7. A wall covered with graffiti
8. A fantasy world

# DESCRIBE AN OBJECT

1. A sentimental possession
2. Something ordinary seen in a new and different way
3. An object regarded as beautiful
4. An object that has symbolic value
5. A scary thing described either objectively or subjectively
6. A childhood favorite toy or possession
7. Something that you really want to own
8. A deserted or abandoned home or building

# A Pen by the Phone

Debra Anne Davis

*Debra Anne Davis was born in southern California. She received her B.A. in American Studies from the University of California at Santa Cruz and an M.F.A. from the Nonfiction Writing Program at the University of Iowa. She has published essays in literary journals; her published work is online at* **www.debraannedavis.com.** *Davis is currently working on a memoir. "A Pen by the Phone" first appeared in the* Redwood Coast Review *in 2004.*

    **On Writing:** *Davis observes: "I love to write. Some of the happiest moments and hours of my life have been spent with a pen in hand, with my fingers curved over a keyboard. I'm actually a pretty lazy person, so I don't think I would bother writing (it is a lot of hard work and does take a lot of time and energy) if I didn't enjoy it. The hard part, though, is rejection. Writing is one thing; publishing, or trying to publish, is another. I would say I have 'stacks' of rejection slips from journals, agents, and editors—but I tend to throw them away, so there are no physical stacks. The mental ones, though, do weigh on one. I think this is probably true of all authors. And this is why I chose to write about this here, because I want to send a message to the reader of this anthology. You've probably heard it before, but I'll say it again anyway—and maybe it will stick: Trust yourself. If you want to be a writer, write, and send your writing out knowing that much of it will be rejected. It is not you who is being rejected when this happens. What has happened is this. You have joined a club, largely anonymous, physically disconnected but bound by the long traditions of civilizations, by the love of literature. You are a writer now; enjoy your moments and hours."*

## Before Reading

**Connecting:** Think about one of your parents or grandparents. If you had to isolate one quality about one of them, something that you will always remember about him or her, what would it be?

**Anticipating:** What has Davis's father come to represent to her? How is that trait or quality described in the essay?

1   **M**y father was an avid reader. And a quiet person. But not an especially solitary soul. And he was a fairly large man. So, through much of my youth, there was this comforting sight: Dad reading. Lying flat on his back on the

family couch, a book or folded-back magazine held straight over his head by an arm bent 30 degrees at the elbow, his belly a small hill against the tapestry landscape. Noise and commotion did not faze him. He read science books mostly, books about the planets or earthquakes or nutrition, *Psychology Today* and *Scientific American* (though we'd tried a couple of times, my sister Lisa and I could not understand a single word of that publication; the pictures weren't even all that interesting—yet it could absorb Dad's attention for hours). That's how he read the evening newspaper and *Newsweek*, too. That was where he felt comfortable, reading amidst the mild chaos of his family.

2      There's a family story about Dad's reading. Though I don't remember it happening, I do play a key role in the story. My sister Beth is 13 years older than I am. One night she was at her part-time job as an usher at a movie theater. I was at home playing with, presumably, my stuffed animals and dolls. Dad was, of course, reading. I guess at some point I decided it would be fun to brush his hair. I got a brush and some of my little plastic barrettes, green, pink, yellow. I brushed and styled Dad's hair. He continued reading. Mom (as the story goes) came in and reminded him that he needed to pick Beth up at work. So he left to go get her. Poor Beth. Sixteen years old and completely mortified when her father drove up with a rainbow of barrettes covering his tangled hair.

3      This story is told as such stories are, because it contains that humorous central image: a grown man wearing little girl hair accessories. But the central part of it is, I think, not that Dad had gone out in public like that but that he didn't even realize what he looked like. That he was so unselfconscious, so satisfied with each moment he was living that he could become absolutely absorbed in an article about telescopes or moon rockets—and not even notice a 3-year-old pulling on his hair, snapping barrettes into place, patting her handiwork into perfection. My yanking on his hair didn't bother him because he was completely content in that place at that time. He was there, I was there, his reading lamp was on, the house was warm, and all was right with the universe. (It's too bad, I suppose, that Beth wasn't able to have quite the same perspective on things that night.)

4      My father did have one request in life. All he ever wanted was *a pen by the phone*. A simple demand, as demands of patriarchs go, yes—but one we couldn't seem to honor. It would even cause him to raise his voice. He'd answer the phone in the kitchen; it would be for someone else and he'd want to take a message. Yet this quick task, this basic courtesy was impossible for him to perform. For there was No Pen By the Phone! Never a pen, right there by the phone. He would complain of this, loudly.

5      He'd pick up a bag of one dozen pens the next time he was at the drugstore buying aspirin, staples, chocolate bars. He'd put several of the pens in a cup by the phone. And, slowly or quickly, they'd disappear. We, his children and his wife, would take them. We weren't intentional thieves, just thoughtless kleptomaniacs. Frankly, though I do remember his harangues about the incredible and constant dearth of pens-by-the-phone, I have no recollection of ever having taken one. No memory of that whatsoever. Perhaps they got up

and walked off on their own? Or perhaps I was too busy with the million other things I was doing at the moment to notice that I was also stealing the Pen that should stay By the Phone. And that I was not honoring the one clear and uncomplicated plea he had, a basic plan that would have made life better for all of us.

6      My father taught me simplicity, to live well in the ordinary moments of life—but he didn't know he taught me this. He taught this lesson purely by example, not by design, and so I learned it better than most lessons I've learned. He read and looked so serene, so at home with the time and space he was inhabiting; It didn't take much: a soft sofa, a monthly magazine.

7      My father was one of the few truly content people I have ever known. He had the same basic needs we all have—food, shelter, love—but few wants. He required only a space to himself, intellectual stimulation, entertainment— and he got these in such a gentle way. The rest of us, living our busy, full, often disappointing and sometimes devastating lives required so much more. Or felt that we did.

8      Looking back on all this, I wonder if I might be able to live more as my father did. He has been gone now seven years, and we all miss him, his presence, his wisdom, his stacks of incomprehensible books and magazines next to the couch. I learned from watching him that we need not search for serenity, that peace comes unbidden if we prepare a small space and a little time to receive it. Perhaps now I will be able not just to appreciate the way he lived his life but also to follow his example, to find my own precious and quiet bliss in the life I already have. To read and read and read on my couch at home and to wish only for a simple pen by the phone.

## Questions on Subject and Purpose

1.  What quality or characteristic of her father does Davis focus on in the essay?
2.  What might be appealing about those characteristics of her father in the twenty-first century?
3.  Why might Davis have chosen to write the essay?

## Questions on Strategy and Audience

1.  How much of a description of her father does Davis give?
2.  How does Davis structure her essay?
3.  What could Davis assume about her audience?

## Questions on Vocabulary and Style

1.  At three points in the essay (paragraphs 1, 2, and 3), Davis introduces material that is enclosed within parentheses. Why use parentheses? How would you describe the information that is contained with them?
2.  Why "a pen by the phone"? What is the significance of that demand?

3. Be prepared to define the following words: *avid* (paragraph 1), *mortified* (2), *patriarch* (4), *kleptomaniac* (5), *harangue* (5), *dearth* (5).

## Writing Suggestions

1. **For Your Journal or Blog.** Make a list of your relatives or friends and jot down next to their names an activity, an emotion, or a behavior that you instinctively connect with each one.

2. **For a Paragraph.** Look back through your journal or blog writing. Do you see one person who might be the focus of a descriptive paragraph? Focus on a physical attribute, a characteristic expression or behavior, an obsession, a mannerism, whatever. You can treat the subject sympathetically, comically, critically, lovingly. Write a descriptive paragraph about this person to capture that particular quality.

3. **For an Essay.** Davis sees in her father a trait or quality that is probably not common among most parents today—simplicity and contentment. Those might or might not be words that you would apply to your own parents or stepparents. Write a descriptive essay in which you describe a relative or friend in terms of his or her distinctive quality. If you have difficulty writing about a family member, perhaps you could choose a public figure or even a teacher. The goal, however, is not only to describe this person through the characteristic or quality, but also to connect the person's personality to our culture today. Maybe, for example, the person is highly competitive, materialistic, always multitasking.

4. **For Research.** Scholars debate the impact of work on Americans' leisure time. In a recent book, for example, one author notes that Americans average only sixteen hours of leisure a week, and they are working longer hours than people did forty years ago. Other studies, such as the U.S. government's "America Time-Use Survey," to dispute some of those claims. Research the problem through print and online sources, and present your conclusions in a researched essay. You can use personal examples or descriptions of people you know in your essay as well.

## For Further Study

**Focusing on Grammar and Writing.** Davis uses some sentence fragments in her essay. See how many you can find. Why is each a fragment and not a complete sentence? Rewrite each fragment as a complete sentence.

**Working Together.** Divide into two large groups and then into smaller teams within each group. One set of teams will work with the scene in paragraph 2; the other with the scene in 4. Both scenes are summaries. Dramatize each scene by including characters interacting with some dialogue. The teams should compare their results. What happens to the essay when these changes are made?

**Seeing Other Modes at Work.** The essay also involves narration.

**Finding Connections.** The essay could be effectively paired with any of the essays in Chapter 2 to compare the use of narrative strategies. Another excellent pairing involving a memory of a father is Scott Russell Sanders's "The Inheritance of Tools," in this chapter.

**Exploring the Web.** Davis maintains her own Website on which you can read a number of her essays. See the URL in the headnote to this essay.

# The Way to Rainy Mountain

N. Scott Momaday

*Navarre Scott Momaday was born in Lawton, Oklahoma, in 1934. He earned a B.A. from the University of New Mexico and a Ph.D. in English from Stanford University. Professor of English, artist, editor, poet, and novelist, Momaday is above all a storyteller committed to pre-serving and interpreting the rich oral history of the Kiowa Indians. His work includes a book of Kiowa folktales,* The Journey of Tai-me *(1967), which he revised as* The Way to Rainy Mountain *(1969), and the Pulitzer Prize-winning novel* House Made of Dawn *(1968). In 2007 he was awarded the National Medal of Arts. His most recent book is a col-lection of three plays (2007).*

*This essay originally appeared in the magazine* The Reporter *in 1967, but Momaday revised it and used it as the introduction to* The Way to Rainy Mountain.

**On Writing:** *Momaday commented: "There's a lot of frustration in writing. I heard an interview with a writer not long ago in which the interviewer said, tell me, is writing difficult? And the writer said, oh, no…no, of course not. He said, 'All you do is sit down at a typewriter, you put a page in it, and then you look at it until beads of blood appear on your forehead. That's all there is to it.' There are days like that."*

## Before Reading

**Connecting:** In what way does one of your relatives, perhaps a grandparent or a great-grandparent, connect you to a part of your family's past?

**Anticipating:** How and why does Momaday interlink descrip-tions of the landscape with descriptions of his grandmother?

1   **A** single knoll rises out of the plain in Oklahoma, north and west of the Wichita Range. For my people, the Kiowas, it is an old landmark, and they gave it the name Rainy Mountain. The hardest weather in the world is there. Winter brings blizzards, hot tornadic winds arise in the spring, and in summer the prairie is an anvil's edge. The grass turns brittle and brown, and it cracks beneath your feet. There are green belts along the rivers and creeks, linear groves of hickory and pecan, willow and witch hazel. At a distance in July or August the steaming foliage seems almost to writhe in fire. Great green and yellow grasshoppers are everywhere in the tall grass, popping up like corn to sting the flesh, and tortoises crawl about on the red earth, going nowhere in

the plenty of time. Loneliness is an aspect of the land. All things in the plain are isolate; there is no confusion of objects in the eye, but one hill or one tree or one man. To look upon that landscape in the early morning, with the sun at your back, is to lose the sense of proportion. Your imagination comes to life, and this, you think, is where Creation was begun.

2        I returned to Rainy Mountain in July. My grandmother had died in the spring, and I wanted to be at her grave. She had lived to be very old and at last infirm. Her only living daughter was with her when she died, and I was told that in death her face was that of a child.

3        I like to think of her as a child. When she was born, the Kiowas were living the last great moment of their history. For more than a hundred years they had controlled the open range from the Smoky Hill River to the Red, from the headwaters of the Canadian to the fork of the Arkansas and Cimarron. In alliance with the Comanches, they had ruled the whole of the southern Plains. War was their sacred business, and they were among the finest horsemen the world has ever known. But warfare for the Kiowas was preeminently a matter of disposition rather than of survival, and they never understood the grim, unrelenting advance of the U.S. Cavalry. When at last, divided and ill-provisioned, they were driven onto the Staked Plains in the cold rains of autumn, they fell into panic. In Palo Duro Canyon they abandoned their crucial stores to pillage and had nothing then but their lives. In order to save themselves, they surrendered to the soldiers at Fort Sill and were imprisoned in the old stone corral that now stands as a military museum. My grandmother was spared the humiliation of those high gray walls by eight or ten years, but she must have known from birth the affliction of defeat, the dark brooding of old warriors.

4        Her name was Aho, and she belonged to the last culture to evolve in North America. Her forebears came down from the high country in western Montana nearly three centuries ago. They were a mountain people, a mysterious tribe of hunters whose language has never been positively classified in any major group. In the late seventeenth century they began a long migration to the south and east. It was a journey toward the dawn, and it led to a golden age. Along the way the Kiowas were befriended by the Crows, who gave them the culture and religion of the Plains. They acquired horses, and their ancient nomadic spirit was suddenly free of the ground. They acquired Tai-me, the sacred Sun Dance doll, from that moment the object and symbol of their worship, and so shared in the divinity of the sun. Not least, they acquired the sense of destiny, therefore courage and pride. When they entered upon the southern Plains they had been transformed. No longer were they slaves to the simple necessity of survival; they were a lordly and dangerous society of fighters and thieves, hunters and priests of the sun. According to their origin myth, they entered the world through a hollow log. From one point of view, their migration was the fruit of an old prophecy, for indeed they emerged from a sunless world.

5        Although my grandmother lived out her long life in the shadow of Rainy Mountain, the immense landscape of the continental interior lay like memory

in her blood. She could tell of the Crows, whom she had never seen, and of the Black Hills, where she had never been. I wanted to see in reality what she had seen more perfectly in the mind's eye, and traveled fifteen hundred miles to begin my pilgrimage.

6      Yellowstone, it seemed to me, was the top of the world, a region of deep lakes and dark timber, canyons and waterfalls. But, beautiful as it is, one might have the sense of confinement there. The skyline in all directions is close at hand, the high wall of the woods and deep cleavages of shade. There is a perfect freedom in the mountains, but it belongs to the eagle and the elk, the badger and the bear. The Kiowas reckoned their stature by the distance they could see, and they were bent and blind in the wilderness.

7      Descending eastward, the highland meadows are a stairway to the plain. In July the inland slope of the Rockies is luxuriant with flax and buckwheat, stonecrop and larkspur. The earth unfolds and the limit of the land recedes. Clusters of trees, and animals grazing far in the distance, cause the vision to reach away and wonder to build upon the mind. The sun follows a longer course in the day, and the sky is immense beyond all comparison. The great billowing clouds that sail upon it are shadows that move upon the grain like water, dividing light. Farther down, in the land of the Crows and Blackfeet, the plain is yellow. Sweet clover takes hold of the hills and bends upon itself to cover and seal the soil. There the Kiowas paused on their way; they had come to the place where they must change their lives. The sun is at home on the plains. Precisely there does it have the certain character of a god. When the Kiowas came to the land of the Crows, they could see the dark lees of the hills at dawn across the Bighorn River, the profusion of light on the grain shelves, the oldest deity ranging after the solstices. Not yet would they veer southward to the caldron of the land that lay below; they must wean their blood from the northern winter and hold the mountains a while longer in their view. They bore Tai-me in procession to the east.

8      A dark mist lay over the Black Hills, and the land was like iron. At the top of a ridge I caught sight of Devil's Tower up-thrust against the gray sky as if in the birth of time the core of the earth had broken through its crust and the motion of the world was begun. There are things in nature that engender an awful quiet in the heart of man; Devil's Tower is one of them. Two centuries ago, because they could not do otherwise, the Kiowas made a legend at the base of the rock. My grandmother said:

> Eight children were there at play, seven sisters and their brother. Suddenly the boy was struck dumb; he trembled and began to run upon his hands and feet. His fingers became claws, and his body was covered with fur. Directly there was a bear where the boy had been. The sisters were terrified; they ran, and the bear after them. They came to the stump of a great tree, and the tree spoke to them. It bade them climb upon it, and as they did so it began to rise into the air. The bear came to kill them, but they were just beyond its reach. It reared against the tree and scored the bark all around with its claws. The seven sisters were borne into the sky, and they became the stars of the Big Dipper.

From that moment, and so long as the legend lives, the Kiowas have kinsmen in the night sky. Whatever they were in the mountains, they could be no more. However tenuous their well-being, however much they had suffered and would suffer again, they had found a way out of the wilderness.

9        My grandmother had a reverence for the sun, a holy regard that now is all but gone out of mankind. There was a wariness in her, and an ancient awe. She was a Christian in her later years, but she had come a long way about, and she never forgot her birthright. As a child she had been to the Sun Dances; she had taken part in those annual rites, and by them she had learned the restoration of her people in the presence of Tai-me. She was about seven when the last Kiowa Sun Dance was held in 1887 on the Washita River above Rainy Mountain Creek. The buffalo were gone. In order to consummate the ancient sacrifice—to impale the head of a buffalo bull upon the medicine tree—a delegation of old men journeyed into Texas, there to beg and barter for an animal from the Goodnight herd. She was ten when the Kiowas came together for the last time as a living Sun Dance culture. They could find no buffalo; they had to hang an old hide from the sacred tree. Before the dance could begin, a company of soldiers rode out from Fort Sill under orders to disperse the tribe. Forbidden without cause the essential act of their faith, having seen the wild herds slaughtered and left to rot upon the ground, the Kiowas backed away forever from the medicine tree. That was July 20, 1890, at the great bend of the Washita. My grandmother was there. Without bitterness, and for as long as she lived, she bore a vision of deicide.

10        Now that I can have her only in memory, I see my grandmother in the several postures that were peculiar to her: standing at the wood stove on a winter morning and turning meat in a great iron skillet; sitting at the south window, bent above her beadwork, and afterwards, when her vision failed, looking down for a long time into the fold of her hands; going out upon a cane, very slowly as she did when the weight of age came upon her; praying. I remember her most often at prayer. She made long, rambling prayers out of suffering and hope, having seen many things. I was never sure that I had the right to hear, so exclusive were they of all mere custom and company. The last time I saw her she prayed standing by the side of her bed at night, naked to the waist, the light of a kerosene lamp moving upon her dark skin. Her long, black hair, always drawn and braided in the day, lay upon her shoulders and against her breasts like a shawl. I do not speak Kiowa, and I never understood her prayers, but there was something inherently sad in the sound, some merest hesitation upon the syllables of sorrow. She began in a high and descending pitch, exhausting her breath to silence; then again and again—and always the same intensity of effort, of something that is, and is not, like urgency in the human voice. Transported so in the dancing light among the shadows of her room, she seemed beyond the reach of time. But that was illusion; I think I knew then that I should not see her again.

11        Houses are like sentinels in the plain, old keepers of the weather watch. There, in a very little while, wood takes on the appearance of great age. All colors wear soon away in the wind and rain, and then the wood is burned gray

and the grain appears and the nails turn red with rust. The windowpanes are black and opaque; you imagine there is nothing within, and indeed there are many ghosts, bones given up to the land. They stand here and there against the sky, and you approach them for a longer time than you expect. They belong in the distance; it is their domain.

12        Once there was a lot of sound in my grandmother's house, a lot of coming and going, feasting and talk. The summers there were full of excitement and reunion. The Kiowas are a summer people; they abide the cold and keep to themselves, but when the season turns and the land becomes warm and vital they cannot hold still; an old love of going returns upon them. The aged visitors who came to my grandmother's house when I was a child were made of lean and leather, and they bore themselves upright. They wore great black hats and bright ample shirts that shook in the wind. They rubbed fat upon their hair and wound their braids with strips of colored cloth. Some of them painted their faces and carried the scars of old and cherished enmities. They were an old council of warlords, come to remind and be reminded of who they were. Their wives and daughters served them well. The women might indulge themselves; gossip was at once the mark and compensation of their servitude. They made loud and elaborate talk among themselves, full of jest and gesture, fright and false alarm. They went abroad in fringed and flowered shawls, bright beadwork and German silver. They were at home in the kitchen, and they prepared meals that were banquets.

13        There were frequent prayer meetings, and great nocturnal feasts. When I was a child I played with my cousins outside, where the lamplight fell upon the ground and the singing of the old people rose up around us and carried away into the darkness. There were a lot of good things to eat, a lot of laughter and surprise. And afterwards, when the quiet returned, I lay down with my grandmother and could hear the frogs away by the river and feel the motion of the air.

14        Now there is a funeral silence in the rooms, the endless wake of some final word. The walls have closed in upon my grandmother's house. When I returned to it in mourning, I saw for the first time in my life how small it was. It was late at night, and there was a white moon, nearly full. I sat for a long time on the stone steps by the kitchen door. From there I could see out across the land; I could see the long row of trees by the creek, the low light upon the rolling plains, and the stars of the Big Dipper. Once I looked at the moon and caught sight of a strange thing. A cricket had perched upon the handrail, only a few inches away from me. My line of vision was such that the creature filled the moon like a fossil. It had gone there, I thought, to live and die, for there, of all places, was its small definition made whole and eternal. A warm wind rose up and purled like the longing within me.

15        The next morning I awoke at dawn and went out on the dirt road to Rainy Mountain. It was already hot, and the grasshoppers began to fill the air. Still, it was early in the morning, and the birds sang out of the shadows. The long yellow grass on the mountain shone in the bright light, and a scissortail hied above the land. There, where it ought to be, at the end of a long and

legendary way, was my grandmother's grave. Here and there on the dark stones were ancestral names. Looking back once, I saw the mountain and came away.

## Questions on Subject and Purpose

1. What event triggers Momaday's essay?
2. How many "journeys" are involved in Momaday's story?
3. Why might Momaday have titled the essay "The Way to Rainy Mountain"? Why not, for example, refer more specifically to the event that has brought him back?

## Questions on Strategy and Audience

1. Why might Momaday retell the legend of the "seven sisters" (paragraph 8)? How does that fit into his essay?
2. How much descriptive detail does Momaday give of his grandmother? Go through the essay and isolate each physical detail.
3. What expectations might Momaday have of his audience? How might those expectations affect the essay?

## Questions on Vocabulary and Style

1. Identify the figure of speech used in each of these descriptions:
   a. "in summer the prairie is an anvil's edge" (paragraph 1)
   b. "the highland meadows are a stairway to the plain" (7)
   c. "the land was like iron" (8)
   d. "houses are like sentinels in the plain" (11)
2. Between the essay's first appearance in a magazine and its inclusion in a book of essays two years later, Momaday added two new paragraphs, now 6 and 7. What do these paragraphs add to the essay?
3. Be prepared to define the following words: *knoll* (paragraph 1), *writhe* (1), *pillage* (3), *nomadic* (4), *luxuriant* (7), *lees* (7), *solstices* (7), *veer* (7), *tenuous* (8), *deicide* (9), *enmities* (12), *purled* (14), *hied* (15).

## Writing Suggestions

1. **For Your Journal or Blog.** What memories do you have of a grandparent or a great-grandparent? When you think of that person, what comes to mind? In your journal or blog make a list of those memories—sights, sounds, smells, associations of any sort.
2. **For a Paragraph.** In a substantial paragraph, analyze the effects that Momaday achieved by adding paragraphs 6 and 7 to the essay.
3. **For an Essay.** Momaday once told an interviewer, "I believe that the Indian has an understanding of the physical world and of the earth as a spiritual entity that is his, very much his own. The non-Indian can benefit a good deal by having that perception revealed to him." What do such perceptions reveal to the non-Indian?

4. **For Research.** What part have geography and other aspects of the natural world played in determining who you are? If you had to undertake a "pilgrimage" to a place or a geographical location or to retrace a migration, where would you go? What were the stages on the journey? Research part of your own family history, and write a research paper in which you trace that journey for a reader. You might want to start by talking with relatives. Then use research—in the library, in archives, in electronic databases, in atlases, in talks with people—to fill out the story for your reader. Be sure to acknowledge all of your sources.

## For Further Study

**Focusing on Grammar and Writing.** Teachers often urge students to explore a variety of sentence types, not to rely, for example, on writing strings of simple sentences. Look at paragraph 10 in Momaday's essay. The long first sentence, a complex series of parallel clauses introduced by a colon and separated by semicolons, ends with a single participle, *praying*. That long sentence is followed a simple sentence that grows out of that participle. The remainder of the paragraph shows other patterns at work: long, compound sentences held together with coordinating conjunctions and complex sentences containing dependent clauses. How do the sentences' structures reflect their meaning? What does Momaday gain by varying his sentence structures? What does this suggest about your own writing?

**Working Together.** Divide into small groups; each group take a block of paragraphs to examine. Go through that block and locate all the uses of simile and metaphor (see Glossary and Ready Reference). Are there sections of the essay in which such devices do not occur? Where do the similes and metaphors tend to congregate? Why in those places and not others? Present your findings to the class as a whole.

**Seeing Other Modes at Work.** Momaday's essay involves a cause-and-effect strategy as well. He explain how the Kiowa people moved from the mountains to the Plains, how their gods changed, and how they suffered.

**Finding Connections.** Good pairings are with Debra Anne Davis's "A Pen by the Phone" and Scott Russell Sanders's "The Inheritance of Tools" (both in this chapter).

**Exploring the Web.** Among the many Web resources for Momaday is a long, detailed interview with him that includes extensive audio clips.

# Nameless, Tennessee

William Least Heat Moon

*William Least Heat Moon was born William Trogdon in Missouri in 1939 and earned a Ph.D. in English from the University of Missouri in 1973. Trogdon's father created his pen name in memory of their Sioux forefather. His books include* Blue Highways: A Journey into America *(1982),* PrairyErth *(1991), and* River-Horse: A Voyage Across America *(1999), an account of his 5,000-mile journey across America's waterways from New York harbor to the Pacific Ocean. The following essay is from* Blue Highways, *an account of Least Heat Moon's 14,000-mile journey through American backroads in a converted van called* Ghost Dancing. *Its title refers to the blue ink used by map publisher Rand McNally to indicate smaller, or secondary, roads.*

**On Writing:** *Asked about his writing, Least Heat Moon observed: "Woody Allen once said the hardest thing in writing is going from nothing to something. And I think he's right. I struggle so much getting that first draft down. My writing draws so much upon every bit that I am, that I feel drained when I finish a book, and it's years before I'm ready to write again."*

## Before Reading

**Connecting:** If you could get in an automobile and drive off, and time, money, and responsibilities posed no obstacles, where would you go?

**Anticipating:** "Nameless, Tennessee" does more than just faithfully record everything Least Heat Moon saw while visiting the Wattses. The narrative has a central focus that controls the selection of detail. What is that focus?

1    Nameless, Tennessee, was a town of maybe ninety people if you pushed it, a dozen houses along the road, a couple of barns, same number of churches, a general merchandise store selling Fire Chief gasoline, and a community center with a lighted volleyball court. Behind the center was an open-roof, rusting metal privy with PAINT ME on the door, in the hollow of a nearby oak lay a full pint of Jack Daniel's Black Label. From the houses, the odor of coal smoke.

2    Next to a red tobacco barn stood the general merchandise with a poster of Senator Albert Gore, Jr., smiling from the window. I knocked. The door opened partway. A tall, thin man said, "Closed up. For good," and started to shut the door.

3    "Don't want to buy anything. Just a question for Mr. Thurmond Watts."

4    The man peered through the slight opening. He looked me over. "What question would that be?"

5    "If this is Nameless, Tennessee, could he tell me how it got that name?"

6    The man turned back into the store and called out, "Miss Ginny! Somebody here wants to know how Nameless come to be Nameless."

7    Miss Ginny edged to the door and looked me and my truck over. Clearly, she didn't approve. She said, "You know as well as I do, Thurmond. Don't keep him on the stoop in the damp to tell him." Miss Ginny, I found out, was Mrs. Virginia Watts, Thurmond's wife.

8    I stepped in and they both began telling the story, adding a detail here, the other correcting a fact there, both smiling at the foolishness of it all. It seems the hilltop settlement went for years without a name. Then one day the Post Office Department told the people if they wanted mail up on the mountain they would have to give the place a name you could properly address a letter to. The community met; there were only a handful, but they commenced debating. Some wanted patriotic names, some names from nature, one man recommended in all seriousness his own name. They couldn't agree, and they ran out of names to argue about. Finally, a fellow tired of the talk; he didn't like the mail he received anyway. "Forget the durn Post Office," he said. "This here's a nameless place if I ever seen one, so leave it be." And that's just what they did.

9    Watts pointed out the window. "We used to have signs on the road, but the Halloween boys keep tearin' them down."

10    "You think Nameless is a funny name," Miss Ginny said. "I see it plain in your eyes. Well, you take yourself up north a piece to Difficult or Defeated or Shake Rag. Now them are silly names."

11    The old store, lighted only by three fifty-watt bulbs, smelled of coal oil and baking bread. In the middle of the rectangular room, where the oak floor sagged a little, stood an iron stove. To the right was a wooden table with an unfinished game of checkers and a stool made from an apple-tree stump. On shelves around the walls sat earthen jugs with corncob stoppers, a few canned goods, and some of the two thousand old clocks and clockworks Thurmond Watts owned. Only one was ticking, the others he just looked at. I asked how long he'd been in the store.

12    "Thirty-five years, but we closed the first day of the year. We're hopin' to sell it to a churchly couple. Upright people. No athians."

13    "Did you build this store?"

14    "I built this one, but it's the third general store on the ground. I fear it'll be the last. I take no pleasure in that. Once you could come in here for a gallon of paint, a pickle, a pair of shoes, and a can of corn."

15    "Or horehound candy," Miss Ginny said. "Or corsets and salves. We had cough syrups and all that for the body. In season, we'd buy and sell blackberries and walnuts and chestnuts, before the blight got them. And outside, Thurmond milled corn and sharpened plows. Even shoed a horse sometimes."

16    "We could fix up a horse or a man or a baby," Watts said.

17    "Thurmond, tell him we had a doctor on the ridge in them days."

18    "We had a doctor on the ridge in them days. As good as any doctor alivin'. He'd cut a crooked toenail or deliver a woman. Dead these last years."

19    "I got some bad ham meat one day," Miss Ginny said, "and took to vomitin'. All day, all night. Hangin' on the drop edge of yonder. I said to Thurmond, 'Thurmond, unless you want shut of me, call the doctor.'"

20    "I studied on it," Watts said.

21    "You never did. You got him right now. He come over and put three drops of iodeen in half a glass of well water. I drank it down and the vomitin' stopped with the last swallow. Would you think iodeen could do that?"

22    "He put Miss Ginny on one teaspoon of spirits of ammonia in well water for her nerves. Ain't nothin' works better for her to this day."

23    "Calms me like the hand of the Lord."

24    Hilda, the Wattses' daughter, came out of the backroom. "I remember him," she said. "I was just a baby. Y'all were talkin' to him, and he lifted me up on the counter and gave me a stick of Juicy Fruit and a piece of cheese."

25    "Knew the old medicines," Watts said. "Only drugstore he needed was a good kitchen cabinet. None of them anteebeeotics that hit you worsen your ailment. Forgotten lore now, the old medicines, because they ain't profit in iodeen."

26    Miss Ginny started back to the side room where she and her sister Marilyn were taking apart a duck-down mattress to make bolsters. She stopped at the window for another look at Ghost Dancing. "How do you sleep in that thing? Ain't you all cramped and cold?"

27    "How does the clam sleep in his shell?" Watts said in my defense.

28    "Thurmond, get the boy a piece of buttermilk pie afore he goes on."

29    "Hilda, get some buttermilk pie." He looked at me. "You like good music?" I said I did. He cranked up an old Edison phonograph, the kind with the big morning-glory blossom for a speaker, and put on a wax cylinder. "This will be 'My Mother's Prayer,'" he said.

30    While I ate buttermilk pie, Watts served as disc jockey of Nameless, Tennessee. "Here's 'Mountain Rose.'" It was one of those moments that you know at the time will stay with you to the grave: the sweet pie, the gaunt man playing the old music, the coals in the stove glowing orange, the scent of kerosene and hot bread. "Here's 'Evening Rhapsody.'" The music was so heavily romantic we both laughed. I thought: It is for this I have come.

31    Feathered over and giggling, Miss Ginny stepped from the side room. She knew she was a sight. "Thurmond, give him some lunch. Still looks hungry."

32    Hilda pulled food off the woodstove in the backroom: home-butchered and canned whole-hog sausage, home-canned June apples, turnip greens, cole slaw, potatoes, stuffing, hot cornbread. All delicious.

33    Watts and Hilda sat and talked while I ate. "Wish you would join me."

34    "We've ate," Watts said. "Cain't beat a woodstove for flavorful cookin'."

35    He told me he was raised in a one-hundred-fifty-year-old cabin still standing in one of the hollows. "How many's left," he said, "that grew up in a log cabin? I ain't the last surely, but I must be climbin' on the list."

36    Hilda cleared the table. "You Watts ladies know how to cook."

37    "She's in nursin' school at Tennessee Tech. I went over for one of them football games last year there at Coevul." To say *Cookeville*, you let the word collapse in upon itself so that it comes out "Coevul."

38    "Do you like football?" I asked.

39    "Don't know. I was so high up in that stadium, I never opened my eyes."

40    Watts went to the back and returned with a fat spiral notebook that he set on the table. His expression had changed. "Miss Ginny's *Deathbook*."

41    The thing startled me. Was it something I was supposed to sign? He opened it but said nothing. There were scads of names written in a tidy hand over pages incised to crinkliness by a ball-point. Chronologically, the names had piled up: Wives, grandparents, a stillborn infant, relatives, friends close and distant. Names, names. After each, the date of the unknown finally known and transcribed. The last entry bore yesterday's date.

42    "She's wrote out twenty years' worth. Ever day she listens to the hospital report on the radio and puts the names in. Folks come by to check a date. Or they just turn through the books. Read them like a scrapbook."

43    Hilda said, "Like Saint Peter at the gates inscribin' the names."

44    Watts took my arm. "Come along." He led me to the fruit cellar under the store. As we went down, he said, "Always take a newborn baby upstairs afore you take him downstairs, otherwise you'll incline him downwards."

45    The cellar was dry and full of cobwebs and jar after jar of home-canned food, the bottles organized as a shopkeeper would: sausage, pumpkin, sweet pickles, tomatoes, corn relish, blackberries, peppers, squash, jellies. He held a hand out toward the dusty bottles. "Our tomorrows."

46    Upstairs again, he said, "Hope to sell the store to the right folk. I see now, though, it'll be somebody offen the ridge. I've studied on it, and maybe it's the end of our place." He stirred the coals. "This store could give a comfortable livin', but not likely get you rich. But just gettin' by is dice rollin' to people nowadays. I never did see my day guaranteed."

47    When it was time to go, Watts said, "If you find anyone along your ways wants a good store—on the road to Cordell Hull Lake—tell them about us."

48    I said I would. Miss Ginny and Hilda and Marilyn came out to say goodbye. It was cold and drizzling again. "Weather to give a man the weary dismals," Watts grumbled. "Where you headed from here?"

49    "I don't know."

50    "Cain't get lost then."

51    Miss Ginny looked again at my rig. It had worried her from the first as it had my mother. "I hope you don't get yourself kilt in that durn thing gallivantin' around the country."

52    "Come back when the hills dry off," Watts said. "We'll go lookin' for some of them round rocks all sparkly inside."

53    I thought a moment. "Geodes?"

54    "Them's the ones. The country's properly full of them."

## Questions on Subject and Purpose

1. At one point in the narrative (paragraph 30), Least Heat Moon remarks, "I thought: It is for this I have come." What does he seem to be suggesting? What is the "this" that he finds in Nameless?

2. Why do "Miss Ginny's *Deathbook*" (paragraph 40) and the "fruit cellar" (44) seem appropriate details?

3. What might have attracted Least Heat Moon to this place and these people? What does he want you to sense? Is there anything in his description and narrative that suggests how he feels about Nameless?

## Questions on Strategy and Audience

1. After you have read the selection, describe each member of the Watts family. Describe the exterior and interior of their store. Then carefully go through the selection and see how many specific descriptive details the author uses. List them.

2. What devices other than direct description does Least Heat Moon use to create the sense of place and personality? Make a list, and be prepared to tell how those devices work.

3. How is the narrative arranged? Is the order just spatial and chronological?

4. This selection is taken from *Blue Highways: A Journey into America*, a bestseller for nearly a year. Why would a travel narrative full of stories such as this be so appealing to an American audience?

## Questions on Vocabulary and Style

1. Least Heat Moon attempts to reproduce the pronunciation of some words— for example, *athians* (paragraph 12), *iodeen* (21), and *anteebeeotics* (25). Make a list of all such phonetic spellings. Why does Least Heat Moon do this? Do you think he captures all of the Wattses' accent or just some part of it? Is the device effective?

2. Examine how Least Heat Moon uses dialogue in his description. How are the Wattses revealed by what they say? How much of what was actually said during the visit is recorded? Can you find specific points in the story where Least Heat Moon obviously omits dialogue?

3. Try to define or explain the following words and phrases: *horehound candy* (paragraph 15), *bolsters* (26), *buttermilk pie* (28), *incised to crinkliness by a ballpoint* (41), *weary dismals* (48), *gallivantin' around* (51).

## Writing Suggestions

1. **For Your Journal or Blog.** Have you ever encountered or experienced a person, a place, or an event that seemed cut off from the modern world? In your journal or blog, try to recall a few such experiences.

2. **For a Paragraph.** Virtually every campus has a building or a location that has acquired a strange or vivid name (for example, the cafeteria in the Student

Center known as "The Scrounge"). In a paragraph, describe such a place to a friend who has never seen it. Remember to keep a central focus—you want to convey an atmosphere more than a verbal photograph.

3. **For an Essay.** Look for an unusual business in your town or city (a barber shop, a food co-op, a delicatessen or diner, a secondhand clothing store, a specialized boutique). In an essay, describe the place. Make sure you have a focus—a central impression or thesis—that will govern your selection of details. It will probably work best if you also include some descriptions of people and dialogue.

4. **For Research.** Least Heat Moon is fascinated by unusual names and often drives considerable distances to visit towns with names such as Dime Box, Hungry Horse, Liberty Bond, Ninety-Six, and Tuba City. Choose an unusual place name (town, river, subdivision, topographical feature) from your home state and research the origin of the name. A reference librarian can show you how to locate source materials. If possible, contact your local historical society or public library for help or interview some knowledgeable local residents. Using your research, write an essay about how that name was chosen. Remember to document your sources.

## For Further Study

**Focusing on Grammar and Writing.** Writing dialogue is never easy, but there are times when dialogue is extremely effective. Select a group of paragraphs from the essay and rewrite them using no dialogue. You could simply have your narrator indirectly report what was said. What is lost when the dialogue is removed? What does this suggest about the effectiveness of dialogue? Study the dialogue that Least Heat Moon writes. What can you learn from him?

**Working Together.** Working in small groups, divide the essay into blocks of paragraphs. Take turns reading the story aloud and time it as you do. Presumably, Least Heat Moon's visit lasted several hours. How much time elapses in the dialogue? As you read, look for places in the narrative where time is abridged or when actions are clearly omitted. What does that reveal about artfully telling a story?

**Seeing Other Modes at Work.** The essay is also a narrative. How does Least Heat Moon structure his narrative?

**Finding Connections.** An interesting comparison in creating character is with Debra Anne Davis's "A Pen by the Phone" (this chapter). Davis, for example, uses no dialogue at all.

**Exploring the Web.** Want to read an excerpt from Least Heat Moon's *River-Horse*, an account of a 5,000-mile water voyage across America in a small boat named *Nikawa*? Is there really a Nameless, Tennessee? Visit the Web.

# The Village Watchman

Terry Tempest Williams

*Terry Tempest Williams (1955–), a fifth-generation Mormon, grew up within sight of Great Salt Lake. Williams has written and edited a number of books including* Red: Passion and Patience in the Desert *(2001) and* The Open Space of Democracy *(2004). Her most recent book is* Mosaic: Finding Beauty in a Broken Word *(2008).*

*"The Village Watchman" first appeared in* Between Friends *(1994), a collection of essays; it was reprinted in her collection of essays titled* An Unspoken Hunger *(1994).*

**On Writing:** *A writer deeply concerned about environmental issues, Williams has observed that she writes "through my biases of gender, geography, and culture, that I am a woman whose ideas have been shaped by the Colorado Plateau and the Great Basin, that these ideas are then sorted out through the prism of my culture—and my culture is Mormon. Those tenets of family and community that I see at the heart of that culture are then articulated through story."*

## Before Reading

**Connecting:** In her essay, Williams writes of our attitude toward people who are "mentally disabled or challenged": "We see them for who they are not, rather than for who they are." What does that sentence mean to you?

**Anticipating:** Williams is writing about her memories of her uncle. Of the many memories that she has, why might she select the ones that she does? How does each included detail or incident affect our sense of Alan?

1   **S**tories carved in cedar rise from the deep woods of Sitka. These totem poles are foreign to me, this vertical lineage of clans: Eagle, Raven, Wolf, and Salmon. The Tlingit craftsmen create a genealogy of the earth, a reminder of mentors, a reminder that we come into this world in need of proper instruction. I sit on the soft floor of this Alaskan forest and feel the presence of Other. The totem before me is called "Wolf Pole" by locals. The Village Watchman sits on top of Wolf's head with his knees drawn to his chest, his hands holding them tight against his body. He wears a red and black striped hat. His eyes are direct, deep set, painted blue.

2   The expression on his face reminds me of a man I loved, a man who was born into this world feet first. "Breech," my mother told me of her brother's

birth. "Alan was born feet first. As a result, his brain was denied oxygen. He is special." As a child, I was impressed by this information. I remember thinking that fish live underwater. Maybe Alan had gills, maybe he didn't need a face-first gulp of air like the rest of us. The amniotic sea he had floated in for nine months delivered him with a fluid memory. He knew something. Other.

3      There is a story of a boy who was kidnapped from his village by the Salmon People. He was taken from his family to learn the ways of water. When he returned many years later to his home, he was recognized by his own as a holy man privy to the mysteries of the unseen world. Twenty years after my uncle's death, I wonder if Alan could have been that boy.

4      But our culture tells a different story, more alien. My culture calls people of such births retarded, handicapped, mentally disabled or challenged. We see them for who they are not, rather than for who they are.

5      My grandmother, Lettie Romney Dixon, wrote in her journal, "It wasn't until Alan was 16 months old that a busy doctor cruelly broke the news to us. Others may have suspected our son's limitations but to those of us who loved him so unquestionably, lightning struck without warning. I hugged my sorrow to myself. I felt abandoned and lost. I wouldn't accept the verdict. Then we started the trips to a multitude of doctors. Most of them were kind and explained that our child was like a car without brakes, like an electric wire without insulation. They gave us no hope for a normal life."

6      Normal. Latin: *normalis; norma*, a rule: conforming with or constituting an accepted standard, model, or pattern, especially corresponding to the median or average of a large group in type, appearance, achievement, function, or development.

7      Alan was not normal. He was unique; one and only; single; sole; unusual; extraordinary; rare. His emotions were not measured, his curiosity not bridled. In a sense, he was wild like a mustang in the desert, and like most wild horses, he was eventually rounded up.

8      He was unpredictable. He created his own rules and they changed from moment to moment. Alan was 12 years old, hyperactive, mischievous, easily frustrated, and unable to learn in traditional ways. The situation was intensified by his seizures. Suddenly, without warning, he would stiffen like a rake, fall forward, and crash to the ground, hitting his head. My grandparents could not keep him home any longer. They needed professional guidance and help. In 1957, they reluctantly placed their youngest child in an institution for handicapped children called the American Fork Training School. My grandmother's heart broke for the second time.

9      Once again, from her journal: "Many a night my pillow is wet from tears of sorrow and senseless dreamings of 'if things had only been different,' or wondering if he is tucked in snug and warm, if he is well and happy, if the wind still bothers him. . . ."

10     The wind may have continued to bother Alan: certainly the conditions he was living under were less than ideal, but there was much about his private life his family never knew. What we did know was that Alan had an enormous capacity for adaptation. We had no choice but to follow him.

11    I followed him for years.

12    Alan was ten years my senior. In my mind, he was mythic. Everything I was taught not to do, Alan did. We were taught to be polite, to not express displeasure or anger in public. Alan was sheer, physical expression. Whatever was on his mind he vocalized and usually punctuated with colorful speech. We would go bowling as a family on Sundays. Each of us would take our turn, hold the black ball to our chest, take a few steps, swing our arm back, forward, glide, and release. The ball would roll down the alley, hit a few pins; we would wait for the ball to return, and then take our second run. Little emotion was shown. When it was Alan's turn, it was an event. Nothing subtle. His style was Herculean. Big man. Big ball. Big roll. Big bang. Whether it was a strike or a gutter ball, he clapped his hands, spun around on the floor, slapped his thighs, and cried, "Goddamn! Did you see that one? Send me another ball, sweet Jesus!" And the ball was always returned.

13    I could count on my uncle for a straight answer. He taught me that one of the remarkable aspects of being human was to hold opposing views in our mind at once.

14    "How are you doing?" I would ask.

15    "Ask me how I am feeling?" he answered.

16    "Okay, how are you feeling?"

17    "Today? Right now?"

18    "Yes."

19    "I am very happy and very sad."

20    "How can you be both at the same time?" I asked in all seriousness, a girl of nine or ten.

21    "Because both require each other's company. They live in the same house. Didn't you know?"

22    We would laugh and then go on to another topic. Talking to my uncle was always like entering a maze of riddles. Ask a question. Answer with a question and see where it leads you.

23    My younger brother Steve and I spent a lot of time with Alan. He offered us shelter from the conventionality of a Mormon family. At our home during Christmas, he would direct us in his own nativity plays. "More—" he would say to us, making wide gestures with his hands. "Give me more of yourself." He was not like anyone we knew. In a culture where we were taught to be seen and not heard, Alan was our mirror.

24    We could be different, too. His unquestioning belief in us as children, as human beings, was in startling contrast to the way we saw the public react to him. It hurt us. We could never tell if it hurt him.

25    Each week, Steve and I would accompany our grandparents south to visit Alan. It was an hour's drive to the school from Salt Lake City, mostly through farmlands. We would enter the grounds, pull into the parking lot to a playground filled with huge papier-mâché storybook figures (a 20-foot pied piper, a pumpkin carriage with Cinderella inside, the old woman who lived in a shoe), and nine times out of ten, Alan would be standing outside his dormitory waiting for us. We would get out of the car and he would run toward us and throw his powerful arms around us. His hugs cracked my back and at

times I had to fight for my breath. My grandfather would calm him down by simply saying, "We're here, son. You can relax now."

26      Alan was a formidable man, now in his early twenties, stocky and strong. His head was large, with a protruding forehead that bore many scars, a line-by-line history of seizures. He always had on someone else's clothes—a tweed jacket too small, brown pants too big, a striped golf shirt that didn't match. He showed us that appearances didn't matter, personality did. If you didn't know him, he could look frightening. It was an unspoken rule in our family that the character of others was gauged by how they treated Alan. The only consistent thing about his attire was that he always wore a silver football helmet from Olympus High School, where my grandfather was coach. It was a loving, practical solution to protect Alan when he fell.

27      "Part of the team," my grandfather would say as he slapped Alan affectionally on the back, "You're a Titan, son, and I love you."

28      The windows to the dormitory were dark, reflecting Mount Timpanogos to the east. It was hard to see inside, but I knew what the interior held. It looked like an abandoned gymnasium without bleachers, filled with hospital beds. The stained white walls and yellow-waxed floors offered no warmth. The stench was nauseating: sweat and urine trapped in the oppression of stale air. I recall the dirty sheets, the lack of privacy, and the almond-eyed children who never rose from their beds. And then I would turn around and face Alan's cheerfulness, the open and loving manner in which he would introduce me to his friends, the pride he exhibited as he showed me around his home. I kept thinking, "Doesn't he see how bad this is, how poorly they are being treated?" His words would return to me: "I am very happy and very sad."

29      For my brother and me, Alan was guide, elder. He was fearless. But neither one of us will ever be able to escape the image of Alan kissing his parents good-bye after an afternoon with family and slowly walking back to his dormitory. Before we drove away, he would turn toward us, take off his silver helmet, and wave. The look on his face haunts me still.

30      Alan liked to talk about God. Perhaps it was in these private conversations that our real friendship was forged.

31      "I know Him," he would say when all the adults were gone.

32      "You do?" I asked.

33      "I talk to Him every day."

34      "How?"

35      "I talk to Him in my prayers. I listen and then I hear His voice."

36      "What does He tell you?"

37      "He tells me to be patient. He tells me to be kind. He tells me that He loves me."

38      In Mormon culture, children are baptized as members of the Church of Jesus Christ of Latter-day Saints when they turn 8 years old. Alan had never been baptized because my grandparents believed it should be his choice, not something simply taken for granted. When he turned 22, he expressed a sincere desire to join the church. A date was set immediately.

39    The entire Dixon clan convened in the Lehi chapel, a few miles north of the group home where Alan was then living. We were there to support and witness his conversion. As we walked toward the meetinghouse where this sacred rite was to be performed, Alan had a violent seizure. My grandfather and uncle Don, Alan's elder brother, dropped down with him, holding his head and body as every muscle thrashed on the pavement like a school of netted fish brought on deck. I didn't want to look, but to walk away would have been worse. We stayed with him, all of us.

40    "Talk to God,—" I heard myself saying under my breath. "I love you, Alan."

41    "Can you hear me, darling?" It was my grandmother, holding her son's hand.

42    By now, many of us were gathered on our knees around him, our trembling hands on his rigid body.

43    Alan opened his eyes. "I want to be baptized," he said. The men helped him to his feet. The gash on his left temple was deep. Blood dripped down the side of his face. My mother had her arm around my grandmother's waist. Shaken, we all followed him inside.

44    Alan's father and brother stopped the bleeding and bandaged the pressure wound, then helped him change into the designated white garments for baptism. He entered the room with great dignity and sat on the front pew with a dozen or more 8-year-old children seated on either side. Row after row of family sat behind him.

45    "Alan Romney Dixon." His name was called by the presiding bishop. Alan rose from the pew and met his brother Don, also dressed in white, who took his hand and led him down the blue-tiled stairs into the baptismal font filled with water. They faced the congregation. Don raised his right arm to the square in the gesture of a holy oath as Alan placed his hands on his brother's left forearm. The sacred prayer was offered in the name of the Father, the Son, and the Holy Ghost, after which my uncle put his right hand behind Alan's shoulder and gently lowered him into the water for a baptism by complete immersion.

46    Alan emerged from the holy waters like an angel.

47    Six years later, I found myself sitting with my uncle at a hospital where he was being treated for a severe ear infection. I was 18. He was 28.

48    "Alan," I asked, "what is it really like to live inside your body?"

49    He crossed his legs and placed both hands on the arms of the chair. His brown eyes were piercing.

50    "I can't tell you what it's like except to say I feel pain for not being seen as the person I am."

51    A few days later, Alan died—alone, unique, one and only, single—in American Fork, Utah.

52    The Village Watchman sits on top of his totem with Wolf and Salmon. It is beginning to rain in the forest. I find it curious that this spot in southeast Alaska has brought me back into relation with my uncle, this man who came into the world feet first. He reminds me of what it means to live and love with a broken heart; how nothing is sacred, how everything is sacred. He was a weather vane, at once a storm and a clearing.

53      Shortly after his death, Alan appeared to me in a dream. We were standing in my grandmother's kitchen. He was leaning against the white stove with his arms folded.

54      "Look at me now, Terry," he said, smiling. "I'm normal—perfectly normal." And then he laughed. We both laughed.

55      He handed me his silver football helmet, which was resting on the counter, kissed me, and opened the back door.

56      "Do you recognize who I am?"

57      On this day in Sitka, I remember.

## Questions on Subject and Purpose

1. What associations do you have with the word *normal?* Does Williams's definition (paragraph 6) challenge those associations?

2. In two places (paragraphs 5 and 9), Williams quotes from her grandmother's journal. What is the effect of these quotations?

3. Why would a reader be interested in a tribute to her uncle? Do you find the story moving?

## Questions on Strategy and Audience

1. Why does Williams begin and end with the references to the totem poles in Alaska?

2. At several places, Williams reproduces—or rather re-creates—conversations she had with Alan (paragraphs 14–21, 31–37, and 48–50). Why? What is the effect of these sections?

3. What expectations might Williams have about her audience and their reaction to Alan?

## Questions on Vocabulary and Style

1. At a number of points in the essay, Williams quotes Alan. What do these quotations add to her description?

2. What is the effect of Alan's question, "Do you recognize am?" (paragraph 56)?

3. Be prepared to define the following words: *privy* (paragraph 3) and *convened* (39).

## Writing Suggestions

1. **For Your Journal or Blog.** Select a vivid memory that involves a family member or a close friend who touched your life. In your journal or blog, describe for yourself what you remember. Do not worry about being too focused. Concentrate on recovering memories.

2. **For a Paragraph.** In a paragraph, try to "capture" that person. Remember that your description needs a central focus or purpose. Why are you writing about this person? What is important for the reader to know about this person? Select details to reveal the person to your reader rather than telling the reader what to think.

3. **For an Essay.** In writing about Alan, Williams achieves two purposes: she memorializes her uncle, and she comments on society's perceptions of persons who are "mentally disabled or challenged." Try for a similar effect in an essay about someone who has touched your life. Remember, essay needs to have a dual purpose or thesis.

4. **For Research.** Explore our society's reactions to people who are, to use Williams's words, "retarded, handicapped, mentally disabled or challenged." How does society see such people? How are they treated or portrayed? This is a large subject, so you will need to find a way to focus your research and writing. You could concentrate on changes in reaction over time (early twentieth century versus early twenty-first century), portrayals (or their lack) in the popular media, family attitudes versus outsiders' attitudes, or reactions to a specific disability (such as Down syndrome). Textbooks might be a place to start. You will need to establish a list of possible subject headings and key words before you start searching library resources, online databases, and the Web. Remember to document your sources, including any information that you obtain through interviews.

## For Further Study

**Focusing on Grammar and Writing.** Select some of the longer paragraphs in Williams's essay. Look carefully at the first sentence in each paragraph. How does that sentence control the details that follow? Even though many of Williams's paragraphs are narrative in nature, she still forecasts their structure through those first sentences. What does this suggest about your own paragraphs in your essay?

**Working Together.** Divide into small groups. Each group should choose one of the following to examine:

1. The story of the boy kidnapped by the Salmon People (paragraph 3)
2. The scene in the bowling alley (12)
3. The papier-mâché storybook figures (25)
4. The dormitory (28)
5. Alan's conversations with God (30–37)
6. Williams's dream after Alan's death (53–56)

What does each section or detail contribute to the essay? What does each add to the story of Alan?

**Seeing Other Modes at Work.** The essay employs a range of other strategies or modes, including narration (throughout), definition (paragraph 6), comparison and contrast (5, 7, 12), and persuasion (throughout).

**Finding Connections.** The essay can be paired with William Least Heat Moon's "Nameless Tennessee" for a comparison on creating and revealing character, or with Scott Russell Sanders's "The Inheritance of Tools" for a comparison on how the death of a loved one is handled. Both essays are in this chapter.

**Exploring the Web.** Sites dealing with Williams and her writing and sites about specific genetic or birth conditions can be found on the Web.

# The Inheritance of Tools

Scott Russell Sanders

*Born in Memphis, Tennessee, in 1945, Scott Russell Sanders received a Ph.D. from Cambridge University. Currently a professor of English at Indiana University, Sanders is a novelist, an essayist, and a science fiction writer. He has contributed fiction and essays to many journals and magazines and has published numerous books including,* A Private History of Awe *(2006).*

*Sanders writes often about his childhood and his efforts to "ground" himself. In another of his collections of essays,* Secrets of the Universe *(1991), Sanders describes growing up with an alcoholic father, noting that he "wants to drag into the light what eats at me—the fear, the guilt, the shame—so that my own children may be spared."*

**On Writing:** *Commenting on the development of his writing style from academic prose to creative writing and essays, Sanders observed: "I flouted rules I learned about writing in school. I played with sound, strung images together line after line, flung out metaphors by the handful. Sin of sins, I even mixed metaphors, the way any fertile field will sprout dozens of species of grass and flower and fern. I let my feelings and opinions show. . . . I drew shamelessly on my own life. I swore off jargon and muddle and much. I wrote in the active voice."*

## Before Reading

**Connecting:** Can you think of something that you learned how to do from a family member or friend?

**Anticipating:** In what ways is "The Inheritance of Tools" an appropriate title for the essay? What is the essay about?

1  **A**t just about the hour when my father died, soon after dawn one February morning when ice coated the windows like cataracts, I banged my thumb with a hammer. Naturally I swore at the hammer, the reckless thing, and in the moment of swearing I thought of what my father would say: "If you'd try hitting the nail it would go in a whole lot faster. Don't you know your thumb's not as hard as that hammer?" We both were doing carpentry that day, but far apart. He was building cupboards at my brother's place in Oklahoma; I was at home in Indiana putting up a wall in the basement to make a bedroom for my daughter. By the time my mother called with news of his death—the long distance wires whittling her voice until it seemed too thin to bear the weight of what she had to say—my thumb was swollen. A week or so later a white scar in the shape

of a crescent moon began to show above the cuticle, and month by month it rose across the pink sky of my thumbnail. It took the better part of a year for the scar to disappear, and every time I noticed it I thought of my father.

2    The hammer had belonged to him, and to his father before him. The three of us have used it to build houses and barns and chicken coops, to upholster chairs and crack walnuts, to make doll furniture and book shelves and jewelry boxes. The head is scratched and pockmarked, like an old plowshare that has been working rocky fields, and it gives off the sort of dull sheen you see on fast creek water in the shade. It is a finishing hammer, about the weight of a bread loaf, too light, really, for framing walls, too heavy for cabinetwork, with a curved claw for pulling nails, a rounded head for pounding, a fluted neck for looks, and a hickory handle for strength.

3    The present handle is my third one, bought from a lumberyard in Tennessee down the road from where my brother and I were helping my father build his retirement house. I broke the previous one by trying to pull sixteen-penny nails out of floor joists—a foolish thing to do with a finishing hammer, as my father pointed out. "You ever hear of a crowbar?" he said. No telling how many handles he and my grandfather had gone through before me. My grandfather used to cut down hickory trees on his farm, saw them into slabs, cure the planks in his hayloft, and carve handles with a drawknife. The grain in hickory is crooked and knotty, and therefore rough, hard to split, like the grain in the two men who owned this hammer before me.

4    After proposing marriage to a neighbor girl, my grandfather used this hammer to build a house for his bride on a stretch of river bottom in northern Mississippi. The lumber for the place, like the hickory for the handle, was cut on his own land. By the day of the wedding he had not quite finished the house, and so right after the ceremony he took his wife home and put her to work. My grandmother had worn her Sunday dress for the wedding, with a fringe of lace tacked on around the hem in honor of the occasion. She removed this lace and folded it away before going out to help my grandfather nail siding on the house. "There she was in her good dress," he told me some fifty-odd years after that wedding day, "holding up them long pieces of clapboard while I hammered, and together we got the place covered up before dark." As the family grew to four, six, eight, and eventually thirteen, my grandfather used this hammer to enlarge his house room by room, like a chambered nautilus expanding his shell.

5    By and by the hammer was passed along to my father. One day he was up on the roof of our pony barn nailing shingles with it, when I stepped out the kitchen door to call him for supper. Before I could yell, something about the sight of him straddling the spine of that roof and swinging the hammer caught my eye and made me hold my tongue. I was five or six years old, and the world's commonplaces were still news to me. He would pull a nail from the pouch at his waist, bring the hammer down, and a moment later the *thunk* of the blow would reach my ears. And that is what had stopped me in my tracks and stilled my tongue, that momentary gap between seeing and hearing the blow. Instead of yelling from the kitchen door, I ran to the barn and climbed

two rungs up the ladder—as far as I was allowed to go—and spoke quietly to my father. On our walk to the house he explained that sound takes time to make its way through air. Suddenly the world seemed larger, the air more dense, if sound could be held back like any ordinary traveler.

6        By the time I started using this hammer, at about the age when I discovered the speed of sound, it already contained houses and mysteries for me. The smooth handle was one my grandfather had made. In those days I needed both hands to swing it. My father would start a nail in a scrap of wood, and I would pound away until I bent it over.

7        "Looks like you got ahold of some of those rubber nails," he would tell me. "Here, let me see if I can find you some stiff ones." And he would rummage in a drawer until he came up with a fistful of more cooperative nails. "Look at the head," he would tell me. "Don't look at your hands, don't look at the hammer. Just look at the head of that nail and pretty soon you'll learn to hit it square."

8        Pretty soon I did learn. While he worked in the garage cutting dovetail joints for a drawer or skinning a deer or tuning an engine, I would hammer nails. I made innocent blocks of wood look like porcupines. He did not talk much in the midst of his tools, but he kept up a nearly ceaseless humming, slipping in and out of a dozen tunes in an afternoon, often running back over the same stretch of melody again and again, as if searching for a way out. When the humming did cease, I knew he was faced with a task requiring great delicacy or concentration, and I took care not to distract him.

9        He kept scraps of wood in a cardboard box—the ends of two-by-fours, slabs of shelving and plywood, odd pieces of molding—and everything in it was fair game. I nailed scraps together to fashion what I called boats or houses, but the results usually bore only faint resemblance to the visions I carried in my head. I would hold up these constructions to show my father, and he would turn them over in his hands admiringly, speculating about what they might be. My cobbled-together guitars might have been alien spaceships, my barns might have been models of Aztec temples, each wooden contraption might have been anything but what I had set out to make.

10       Now and again I would feel the need to have a chunk of wood shaped or shortened before I riddled it with nails, and I would clamp it in a vise and scrape at it with a handsaw. My father would let me lacerate the board until my arm gave out, and then he would wrap his hand around mine and help me finish the cut, showing me how to use my thumb to guide the blade, how to pull back on the saw to keep it from binding, how to let my shoulder do the work.

11       "Don't force it," he would say, "just drag it easy and give the teeth a chance to bite."

12       As the saw teeth bit down, the wood released its smell, each kind with its own fragrance, oak or walnut or cherry or pine—usually pine because it was the softest, easiest for a child to work. No matter how weathered and gray the board, no matter how warped and cracked, inside there was this smell waiting, as of something freshly baked. I gathered every smidgen of sawdust and stored

it away in coffee cans, which I kept in a drawer of the workbench. When I did not feel like hammering nails I would dump my sawdust on the concrete floor of the garage and landscape it into highways and farms and towns, running miniature cars and trucks along miniature roads. Looming as huge as a colossus, my father worked over and around me, now and again bending down to inspect my work, careful not to trample my creations. It was a landscape that smelled dizzyingly of wood. Even after a bath my skin would carry the smell, and so would my father's hair, when he lifted me for a bedtime hug.

13      I tell these things not only from memory but also from recent observation, because my own son now turns blocks of wood into nailed porcupines, dumps cans full of sawdust at my feet and sculpts highways on the floor. He learns how to swing a hammer from the elbow instead of the wrist, how to lay his thumb beside the blade to guide a saw, how to tap a chisel with a wooden mallet, how to mark a hole with an awl before starting a drill bit. My daughter did the same before him, and even now, on the brink of teenage aloofness, she will occasionally drag out my box of wood scraps and carpenter something. So I have seen my apprenticeship to wood and tools reenacted in each of my children, as my father saw his own apprenticeship renewed in me.

14      The saw I use belonged to him, as did my level and both of my squares, and all four tools had belonged to his father. The blade of the saw is the bluish color of gun barrels, and the maple handle, dark from the sweat of hands, is inscribed with curving leaf designs. The level is a shaft of walnut two feet long, edged with brass and pierced by three round windows in which air bubbles float in oil-filled tubes of glass. The middle window serves for testing if a surface is horizontal, the others for testing if a surface is plumb or vertical. My grandfather used to carry this level on the gun-rack behind the seat in his pickup, and when I rode with him I would turn around to watch the bubbles dance. The larger of the two squares is called a framing square, a flat steel elbow, so beat up and tarnished you can barely make out the rows of numbers that show how to figure the cuts on rafters. The smaller one is called a try square, for marking right angles, with a blued steel blade for the shank and a brass-faced block of cherry for the head.

15      I was taught early on that a saw is not to be used apart from a square: "If you're going to cut a piece of wood," my father insisted, "you owe it to the tree to cut it straight."

16      Long before studying geometry, I learned there is a mystical virtue in right angles. There is an unspoken morality in seeking the level and the plumb. A house will stand, a table will bear weight, the sides of a box will hold together only if the joints are square and the members upright. When the bubble is lined up between two marks etched in the glass tube of a level, you have aligned yourself with the forces that hold the universe together. When you miter the corners of a picture frame, each angle must be exactly forty-five degrees, as they are in the perfect triangles of Pythagoras, not a degree more or less. Otherwise the frame will hang crookedly, as if ashamed of itself and of its maker. No matter if the joints you are cutting do not show. Even if you are butting two pieces of wood together inside a cabinet, where no one except a

wrecking crew will ever see them, you must take pains to insure that the ends are square and the studs are plumb.

17      I took pains over the wall I was building on the day my father died. Not long after that wall was finished—paneled with tongue-and-groove boards of yellow pine, the nail holes filled with putty and the wood all stained and sealed—I came close to wrecking it one afternoon when my daughter ran howling up the stairs to announce that her gerbils had escaped from their cage and were hiding in my brand new wall. She could hear them scratching and squeaking behind her bed. Impossible! I said. How on earth could they get inside my drum-tight wall? Through the heating vent, she answered. I went downstairs, pressed my ear to the honey-colored wood, and heard the *scritch scritch* of tiny feet.

18      "What can we do?" my daughter wailed. "They'll starve to death, they'll die of thirst, they'll suffocate."

19      "Hold on," I shouted, "I'll think of something."

20      While I thought and she fretted, the radio on her bedside table delivered us the headlines. Several thousand people had died in a city in India from a poisonous cloud that had leaked overnight from a chemical plant. A nuclear-powered submarine had been launched. Rioting continued in South Africa. An airplane had been hijacked in the Mediterranean. Authorities calculated that several thousand homeless people slept on the streets within sight of the Washington Monument. I felt my usual helplessness in face of all these calamities. But here was my daughter weeping because her gerbils were holed up in a wall. This calamity I could handle.

21      "Don't worry," I told her. "We'll set food and water by the heating vent and lure them out. And if that doesn't do the trick, I'll tear the wall apart until we find them."

22      She stopped crying and gazed as me. "You'd really tear it apart? Just for my gerbils? The *wall?*" Astonishment slowed her down only for a second, however, before she ran to the workbench and began tugging at drawers, saying, "Let's see, what'll we need? Crowbar. Hammer. Chisels. I hope we don't have to use them—but just in case."

23      We didn't need the wrecking tools. I never had to assault my handsome wall, because the gerbils eventually came out to nibble at a dish of popcorn. But for several hours I studied the tongue-and-groove skin I had nailed up on the day of my father's death, considering where to begin prying. There were no gaps in that wall, no crooked joints.

24      I had botched a great many pieces of wood before I mastered the right angle with a saw, botched even more before I learned to miter a joint. The knowledge of these things resides in my hands and eyes and the webwork of muscles, not in the tools. There are machines for sale—powered miter boxes and radial-arm saws, for instance—that will enable any casual soul to cut proper angles in boards. The skill is invested in the gadget instead of the person who uses it, and this is what distinguishes a machine from a tool. If I had to earn my keep by making furniture or building houses, I suppose I would buy powered saws and pneumatic nailers; the need for speed would drive me to it.

But since I carpenter only for my own pleasure or to help neighbors or to re-make the house around the ears of my family, I stick with hand tools. Most of the ones I own were given to me by my father, who also taught me how to wield them. The tools in my work-bench are a double inheritance, for each hammer and level and saw is wrapped in a cloud of knowing.

25      All of these tools are a pleasure to look at and to hold. Merchants would never paste NEW NEW NEW! signs on them in stores. Their designs are old because they work, because they serve their purpose well. Like folksongs and aphorisms and the grainy bits of language, these tools have been pared down to essentials. I look at my claw hammer, the distillation of a hundred genera-tions of carpenters, and consider that it holds up well beside those other classics— Greek vases, Gregorian chants, *Don Quixote*, barbed fish hooks, candles, spoons. Knowledge of hammering stretches back to the earliest humans who squatted beside fires chipping flints. Anthropologists have a lovely name for those unworked rocks that served as the earliest hammers. *Dawn stones*, they are called. Their only qualification for the work, aside from hardness, is that they fit the hand. Our ancestors used them for grinding corn, tapping awls, smashing bones. From dawn stones to this claw hammer is a great leap in time, but no great distance in design or imagination.

26      On that iced-over February morning when I smashed my thumb with the hammer, I was down in the basement framing the wall that my daughter's gerbils would later hide in. I was thinking of my father, as I always did when-ever I built anything, thinking how he would have gone about the work, hear-ing in memory what he would have said about the wisdom of hitting the nail instead of my thumb. I had the studs and plates nailed together all square and trim, and was lifting the wall into place when the phone rang upstairs. My wife answered, and in a moment she came to the basement door and called down softly to me. The stillness in her voice made me drop the framed wall and hurry upstairs. She told me my father was dead. Then I heard the details over the phone from my mother. Building a set of cupboards for my brother in Oklahoma, he had knocked off work early the previous afternoon because of cramps in his stomach. Early this morning, on his way into the kitchen of my brother's trailer, maybe going for a glass of water, so early that no one else was awake, he slumped down on the linoleum and his heart quit.

27      For several hours I paced around inside my house, upstairs and down, in and out of every room, looking for the right door to open and knowing there was no such door. My wife and children followed me and wrapped me in arms and backed away again, circling and staring as if I were on fire. Where was the door, the door, the door? I kept wondering. My smashed thumb turned purple and throbbed, making me furious. I wanted to cut it off and rush outside and scrape away the snow and hack a hole in the frozen earth and bury the shameful thing.

28      I went down into the basement, opened a drawer in my workbench, and stared at the ranks of chisels and knives. Oiled and sharp, as my father would have kept them, they gleamed at me like teeth. I took up a clasp knife, pried out the longest blade and tested the edge on the hair of my forearm. A tuft

came away cleanly, and I saw my father testing the sharpness of tools on his own skin, the blades of axes and knives and gouges and hoes, saw the red hair shaved off in patches from his arms and the backs of his hands. "That will cut bear," he would say. He never cut a bear with his blades, now my blades, but he cut deer, dirt, wood. I closed the knife and put it away. Then I took up the hammer and went back to work on my daughter's wall, snugging the bottom plate against a chalk line on the floor, shimming the top plate against the joists overhead, plumbing the studs with my level, making sure before I drove the first nail that every line was square and true.

## Questions on Subject and Purpose

1. What is the subject of Sanders's essay? Is it tools? His father's death?
2. Is Sanders's father or grandfather (or his children) ever described in the story? How are they revealed to the reader?
3. What "door" (paragraph 27) is Sanders searching for?
4. What exactly has Sanders inherited from his father?

## Questions on Strategy and Audience

1. How does Sanders use time to structure his essay? Is the story told in chronological order?
2. What is the function of each of the following episodes or events in the essay?
   a. The sore thumb
   b. "A mystical virtue in right angles" (paragraph 16)
   c. The wall he was building
3. What expectations does Sanders seem to have about his audience?

## Questions on Vocabulary and Style

1. How much dialogue does Sanders use in the story? What does the dialogue contribute?
2. Throughout the essay, Sanders makes use of many effective similes and metaphors. Make a list of six such devices. What does each contribute to the essay? How fresh and arresting are these images?
3. Be able to define each of the following words or phrases: *plowshare* (paragraph 2), *sixteen-penny nails* (3), *chambered nautilus* (4), *rummage* (7), *lacerate* (10), *smidgen* (12), *plumb* (14), *miter* (24), *aphorisms* (25), *shimming* (28)

## Writing Suggestions

1. **For Your Journal ro Blog.** The word *inheritance* may suggest money or property bequeathed to a descendent. But you can "inherit" many things that are far less tangible. In your journal or blog, explore what you might have inherited from someone in your family—perhaps a talent, an interest, an ability, or an obsession.

2. **For a Paragraph.** Study the childhood scenes or episodes that Sanders includes in his essay—for example, calling his father to supper (paragraph 5), hammering nails (6–9), landscaping with sawdust (12). Notice how Sanders re-creates sensory experiences. Then in a paragraph, re-create a similar experience from your childhood. Remember to evoke sensory impressions for your reader—sight, sound, smell, touch.

3. **For an Essay.** Think about a skill, talent, or habit that you have learned from or share with a family member. In addition to the ability or trait, what else have you "inherited"? How does it affect your life? In an essay, describe the inheritance and its effect on you.

4. **For Research.** The passing on of traditional crafts or skills is an important part of cultural tradition. Choose a society that interests you, and find a particular craft that is preserved from one generation to another. It might also be something that has been preserved in your family's religious or ethnic heritage. In a research paper, document the nature of the craft and the methods by which the culture ensures its transmission. What is important about this craft? What does it represent to that society? Why bother to preserve it?

## For Further Study

1. **Focusing on Grammar and Writing.** Sanders often uses dashes to insert material into his sentences and to add material to the ends of sentences. Make a list of each use, and on the basis of that sample, write some "rules" for the use of the dash in writing. What other punctuation alternatives could Sanders have used in each case? Could he have used commas? Parentheses? What would have been the difference?

2. **Working Together.** Working in small groups, choose a block of paragraphs from the essay. Starting with a definition of simile and metaphor (see Glossary and Ready Reference), how many similes and metaphors can you find in the block you are analyzing? What do those images have in common? Discuss your findings with the class as a whole.

3. **Seeing Other Modes at Work.** In addition to narration, Sanders uses comparison and contrast, particularly to draw the relationship between two generations of fathers and children.

4. **Finding Connections.** The impact of a relative's death is also the subject of Terry Tempest Williams's "The Village Watchman" in this chapter.

5. **Exploring the Web.** Another view of Sanders's relationship with his father can be found in his essay "Under the Influence," which can be read online.

# 4

# DIVISION AND CLASSIFICATION

## 🔑 ❓ KEY QUESTIONS

**Getting Ready to Write**
What is division?
What is classification?
How do you choose a subject?

**Writing**
How do you divide or classify a subject?
*Defining a purpose*
*Making your classification or division complete*
*Using parallelism*
How do you structure a division or classification essay?

**Revising**
How do you revise a division or classification essay?
*Having a clear purpose*
*Keeping the analysis logically structured*
*Making sure the categories or parts are proportionally developed*
*Checking for parallelism one more time*
*Student Essay*
*Evan James, "Riding the Rails: The American 'Hobo'"*
*Some Things to Remember About Writing Division and Classification*
*Seeing Division and Classification in Other Contexts*
**As a literary strategy**
*Aurora Levins Morales, "Child of the Americas"*
**As a critical reading strategy**
*Mark Lester, from Grammar in the Classroom*
**As a visual strategy**
*Photograph of buttons*
*Additional Writing Suggestions for Classification and Division*

## GETTING READY TO WRITE

Division and classification are closely related methods of analysis. To remember the difference, ask yourself whether you are analyzing a single thing by dividing it into its constituent parts, or analyzing two or more things by sorting them into related categories.

### What Is Division?

Division occurs when a single subject is subdivided into its parts. To cut a pizza into slices, to list the ingredients in a box of cereal, or to create a pie chart is to perform a division. The key is that you start with a single thing.

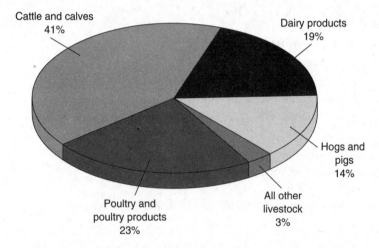

Cattle and calves
41%

Dairy products
19%

Hogs and
pigs
14%

All other
livestock
3%

Poultry and
poultry products
23%

The ideal visual for division is a pie chart. A whole is divided into parts. Here, for example, is a U.S. Department of Agriculture chart on the value of livestock and poultry sold in the United States.
*U.S. Department of Agriculture, National Agricultural Statistics Services.*

Writers can also divide a subject. In the following excerpt from a "chemistry primer" for people interested in cooking, Harold McGee uses division twice—first to subdivide the atom into its smaller constituent particles and second to subdivide the "space" within the atom into two areas (nucleus and shell):

An atom is the smallest particle into which an element can be subdivided without losing its characteristic properties. The atom too is divisible into smaller particles, electrons, protons, and neutrons, but these are the building blocks of all atoms, no matter of what element. The different properties of the elements are due to the varying combinations of subatomic particles contained in their atoms. The Periodic Table arranges the elements in the order of the number of protons contained in one atom of each element. That number is called the atomic number.

The atom is divided into two regions: the nucleus, or center in which the protons and neutrons are located, and a surrounding "orbit," or more accurately a "cloud" or "shell," in which the electrons move continuously. Both protons and neutrons weigh about 2000 times as much as electrons, so practically all of an atom's mass is concentrated in the nucleus.

Similarly, David Bodanis in "What's in Your Toothpaste?" uses division to structure a discussion of toothpaste; he analyzes its composition, offering some surprising insight into the "ingredients" we brush with every morning. Barbara Ehrenreich in "In Defense of Talk Shows" also uses division when she analyzes the distinctive features that different television talk shows exhibit. She treats each show—hosted by people such as Montel Williams or Jerry Springer—as a single subject that can be divided or analyzed into its component parts. Ehrenreich does not classify television talk shows; rather, she analyzes the common characteristics that such shows share.

Division, then, is used to show the components of a larger subject. Division helps the reader understand a complex whole by considering it in smaller units.

## What Is Classification?

Classification, instead of starting with a single subject and subdividing it into smaller units, begins with two or more items that are then grouped or classified into categories. Newspapers, for example, contain "classified" sections in which advertisements for the same type of goods or services are grouped or classified together.

A classification must have at least two categories. Depending on how many items you start with and how different they are, however, you may end up with quite a few categories. Consider the books in your school's library—they are arranged or classified in some way so that they can be easily found. Many schools use the Library of Congress Classification System, which organizes books by subject matter. The sciences, especially the biological sciences, make extensive use of classification. Remember the taxonomic classification you learned in high school biology? It begins by setting up five kingdoms (animals, plants, monera, fungi, and protista) and then moves downward to increasingly narrower categories (defined as phylum or division, class, order, family, genus, species).

- A–GENERAL WORKS
- B–PHILOSOPHY, PSYCHOLOGY, RELIGION
- C–AUXILIARY SCIENCES OF HISTORY
- D–HISTORY (GENERAL) AND HISTORY OF EUROPE
- E–HISTORY: AMERICA
- F–HISTORY: AMERICA
- G–GEOGRAPHY, ANTHROPOLOGY, RECREATION
- H–SOCIAL SCIENCES
- J–POLITICAL SCIENCE
- K–LAW
- L–EDUCATION
- M–MUSIC AND BOOKS ON MUSIC
- N–FINE ARTS
- P–LANGUAGE AND LITERATURE
- Q–SCIENCE
- R–MEDICINE
- S–AGRICULTURE
- T–TECHNOLOGY
- U–MILITARY SCIENCE
- V–NAVAL SCIENCE
- Z–BIBLIOGRAPHY, LIBRARY SCIENCE, INFORMATION RESOURCES (GENERAL)

In the Library of Congress Classification System, books are first organized by "main classes" or by what we might call "subjects." Each class is assigned a letter of the alphabet. If you are familiar with the Library of Congress's system, you can browse the sections knowing that books on these subjects will be grouped together.

Most classifications outside of the sciences are not as precisely and hierarchically defined. For example, E. B. White uses classification to discuss three different groups of people who make up New York City:

> There are roughly three New Yorks. There is, first, the New York of the man or woman who was born here, who takes the city for granted and accepts its size and its turbulence as natural and inevitable. Second, there is the New York of the commuter—the city that is devoured by locusts each day and spat out each night. Third, there is the New York of the person who was born somewhere else and came to New York in quest of something. Of these three trembling cities the greatest is the last—the city of final destination, the city that is a goal.

In this chapter, Bernard R. Berelson's classification of the reasons people want children is precisely and logically ordered. Notice how the organizational pattern is supported by the essay's title, "The Value of Children: A Taxonomical Essay," and by the headings.

**IN THE READINGS, LOOK FOR**

|  | **Division or Classification?** |
| --- | --- |
| David Bodanis, "What's in Toothpaste?" | A whole subdivided into ingredients |
| Barbara Ehrenreich, "Talk Shows" | A group (talk shows) analyzed by shared features |
| Pico Iyer, "This Is Who I Am" | Two sides of self |
| Judith Ortiz Cofer, "Latin Woman" | Stereotypes of the "Latin woman" |
| Bernard R. Berelson, "Value of Children" | Reasons why people want children |
| Deborah Tannen, "What Do You Mean?" | Areas of communication difficulties for men and women |

## How Do You Choose a Subject?

Division and classification are tools to help readers understand a subject. In that sense, part of the purpose of both is to inform readers. Readers will understand the whole better if they know how that whole can be divided, how it can be broken apart into small units. If the question is where do our tax dollars go, a division into small units—such as can be found in a pie chart—makes a complex, huge whole seem a little more manageable. Division also allows comparison of the relative size of each slice. Similarly, if readers are faced with many "things," a classification scheme helps organize those things into more understandable and smaller categories. Think about the classified advertisements in a newspaper. If there were no structure or order to the advertisements, you would have to look through page after page to find the advertisements that relate to the specific subject for which you are looking.

Both division and classification impose order. The purpose of each is to make things clearer and more understandable. Naturally then, each of these methods of analysis should be clearly and logically structured.

That primary informative purpose also suggests care in choosing a topic. Consider how interesting or informative the subject might be to a reader. Avoid the obvious approach to the obvious topic. Every teacher has read a classification essay placing teachers into groups based solely on the grade level at which they teach: elementary school teachers teach in elementary school, middle school teachers teach in middle school, and high school teachers teach in high school. Yes, the classification scheme is complete and accurate. Such a subject and approach, however, are likely to lead you into writing that is boring and simply not worth your time or your reader's. No subject is inherently bad, but if you choose to write about something obvious, find an interesting angle from which to approach it. Always ask, "Will my reader learn something or be entertained by what I plan to write?"

## IN THE READINGS, LOOK FOR

**Purpose and Audience**

David Bodanis, "What's in Toothpaste?"

What is new or interesting about
the topic?

Barbara Ehrenreich, "Talk Shows"

What can Ehrenreich assume
about her audience?

Pico Iyer, "This Is Who I Am"

Why might a reader care or what
might be learned?

Judith Ortiz Cofer, "Latin Woman"

What does the reader learn?

Bernard R. Berelson, "Value of Children"

To whom is Berelson writing?

Deborah Tannen, "What Do You Mean?"

What value might this have for
readers?

## PREWRITING TIPS FOR WRITING DIVISION AND CLASSIFICATION

1. Make a list of possible subjects for division and classification. Try out each idea on peer readers. Pay attention to their reactions to the subjects.

2. Consider what types of information you might need in order to divide or classify. Do you need to research the topic, or can you divide or classify with the information you already have?

3. Jot down a purpose statement for each possible topic. Why are you writing about this? Is your purpose purely informative? Does your topic have a persuasive value? Test your purpose statement on peer readers.

4. Think about your audience. What do they already know about your subject? Are you planning to tell them something that is obvious? Is your subject too complex or technical to handle in a short paper?

5. Brainstorm a tentative structure for the division and classification. That will help you as you gather and begin to organize the information.

## WRITING

### How Do You Divide or Classify a Subject?

Both division and classification involve separation into parts—either dividing a whole into pieces or sorting many things into related groups or categories. As a writer, you have to find ways in which to divide or group the subject of your essay. Those ways can be objective and formal, such as the classification schemes used by biologists or by Bernard R. Berelson in "The Value of Children: A Taxonomical Essay," or they can be subjective and informal like Judith Ortiz Cofer in "The Myth of the Latin Woman." Either way, several tasks are particularly important.

**Defining a Purpose**    You subdivide or categorize for a reason or purpose, and your division or classification should be made with that end in mind. For example, Bernard R. Berelson in "The Value of Children" places people's reasons for wanting children into six categories: biological, cultural, political, economic, familial, and personal. His purpose is to explain the various factors that motivate people—all people, in all cultures, over all time—to want children. Berelson does not include, for example, a category labeled "accidental," for such a heading would be irrelevant to his stated purpose. There is a significant difference, after all, between why people *want* children and why people *have* children.

**Making Your Classification or Division Complete**    Your division or classification must be complete—you cannot omit pieces or leave items unclassified. How complete your classification will be depends on your purpose. Berelson, for example, sets out to be exhaustive, to isolate all the reasons people at any time and in every place have wanted children. As a result, he includes some categories that are essentially irrelevant for most Americans. Probably few Americans want or have children for political reasons, that is, because their government encourages them or forbids them to have children. In some societies or in certain times, however, political reasons have been important. Therefore, Berelson must include that category as well.

**Using Parallelism**    The categories or subdivisions you establish need to be parallel in form. In mathematical terms, the categories should share a lowest common denominator. A simple and fairly effective test for parallelism is to see whether your categories are all phrased in similar grammatical terms. Berelson, for example, defines his categories (the reasons for wanting children) in exactly parallel form:

    Biological
    Cultural
    Political
    Economic
    Familial
    Personal
        Personal power
        Personal competence
        Personal status
        Personal extension
        Personal experience
        Personal pleasure

Do not establish a catchall category that you label something such as "other." When Berelson is finished with his classification scheme, no reasons for wanting children are left out: everything fits into one of the six subdivisions. Finally, your categories or subdivisions should be mutually exclusive; that is, items should belong in only one category.

## How Do You Structure a Division or Classification Essay?

The body of your division or classification essay will have as many parts as you have subdivisions or categories. Each subdivision or category can probably be treated in a single paragraph or in a group of related paragraphs. Deborah Tannen in "But What Do You Mean?" uses typographical devices (centered, numbered, boldface headings) to mark the categories of communication misunderstanding on which she is focusing; the seven areas analyzed in her essay are roughly proportional in length and detail. Bernard Berelson also uses typographical devices to convey a clear sense of how his essay is organized. The headings promote clarity. Not every essay will be so evenly and perfectly divided. Judith Ortiz Cofer's "The Myth of the Latin Woman" uses narrative examples to establish and explore the common stereotypes of the "Latin woman" that she has encountered. Though the essay has a clear, chronological structure, Cofer analyzes the myth in sections of varying length.

Once you have decided how many subdivisions or categories you will have and how long each one will be, you have to decide how to order those parts or categories. Some subjects invite, imply, or even demand a particular order. For example, if you were classifying films using the ratings established by the motion picture industry, you would essentially have to follow the G, PG, PG-13, R, and NC-17 sequence; you could begin at either end, but it would not make sense to begin with one of the middle categories. Having an order underlying your division or classification can be a great help for both you and your reader. It allows you to know where to place each section, dictating the order you will follow. Bernard Berelson, for example, in "The Value of Children," arranges the reasons that people have children in an order that "starts with chemistry and proceeds to spirit" (paragraph 3). That is, he first deals with the biological reasons for wanting children and moves finally to the most spiritual of reasons—love.

Sometimes your subject does not demand a certain order and you must devise your organizational scheme. Deborah Tannen in "But What Do You Mean?" identifies seven categories or areas in which the communication rituals of women and men differ. The arrangement or order in which the seven are analyzed is not inevitable. This is a decision that Tannen makes, for there is no clear reason why "apologies" must come first, "praise" must be fifth, and "jokes" last.

## IN THE READINGS, LOOK FOR

**Structure**

David Bodanis, "What's in Toothpaste?"  What principle of order is used in subdividing the ingredients?

Barbara Ehrenreich, "Talk Shows"  How is the essay divided and why does it not use subheadings?

Pico Iyer, "This Is Who I Am"  Is the essay clearly divided between the two selves he is? Why or why not?

Judith Ortiz Cofer, "Latin Woman"  How does narrative help provide structure for the classification of the "myths"?

Bernard R. Berelson, "Value of Children"  What is the role and impact of the typographical devices in the structure of the essay?

Deborah Tannen, "What Do You Mean?"  Can you see any reason why the areas of miscommunication might be ordered in this way?

## DRAFTING TIPS FOR WRITING DIVISION AND CLASSIFICATION

1.  Look again at your subject and make sure that your approach is either division or classification.

2.  Narrow your subject if necessary. Can your subject and your approach be handled in the amount of space you have available?

3.  Make sure that the number of parts or categories in your essay is manageable. You cannot subdivide into a dozen pieces or a dozen categories and keep your paper a reasonable length. As a rough rule, in a two- to four-page essay, do not have more than six parts or categories. If you have more, see if they can be grouped under larger headings.

4.  Establish a logical organizational pattern. Once you have selected your subdivisions or categories, write each one on a separate index card. Reorder the cards several times to see how many arrangements might be possible.

5.  Verify that your subdivisions or categories account for all or most of your subject. You should not have items that do not fit into your scheme. This is especially important if your analysis is objective rather than subjective.

# REVISING

## How Do You Revise a Division or Classification Essay?

A primary purpose for both division and classification is to help the reader analyze or organize information about a single topic or about a number of related items. It is vital, therefore, that the information be presented clearly and logically. When you have a draft of your essay and are beginning to revise, remember that the clarity and accuracy of your presentation are fundamental to an effective essay. Ask a peer reader, a writing tutor, or your instructor to look closely at those two issues. Does your paper make the subject or topic easier to understand? If your reader does not think so, you must address that problem.

When revising a division or classification essay, pay particular attention to the following areas: purpose, structure, proportional development, and parallelism.

**Having a Clear Purpose**   Why have you chosen this particular subject? Check again to make sure that it is not so common or obvious that your readers are likely to be bored. Also, make sure that the subject is not so large or complicated that you cannot treat it adequately in the space you have available. Ask yourself again what your audience is likely to know about the topic, and be wary of either end of the spectrum—too much or too little knowledge. As you revise, look back to your purpose statement and use it to test what you have written.

**Keeping the Analysis Logically Structured**   The order in which you present information in a division or classification is important. Do you move from the largest unit to the smallest, or in the other direction? The subdivisions or categories must be presented in an order that makes logical sense for the subject. You cannot jump around without a clear rationale. What principle have you used as you move from section to section? Is that principle clearly stated and consistently followed?

If your paper is logically structured and ordered, it will need only a minimum of stage or step markers (for example, "first," "next") or transitional words or phrases ("the next category," "finally"). Coherence in a paper is best achieved by a clearly articulated, logical presentation of the material. For help with stage or step markers and transitional words and phrases, consult the Glossary and Ready Reference at the back of this text.

**Making Sure the Categories or Parts Are Proportionally Developed**   Some of the subdivisions might represent a larger part of the whole than other subdivisions. Likewise, some of the categories in the classification might contain many more items than others. The principle of proportion does not mean that the parts must be equal in content. Rather, it means that you need to present each subdivision and each category in approximately the same amount of space. You should not give one category or subdivision a page and a half of your paper and another only three sentences.

Avoid subdividing or classifying in too great a detail. Your organizational scheme needs to account for the whole subject; that is, you should not have items that do not fit into your division or classification scheme. If you have a hundred objects on the table that you are placing into categories, your scheme must accommodate them all; you cannot have ten left over that do not fit into the scheme. Similarly, avoid catchall categories labeled "other" or "miscellaneous."

**Checking for Parallelism One More Time**    Subdivisions and categories need to be worded in parallel form; that is, they need to be cast into the same grammatical forms. Similar forms make it easy for the reader to see the relationships between the parts. Look back at the headings that are used in this chapter. The largest subdivisions are phrased in parallel form: "Getting Ready to Write," "Writing," and "Revising." At the next level, headings are all written as questions: "How do you . . . ?". The third level of headings (where you are reading now) consists of identically structured clauses "having a clear purpose," "keeping the analysis," "making sure," and "checking for parallelism". Parallelism is an easy way to signal your paper's structure to your readers and an excellent way to promote clarity. Help with parallelism can be found in the Glossary and Ready Reference at the back of this text.

## REVISING TIPS FOR WRITING DIVISION AND CLASSIFICATION

1.   Once you have a draft, write out a several-sentence summary of your essay. Ask some peers to read just that summary. Do they find your subject and approach interesting? Remember, there are no bad subjects, just bad approaches to subjects. Do you need to reconsider your approach?

2.   Look again at how you organized the body of your essay. Why did you begin and end where you did? Did you move from largest to smallest? Most important to least? What is your principle of order?

3.   Have you accounted for everything in your division and classification? Is there anything that does not fall into the subdivisions or categories you have established?

4.   Make sure you followed the principle of proportion.

5.   Check the clarity of your order. Can your reader clearly tell when you have moved from one subdivision or category to another? Have you paragraphed the paper or added subheadings to make that structure clear? Have you used step markers or transitions? Is everything parallel in grammatical form?

6.   Look again at your introduction. Have you tried to catch your reader's attention? Have you written a clear statement of what this paper is about and what your reader can expect to find in it?

## STUDENT ESSAY

Evan James chose to write his term paper for his introductory American studies course on the hobo in America. He read widely about the phenomenon, so he had plenty of information, but he was having trouble getting started and getting organized. He took his draft to the Writing Center.

### First Draft

Hobos

Among the many social problems that the United States faced at the turn of this past century was that of the "hobo." My interest in hobos came about because of the book <u>The Ways of the Hobo</u> that we read. The term <u>hobo</u>, the dictionary says, was probably derived from the greeting "Ho! Beau!" commonly used by vagrants to greet each other, although other possibilities have been suggested as well. The number of hobos in the United States at the turn of the century was large because of soldiers returning from the Civil War and because increasing mechanization had reduced the number of jobs in factories and businesses. In fact, the unemployment rate in the late 1800s ran as high as 40% of the workforce. We think that unemployment rates of 6% are unacceptable today!

Actually hobos were careful about how they referred to themselves. Today, for example, we might use the words <u>hobo</u>, <u>tramp</u>, and <u>bum</u> interchangeably. I was surprised to learn that among the hobos themselves, the distinctions were clear. A hobo was a migrant worker, a tramp was a migrant nonworker, and a bum was a nonmigrant nonworker.

### Comments

When the tutor asked about the problems Evan saw in his essay, Evan listed a couple: he thought the introduction was flat and boring and the essay didn't move smoothly from sentence to sentence ("I think I just jump around from idea to idea"). The tutor and Evan collaborated on a list of the qualities that make a good introduction. They also discussed how writers can group information and make transitions. In the process of revising, Evan found a stronger, more interesting way to begin, and he reparagraphed and developed his opening paragraphs to reflect an analysis both by division and by cause and effect.

## Revised Draft

Riding the Rails: The American Hobo

Although homelessness and vagrancy might seem to be a distinctively modern phenomenon, the problem is probably less acute today (in terms of percentage of our total population) than it was at the turn of the twentieth century. At that time, a series of factors combined to create a large migratory population comprised almost exclusively of young males.

The Civil War was an uprooting experience for thousands of young men. Many left home in their teenage years, had acquired no job skills during their military service, and had grown accustomed to the nomadic life of the soldier—always on the move, living off the land, sleeping in the open. As the armies disbanded, many young men chose not to return home but to continue wandering the countryside.

Even if these former soldiers had wanted to work, few jobs were available to absorb the thousands of men who were mustered out. Increasingly, mechanization in the last decades of the 1800s brought the loss of jobs. In a world before unemployment benefits and social welfare, unemployment encouraged migration. The problem worsened in the 1870s when the country spiraled into a depression. Businesses failed, construction sagged, and the unemployment rate soared to an estimated 40%. Men, looking for work, took to the road.

Such men were called by a variety of names. One was hobo. The origin of that word is unknown. It has been suggested that hobo might be a shortened form of the Latin phrase homo bonus ("good man") or derived from the greeting "Ho! Beau!" commonly used among vagrants (dictionaries favor this suggestion). Other possibilities include a shortened form of the phrase "homeward bound" or "hoe boy," a term used in the eighteenth century for migrant farm workers.

Strictly speaking, not everyone who took to the road should be called a hobo. "Real" hobos were quick to insist on a series of distinctions. The words hobo, tramp, and bum were not interchangeable. By definition within the hobo community, the term hobo referred to a migrant worker, tramp to a migrant nonworker, and bum to a nonmigrant nonworker.

Obviously, the motives of the men traveling the road varied widely. Some were in search of work—migrant agricultural workers were an accepted fact by the turn of the century. Others were fleeing from the law, from family responsibilities, from themselves. Many were alcoholics; some were mentally impaired. All, though, were responding to a version of the American myth—the hope that a better future lay somewhere (geographically) ahead and that, meanwhile, the open road was the place to be.

## SOME THINGS TO REMEMBER WHEN WRITING DIVISION AND CLASSIFICATION

1. In choosing a subject for division or classification, ask yourself, first, what is my purpose? and second, will my reader learn something or be entertained by my paper?
2. Remember that your subdivision or classification should reflect your purpose; that is, the number of categories or parts is related to what you are trying to do.
3. Make sure that your division or classification is complete. Do not omit any pieces or items. Account for everything.
4. Take care that the parts or categories are phrased in parallel form.
5. Avoid a category labeled something such as "other" or "miscellaneous."
6. Remember to make your categories or subdivisions mutually exclusive.
7. Once you have established your subdivisions, check to see whether there is an order implied or demanded by your subject.
8. As you move from one subdivision to another, provide markers for the reader so that the parts are clearly labeled.

## SEEING DIVISION AND CLASSIFICATION IN OTHER CONTEXTS

### As a literary strategy

Like many Americans, Aurora Levins Morales sees in herself the different cultures and races that have made her "a child of the Americas." In her poem she uses division to analyze those diverse threads.

# Child of the Americas

Aurora Levins Morales

I am a child of the Americas,
a light-skinned mestiza of the Caribbean,
a child of many diaspora, born into this continent at a crossroads.

I am a U.S. Puerto Rican Jew,
a product of the ghettos of New York I have never known.
An immigrant and the daughter and granddaughter of immigrants.
I speak English with passion: it's the tone of my consciousness,
a flashing knife blade of crystal, my tool, my craft,

I am Caribeña, island grown. Spanish is in my flesh,
ripples from my tongue, lodges in my hips:
the language of garlic and mangoes,
the singing of my poetry, the flying gestures of my hands.
I am of Latinoamerica, rooted in the history of my continent:
I speak from that body.

I am not africa. Africa is in me, but I cannot return.
I am not taína. Taíno is in me, but there is no way back.
I am not european. Europe lives in me, but I have no home there.

I am new. History made me. My first language was spanlish
I was born at the crossroads
and I am whole.

## Discussion Questions

1. Why might Morales have titled her poem, "Child of the Americas"? Why the plural "Americas"?
2. How many different cultures does Morales identify as being a part of who she is? How does she order those cultures? Which is most predominant and why? What are the elements that she values?
3. What does Morales see as the contribution each culture has made to the person she is today?
4. What might she mean by "I am new. History made me"?
5. How does Morales use classification and division as a structural device in the poem?

## Writing Suggestions

1. In one sense everyone living in the United States is descended from immigrants. It is just a question of when our ancestors came here. Moreover, most people, like Morales, are a mixture of peoples from different cultures and races. Think

about your own ancestry—check with your grandparents or someone in your family who has traced the family's history. In an essay, explore your identity.

2. Most of us have different, even conflicting, elements in our personalities— that, we might argue, is what makes us interesting. Think about the defining elements/values/talents/behaviors/obsessions that combine in you. In an essay, separate out those different elements.

# AS A CRITICAL READING STRATEGY

The following excerpt is taken from Mark Lester's *Grammar in the Class-room*, a college text intended for prospective teachers of grammar. Since the purpose of a textbook is to explain a subject to students, clarity of presentation is especially important. You do not demand to be entertained by a textbook; you expect to have material presented as clearly and simply as possible. Notice how Lester uses classification to explain how traditional grammar classifies sentences by purpose. Notice as well how Lester uses typographical devices and parallelism to promote the clarity and simplicity of the material.

As you read, remember what you have learned about how to write using division or classification—and how that knowledge can help you as a reader.

- Division and classification are used to present information in a clear and organized fashion. Their primary purpose is to inform and clarify, not to entertain or persuade.
- Division and classification involve either dividing a subject into its constituent parts or sorting things into related categories—making order where there appears to be chaos.
- The parts or categories in division and classification must allow for completeness. Nothing should be left over; you should be able to place every part within a division or classification of the broader subject.
- The parts or categories in division and classification must be arranged in a logical order.
- Division and classification make extensive use of parallelism (using the same grammatical structure for statements about related aspects of the parts or categories).
- Division and classification both lend themselves to visual displays and in fact might best be shown through a visual arrangement or device.

### Classifying Sentences By Purpose

Topic sentence— announces how the subject will be broken into categories

In traditional grammar, sentences are classified in a fourfold manner depending upon the purpose of the sentence. The following are the four types of sentences.

Typographical devices—
spacing and numbering
promote clarity

1. **Declarative:** <u>A declarative sentence</u> makes a statement. Declarative sentences are punctuated with a period.

   John went away.

Parallelism
  **a.** Spacing
  **b.** Bold face
  **c.** Numbering
  **d.** Sentence structures
  **e.** Order of sentences
  **f.** Examples

2. **Imperative:** <u>An imperative sentence</u> gives a command or makes a request. Imperative sentences must have an understood *you* as subject. Imperative sentences may be punctuated with either a period or an exclamation point.

   Go away.
   Come here!
   Stop it!

Classification is complete

These are the only four
ways in which sentences can
be classified by purpose in
traditional grammar

3. **Interrogative:** <u>An interrogative sentence</u> asks a question. Interrogative sentences must be punctuated with a question mark.

   Did John go away?
   Where are you?

4. **Exclamatory:** <u>An exclamatory sentence</u> expresses strong feeling. Exclamatory sentences are declarative sentences with an exclamation point. Remember that imperative sentences can have exclamation points too. The difference is that imperative sentences must always have an understood *you* as subject; exclamatory sentences can never have an understood *you* as subject. Exclamatory sentences *must* be punctuated with an exclamation point.

   John went away!
   Sally has no cavities!

## AS A VISUAL STRATEGY

Division and classification are both strongly rooted in the visual. Division takes a single subject and breaks it into its parts. Typically, division might be represented by a list or table—here are the ingredients or the subdivisions of this subject. Pie charts are visual displays of division. The whole is a circle or a pie; the wedges in the pie show how the whole is divided into its constituent parts. On the other hand, classification takes many related items and imposes order on them, arranging or sorting them into groups that can clearly be differentiated. For example, scientists attempting to catalog plants, animals, and insects establish elaborate classification schemes or taxonomies to group and separate, seeing both similarities and differences among the related items. The following photograph shows an assortment of buttons—all have the same function (that is, all are buttons), but they come in a variety of shapes and sizes.

# WRITING ABOUT IMAGES

1. Study the photograph; then devise a classification scheme for the buttons—that is, sort them into groups based on the characteristics that they share and those that they do not. In an essay, first, explain how and why the buttons could be classified, and second, suggest the reasons why such a classification scheme might prove particularly helpful.

2. Look carefully at your Facebook or MySpace page or that of a friend. Think about how the information that is presented—such as the images, the photos of friends, the linked music, the design or wallpaper—might be organized under a division scheme. What subdivisions are included? What does the content and its visual arrangement suggest about you or the person whose page it is?

3. Locate print advertisements for types of products that people your age use or consume, for example, advertisements for cell phones or cell phone service, for tobacco or alcoholic products, for clothes or personal accessories, for sports equipment, for automobiles or bikes. Magazines would be a good source, especially magazines that are targeted at an audience of a particular age or with a similar set of interests. Locate at least ten advertisements for different types of products. Using those images, write an essay in which you classify the advertisements according to how they appeal to you as a potential consumer.

# ADDITIONAL WRITING SUGGESTIONS FOR DIVISION AND CLASSIFICATION

Remember that division takes a whole and separates it into meaningful subdivisions. Classification takes many things and sorts them into categories as a means of ordering them and making them easier to understand. Both division and classification are done for a purpose, and both often make use of visual devices (for example, charts or typographical devices) to help readers grasp the organizational pattern. Keeping a purpose in mind and using visuals if you wish, try writing about one of the following topics:

## DIVISION

1. Freshman class (as a whole) at your college or university
2. Way in which players on a team or in a band might be subdivided by roles
3. Organizational structure of a club or a business
4. Total cost of a year at your college or university/cost of a year for you (humorous)
5. Distribution of federal tax dollars
6. Composition (ingredients) of a prepared food that you regularly consume
7. Your stages in the writing process (try as a humorous essay)
8. A well-balanced meal (serious or humorous)
9. Responsibilities of your job (part-time or full-time)
10. Characteristics of your "ideal" job

## CLASSIFICATION

1. Television talk or reality shows
2. Items found in a drawer, pocket, backpack, or purse
3. E-mails received
4. Excuses for bad behavior/lateness/missing class/not being prepared for class
5. Ways in which you waste time
6. Ways to procrastinate when you have to write a paper
7. Places to eat on campus or in town
8. People you regard as friends or enemies
9. Excuses for smoking or for not exercising more or eating less
10. Possible first-date activities

# What's in Your Toothpaste

David Bodanis

*Raised in Chicago, David Bodanis earned a degree in mathematics from the University of Chicago and did postgraduate work in theoretical biology and population genetics. He traveled to London and then to Paris, where he began his journalism career as a copyboy at the* International Herald Tribune. *Bodanis has a special talent for explaining complex concepts in simple, yet entertaining, language. His most recent book is* Passionate Minds: The Great Love Affair of the Enlightenment *(2006).*

*This essay is excerpted from* The Secret House *(1986). One reviewer noted: "The book explores the gee-whiz science that sits unnoticed under every homeowner's nose." If you are appalled to discover what is in your toothpaste, you ought to read Bodanis's account of some mass-produced ice cream that contains "leftover cattle parts that no one else wants."*

**On Writing:** *Asked about the start of his writing career, Bodanis replied: "I failed my writing exam at the University of Chicago, but it was fair. I didn't know how to write, didn't know the basics of structure." Later, he got a job at the* Herald Tribune *in Paris. "The people there taught practical writing. And I read books, and I felt that writing was a skill to learn, I never thought of it as a career."*

## Before Reading

**Connecting:** Most of us are well aware of the toxic nature of some common products, but there are many others that we assume are safe and maybe even good for us. Think about the things that you use, eat, or drink every day. Which ones have you never worried about?

**Anticipating:** Is Bodanis being fair and objective in his essay? How can you judge?

1    **I**nto the bathroom goes our male resident, and after the most pressing need is satisfied it's time to brush the teeth. The tube of toothpaste is squeezed, its pinched metal seams are splayed, pressure waves are generated inside, and the paste begins to flow. But what's in this toothpaste, so carefully being extruded out?

2    Water mostly, 30 to 45 percent in most brands: ordinary, everyday simple tap water. It's there because people like to have a big gob of toothpaste to spread on the brush, and water is the cheapest stuff there is when it comes to

making big gobs. Dripping a bit from the tap onto your brush would cost virtually nothing; whipped in with the rest of the toothpaste the manufacturers can sell it at a neat and accountant-pleasing $2 per pound equivalent. Toothpaste manufacture is a very lucrative occupation.

3     Second to water in quantity is chalk: exactly the same material that schoolteachers use to write on blackboards. It is collected from the crushed remains of long-dead ocean creatures. In the Cretaceous seas chalk particles served as part of the wickedly sharp outer skeleton that these creatures had to wrap around themselves to keep from getting chomped by all the slightly larger other ocean creatures they met. Their massed graves are our present chalk deposits.

4     The individual chalk particles—the size of the smallest mud particles in your garden—have kept their toughness over the aeons, and now on the toothbrush they'll need it. The enamel outer coating of the tooth they'll have to face is the hardest substance in the body—tougher than skull, or bone, or nail. Only the chalk particles in toothpaste can successfully grind into the teeth during brushing, ripping off the surface layers like an abrading wheel grinding down a boulder in a quarry.

5     The craters, slashes, and channels that the chalk tears into the teeth will also remove a certain amount of build-up yellow in the carnage, and it is for that polishing function that it's there. A certain amount of unduly enlarged extra-abrasive chalk fragments tear such cavernous pits into the teeth that future decay bacteria will be able to bunker down there and thrive; the quality control people find it almost impossible to screen out these errant super-chalk pieces, and government regulations allow them to stay in.

6     In case even the gouging doesn't get all the yellow off, another substance is worked into the toothpaste cream. This is titanium dioxide. It comes in tiny spheres, and it's the stuff bobbing around in white wall paint to make it come out white. Splashed around onto your teeth during the brushing it coats much of the yellow that remains. Being water soluble it leaks off in the next few hours and is swallowed, but at least for the quick glance up in the mirror after finishing it will make the user think his teeth are truly white. Some manufacturers add optical whitening dyes—the stuff more commonly found in washing machine bleach—to make extra sure that that glance in the mirror shows reassuring white.

7     These ingredients alone would not make a very attractive concoction. They would stick in the tube like a sloppy white plastic lump, hard to squeeze out as well as revolting to the touch. Few consumers would savor rubbing in a mixture of water, ground-up blackboard chalk, and the whitener from latex paint first thing in the morning. To get around that finicky distaste the manufacturers have mixed in a host of other goodies.

8     To keep the glop from drying out, a mixture including glycerine glycol—related to the most common car antifreeze ingredient—is whipped in with the chalk and water, and to give *that* concoction a bit of substance (all we really have so far is wet colored chalk) a large helping is added of gummy molecules from the seaweed *Chondrus Crispus*. This seaweed ooze spreads in among the chalk,

paint, and antifreeze, then stretches itself in all directions to hold the whole mass together. A bit of paraffin oil (the fuel that flickers in camping lamps) is pumped in with it to help the moss ooze keep the whole substance smooth.

9       With the glycol, ooze, and paraffin we're almost there. Only two major chemicals are left to make the refreshing, cleansing substance we know as toothpaste. The ingredients so far are fine for cleaning, but they wouldn't make much of the satisfying foam we have come to expect in the morning brushing.

10      To remedy that every toothpaste on the market has a big dollop of detergent added too. You've seen the suds detergent will make in a washing machine. The same substance added here will duplicate that inside the mouth. It's not particularly necessary, but it sells.

11      The only problem is that by itself this ingredient tastes, well, too like detergent. It's horribly bitter and harsh. The chalk put in toothpaste is pretty foul-tasting too for that matter. It's to get around that gustatory discomfort that the manufacturers put in the ingredient they tout perhaps the most of all. This is the flavoring, and it has to be strong. Double rectified peppermint oil is used—a flavorer so powerful that chemists know better than to sniff it in the raw state in the laboratory. Menthol crystals and saccharin or other sugar simulators are added to complete the camouflage operation.

12      Is that it? Chalk, water, paint, seaweed, antifreeze, paraffin oil, detergent, and peppermint? Not quite. A mix like that would be irresistible to the hundreds of thousands of individual bacteria lying on the surface of even an immaculately cleaned bathroom sink. They would get in, float in the water bubbles, ingest the ooze and paraffin, maybe even spray out enzymes to break down the chalk. The result would be an uninviting mess. The way manufacturers avoid that final obstacle is by putting something in to kill the bacteria. Something good and strong is needed, something that will zap any accidentally intrudant bacteria into oblivion. And that something is formaldehyde—the disinfectant used in anatomy labs.

13      So it's chalk, water, paint, seaweed, antifreeze, paraffin oil, detergent, peppermint, formaldehyde, and fluoride (which can go some way towards preserving children's teeth)—that's the usual mixture raised to the mouth on the toothbrush for a fresh morning's clean. If it sounds too unfortunate, take heart. Studies show that thorough brushing with just plain water will often do as good a job.

## Questions on Subject and Purpose

1.  Bodanis explains to the reader what toothpaste is composed of. Is his description objective? Could it appear, for example, in an encyclopedia?

2.  After reading the essay, you might feel that Bodanis avoids certain crucial issues about the composition of toothpaste. Does he raise for you any questions that he does not answer?

3.  What might Bodanis's purpose be? Is he arguing for something? Is he attacking something?

## Questions on Strategy and Audience

1. How does Bodanis seem to arrange or order his division?
2. Bodanis gives the most space (three paragraphs) to chalk. Why? What is his focus in the section?
3. What could Bodanis expect about his audience?

## Questions on Vocabulary and Style

1. How would you characterize the tone of the essay?
2. Bodanis links most of the ingredients to their use in another product. Find these links, and be prepared to comment on the effect that these linkages have on the reader.
3. Be prepared to define the following words: *splayed* (paragraph 1), *extruded* (1), *lucrative* (2), *aeons* (4), *abrading* (4), *carnage* (5), *errant* (5), *finicky* (7), *dollop* (10), *gustatory* (11), *tout* (11), *intrudant* (12).

## Writing Suggestions

1. **For Your Journal or Blog.** Over a period of several days, keep a list of every product that you use or consume—everything from a lip balm to cosmetics to after-shave or cologne to mouthwash to chewing gum. When you really think about it, which ones would you like to know more about?
2. **For a Paragraph.** Select a common food or beverage and subdivide it into its constituent parts. Use the contents label on the package as a place to start. You could use either the list of ingredients or the nutrition information. Present your division in a paragraph. Do not just describe what you find; rather, develop an attitude or thesis toward those findings. Bodanis, for example, certainly expresses (or implies) how he feels about what he finds in toothpaste.
3. **For an Essay.** Americans exhibit widely differing attitudes toward the food they eat, in large part because they have the greatest choice of any people in the world. In an essay, classify the American eater. You can approach your subject from a serious or a comic point of view. Do not just describe types; your essay should either state or imply your feelings or judgments about your findings. Try to establish four to six categories.
4. **For Research.** Americans have become increasingly concerned about the additives that are put into food. Research the nature of food additives. How many are there? In general, what do they do? Develop a classification scheme to explain the largest groups or subdivisions. Be sure to adopt a stand or thesis about the use of such additives; also be sure to document your sources.

## For Further Study

**Focusing on Grammar and Writing.** Bodanis uses summary sentences at times to repeat or reinforce the points that he has made so far—examples occur in paragraphs 7, 8, 9, 12, and 13. Why might he keep doing this? What is the effect of such summary or repetition? When might you use such a strategy in your own writing?

**Working Together.** Throughout the essay, Bodanis links the ingredients in toothpaste to other products in which they can be found. Divide into small groups and choose one of the following ingredients to examine: water (paragraph 1); chalk (2–5); titanium dioxide (6); glycerine, glycol, seaweed, and paraffin oil (8); detergent (10); peppermint oil (11), and formaldehyde (12). How does Bodanis, in listing the ingredients, manage at the same time to shock the reader? Pay attention to word choice and analogy.

**Seeing Other Modes at Work.** The essay could easily be turned into a persuasive essay. What elements of persuasion does the essay already contain? What would have to be added?

**Finding Connections.** An interesting pairing can be made on the basis of tone. In what ways, for example, are the tones of Bodanis's essay and Judy Brady's "I Want a Wife" (Chapter 8) similar?

**Exploring the Web.** Shocked to find out what is in your toothpaste? That is nothing compared to the ingredients in a jar of baby food! Read a description from Bodanis's *The Secret Family* on the Web.

# In Defense of Talk Shows

Barbara Ehrenreich

*Born in Butte, Montana, in 1941, Barbara Ehrenreich earned her Ph.D. in biology at Rockefeller University. After a period of university teaching, Ehrenreich turned to writing full time. A prolific writer, Ehrenreich's most recent book is* Dancing in the Streets: A History of Collective Joy *(2007).*

**On Writing:** *Ehrenreich writes regularly for* The Progressive *and a wide range of other magazines, including* Time, *where "In Defense of Talk Shows" first appeared. Commenting on writing essays for magazines, she observed: "I don't see myself as writing polemics where I'm just trying to beat something into people's heads. An essay is like a little story, a short story, and I will obsess about what is the real point, what are the real connections, a long time before I ever put finger to keyboard."*

## Before Reading

**Connecting:** Do you ever watch talk shows such as the ones that Ehrenreich mentions? What attracts you to them?

**Anticipating:** To what extent is the essay a "defense" of talk shows?

1   **U**p until now, the targets of Bill (*The Book of Virtues*) Bennett's crusades have at least been plausible sources of evil. But the latest victim of his wrath—TV talk shows of the Sally Jessy Raphael variety—are in a whole different category from drugs and gangsta rap. As anyone who actually watches them knows, the talk shows are one of the most excruciatingly moralistic forums the culture has to offer. Disturbing and sometimes disgusting, yes, but their very business is to preach the middle-class virtues of responsibility, reason and self-control.

2   Take the case of Susan, recently featured on *Montel Williams* as an example of a woman being stalked by her ex-boyfriend. Turns out Susan is also stalking the boyfriend and—here's the sexual frisson—has slept with him only days ago. In fact Susan is neck deep in trouble without any help from the boyfriend: She's serving a yearlong stretch of home incarceration for assaulting another woman, and home is the tiny trailer she shares with her nine-year-old daughter.

3   But no one is applauding this life spun out of control. Montel scolds Susan roundly for neglecting her daughter and failing to confront her role in the mutual stalking. A therapist lectures her about this unhealthy "obsessive kind of love." The studio audience jeers at her every evasion. By the end Susan has lost her cocky charm and dissolved into tears of shame.

4       The plot is always the same. People with problems—"husband says she looks like a cow," "pressured to lose her virginity or else," "mate wants more sex than I do"—are introduced to rational methods of problem solving. People with moral failings—"boy crazy," "dresses like a tramp," "a hundred sex partners"—are introduced to external standards of morality. The preaching—delivered alternately by the studio audience, the host and the ever present guest therapist—is relentless. "This is wrong to do this," Sally Jessy tells a cheating husband. "Feel bad?" Geraldo asks the girl who stole her best friend's boyfriend. "Any sense of remorse?" The expectation is that the sinner, so hectored, will see her way to reform. And indeed, a Sally Jessy update found "boy crazy," who'd been a guest only weeks ago, now dressed in schoolgirlish plaid and claiming her "attitude [had] changed"—thanks to the rough-and-ready therapy dispensed on the show.

5       All right, the subjects are often lurid and even bizarre. But there's no part of the entertainment spectacle, from *Hard Copy* to *Jade*, that doesn't trade in the lurid and bizarre. At least in the talk shows, the moral is always loud and clear: Respect yourself, listen to others, stop beating on your wife. In fact it's hard to see how *The Bill Bennett Show*, if there were to be such a thing, could deliver a more pointed sermon. Or would he prefer to see the feckless Susan, for example, tarred and feathered by the studio audience instead of being merely booed and shamed?

6       There is something morally repulsive about the talks, but it's not anything Bennett or his co-crusader Senator Joseph Lieberman has seen fit to mention. Watch for a few hours, and you get the claustrophobic sense of lives that have never seen the light of some external judgment, of people who have never before been listened to, and certainly never been taken seriously if they were. "What kind of people would let themselves be humiliated like this?" is often asked, sniffily, by the shows' detractors. And the answer, for the most part, is people who are so needy—of social support, of education, of material resources and self-esteem—that they mistake being the center of attention for being actually loved and respected.

7       What the talks are about, in large part, is poverty and the distortions it visits on the human spirit. You'll never find investment bankers bickering on *Rolonda*, or the host of *Gabrielle* recommending therapy to sobbing professors. With few exceptions the guests are drawn from trailer parks and tenements, from bleak streets and narrow, crowded rooms. Listen long enough, and you hear references to unpaid bills, to welfare, to twelve-hour workdays and double shifts. And this is the real shame of the talks: that they take lives bent out of shape by poverty and hold them up as entertaining exhibits. An announcement appearing between segments of *Montel* says it all: The show is looking for "pregnant women who sell their bodies to make ends meet."

8       This is class exploitation, pure and simple. What next—"homeless people so hungry they eat their own scabs"? Or would the next step be to pay people outright to submit to public humiliation? For $50 would you confess to adultery in your wife's presence? For $500 would you reveal your thirteen-year-old's girlish secrets on *Ricki Lake*? If you were poor enough, you might.

9        It is easy enough for those who can afford spacious homes and private therapy to sneer at their financial inferiors and label their pathetic moments of stardom vulgar. But if I had a talk show, it would feature a whole different cast of characters and category of crimes than you'll ever find on the talks: "CEOs who rake in millions while their employees get downsized" would be an obvious theme, along with "Senators who voted for welfare and Medicaid cuts"—and, if they'll agree to appear, "well-fed Republicans who dithered about talk shows while trailer-park residents slipped into madness and despair."

## Questions on Subject and Purpose

1. Write a thesis statement—or find one—for the essay.
2. According to Ehrenreich, why would people agree to appear on these talk shows?
3. What makes such shows "morally repulsive" (paragraph 6)?

## Questions on Strategy and Audience

1. How does Ehrenreich divide or analyze the distinctive common features of the talk shows?
2. Why are such shows popular?
3. What expectations does Ehrenreich seem to have about her audience?

## Questions on Vocabulary and Style

1. In paragraphs 4 and 5, Ehrenreich uses an extended metaphor to explain the pattern that the shows follow. What is that metaphor? (Check the Glossary and Ready Reference for a definition of *metaphor*.)
2. How would you characterize the tone of the rhetorical questions that Ehrenreich asks in paragraph 8? (Check the Glossary and Ready Reference for a definition of *tone*.)
3. Be prepared to define the following words: *excruciatingly* (paragraph 1), *frisson* (2), *hectored* (4), *lurid* (5), *feckless* (5), *dithered* (9).

## Writing Suggestions

1. **For Your Journal or Blog.** All forms of media—compact discs, software programs, magazines, books, television or radio shows, even Websites—try to mimic whatever has been successful. For example, if one television show about "friends" or a new prime-time game show is popular, expect next season to see several other imitators. Select one medium, and make notes in your journal or blog about the similarities that you see among the items that belong in that category.
2. **For a Paragraph.** Expand your observations from your journal or blog into a paragraph. Try for the same type of analysis or division that Ehrenreich achieves. Focus your paragraph around a single shared element.

3. **For an Essay.** Expand your paragraph analysis or division into a full essay. You are analyzing the elements that a series of similar media products share—for example, the common elements of television cooking shows or of magazines intended for teenage girls. Remember, the choice of medium is yours: software programs, magazines, advertisements, Websites. You will probably want to analyze three or four shared elements. How do these shared elements work together? To what purpose or goal do all of these things contribute?

4. **For Research.** Test your analysis by checking research done on the subject. Using the resources of your library, and perhaps of online databases and the Web, see what other writers have said. Remember that information will appear in communication journals, marketing and business journals, trade papers for that particular medium, and scholarly and general journals and magazines. A keyword search might be a good place to begin. If you are having trouble gathering information, ask a reference librarian for help.

## For Further Study

**Focusing on Grammar and Writing.** Assuming a spectrum from formal to informal, where would you place Ehrenreich's essay on the scale? Identify those features in her prose (such as word choice and sentence structure) that support your opinion. Under what circumstances do you want your writing to be formal? When can it be informal?

**Working Together.** Working in small groups, examine one of the following paragraphs: 2, 4, 5, or 7. Each group should report on how Ehrenreich uses language, detail, and sentence structure in the paragraph.

**Seeing Other Modes at Work.** In paragraph 9 Ehrenreich uses comparison and contrast to introduce the types of guests she would invite to her talk show. The essay also exhibits persuasion.

**Finding Connections.** An interesting pairing is Lars Eighner's "My Daily Dives into the Dumpster" (Chapter 6).

**Exploring the Web.** Did you know that most talk shows have extensive Websites where you can see additional photographs, watch video clips, and explore other special features. Check the Web.

# This Is Who I Am When No One Is Looking

Pico Iyer

> *Pico Iyer (1957–) was, as he writes, "born, as the son of Indian parents, in England, [and] moved to America at seven." One of the country's foremost travel writers, Iyer is the author of a number of books, including several about spiritual issues and his search for silence. His most recent book,* The Open Road *(2008), tells the story of his meetings with the fourteenth Dalai Lama over 30 years. This essay was originally published in* Portland *magazine, a publication of the University of Portland, Oregon, in 2006.*
>
> **On Writing:** *Iyer comments: "Writing should be an act of communication more than of mere self-expression—a telling of a story rather than a flourishing of skills. . . . Writing . . . should, ideally, be as spontaneous and urgent as a letter to a lover, or a message to a friend who has just lost a parent. And because of the ways a writer is obliged to tap in private the selves that even those closest to him never see, writing is, in the end, that oddest of anomalies: an intimate letter to a stranger."*

## Before Reading

**Connecting:** Have you ever thought that the "real" you is someone that few, if any, people ever see?

**Anticipating:** Iyer is a global traveler who has written much about his experiences traveling. What is it that he is searching for on this "journey"?

1 **O**nce every three or four months, for much of my adult life now, I've gotten in my car in my mother's house in the dry hills of California, above the sea, and driven up the road, past the local yoga foundation, past the community of local sixties refugees, past the mock-Danish tourist town and the vineyards, past where Ronald Reagan used to keep his Western White House and where Michael Jackson sat imprisoned in his Neverland, past a lighthouse, past meadows of dormant cows, to another little room a thousand feet above the ocean, in the dry hills, where deer come out to graze at dusk and mountain lions come out, too, to stalk our urban fantasies.

2 There is a sign on the main highway down below—hanging from a large cross—and there is a saint's name on the door of the little room I enter,

underneath the number. But the names are all forgotten here, especially my own, and when I step into the little "cell" than awaits me—narrow bed huddled up against one wall, closet and bathroom, wide blond-wood desk overlooking a garden that overlooks the sea—I really don't know or care what "Catholic" means, or hermitage, or monastery, or Big Sur.

3    There are crosses in this place, and hooded men singing the psalms at dawn (at noon, at dusk, at sunset), and there's a cross on the wall above the bed. But I go not because of all the trappings of the chapel I had to attend twice a day every school day of my adolescence, but in spite of it. I go to disappear into the silence.

4    My friends assume, I'm sure, that I go to the monastery to catch my breath, to be away from the phone, to drink in one of the most beautiful stretches of coastline in the world. What I can't tell them—what they don't want to hear—is that I go to the monastery to become another self, the self that we all are if only we choose to unpack our overstuffed lives and leave our selves at home.

5    In my cell I read novels in the ringing silence, and they are novels, often, of infidelity. In the best of them, the ones by Sue Miller, say, there is a palpable, quickening sense of the excitement of betraying others and your daily self in the world you know. I read these with recognition. This shadow story is as close to us as our dreams. All the great myths are about it, the stories of Shakespeare and Aeschylus and Homer are about it, as are our romance novels and our letters to Aunt Agony, but here in the monastery I'm committing a deeper infidelity, against the life I know and the values by which we are supposed to live. I am being disloyal in the deepest way to the assumptions of the daily round, and daring to lay claim to a mystery at the heart of me.

6    I step into my cell, and I step into the realest life I know. My secret life, as Leonard Cohen calls it, also happens to be my deepest and my best life. There is no will involved, no choice; this other world, and self, are waiting for me like the clothes I never thought to ask for.

7    I'm not a Benedictine monk, and I attend none of the services held day in, day out, four times a day, while I'm in my little room. If I make the mistake of attending one because of my longing to be good, my wish to pay, in some way, the kind monks for making the silence available to me, I soon run out again. The presence of the fifteen kindly souls in hoods, singing, takes me back, somehow, to the world, the self I've come here to escape; the words in the psalms are all of war, and I notice which face looks kind and which one bitter.

8    No, the flight is to something much larger than a single text or doctrine. It's to—this the word I otherwise shy from—eternity. I step into a place that never changes, and with it that part of me, that ground in me, that belongs to what is changeless. There is a self at the core of us—what some call "Christ," others the "Buddha nature," and poets refer to as the immortal soul—that is simply part of the nonshifting nature of the universe. Not in any exalted way: just like the soil or sky or air. It does not fit into our everyday notions any more

than sky fits into a bed. But I steal into this better world as into a secret love, and there, as in the best of loves, I feel I am known in a way I know is true.

9      Thomas Merton put this best, not because he was a Christian, or even because he was a monk, but because he fell in love with silence. And he made the pursuit of that real life his lifelong mission. He knew, he saw, that it was akin to the earthly love we feel, and that the heightening, the risking up to a higher place, the making sense of things—above all, the dissolution of the tiny self we know—when we fall in love is our closest approximation to this state, as certain drugs can give us an indication of what lies beyond. But it is only an approximation, a momentary glimpse, like snapshots of a sunset where we long to live forever.

10      I wouldn't call this a pilgrimage, because, as Merton says, again, I'm not off to find myself; only to lose myself. I'm not off in search of anything; in fact, only—the words sound fanciful—the sense of being found. You could say it's not a pilgrimage because there's no movement involved after I step out of my car, three hours and fifteen minutes north of my mother's house, and I don't pay any of the religious dues when I arrive. But all the movements and journeys I have taken around the world are underwritten, at heart, by this: this is who I am when nobody is looking. This is who I'm not, because the petty, struggling, ambitious "I" is gone. I am as still, as timeless as the plate of sea below me.

11      I keep quiet about this journey, usually because it sounds as strange to other people, or to myself, as a piece of silence brought to a shopping mall. If they have an equivalent—and they surely do, in meditation, in sky-diving, in running, in sex—they will know what I'm talking of, and substitude their own terms; everyone knows at moments she has a deeper, purer self within, something that belongs to what stands out of time and space, and when she falls in love, she rises to that eternal candle in another, and to the self that is newly seen in her. But it belongs to a different order from the words we throw around at home. When we fall in love, when we enter a room with our beloved, we know that we can't really speak of it to anyone else. The point, the very beauty of it, is that it admits us into the realm of what cannot be said.

12      So when I come down to the monastery, I tell my friends that monks watch the film *A Fish Called Wanda* in the cloister. That most of the visitors are female, and very down to earth. The monks sell fruitcake and greeting cards and cassettes in the hermitage bookstore; they have Alcoholics Anonymous meetings once a week, and a sweet woman now lives on the property, helping care for the rooms. The monastery has a website and a fax number. There's a workout room in the "enclosure" for the monks; visiting it once, I came upon books by the Hollywood producer Robert Evans and by Woody Allen.

13      Everyone feels better when I assure them it's a mortal place, with regular human beings, balding, divorced, confused, with a mailing address I can send packages to. The infidelity sounds less glaring if I phrase it thus. But I can say all this only because I know I'm not talking about what I love and find; because this is the place where all seeking ends.

## Questions on Subject and Purpose

1. Iyer reads novels in his cell about infidelity (paragraph 5), likening what he is doing to being unfaithful or disloyal. What does he mean?

2. At the end of the essay, Iyer confesses what he tells his friends about the monastery. Why, and in what sense is this also infidelity?

3. Relatively few people withdraw to monasteries for even brief stays. Iyer is not trying to promote the benefits from withdrawing from the world for a period of time. What then might be the reason he writes of his experience?

## Questions on Strategy and Audience

1. What structural strategy does Iyer use in his opening paragraph?

2. What oppositions or divisions structure the essay?

3. How do Iyer's comments in On Writing shed light on this essay?

## Questions on Vocabulary and Style

1. Iyer is a travel writer who writes about the places he visits. Do you see any parallels between that type of writing and this essay?

2. In paragraph 5, Iyer mentions the "ringing silence"? How can silence ring?

3. What does the word *eternity* suggest to you? Is that word ever part of your thoughts?

## Writing Suggestions

1. **For Your Journal or Blog.** Put in more familiar terms, do you ever have the desire to "get away from it all"? If you do, what do you do? Do you go to a certain place? Seek a certain experience? What exactly is the "it" from which you are trying to get away? How do feel when you have "escaped"? If you have not felt that need, why not? Explore the concept—positively or negatively—in your journal or blog.

2. **For a Paragraph.** Do you ever feel that there is some aspect of you that is not publicly accessible, that you do not readily share with others? In a paragraph, explore a sense of yourself as two different persons or as wearing two different faces. What are those different persons or faces?

3. **For an Essay.** Unfortunately part of the appeal of recreational drugs and alcohol might have something to do with the experiences and the needs about which Iyer is writing: the desire to get away from pressures, to obliterate temporarily self and even consciousness. In an essay, interview a series of peers and ask them how they transcend or escape the pressures of day-to-day life. Construct a classification that explains the responses you found.

4. **For Research.** Yoga and various forms of meditation are increasingly important in the United States. To what extent do these types of practices achieve or mirror the type of experience that Iyer has? Research the topic and in an essay explain the nature and benefits of such experiences.

## For Further Study

**Focusing on Grammar and Writing.** What is a *metaphor*? Check the Glossary and Ready Reference if you are not certain. How many metaphors can you find in the essay?

**Working Together.** Split into pairs and interview one another about how each person seeks to escape pressures—see the essay topic under Writing Suggestions. Do this a number of times to get a significant body of responses. You can use the information you gathered from interviews as part of the evidence for your paper.

**Seeing Other Modes at Work.** Iyer uses an underlying narrative to help structure the essay—from the trip up into the mountains in the opening paragraph to when he "comes down" from the monastery (paragraph 12).

**Finding Connections.** A possible pairing would be with N. Scott Momaday's "The Way to Rainy Mountain" (Chapter 3).

**Exploring the Web.** Travel agencies promote vacations as a way to escape. What they suggest as escapes, however, are quite different from what Iyer does. Research the "escape" vacations that are advertised on the Web. Gather a series of examples and classify them in terms of types of destinations and activities. Present your findings in an essay that uses some visuals as well.

# The Myth of the Latin Woman: I Just Met a Girl Named Maria

Judith Ortiz Cofer

*Judith Ortiz Cofer was born in Puerto Rico in 1952. Her family settled in Patterson, New Jersey, in 1954, but frequently returned to the Island. Cofer is currently a professor of English and creative writing at the University of Georgia. She is the author of* Woman in Front of the Sun: On Becoming a Writer *(2000).*

**On Writing:** *Cofer comments about living in and writing about two cultures:* "The very term 'bilingual' tells you I have two worlds. At least now, they're very strictly separated, but when I was growing up it was a constant shift back and forth. I think my brain developed a sense of my world and my reality as being composed of two halves. But I'm not divided in them. I accept them, and I think they have basically been the difference that has allowed me to write things that are not like anybody else's."

## Before Reading

**Connecting:** Have you ever been treated as a stereotype? Have people ever expected certain things of you (good or bad) because of how you were classified in their eyes?

**Anticipating:** What expectations would you have of a "Latin woman"? Or a "Latin man"? Do those expectations coincide with those about which Cofer writes?

1   **O**n a bus trip to London from Oxford University where I was earning some graduate credits one summer, a young man, obviously fresh from a pub, spotted me and as if struck by inspiration went down on his knees in the aisle. With both hands over his heart he broke into an Irish tenor's rendition of "Maria" from *West Side Story.* My politely amused fellow passengers gave his lovely voice the round of gentle applause it deserved. Though I was not quite as amused, I managed my version of an English smile: no show of teeth, no extreme contortions of the facial muscles—I was at this time of my life practicing reserve and cool. Oh, that British control, how I coveted it. But "Maria" had followed me to London, reminding me of a prime fact of my life: you can leave the island, master the English language, and travel as far as you can, but if you are a Latina, especially one like me who so obviously belongs to Rita Moreno's gene pool, the island travels with you.

2       This is sometimes a very good thing—it may win you that extra minute of someone's attention. But with some people, the same things can make *you* an island—not a tropical paradise but an Alcatraz, a place nobody wants to visit. As a Puerto Rican girl living in the United States and wanting like most children to "belong," I resented the stereotype that my Hispanic appearance called forth from many people I met.

3       Growing up in a large urban center in New Jersey during the 1960s, I suffered from what I think of as "cultural schizophrenia." Our life was designed by my parents as a microcosm of their *casas* on the island. We spoke in Spanish, ate Puerto Rican food bought at the *bodega*, and practiced strict Catholicism at a church that allotted us a one-hour slot each week for mass, performed in Spanish by a Chinese priest trained as a missionary for Latin America.

4       As a girl I was kept under strict surveillance by my parents, since my virtue and modesty were, by their cultural equation, the same as their honor. As a teenager I was lectured constantly on how to behave as a proper *señorita*. But it was a conflicting message I received, since the Puerto Rican mothers also encouraged their daughters to look and act like women and to dress in clothes our Anglo friends and their mothers found too "mature" and flashy. The difference was, and is, cultural; yet I often felt humiliated when I appeared at an American friend's party wearing a dress more suitable to a semi-formal than to a playroom birthday celebration. At Puerto Rican festivities, neither the music nor the colors we wore could be too loud.

5       I remember Career Day in our high school, when teachers told us to come dressed as if for a job interview. It quickly became obvious that to the Puerto Rican girls "dressing up" meant wearing their mother's ornate jewelry and clothing, more appropriate (by mainstream standards) for the company Christmas party than as daily office attire. That morning I had agonized in front of my closet, trying to figure out what a "career girl" would wear. I knew how to dress for school (at the Catholic school I attended, we all wore uniforms), I knew how to dress for Sunday mass, and I knew what dresses to wear for parties at my relatives' homes. Though I do not recall the precise details of my Career Day outfit, it must have been a composite of these choices. But I remember a comment my friend (an Italian American) made in later years that coalesced my impressions of that day. She said that at the business school she was attending, the Puerto Rican girls always stood out for wearing "everything at once." She meant, of course, too much jewelry, too many accessories. On that day at school we were simply made the negative models by the nuns, who were themselves not credible fashion experts to any of us. But it was painfully obvious to me that to the others, in their tailored skirts and silk blouses, we must have seemed "hopeless" and "vulgar." Though I now know that most adolescents feel out of step much of the time, I also know that for the Puerto Rican girls of my generation that sense was intensified. The way our teachers and classmates looked at us that day in school was just a taste of the cultural clash that awaited us in the real world, where prospective employers and men on the street would often misinterpret our tight skirts and jingling bracelets as a "come-on."

6    Mixed cultural signals have perpetuated certain stereotypes—for example, that of the Hispanic woman as the "hot tamale" or sexual firebrand. It is a one-dimensional view that the media have found easy to promote. In their special vocabulary, advertisers have designated "sizzling" and "smoldering" as the adjectives of choice for describing not only the foods but also the women of Latin America. From conversations in my house I recall hearing about the harassment that Puerto Rican women endured in factories where the "bossmen" talked to them as if sexual innuendo was all they understood, and worse, often gave them the choice of submitting to their advances or being fired.

7    It is custom, however, not chromosomes, that leads us to choose scarlet over pale pink. As young girls, it was our mothers who influenced our decisions about clothes and colors—mothers who had grown up on a tropical island where the natural environment was a riot of primary colors, where showing your skin was one way to keep cool as well as to look sexy. Most important of all, on the island, women perhaps felt freer to dress and move more provocatively since, in most cases, they were protected by the traditions, mores, and laws of a Spanish/Catholic system of morality and machismo whose main rule was: *You may look at my sister, but if you touch her I will kill you.* The extended family and church structure could provide a young woman with a circle of safety in her small pueblo on the island; if a man "wronged" a girl, everyone would close in to save her family honor.

8    My mother has told me about dressing in her best party clothes on Saturday nights and going to the town's plaza to promenade with her girlfriends in front of the boys they liked. The males were thus given an opportunity to admire the women and to express their admiration in the form of *piropos:* erotically charged street poems they composed on the spot. (I have myself been subjected to a few *piropos* while visiting the island, and they can be outrageous, although custom dictates that they must never cross into obscenity.) This ritual, as I understand it, also entails a show of studied indifference on the woman's part; if she is "decent," she must not acknowledge the man's impassioned words. So I do understand how things can be lost in translation. When a Puerto Rican girl dressed in her idea of what is attractive meets a man from the mainstream culture who has been trained to react to certain types of clothing as a sexual signal, a clash is likely to take place. I remember the boy who took me to my first formal dance leaning over to plant a sloppy, over-eager kiss painfully on my mouth; when I didn't respond with sufficient passion, he remarked resentfully: "I thought you Latin girls were supposed to mature early," as if I were expected to *ripen* like a fruit or vegetable, not just grow into womanhood like other girls.

9    It is surprising to my professional friends that even today some people, including those who should know better, still put others "in their place." It happened to me most recently during a stay at a classy metropolitan hotel favored by young professional couples for weddings. Late one evening after the theater, as I walked toward my room with a colleague (a woman with whom I was coordinating an arts program), a middle-aged man in a tuxedo, with a young girl in satin and lace on his arm, stepped directly into our path. With his champagne glass extended toward me, he exclaimed "Evita!"

10       Our way blocked, my companion and I listened as the man half-recited, half-bellowed "Don't Cry for Me, Argentina." When he finished, the young girl said: "How about a round of applause for my daddy?" We complied, hoping this would bring the silly spectacle to a close. I was becoming aware that our little group was attracting the attention of the other guests. "Daddy" must have perceived this too, and he once more barred the way as we tried to walk past him. He began to shout-sing a ditty to the tune of "La Bamba"—except the lyrics were about a girl named Maria whose exploits rhymed with her name and gonorrhea. The girl kept saying "Oh, Daddy" and looking at me with pleading eyes. She wanted me to laugh along with the others. My companion and I stood silently waiting for the man to end his offensive song. When he finished, I looked not at him but at his daughter. I advised her calmly never to ask her father what he had done in the army. Then I walked between them and to my room. My friend complimented me on my cool handling of the situation, but I confessed that I had really wanted to push the jerk into the swimming pool. This same man—probably a corporate executive, well-educated, even worldly by most standards—would not have been likely to regale an Anglo woman with a dirty song in public. He might have checked his impulse by assuming that she could be somebody's wife or mother, or at least *somebody* who might take offense. But, to him, I was just an Evita or a Maria: merely a character in his cartoon-populated universe.

11       Another facet of the myth of the Latin woman in the United States is the menial, the domestic—Maria the housemaid or countergirl. It's true that work as domestics, as waitresses, and in factories is all that's available to women with little English and few skills. But the myth of the Hispanic menial—the funny maid, mispronouncing words and cooking up a spicy storm in a shiny California kitchen—has been perpetuated by the media in the same way that "Mammy" from *Gone with the Wind* became America's idea of the black woman for generations. Since I do not wear my diplomas around my neck for all to see, I have on occasion been sent to that "kitchen" where some think I obviously belong.

12       One incident has stayed with me, though I recognize it as a minor offense. My first public poetry reading took place in Miami, at a restaurant where a luncheon was being held before the event. I was nervous and excited as I walked in with notebook in hand. An older woman motioned me to her table, and thinking (foolish me) that she wanted me to autograph a copy of my newly published slender volume of verse, I went over. She ordered a cup of coffee from me, assuming I was the waitress. (Easy enough to mistake my poems for menus, I suppose.) I know it wasn't an intentional act of cruelty. Yet of all the good things that happened later, I remember that scene most clearly, because it reminded me of what I had to overcome before anyone would take me seriously. In retrospect I understand that my anger gave my reading fire. In fact, I have almost always taken any doubt in my abilities as a challenge, the result most often being the satisfaction of winning a convert, of seeing the cold, appraising eyes warm to my words, the body language change, the smile that indicates I have opened some avenue for communication. So that day as I read, I looked directly at that woman. Her lowered eyes told me she was

embarrassed at her faux pas, and when I willed her to look up at me, she graciously allowed me to punish her with my full attention. We shook hands at the end of the reading and I never saw her again. She has probably forgotten the entire incident, but maybe not.

13     Yet I am one of the lucky ones. There are thousands of Latinas without the privilege of an education or the entrees into society that I have. For them life is a constant struggle against the misconceptions perpetuated by the myth of the Latina. My goal is to try to replace the old stereotypes with a much more interesting set of realities. Every time I give a reading, I hope the stories I tell, the dreams and fears I examine in my work, can achieve some universal truth that will get my audience past the particulars of my skin color, my accent, or my clothes.

14     I once wrote a poem in which I called all Latinas "God's brown daughters." This poem is really a prayer of sorts, offered upward, but also, through the human-to-human channel of art, outward. It is a prayer for communication and for respect. In it, Latin women pray "in Spanish to an Anglo God/with a Jewish heritage," and they are "fervently hoping/that if not omnipotent, /at least He be bilingual."

## Questions on Subject and Purpose

1. What exactly is a stereotype? Where does the word *stereotype* come from?
2. What are the stereotypes or "myths" of the Latin woman that Cofer has experienced?
3. What is Cofer's announced goal in writing?

## Questions on Strategy and Audience

1. At what point in time does the essay begin? Why does Cofer start with this example?
2. How does Cofer use time or chronology as a structural device in her essay?
3. Who does Cofer imagine as her reader? How can you tell?

## Questions on Vocabulary and Style

1. What does Cofer mean when she writes, "It is custom, however, not chromosomes, that leads us to choose scarlet over pale pink"?
2. What does *machismo* (paragraph 7) mean?
3. Be prepared to define the following words: *coveted* (paragraph 1), *microcosm* (3), *coalesced* (5), *innuendo* (6), *mores* (7), *regale* (10), *menial* (11), *faux pas* (12).

## Writing Suggestions

1. **For Your Journal or Blog.** Probably most people have in one way or another been stereotyped by someone else. Stereotyping is not reserved only for individuals from particular races or cultures. Think about the wide range of stereotypes that exists in our culture, based on gender, age, physical appearance, hair or clothing styles, language dialects, or geography. In your journal or blog, make a list of such stereotypes. Focus on those that have been applied to you or on those that you have consciously or unconsciously applied to others.

2. **For a Paragraph.** Using your journal or blog writing as a prewriting exercise, take one of the stereotypes and in a paragraph develop one aspect of that stereotype. Show how it is evidenced by others or by yourself.

3. **For an Essay.** Expand your paragraph into an essay. Remember that you are fully exploring a stereotype that you have encountered or that you apply to others. Stereotypes are everywhere—they are not encountered solely by people from different cultures, races, or religions. For example, has anyone ever considered you a "dumb blonde" or a "nerd" or a "jock"? What aspects of personality do people expect when they see you as a stereotype (or do you expect when you see someone else as a stereotype)? Classify these reactions.

4. **For Research.** Think about the stereotypes that Americans commonly hold about people from another culture. Cultural differences sometimes produce a great deal of misunderstanding. Select a culture (or some aspect of that culture) that seems to be widely misunderstood by most Americans. Research the cultural differences, and present your findings in an essay. One excellent source of information would be interviews with students from other countries and cultures. Where do they see those misunderstandings occurring most frequently? Your library, online databases, and the Web can also be good sources of information when you are able to narrow your search with appropriate specific subjects and key words. Be sure to document all of your sources and to ask permission of any interviewees.

## For Further Study

**Focusing on Grammar and Writing.** Cofer uses a number of parentheses in her writing. What are the rules that govern the use of parentheses? How do they differ from a pair of commas or a pair of dashes? Look closely at how Cofer uses parentheses. Can you construct some rules or suggestions for their use based on her sentences? Under what circumstances might you enclose material within parentheses in your writing?

**Working Together.** Divide into small groups. Each group should choose one of the following assignments:

1. Explain why the men break into song—"Maria," "Don't Cry for Me, Argentina," "La Bamba."
2. Analyze the Career Day experience.
3. Explain why the young men perform *piropos*.
4. Analyze the confrontation with the man and his daughter in the "classy" hotel (paragraphs 9 and 10).
5. Analyze the concluding paragraph.

   What does each section or detail contribute to the essay?

**Seeing Other Modes at Work.** The essay uses narration to follow a Puerto Rican female from girlhood to adulthood.

**Finding Connections.** An interesting pairing is with Janice Mirikitani's "Recipe" (Chapter 6).

**Exploring the Web.** A listing of sites dealing with Cofer and her writing can be found on the Web. A good place to start is at Cofer's own Website: www.english.uga.edu/~jcofer

# The Value of Children: A Taxonomical Essay

Bernard R. Berelson

*Bernard R. Berelson (1912–1979) was born in Spokane, Washington, and received a Ph.D. from the University of Chicago. He divided his time between the academic world and the world of international development assistance. In 1962, he joined the Population Council, eventually serving as its president until his retirement in 1974. Berelson published extensively on population policy and the prospects for fertility declines in developing countries.*

*Berelson's concern with population policy is obvious in this essay reprinted from the* Annual Report *of the Population Council. Using a clear scheme of classification, Berelson analyzes the reasons why people want children.*

## Before Reading

**Connecting:** The phrase "the value of children" might seem a little unusual. What, for example, was your "value" to your parents? If you have children, in what sense do they have "value" to you?

**Anticipating:** Despite the many reasons for having or wanting children, people in many societies today consciously choose to limit the number of children that they have. How might Berelson explain this phenomenon?

1 **W**hy do people want children? It is a simple question to ask, perhaps an impossible one to answer.

2 Throughout most of human history, the question never seemed to need a reply. These years, however, the question has a new tone. It is being asked in a nonrhetorical way because of three revolutions in thought and behavior that characterize the latter decades of the twentieth century: the vital revolution in which lower death rates have given rise to the population problem and raise new issues about human fertility; the sexual revolution from reproduction; and the women's revolution, in which childbearing and -rearing no longer are being accepted as the only or even the primary roles of half the human race. Accordingly, for about the first time, the question of why people want children now can be asked, so to speak, with a straight face.

3 "Why" questions of this kind, with simple surfaces but profound depths, are not answered or settled; they are ventilated, explicated, clarified. Anything

as complex as the motives for having children can be classified in various ways, and any such taxonomy has an arbitrary character to it. This one starts with chemistry and proceeds to spirit.

## The Biological

4 Do people innately want children for some built-in reason of physiology? Is there anything to maternal instinct, or parental instinct? Or is biology satisfied with the sex instinct as the way to assure continuity?

5      In psychoanalytic thought there is talk of the "child-wish," the "instinctual drive of physiological cause," "the innate femaleness of the girl direct(ing) her development toward motherhood," and the wanting of children as "the essence of her self-realization," indicating normality. From the experimental literature, there is some evidence that man, like other animals, is innately attracted to the quality of "babyishness."

6      If the young and adults of several species are compared for differences in bodily and facial features, it will be seen readily that the nature of the difference is apparently the same almost throughout the phylogenetic scale. Limbs are shorter and much heavier in proportion to the torso in babies than in adults. Also, the head is proportionately much larger in relation to the body than is the case with adults. On the face itself, the forehead is more prominent and bulbous; the eyes large and perhaps located as far down as below the middle of the face, because of the large forehead. In addition, the cheeks may be round and protruding. In many species there is also a greater degree of overall fatness in contrast to normal adult bodies. . . . In man, as in other animals, social prescriptions and customs are not the sole or even primary factors that guarantee the rearing and protection of babies. This seems to indicate that the biologically rooted releaser of babyishness may have promoted infant care in primitive man before societies ever were formed, just as it appears to do in many animal species. Thus this releaser may have a high survival value for the species of man.[*]

7      In the human species the question of social and personal motivation distinctively arises, but that does not necessarily mean that the biology is completely obliterated. In animals the instinct to reproduce appears to be all; in humans is it something?

## The Cultural

8 Whatever the biological answer, people do not want all the children they physically can have—no society, hardly any woman. Everywhere social traditions and social pressures enforce a certain conformity to the approved childbearing pattern, whether large numbers of children in Africa or small numbers in Eastern

---

[*]Eckhard H. Hess, "Ethology and Developmental Psychology," in Paul H. Musser, ed., *Carmichael's Manual of Child Psychology*, Vol. 1 (New York: Wiley, 1970), pp. 20–21.

Europe. People want children because that is "the thing to do"—culturally sanctioned and institutionally supported, hence about as natural as any social behavior can be.

9    Such social expectations, expressed by everyone toward everyone, are extremely strong in influencing behavior even on such an important element in life as childbearing and on whether the outcome is two children or six. In most human societies, the thing to do gets done, for social rewards and punishments are among the most powerful. Whether they produce lots of children or few and whether the matter is fully conscious or not, the cultural norms are all the more effective if, as often, they are rationalized as the will of God or the hand of fate.

## The Political

10   The cultural shades off into political considerations: reproduction for the purposes of a higher authority. In a way, the human responsibility to perpetuate the species is the grandest such expression—the human family pitted politically against fauna and flora—and there always might be people who partly rationalize their own childbearing as a contribution to that lofty end. Beneath that, however, there are political units for whom collective childbearing is or has been explicitly encouraged as a demographic duty—countries concerned with national glory or competitive political position; governments concerned with the supply of workers and soldiers; churches concerned with propagation of the faith or their relative strength; ethnic minorities concerned with their political power; linguistic communities competing for position; clans and tribes concerned over their relative status within a larger setting. In ancient Rome, according to the Oxford English Dictionary, the proletariat—from the root *proles*, for progeny—were "the lowest class of the community, regarded as contributing nothing to the state but offspring": and a proletaire was "one who served the state not with his property but only with his offspring." The world has changed since then, but not all the way.

## The Economic

11   As the "new home economics" is reminding us in its current attention to the microeconomics of fertility, children are economically valuable. Not that that would come as a surprise to the poor peasant who consciously acts on the premise, but it is clear that some people want children or not for economic reasons.

12   Start with the obvious case of economic returns from children that appears to be characteristic of the rural poor. To some extent, that accounts for their generally higher fertility than that of their urban and wealthier counterparts: labor in the fields; hunting, fishing, animal care; help in the home and with the younger children; dowry and "bride-wealth"; support in later life (the individualized system of social security).

13   The economics of the case carries through on the negative side as well. It is not publicly comfortable to think of children as another consumer

durable, but sometimes that is precisely the way parents do think of them, before conception: another child or a trip to Europe; a birth deferred in favor of a new car, the $n$th child requiring more expenditure on education or housing. But observe the special characteristics of children viewed as consumer durables: they come only in whole units; they are not rentable or returnable or exchangeable or available on trial; they cannot be evaluated quickly; they do not come in several competing brands or products; their quality cannot be pretested before delivery; they usually are not available for appraisal in large numbers in one's personal experience; they themselves participate actively in the household's decisions. And in the broad view, both societies and families tend to choose standard of living over number of children when the opportunity presents itself.

## The Familial

14  In some societies people want children for what might be called familial reasons: to extend the family line or the family name; to propitiate the ancestors; to enable the proper functioning of religious rituals involving the family (e.g., the Hindu son needed to light the father's funeral pyre, the Jewish son needed to say Kaddish for the dead father). Such reasons may seem thin in the modern, secularized society but they have been and are powerful indeed in other places.

15  In addition, one class of family reasons shares a border with the following category, namely, having children in order to maintain or improve a marriage: to hold the husband or occupy the wife; to repair or rejuvenate their marriage; to increase the number of children on the assumption that family happiness lies that way. The point is underlined by its converse: in some societies the failure to bear children (or males) is a threat to the marriage and a ready cause for divorce.

16  Beyond all that is the profound significance of children to the very institution of the family itself. To many people, husband and wife alone do not seem a proper family—they need children to enrich the circle, to validate its family character, to gather the redemptive influence of offspring. Children need the family, but the family seems also to need children, as the social institution uniquely available, at least in principle, for security, comfort, assurance, and direction in a changing, often hostile, world. To most people, such a home base, in the literal sense, needs more than one person for sustenance and in generational extension.

## The Personal

17  Up to here the reasons for wanting children primarily refer to instrumental benefits. Now we come to a variety of reasons for wanting children that are supposed to bring direct personal benefits.

18  *Personal Power.* As noted, having children sometimes gives one parent power over the other. More than that, it gives the parents power over the child(ren)—in many cases, perhaps most, about as much effective power as they ever will have

the opportunity of exercising on an individual basis. They are looked up to by the child(ren), literally and figuratively, and rarely does that happen otherwise. Beyond that, having children is involved in a wider circle of power:

19    In most simple societies the lines of kinship are the lines of political power, social prestige and economic aggrandizement. The more children a man has, the more successful marriage alliances he can arrange, increasing his own power and influence by linking himself to men of greater power or to men who will be his supporters. . . . In primitive and peasant societies, the man with few children is the man of minor influence and the childless man is virtually a social nonentity.*

20    *Personal Competence.* Becoming a parent demonstrates competence in an essential human role. Men and women who are closed off from other demonstrations of competence, through lack of talent or educational opportunity or social status, still have this central one. For males, parenthood is thought to show virility, potency, *machismo.* For females it demonstrates fecundity, itself so critical to an acceptable life in many societies.

21    *Personal Status.* Everywhere parenthood confers status. It is an accomplishment open to all, or virtually all, and realized by the overwhelming majority of adult humankind. Indeed, achieving parenthood surely must be one of the two most significant events in one's life—that and being born in the first place. In many societies, then and only then is one considered a real man or a real woman.

22    Childbearing is one of the few ways in which the poor can compete with the rich. Life cannot make the poor man prosperous in material goods and services but it easily can make him rich with children. He cannot have as much of anything else worth having, except sex, which itself typically means children in such societies. Even so, the poor still are deprived by the arithmetic; they have only two or three times as many children as the rich whereas the rich have at least forty times the income of the poor.

23    *Personal Extension.* Beyond the family line, wanting children is a way to reach for personal immortality—for most people, the only way available. It is a way to extend oneself indefinitely into the future. And short of that, there is simply the physical and psychological extension of oneself in the children, here and now—a kind of narcissism: there they are and they are mine (or like me).

24    *Look in thy glass and tell the face thou viewest,*
       *Now is the time that face should form another;*
       *But if thou live, remember'd not to be,*
       *Die single, and thine image dies with thee.*

                                    —Shakespeare's Sonnets, III

25    *Personal Experience.* Among all the activities of life, parenthood is a unique experience. It is a part of life, or personal growth, that simply cannot be experienced in any other way and hence is literally an indispensable element of the

---

*Burton Benedict, "Population Regulation in Primitive Societies," in Anthony Ellison, *Population Control* (London: Penguin, 1970), pp. 176–77.

full life. The experience has many profound facets: the deep curiosity as to how the child will turn out; the renewal of self in the second chance; the reliving of one's own childhood; the redemptive opportunity; the challenge to shape another human being; the sheer creativity and self-realization involved. For a large proportion of the world's women, there was and probably still is nothing else for the grown female to do with her time and energy, as society defines her role. And for many women, it might be the most emotional and spiritual experience they ever have and perhaps the most gratifying as well.

26      *Personal Pleasure.* Last, but one hopes not least, in the list of reasons for wanting children is the altruistic pleasure of having them, caring for them, watching them grow, shaping them, being with them, enjoying them. This reason comes last on the list but it is typically the first one mentioned in the casual inquiry: "because I like children." Even this reason has its dark side, as with parents who live through their children, often to the latter's distaste and disadvantage. But that should not obscure a fundamental reason for wanting children: love.

27      There are, in short, many reasons for wanting children. Taken together, they must be among the most compelling motivations in human behavior: culturally imposed, institutionally reinforced, psychologically welcome.

## Questions on Subject and Purpose

1.  What is "the value of children"? How many different values does Berelson cite?
2.  Berelson gives positive, negative, and neutral reasons for wanting children. Is the overall effect of the essay positive, negative, or neutral?
3.  Which of Berelson's reasons seem most relevant in American society today? Which seem least relevant?

## Questions on Strategy and Audience

1.  How does Berelson organize his classification? Can you find an explicit statement of organization?
2.  Could the classification have been organized in a different way? Would that have changed the essay in any way?
3.  How effective is Berelson's introduction? His conclusion? Suggest other ways in which the essay could have begun or ended.

## Questions on Vocabulary and Style

1.  Berelson asks a number of rhetorical questions (see Glossary and Ready Reference). Why does he ask them? Does he answer them? Does he "ventilate," "explicate," and "clarify" them (paragraph 3)?
2.  Describe the tone of Berelson's essay—what does he sound like? Be prepared to support your statement with some specific illustrations from the text.
3.  Be prepared to define the following words: *taxonomy* (paragraph 3), *physiology* (4), *phylogenetic* (6), *bulbous* (6), *sanctioned* (8), *fauna and flora* (10), *demographic* (10), *consumer durable* (13), *propitiate* (14), *sustenance* (16), *aggrandizement* (19), *nonentity* (19), *machismo* (20), *fecundity* (20), *narcissism* (23).

## Writing Suggestions

1. **For Your Journal or Blog.** In your journal or blog, explore the reasons why you do or do not want to have children. Would you choose to limit the number of children you have? Why or why not?

2. **For a Paragraph.** Using your journal or blog writing as a starting point, in a paragraph classify the reasons for your decision. Focus on two or three reasons at most, and be sure to have some logical order to your arrangement.

3. **For an Essay.** Few issues are so charged in American society today as abortion. In an essay, classify the reasons why people are either pro-choice or pro-life. Despite your personal feelings on the topic, try in your essay to be as objective as possible. Do not write an argument for or against abortion or a piece of propaganda.

4. **For Research.** Studies have shown that as countries become increasingly industrialized, their population growth declines. In 2006, the average population growth rate for the world was 1.17 percent. China's growth was 0.58 percent; India's 1.46 percent; Liberia's 4.50 percent. In a research paper, explore how and why increasingly industrialized societies have changed their views on the value of children. Another possibility would be to examine those countries showing the greatest growth rates. What do they have in common and what might explain their higher numbers? Be sure to document your sources wherever appropriate.

## For Further Study

**Focusing on Grammar and Writing.** Berelson uses several different typographical devices to signal the structure of his essay (spacing to separate subdivisions, bold-faced headings, indented italic headings). Such devices are common in magazines and newspapers. What do such devices do? Are they helpful to you as a reader? In what ways? Under what circumstances? Might it be appropriate for you to use typographical devices in your writing?

**Working Together.** Finding the right order for categories within a classification scheme is important. Starting as a class, come up with some possible choices for a classification—such as evening television shows, types of music, bottles or cans of drinks found in a convenience store, newspapers, Hollywood films. Once you have generated possible topics, divide into small groups. Each group should work on constructing a classification scheme for its topic and a rationale for the order in which the categories will be presented. Each group should then report to the class as a whole.

**Seeing Other Modes at Work.** Within each of the categories that he establishes, Berelson also uses cause and effect. How, for example, within the category "familial," would a cause-and-effect analysis be made?

**Finding Connections.** Judy Brady's "I Want a Wife" (Chapter 8) makes an effective pairing. How might Berelson rewrite Brady's essay? Brady's essay involves a classification scheme as well.

**Exploring the Web.** Is the world still facing a population explosion? Have birthrates stabilized? Declined? What type of population growth will the world see during this century? Use the Web to research the topic.

# But What Do You Mean?

Deborah Tannen

*Deborah Tannen received her Ph.D. from the University of California, Berkeley. She is currently a University Professor at Georgetown University and has published widely on interpersonal communication, including a number of books intended for the general reader. Her most recent book is* You're Wearing That?: Understanding Mothers and Daughters in Conversation *(2006).*

*The selection is taken from her* Talking from 9 to 5: Women and Men at Work *published in 1994. Tannen focuses on the differences between women's and men's verbal interactions within the world of business.*

**On Writing:** *Tannen has remarked about her writing: "My style is considered very conversational and informal by academics. You could probably pick up any academic article of mine and read it. But it reads very differently from the popular writing. It's quite typical in academic writing to take a small piece of data and analyze everything you can about it. An academic piece might stay with a transcript of a single conversation, including more of the theoretical background, and making reference to other people's work. Publishers advised me in my popular writing to reduce the level of focus and detail, to bring in more sweep and more characters."*

## Before Reading

**Connecting:** Tannen's essay deals with the different ways in which men and women communicate. Can you think of a time you felt frustrated when trying to talk with someone of the opposite sex at work? In a social setting?

**Anticipating:** Of the observations made by Tannen in the essay, which seems the most familiar to you? Which seems the least familiar? Why might that be?

1　Conversation is a ritual. We say things that seem obviously the thing to say, without thinking of the literal meaning of our words, any more than we expect the question "How are you?" to call forth a detailed account of aches and pains.

2　　Unfortunately, women and men often have different ideas about what's appropriate, different ways of speaking. Many of the conversational rituals common among women are designed to take the other person's feelings into account, while many of the conversational rituals common among men are designed to maintain the one-up position, or at least avoid appearing one-down. As a result, when men and women interact—especially at work—it's often women who are at the disadvantage. Because women are not trying to avoid the one-down position, that is unfortunately where they may end up.

3    Here, the biggest areas of miscommunication.

# 1. Apologies

4    Women are often told they apologize too much. The reason they're told to stop doing it is that, to many men, apologizing seems synonymous with putting oneself down. But there are many times when "I'm sorry" isn't self-deprecating, or even an apology; it's an automatic way of keeping both speakers on an equal footing. For example, a well-known columnist once interviewed me and gave me her phone number in case I needed to call her back. I misplaced the number and had to go through the newspaper's main switchboard. When our conversation was winding down and we'd both made ending-type remarks, I added, "Oh, I almost forgot—I lost your direct number, can I get it again?" "Oh, I'm sorry," she came back instantly, even though she had done nothing wrong and *I* was the one who'd lost the number. But I understood she wasn't really apologizing; she was just automatically reassuring me she had no intention of denying me her number.

5    Even when "I'm sorry" is an apology, women often assume it will be the first step in a two-step ritual: I say "I'm sorry" and take half the blame, then you take the other half. At work, it might go something like this:

> A: When you typed this letter, you missed this phrase I inserted.
> B: Oh, I'm sorry. I'll fix it.
> A: Well, I wrote it so small it was easy to miss.

6    When both parties share blame, it's a mutual face-saving device. But if one person, usually the woman, utters frequent apologies and the other doesn't, she ends up looking as if she's taking the blame for mishaps that aren't her fault. When she's only partially to blame, she looks entirely in the wrong.

7    I recently sat in on a meeting at an insurance company where the sole woman, Helen, said "I'm sorry" or "I apologize" repeatedly. At one point she said, "I'm thinking out loud. I apologize." Yet the meeting was intended to be an informal brainstorming session, and *everyone* was thinking out loud.

8    The reason Helen's apologies stood out was that she was the only person in the room making so many. And the reason I was concerned was that Helen felt the annual bonus she had received was unfair. When I interviewed her colleagues, they said that Helen was one of the best and most productive workers—yet she got one of the smallest bonuses. Although the problem might have been outright sexism, I suspect her speech style, which differs from that of her male colleagues, masks her competence.

9      Unfortunately, not apologizing can have its price too. Since so many women use ritual apologies, those who don't may be seen as hard-edged. What's important is to be aware of how often you say you're sorry (and why), and to monitor your speech based on the reaction you get.

## 2. Criticism

10  A woman who cowrote a report with a male colleague was hurt when she read a rough draft to him and he leapt into a critical response—"Oh, that's too dry! You have to make it snappier!" She herself would have been more likely to say, "That's a really good start. Of course, you'll want to make it a little snappier when you revise."

11      Whether criticism is given straight or softened is often a matter of convention. In general, women use more softeners. I noticed this difference when talking to an editor about an essay I'd written. While going over changes she wanted to make, she said, "There's one more thing. I know you may not agree with me. The reason I noticed the problem is that your other points are so lucid and elegant." She went on hedging for several more sentences until I put her out of her misery: "Do you want to cut that part!" I asked—and of course she did. But I appreciated her tentativeness. In contrast, another editor (a man) I once called summarily rejected my idea for an article by barking, "Call me when you have something new to say."

12      Those who are used to ways of talking that soften the impact of criticism may find it hard to deal with the right-between-the-eyes style. It has its own logic, however, and neither style is intrinsically better. People who prefer criticism given straight are operating on an assumption that feelings aren't involved: "Here's the dope. I know you're good; you can take it."

## 3. Thank-Yous

13  A woman manager I know starts meetings by thanking everyone for coming, even though it's clearly their job to do so. Her "thank-you" is simply a ritual.

14      A novelist received a fax from an assistant in her publisher's office; it contained suggested catalog copy for her book. She immediately faxed him her suggested changes and said, "Thanks for running this by me," even though her contract gave her the right to approve all copy. When she thanked the assistant, she fully expected him to reciprocate: "Thanks for giving me such a quick response." Instead, he said, "You're welcome." Suddenly, rather than an equal exchange of pleasantries, she found herself positioned as the recipient of a favor. This made her feel like responding, "Thanks for nothing!"

15      Many women use "thanks" as an automatic conversation starter and closer; there's nothing literally to say thank you for. Like many rituals typical of women's conversation, it depends on the goodwill of the other to restore the balance. When the other speaker doesn't reciprocate, a woman may feel

like someone on a seesaw whose partner abandoned his end. Instead of balancing in the air, she has plopped to the ground, wondering how she got there.

## 4. Fighting

16 Many men expect the discussion of ideas to be a ritual fight—explored through verbal opposition. They state their ideas in the strongest possible terms, thinking that if there are weaknesses someone will point them out, and by trying to argue against those objections, they will see how well their ideas hold up.

17 Those who expect their own ideas to be challenged will respond to another's ideas by trying to poke holes and find weak links—as a way of *helping*. The logic is that when you are challenged you will rise to the occasion: Adrenaline makes your mind sharper, you get ideas and insights you would not have thought of without the spur of battle.

18 But many women take this approach as a personal attack. Worse, they find it impossible to do their best work in such a contentious environment. If you're not used to ritual fighting, you begin to hear criticism of your ideas as soon as they are formed. Rather than making you think more clearly, it makes you doubt what you know. When you state your ideas, you hedge in order to fend off potential attacks. Ironically, this is more likely to *invite* attack because it makes you look weak.

19 Although you may never enjoy verbal sparring, some women find it helpful to learn how to do it. An engineer who was the only woman among four men in a small company found that as soon as she learned to argue she was accepted and taken seriously. A doctor attending a hospital staff meeting made a similar discovery. She was becoming more and more angry with a male colleague who'd loudly disagreed with a point she'd made. Her better judgment told her to hold her tongue, to avoid making an enemy of this powerful senior colleague. But finally she couldn't hold it in any longer, and she rose to her feet and delivered an impassioned attack on his position. She sat down in a panic, certain she had permanently damaged her relationship with him. To her amazement, he came up to her afterward and said, "That was a great rebuttal. I'm really impressed. Let's go out for a beer after work and hash out our approaches to this problem."

## 5. Praise

20 A manager I'll call Lester had been on his new job six months when he heard that the women reporting to him were deeply dissatisfied. When he talked to them about it, their feelings erupted; two said they were on the verge of quitting because he didn't appreciate their work, and they didn't want to wait to be fired. Lester was dumbfounded: He believed they were doing a fine job. Surely, he thought, he had said nothing to give them the impression he didn't

like their work. And indeed he hadn't. That was the problem. He had said *nothing*—and the women assumed he was following the adage "If you can't say something nice, don't say anything." He thought he was showing confidence in them by leaving them alone.

21      Men and women have different habits in regard to giving praise. For example, Deirdre and her colleague William both gave presentations at a conference. Afterward, Deirdre told William, "That was a great talk!" He thanked her. Then she asked, "What did you think of mine?" and he gave her a lengthy and detailed critique. She found it uncomfortable to listen to his comments. But she assured herself that he meant well, and that his honesty was a signal that she, too, should be honest when he asked for a critique of his performance. As a matter of fact, she had noticed quite a few ways in which he could have improved his presentation. But she never got a chance to tell him because he never asked—and she felt put down. The worst part was that it seemed she had only herself to blame, since she *had* asked what he thought of her talk.

22      But had she really asked for his critique? The truth is, when she asked for his opinion, she was expecting a compliment, which she felt was more or less required following anyone's talk. When he responded with criticism, she figured, "Oh, he's playing 'Let's critique each other' "—not a game she'd initiated, but one which she was willing to play. Had she realized he was going to criticize her and not ask her to reciprocate, she would never have asked in the first place.

23      It would be easy to assume that Deirdre was insecure, whether she was fishing for a compliment or soliciting a critique. But she was simply talking automatically, performing one of the many conversational rituals that allow us to get through the day. William may have sincerely misunderstood Deirdre's intention—or may have been unable to pass up a chance to one-up her when given the opportunity.

## 6. Complaints

24  "Troubles talk" can be a way to establish rapport with a colleague. You complain about a problem (which shows that you are just folks) and the other person responds with a similar problem (which puts you on equal footing). But while such commiserating is common among women, men are likely to hear it as a request to *solve* the problem.

25      One woman told me she would frequently initiate what she thought would be pleasant complaint-airing sessions at work. She'd talk about situations that bothered her just to talk about them, maybe to understand them better. But her male office mate would quickly tell her how she could improve the situation. This left her feeling condescended to and frustrated. She was delighted to see this very impasse in a section in my book *You Just Don't Understand*, and showed it to him. "Oh," he said, "I see the problem. How can we solve it?" Then they both laughed, because it had happened again: He

short-circuited the detailed discussion she'd hoped for and cut to the chase of finding a solution.

Sometimes the consequences of complaining are more serious: A man might take a woman's lighthearted griping literally, and she can get a reputation as a chronic malcontent. Furthermore, she may be seen as not up to solving the problems that arise on the job.

## 7. Jokes

I heard a man call in to a talk show and say, "I've worked for two women and neither one had a sense of humor. You know, when you work with men, there's a lot of joking and teasing." The show's host and the guest (both women) took his comment at face value and assumed the women this man worked for were humorless. The guest said, "Isn't it sad that women don't feel comfortable enough with authority to see the humor?" The host said, "Maybe when more women are in authority roles, they'll be more comfortable with power." But although the women this man worked for *may* have taken themselves too seriously, it's just as likely that they each had a terrific sense of humor, but maybe the humor wasn't the type he was used to. They may have been like the woman who wrote to me: "When I'm with men, my wit or cleverness seems inappropriate (or lost!) so I don't bother. When I'm with my women friends, however, there's no hold on puns or cracks and my humor is fully appreciated."

The types of humor women and men tend to prefer differ. Research has shown that the most common form of humor among men is razzing, teasing, and mock-hostile attacks, while among women it's self-mocking. Women often mistake men's teasing as genuinely hostile. Men often mistake women's mock self-deprecation as truly putting themselves down.

Women have told me they were taken more seriously when they learned to joke the way the guys did. For example, a teacher who went to a national conference with seven other teachers (mostly women) and a group of administrators (mostly men) was annoyed that the administrators always found reasons to leave boring seminars, while the teachers felt they had to stay and take notes. One evening, when the group met at a bar in the hotel, the principal asked her how one such seminar had turned out. She retorted, "As soon as you left, it got much better." He laughed out loud at her response. The playful insult appealed to the men—but there was a trade-off. The women seemed to back off from her after this. (Perhaps they were put off by her using joking to align herself with the bosses.)

There is no "right" way to talk. When problems arise, the culprit may be style differences—and *all* styles will at times fail with others who don't share or understand them, just as English won't do you much good if you try to speak to someone who knows only French. If you want to get your message across, it's not a question of being "right": it's a question of using language that's shared—or at least understood.

## Questions on Subject and Purpose

1. What does Tannen mean by her first sentence, "Conversation is a ritual."
2. Early in the essay, Tannen remarks that women and men have different goals or values in their conversation. What are they?
3. Why might it be important for both women and men in the workplace to understand how they miscommunicate? Who would be particularly interested in reading the book from which this essay is taken?

## Questions on Strategy and Audience

1. What types of evidence or examples does Tannen use in her essay?
2. Why use these little scenes—including giving names to the people involved? Why not just simply list the problem areas?
3. Judging simply from the text of the essay, who does Tannen imagine as her primary reader? On what basis do you make that judgment?

## Questions on Vocabulary and Style

1. Why might Tannen have chosen to introduce herself into the scenes using a first-person pronoun ("I")?
2. How often in the essay does Tannen address her readers as "you"? What is the effect of using this pronoun?
3. Be prepared to define the following words: *self-deprecating* (paragraph 4), *intrinsically* (12), *reciprocate* (14), *contentious* (18), *rapport* (24), *commiserating* (24), *retorted* (29).

## Writing Suggestions

1. **For Your Journal or Blog.** In preparation for writing, keep a list of times during the next few days in which you noticed differences between the conversational styles of men and women in social interactions. In addition to observing and listening, ask friends of both sexes for examples of conflict, misunderstanding, or hurt feelings. Given Tannen's research, it is more likely that women will perceive problems than men.
2. **For a Paragraph.** Using the information that you gathered, create a scene like one of Tannen's in which you dramatize a misunderstanding between a young man and a young woman.
3. **For an Essay.** Think about other situations in which our speech is simply ritualistic—that what we say is almost programmed. Text messaging is particularly rich in such automatically written responses that we insert without any thought (for example, LOL). Classify the types of automatic responses used in texting; how might they be classified in terms of context or meaning?
4. **For Research.** Tannen writes: "The types of humor women and men tend to prefer differ." Research the differences between what men and women find funny. What are the differences? In jokes? In television shows or films? In books or comics? In stand-up comedy? Offer a classification scheme similar to Tannen's. Be sure to document your sources.

## For Further Study

**Focusing on Grammar and Writing.** What role does parallelism play in this essay? Think particularly of the larger structures in the essay.

**Working Together.** Break into small groups by gender and brainstorm some situations in which you or a friend have experienced a misunderstanding in a social or dating situation. Use this brainstorming session as a preliminary exercise for the journal/blog and paragraph writing suggestions.

**Seeing Other Modes at Work.** In the essay Tannen uses narration to relate situations and comparison and contrast to show how women and men use language in different ways.

**Finding Connections.** A pairing would be Allison Perkins's "Mission Iraq" (Chapter 2).

**Exploring the Web.** Are there differences between the ways in which women/girls and men/boys learn? What are the arguments in favor of separating the sexes in school systems—elementary, middle, high, college? Do some instructional methods work better with one sex than with the other? You will need to narrow your research topic; choose an aspect of classroom education and research it on the Web and in online sources. Use a classification scheme to organize your information.

# 5

# COMPARISON AND CONTRAST

# GETTING READY TO WRITE

## What Is Comparison and Contrast?

Whenever you decide between two alternatives, you engage in comparison and contrast. Which DVD player is the best value or has the most attractive set of features? Which professor's section of Introductory Sociology should you register for in the spring semester? In both cases, you make a selection by comparing alternatives on a series of relevant points and then deciding which has the greatest advantages.

In comparison and contrast, subjects are set in opposition in order to reveal similarities and differences. Comparison involves finding similarities among two or more things, people, or ideas; contrast involves finding differences. Comparison and contrast writing tasks can involve then, three activities: emphasizing similarities, emphasizing differences, or emphasizing both.

Visual images can illustrate comparison and contrast. Look at the Venn diagram, which shows two or more subjects that share some, but not all, things.

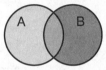

In a cartoon originally published in the *Utne Reader*, the Tour de France (the famous bicycle race) is compared with a Tour de U.S.A. (which does not exist). By changing the background and the bikers' eyes, the artist creates a vivid contrast.

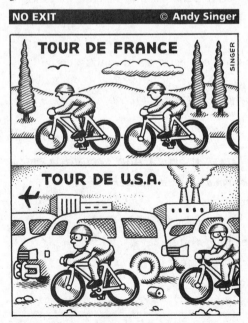

Biking is a popular recreation in the United States, but not always a safe sport in America's urbanized areas. *Andy Singer*

Comparison and contrast often involves visual displays of similarities and differences—things such as lists, tables, and charts—but it also occurs with just words. John Fischer uses comparison in this paragraph to emphasize the similarities between Ukrainians and Texans:

> The Ukrainians are the Texans of Russia. They believe they can fight, drink, ride, sing, and make love better than anyone else in the world, and if pressed will admit it. Their country, too, was a borderland—that's what Ukraine means—and like Texas it was settled by outlaws, horse thieves, land-hungry farmers, and people who hadn't made a go of it somewhere else. Some of these hard cases banded together, long ago, to raise hell and livestock. They called themselves Cossacks, and they would have felt right at home in any Western movie. Even today the Ukrainians cherish a wistful tradition of horsemanship, although most of them would feel as uncomfortable in a saddle as any Dallas banker. They still like to wear knee-high boots and big, furry hats, made of gray or Persian lamb, which is the local equivalent of the Stetson.

Fischer emphasizes only similarities. He tries to help his readers understand a foreign country by likening it to a place far more familiar to most Americans. Fischer concentrates on four similarities:

Ukrainians and Texans:

1. Believe that they are good at fighting, drinking, singing, making love
2. Are descended from people willing to take risks
3. Cherish a tradition of horsemanship
4. Wear high boots and big hats

Henry Petroski, in his essay "The Gleaming Silver Bird and the Rusty Iron Horse," contrasts air travel and train travel, emphasizing their differences:

> The airplane lets us fly and forget. We are as gods, even in coach class, attended by young, smiling stewards and stewardesses who bring us food, drink, and entertainment. From the window of the airplane we marvel at the cities far beneath us, at the great land formations and waterways, and at the clouds. Political boundaries are forgotten, and the world is one. Everything is possible.
>
> Nothing is forgotten on the train, however. The right of way is strewn with the detritus of technology, and technology's disruptiveness is everywhere apparent. Outside the once-clean picture window of the train, which has probably slowed down to pass over a deteriorating roadbed under repair, one sees not heaven in the clouds but the graveyards of people and machines. One cannot help but notice how technology has changed the land and the lives of those who live beside the rails. The factory abandoned is a blight not easily removed; the neglected homes of myriad factory (and railroad?) workers are not easily restored.

Petroski treats his two subjects in two separate paragraphs, emphasizing their differences. A simple outline of the paragraphs would look like this:

*Airplanes*

1. We are as gods, passing over the earth—we see only the "big" picture, the world at a distance.
2. The view is an optimistic one—differences are eliminated.

*Trains*

1. We see through the dirty train windows all of the decay and deterioration that borders railroad tracks. We see the "grimy" details, not the "big" picture.

2. The view is a pessimistic one—we are constantly reminded of the "cost" of technology.

Like every writing task, comparison and contrast is done to achieve a particular purpose. In practical situations, you use it to help make a decision. You compare DVD players or college professors in order to make an intelligent choice. In academic situations, comparison and contrast allows you to analyze two or more subjects carefully and thoroughly on the basis of a series of shared similarities or differences.

 **IN THE READINGS, LOOK FOR**

| | **Comparison and contrast** |
|---|---|
| Alice Mathias, "Fakebook" | One Website, two groups of users with quite different intentions |
| William Zinsser, "The Transaction" | Contradictory answers to the same questions |
| David Sedaris, "Remembering My Childhood" | Funny account of two very different childhoods |
| Suzanne Britt, "Neat vs Sloppy" | Comic exaggeration of two different stereotypes of people |
| Danzy Senna, "Color of Love" | Similarities and differences with a family member |
| Meghan Daum, "Virtual Love" | Two "romances" with one person |

## How Do You Choose a Subject?

Many times, especially on examinations in academic courses, the subject for comparison and contrast is chosen for you. On an economics examination you are asked, "What are the main differences between the public and private sectors?" In political science you are to "compare the political platforms of the Republican and Democratic parties in the last presidential election." At other times, however, you must choose the subject for comparison and contrast.

The choice of subject is crucial. Try to limit your paragraph or essay to subjects that have obvious similarities or differences. Alice Mathias contrasts how she and her peers playfully use Facebook with how serious adults seek to use it as a networking tool. William Zinsser compares his writing process to Dr. Brock's. David Sedaris contrasts his friend's exotic, or at least unusual childhood experiences, to his own ordinary ones. Suzanne Britt contrasts "sloppy" and "neat" people; Danzy Senna compares and contrasts herself with her grandmother; and Meghan Daum is shocked to find that her "virtual love" Pete is much better than the "real" Pete.

Two other cautions are also important. First, be sure that you have a reason for making the comparison or contrast. You want to reveal something new or important to give your comparison or contrast an interesting thesis. Meghan Daum begins a "virtual," that is, electronic online, relationship with an admirer named Pete. The romance flourishes until she meets the "real" Pete. Although the two have an electronic, but "old-fashioned kind of courtship," although neither had lied or pretended to be someone else, although the two "real" people are the same as the two "virtual" people, the romance dies instantly when they meet each other in person. Daum uses comparison and contrast to make a point not just about this one relationship, but about our needs and our frustrations in trying to establish lasting relationships in contemporary society. She comments, "our need to worship somehow fuses with our need to be worshiped."

Second, limit your comparison and contrast to important points; do not try to cover everything. Obviously David Sedaris and his friend Hugh had very different childhoods, but Sedaris concentrates on a limited number of funny experiences.

---

 **IN THE READINGS, LOOK FOR**

|  | **Choice of subjects** |
|---|---|
| Alice Mathias, "Fakebook" | Facebook and its users |
| William Zinsser, "The Transaction" | Advice from a classic "informal guide" to writing |
| David Sedaris, "Remembering My Childhood" | Comic contrast of two childhoods |
| Suzanne Britt, "Neat vs. Sloppy" | Comic exploration of two stereotypes |
| Danzy Senna, "Color of Love" | Exploring identity through family |
| Meghan Daum, "Virtual Love" | Online dating and romance |

---

## Must You Always Find Both Similarities and Differences?

You can compare and contrast only if there is some basic similarity between two subjects: John Fischer compares two groups of people—Ukrainians and Texans; Henry Petroski compares two modes of transportation—the airplane and the railroad. There is no point in comparing two totally unrelated subjects; for example, the mind could be compared to a computer since both process information, but there would be no reason to compare a computer and a piece of fruit. Remember, too, that some similarities are obvious and hence are not worth writing about. It would be pointless for William Zinsser to observe that both he and Dr. Brock write on word processors, use dictionaries, or work best in a quiet room. Some similarities, however, are important and should be mentioned. Danzy Senna sees a number of similarities between herself and her grandmother—both are writers, both are strong-willed and outspoken women. At the same time, Senna is struck by the differences in their backgrounds and expectations.

Once you have chosen your subject, make a list of possible points of comparison and contrast. Be sure that those points are shared. Zinsser, for example, organizes his comparison and contrast around six questions. To each of the six, Zinsser gives first Dr. Brock's response and then his own. The contrast depends on the two responses to each to the six questions. If Brock had answered only one group of three and Zinsser a different group of three, the contrast would not have worked.

Be careful when you create analogies, similes, and metaphors. If you try to be too clever, your point will seem forced. But do not avoid such devices altogether. Used sparingly, these compressed comparisons can be evocative and effective.

## PREWRITING TIPS FOR WRITING COMPARISON AND CONTRAST

1.  Jot down ideas on subjects that might be compared or contrasted. Remember, comparison involves finding similarities among two or more things—typically things that initially appear to be different. Contrast involves finding differences among things that seem quite similar.

2.  Under each possible subject, make a list of similarities or of differences. Do not worry about an order, just generate ideas.

3.  Go back over your lists and make sure that the similarities or differences are important enough to write about. The idea is not to generate as many similarities or differences as possible, but to find interesting and significant points.

4.  Narrow down to a possible topic and then explain in one sentence (a thesis) why you are making this comparison or contrast.

5.  Check your list to see that all of the items on it are phrased in parallel form. Check the Glossary and Ready Reference at the back of this text for examples of parallelism.

## WRITING

### How Do You Structure a Comparison and Contrast Essay?

Comparison and contrast is not only an intellectual process, but it is also a structural pattern that can be used to organize paragraphs and essays. In comparing and contrasting two subjects, three organizational models are available.

*Subject by Subject (all of subject A, then all of subject B)*

SUBJECT A

Point 1
Point 2
Point 3

SUBJECT B

Point 1
Point 2
Point 3

The subject-by-subject pattern works best for short essays. All of subject A is treated in a paragraph or two; all of subject B is treated in another group of paragraphs. The points of comparison or contrast are presented in the same order and in the same grammatical form in each of the paragraphs. If your paper is fairly long and if the points of comparison and contrast are somewhat complicated, the subject-by-subject pattern might not be appropriate. In a longer, multipage paper, it is potentially more difficult for your reader to remember the analysis of subject A when reading the analysis of subject B.

*Point by Point (point 1 in A, then point 1 in B)*

SUBJECT A, POINT 1/ SUBJECT B, POINT 1
SUBJECT A, POINT 2/ SUBJECT B, POINT 2
SUBJECT A, POINT 3/ SUBJECT B, POINT 3

William Zinsser's comparison of his writing process with that of Dr. Brock's uses a point-by-point pattern of contrast. The two authors take turns responding to a series of six questions asked by students. The essay then follows a pattern that can be described as A1B1, A2B2, A3B3, A4B4, A5B5, A6B6. In replying to the fourth question, for example, about whether or not feeling "depressed or unhappy" will affect their writing, Brock and Zinsser reply:

"Probably it will," Dr. Brock replied. "Go fishing. Take a walk."
"Probably it won't," I said. "If your job is to write every day, you learn to do it like any other job."

The point-by-point, or alternating, pattern emphasizes the individual points of comparison or contrast rather than the subject as a whole. In college courses, students who use this pattern usually write a group of sentences or a paragraph for each point, alternating between subject A and subject B. If you use the alternating pattern, you must decide how to order your points—for instance, by beginning or by ending with the strongest or most significant.

*Mixed Sequence (includes subject by subject and point by point)*

SUBJECT A

POINT 1
POINT 2

SUBJECT B

POINT 1
POINT 2

SUBJECT A, POINT 3/ SUBJECT B, POINT 3

In longer pieces of writing, authors typically mix the subject-by-subject and the point-by-point patterns. Such an arrangement provides variety and can make the points of comparison or contrast much more vivid for the reader.

Much of the examination writing that you do in college probably should be organized in the subject-by-subject or point-by-point patterns, because these are the clearest structures for short responses. Many of the essays you encounter in magazines and newspapers use the mixed pattern in order to achieve flexibility and variety.

---

### IN THE READINGS, LOOK FOR

| | Primary organization of essay |
|---|---|
| Alice Mathias, "Fakebook" | Subject-by-subject, online community theater versus social networking tool |
| William Zinsser, "The Transaction" | Point-by-point, but what is different about paragraphs 9 through 11? |
| David Sedaris, "Remembering My Childhood" | Point-by-point, contrasting types of experiences |
| Suzanne Britt, "Neat vs. Sloppy" | Subject-by-subject, "sloppy" then "neat" |
| Danzy Senna, "Color of Love" | Subject-by-subject—generational similarities and differences |
| Meghan Daum, "Virtual Love" | Subject-by-subject—"virtual" Pete then "real" Pete |

---

## How Do You Use Analogy, Metaphor, and Simile?

Writing a comparison often involves constructing an analogy, that is, an extended comparison in which something complex or unfamiliar is likened to something simple or familiar. The reason for making the analogy is to help the reader more easily understand or visualize the more complex or unfamiliar subject. For example, if you are trying to explain how the hard disk on your computer is organized, you might use the analogy of a file cabinet. The hard disk, you write, is the file cabinet itself, which is partitioned into directories (the file drawers), each of which contains subdirectories (the hanging folders), which in turn contain the individual files (the manila folders in which the individual documents are stored). The way in which your software program displays your files (and the icons it uses) suggests this metaphor.

Analogies are also used to provide a new way of seeing something. J. Anthony Lukas, for example, explains his attraction to the game of pinball by an analogy:

> Pinball is a metaphor for life, pitting man's skill, nerve, persistence, and luck against the perverse machinery of human existence. The playfield is rich with rewards: targets that bring huge scores, bright lights, chiming bells, free balls, and extra games. But it is replete with perils, too: culs-de-sac, traps, gutters, and gobble holes down which the ball may disappear forever.

This analogy does not seek to explain the unfamiliar. Probably every reader has seen a pinball machine. Rather, the analogy invites the reader to see the game in a fresh way. The suggested similarity might help the reader understand why arcade games such as pinball have a particular significance or attraction.

Two common forms of analogy used frequently in writing are metaphor and simile. A *metaphor* identifies one thing with another. When Henry Petroski contrasts air travel and train travel, he uses metaphor—the airplane is a "silver bird" and the train is an "iron horse." A *simile*, as its name suggests, is also a comparison based on a point or points of similarity. A simile differs from a metaphor by using the word *like* or *as* to link the two things being compared. In a sense, a simile suggests, rather than directly establishes, the comparison. On the February morning when his father died, Scott Russell Sanders in "The Inheritance of Tools" (Chapter 3) saw that the ice "coated the windows like cataracts." Seventeenth-century poet Robert Herrick found a witty similarity: "Fain would I kiss my Julia's dainty leg, / Which is as white and hairless as an egg."

 **DRAFTING TIPS FOR WRITING COMPARISON AND CONTRAST**

1. Decide on whether the best organizational strategy will be subject-by-subject, point-by-point, or a mix of the two. Plan the organizational strategy of your paper with an outline.

2. Decide on a rationale for the ordering the points of comparison or contrast. What will come first and why? Why will come last and why? Try different orders.

3. Rate each point of comparison or contrast. Is each one really significant or interesting? Eliminate any points that seem minor or trivial.

4. Check to see if your paragraphing in the essay reveals the structure of the essay. Can your reader clearly see your organizational plan?

5. Find a peer reader, tutor, or your instructor to read your draft. Ask for suggestions about how the paper might be improved. Consider each suggestion.

# REVISING

## How Do You Revise a Comparison and Contrast Essay?

Comparison and contrast is intended to isolate similarities and differences between two or more subjects. It is a fundamental process by which the mind understands things. Like all writing tasks, comparison and contrast writing is done for a purpose—in this instance, to help the reader make a choice or to help the reader clarify and understand the subject. Although comparison and contrast writing can be funny and entertaining, generally it has a serious, informative purpose. For that reason, make sure your comparison and contrast essay is clearly and logically organized. When revising a comparison and contrast essay, pay particular attention to the following cautions: avoid the obvious and keep the analysis logically structured.

**Avoiding the Obvious**    Your paper needs to be both informative and interesting enough to hold your readers' attention. Do not compare and contrast points that are obvious. When John McPhee compares Florida and California oranges (see the heading As a Critical Reading Strategy), he focuses only on the differences that are important, explaining why oranges from two different states are so different. He contrasts them on the thickness of their skins, on their juiciness, and on the ease of peeling and separating segments. Readers tire easily of essays that offer only the obvious. Think again about what you have chosen to write. Ask a peer reader to assess your essay's interest. Does it tell readers only what they already know? Are the points of comparison and contrast significant or trivial? If there is a problem, you need to change your points of similarity or contrast or find a new subject.

**Keeping the Analysis Logically Structured**    In addition to considering three organizational patterns (subject-by-subject, point-by-point, and mixed) in comparison and contrast writing, rememeber three organizational principles: The points of comparison and contrast must be (1) identical in both subjects, (2) taken in the same order, and (3) phrased in parallel grammatical form. You will guarantee a clear, organized, easily followed essay if you adhere to these three principles.

If you are using the subject-by-subject pattern, it is fairly easy to signal to your reader when you have finished one subject and started another. Typically, the essay will be divided by paragraphs in a way that marks the switch from one subject to another. If you are using the point-by-point or a mixed method, you will need to provide step or sequence markers for your reader to signal when you are moving to the next point. Have you called out the points (for example, *first, second, next, then*) or used transitional words or phrases to signal the transition? Ask a peer reader if your essay is easy to follow; if not, identify the areas that are confusing.

Parallel structures—that is, items that are phrased in grammatically similar ways—are also important. Underline each of the points you are using. Have you cast those points in grammatical structures that are parallel in form?

For help with parallelism, check the Glossary and Ready Reference at the back of this text.

Have you arranged the points of comparison and contrast in an order that makes sense? If the points are of the same relative importance, you can be flexible in ordering them. If the points can be arranged from greater to lesser significance, then you need to arrange them in a descending or an ascending order. Decide whether you want to start with the most significant difference or end with it.

---

## IN THE READINGS, LOOK FOR

| | **Analogies, transitions, and arrangement** |
|---|---|
| Alice Mathias, "Fakebook" | Trace the use of the metaphor of Facebook as "online community theater" |
| William Zinsser, "The Transaction" | Notice how paragraphing signals arrangement |
| David Sedaris, "Remembering My Childhood" | Notice transitions from one narrative episode to another |
| Suzanne Britt, "Neat vs. Sloppy" | Analyze why there is no concluding paragraph |
| Danzy Senna, "Color of Love" | Explain where the essay ends and why there |
| Meghan Daum, "Virtual Love" | Notice use of analogies—similes and metaphors |

---

## REVISING TIPS FOR WRITING COMPARISON AND CONTRAST

1. Assess the significance of your subject and your approach to it. Do not waste your readers' time on the obvious or the trivial.

2. Experiment with the paper's organizational strategy. Could it be arranged in another way? Could the points be put in a different order? Experiment with changes.

3. Look again at your introduction. Ask friends to read it. Does it make them want to keep reading? If not, rewrite your opening.

4. Honestly evaluate your conclusion. Did you just stop or did you really write a conclusion? Does your final paragraph seem to emphasize the points you are making in the essay? Does it reinforce your thesis?

5. Check your title. Every paper needs a real title—not something descriptive such as "Comparison and Contrast Essay." If necessary, write several other titles before choosing a final one.

# STUDENT ESSAY

## Sample Student Essay

As part of the library research paper unit in freshman English, Alicia Gray's class had been talking about searching their school's online library catalog for relevant books. The instructor had mentioned a number of times that card catalogs could be searched for both subjects and keywords—the software program allowed for both. To give the students practice in both kinds of searches, Meghan, their instructor, gave them a worksheet to do for homework. On the way out of class, Alicia stopped and remarked to her instructor, "I always just do a keyword search," she said, "and it always seems like I find plenty of material. Since we have the capability to do a keyword search, isn't doing a subject search just unnecessary and even old-fashioned?" "Do the worksheet," Meghan replied. "Maybe you could compare and contrast the two methods for your essay, which is due next week." A week later, Alicia brought to class the following rough draft of her essay comparing keyword and subject searches.

## First Draft

Subject vs. Keyword Searches

When it is time to start gathering information for your research paper in Freshman English, you will need to consult our Library's on-line catalog. The card catalog is a listing of the books that our library holds. Those books are cataloged, or listed, by author, title, subject, and keyword. Since normally we start by looking for books about our intended topic—rather than for specific titles by specific authors—we must start with either subject searches or keyword searches. What exactly is the difference between these two types of searches and how do you know when to use each?

When librarians refer to a "subject" search, they mean something quite specific and different from a "keyword." The term subject in library catalogs refers to a large listing of subject headings that are used by the Library of Congress to catalog a book. In fact, if you want to do a subject search in a library catalog, you don't start with the catalog itself. Instead you go to a multivolume series of books entitled the <u>Library of Congress Subject Headings.</u> Those books list alphabetically the various headings under which the Library of Congress files books. That listing is complete with cross-references, that is, with references to broader terms and to narrower, more specific terms. When catalogers at the Library of Congress look at new books, they do not just randomly assign a heading or a group of headings to the book, nor do they take the heading from a word in the book's title. Instead, they choose a heading or headings from the published list.

The principle behind the subject headings is to group related books under one heading. So instead of filing books about "the death penalty," "capital punishment," "death by lethal injection" under three separate subject headings, the Library of Congress uses a single subject heading ("capital punishment") and then provides cross-references from any other synonymous terms. The subject heading can also be followed by a whole series of other headings (for example, "capital punishment—history"). These other, more specific headings are very important because the Library of Congress always tries to assign the most specific subject heading to a book that it can. You never want to look under a large general heading if a more specific one is used. And how do you know if a more specific heading exists? You need to check the printed collection of headings currently in use. Subject headings impose a control on the vocabulary words used for headings.

In contrast, keyword searches look for words that are present somewhere in the book's record—typically in its title or subtitle, its author, its publisher. A keyword search retrieves information only when that word or group of words that you have entered appear in a record. That means there is no attempt at controlling the vocabulary. A book that had the phrase "the death penalty" somewhere in the title could be retrieved only if you typed in the keywords "death" and "penalty." A book on the same subject that used "capital punishment" would never appear—and keyword searches do not suggest related synonyms to you. Moreover, the presence of the keywords would not necessarily mean that the book would be about the "death penalty" in the sense of "capital punishment." The words could appear in the title of novel or a collection of poems; they could refer to vastly different and unrelated circumstances—"the death penalty in ancient Rome." And, if you don't indicate the relationship (for example, immediately next to each other) that the two (or more) terms are to have, you'll end up retrieving a mountain of records that have the terms "death" and "penalty" somewhere in the record (for example, "The Penalty of Life: The Death of John Sayce").

Keyword searches have an advantage in that they can be used to find the very specific words for which you might be looking. Maybe those words haven't yet been added to the subject headings. Since subject headings depend on printed lists, subject headings are slow to react to new fields of study or new technologies.

## Comments

Alicia shared the opening paragraphs of her rough draft with a classmate during in-class peer editing. The instructor had asked the students to concentrate on the organizational pattern used in the body of the essay and on the introduction. After reading Alicia's paper, her partner Sara LaBarca offered some advice on revising the draft. "You have lots of information," she said, "but your main pattern of development is subject-by-subject except for the fifth paragraph where you switch to point-by-point. Maybe you should try doing more with the point-to-point; otherwise, by the time your readers come to the second half of your essay, they might forget the contrasts you established in the first half."

"I also think you need a strong introduction," she added. "You have a good thesis statement, but, well, frankly, I found the opening paragraph a little boring." Alicia tried to take Sara's advice and revised the opening of her essay and reorganized the body.

## Revised Draft

### Minimizing the Guesswork in a Library Search

The Cecil County Community College Library has twenty books dealing with the death penalty, but unless you pay attention to the next couple of pages, you will never find most of them. Why? Because no single search strategy will lead you to all twenty books.

Looking for book sources is more complicated than you might think. A successful search will require two different types of searches—a subject and a keyword search. They are very different kinds of searches with different rules and results. But to maximize your sources for a quality research paper, you will need to know how to do both.

In both subject and keyword searches, you are looking for single words or phrases that will lead you to the books you need. Those subject or keyword terms come from two different places. The term subject in library catalogs refers to a large alphabetized listing of subject headings that are assigned by the Library of Congress when cataloging a book. You find an appropriate heading not by guessing as you stand at a computer terminal, but by looking in a multivolume series of books entitled Library of Congress Subject Headings. When catalogers at the Library of Congress look at new books, they do not just randomly assign a heading or a group of headings to the book, nor do they necessarily take the heading from a word in the book's title. Instead, they choose a heading or headings from the published list. A keyword, on the other hand, is a significant word, generally a noun, that is typically in a book's title or subtitle. Unlike a subject search where the categories are "controlled" (that is, someone has predetermined what subject headings will be used), a keyword search is, in one sense, guesswork. You think of an important word or phrase that might describe the topic about which you want information and you try that. Just like any time you guess, though, there are risks. A keyword search retrieves information only when that word or group of words that you have entered appears in a record.

"If I have the choice of having to look things up in a set of books or of just guessing, I'll guess," you might reply. But before you reject subject searches, consider the problem of synonyms—that is, words or phrases that mean roughly the same thing. A controlled subject search groups related books under one heading. So instead of filing books about "the death penalty," "capital punishment," and "death by lethal injection" under three separate subject headings, the Library of Congress uses a single subject heading ("capital punishment") and then provides cross-references from any other synonymous terms. In contrast, you can only retrieve a book in a keyword search if it has those specific words somewhere in its record. A book that had the phrase "the death penalty" somewhere in the title could be retrieved only if you typed in the keywords "death" and "penalty." A book on the same subject that used "capital punishment" would never appear, and keyword searches do not suggest related synonyms to you. Moreover, the presence of the keywords would not necessarily mean that the book would be about the "death penalty" in the sense of "capital punishment." The words could appear in the title of a novel or a collection of poems; they could refer to vastly different and unrelated circumstances— "the death penalty in ancient Rome." And, if you don't indicate the relationship (for example, immediately next to each other) that the two (or more) terms are to have, you'll end up retrieving a mountain of records that have the terms "death" and "penalty" somewhere in the record (for example, "The Penalty of Life: The Death of John Sayce").

Keyword searches have some distinct advantages, however. Since subject searches are controlled, the Library of Congress tries to find existing appropriate terms under which to file books—even if they end up having to use more general terms. Although new subject headings are regularly added to the lists, emerging fields and technologies are rarely represented adequately in the subject headings. On the other hand, since keywords do not depend on any pre-existing published categories and since no one has tried to classify those keywords into categories, keywords can be the best way to look for books on new and emerging subjects. In that sense, a keyword can be far more precise (if you guess the right one!) than a subject heading.

## SOME THINGS TO REMEMBER WHEN WRITING COMPARISON AND CONTRAST

1. Limit your comparison and contrast to subjects that can be adequately developed in a paragraph or an essay.
2. Make sure that the subjects you are comparing and contrasting have some basic similarities. Make a list of similarities and differences before you begin to write.
3. Decide why the comparison or contrast is important. What does it reveal? Remember to make the reason clear to the reader.
4. Decide what points of comparison or contrast are the most important or the most revealing. In general, omit any points of comparison that would be obvious to anybody.
5. Decide which of the three patterns of comparison and contrast best fits your purpose: subject-by-subject, point-by-point, or mixed.
6. Remember to make clear to your reader when you are switching from one subject to another or from one point of comparison to another.

## SEEING COMPARISON AND CONTRAST IN OTHER CONTEXTS

### As a Literary Strategy

Poet Martin Espada uses comparison and contrast to structure his poem "Coca-Cola and Coco Frio." As you read the poem, notice the points of comparison and contrast that Espada develops and think about what the comparison and contrast is intended to reveal.

# Coca-Cola and Coco Frio

Martin Espada

*On his first visit to Puerto Rico,*
*island of family folklore,*
*the fat boy wandered*
*from table to table*
*with his mouth open.*
*At every table, some great-aunt*
*would steer him with cool-spotted hands*
*to a glass of Coca-Cola.*
*One even sang to him, in all the English*
*she could remember, a Coca-Cola jingle*
*from the forties. He drank obediently, though*
*he was bored with this portion, familiar*
*from soda fountains in Brooklyn.*

*Then, at a roadside stand off the beach, the fat boy*
*opened his mouth to coco frio, a coconut*
*chilled, then scalped by a machete*
*so that a straw could inhale the clear milk.*
*The boy tilted the green shell overhead*
*and drooled coconut milk down his chin;*
*suddenly, Puerto Rico was not Coca-Cola*
*or Brooklyn, and neither was he.*

*For years afterwards, the boy marveled at an island*
*where the people drank Coca-Cola*
*and sang jingles from World War II*
*in a language they did not speak,*
*while so many coconuts in the trees*
*sagged heavy with milk, swollen*
*and unsuckled.*

## Discussion Questions

1. How does Espada organize his comparison and contrast in the poem? In what ways are the two drinks similar? In what ways are they different?
2. What is it about the two drinks that catches Espada's attention? Why might he have written the poem? What is he trying to reveal?
3. What does the boy discover? How does the comparison and contrast lead to that discovery?

4. What image is developed in the final two lines of the poem? What is that image called? How is it also an example of comparison and contrast?

5. What is the significance of the word "unsuckled" in the final line? Who should consume the nourishment that the coconuts supply? Why?

## Writing Suggestions

Espada uses something from American popular culture to comment on the "island of [his] family folklore." Think about conflicts you have experienced between how something is done in your culture and how it is done in another. The conflicts, for example, could result from differences in culture, in age, in religion, in values, in expectations, or in social or economic backgrounds. As a departure point, consider the following possible conflicts:

a. Between you and your parents
b. Between you and your grandparents
c. Between you and your siblings

# As a Critical Reading Strategy

The following paragraph is taken from John McPhee's nonfiction book *Oranges*. McPhee is a writer fascinated by details, and *Oranges* contains just about everything you might ever want to know about the fruit. As McPhee indicates, domestically grown oranges typically come from either Florida or California. You might think first of the differences between seeded and unseeded (or navel) oranges, but as McPhee points out, the oranges grown in these two climates differ significantly.

As you read, remember what you have learned about how to write using comparison and contrast and how that knowledge might help you as a reader.

- Comparison finds similarities among things that appear to be different. An analogy—likening an unfamiliar thing to a familiar one—is a form of comparison.

- Contrast finds differences among things that appear to be similar. Any time we look at the features of a service or a product before we purchase it, we are making a contrast.

- The primary purpose of comparison and contrast is to explain or clarify.

- Comparison and contrast has three possible organizational patterns. The subjects are treated one at a time (subject by subject), or the points of similarity and difference between the subject are treated one at a time (point by point). In longer essays, a mixed pattern—a bit of both—is sometimes used.

- The points of comparison and contrast are typically arranged in an order that reflects their relative importance.

- The points of comparison and contrast are phrased in parallel form—identical grammatical forms.

The paragraph focuses on points of contrast—the similarities are obvious: both are oranges

Florida
1. Tight skin
2. Heavy with juice
3. Harder to peel

California
1. Thicker skin
2. Not as juicy
3. Easier to peel

Comparison of growing conditions

Florida—abundant rain
California—irrigation

Comparison of amount of oranges grown

An orange grown in Florida usually has a <u>thin and tightly fitting skin</u> and it is also <u>heavy with juice</u>. [Californians say that if you want to eat a Florida orange, you have to get into a bathtub first]. California oranges are <u>light in weight</u> and have <u>thick skins</u> that <u>break easily and come off in chunks</u>. The flesh inside is <u>marvelously sweet</u>, and the <u>segments almost separate themselves</u>. [In Florida, it is said that you can run over a California orange with a ten-ton truck and not even wet the pavement.] The differences from which these hyperboles arise will prevail in the two states even if the type of orange is the same. In arid climates, like California's, oranges develop a thick albedo, which is the white part of the skin. Florida is one of the two or three most rained-upon states in the United States. California uses the Colorado River and similarly impressive sources to irrigate its oranges, but of course irrigation can only do so much. The annual difference in rainfall between the Florida and California orange-growing areas is one million one hundred and forty-thousand gallons per acre. For years, California was the leading orange-growing state, but Florida surpassed California in 1942 and grows three times as many oranges now. California oranges, for their part, can safely be called three times as beautiful.

## As a Visual Strategy

Comparison and contrast frequently can be visually displayed. The "extreme makeovers" of people or houses popular on television are, at their core, comparison and contrast, more popularly phrased as "before and after." Comparison stresses similarities—despite the extreme physical makeovers, the people (their personalities, qualities, abilities, knowledge) have not changed. Even when the original house is torn down, the new house still is a house and fulfills the same function. In that sense, contrasts that highlight differences are what are visually emphasized. The following two photographs provoke painful memories for many Americans—the twin towers of the World Trade Center before and after the tragedy of 9/11.

## WRITING ABOUT IMAGES

1. Study the two photographs—a before and an after. Then, using comparison and contrast, write an essay in which you focus on the similarities or differences between pre-9/11 and post-9/11 America. Has anything changed in our culture? What and why?

2. Search magazines for examples of visual advertisements that promote the same type of product to men and women (for example, clothing or shoes, watches, perfumes and colognes, food or drink). What do the advertisements have in common? How are they different? What do the advertisements suggest about how products are made appealing to different genders? Include your visuals with your essay.

3. Locate some photographs of you (or of a friend or a family member) that are separated by at least ten years. What is the same about this person and what has changed? Use the photographs as a memory aid to recover that earlier person—what he or she wanted, thought about, hoped for. Photocopy the photos or digitize them and include them with your essay.

## ADDITIONAL WRITING SUGGESTIONS FOR COMPARISON AND CONTRAST

Remember that comparison finds similarities while contrast finds differences. Regardless of which you are doing, also remember to focus on the significant and not the obvious or trivial. Have a reason or purpose for making this comparison or contrast.

## Comparison

1. Playing a sport and working for a company or being in the military
2. A buffet in a restaurant and your school's undergraduate course offerings
3. Lessons learned as a child and adult experiences
4. Skateboarding and snowboarding or skiing
5. Something technical and something simple (develop an analogy)
6. A particular video game and life
7. Characteristics that achievers share (regardless of gender, race, or economic background)
8. Similarities among those who are seen by our culture as "celebrities" or "stars"
9. Qualities that make someone in our culture a "hero"
10. Life as a jungle and life as a beach

## Contrast

1. Facebook and MySpace
2. Texting or instant messaging and telephone calls
3. Meat eaters and vegans
4. Early riser and late sleepers (humorous)
5. E-mailing and letter writing
6. Two different popular diet plans or two different types of exercise
7. Two gaming systems
8. Off-campus housing and dormitories
9. Two different types of music (for example, rap and punk rock)
10. Your generation and your parents' or grandparents' generation

# The Fakebook Generation

Alice Mathias

*Alice Mathias is a 2007 graduate of Dartmouth. While in college, she was a columnist for* The Dartmouth Mirror *and was invited by* The New York Times *to write for an online blog called "The Graduates,"* The Times *chose eight college seniors, who wrote for their school's newspaper, to reflect on the "prospects of graduating from college today." This essay originally appeared as a op-ed piece in* The New York Times *in October 2007.*

*In early 2008, MySpace membership reached 225 million (up from 20 million in 2005), while Facebook grew 550 percent a year, each year between 2005 and 2008.*

**On Writing:** *Mathias observed, "People from all over the country are giving me input about my blog post on Facebook. It shows how the world is so big, yet so connected."*

## Before Reading

**Connecting:** Do you have a Facebook page? What have you put on it and why? How do you use Facebook?

**Anticipating:** Mathias argues that she and her friends saw Facebook as playing a particular role in their lives, a role that was different from that of adult users. Do you agree with her description of how Facebook is used by college students?

1   The time-chugging Web site Facebook.com first appeared during my freshman year as the exclusive domain of college students. This spring, Facebook opened its pearly gates, enabling myself and other members of the class of '07 to graduate from our college networks into those of the real world.

2   In no time at all, the Web site has convinced its rapidly assembling adult population that it is a forum for genuine personal and professional connections. Its founder, Mark Zuckerberg, has even declared his quest to chart a "social graph" of human relationships the way that cartographers once charted the world.

3   Just a warning: if you're planning on following the corner of this map that's been digitally doodled by my 659 Facebook friends, you are going to end up in the middle of nowhere. All the rhetoric about human connectivity misses the real reason this popular online study buddy has so distracted college students for the past four years.

4      Facebook did not become popular because it was a functional tool—after all, most college students live in close quarters with the majority of their Facebook friends and have no need for social networking. Instead, we log into the Web site because it's entertaining to watch a constantly evolving narrative starring the other people in the library.

5      I've always thought of Facebook as online community theater. In costumes we customize in a backstage makeup room—the Edit Profile page, where we can add a few Favorite Books or touch up our About Me section— we deliver our lines on the very public stage of friends' walls or photo albums. And because every time we join a network, post a link or make another friend it's immediately made visible to others via the News Feed, every Facebook act is a soliloquy to our anonymous audience.

6      It's all comedy: making one another laugh matters more than providing useful updates about ourselves, which is why entirely phony profiles were all the rage before the grown-ups signed in. One friend announced her status as In a Relationship with Chinese Food, whose profile picture was a carry-out box and whose personal information personified the cuisine of China.

7      We even make a joke out of how we know one another—claiming to have met in "Intro to Super Mario Re-enactments," which I seriously doubt is a real course at Wesleyan, or to have lived together in a "spay and neuter clinic" instead of the dorm. Still, these humor bits often reveal more about our personalities and interests than any honest answers.

8      Facebook administrators have since exiled at least the flagrantly fake profiles, the Greta Garbos and the I Can't Believe It's Not Butters, in an effort to have the site grow up from a farce into the serious social networking tool promised to its new adult users, who earnestly type in their actual personal information and precisely label everyone they know as former co-workers or current colleagues, family members or former lovers.

9      But does this more reverent incarnation of Facebook actually enrich adult relationships? What do these constellations of work colleagues and long-lost friends amount to? An online office mixer? A reunion with that one other guy from your high school who has a Facebook profile? Oh! You get to see pictures of your former college sweetheart's family! (Only depressing possibilities are coming to mind for some reason.)

10     My generation has long been bizarrely comfortable with being looked at, and as performers on the Facebook stage, we upload pictures of ourselves cooking dinner for our parents or doing keg stands at last night's party; we are reckless with our personal information. But there is one area of privacy that we won't surrender: the secrecy of how and whom we search.

11     A friend of mine was recently in a panic over rumors of a hacker application that would allow Facebook users to see who's been visiting their profiles. She'd spent the day ogling a love interest's page and was horrified at the idea that he knew she'd been looking at him. But there's no way Facebook would allow such a program to exist: the site is popular largely because

it enables us to indulge our gazes anonymously. (We might feel invulnerable in the spotlight, but we don't want to be caught sitting in someone else's audience.) If our ability to privately search is ever jeopardized, Facebook will turn into a ghost town.

12      Facebook purports to be a place for human connectivity, but it's made us more wary of real human confrontation. When I was in college, people always warned against the dangers of "Facebook stalking" at a library computer—the person whose profile you're perusing might be right behind you. Dwelling online is a cowardly and utterly enjoyable alternative to real interaction.

13      So even though Facebook offers an elaborate menu of privacy settings, many of my friends admit that the only setting they use is the one that prevents people from seeing that they are Currently Logged In. Perhaps we fear that the Currently Logged In feature advertises to everyone else that we (too!) are Currently Bored, Lustful, Socially Unfulfilled or Generally Avoiding Real Life.

14      For young people, Facebook is yet another form of escapism; we can turn our lives into stage dramas and relationships into comedy routines. Make believe is not part of the postgraduate Facebook user's agenda. As more and more older users try to turn Facebook into a legitimate social reference guide, younger people may follow suit and stop treating it as a circus ring. But let's hope not.

## Questions on Subject and Purpose

1. The term Op-ed refers to material that appears in newspapers usually opposite the editorial page. Content ranges widely, but the idea is to get expressions of different opinions and viewpoints. How does this essay meet that definition?
2. What is Mathias suggesting by titling the essay "The Fakebook Generation"?
3. To what extent could there be a persuasive element in what Mathias is saying—not an overt one, but one that could justify the article being rewritten for a business magazine?

## Questions on Strategy and Audience

1. What is the main contrast that Mathias makes in the essay?
2. Throughout the essay, Mathias develops an extended metaphor to describe how she and her generation saw Facebook. What is that metaphor? For a definition of the term, check the Glossary and Ready Reference at the back of this text.
3. How might Mathias have imagined her audience for this essay?

## Questions on Vocabulary and Style

1. What might govern Mathias's choice of the phrase "the time-chugging" Website?
2. How would you describe the "voice" that Mathias projects in the essay? What contributes to or creates that voice? Would you say the essay is formal or informal? Why?

3. Be prepared to define the following words: *cartographers* (2), *soliloquy* (5), *flagrantly* (8), *farce* (8), *incarnation* (9), *purports* (12).

## Writing Suggestions

1. **For Your Journal or Blog.** Your parents have asked if they can be your "friends" in cyberspace. How would you react to that request? What would you say in reply? In your journal or blog speculate on such a possibility. Would you be concerned that your parents might not understand something about either your use of the space or the things that you include? How might their view differ from yours?

2. **For a Paragraph.** Expand your thoughts into a paragraph (or a letter) in which you reply thoughtfully to your parents' request.

3. **For an Essay.** Mathias observes toward the end of the essay: "Dwelling online is a cowardly and utterly enjoyable alternative to real interaction" (paragraph 12). That sentiment is often echoed about teenagers and young adults who game. Compare and contrast two worlds—dwelling online and dwelling in a face-to-face social community.

4. **For Research.** Many users would draw a distinction between those who use MySpace and those who use Facebook. Do some research on the subject—especially in online sources and interviews—and in a documented essay compare the two sites, their users, and their contents.

## For Further Study

**Focusing on Grammar and Writing.** Four times in the essay, Mathias uses a colon. Check colon usage in the Glossary and Ready Reference and then look at each use in the essay. Why does she use a colon in these situations? Could any other mark of punctuation have been substituted?

**Working Together.** Split into small groups and, prior to a discussion of the essay, share if and how you participate in Facebook or similar online sites. Do you agree with Mathias's observations? If not, why not? If you have a MySpace or Facebook profile, what do you include on it and why?

**Seeing Other Modes at Work.** Cause and effect is also used in the essay to explain the popularity of Facebook among students.

**Finding Connections.** For links to popular culture, pairings would include Andres Martin's "On Teenagers and Tattoos" and Natalie Angier's "Drugs, Sports, Body Image and G.I. Joe" (both in Chapter 7). Meghan Daum's "Virtual Love" in this chapter is also related.

**Exploring the Web.** Facebook and MySpace have grown phenomenally in their relatively short life span (see headnote to the essay). Are the sites fundamentally changing as more people join? Both sites are widely written about—on the Web and in online databases of articles accessible through your college's library. Using the information that you gather, compare one of the sites as it was in its earliest days to what it is today. Be sure to provide proper documentation for your information.

# The Transaction:
# Two Writing Processes

William Zinsser

*William Zinsser (1922–) has been an editor, critic, editorial writer, college teacher, and writing consultant. He is the author of many books including* On Writing Well: An Informal Guide to Writing Nonfiction *(sixth edition, 1998), a textbook classic of which* The New York Times *wrote: "It belongs on any shelf of serious reference works for writers."*

**On Writing:** *As someone who earns his living as a writer, Zinsser sees writing as hard work. "The only way to learn to write," he has observed, "is to force yourself to produce a certain number of words on a regular basis." In an interview, he once remarked: "I don't think writing is an art. I think sometimes it's raised to an art, but basically it's a craft, like cabinet making or carpentry."*

## Before Reading

**Connecting:** If you had to describe your writing process to a group of younger students, what would you say?

**Anticipating:** Why should writing seem so easy to Brock and so difficult to Zinsser? If he finds it so difficult, why does Zinsser continue to write?

1    **A** school in Connecticut once held "a day devoted to the arts," and I was asked if I would come and talk about writing as a vocation. When I arrived I found that a second speaker had been invited—Dr. Brock (as I'll call him), a surgeon who had recently begun to write and had sold some stories to magazines. He was going to talk about writing as an avocation. That made us a panel, and we sat down to face a crowd of students and teachers and parents, all eager to learn the secrets of our glamorous work.

2    Dr. Brock was dressed in a bright red jacket, looking vaguely bohemian, as authors are supposed to look, and the first question went to him. What was it like to be a writer?

3    He said it was tremendous fun. Coming home from an arduous day at the hospital, he would go straight to his yellow pad and write his tensions away. The words just flowed. It was easy. I then said that writing wasn't easy and wasn't fun. It was hard and lonely, and the words seldom just flowed.

4    Next Dr. Brock was asked if it was important to rewrite. Absolutely not, he said. "Let it all hang out," he told us and whatever form the sentences take

will reflect the writer at his most natural. I then said that rewriting is the essence of writing. I pointed out that professional writers rewrite their sentences repeatedly over and over and then rewrite what they have rewritten.

5    "What do you do on days when it isn't going well?" Dr. Brock was asked. He said he just stopped writing and put the work aside for a day when it would go better. I then said that the professional writer must establish a daily schedule and stick to it. I said that writing is a craft, not an art, and that the man who runs away from his craft because he lacks inspiration is fooling himself. He is also going broke.

6    "What if you're feeling depressed or unhappy?" a student asked. "Won't that affect your writing?"

7    Probably it will, Dr. Brock replied. Go fishing. Take a walk. Probably it won't, I said. If your job is to write every day, you learn to do it like any other job.

8    A student asked if we found it useful to circulate in the literary world. Dr. Brock said he was greatly enjoying his new life as a man of letters, and he told several stories of being taken to lunch by his publisher and his agent at Manhattan restaurants where writers and editors gather. I said that professional writers are solitary drudges who seldom see other writers.

9    "Do you put symbolism in your writing?" a student asked me.

10    "Not if I can help it," I replied. I have an unbroken record of missing the deeper meaning in any story, play or movie, and as for dance and mime, I have never had any idea of what is being conveyed.

11    "I *love* symbols!" Dr. Brock exclaimed, and he described with gusto the joys of weaving them through his work.

12    So the morning went, and it was a revelation to all of us. At the end Dr. Brock told me he was enormously interested in my answers—it had never occurred to him that writing could be hard. I told him I was just as interested in *his* answers—it had never occurred to me that writing could be easy. Maybe I should take up surgery on the side.

13    As for the students, anyone might think we left them bewildered. But in fact we probably gave them a broader glimpse of the writing process than if only one of us had talked. For there isn't any "right" way to do such personal work. There are all kinds of writers and all kinds of methods, and any method that helps you to say what you want to say is the right method for you. . . .

## Questions on Subject and Purpose

1. Zinsser uses contrast to make a point about how people write. What is that point?
2. How effective is the beginning? Would the effect have been lost if Zinsser had opened with a statement similar to his final sentence?
3. What process do you use when you write? Does it help in any way to know what other people do? Why? Why not?

## Questions on Strategy and Audience

1. Which method of development does Zinsser use for his example? How many points of contrast does he make?
2. Would it have made any difference if Zinsser had used another pattern of development? Why?
3. How effective are the short paragraphs? Should they be longer?

## Questions on Vocabulary and Style

1. What makes Zinsser's story humorous? Try to isolate several aspects of humor.
2. Zinsser uses a number of parallel structures in his narrative. Make a list of them, and be prepared to show how they contribute to the narrative's effectiveness.
3. Be prepared to define the following words: *avocation* (paragraph 1), *bohemian* (2), *arduous* (3), *drudge* (8), *mime* (10), *gusto* (11).

## Writing Suggestions

1. **For Your Journal or Blog.** How do you feel about writing? How do you feel about having other people read your writing? Is writing a source of great anxiety? Of pleasure? In your journal or blog, explore those feelings.
2. **For a Paragraph.** Using the details provided by Zinsser, rewrite the narrative using a subject-by-subject pattern. Choose either writer, and put together his advice in a single paragraph. Be sure to formulate a topic sentence that will control the paragraph.
3. **For an Essay.** Let's be honest—writing instructors and textbooks offer one view of the writing process, but the practices of most writers can differ sharply. Prewriting and revising get squeezed out when a paper is due and only one night is available. In an essay, compare and contrast your typical behavior as a writer with the process outlined in this text. Do not be afraid to be truthful.
4. **For Research.** Compare the creative processes of two or more artists. You can choose painters, musicians, dancers, writers, actors—anyone involved in the creative arts. Check your library's catalog and the various periodical indexes and electronic databases for books and articles about the creative work of each person. Try to find interviews or statements in which the artists talk about how they work. If you are having trouble finding information, ask a reference librarian to help you. Be sure to document your sources.

## For Further Study

**Focusing on Grammar and Writing.** Rewrite paragraph 12 in the essay, casting it into simple sentences, each of which is followed by a period. What is the difference between the new paragraph and the one that Zinsser originally wrote? How does the punctuation of the original help reflect and emphasize Zinsser's meaning?

**Working Together.** What would be the result of reparagraphing Zinsser's essay? Would it change the essay? Would it be more or less effective? Divide into small groups and reparagraph the entire essay. Is there general agreement on where that new paragraphing could occur? Compare results.

**Seeing Other Modes at Work.** As the subtitle of the selection notes, Zinsser's piece is also a process narrative. How might either Zinsser or Dr. Brock describe his own writing process?

**Finding Connections.** A good pairing is with Nora Ephron's "Revision and Life" and with Walter Mosley's "For Authors, Fragile Ideas Need Loving Every Day" (both in Chapter 6).

**Exploring the Web.** Interested in finding online help for your writing? Search the Web for online writing centers.

# Remembering My Childhood on the Continent of Africa

David Sedaris

*David Sedaris (1956–) is a frequent contributor to Public Radio International's* This American Life. *In 2001, he received the Thurber Prize for American humor and* Time *magazine named him Humorist of the Year. His essays appear in* Esquire *and* The New Yorker *and he has published three best-selling collections of them:* Naked, Me Talk Pretty One Day, *and* Dress Your Family in Corduroy and Denim. *His fourth collection,* When You Are Engulfed in Flames, *appeared in 2008.*

*This essay was originally published in the collection* Me Talk Pretty One Day *(2000).*

**On Writing:** *Many years ago Sedaris began keeping the diaries from which he develops much of his writing. On* www.slate.com *he commented: "The earliest diaries . . . tell me not who I was, but who I wanted to be. That person wore a beret and longed to ride a tandem bicycle with Laura Nyro. He wanted to arrive at parties on the back of a camel and sketch the guests, capturing the look of wonder on their faces as they admired his quiet, unassuming celebrity."*

## Before Reading

**Connecting:** Have you ever wished that your life up to this point had been more exciting or more exotic? Or maybe that it was more conventional and comfortable?

**Anticipating:** Is there ever a moment in the essay in which you think Sedaris might be embellishing or inventing details in either Hugh's life or his own?

1   **W**hen Hugh was in the fifth grade, his class took a field trip to an Ethiopian slaughterhouse. He was living in Addis Ababa at the time, and the slaughterhouse was chosen because, he says, "it was convenient."

2   This was a school system in which the matter of proximity outweighed such petty concerns as what may or may not be appropriate for a busload of eleven-year-olds. "What?" I asked. "Were there no autopsies scheduled at the local morgue? Was the federal prison just a bit too far out of the way?"

3       Hugh defends his former school, saying, "Well, isn't that the whole point of a field trip? To see something new?"

4       "Technically yes, but. . . ."

5       "All right then," he says. "So we saw some new things."

6       One of his field trips was literally a trip to a field where the class watched a wrinkled man fill his mouth with rotten goat meat and feed it to a pack of waiting hyenas. On another occasion they were taken to examine the bloodied bedroom curtains hanging in the palace of the former dictator. There were tamer trips, to textile factories and sugar refineries, but my favorite is always the slaughterhouse. It wasn't a big company, just a small rural enterprise run by a couple of brothers operating out of a low-ceilinged concrete building. Following a brief lecture on the importance of proper sanitation, a small white piglet was herded into the room, its dainty hooves clicking against the concrete floor. The class gathered in a circle to get a better look at the animal, who seemed delighted with the attention he was getting. He turned from face to face and was looking up at Hugh when one of the brothers drew a pistol from his back pocket, held it against the animal's temple, and shot the piglet, execution-style. Blood spattered, frightened children wept, and the man with the gun offered the teacher and bus driver some meat from a freshly slaughtered goat.

7       When I'm told such stories, it's all I can do to hold back my feelings of jealousy. An Ethiopian slaughterhouse. Some people have all the luck. When I was in elementary school, the best we ever got was a trip to Old Salem or Colonial Williamsburg, one of those preserved brick villages where time supposedly stands still and someone earns his living as a town crier. There was always a blacksmith, a group of wandering patriots, and a collection of bonneted women hawking corn bread or gingersnaps made "the old-fashioned way." Every now and then you might come across a doer of bad deeds serving time in the stocks, but that was generally as exciting as it got.

8       Certain events are parallel, but compared with Hugh's, my childhood was unspeakably dull. When I was seven years old, my family moved to North Carolina. When he was seven years old, Hugh's family moved to the Congo. We had a collie and a house cat. They had a monkey and two horses named Charlie Brown and Satan. I threw stones at stop signs. Hugh threw stones at crocodiles. The verbs are the same, but he definitely wins the prize when it comes to nouns and objects. An eventful day for my mother might have involved a trip to the dry cleaner or a conversation with the potato-chip deliveryman. Asked one ordinary Congo afternoon what she'd done with her day, Hugh's mother answered that she and a fellow member of the Ladies' Club had visited a leper colony on the outskirts of Kinshasa. No reason was given for the expedition, though chances are she was staking it out for a future field trip.

9       Due to his upbringing, Hugh sits through inane movies never realizing that they're often based on inane television shows. There were no poker-faced sitcom martians in his part of Africa, no oil-rich hillbillies or aproned brides trying to wean themselves from the practice of witchcraft. From time to time a movie would arrive packed in a dented canister, the film scratched and faded

from its slow trip around the world. The theater consisted of a few dozen folding chairs arranged before a bedsheet or the blank wall of a vacant hangar out near the airstrip. Occasionally a man would sell warm soft drinks out of a cardboard box, but that was it in terms of concessions.

10      When I was young, I went to the theater at the nearby shopping center and watched a movie about a talking Volkswagen. I believe the little car had a taste for mischief but I can't be certain, as both the movie and the afternoon proved unremarkable and have faded from my memory. Hugh saw the same movie a few years after it was released. His family had left the Congo by this time and were living in Ethiopia. Like me, Hugh saw the movie by himself on a weekend afternoon. Unlike me, he left the theater two hours later, to find a dead man hanging from a telephone pole at the far end of the unpaved parking lot. None of the people who'd seen the movie seemed to care about the dead man. They stared at him for a moment or two and then headed home, saying they'd never seen anything as crazy as that talking Volkswagen. His father was late picking him up, so Hugh just stood there for an hour, watching the dead man dangle and turn in the breeze. The death was not reported in the newspaper, and when Hugh related the story to his friends, they said, "You saw the movie about the talking car?"

11      I could have done without the flies and the primitive theaters, but I wouldn't have minded growing up with a houseful of servants. In North Carolina it wasn't unusual to have a once-a-week maid, but Hugh's family had houseboys, a word that never fails to charge my imagination. They had cooks and drivers, and guards who occupied a gatehouse, armed with machetes. Seeing as I had regularly petitioned my parents for an electric fence, the business with the guards strikes me as the last word in quiet sophistication. Having protection suggests that you are important. Having that protection paid for by the government is even better, as it suggests your safety is of interest to someone other than yourself.

12      Hugh's father was a career officer with the US State Department, and every morning a black sedan carried him off to the embassy. I'm told it's not as glamorous as it sounds, but in terms of fun for the entire family, I'm fairly confident that it beats the sack race at the annual IBM picnic. By the age of three, Hugh was already carrying a diplomatic passport. The rules that applied to others did not apply to him. No tickets, no arrests, no luggage search: He was officially licensed to act like a brat. Being an American, it was expected of him, and who was he to deny the world an occasional tantrum?

13      They weren't rich, but what Hugh's family lacked financially they more than made up for with the sort of exoticism that works wonders at cocktail parties, leading always to the remark "That sounds fascinating." It's a compliment one rarely receives when describing an adolescence spent drinking Icees at the North Hills Mall. No fifteen-foot python ever wandered onto my school's basketball court. I begged, I prayed nightly, but it just never happened. Neither did I get to witness a military coup in which forces sympathetic to the colonel arrived late at night to assassinate my next-door neighbor. Hugh had been at the Addis Ababa teen club when the electricity was cut off and soldiers

arrived to evacuate the building. He and his friends had to hide in the back of a jeep and cover themselves with blankets during the ride home. It's something that sticks in his mind for one reason or another.

14       Among my personal highlights is the memory of having my picture taken with Uncle Paul, the legally blind host of a Raleigh children's television show. Among Hugh's is the memory of having his picture taken with Buzz Aldrin on the last leg of the astronaut's world tour. The man who had walked on the moon placed his hand on Hugh's shoulder and offered to sign his autograph book. The man who led Wake County schoolchildren in afternoon song turned at the sound of my voice and asked, "So what's your name, princess?"

15       When I was fourteen years old, I was sent to spend ten days with my maternal grandmother in western New York State. She was a small and private woman named Billie, and though she never came right out and asked, I had the distinct impression she had no idea who I was. It was the way she looked at me, squinting through her glasses while chewing on her lower lip. That, coupled with the fact that she never once called me by name. "Oh," she'd say, "are you still here?" She was just beginning her long struggle with Alzheimer's disease, and each time I entered the room, I felt the need to reintroduce myself and set her at ease. "Hi, it's me. Sharon's boy, David. I was just in the kitchen admiring your collection of ceramic toads." Aside from a few trips to summer camp, this was the longest I'd ever been away from home, and I like to think I was toughened by the experience.

16       About the same time I was frightening my grandmother, Hugh and his family were packing their belongings for a move to Somalia. There were no English-speaking schools in Mogadishu, so, after a few months spent lying around the family compound with his pet monkey, Hugh was sent back to Ethiopia to live with a beer enthusiast his father had met at a cocktail party. Mr. Hoyt installed security systems in foreign embassies. He and his family gave Hugh a room. They invited him to join them at the table, but that was as far as they extended themselves. No one ever asked him when his birthday was, so when the day came, he kept it to himself. There was no telephone service between Ethiopia and Somalia, and letters to his parents were sent to Washington and then forwarded on to Mogadishu, meaning that his news was more than a month old by the time they got it. I suppose it wasn't much different than living as a foreign-exchange student. Young people do it all the time, but to me it sounds awful. The Hoyts had two sons about Hugh's age who were always saying things like "Hey that's *our* sofa you're sitting on" and "Hands off that ornamental stein. It doesn't belong to you."

17       He'd been living with these people for a year when he overheard Mr. Hoyt tell a friend that he and his family would soon be moving to Munich, Germany, the beer capital of the world.

18       "And that worried me," Hugh said, "because it meant I'd have to find some other place to live."

19       Where I come from, finding shelter is a problem the average teenager might confidently leave to his parents. It was just something that came with

having a mom and a dad. Worried that he might be sent to live with his grandparents in Kentucky, Hugh turned to the school's guidance counselor, who knew of a family whose son had recently left for college. And so he spent another year living with strangers and not mentioning his birthday. While I wouldn't have wanted to do it myself, I can't help but envy the sense of fortitude he gained from the experience. After graduating from college, he moved to France knowing only the phrase "Do you speak French?"—a question guaranteed to get you nowhere unless you also speak the language.

20      While living in Africa, Hugh and his family took frequent vacations, often in the company of their monkey. The Nairobi Hilton, some suite of high-ceilinged rooms in Cairo or Khartoum: These are the places his people recall when gathered at a common table. "Was that the summer we spent in Beirut or, no, I'm thinking of the time we sailed from Cyprus and took the *Orient Express* to Istanbul."

21      Theirs was the life I dreamt about during my vacations in eastern North Carolina. Hugh's family was hobnobbing with chiefs and sultans while I ate hush puppies at the Sanitary Fish Market in Morehead City, a beach towel wrapped like a hijab around my head. Someone unknown to me was very likely standing in a muddy ditch and dreaming of an evening spent sitting in a clean family restaurant, drinking iced tea and working his way through an extra-large seaman's platter, but that did not concern me, as it meant I should have been happy with what I had. Rather than surrender to my bitterness, I have learned to take satisfaction in the life that Hugh has led. His stories have, over time, become my own. I say this with no trace of a kumbaya. There is no spiritual symbiosis; I'm just a petty thief who lifts his memories the same way I'll take a handful of change left on his dresser. When my own experiences fall short of the mark, I just go out and spend some of his. It is with pleasure that I sometimes recall the dead man's purpled face or the report of the handgun ringing in my ears as I studied the blood pooling beneath the dead white piglet. On the way back from the slaughterhouse, we stopped for Cokes in the village of Mojo, where the gas-station owner had arranged a few tables and chairs beneath a dying canopy of vines. It was late afternoon by the time we returned to school, where a second bus carried me to the foot of Coffeeboard Road. Once there, I walked through a grove of eucalyptus trees and alongside a bald pasture of starving cattle, past the guard napping in his gatehouse, and into the waiting arms of my monkey.

## Questions on Subject and Purpose

1.  Why does Sedaris title the essay "Remembering My Childhood on the Continent of Africa" when it was Hugh's childhood and not his?
2.  Identify one experience or detail in the essay which you doubt ever really happened. Why that one?
3.  If the three major purposes for writing are to entertain, to inform, and to persuade, which seems to be the purpose in this essay?

## Questions on Strategy and Audience

1. What is the effect of starting the essay with the long and detailed example of the field trip to the Ethiopian slaughterhouse (paragraphs 1–6)?

2. What is comic about the use of words and phrases such "princess" (paragraph 14), "ceramic toads" (15), and "into the waiting arms of my monkey" (21).

3. What could Sedaris expect of his audience?

## Questions on Vocabulary and Style

1. At several points in the essay, Sedaris uses dialogue. Why? What is the effect of this device in the essay?

2. Toward the end of the essay, Sedaris writes, "I'm just a petty thief who lifts his memories the same way I'll take a handful of change left on his dresser" (paragraph 21). What figure of speech is Sedaris using in that sentence?

3. Be prepared to define the following words: *inane* (paragraph 9), *hobnobbing* (21), *hijab* (21), *kumbaya* (21), *symbiosis* (21).

## Writing Suggestions

1. **For Your Journal or Blog.** Can you remember a time when you envied the experiences or lifestyle of someone else? Try to recall a specific experience and contrast it with a moment from your own life. Your writing does not have to be funny—it can be quite serious.

2. **For a Paragraph.** Be honest, have you ever "borrowed" someone else's experience to make your life sound more exciting and interesting? Can you imagine doing so? What would be appealing and why? In a paragraph, explore the possibility and then comment on why you are envious of that experience.

3. **For an Essay.** Think of a time in which you found yourself in a very different environment, away from home and from your immediate family. Maybe it was a summer camp, a stay with grandparents, a high school trip, a study abroad experience, or freshman year living in a dormitory. In an essay, compare and contrast your usual environment and the different experience. Treat your subject either comically or seriously. What was it like to find yourself in that different environment? What did you discover, learn, or feel?

4. **For Research.** Colleges and universities increasingly offer or even require study abroad programs, cooperative or intern experiences, service-learning partnerships. How do such experiences affect those who participate in them? Are they valuable experiences? If so, in what way? Are there dangers or risks involved? Research how these learning experiences complement typical classroom experiences.

## For Further Study

**Focusing on Grammar and Writing.** Look carefully at paragraph 8. How does Sedaris use parallelism to structure that paragraph? If you are uncertain about the term parallelism consult the Glossary and Ready Reference at the back of this text.

**Working Together.** What makes Sardaris's essay funny? Divide into small groups; each group should compile a list of remarks (or events or descriptions) that contribute to the humor of the essay. Then, each group should focus on a single item and suggest reasons for why it is funny. What is it that Sedaris does to create the humor of the essay?

**Seeing Other Modes at Work.** Sedaris uses narrative throughout the essay to contrast his childhood experiences with Hugh's.

**Finding Connections.** It is not easy to be funny in writing, but several essays could be paired with Sedaris's for a comparison of comic strategies. Good possibilities include Maya Angelou's "Sister Monroe" (Chapter 2), David Bodanis's "What's in Your Toothpaste?" (4), Suzanne Britt's "Neat People vs. Sloppy People" (5), and Judy Brady's "I Want a Wife" (8).

**Exploring the Web.** What is childhood like in another country? Pick a country—one quite different from your own, perhaps the country in which your parents or grandparents grew up. What is childhood like there now? What experiences and conditions would you have faced if you had grown up in such a world? As you start thinking about the topic, you might want to read Tom Haines's "Facing Famine" (Chapter 2).

# Neat People vs. Sloppy People

Suzanne Britt

*Suzanne Britt was born in Winston-Salem, North Carolina, and currently teaches writing and literature courses at Meredith College in Raleigh, North Carolina. She has published essays in a number of newspapers and magazines and has published several collections of essays and a college writing textbook,* A Writer's Rhetoric *(1988). "Neat People vs. Sloppy People" first appeared in her collection* Show and Tell *(1983).*

## Before Reading

**Connecting:** Are you a neat or a sloppy person? Sometimes a little of both?

**Anticipating:** As you read, think about how Britt organizes her essay. What types of structures does she use?

1   I've finally figured out the difference between neat people and sloppy people. The distinction is, as always, moral. Neat people are lazier and meaner than sloppy people.

2   Sloppy people, you see, are not really sloppy. Their sloppiness is merely the unfortunate consequence of their extreme moral rectitude. Sloppy people carry in their mind's eye a heavenly vision, a precise plan, that is so stupendous, so perfect, it can't be achieved in this world or the next.

3   Sloppy people live in Never-Never Land. Someday is their métier. Someday they are planning to alphabetize all their books and set up home catalogs. Someday they will go through their wardrobes and mark certain items for tentative mending and certain items for passing on to relatives of similar shape and size. Someday sloppy people will make family scrapbooks into which they will put newspaper clippings, postcards, locks of hair, and the dried corsage from their senior prom. Someday they will file everything on the surface of their desks, including the cash receipts from coffee purchases at the snack shop. Someday they will sit down and read all the back issues of *The New Yorker*.

4   For all these noble reasons and more, sloppy people never get neat. They aim too high and wide. They save everything, planning someday to file, order, and straighten out the world. But while these ambitious plans take clearer and clearer shape in their heads, the books spill from the shelves onto the floor, the clothes pile up in the hamper and closet, the family mementos

accumulate in every drawer, the surface of the desk is buried under mounds of paper, and the unread magazines threaten to reach the ceiling.

5        Sloppy people can't bear to part with anything. They give loving attention to every detail. When sloppy people say they're going to tackle the surface of a desk, they really mean it. Not a paper will go unturned; not a rubber band will go unboxed. Four hours or two weeks into the excavation, the desk looks exactly the same, primarily because the sloppy person is meticulously creating new piles of papers with new headings and scrupulously stopping to read all the old book catalogs before he throws them away. A neat person would just bulldoze the desk.

6        Neat people are bums and clods at heart. They have cavalier attitudes toward possessions, including family heirlooms. Everything is just another dust-catcher to them. If anything collects dust, it's got to go and that's that. Neat people will toy with the idea of throwing the children out of the house just to cut down on the clutter.

7        Neat people don't care about process. They like results. What they want to do is get the whole thing over with so they can sit down and watch the rasslin' on TV. Neat people operate on two unvarying principles: Never handle any item twice, and throw everything away.

8        The only thing messy in a neat person's house is the trash can. The minute something comes to a neat person's hand, he will look at it, try to decide if it has immediate use and, finding none, throw it in the trash.

9        Neat people are especially vicious with mail. They never go through their mail unless they are standing directly over a trash can. If the trash can is beside the mailbox, even better. All ads, catalogs, pleas for charitable contributions, church bulletins, and money-saving coupons go straight into the trash can without being opened. All letters from home, postcards from Europe, bills, and paychecks are opened, immediately responded to, then dropped in the trash can. Neat people keep their receipts only for tax purposes. That's it. No sentimental salvaging of birthday cards or the last letter a dying relative ever wrote. Into the trash it goes.

10       Neat people place neatness above everything, even economics. They are incredibly wasteful. Neat people throw away several toys every time they walk through the den. I knew a neat person once who threw away a perfectly good dish drainer because it had mold on it. The drainer was too much trouble to wash. And neat people sell their furniture when they move. They will sell a La-Z-Boy recliner while you are reclining in it.

11       Neat people are no good to borrow from. Neat people buy everything in expensive little single portions. They get their flour and sugar in two-pound bags. They wouldn't consider clipping a coupon, saving a leftover, reusing plastic nondairy whipped cream containers, or rinsing off tin foil and draping it over the unmoldy dish drainer. You can never borrow a neat person's newspaper to see what's playing at the movies. Neat people have the paper all wadded up and in the trash by 7:05 A.M.

12       Neat people cut a clean swath through the organic as well as the inorganic world. People, animals, and things are all one to them. They are so insensitive.

After they've finished with the pantry, the medicine cabinet, and the attic, they will throw out the red geranium (too many leaves), sell the dog (too many fleas), and send the children off to boarding school (too many scuff-marks on the hardwood floors).

## Questions on Subject and Purpose

1. Is Britt a neat or a sloppy person? How do you know?
2. If you are sloppy or neat, are you offended by anything in the essay? Do you regard this as an unfair criticism of you? Why or why not?
3. What might Britt's purpose be in writing the essay?

## Questions on Strategy and Audience

1. How does Britt structure her essay? Is it subject by subject or point by point?
2. Is this essay comparison or contrast? Or both?
3. What can Britt assume about her audience? What does she expect of her audience?

## Questions on Vocabulary and Style

1. How would you describe the tone (see Glossary and Ready Reference) of the essay?
2. What is the effect of the repetition of the phrases "sloppy people" and "neat people" at the start of so many sentences in the essay?
3. Be prepared to define the following words: *rectitude* (paragraph 2), *métier* (3), *meticulously* (5), *scrupulously* (5), *cavalier* (6), *swath* (12).

## Writing Suggestions

1. **For Your Journal or Blog.** Brainstorm about some other possible pairings of people. Remember that you are not classifying people, so your pairings do not need to include all people. Consider both serious topics and humorous ones.
2. **For a Paragraph.** Choose one of the topics from your journal or blog writing and explore it in a paragraph. Concentrate on a single point of comparison and contrast.
3. **For an Essay.** Expand your paragraph into an essay. Compare or contrast a pairing of people (for example, late people and early people; PC users and MAC users; morning people and night people). Compare or contrast on a number of points, not just a single one. You can try a humorous or serious approach.
4. **For Research.** What do we know about neatness and sloppiness? What makes a person one or the other? Is it just an attitude or behavior that could be changed, or is it more deeply ingrained in personality? What does research tell us? Using Web sources, interviews, and print sources, see what evidence exists about why a person might be neat or sloppy.

## For Further Study

**Focusing on Grammar and Writing.** Look closely at the opening sentences of each of Britt's paragraphs. What role do these topic sentences play in the paragraph? How do such sentences help you as a reader?

**Working Together.** Divide into small groups. Each should consider whether it is possible to exhibit some of the characteristics of both groups in the essay (sloppy and neat). What would happen if a third group—a group that exhibited both sloppy and neat traits—were added to the essay? What might such a section look like, and what might it add or detract from the essay?

**Seeing Other Modes at Work.** Both sections of the essay show elements of definition as well. Sloppy and neat people are defined by the ways in which they react to certain situations.

**Finding Connections.** Good pairings on the nature of humor writing include David Sedaris's "Remembering My Childhood on the Continent of Africa" (this chapter), Judy Brady's "I Want a Wife" (Chapter 8), and Jonathan Swift's "A Modest Proposal" (Chapter 10).

**Exploring the Web.** Tempted to send an electronic postcard to a "sloppy" friend? You can do so on the Web. Not everyone finds the essay funny. One reader replied, "The essay was painful to read, like a Klan pamphlet or a Homophobic newsletter."

# The Color of Love

Danzy Senna

*Danzy Senna (1970–) is a graduate of Stanford University with an M.F.A. from the University of California, Irvine. The daughter of a white mother and a black father, Senna is particularly interested in multiracial identity in the United States, which she explores in her first novel,* Caucasia *(1998). "The Color of Love" first appeared in* O, The Oprah Magazine.

**On Writing:** *In an interview, Senna commented: "I'm not interested in memoir, or purely autobiographical writing. I'm more interested in what might have happened than what really did."*

## Before Reading

**Connecting:** "The Color of Love" focuses on the conflict between Senna and her grandmother. Are there some fundamental ways in which you and a grandparent are opposites?

**Anticipating:** Is the conflict between Senna and her grandmother ever resolved in the essay? Why or why not?

1    We had this much in common: We were both women, and we were both writers. But we were as different as two people can be and still exist in the same family. She was ancient—as white and dusty as chalk—and spent her days seated in a velvet armchair, passing judgments on the world below. She still believed in noble bloodlines; my blood had been mixed at conception. I believed there was no such thing as nobility or class or lineage, only systems designed to keep some people up in the big house and others outside, in the cold.

2    She was my grandmother. She was Irish but from that country's Protestant elite, which meant she seemed more British than anything. She was an actress, a writer of plays and novels and still unmarried in her thirties when she came to America to visit. One night while in Boston, she went to a dinner party, where she was seated next to a young lawyer with blood as blue as the ocean. Her pearl earring fell in his oyster soup—or so the story goes—and they fell in love. My grandmother married that lawyer and left her native Ireland for New England.

3    How she came to have black grandchildren is a story of opposites. It was 1968 in Boston when her daughter—my mother—a small, blonde Wasp poet, married my father, a tall and handsome black intellectual, in an act that was as rebellious as it was hopeful. The products of that unlikely union—my older

sister, my younger brother and I—grew up in urban chaos, in a home filled with artists and political activists. The old lady across the river in Cambridge seemed to me an endangered species. Her walls were covered with portraits of my ancestors, the pale and dead men who had conquered Africa and built Boston long before my time. When I visited, their eyes followed me from room to room with what I imagined to be an expression of scorn. Among the portraits sat my grandmother, a bird who had flown in to remind us all that there had indeed been a time when lineage and caste meant something. To me, young and dark and full of energy, she was the missing link between the living and the dead.

4    But her blood flowed through me, whether I liked it or not. I grew up to be a writer, just like her. And as I struggled to tell my own stories—about race and class and post–civil rights America—I wondered who my grandmother had been before, in Dublin, when she was friend and confidante to literary giants such as William Butler Yeats and Samuel Beckett. Once, while snooping in her bedroom, I discovered her novels, the ones that had been published in Ireland when she was my age. I stared at her photograph on the jacket and wondered about the young woman who wore a mischievous smile. Had she ever worried about becoming so powerful that no man would want her? Did she now feel that she had sacrificed her career and wild Irishwoman dreams to become a wife and mother and proper Bostonian?

5    I longed to know her—to love her. But the differences between us were real and alive, and they threatened to squelch our fragile connection. She was an alcoholic. In the evening, after a few glasses of gin, she could turn vicious. Though she held antiquated racist views, my grandmother would still have preferred to see my mother married and was saddened when my parents split in the seventies. She believed that a woman without a man was pitiable. The first question she always asked me when she saw me: "Do you have a man?" The second question: "What is he?" That was her way of finding out his race and background. She looked visibly pleased if he was a Wasp, neutral if he was Jewish and disappointed if he was black.

6    My mother ignored her hurtful comments but felt them just the same. She spent her visits to my grandmother's house slamming dishes in the kitchen, hissing her anger just out of hearing range, then raving, on the drive home, about what awful thing her mother had said this time. Like my mother, I knew the rule: I was not to disrespect elders. She was old and gray and would soon be gone. But I had inherited my grandmother's short temper. When I got angry, even as a child, I felt as if blood were rushing around in my head, red waves battering the shore. Words spilled from my mouth—cutting, vicious words that I regretted.

7    One autumn day in Cambridge, at my grandmother's place, I lost my temper. I was home from college for the holidays, staying in her guest room. I woke from a nap to the sound of her enraged voice shouting at what I could only imagine was the television.

8    "Idiot! You damn fool!" she bellowed. "You stupid, stupid woman!" It has to be *Jeopardy!*, I thought. She must be yelling at those tiny contestants on

the screen. She knows the answers to those questions better than they do. But when the shouting went on for a beat too long, I went to the top of the stairs and looked down into the living room. She was speaking to a real person: her cleaning lady, a Greek woman named Mary, who was on her hands and knees, nervously gathering the shards of a broken vase. My grandmother stood over her, hands on hips, cursing.

9      "You fool," my grandmother repeated. "How in bloody hell could you have done something so stupid?"

10     "Grandma." I didn't shout her name but said it loudly enough that she, though hard of hearing, glanced up.

11     "Oh, darling!" she piped, suddenly cheerful. "Would you like a cup of tea? You must be dreadfully tired."

12     Mary was on her feet again. She smiled nervously at me, then rushed into the kitchen with the pieces of the broken vase.

13     I told myself to be a good girl, to be polite. But something snapped. I marched down the stairs, and even she noticed something on my face that made her sit in her velvet chair.

14     "Don't you ever talk to her that way," I shouted. "Where do you think you are? Slavery was abolished long ago."

15     I stood over her, tall and long-limbed, daring her to speak. My grandmother shook her head. "It's about race, isn't it?"

16     "Race?" I said, baffled. "Mary's white. This is about respect—treating other human beings with respect."

17     She wasn't hearing me. All she saw was color. "The tragedy about you," she said soberly, "is that you are mixed." I felt those waves in my head: "Your tragedy is that you're old and ignorant," I spat. "You don't know the first thing about me."

18     She cried into her hands. She seemed diminished, a little old woman. She looked up only to say, "You are a cruel girl."

19     I left her apartment trembling yet feeling exhilarated by what I had done. But my elation soon turned to shame. I had taken on an old lady. And for what? Her intolerance was, at her age, deeply entrenched. My rebuttals couldn't change her.

20     Yet that fight marked the beginning of our relationship. I've since decided that when you cease to express anger toward those who have hurt you, you are essentially giving up on them. They are dead to you. But when you express anger, it is a sign that they still matter, that they are worth the fight.

21     After that argument, my grandmother and I began a conversation. She seemed to see me clearly for the first time, or perhaps she, a "cruel girl" herself, had simply met her match. And I no longer felt she was a relic. She was a living, breathing human being who deserved to be spoken to as an equal.

22     I began visiting her more. I would drive to Cambridge and sit with her, eating mixed nuts and sipping ginger ale, regaling her with tales of my latest love drama or writing project. In her presence, I was proudly black and young and political, and she was who she was: subtly racist, terribly elitist and awfully funny. She still said things that angered me: She bemoaned my mother's

marriage to my father, she said that I should marry not for love but for money, and she told me that I needn't identify as black, since I didn't look it. I snapped back at her. But she, with senility creeping in, didn't seem to hear me; each time I came, she said the same things.

23    Last summer I went into hiding to work on my second novel at a writers' retreat in New Hampshire. The place was a kind of paradise for creative souls, a hideaway where every writer had his or her own cabin in the woods with no phone or television—no distractions to speak of. But I was miserable. I could not write. Even the flies outside my window seemed to whisper, "Go out and play. Forget the novel. Leave it till tomorrow."

24    I woke one morning at four, the light outside my window still blue. I felt panic and sadness, though I didn't know why I got up, dressed and went outside for a walk through the forest. But the panic persisted, and I began to cry. I assumed that my writer's block had seized me suddenly.

25    That night I ate dinner in the main house and received a call on the pay phone from my mother. She told me my grandmother had fallen and broken her leg. But that wasn't all; she had subsequently suffered a heart attack. Her other organs were failing. I had to hurry if I wanted to say good-bye.

26    I drove to Boston that night, not believing that we could be losing her. She would make it. I was certain. Sure, she was ninety-two, frail, unable to walk steadily. But she was lucid, and her tongue was as sharp as ever. Somehow I had imagined her as indestructible, made immortal by power and cruelty and wit.

27    The woman I found in the hospital bed was barely recognizable. My grandmother had always been fussy about her appearance. She never showed her face without makeup. Even in the day, when it was just she and the cleaning lady, she dressed as if she were ready for a cocktail party. At night she usually had cocktail parties; doddering old men hovered around her, sipping Scotch and bantering about theater and politics.

28    My grandmother's face had swollen to twice its normal size, and tubes came out of her nose. She had struggled so hard to pull them out that the nurses had tied her wrists to the bed rails. Her hair was gray and thin. Her body was withered and bruised, barely covered by the green hospital gown.

29    Her hazel eyes were all that was still recognizable, but the expression in them was different from any I had ever seen on her—terror. She was terrified to die. She tried to rise when she saw me, and her eyes pleaded with me to help her, to save her, to get her out of this mess. I stood over her, and I felt only one thing: overwhelming love. Not a trace of anger. That dark gray rage I'd felt toward her was gone as I stroked her forehead and told her she would be okay, even knowing she would not.

30    For two days, my mother, her sisters and I stood beside my grandmother, singing Irish ballads and reading passages to her from the works of her favorite novelist, James Joyce. For the first time, she could not talk. At one point, she gestured wildly for pen and paper. I brought her the pen and the paper and held them up for her, but she was too weak for even that. What came out was only a faint, incomprehensible line.

31     In death we are each reduced to our essence: the spirit we are when we are born. The trappings we hold on to our whole lives—our race, our money, our sex, our age, our politics—become irrelevant. My grandmother became a child in that hospital bed, a spirit about to embark on an unknown journey, terrified and alone, no matter how many of us were crowded around her. In the final hours, even her skin seemed to lose its wrinkles and take on a waxy glow. Then, finally, the machines around us went silent as she left us behind to squabble in the purgatory of the flesh.

## Questions on Subject and Purpose

1. In what sense is this a comparison and contrast essay? What is being compared and contrasted?
2. Why might Senna have titled the essay "The Color of Love"? Does love have a color?
3. Does the essay transcend the personal? That is, do you as a reader feel that Senna's experience is relevant to you?

## Questions on Strategy and Audience

1. What shift occurs in the essay in paragraphs 7 through 19?
2. What is the significance of the scene that occurs in paragraphs 7 through 19?
3. In what way is the writing of the essay similar to the fight between Senna and her grandmother?

## Questions on Vocabulary and Style

1. What is your sense of the narrator? Do you find her sympathetic?
2. What is the effect of the use of dialogue in paragraphs 7 through 19?
3. Be prepared to define the following words: *antiquated* (paragraph 5), *shards* (8), *elation* (19), *regaling* (22), *lucid* (26), *doddering* (27).

## Writing Suggestions

1. **For Your Journal or Blog.** What generational conflicts have you experienced within your own family? Are there conflicts between you and your grandparents, between your parents and your grandparents, between you and your parents? Jot down some ideas and possible scenes in your journal or blog. Try to think not only about an issue on which the two disagree, but also about a possible scene where that disagreement is clearly revealed.
2. **For a Paragraph.** Using your journal or blog as a departure point, create for the reader that conflict in a paragraph. Do not just *tell* the reader; try also to *show* how the two sides revealed their differences.
3. **For an Essay.** Expand your paragraph into an essay. Remember that conflicts are likely to be rooted in a set of values or a particular expectation. Even if you feel that one side is completely wrong, it is at least possible to understand why

the person feels the way that he or she does. Remember, your experience is probably not unique—most of your readers have experienced similar things. Like Senna, try to include at least one dramatized scene with some dialogue.

4. **For Research.** Select one or more significant differences or conflicts between generations. Look for a charged issue, for example, race relations, attitudes toward sex or money, views of gender roles, work ethics. What are the significant factors or experiences that fuel those conflicts? What can you learn from research and interviews? What explains the differences between the two generations and their attitudes toward the subject?

## For Further Study

**Focusing on Grammar and Writing.** Choose one of the paragraphs in the essay (good choices include paragraphs 1, 3, 4, 5, 6, 29), and look closely at how Senna punctuates her sentences. Using a grammar handbook, try to find the reasons why each mark is appropriate in its particular context. When do you use a colon, a semicolon, a dash? What are the most common uses of the comma? What does the variety of Senna's punctuation suggest about your own writing? Do you use a variety of punctuation marks?

**Working Together.** Divide into small groups. Each group should choose one of the following details from the story. What does each detail contribute to the essay?

a. The portraits of Senna's ancestors (paragraph 3)
b. The grandmother's sudden change of tone when Senna comes downstairs (11)
c. Senna's experience at the writers' retreat (23 and 24)
d. The physical appearance of her grandmother in the hospital (27—29)
e. The grandmother's unsuccessful attempt to write something down (30)

**Seeing Other Modes at Work.** Senna's essay depends upon a narrative structure and could be used as an example of narration.

**Finding Connections.** N. Scott Momaday's "The Way to Rainy Mountain" (Chapter 3) also deals with a relationship to a grandparent.

**Exploring the Web.** Read an interview with Senna, check out reviews of her book, and locate additional information—all can be found on the Web.

# Virtual Love

Meghan Daum

*Meghan Daum graduated from Vassar College and earned an M.F.A. at Columbia University. Her essays and articles have appeared in* The New Yorker, The New York Times Book Review, GQ, Vogue *and* Self, *among others, and have been collected in* My Misspent Youth *(2001). "Virtual Love" first appeared in* The New Yorker. *Her first novel,* The Quality of Life Report, *appeared in 2003.*

**On Writing:** *Asked about her writing, Daum commented: "The subjects that I find most fascinating concern ideas or events that have not only affected me personally but seem to resonate with the culture at large. Though I am often called a 'confessional' writer, I am less interested in 'confessing' than in using specific experiences as a tool for looking at more general or abstract phenomena in the world. The key to writing about yourself without falling into solipsism is to explore issues that transcend the merely personal and shed a new light on the experiences that many of us share. It also helps to have a sense of humor and respect for the absurdity of life by not taking yourself too seriously."*

## Before Reading

**Connecting:** Do you think that it is possible to "fall in love" with someone that you have never met face to face?

**Anticipating:** What is it about this "virtual" relationship that attracts Daum?

1    It was last November; fall was drifting away into an intolerable chill. I was at the end of my twenty-sixth year, and was living in New York City, trying to support myself as a writer, and taking part in the kind of urban life that might be construed as glamorous were it to appear in a memoir in the distant future. At the time, however, my days felt more like a grind than like an adventure: hours of work strung between the motions of waking up, getting the mail, watching TV with my roommates, and going to bed. One morning, I logged on to my America Online account to find a message under the heading "is this the real meghan daum?" It came from someone with the screen name PFSlider. The body of the message consisted of five sentences, written entirely in lower-case letters, of perfectly turned flattery: something about PFSlider's admiration of some newspaper and magazine articles I had published over the last year and a half, something about his

resulting infatuation with me, and something about his being a sportswriter in California.

2      I was engaged for the thirty seconds that it took me to read the message and fashion a reply. Though it felt strange to be in the position of confirming that I was indeed "the real meghan daum," I managed to say, "Yes, it's me. Thank you for writing." I clicked the "Send Now" icon, shot my words into the void, and forgot about PFSlider until the next day, when I received another message, this one headed "eureka."

3      "wow, it is you," he wrote, still in lower case. He chronicled the various conditions under which he'd read my few-and-far-between articles—a board-walk in Laguna Beach, the spring-training pressroom for a baseball team that he covered for a Los Angeles newspaper. He confessed to having a crush on me. He referred to me as "princess daum." He said he wanted to have lunch with me during one of his two annual trips to New York.

4      The letter was outrageous and endearingly pathetic, possibly the practical joke of a friend trying to rouse me out of a temporary writer's block. But the kindness pouring forth from my computer screen was bizarrely exhilarating, and I logged off and thought about it for a few hours before writing back to express how flattered and "touched"—this was probably the first time I had ever used that word in earnest—I was by his message.

5      I am not what most people would call a computer person. I have no interest in chat rooms, newsgroups, or most Websites. I derive a palpable thrill from sticking a letter in the United States mail. But I have a constant low-grade fear of the telephone, and I often call people with the intention of getting their answering machines. There is something about the live voice that I have come to find unnervingly organic, as volatile as live television. E-mail provides a useful antidote for my particular communication anxieties. Though I generally send and receive only a few messages a week, I take comfort in their silence and their boundaries.

6      PFSlider and I tossed a few innocuous, smart-assed notes back and forth over the week following his first message. Let's say his name was Pete. He was twenty-nine, and single. I revealed very little about myself, relying instead on the ironic commentary and forced witticisms that are the conceit of so many E-mail messages. But I quickly developed an oblique affection for PFSlider. I was excited when there was a message from him, mildly depressed when there wasn't. After a few weeks, he gave me his phone number. I did not give him mine, but he looked it up and called me one Friday night. I was home. I picked up the phone. His voice was jarring, yet not unpleasant. He held up more than his end of the conversation for an hour, and when he asked permission to call me again I granted it, as though we were of an earlier era.

7      Pete—I could never wrap my mind around his name, privately thinking of him as PFSlider, "E-mail guy," or even "baseball boy"—began phoning me two or three times a week. He asked if he could meet me, and I said that that would be O.K. Christmas was a few weeks away, and he told me that he would be coming back East to see his family. From there, he would take a short flight to New York and have lunch with me.

8      "It is my off-season mission to meet you," he said.

9   "There will probably be a snowstorm," I said.

10  "I'll take a team of sled dogs," he answered.

11  We talked about our work and our families, about baseball and Bill Clinton and Howard Stern and sex, about his hatred for Los Angeles and how much he wanted a new job. Sometimes we'd find each other logged on simultaneously and type back and forth for hours.

12  I had previously considered cyber-communication an oxymoron, a fast road to the breakdown of humanity. But, curiously, the Internet—at least in the limited form in which I was using it—felt anything but dehumanizing. My interaction with PFSlider seemed more authentic than much of what I experienced in the daylight realm of living beings. I was certainly putting more energy into the relationship than I had put into many others. I also was giving Pete attention that was by definition undivided, and relishing the safety of the distance between us by opting to be truthful instead of doling out the white lies that have become the staple of real life. The outside world—the place where I walked around avoiding people I didn't want to deal with, peppering my casual conversations with half-truths, and applying my motto "Let the machine take it" to almost any scenario—was sliding into the periphery of my mind.

13  For me, the time on-line with Pete was far superior to the phone. There were no background noises, no interruptions from "call waiting," no long-distance charges. Through typos and misspellings, he flirted maniacally. "I have an absurd crush on you," he said. "If I like you in person, you must promise to marry me." I was coy and conceited, telling him to get a life, baiting him into complimenting me further, teasing him in a way I would never have dared to do in person, or even on the phone. I would stay up until 3 A.M. typing with him, smiling at the screen, getting so giddy that when I quit I couldn't fall asleep. I was having difficulty recalling what I used to do at night. It was as if he and I lived together in our own quiet space—a space made all the more intimate because of our conscious decision to block everyone else out. My phone was tied up for hours at a time. No one in the real world could reach me, and I didn't really care.

14  Since my last serious relationship, I'd had the requisite number of false starts and five-night stands, dates that I wasn't sure were dates, and emphatically casual affairs that buckled under their own inertia. With PFSlider, on the other hand, I may not have known my suitor, but, for the first time in my life, I knew the deal: I was a desired person, the object of a blind man's gaze. He called not only when he said he would call but unexpectedly, just to say hello. He was protected by the shield of the Internet; his guard was not merely down but nonexistent. He let his phone bill grow to towering proportions. He told me that he thought about me all the time, though we both knew that the "me" in his mind consisted largely of himself. He talked about me to his friends, and admitted it. He arranged his holiday schedule around our impending date. He managed to charm me with sports analogies. He didn't hesitate. He was unblinking and unapologetic, all nerviness and balls to the wall.

15  And so PFSlider became my everyday life. All the tangible stuff fell away. My body did not exist. I had no skin, no hair, no bones. All desire had converted itself into a cerebral current that reached nothing but my frontal lobe. There

was no outdoors, no social life, no weather. There was only the computer screen and the phone, my chair, and maybe a glass of water. Most mornings, I would wake up to find a message from PFSlider, composed in Pacific time while I slept in the wee hours. "I had a date last night," he wrote. "And I am not ashamed to say it was doomed from the start because I couldn't stop thinking about you."

16   I fired back a message slapping his hand. "We must be careful where we tread," I said. This was true but not sincere. I wanted it, all of it. I wanted un-fettered affection, soul-mating, true romance. In the weeks that had elapsed since I picked up "is this the real meghan daum?" the real me had undergone some kind of meltdown—a systemic rejection of all the savvy and independ-ence I had worn for years, like a grownup Girl Scout badge.

17   Pete knew nothing of my scattered, juvenile self, and I did my best to keep it that way. Even though I was heading into my late twenties, I was still a child, ignorant of dance steps and health insurance, a prisoner of credit-card debt and student loans and the nagging feeling that I didn't want anyone to find me un-til I had pulled myself into some semblance of an adult. The fact that Pete had literally seemed to discover me, as if by turning over a rock, lent us an aura of fate which I actually took half-seriously. Though skepticism seemed like the ob-vious choice in this strange situation, I discarded it precisely because it was the obvious choice, because I wanted a more interesting narrative than cynicism would ever allow. I was a true believer in the urban dream: the dream of years of struggle, of getting a break, of making it. Like most of my friends, I wanted someone to love me, but I wasn't supposed to need it. To admit to loneliness was to smack the face of progress, to betray the times in which we lived. But PFS-lider derailed me. He gave me all of what I'd never even realized I wanted.

18   My addiction to PFSlider's messages indicated a monstrous narcissism, but it also revealed a subtler desire, which I didn't fully understand at that time. My need to experience an old-fashioned kind of courtship was stronger than I had ever imagined. And the fact that technology was providing an avenue for such archaic discourse was a paradox that both fascinated and repelled me. Our relationship had an epistolary quality that put our communication closer to the eighteenth century than to the impending millennium. Thanks to the computer, I was involved in a well-defined courtship, a neat little space in which he and I were both safe to express the panic and the fascination of our mutual affection. Our interaction was refreshingly orderly, noble in its vigor, dignified despite its shamelessness. It was far removed from the randomness of real-life relation-ships. We had an intimacy that seemed custom-made for our strange, lonely times. It seemed custom-made for me.

19   The day of our date, a week before Christmas, was frigid and sunny. Pete was sitting at the bar of the restaurant when I arrived. We shook hands. For a split second, he leaned toward me with his chin, as if to kiss me. He was shorter than I had pictured, though he was not short. He struck me as clean-cut. He had very nice hands. He wore a very nice shirt. We were seated at a very nice table. I scanned the restaurant for people I knew, saw none, and couldn't de-cide how I felt about that.

20    He talked, and I heard nothing he said. I stared at his profile and tried to figure out whether I liked him. He seemed to be saying nothing in particular, but he went on forever. Later, we went to the Museum of Natural History and watched a science film about storm chasers. We walked around looking for the dinosaurs, and he talked so much that I wanted to cry. Outside, walking along Central Park West at dusk, through the leaves, past the yellow cabs and the splendid lights of Manhattan at Christmas, he grabbed my hand to kiss me and I didn't let him. I felt as if my brain had been stuffed with cotton. Then, for some reason, I invited him back to my apartment. I gave him a few beers and finally let him kiss me on the lumpy futon in my bedroom. The radiator clanked. The phone rang and the machine picked up. A car alarm blared outside. A key turned in the door as one of my roommates came home. I had no sensation at all—only a clear conviction that I wanted Pete out of my apartment. I wanted to hand him his coat, close the door behind him, and fight the ensuing emptiness by turning on the computer and taking comfort in PFSlider.

21    When Pete finally did leave, I berated myself from every angle: for not kissing him on Central Part West, for letting him kiss me at all, for not liking him, for wanting to like him more than I had wanted anything in such a long time. I was horrified by the realization that I had invested so heavily in a made-up character—a character in whose creation I'd had a greater hand than even Pete himself. How could I, a person so self-congratulatingly reasonable, have been sucked into a scenario that was more akin to a television talk show than to the relatively full and sophisticated life I was so convinced I led? How could I have received a fan letter and allowed it to go this far?

22    The next day, a huge bouquet of FTD flowers arrived from him. No one had ever sent me flowers before. I forgave him. As human beings with actual flesh and hand gestures and Gap clothing, Pete and I were utterly incompatible, but I decided to pretend otherwise. He returned home and we fell back into the computer and the phone, and I continued to keep the real world safely away from the desk that held them. Instead of blaming him for my disappointment, I blamed the earth itself, the invasion of roommates and ringing phones into the immaculate communication that PFSlider and I had created.

23    When I pictured him in the weeks that followed, I saw the image of a plane lifting off over an overcast city. PFSlider was otherworldly, more a concept than a person. His romance lay in the notion of flight, the physics of gravity defiance. So when he offered to send me a plane ticket to spend the weekend with him in Los Angeles I took it as an extension of our blissful remoteness, a three-dimensional E-mail message lasting an entire weekend.

24    The temperature of the runway at J.F.K. was seven degrees Fahrenheit. Our DC-10 sat for three hours waiting for deicing. Finally, it took off over the frozen city, and the ground below shrank into a drawing of itself. Phone calls were made, laptop computers were plopped onto tray tables. The recirculating air dried out my contact lenses. I watched movies without the sound and told myself that they were probably better that way. Something about the plastic interior of the fuselage and the plastic forks and the din of the air and the engines was soothing and strangely sexy.

25    Then we descended into LAX. We hit the tarmac, and the seat-belt signs blinked off. I hadn't moved my body in eight hours, and now I was walking through the tunnel to the gate, my clothes wrinkled, my hair matted, my hands shaking. When I saw Pete in the terminal, his face seemed to me just as blank and easy to miss as it had the first time I'd met him. He kissed me chastely. On the way out to the parking lot, he told me that he was being seriously considered for a job in New York. He was flying back there next week. If he got the job, he'd be moving within the month. I looked at him in astonishment. Something silent and invisible seemed to fall on us. Outside, the wind was warm, and the Avis and Hertz buses ambled alongside the curb of Terminal 5. The palm trees shook, and the air seemed as heavy and palpable as Pete's hand, which held mine for a few seconds before dropping it to get his car keys out of his pocket. He stood before me, all flesh and preoccupation, and for this I could not forgive him.

26    Gone were the computer, the erotic darkness of the telephone, the clean, single dimension of Pete's voice at 1 A.M. It was nighttime, yet the combination of sight and sound was blinding. It scared me. It turned me off. We went to a restaurant and ate outside on the sidewalk. We strained for conversation, and I tried not to care that we had to. We drove to his apartment and stood under the ceiling light not really looking at each other. Something was happening that we needed to snap out of. Any moment now, I thought. Any moment and we'll be all right. These moments were crowded with elements, with carpet fibers and automobiles and the smells of everything that had a smell. It was all wrong. The physical world had invaded our space.

27    For three days, we crawled along the ground and tried to pull ourselves up. We talked about things that I can no longer remember. We read the Los Angeles *Times* over breakfast. We drove north past Santa Barbara to tour the wine country. I felt like an object that could not be lifted, something that secretly weighed more than the world itself. Everything and everyone around us seemed imbued with a California lightness. I stomped around the countryside, an idiot New Yorker in my clunky shoes and black leather jacket. Not until I studied myself in the bathroom mirror of a highway rest stop did I fully realize the preposterousness of my uniform. I was dressed for war. I was dressed for my regular life.

28    That night, in a tiny town called Solvang, we ate an expensive dinner. We checked into a Marriott and watched television. Pete talked at me and through me and past me. I tried to listen. I tried to talk. But I bored myself and irritated him. Our conversation was a needle that could not be threaded. Still, we played nice. We tried to care, and pretended to keep trying long after we had given up. In the car on the way home, he told me that I was cynical, and I didn't have the presence of mind to ask him just how many cynics he had met who would travel three thousand miles to see someone they barely knew.

29    Pete drove me to the airport at 7 A.M. so I could make my eight-o'clock flight home. He kissed me goodbye—another chaste peck that I recognized from countless dinner parties and dud dates. He said that he'd call me in a few days when he got to New York for his job interview, which we had discussed only in passing and with no reference to the fact that New York was where I happened to live. I returned home to frozen January. A few days later, he came

to New York, and we didn't see each other. He called me from the plane taking him back to Los Angeles to tell me, through the static, that he had got the job. He was moving to my city.

30   PFSlider was dead. There would be no meeting him in distant hotel lobbies during the baseball season. There would be no more phone calls or E-mail messages. In a single moment, Pete had completed his journey out of our mating dance and officially stepped into the regular world—the world that gnawed at me daily, the world that fostered those five-night stands, the world where romance could not be sustained, because so many of us simply did not know how to do it. Instead, we were all chitchat and leather jackets, bold proclaimers of all that we did not need. But what struck me most about this affair was the unpredictable nature of our demise. Unlike most cyberromances, which seem to come fully equipped with the inevitable set of misrepresentations and false expectations, PFSlider and I had played it fairly straight. Neither of us had lied. We'd done the best we could. Our affair had died from natural causes rather than virtual ones.

31   Within a two-week period after I returned from Los Angeles, at least seven people confessed to me the vagaries of their own E-mail affairs. This topic arose, unprompted, in the course of normal conversation. I heard most of these stories in the close confines of smoky bars and crowded restaurants, and we all shook our heads in bewilderment as we told our tales, our eyes focussed on some point in the distance. Four of these people had met their correspondents, by travelling from New Haven to Baltimore, from New York to Montana, from Texas to Virginia, and from New York to Johannesburg. These were normal people, writers and lawyers and scientists. They were all smart, attractive, and more than a little sheepish about admitting just how deeply they had been sucked in. Mostly, it was the courtship ritual that had seduced us. E-mail had become an electronic epistle, a yearned-for rule book. It allowed us to do what was necessary to experience love. The Internet was not responsible for our remote, fragmented lives. The problem was life itself.

32   The story of PFSlider still makes me sad, not so much because we no longer have anything to do with each other but because it forces me to see the limits and the perils of daily life with more clarity than I used to. After I realized that our relationship would never transcend the screen and the phone—that, in fact, our face-to-face knowledge of each other had permanently contaminated the screen and the phone—I hit the pavement again, went through the motions of everyday life, said hello and goodbye to people in the regular way. If Pete and I had met at a party, we probably wouldn't have spoken to each other for more than ten minutes, and that would have made life easier but also less interesting. At the same time, it terrifies me to admit to a firsthand understanding of the way the heart and the ego are snarled and entwined like diseased trees that have folded in on each other. Our need to worship somehow fuses with our need to be worshipped. It upsets me still further to see how inaccessibility can make this entanglement so much more intoxicating. But I'm also thankful that I was forced to unpack the raw truth

of my need and stare at it for a while. It was a dare I wouldn't have taken in three dimensions.

33    The last time I saw Pete, he was in New York, three thousand miles away from what had been his home, and a million miles away from PFSlider. In a final gesture of decency, in what I later realized was the most ordinary kind of closure, he took me out to dinner. As the few remaining traces of affection turned into embarrassed regret, we talked about nothing. He paid the bill. He drove me home in a rental car that felt as arbitrary and impersonal as what we now were to each other.

34    Pete had known how to get me where I lived until he came to where I lived: then he became as unmysterious as anyone next door. The world had proved to be too cluttered and too fast for us, too polluted to allow the thing we'd attempted through technology ever to grow in the earth. PFSlider and I had joined the angry and exhausted living. Even if we met on the street, we wouldn't recognize each other, our particular version of intimacy now obscured by the branches and bodies and falling debris that make up the physical world.

## Questions on Subject and Purpose

1.  What is a "virtual" love?
2.  In paragraph 18, Daum writes, "My need to experience an old-fashioned kind of courtship was stronger than I had ever imagined." How could an Internet romance be old-fashioned?
3.  What is Daum saying or implying about "real" relationships in our society?

## Questions on Strategy and Audience

1.  What is the central contrast in Daum's essay?
2.  The essay can be roughly divided into half. Where does the second half of the essay begin? What is the event that begins the second half?
3.  Realistically, how large is Daum's audience? That is, to whom is she writing? How did you react to her essay?

## Questions on Vocabulary and Style

1.  In paragraph 12, Daum writes: "I had previously considered cyber-communication an oxymoron." What is an *oxymoron*? What does she mean by that sentence?
2.  Pete accuses Daum of being "cynical" (paragraph 28). What does that mean?
3.  Be prepared to define the following words: *construed* (paragraph 1), *palpable* (5), *volatile* (5), *innocuous* (6), *conceit* (6), *periphery* (12), *unfettered* (16), *archaic* (18), *epistolary* (18), *berated* (21), *imbued* (27), *demise* (30), *vagaries* (31).

## Writing Suggestions

1.  **For Your Journal or Blog.** Think about the times in your relationships—with a family member, a close friend, someone you were dating, someone to whom you might have been engaged or even married—when you suddenly realized

something about the other person that really changed the way in which you "saw" that person. It could be a change for the better or for the worse. What you are looking for basically is a contrast, a before and an after. In your journal or blog, first, make a list of possible subjects and, second, write two sentences for each about the before and after experience.

2. **For a Paragraph.** Using your journal or blog as a prewriting exercise, explore one of these before-and-after situations in a paragraph.

3. **For an Essay.** Expand your paragraph writing into an essay. Look at the guidelines for the assignment in exercise 1. Remember, you are basically working on a contrast—what you had thought or assumed before and the reality that you discovered after.

4. **For Research.** The remarkable thing about Daum's "virtual" relationship was that it was honest—neither person pretended to be different from whom they were; neither "doled out white lies." Why do people often change their identities or their personalities in cyberspace? Research the problem. Explore the contrasts that occur between people's real-life identities and personalities and the virtual identities and personalities they assume. What do we know about these contrasts? Why do they occur? You might find that databases of articles are better sources for information than your school's online library catalog. Check with a reference librarian for search strategy suggestions. Be sure to document any direct quotations, paraphrases, or ideas that you take from your sources.

## For Further Study

**Focusing on Grammar and Writing.** At several points in the essay, Daum intentionally repeats the same sentence structure: the final three sentences in paragraph 3; the first three sentences in paragraph 5; the final nine sentences in paragraph 14. See if you can locate other examples. Specifically, what types of opening structures does Daum repeat and why? Usually, teachers caution students about repeating the same types of sentences. Are they effective here? If so, why? What does this suggest about your own writing?

**Working Together.** Divide into small groups and choose one of the following details from the story. What does each detail contribute to the essay?

   a. The small bits of direct quotation that Daum uses (for example, paragraphs 2, 8–10)

   b. The huge bouquet of flowers that Pete sends (22)

   c. Daum's realization that she was "dressed for war" (27)

   d. Pete's move to New York City (concentrate on 30)

   e. Daum's final dinner with Pete (33)

**Seeing Other Modes at Work.** Daum's essay is also a personal experience narrative. It follows her relationship with Pete linearly from its beginning to its end.

**Finding Connections.** An interesting pairing could be made with Judy Brady's "I Want a Wife" (Chapter 8).

**Exploring the Web.** Read more about online romances and locate additional online essays by Daum by going to the Web. Daum maintains her own Website (www.meghandaun.com) on which you can read the weekly op-ed column she writes for *The Los Angeles Times*.

# 6

# PROCESS

---

## 🔑 ❓ KEY QUESTIONS

**Getting Ready to Write**
What is process?
How do you choose a process subject?

**Writing**
How do you structure a process essay?

**Revising**
How do you revise a process essay?
    *Choosing an interesting and manageable subject*
    *Checking for logical organization*
    *Writing an appropriate beginning and ending*

*Student Essay*
    *Julie Anne Halbfish, "How to Play Dreidel"*

*Some Things to Remember About Writing Process*

*Seeing Process in Other Contexts*

**As a literary strategy**
    *Janice Mirikitani, "Recipe"*

**As a critical reading strategy**
    *www.careerwomen.com, "Getting the Interview"*

**As a visual strategy**
    *Photograph of distorted mirror image*

*Additional Writing Suggestions for Process*

# GETTING READY TO WRITE

## What Is Process?

What do each of the following have in common?

> A recipe in a cookbook
> A textbook discussion of how the body converts food into energy and fat
> Directions on how to install a CD changer in your car
> An online explanation of why earthquakes occur

Each is a process analysis—either a set of directions for how to do something (make lasagna or install a CD changer) or a description of how something happens or is done (food is converted or the earth "quakes"). These two different types of process writing have two different purposes.

The function of a set of directions is to allow the reader to duplicate the process. For example, *The Amy Vanderbilt Complete Book of Etiquette* offers the following step-by-step advice to the young executive woman about how to handle paying for a business lunch or dinner.

> No one likes a man who is known never to pick up a check. In today's world, people are going to feel the same about a woman who is known never to pick up a tab. The woman executive is going to have to learn to pay gracefully when it's her turn.
>
> In order to save embarrassment all around, who will pay for the next business lunch should be decided without question in advance. If it's a woman's turn, she should make it very clear over the telephone or face to face when the appointment is made that she will be paying. She has only to say with a smile that it really is her turn. She should name the time and the place, call the restaurant, and make the reservation in her name.
>
> At the end of lunch she should unobtrusively ask for the bill, add the waiter's tip to the total without an agonizing exercise in mathematics, and then use her credit card or sign her name and her company's address to the back of the check (if she has a charge account there). If she does this quietly, no one around them need be aware of her actions.

Several readings in this chapter similarly offer advice or instructions. Lars Eighner in "My Daily Dives in the Dumpster" describes how he "dives" into dumpsters and what the process eventually taught him about life and human acquisitiveness. Walter Mosley in "For Authors, Fragile Ideas Need Loving Every Day" shares with his readers advice on what it takes to write a novel— daily work. Charlie Drozdyk in "Into the Loop" offers advice to soon-to-graduate college students on how to "get the job you want after graduation."

Not every example of process is a set of directions about how to do something. Process can also be used to tell the reader how something happens or is made. Harold McGee, for example, explains to his readers how chewing gum, a quintessential American product, is made. McGee's paragraph is not a recipe. Instead, its function is to provide a general view of the manufacturing process.

Today chewing gum is made mostly of synthetic polymers, especially styrenebutadiene rubber and polyvinyl acetate, though 10 to 20% of some brands is still accounted for by chicle or jelutong, a latex from the Far East. The crude gum base is first filtered, dried, and then cooked in water until syrupy. Powdered sugar and corn syrup are mixed in, then flavorings and softeners—vegetable oil derivatives that make the gum easier to chew—and the material is cooked, kneaded to an even, smooth texture, cut, rolled thin, and cut again into strips, and packaged. The final produce is about 60% sugar, 20% corn syrup, and 20% gum materials.

Nora Ephron in "Revision and Life" describes her own revising process; David Brooks describes the process through which martyrdom has become an end rather than a means in the Arab-Israeli conflict; Jennifer Kahn describes the process through which organs are "harvested" from a dead donor for transplantation. None of these essays is meant to describe a process that we are to perform or imitate. Ephron describes her own process of revision as also a process of maturing or aging. Brooks attempts to explain a phenomenon that many Americans do not understand. Kahn writes as an observer who has come to watch a procedure about which she, like the reader, knows very little.

 ## IN THE READINGS, LOOK FOR

| | Nature of the process narrative |
|---|---|
| Lars Eighner, "My Daily Dives" | How he does it and what he has learned |
| Nora Ephron, "Revision and Life" | What the links are between life and revision |
| Walter Mosley, "For Authors" | How to write and live |
| David Brooks, "Culture of Martyrdom" | Why there are suicide bombers |
| Charlie Drozdyk, "Into the Loop" | How to get a job after graduation |
| Jennifer Kahn, "Stripped for Parts" | How organs are "harvested" and the process of dying |

## How Do You Choose a Process Subject?

Choosing a subject is not a problem if you have been given a specific assignment, for example, to describe how a congressional bill becomes a law, how a chemistry experiment was performed, how to write an "A" paper for your English course. Often, however, you have to choose your own subject. Two considerations are crucial to that decision.

First, choose a subject that can be adequately described or analyzed in the space you have available. When Nora Ephron in "Revision and Life" traces her revision process, she isolates three decades of her life—her 20s, 30s, and 40s. She alternates paragraphs dealing with her evolving attitudes toward revision with paragraphs establishing links between revision and life. At 20, she revised nothing; at 40, she is increasingly drawn to revision. Ephron does not try to identify every change that occurred during these three decades. Instead, she confines her analysis to the major periods.

Second, in a process analysis, as in any other writing assignment, identify the audience to whom you are writing. What does that audience already know about your subject? Are you writing to a general audience, an audience of your fellow classmates, or a specialized audience? You do not want to bore your reader with the obvious, nor do you want to lose your reader in a tangle of unfamiliar terms and concepts. Your choice of subject and certainly your approach to it should be determined by your audience. Charlie Drozdyk's essay on job-seeking strategies for young college students appeared in *Rolling Stone* magazine; to appeal to readers of this publication, he focused on interviewing people who held relatively "glamorous" positions in publishing, on Wall Street, in advertising, in fashion design, in interior design, and in television. David Brooks's "The Culture of Martyrdom" appeared in *Atlantic Monthly*, a literary magazine aimed at older, sophisticated readers. Brooks writes to an American audience, an audience who is puzzled by the suicide bombings in the Middle East, but an audience probably more sympathetic to the Israelis than to the Palestinians. Identifying your audience—what they might be interested in, what they already know—will help in both selecting a subject and in deciding how or what to write about it.

---

 **IN THE READINGS, LOOK FOR**

|  | **Audience** |
| --- | --- |
| Lars Eighner, "My Daily Dives" | Surely not would-be dumpster divers |
| Nora Ephron, "Revision and Life" | College writers |
| Walter Mosley, "For Authors" | Aspiring writers |
| David Brooks, "Culture of Martyrdom" | Adults seeking to understand another culture |
| Charlie Drozdyk, "Into the Loop" | Graduating college students |
| Jennifer Kahn, "Stripped for Parts" | Everyone, but not likely to appeal to all, especially would-be organ donors |

## PREWRITING TIPS FOR WRITING PROCESS

1. Brainstorm some possible topics that lend themselves to a process narrative—how something is done, how to make something, the stages in which something occurred, or your plan for handling a situation. Do not commit too quickly to a particular topic; allow a couple of days for just thinking about possibilities.

2. Answer these questions: Why am I writing about this? What purpose do I have in mind? Am I trying to inform? Entertain? Persuade? Remember that an essay needs a purpose.

3. Define your audience and think about what they might already know about the subject. If your audience is very familiar with the subject, they are likely to be bored. If the subject is too technical or requires much prior knowledge, the audience will not understand.

4. Think about the steps or stages in the process that you are describing. Remember that you probably need between three and six. If the process involves fewer than three, it might be too simple to justify an essay; if it has more than six, it might be too complicated. This is not an unbreakable rule; use it for guidance.

5. Consider how your steps or stages might be ordered. Is there an obvious place at which to start? To end? What about the middle steps in the process? If you have options about order, experiment with some alternatives to see what might work best.

## WRITING

### How Do You Structure a Process Essay?

If you have ever tried to assemble something from a set of directions, you know how important it is that each step or stage in the process be clearly defined and properly placed in the sequence. Because process always involves a series of events or steps that must be done in proper order, the fundamental structure for a process paragraph or essay will be chronological (what occurs first in time).

Begin your planning by making a list of the various steps in the process. Once your list seems complete, arrange the items in the order in which they are performed or in which they occur. Check to make sure that nothing has been omitted or misplaced. If your process is a description of how to do or make something, check your arranged list by performing the process according to the directions you have assembled so far. This ordered list will serve as the outline for your process paper.

"Some assembly required." Most of us have come to fear those words. Directions—the most common form of process writing—must be clear and correctly ordered. The success of a set of directions is always easy to measure—did they work?
*www.CartoonStock.com*

Converting your list or outline into a paragraph or an essay is the next step. Be sure that all the phrases on your outline have been turned into complete sentences and that any technical terms have been carefully explained. You will need some way of signaling to your reader each step or stage in the process. On your list, you probably numbered the steps, but in your paragraph or essay you generally cannot use such a device. More commonly, process papers employ various types of step or time markers to indicate order. Step markers like *first*, *second*, and *third* can be used at the beginning of sentences or paragraphs devoted to each individual stage. Time markers like *begin*, *next*, *in three minutes*, or *while this is being done* remind the reader of the proper chronological sequence.

## 🔍 IN THE READINGS, LOOK FOR

**Structuring middles**

Lars Eighner, "My Daily Dives"

Nora Ephron, "Revision and Life"

What are the four parts of the essay?

What role does time play in the essay's organization?

**DRAFTING TIPS FOR WRITING PROCESS**

1. Be sure to include each step necessary to perform or understand the process. Are those steps and stages in a logical or chronological order? Could you construct a flowchart or a timeline outlining those steps?

2. Have you clearly marked the steps or stages? Have you used sequence markers (for example, *first, then*)? Have you put each stage in a separate paragraph? Does the appearance of the text on the printed page help explain the sequence to be followed?

3. Have you used any words or phrases that your audience might not understand? Be sure to provide a parenthetical definition after that word or phrase.

4. Check to see if your steps or stages are phrased in parallel form (for a definition see the Glossary and Ready Reference). Use a marker to underline the start of each new step or stage. Look at the sentences you have underlined. Are they parallel in grammatical form?

5. Once you have a complete draft, find someone who will read your essay and offer honest advice. Perhaps a classmate? Visit your school writing lab or center. Look for readers and listen to what they say.

## REVISING

### How Do You Revise a Process Essay?

Many writers revise as they write, and even if you do so, "re-see" your paper once again when you have a complete, finished draft. Ideally, you should allow some time to elapse between finishing the draft and looking again at what you have written. If you try to revise too soon, you may see what you want to see and not what you actually wrote. As you look again at your finished draft, remember that process is primarily written for an informative purpose. A how-to-do-it process essay is successful if the reader can reproduce the process you describe without error and with the same result. A here-is-how-it works process narrative is intended to explain how something is done with no intention of having the reader reproduce the process. Either way, the key element in process writing is clarity.

When revising a process essay, pay particular attention to the following areas: choosing an interesting and manageable subject, checking for logical organization, and writing an appropriate beginning and ending.

**Choosing an Interesting and Manageable Subject**     Revision should always begin by looking critically at the essay as a whole. First ask yourself about your choice of subject. Was it too simple? Was it too complicated? Does your draft have three very short body paragraphs or twelve long ones? In either case, unless you have an unusual approach to a simple subject, your audience is likely to be bored. For example, a simple process such as how to make a peanut butter and jelly sandwich or how to put gasoline in your car is probably not a good choice. On the other hand, a complex process is likely to be too long and too detailed for an essay in a writing class.

Second, define your imagined reader. How much prior knowledge is the reader likely to have about your subject? Are you expecting too little or too much of your reader? If you have used technical words and concepts, make sure to provide definitions for them, enclosed with parentheses or set off with commas. Depending on your subject and what your instructor wants, you might want to use visuals in your essay. Often pictures are more effective than words in showing how something is done.

Third, assess again your purpose in the essay. Are you giving directions so the reader might be able to duplicate the process? Or are you trying to describe a process so the reader understands how it works?

**Checking for Logical Organization**     Because process essays are either directions on how to do something or descriptions of how something happens, they must be clearly organized into steps or stages. Think of the directions in a cookbook or a repair manual. The steps of the process must be arranged in a logical, and often chronological, order: first do this, then this, finally this. The steps in the process must be clearly marked off—by being placed in separate paragraphs or sentences, by the use of place and sequence markers (*first, next, finally*), or by numbering (*first* or 1.). Sometimes each step is illustrated with a diagram or a photograph.

The steps must then be arranged in the right order so that the process will work and will produce the same result each time. A good test of logical ordering is to ask a friend to follow the directions that you have given to see if they are clear, comprehensive, and in the right order.

Parallelism—that is, placing words, phrases, and clauses in the steps or sequence in a similar grammatical form—is extremely important in process writing. For more information and examples, check the Glossary and Ready Reference at the back of this text.

**Writing an Appropriate Beginning and Ending**     Readers choose to read process essays when they need the information that the essay provides. If you are trying to add a double major or a minor, you are motivated to read how to do it. If you are learning about how a solar panel creates electricity, you are motivated to read about the process. Do not assume, however, that your reader will read regardless of what you say or how you say it. An introduction to a process essay identifies the subject, but it should try to catch readers' attention as well. In a sense, you are trying to persuade your readers to read your essay. What is important or interesting about this process? How will your readers benefit from knowing this?

Conclusions also pose challenges in process writing. Typically, you do not want simply to summarize the steps or stages in the process. That repetition would be boring and unnecessary. Instead, try suggesting what is important about this knowledge, why it might be useful, or what might be learned through studying the process.

---

 ## IN THE READINGS, LOOK FOR

**Introductions and conclusions**

| | |
|---|---|
| Lars Eighner, "My Daily Dives" | What is the effect of the final sentence? |
| Nora Ephron, "Revision and Life" | How does the conclusion reflect the author's revising practice? |
| Walter Mosley, "For Authors" | How is the first sentence also a summary? |
| David Brooks, "Culture of Martyrdom" | What strategy is used in the introduction? |
| Charlie Drozdyk, "Into the Loop" | Why is there no summary conclusion? |
| Jennifer Kahn, "Stripped for Parts" | What about the introduction catches your attention? |

---

 ## REVISING TIPS FOR WRITING PROCESS

1. Use the feedback provided by a peer reader, your instructor, or a tutor to revise your essay. Pay attention to their criticisms and suggestions.

2. Provide an answer to the following prompts: My purpose is? My intended audience is? My readers will be interested in this subject because?

3. Look again at your introduction and conclusion. Do you catch your readers' attention in your introduction? Do you have a clear statement of purpose? Does your conclusion simply repeat the steps or stages in the process? Consider another type of ending: stress the importance or value of the process, raise a thought-provoking idea.

4. Never underestimate the power of a good title. Write several titles for your paper. Ask friends to evaluate each one.

5. Remember to proofread one final time. See the advice on proofreading offered earlier in this text in How to Revise an Essay.

## STUDENT ESSAY

As part of her student-teaching assignment, Julie Anne Halbfish was asked by her cooperating teacher to write a set of directions on how to play dreidel, a game associated with the Jewish holiday Hanukkah. Most of the students in the seventh-grade class in which Julie was student-teaching had never played the game.

### First Draft

#### How to Play Dreidel

A dreidel is a small top with four sides. On each side is a Hebrew letter. The letters correspond to the first letters in each word of the Hebrew phrase "Nes gadol haya sham," which means "A great miracle happened there." That phrase refers to the military victory of the Maccabees over the Greeks and the story of the small jug of olive oil that burned for eight days. The corresponding Hebrew letters on the dreidel are called nun [ ﬞ ], gimel [ ﬞ ], hay [ה], and shin [ש].

Many people have heard the Hanukkah song "Dreidel," but most are unfamiliar with how to play the traditional children's game of the same name. The rules are actually quite simple.

To start the game, every player receives ten pieces of "money" (usually peanuts, candies, pennies, or anything else the players choose to play for) and a dreidel. Each player puts two pieces of money into the "pot" and then spins the dreidel. When the dreidel stops spinning, the letter that is on the side facing up determines how many pieces the player takes from or adds to the pot. If the dreidel lands on nun, the player takes nothing. If it lands on gimel, the player takes all of the pot. If the dreidel lands on hay, the player receives half of the pot. Finally, if the dreidel lands on shin, the player must put two additional pieces into the pot. After as many rounds of play as the players want, the game ends, and whoever has the most goodies is declared the winner. However, the reason so many people love this game is that everyone ends up with treats to enjoy, so nobody loses.

### Comments

After Julie finished a draft of her essay, she showed her paper to Adam Helenic, a fellow classmate. At first, Adam simply praised the draft—"It's good; it's clear; it's fine, Julie." But Julie would not settle for simple approval. When pushed, Adam made several suggestions. Since many students have heard the dreidel song, he urged her somehow to work at least part of the song into the essay—maybe as an attention-getting introduction. He also suggested that she reorder paragraphs 1 and 2 and that she tighten up her prose in a number of places. When Julie revised her set of directions, she tried to incorporate all of the changes that Adam had suggested. Interestingly, when Julie set out to check her "facts" about the song and the game, she used the Web. She found a computerized dreidel game that you might like to try; several are available online—for example, www.babaganewz.com/dreidel/dreidel.cfm.

## Revised Draft

### How to Play Dreidel

I have a little dreidel,
I made it out of clay.
And when it's dry and ready,
Oh, dreidel I shall play!
It has a lovely body,
With legs so short and thin.
And when it gets all tired,
It drops and then I win.

During Hanukkah, we often hear the "Dreidel" song, but most people have never actually played the traditional children's game to which the song refers. The game is quite simple, and since every player is sure to win something, dreidel is a popular Hanukkah game.

A dreidel is a small, four-sided top, traditionally made out of clay. On each side is a Hebrew letter. The letters correspond to the first letters in each word of the Hebrew phrase "<u>Nes gadol haya sham</u>," which means "A great miracle happened there." That phrase refers to the military victory of the Maccabees over the Greeks and the story of the small jug of olive oil that miraculously burned for eight days. The corresponding Hebrew letters on the dreidel are called <u>nun</u> [נ], <u>gimel</u> [ג], <u>hay</u> [ה], and <u>shin</u> [ש].

To start the game, every player receives ten pieces of "money" (usually peanuts, candies, pennies, or anything else the players choose to play for) and a dreidel. Each player puts two pieces of money into the "pot" and then spins the dreidel. When the dreidel is spinning, the players are encouraged to sing a Hanukkah song or to shout "<u>Gimel</u>!" When the dreidel stops spinning, the letter that is on the side facing up determines how many pieces the player takes from or adds to the pot. If the dreidel lands on <u>nun</u>, the player takes nothing. If it lands on <u>gimel</u>, the player takes all of the pot. If the dreidel lands on <u>hay</u>, the player receives half of the pot. Finally, if the dreidel lands on <u>shin</u>, the player must put two additional pieces into the pot.

After as many rounds of play as the players want, the game ends, and whoever has the most goodies is declared the winner. Whether you win or not, no one really loses since everyone ends up with treats to enjoy.

## SOME THINGS TO REMEMBER WHEN WRITING PROCESS

1. Choose a subject that can be analyzed and described within the space you have available.
2. Remember that process takes one of two forms, reflecting its purpose: either to tell the reader how to do something or to tell the reader how something happens. Make sure you have a purpose clearly in mind before you start your paper.
3. Identify your audience and write to that audience. Ask yourself: Will my audience be interested in what I am writing about? How much does my audience know about this subject?
4. Make a list of the steps or stages in the process.
5. Order or arrange the list, checking to make sure nothing is omitted or misplaced.
6. Convert the list into paragraphs using complete sentences. Remember to define any unfamiliar terms or concepts.
7. Use step or time markers to indicate the proper sequence in the process.
8. Check your process one final time to make sure that nothing has been omitted. If you are describing how to do something, use your paper as a guide to the process. If you are describing how something happens, ask a friend to read your process analysis to see whether it is clear.

## SEEING PROCESS IN OTHER CONTEXTS

### As a Literary Strategy

Janice Mirikitani, a third-generation Japanese American, uses process in her poem "Recipe." As the title and its list of "ingredients" suggests, the poem might at first seem like a set of directions that you would find in a magazine—"how to create the illusion of having round eyes." As you read the poem, think first about how Mirikitani uses the elements of a process analysis to structure her poem.

# Recipe

Janice Mirikitani

> *Round Eyes*
> *Ingredients: scissors, Scotch magic transparent tape.*
> *eyeliner—water based, black.*
> *Optional: false eyelashes.*
> *Cleanse face thoroughly.*
> *For best results, powder entire face, including eyelids.*
> *(lighter shades suited to total effect desired)*
> *With scissors, cut magic tape 1/16" wide, 1/4–1/2" long—depending on*
> *length of eyelid.*
> *Stick firmly onto mid-upper eyelid area*
> *(looking down into handmirror facilitates finding adequate surface)*
> *If using false eyelashes, affix first on lid, folding any excess lid over the base of*
> *eyelash with glue.*
> *Paint black eyeliner on tape and entire lid.*
> *Do not cry.*

## Discussion Questions

1. How do you think that Mirikitani feels about "round eyes"? Is she trying simply to describe how to create that illusion? Is her poem trying to be "helpful"?
2. How would you characterize the tone of the poem? What in the poem provides evidence for your viewpoint?
3. How does the process structure contribute to the poem's effect? For example, what initial expectation did you have about the poem? Did your expectations change as you read? Where?
4. Is there anything in the "steps" of the process that seems unusual?
5. What makes this a poem and not a helpful set of instructions?

## Writing Suggestions

As this poem suggests, process does not have to be used in a simple, expository way. Mirikitani uses it to make a comment about a social issue, about cultural pressure and values. Explore a similar issue using a process model—either a set of directions or a description of how something works. Some possibilities for topics include:

a. Underage drinking or smoking
b. The desire to change your "looks" (for example, hair coloring, body piercing, hair straightening or curling, plastic surgery, purging)
c. The desire to conform to your peers (for example, behavior, dress, attitude)

## AS A CRITICAL READING STRATEGY

Every set of directions, or how-to-do-it, or how-it-is-done-or-produced is a process narrative or analysis. When we read a description of a process, we can expect to see several distinctive features:

- Process is always structured in time, from the first step to the last. In that sense, it is similar to a narrative or story, but unlike a narrative, process does not use flashbacks. That would only confuse the reader.
- The function of process is to allow a reader to duplicate the procedure or to understand the stages or steps. In that sense, process has a practical goal. It is effective only if the reader can follow it.
- To promote clarity, process frequently uses step or stage markers—first do this; then this. Typically, the steps or stages are numbered, or separated by extra space, or divided into paragraphs. The structure and how it is revealed on the printed page clearly emphasizes the steps.
- Process typically uses parallel structures—headings, sentences, and paragraphs are written so that they are grammatically similar in structure. (See Glossary and Ready Reference for examples.)
- Process is always conscious of its audience. Who is the intended audience? How much do they already know about the subject? The intended audience for an introductory biology textbook is obviously different from the audience for a research article published in a scientific journal.

To test your awareness of how process works, review this analysis of an essay taken from the CareerWomen Website (www.careerwomen.com)

| | |
|---|---|
| Note the reference to TV program | **"Getting the Interview Edge 'Apprentice-Style'"** |
| Who is the imagined audience? Young women looking for a job | The popularity of reality TV phenomenon *The Apprentice* provides job seekers new insights on the importance of the interview. While most employers have less than a 15-week |
| What is the purpose? To help them gain an "interview edge" | interview process, many lessons can be learned from how all candidates were evaluated during "The Apprentice." CareerWomen.com asked leading employers and recruiters for their top tips on gaining the interview edge. |
| Starts with preparation—before an interview | **1.** Be prepared<br>Familiarize yourself with the company as well as the position. Get up-to-date on current corporate issues so you can address any questions about |

Steps are in separate numbered, titled paragraphs

direction and opportunity. Develop a list of questions prior to the interview to demonstrate your interest and curiosity about the company. According to one recruiter, "I'm always stunned at how many times someone applies for a new job that they know nothing about or are unqualified for. Be prepared, professional and qualified if you want to go to the next step."

Each block is written in clear, nontechnical language

**2. Be qualified**

Highlight related experience, education and skills. Have solid references that will validate your qualifications. A leading recruiter comments, "Be good at what you do. Create great references by being the best you can at the job you already have."

Moved from preparing to the actual interview

**3. Make a positive impact**

Highlight your strengths and what you uniquely bring to the job opening. Show how you can make a positive impact. Demonstrate interest, insight, initiative and enthusiasm. Do you want the job? A CareerWomen.com employer

Each step uses a quotation to support the advice

suggests, "If you're applying for a marketing job, for example, bring in a sample campaign or ideas. Doing this would demonstrate an extraordinary candidate."

**4. Be professional**

Common courtesies will take you a long way at setting the right professional impression. For example, be sure to turn off the cell phone before the interview. If your interview is over lunch, watch your manners. Most importantly, be on time!

The headings for each paragraph are parallel in structure—"be," "make."

**5. Be a good communicator**

Get to the point quickly and say what needs to be said. A leading employer suggests, "Don't be too talkative or try to act like you know it all." Practice and prepare by

Each paragraph offers some specific examples of the skill or preparation being emphasized

answering sample interview questions found
at sites like CareerWomen.com, and create
responses for different levels within the
organization.

**6.** Follow-up appropriately

*Final advice—the last step in the process*

E-mail a thank you note immediately that
summarizes the interview and your ability to
contribute to the organization. Be sure that
your e-mail address is professional, not
"hotchick@aol.com."

*Process typically doesn't have a summary ending since it would not be necessary*

Additional resources to enhance professional
development and advance women's careers can
be found at CareerWomen.com, including
career development tools, career and
employment news, professional associations
and employment opportunities across the US
with some of the best women-friendly
companies.

### *Looking for process*

1. Look through your textbooks for this semester. Can you find examples of process narratives or analyses? Bring an example to share with the rest of the class.

2. Look for examples of process that you encounter every day. Make a list of situations in which you have had to read about a process before being able to do it—download music, play a new electronic game, operate a feature on your cell phone, fix something on your car or motorcycle.

## AS A VISUAL STRATEGY

Because process involves a series of steps or stages, it is typically represented through or accompanied by a series of photographs or drawings. Instructions for "how to assemble" often are nothing more than a series of illustrations with only a minimal number of words. Even descriptions of how something works or occurs generally use visuals to display the stages of the process. Single illustrations, however, can also suggest a process. Consider the following photograph. The young woman looks at herself in a mirror that is distorted. She sees herself in a distorted way.

## WRITING ABOUT IMAGES

1. The photograph suggests several possible process analyses. Choose one of the following possibilities and, in an essay, describe the process through which it happens or develops:

   **a.** Steps or stages in eating disorders

   **b.** Process by which women (or men) become obsessed by an ideal body shape

   **c.** Steps or stages in healthy weight loss or muscular development or fitness

   **d.** Steps or stages in recovering from an eating disorder or steroid use

   **e.** Steps or stages in developing a healthy body image

2. Flowcharts are the usual visual device through which process is displayed. Locate a flowchart for a common process (perhaps something from another course you are taking or a subject that is related to your major). Textbooks are a good place in which to look, or you can search images on Google. Then write an essay that translates the flowchart into words. Attach a copy of the flowchart to your paper.

3. Crack cocaine has particularly devastating effects on physical health and appearance. Television frequently shows before and after photographs of users. Using Google (www.google.com) or another search engine, locate a series of images or pictures of crack victims over time. In an essay, write about the process by which these effects occur.

## ADDITIONAL WRITING SUGGESTIONS FOR PROCESS

Process writing falls into two categories based on purpose. One type tells the reader how to do or make something; it assumes that the reader wishes to duplicate the process. The second type describes how something works or happened; it assumes that the reader wants to know how or why the process works. With either type of process writing, visual devices are often helpful and occasionally even indispensable.

## HOW-TO-DO-IT

1. How to choose the cell phone plan that is best for you
2. How to fail a course (humorous)
3. How to choose a major
4. How to locate a summer internship in your major
5. How to break up with a partner or how to cope with a breakup
6. How to change a tire on your car
7. How to get in shape or train for a particular event
8. How to choose the best credit card
9. How to buy the "right" piece of sports equipment or clothing
10. How to say no
11. How to treat a common athletic or sports injury
12. How to earn an "A" in a course
13. How to persuade your parents to allow you to study abroad
14. How to plan a perfect party
15. How to find a good roommate

## HOW-IT-WORKS

1. How does text messaging or instant messaging work
2. How do air bags work in automobiles
3. How do cell phones work
4. How are audio or video contents stored on a CD or DVD
5. How are vaccines made
6. How is muscle size increased
7. How does alcohol make you drunk
8. How does a specific weather event (for example, a hurricane, tornado, cyclone) occur
9. How is oil refined
10. How do search engines on the Web work
11. How do hybrid automobiles work
12. How are biofuels made
13. How do cattle contribute to global warming
14. How does aspirin work
15. How can fiber optics transmit information

# My Daily Dives in the Dumpster

Lars Eighner

*Born in 1948, Lars Eighner grew up in Houston, Texas. He attended the University of Texas at Austin but dropped out before graduation to do social work. In the mid-1980s, he lost his job as an attendant at a mental institution, which launched him on a three-year nightmare as a homeless person, with his dog, Lizbeth, as his companion. He later reworked these experiences as a book,* Travels with Lizbeth *(1993), the final manuscript of which was written on a personal computer that Eighner found in a dumpster.*

*__On Writing:__ Advice from Eighner's Website: "The best thing you can do for your writing is to learn to revise effectively. Sure, some natural geniuses may never have to revise a word, but the number of writers who consider themselves geniuses must outnumber the true geniuses by a factor of a thousand. And yes, some writers who practice revision for a long time eventually learn to avoid most mistakes so that their first drafts do not need much revision. But everyone else needs* to revise and revise and revise. *Putting a work through a spelling checker or a grammar checker is not revision. . . . Revision means changing words and phrases and sometimes changing whole sentences and paragraphs. Almost everyone's writing needs this kind of revision."*

## Before Reading

**Connecting:** If you came across someone "diving" into a dumpster, what assumptions would you be likely to make about that person?

**Anticipating:** One would hope that few of Eighner's readers will ever have to dive into dumpsters to survive. What then can readers learn from his essay?

1    I began Dumpster diving about a year before I became homeless.

2    I prefer the term "scavenging" and use the word "scrounging" when I mean to be obscure. I have heard people, evidently meaning to be polite, use the word "foraging," but I prefer to reserve that word for gathering nuts and berries and such, which I do also, according to the season and opportunity.

3    I like the frankness of the word "scavenging." I live from the refuse of others. I am a scavenger. I think it a sound and honorable niche, although if I could I would naturally prefer to live the comfortable consumer life,

perhaps—and only perhaps—as a slightly less wasteful consumer owing to what I have learned as a scavenger.

4     Except for jeans, all my clothes come from Dumpsters. Boom boxes, candles, bedding, toilet paper, medicine, books, a typewriter, a virgin male love doll, change sometimes amounting to many dollars: All came from Dumpsters. And, yes, I eat from Dumpsters too.

5     There are a predictable series of stages that a person goes through in learning to scavenge. At first the new scavenger is filled with disgust and self-loathing. He is ashamed of being seen and may lurk around trying to duck behind things, or he may try to dive at night. (In fact, this is unnecessary, since most people instinctively look away from scavengers.)

6     Every grain of rice seems to be a maggot. Everything seems to stink. The scavenger can wipe the egg yolk off the found can, but he cannot erase the stigma of eating garbage from his mind.

7     This stage passes with experience. The scavenger finds a pair of running shoes that fit and look and smell brand-new. He finds a pocket calculator in perfect working order. He finds pristine ice cream, still frozen, more than he can eat or keep. He begins to understand: People do throw away perfectly good stuff, a lot of perfectly good stuff.

8     At this stage he may become lost and never recover. All the Dumpster divers I have known come to the point of trying to acquire everything they touch. Why not take it, they reason, it is all free. This is, of course, hopeless, and most divers come to realize that they must restrict themselves to items of relatively immediate utility.

9     The finding of objects is becoming something of an urban art. Even respectable, employed people will sometimes find something tempting sticking out of a Dumpster or standing beside one. Quite a number of people, not all of them of the bohemian type, are willing to brag that they found this or that piece in the trash.

10     But eating from Dumpsters is the thing that separates the dilettanti from the professionals. Eating safely involves three principles: using the senses and common sense to evaluate the condition of the found materials; knowing the Dumpsters of a given area and checking them regularly; and seeking always to answer the question, Why was this discarded?

11     Perhaps everyone who has a kitchen and a regular supply of groceries has, at one time or another, eaten half a sandwich before discovering mold on the bread, or has gotten a mouthful of milk before realizing the milk had turned. Nothing of the sort is likely to happen to a Dumpster diver because he is constantly reminded that most food is discarded for a reason.

12     Yet perfectly good food can be found in Dumpsters. Canned goods, for example, turn up fairly often in the Dumpsters I frequent. All except the most phobic people would be willing to eat from a can even if it came from a Dumpster. I have few qualms about dry foods such as crackers, cookies, cereal, chips, and pasta if they are free of visible contaminates and still dry and crisp. Raw fruits and vegetables with intact skins seem perfectly safe to me, excluding, of

course, the obviously rotten. Many are discarded for minor imperfections that can be pared away. Chocolate is often discarded only because it has become discolored as the cocoa butter de-emulsified.

13     I began scavenging by pulling pizzas out of the Dumpster behind a pizza delivery shop. In general, prepared food requires caution, but in this case I knew what time the shop closed and went to the Dumpster as soon as the last of the help left.

14     Because the workers at these places are usually inexperienced, pizzas are often made with the wrong topping, baked incorrectly, or refused on delivery for being cold. The products to be discarded are boxed up because inventory is kept by counting boxes: A boxed pizza can be written off; an unboxed pizza does not exist. So I had a steady supply of fresh, sometimes warm pizza.

15     The area I frequent is inhabited by many affluent college students. I am not here by chance; the Dumpsters are very rich. Students throw out many good things, including food, particularly at the end of the semester and before and after breaks. I find it advantageous to keep an eye on the academic calendar.

16     A typical discard is a half jar of peanut butter—though nonorganic peanut butter does not require refrigeration and is unlikely to spoil in any reasonable time. Occasionally I find a cheese with a spot of mold, which, of course, I just pare off, and because it is obvious why the cheese was discarded, I treat it with less suspicion than an apparently perfect cheese found in similar circumstances. One of my favorite finds is yogurt—often discarded, still sealed, when the expiration date has passed—because it will keep for several days, even in warm weather.

17     I avoid ethnic foods I am unfamiliar with. If I do not know what it is supposed to look or smell like when it is good, I cannot be certain I will be able to tell if it is bad.

18     No matter how careful I am I still get dysentery at least once a month, oftener in warm weather. I do not want to paint too romantic a picture. Dumpster diving has serious drawbacks as a way of life.

19     Though I have a proprietary feeling about my Dumpsters, I don't mind my direct competitors, other scavengers, as much as I hate the sodacan scroungers.

20     I have tried scrounging aluminum cans with an able-bodied companion, and afoot we could make no more than a few dollars a day. I can extract the necessities of life from the Dumpsters directly with far less effort than would be required to accumulate the equivalent value in aluminum. Can scroungers, then, are people who *must* have small amounts of cash—mostly drug addicts and winos.

21     I do not begrudge them the cans, but can scroungers tend to tear up the Dumpsters, littering the area and mixing the contents. There are precious few courtesies among scavengers, but it is a common practice to set aside surplus items: pairs of shoes, clothing, canned goods, and such. A true scavenger hates to see good stuff go to waste, and what he cannot use he leaves in good condition in plain sight. Can scroungers lay waste to everything in their path and will

stir one of a pair of good shoes to the bottom of a Dumpster to be lost or ruined in the muck. They become so specialized that they can see only cans and earn my contempt by passing up change, canned goods, and readily hockable items.

22  Can scroungers will even go through individual garbage cans, something I have never seen a scavenger do. Going through individual garbage cans without spreading litter is almost impossible, and litter is likely to reduce the public's tolerance of scavenging. But my strongest reservation about going through individual garbage cans is that this seems to me a very personal kind of invasion, one to which I would object if I were a homeowner.

23  Though Dumpsters seem somehow less personal than garbage cans, they still contain bank statements, bills, correspondence, pill bottles, and other sensitive information. I avoid trying to draw conclusions about the people who dump in the Dumpsters I frequent. I think it would be unethical to do so, although I know many people will find the idea of scavenger ethics too funny for words.

24  Occasionally a find tells a story. I once found a small paper bag containing some unused condoms, several partial tubes of flavored sexual lubricant, a partially used compact of birth control pills, and the torn pieces of a picture of a young man. Clearly, the woman was through with him and planning to give up sex altogether.

25  Dumpster things are often sad—abandoned teddy bears, shredded wedding albums, despaired-of sales kits. I find diaries and journals. College students also discard their papers; I am horrified to discover the kind of paper that now merits an A in an undergraduate course.

26  Dumpster diving is outdoor work, often surprisingly pleasant. It is not entirely predictable; things of interest turn up every day, and some days there are finds of great value. I am always very pleased when I can turn up exactly the thing I most wanted to find. Yet in spite of the element of chance, scavenging, more than most other pursuits, tends to yield returns in some proportion to the effort and intelligence brought to bear.

27  I think of scavenging as a modern form of self-reliance. After ten years of government service, where everything is geared to the lowest common denominator, I find work that rewards initiative and effort refreshing. Certainly I would be happy to have a sinecure again, but I am not heart-broken to be without one.

28  I find from the experience of scavenging two rather deep lessons. The first is to take what I can use and let the rest go. I have come to think that there is no value in the abstract. A thing I cannot use or make useful, perhaps by trading, has no value, however fine or rare it may be. (I mean useful in the broad sense—some art, for example, I would think valuable.)

29  The second lesson is the transience of material being. I do not suppose that ideas are immortal, but certainly they are longer-lived than material objects.

30  The things I find in Dumpsters, the love letters and rag dolls of so many lives, remind me of this lesson. Many times in my travels I have lost everything

but the clothes on my back. Now I hardly pick up a thing without envisioning the time I will cast it away. This, I think, is a healthy state of mind. Almost everything I have now has already been cast out at least once, proving that what I own is valueless to someone.

31    I find that my desire to grab for the gaudy bauble has been largely sated. I think this is an attitude I share with the very wealthy—we both know there is plenty more where whatever we have came from. Between us are the rat-race millions who have confounded their selves with the objects they grasp and who nightly scavenge the cable channels looking for they know not what.

32    I am sorry for them.

## Questions on Subject and Purpose

1. Is the subject of Eighner's essay simply how to "dive" into a dumpster? What other points does he make?
2. A substantial part of the essay deals with scavenging for food. Why does Eighner devote so much space to this?
3. What larger or more general lesson or truth does Eighner see in his experiences? For example, for whom does Eighner say he feels sorry at the end of the essay?

## Questions on Strategy and Audience

1. In what ways does the essay use process as a writing strategy?
2. What are the "predictable stages" that a scavenger goes through?
3. What assumptions does Eighner make about his audience?

## Questions on Vocabulary and Style

1. Why does Eighner prefer the term *scavenging* to a more ambiguous or better-sounding term?
2. In what way is Eighner's final sentence ironic? Why might he choose to make it a separate paragraph?
3. Be prepared to define the following words: *niche* (paragraph 3), *stigma* (6), *pristine* (7), *bohemian* (9), *dilettanti* (10), *phobic* (12), *qualms* (12), *de-emulsified* (12), *affluent* (15), *proprietary* (19), *sinecure* (27), *transience* (29), *gaudy* (31), *bauble* (31), *sated* (31).

## Writing Suggestions

1. **For Your Journal or Blog.** Suppose that suddenly you found yourself without a full-time job or financial support from your family. What would you do? Using an ordered sequence, plan out the steps that you would take in trying to deal with the situation.
2. **For a Paragraph.** In a world in which many Americans can find only low-paying jobs with no benefits, what advice could you offer to a young high school student today? In a paragraph organized according to a process

structure, address that audience. Be sure to have a specific point or thesis to your paragraph. Try to avoid clichéd answers; just saying "go to college," for example, is not particularly good advice, as many college students are not able to find well-paying, full-time jobs.

3. **For an Essay.** Where are you going in your life, and how do you plan to get there? What are your objectives, goals, or aspirations? Where do you hope to be in ten years? In twenty years? What are you doing now to try to achieve those goals? What should you be doing? In an essay, honestly examine your directions and your actions.

4. **For Research.** With corporate and business "downsizing," many Americans have suddenly found themselves out of work. As advice for those trapped in such a situation, write a guide to the resources available to the newly unemployed. Use a process strategy as a way of providing step-by-step advice to your audience. Contact local and state agencies to see what help is available and how one goes about making an application. Be sure to document your sources—including interviews—wherever appropriate.

## For Further Study

**Focusing on Grammar and Writing.** Locate each instance in which Eighner uses a colon or a semicolon. On the basis of these examples, write a series of rules that govern colon and semicolon usage. How often do you use either mark in your own writing? What does each mark do that cannot be done by another mark of punctuation?

**Working Together.** Working with classmates in small groups, brainstorm responses on how to furnish a dorm room or an apartment with "free" or very inexpensive items. What would the process entail? Make a list of the steps or stages and experiment with using a numbered list, with explicit sequence markers, or with extra white space or paragraphs.

**Seeing Other Modes at Work.** To what extent is Eighner's essay persuasive? If the essay were to be recast to persuade readers about the importance or unimportance of things in life, what could be used in the essay, and what would have to be deleted, changed, or expanded?

**Finding Connections.** Read E. M. Forster's "My Wood" (Chapter 7). In what ways is that essay similar to Eighner's? About what might the two writers agree? Disagree?

**Exploring the Web.** Eighner has a home page on the Web (www.larseighner. com) that includes a wide range of information about his books, his other publications, and a bibliography of articles about him and his work.

# Revision and Life: Take It from the Top—Again

Nora Ephron

*Nora Ephron (1941–) graduated from Wellesley College and worked as a journalist and columnist for the* New York Post, New York *magazine, and* Esquire. *She is also a successful screenplay writer and director whose credits include* Sleepless in Seattle *(1993),* You've Got Mail *(1998), and* Julie and Julia *(2009). "Revision and Life," written in response to an invitation to participate in this textbook, was originally published in* The New York Times Book Review.

**On Writing:** *When asked about the autobiographical influences of her first novel, Ephron replied: "I've always written about my life. That's how I grew up. 'Take notes. Everything is copy.' All that stuff my mother [also a writer] said to us."*

## Before Reading

**Connecting:** When it comes to writing, what does the word *revision* suggest to you?

**Anticipating:** When Ephron observes, "A gift for revision may be a developmental stage," what does she mean?

1 I have been asked to write something for a textbook that is meant to teach college students something about writing and revision. I am happy to do this because I believe in revision. I have also been asked to save the early drafts of whatever I write, presumably to show these students the actual process of revision. This too I am happy to do. On the other hand, I suspect that there is just so much you can teach college students about revision; a gift for revision may be a developmental stage—like a 2-year-old's sudden ability to place one block on top of another—that comes along somewhat later, in one's mid-20s, say; most people may not be particularly good at it, or even interested in it, until then.

2 When I was in college, I revised nothing. I wrote out my papers in longhand, typed them up and turned them in. It would never have crossed my mind that what I had produced was only a first draft and that I had more work to do; the idea was to get to the end, and once you had got to the end you were

finished. The same thinking, I might add, applied in life: I went pell-mell through my four years in college without a thought about whether I ought to do anything differently; the idea was to get to the end—to get out of school and become a journalist.

3      Which I became, in fairly short order. I learned as a journalist to revise on deadline. I learned to write an article a paragraph at a time—and I arrived at the kind of writing and revising I do, which is basically a kind of typing and retyping. I am a great believer in this technique for the simple reason that I type faster than the wind. What I generally do is to start an article and get as far as I can—sometimes no farther in than a sentence or two—before running out of steam, ripping the piece of paper from the typewriter and starting all over again. I type over and over until I have got the beginning of the piece to the point where I am happy with it. I then am ready to plunge into the body of the article itself. This plunge usually requires something known as a transition. I approach a transition by completely retyping the opening of the article leading up to it in the hope that the ferocious speed of my typing will somehow catapult me into the next section of the piece. This does not work—what in fact catapults me into the next section is a concrete thought about what the next section ought to be about—but until I have the thought the typing keeps me busy, and keeps me from feeling something known as blocked.

4      Typing and retyping as if you know where you're going is a version of what therapists tell you to do when they suggest that you try changing from the outside in—that if you can't master the total commitment to whatever change you want to make, you can at least do all the extraneous things connected with it, which make it that much easier to get there. I was 25 years old the first time a therapist suggested that I try changing from the outside in. In those days, I used to spend quite a lot of time lying awake at night wondering what I should have said earlier in the evening and revising my lines. I mention this not just because it's a way of illustrating that a gift for revision is practically instinctive, but also (once again) because it's possible that a genuine ability at it doesn't really come into play until one is older—or at least older than 25, when it seemed to me that all that was required in my life and my work was the chance to change a few lines.

5      In my 30's, I began to write essays, one a month for *Esquire* magazine, and I am not exaggerating when I say that in the course of writing a short essay—1,500 words, that's only six double-spaced typewritten pages—I often used 300 or 400 pieces of typing paper, so often did I type and retype and catapult and recatapult myself, sometimes on each retyping moving not even a sentence farther from the spot I had reached the last time through. At the same time, though, I was polishing what I had already written: as I struggled with the middle of the article, I kept putting the beginning through the typewriter; as I approached the ending, the middle got its turn. (This is a kind of polishing that the word processor all but eliminates, which is why I don't use one. Word processors make it possible for a writer to change the sentences that clearly need changing without having to retype the rest, but I believe that you can't

always tell whether a sentence needs work until it rises up in revolt against your fingers as you retype it.) By the time I had produced what you might call a first draft—an entire article with a beginning, middle and end—the beginning was in more like 45th draft, the middle in 20th, and the end was almost newborn. For this reason, the beginnings of my essays are considerably better written than the ends, although I like to think no one ever notices this but me.

6       As I learned the essay form, writing became harder for me. I was finding a personal style, a voice if you will, a way of writing that looked chatty and informal. That wasn't the hard part—the hard part was that having found a voice, I had to work hard month to month not to seem as if I were repeating myself. At this point in this essay it will not surprise you to learn that the same sort of thing was operating in my life. I don't mean that my life had become harder— but that it was becoming clear that I had many more choices than had occurred to me when I was marching through my 20's. I no longer lost sleep over what I should have said. Not that I didn't care—it was just that I had moved to a new plane of late-night anxiety: I now wondered what I should have done. Whole areas of possible revision opened before me. What should I have done instead? What could I have done? What if I hadn't done it the way I did? What if I had a chance to do it over? What if I had a chance to do it over as a different person? These were the sorts of questions that kept me awake and led me into fiction, which at the very least (the level at which I practice it) is a chance to rework the events of your life so that you give the illusion of being the intelligence at the center of it, simultaneously managing to slip in all the lines that occurred to you later. Fiction, I suppose, is the ultimate shot at revision.

7       Now I am in my 40's and I write screenplays. Screenplays—if they are made into movies—are essentially collaborations, and movies are not a writer's medium, we all know this, and I don't want to dwell on the craft of screenwriting except insofar as it relates to revision. Because the moment you stop work on a script seems to be determined not by whether you think the draft is good but simply by whether shooting is about to begin: if it is, you get to call your script a final draft; and if it's not, you can always write another revision. This might seem to be a hateful way to live, but the odd thing is that it's somehow comforting; as long as you're revising, the project isn't dead. And by the same token, neither are you.

8       It was, as it happens, while thinking about all this one recent sleepless night that I figured out how to write this particular essay. I say "recent" in order to give a sense of immediacy and energy to the preceding sentence, but the truth is that I am finishing this article four months after the sleepless night in question, and the letter asking me to write it, from George Miller of the University of Delaware, arrived almost two years ago, so for all I know Mr. Miller has managed to assemble his textbook on revision without me.

9       Oh, well. That's how it goes when you start thinking about revision. That's the danger of it, in fact. You can spend so much time thinking about how to switch things around that the main event has passed you by. But it doesn't matter. Because by the time you reach middle age, you want more than anything for things not to come to an end; and as long as you're still revising, they don't.

10      I'm sorry to end so morbidly—dancing as I am around the subject of death—but there are advantages to it. For one thing, I have managed to move fairly effortlessly and logically from the beginning of this piece through the middle and to the end. And for another, I am able to close with an exhortation, something I rarely manage, which is this: Revise now, before it's too late.

## Questions on Subject and Purpose

1. For Ephron, how are revision and life connected?
2. Why is fiction the "ultimate shot at revision" (paragraph 6)?
3. Is the essay about how to revise or about something else?

## Questions on Strategy and Audience

1. How does Ephron structure her essay? What principle of order does she follow?
2. What might Ephron mean by her final sentence ("Revise now, before it's too late")?
3. It would have been a simple matter for Ephron to omit the references to this textbook (paragraphs 1 and 8). *The New York Times* audience, for example, would not be interested in knowing these details. Why might she have chosen to include these references in her essay?

## Questions on Vocabulary and Style

1. Have you ever heard the phrase "take it from the top—again"? In what context is it usually used? What might such a figure of speech be called?
2. Ephron refers to her strategy of retyping as a way of "catapulting" herself into the next section. Where does the verb *catapult* come from? What does it suggest?
3. Be prepared to define the following words: *pell-mell* (paragraph 2), *extraneous* (4), *exhortation* (10).

## Writing Suggestions

1. **For Your Journal or Blog.** What obstacles do you face when you try to revise something that you have written? Make a list of the ones that immediately come to mind. Add to your list as you finish each paragraph and essay during this course.
2. **For a Paragraph.** Formulate a thesis about Ephron's process of revision based on this essay. In a paragraph, assert your thesis and support it with appropriate evidence from the essay.
3. **For an Essay.** On the basis of your own experience as a writer and as a student in this course, argue for or against *requiring* revision in a college writing course. Should a student be forced to do it? Does revision always produce a better paper?

4. **For Research.** What role does revision play in the writing process of faculty and staff at your college or university? Interview a range of people—faculty (especially professors in disciplines other than English) and other professional staff members who write as a regular part of their job (for example, librarians, information officers, and admissions officers). Using notes from your interviews, write an essay about the revision practices of these writers. Your essay could be a feature article in the campus newspaper.

## For Further Study

**Focusing on Grammar and Writing.** Information inserted into a sentence can be set off by commas, parentheses, or dashes. In paragraphs 5 and 6, Ephron uses all three marks. Study these paragraphs, and offer an explanation for why Ephron chooses to punctuate each insertion or addition as she does.

**Working Together.** Working in small groups, discuss if and how each of you "revise" an essay. Probably no one works as Ephron did, but what other strategies do writers use? How many ask classmates, friends, or relatives to read their papers? How many are willing to really change the structure of a paper? How many regard revision as changing words and punctuation? Prepare to share your experiences with others in the class.

**Seeing Other Modes at Work.** Ephron uses division to structure the middle of her essay—what revision meant to her at each stage of her life, from her college years to her forties.

**Finding Connections.** A number of essays explore the "knowledge" or "recognition" that comes with age—possible comparisons include Anne Quindlen's "The Name is Mine" (Chapter 1) and Scott Russell Sanders's "The Inheritance of Tools" (Chapter 3).

**Exploring the Web.** Ephron is increasingly known as both a screenwriter and director. You can find detailed Web resources on all of her films, including stills, audio, and video clips. Visit www.imdb.com for information on her film writing and directing. How does this essay explain her interest in filmmaking?

# For Authors, Fragile Ideas Need Loving Every Day

Walter Mosley

*Walter Mosley (1952–), author of dozens of books and winner of many writing awards, is probably best known for his crime fictions, especially a series of historical mysteries that feature Easy Rawlins, a private investigator who lives in Watts, in Los Angeles. Mosley's essay was originally commissioned by* The New York Times *as part of a regular series of articles under the heading "Writers on Writing." John Darnton, a writer and editor for the* Times, *conceived of the series as a place in which writers might talk about the craft of writing. The essays were eventually published in book form under the title* Writers on Writing *(2001).*

**On Writing:** *Darnton reflected on his experiences with writers: "I learned a number of things. Not all writers want to talk about what they do. A lot of them do not meet deadlines. And unlike reporters, they do not accept assignments gracefully—they actually have to want to do it. Beware of interrupting a writer in the middle of his working day: if he appears to want to remain on the line long after you do, that's not a good sign. Some are perfectionists. . . . Some are vain. . . . And all of them are human in one respect: they wanted to hear, right away, what you thought of their work."*

## Before Reading

**Connecting:** Have you ever thought that you have a novel or short story (or poem, play, or film) "inside" of you? Can you imagine yourself as a writer? Why or why not?

**Anticipating:** What is the single most important piece of advice that Mosley offers his readers?

1  If you want to be a writer, you have to write every day. The consistency, the monotony, the certainty, all vagaries and passions are covered by this daily reoccurrence.

2  You don't go to a well once but daily. You don't skip a child's breakfast or forget to wake up in the morning. Sleep comes to you each day, and so does the muse.

3  She comes softly and quietly, behind your left ear or in a corner of the next room. Her words are whispers, her ideas shifting renditions of possibilities that

have not been resolved, though they have occurred and reoccurred a thousand times in your mind. She, or it, is a collection of memories not exactly your own.

4    These reminiscences surface in dreams or out of abstract notions brought on by tastes and excitations, failures and hopes that you experience continually. These ideas have no physical form. They are smoky concepts liable to disappear at the slightest disturbance. An alarm clock or a ringing telephone will dispel a new character; answering the call will erase a chapter from the world.

5    Our most precious ability, the knack of creation, is also our most fleeting resource. What might be fades in the world of necessity.

6    How can I create when I have to go to work, cook my dinner, remember what I did wrong to the people who have stopped calling? And even if I do find a moment here and there—a weekend away in the mountains, say—how can I say everything I need to say before the world comes crashing back with all of its sirens and shouts and television shows?

7    "I know I have a novel in me," I often hear people say. "But how can I get it out?"

8    The answer is, always is, every day.

9    The dream of the writer, of any artist, is a fickle and amorphous thing. One evening you're remembering a homeless man, dressed in clothes that smelled like cheese rinds, who you once stood next to on a street corner in New York. Your memory becomes a reverie, and in this daydream you ask him where he's from. With a thick accent he tells you that he was born in Hungary, that he was a freedom fighter, but that now, here in America, his freedom has deteriorated into the poverty of the streets.

10    You write down a few sentences in your journal and sigh. This exhalation is not exhaustion but anticipation at the prospect of a wonderful tale exposing a notion that you still only partly understand.

11    A day goes by. Another passes. At the end of the next week you find yourself in the same chair, at the same hour when you wrote about the homeless man previously. You open the journal to see what you'd written. You remember everything perfectly, but the life has somehow drained out of it. The words have no art to them; you no longer remember the smell. The idea seems weak, it has dissipated, like smoke.

12    This is the first important lesson that the writer must learn. Writing a novel is gathering smoke. It's an excursion into the ether of ideas. There's no time to waste. You must work with that idea as well as you can, jotting down notes and dialogue.

13    The first day the dream you gathered will linger, but it won't last long. The next day you have to return to tend to your flimsy vapors. You have to brush them, reshape them, breathe into them and gather more.

14    It doesn't matter what time of day you work, but you have to work every day because creation, like life, is always slipping away from you. You must write every day, but there's no time limit on how long you have to write.

15    One day you might read over what you've done and think about it. You pick up the pencil or turn on the computer, but no new words come. That's

fine. Sometimes you can't go further. Correct a misspelling, reread a perplexing paragraph, and then let it go. You have reentered the dream of the work, and that's enough to keep the story alive for another twenty-four hours.

16      The next day you might write for hours; there's no way to tell. The goal is not a number of words or hours spent writing. All you need is to keep your heart and mind open to the work.

17      Nothing we create is art at first. It's simply a collection of notions that may never be understood. Returning every day thickens the atmosphere. Images appear. Connections are made. But even these clearer notions will fade if you stay away more than a day.

18      Reality fights against your dreams, it tries to deny creation and change. The world wants you to be someone known, someone with solid ideas, not blowing smoke. Given a day, reality will begin to scatter your notions; given two days, it will drive them off.

19      The act of writing is a kind of guerrilla warfare; there is no vacation, no leave, no relief. In actuality there is very little chance of victory. You are, you fear, like that homeless man, likely to be defeated by your fondest dreams.

20      But then the next day comes, and the words are waiting. You pick up where you left off, in the cool and shifting mists of morning.

## Questions on Subject and Purpose

1. Mosley says that the "muse" comes every day. What is a muse and where does that idea come from?
2. Would a reader not interested in writing a novel learn anything of value from the essay?
3. How does Mosley see the process of writing? What is it like? It is fun? Easy?

## Questions on Strategy and Audience

1. Although Mosley describes his process of writing, he does not do so in a precise step-by-step way (for example, "first do this, then this"). Why not?
2. The essay first appeared in a newspaper. How might its place of publication have influenced how the essay is paragraphed?
3. Given where the essay originally appeared, what might Mosley be able to assume about his audience?

## Questions on Vocabulary and Style

1. Mosley writes, "The idea seems weak, it has dissipated, like smoke" (paragraph 11) and then, "Writing a novel is gathering smoke" (12). Both are figures of speech—what are they called and what is the difference between them?
2. Mosley has a number of very short sentences (sometimes just two words), but are they all sentences? Are any fragments? How can you tell the difference?
3. Be prepared to define the following words: *vagaries* (paragraph 1), *renditions* (3), *amorphous* (9), *dissipated* (11).

## Writing Suggestions

1. **For Your Journal or Blog.** Think about something at which you are good. It does not matter what it is—a sport, a game, an activity, whatever. Identify what it is and reflect on how you got to be so good at it.

2. **For a Paragraph.** Expand your journal or blog entry into a paragraph. Trace your evolution over time; try to identify at least two milestones in your development.

3. **For an Essay.** Expand your paragraph into an essay. This time direct your paper to readers who are interested in developing a similar skill or ability. Write your essay as a process narrative, tracing out the steps or stages readers would need to move through to acquire this skill or ability.

4. **For Research.** Mosley's Website (www.waltermosley.com) offers extensive reflections on how he revises. Visit the site, take notes, and then in an essay describe the process of rewriting that Mosley follows. Be sure to document all of the direct quotations taken from the Website.

## For Further Study

**Focusing on Grammar and Writing.** Throughout the essay, Mosley uses one particular metaphor when he writes about creative ideas. What is that metaphor (check the Glossary and Ready Reference for a definition) and what is appropriate about it?

**Working Together.** Mosley is primarily talking about writing a novel, although he has written other types of books and many articles as well. How helpful is his advice to you as a student writer in a college course? Divide into small groups and discuss the extent to which what he says might be applied to your own writing.

**Seeing Other Modes at Work.** A fundamental comparison and contrast exists in the essay between the world of everyday "necessity" (paragraph 5) and the world of creativity and memory.

**Finding Connections.** Interesting pairings could be made with William Zinsser's "The Transaction" (Chapter 5) and Nora Ephron's "Revision and Life" (this chapter).

**Exploring the Web.** Walter Mosley has an extensive website at www.waltermosley.com. You can read more there about his reflections on writing under the heading "In His Own Words"; also included is a transcript of an interview.

# The Culture of Martyrdom

David Brooks

*David Brooks, a graduate of the University of Chicago, is a senior editor at* The Weekly Standard, *a contributing editor at* Newsweek, *a correspondent for* Atlantic Monthly, *and a political analyst for* The NewsHour with Jim Lehrer. *His most recent book is* On Paradise Drive: How We Live Now (And Always Have) in the Future Tense *(2004). "The Culture of Martyrdom" appeared in the* Atlantic Monthly *in the summer of 2002.*

**On Writing:** *In the Acknowledgments to* Bobos in Paradise, *Brooks suggests the importance to professional writers of peer readers and editors. He thanks numerous readers of his manuscript for their "valuable advice" and, in particular, his editor, who "seemed to ponder every word" and whose "comments improved it in ways great and small."*

## Before Reading

**Connecting:** What does the word *martyr* mean to you?

**Anticipating:** Throughout the essay Brooks suggests that suicide bombings are an "addiction." Why does he make this analogy? In his mind, what justifies such a link?

1 **S**uicide bombing is the crack cocaine of warfare. It doesn't just inflict death and terror on its victims; it intoxicates the people who sponsor it. It unleashes the deepest and most addictive human passions—the thirst for vengeance, the desire for religious purity, the longing for earthly glory and eternal salvation. Suicide bombing isn't just a tactic in a larger war; it overwhelms the political goals it is meant to serve. It creates its own logic and transforms the culture of those who employ it. This is what has happened in the Arab-Israeli dispute. Over the past year suicide bombing has dramatically changed the nature of the conflict.

2 Before 1983 there were few suicide bombings. The Koran forbids the taking of one's own life, and this prohibition was still generally observed. But when the United States stationed Marines in Beirut, the leaders of the Islamic resistance movement Hizbollah began to discuss turning to this ultimate terrorist weapon. Religious authorities in Iran gave it their blessing, and a wave of suicide bombings began, starting with the attacks that killed about sixty U.S. embassy workers in April of 1983 and about 240 people in the Marine compound at the airport in October. The bombings proved so successful at

driving the United States and, later, Israel out of Lebanon that most lingering religious concerns were set aside.

3      The tactic was introduced into Palestinian areas only gradually. In 1988 Fathi Shiqaqi, the founder of the Palestinian Islamic Jihad, wrote a set of guidelines (aimed at countering religious objections to the truck bombings of the 1980s) for the use of explosives in individual bombings; nevertheless, he characterized operations calling for martyrdom as "exceptional." But by the mid-1990s the group Hamas was using suicide bombers as a way of derailing the Oslo peace process. The assassination of the master Palestinian bomb maker Yahya Ayyash, presumably by Israeli agents, in January of 1996, set off a series of suicide bombings in retaliation. Suicide bombings nonetheless remained relatively unusual until two years ago, after the Palestinian leader Yasir Arafat walked out of the peace conference at Camp David—a conference at which Israel's Prime Minister, Ehud Barak, had offered to return to the Palestinians parts of Jerusalem and almost all of the West Bank.

4      At that point the psychology shifted. We will not see peace soon, many Palestinians concluded, but when it eventually comes, we will get everything we want. We will endure, we will fight, and we will suffer for that final victory. From then on the struggle (at least from the Palestinian point of view) was no longer about negotiation and compromise—about who would get which piece of land, which road or river. The red passions of the bombers obliterated the grays of the peace process. Suicide bombing became the tactic of choice, even in circumstances where a terrorist could have planted a bomb and then escaped without injury. Martyrdom became not just a means but an end.

5      Suicide bombing is a highly communitarian enterprise. According to Ariel Merari, the director of the Political Violence Research Center, at Tel Aviv University, and a leading expert on the phenomenon, in not one instance has a lone, crazed Palestinian gotten hold of a bomb and gone off to kill Israelis. Suicide bombings are initiated by tightly run organizations that recruit, indoctrinate, train, and reward the bombers. Those organizations do not seek depressed or mentally unstable people for their missions. From 1996 to 1999 the Pakistani journalist Nasra Hassan interviewed almost 250 people who were either recruiting and training bombers or preparing to go on a suicide mission themselves. "None of the suicide bombers—they ranged in age from eighteen to thirty-eight—conformed to the typical profile of the suicidal personality," Hassan wrote in *The New Yorker*. "None of them were uneducated, desperately poor, simple-minded, or depressed." The Palestinian bombers tend to be devout, but religious fanaticism does not explain their motivation. Nor does lack of opportunity, because they also tend to be well educated.

6      Often a bomber believes that a close friend or a member of his family has been killed by Israeli troops, and this is part of his motivation. According to most experts, though, the crucial factor informing the behavior of suicide bombers is loyalty to the group. Suicide bombers go through indoctrination processes similar to the ones that were used by the leaders of the Jim Jones and Solar Temple cults. The bombers are organized into small cells and given countless hours of intense and intimate spiritual training. They are instructed

in the details of *jihad*, reminded of the need for revenge, and reassured about the rewards they can expect in the afterlife. They are told that their families will be guaranteed a place with God, and that there are also considerable rewards for their families in this life, including cash bonuses of several thousand dollars donated by the government of Iraq, some individual Saudis, and various groups sympathetic to the cause. Finally, the bombers are told that paradise lies just on the other side of the detonator, that death will feel like nothing more than a pinch.

7    Members of such groups re-enact past operations. Recruits are sometimes made to lie in empty graves, so that they can see how peaceful death will be; they are reminded that life will bring sickness, old age, and betrayal. "We were in a constant state of worship," one suicide bomber (who somehow managed to survive his mission) told Hassan. "We told each other that if the Israelis only knew how joyful we were they would whip us to death! Those were the happiest days of my life!"

8    The bombers are instructed to write or videotape final testimony. (A typical note, from 1995: "I am going to take revenge upon the sons of the monkeys and the pigs, the Zionist infidels and the enemies of humanity. I am going to meet my holy brother Hisham Hamed and all the other martyrs and saints in paradise.") Once a bomber has completed his declaration, it would be humiliating for him to back out of the mission. He undergoes a last round of cleansing and prayer and is sent off with his bomb to the appointed pizzeria, coffee shop, disco, or bus.

9    For many Israelis and Westerners, the strangest aspect of the phenomenon is the televised interview with a bomber's parents after a massacre. These people have just been told that their child has killed himself and others, and yet they seem happy, proud, and—should the opportunity present itself—ready to send another child off to the afterlife. There are two ways to look at this: One, the parents feel so wronged and humiliated by the Israelis that they would rather sacrifice their children than continue passively to endure. Two, the cult of suicide bombing has infected the broader culture to the point where large parts of society, including the bombers' parents, are addicted to the adrenaline rush of vengeance and murder. Both explanations may be true.

10    It is certainly the case that vast segments of Palestinian culture have been given over to the creation and nurturing of suicide bombers. Martyrdom has replaced Palestinian independence as the main focus of the Arab media. Suicide bombing is, after all, perfectly suited to the television age. The bombers' farewell videos provide compelling footage, as do the interviews with families. The bombings themselves produce graphic images of body parts and devastated buildings. Then there are the "weddings" between the martyrs and dark-eyed virgins in paradise (announcements that read like wedding invitations are printed in local newspapers so that friends and neighbors can join in the festivities), the marches and celebrations after each attack, and the displays of things bought with the cash rewards to the families. Woven together, these images make gripping packages that can be aired again and again.

11        Activities in support of the bombings are increasingly widespread. Last year the BBC shot a segment about so-called Paradise Camps—summer camps in which children as young as eight are trained in military drills and taught about suicide bombers. Rallies commonly feature children wearing bombers' belts. Fifth- and sixth-graders have studied poems that celebrate the bombers. At Al Najah University, in the West Bank, a student exhibition last September included a re-created scene of the Sbarro pizzeria in Jerusalem after the suicide bombing there last August: "blood" was splattered everywhere, and mock body parts hung from the ceiling as if blown through the air.

12        Thus suicide bombing has become phenomenally popular. According to polls, 70 to 80 percent of Palestinians now support it—making the act more popular than Hamas, the Palestinian Islamic Jihad, Fatah, or any of the other groups that sponsor it, and far more popular than the peace process ever was. In addition to satisfying visceral emotions, suicide bombing gives average Palestinians, not just PLO elites, a chance to play a glorified role in the fight against Israel.

13        Opponents of suicide bombings sometimes do raise their heads. Over the last couple of years educators have moderated the tone of textbooks to reduce and in many cases eliminate the rhetoric of holy war. After the BBC report aired, Palestinian officials vowed to close the Paradise Camps. Nonetheless, Palestinian children grow up in a culture in which suicide bombers are rock stars, sports heroes, and religious idols rolled into one. Reporters who speak with Palestinians about the bombers notice the fire and pride in their eyes.

14        "I'd be very happy if my daughter killed Sharon," one mother told a reporter from *The San Diego Union-Tribune* last November. "Even if she killed two or three Israelis, I would be happy." Last year I attended a dinner party in Amman at which six distinguished Jordanians—former cabinet ministers and supreme-court justices and a journalist—talked about the Tel Aviv disco bombing, which had occurred a few months earlier. They had some religious qualms about the suicide, but the moral aspect of killing teenage girls—future breeders of Israelis—was not even worth discussing. They spoke of the attack with a quiet sense of satisfaction.

15        It's hard to know how Israel, and the world, should respond to the rash of suicide bombings and to their embrace by the Palestinian people. To take any action that could be viewed as a concession would be to provoke further attacks, as the U.S. and Israeli withdrawals from Lebanon in the 1980s demonstrated. On the other hand, the Israeli raids on the refugee camps give the suicide bombers a propaganda victory. After Yasir Arafat walked out of the Camp David meetings, he became a pariah to most governments, for killing the peace process. Now, amid Israeli retaliation for the bombings, the global community rises to condemn Israel's actions.

16        Somehow conditions must be established that would allow the frenzy of suicide bombings to burn itself out. To begin with, the Palestinian and Israeli populations would have to be separated; contact between them inflames the passions that feed the attacks. That would mean shutting down the vast majority of Israeli settlements in the West Bank and Gaza and creating a buffer zone

between the two populations. Palestinian life would then no longer be dominated by checkpoints and celebrations of martyrdom; it would be dominated by quotidian issues such as commerce, administration, and garbage collection.

17    The idea of a buffer zone, which is gaining momentum in Israel, is not without problems. Where, exactly, would the buffer be? Terrorist groups could shoot missiles over it. But it's time to face the reality that the best resource the terrorists have is the culture of martyrdom. This culture is presently powerful, but it is potentially fragile. If it can be interrupted, if the passions can be made to recede, then the Palestinians and the Israelis might go back to hating each other in the normal way, and at a distance. As with many addictions, the solution is to go cold turkey.

## Questions on Subject and Purpose

1. What is a martyr?
2. What does the phrase "the culture of martyrdom" suggest to you?
3. What purpose or purposes might Brooks have in his essay?

## Questions on Strategy and Audience

1. How effective is Brooks's introduction?
2. How does Brooks use process in his essay?
3. To whom is Brooks writing? What assumptions does he make about his audience? How can you tell?

## Questions on Vocabulary and Style

1. What does the expression "to go cold turkey" mean? From what context is it derived? What might we call such an expression?
2. How appropriate is Brooks's final sentence as a concluding statement for the essay?
3. Be prepared to define the following words: *obliterated* (paragraph 4), *infidels* (8), *visceral* (12), *pariah* (15), *quotidian* (16).

## Writing Suggestions

1. **For Your Journal or Blog.** In your journal or blog, reflect on how you handle conflict—with parents, friends, authority figures, or people you perceive as "enemies." Be honest with yourself. Try to think of specific situations in which you were faced with a conflict. Make a list of several. What did you do in response to that conflict? What should you have done?
2. **For a Paragraph.** Conflict often provokes counterproductive reactions. Someone screams at us; we scream louder in response. Generally, we know how we ought to react, even if we rarely do so. Expand your journal or blog writing into a paragraph. In the paragraph offer advice in a step-by-step process about how to handle a specific type of conflict. Possible situations

might include a quarrel with your parents or with a sibling, a conflict with a teacher over a grade, resentment toward a friend who clearly takes advantage of you, or your response to someone who insults or demeans you.

3. **For an Essay.** "How to Negotiate Conflicts." Expand your paragraph into an essay offering advice to your contemporaries on how to handle a commonly encountered conflict. You might want to imagine that your essay will appear in your college or university newspaper. Remember, you can address serious conflicts such as sexual, racial, or ethnic discrimination, domestic abuse, or criminal and/or immoral behavior.

4. **For Research.** What proposals have been put forth for a settlement of the Arab-Israeli conflict? How have people suggested creating a peace? What are the key steps in such a process? Research the issue. Remember to treat both sides fairly—any resolution must be equally embraced by both sides.

## For Further Study

**Focusing on Grammar and Writing.** What is a topic sentence? Look carefully at Brooks's essay. Do his paragraphs always have topic sentences? Where are they placed in his paragraphs? Are they always the first sentences? How do they help you as a reader? What does Brooks's use of topic sentences suggest about your own writing?

**Working Together.** What is the difference between a *martyr* and a *terrorist*? Working in small groups, brainstorm about your understanding of those two terms. What about the term *insurgent*? What does that mean? If you have a dictionary available, check the dictionary definitions. Is a martyr to one culture or faith a terrorist or insurgent to another culture or faith? What is the impact on the audience of using each word?

**Seeing Other Modes at Work.** Identify those portions of Brooks's essay in which he uses a cause-and-effect structure.

**Finding Connections.** A possible pairing is with Allison Perkins's "Mission Iraq" (Chapter 2).

**Exploring the Web.** The Web offers a wide variety of sources for gathering information about the Arab–Israeli conflict and about suicide bombing. In addition, you can read interviews with Brooks and check out reviews of his most recent book. An op-ed columnist from *The New York Times*, Brooks's editorials can be read on the *Times* Website.

# Into the Loop: How to Get the Job You Want after Graduation

Charlie Drozdyk

*Charlie Drozdyk has had a wide range of job experiences. He has worked for the Big Apple Circus and the Brooklyn Academy of Music. He has also been theater manager at the Criterion Center on Broadway, a researcher at CBS, a director of development for a film production company, a producer of videos, and a talent agent. He is the author of* Hot Jobs Handbook *(1994) and* Jobs That Don't Suck *(1998). This essay originally appeared in* Rolling Stone *magazine.*

## Before Reading

**Connecting:** At this point, what expectations do you have about your first job after college?

**Anticipating:** What seems like the most surprising piece of information or advice in the essay?

1   **W**hen Benjamin Braddock, Dustin Hoffman's bewildered twenty-something hero in *The Graduate*, finished college, he was hit with a mind-numbing barrage of good wishes from well-meaning friends. Who can forget that single depressing word of advice that sent Benjamin into catatonic shock—*plastics?* It was no wonder he wound up sleeping with his girlfriend's mother and hanging out all summer at the bottom of his parents' swimming pool.

2   In 1995, 1.38 million college graduates will find themselves in Benjamin's shoes. They might not share *all* of his summer adventures, but with the flip of a tassel, they will soon find themselves at the bottom of the employment pool. Whom are they going to listen to?

3   The truth is, Benjamin had it pretty good back in 1967. Not only were jobs being created as fast as the labor force would grow, but once a job seeker got a foot in the door at an IBM or a Grey Advertising, he or she could expect to stroll the halls for some 40 years while waiting for the gold watch. Unfortunately, the Fortune 500 companies that 20 years ago employed one in five of all Americans now employ fewer than one in 10.

4   It's called corporate downsizing, and it's not over yet. In 1994 the largest U.S. companies dropped around 700,000 employees. But in spite of

that, unemployment numbers are actually shrinking. The big guys may be busy handing out pink slips, but small employers are even busier signing up new hires.

5          But beware of *under*employment. Among the 30 fastest-growing occupations, 21 require no college degree. In fact, the 10 occupations that will pour the greatest number of jobs into the economy, in order, are salespeople (retail), registered nurses, cashiers, general office clerks, truck drivers, waiters/waitresses, nursing aides, janitors/cleaners, food-preparation workers and systems analysts. It is the service industry that will contribute the bulk—approximately two-thirds—of all new jobs.

6          So the question is, How can the class of 1995 put to use the $140 billion it spent on higher education last year? The graduates didn't spend five years—the average amount of time it now takes to get a B.A.—to land a job that doesn't require a college degree. Or did they? Well, the sad truth is that 25 percent of the class of 1995 will be working at jobs that don't require a college diploma.

7          They could always stay on campus. If you're planning on getting a master's degree, the odds of not using your education in a career will drop to 10 percent. For Ph.D.s the odds drop to a 4 percent chance. As you can see, the burger-flipping probability decreases with degrees earned. For those who are thinking about postponing the inevitable job thing, that's good news.

8          For anyone else eager to get on with a career, including Benjamin, if you're still looking, I've talked to plenty of people who have advice. And they're not talking plastics.

9          But before diving into how to get a job, there's one thing to keep in mind, and it's this: Bosses hate hiring people; in fact, they loathe and generally resent the entire process. Put yourself in a boss's shoes. The person they hired two years, or may be just six months ago, has quit, and now they have to dig through the résumés on their desks and meet with a bunch of random strangers all over again. Or not. What they usually do is toss those résumés in the old circular file and call their friends and business associates, asking them if they know of anyone who's looking for a job.

10         This is exactly how Lauren Marino, a book editor at Hyperion (a trade-book publishing company owned by Disney), hired her assistant. She called the literary agencies she works with on a daily basis and asked her contacts if they knew anyone who was looking for a job. "Not only do they know the business already," she says, "but if someone I know recommends them, then it's not going to be a complete waste of time meeting with them."

11         So how do you get to be the person who is recommended? Get in the loop. You will never even hear of most of the job openings out there if you're not in the loop. Once you get your first job, however, you're automatically in the loop. In many companies, workers are paid to talk to people at different companies all day. And it will instantly start to make sense how the average worker manages to change jobs 7.5 times between the ages of 18 and 30. As obnoxious as the word sounds, it's all about *networking*.

12         For recent graduates without the benefits of business contacts and associates, instant entry into the loop is through a connection. For a lot of people,

the word *connection* is as loathsome as that other word. Friends will snivel, "Hey, man, he only got that job because he knows somebody." Absolutely. It's how the game works. So don't discount anyone as a connection—your neighbor, your parents' friends, your baby sitter from 10 years ago. Ask them if they know anyone—or know anyone who knows anyone—who works in the industry into which you want to get. Meet with as many people as you can for a five-minute informational interview, and then go in there and pick their brains: Are they hiring? Do they know anyone who is? (But let them think you're there to simply learn what they do. They know why you're really there.)

13    Don't worry that you'll be bugging them. As Bill Wright-Swadel, director of career services at Dartmouth College, says, "Most people who have an expertise love to talk about the things that they're knowledgeable about." Contacts aren't just about getting an interview, though. Once you've interviewed somewhere, find out if any alumni from your college work there—or any friend of a friend. Call that person, say you've just interviewed and ask him to make a call on your behalf. Basically, it's just someone giving testament that you're *one of them*. It's standard networking procedure—but something often ignored.

14    "People don't know how to network," says David McNulty, a recruiter for Smith Barney. "If you want to get hired by a Wall Street firm, you should find out who went to your school and who works in the firm and call them."

15    Melissa Statmore, human-resources manager at J. Walter Thompson advertising, agrees. "Use any connections you have," she says. "We love referrals. They're taken very seriously."

## Recruiting Roulette

16  Say, however, that you've got no connections. You've just crawled out from under the rock of your undergraduate studies, your parents live in Tibet, and you have no friends. There's always recruiting, right? Yes and no. Finding a job by interviewing with firms that show up on your campus is like getting a job through the want ads—it's a passive take-what's-being-thrown-in-front-of-you-approach. And considering that employers will visit an average of 7.4 fewer campuses in 1995 than they did in 1994, it's also a somewhat dying approach.

17    If you're at one of the Ivy League schools, the University of Virginia, Stanford, Michigan or about a dozen select others, and if you want to work for Smith Barney, you're lucky—the company will visit your school. And if you want to work for J. Walter Thompson, and if you're at Amherst, Yale, Colby or Bates, to name a random few, you're also in luck. My senior year at school—not among the chosen few—I remember seeing recruiters from a railroad, a pharmaceutical firm and a company that had something to do with socks and underwear.

18    Even though it's March, and you haven't scored a job via recruiting with some company you never really wanted to work for in the first place, don't worry about it—you're probably better off. Remember Lauren Marino, the editor who was looking for an assistant? When Marino was about to graduate, she interviewed on campus with a printing company based in Tennessee and was offered a job. The company then had to rescind the offer because of a hiring

freeze, and Marino was forced to continue searching. If the offer hadn't been rescinded, instead of loving her life as a book editor (at only 27) in New York, she would be destined, as she puts it, to be "living in Kingsport, Tenn., a member of the Junior League and would have 10 kids."

## Intern Into the Loop

19  So don't fret that you blew off that recruiter. Truth is, if you're about to graduate, it may not be you they're after. The new trend in recruiting is lassoing sophomores and juniors as interns, giving them a summer or semester of experience and then hiring them as soon as they're done with school. This gives the company a chance to see if they fit in and saves time and money in training.

20      But just because you're about to graduate doesn't mean you can't still intern. In fact, you probably should. In a survey by the College Placement Council, employers say that three out of 10 new hires will be former interns. Christian Breheney is part of that 30 percent. Right before she was about to graduate a semester early from Johns Hopkins and armed with her Spanish major, she saw a flier on a bulletin board and ripped it off the wall. After she was offered the nonpaying internship at *Late Night with David Letterman*, she put the flier back up.

21      Some of her friends thought that Breheney's decision to work for free was questionable. After all, she was about to be a college graduate. Her plan worked, though. After four months of commuting from New Jersey five days a week, working from 10 A.M. to 7 P.M., she got her break. A receptionist quit, and Breheney got the job. How? "If you're well liked and make a good impression, you can get hired right off of your internship," she says. Which is something that happens quite often, apparently, as she lists about a dozen full timers who started as interns.

22      Two years later and now the assistant to the head writer at the *Late Show with David Letterman*, Breheney has yet to send out a single résumé. It's just been a matter of "moving up that ladder," she says gleefully.

## Temp Into the Loop

23  The cost-effective benefits in hiring interns—pretrained, proven commodities— are the same reason that temps (temporary employees who are hired to fill in when needed) are landing full-time jobs at the companies where they're assigned. Thirty-eight percent of all temporary workers are offered full-time employment while on an assignment.

24      Temping has become a recruiting technique in itself, not just a means of replacing somebody when he or she is out sick. It's becoming known as "temping to perm." As Jules Young, president of Friedman Personnel Agency, in West Hollywood, Calif., says: "Temping is like living with someone before you marry them. A lot of placement is based on chemistry between the people you're going to work with. That's why a temp is a good way to go—because it gives the employer a chance to check out whether the chemistry matches."

25    At many large companies like Nike or Paramount Pictures—as well as most of the faster-growing small companies (200 employees or fewer) that by the year 2000 will employ 85 percent of all Americans—a great way in, and a fairly common one, is through temping. The best way to go is to call the company you want to work for and ask which temp agency they use. Then call that agency, go in and pass its typing test and boom! You're in the door. Get familiar with some of the more popular computer programs (WordPerfect, Microsoft Word, Excel and Lotus 1-2-3)—the agencies are going to be looking for them.

## The Personnel Myth

26    We're practically programmed to do it. We make a list of the companies we want to work for, write a standard cover letter (changing the name of the company and the person to whom we're sending it, of course) and drop that and a résumé in the mailbox. A hundred letters sent to 100 personnel departments. Probability alone suggests that at least one or two interviews will come out of it, right? Not likely. You know how many résumés Nike got in 1994? More than 23,000. It hired 511 people. Smith Barney hired around 80 people last year from a pool of applicants that numbered about 10,000. Do the math: The odds aren't good.

27    When Lauren Marino decided to go into publishing, she sent résumés to every publishing house in New York. You know how many interviews she got? Zero. As she realizes now, "That was a huge waste of my time. Personnel departments don't hire anybody. The only way to get an editorial job in publishing is by knowing somebody or by sending a letter directly to the editor."

28    Although it's not a rule to live by, most people don't use their company's personnel departments for a job search. If you want to work at a company, pinpoint which department you want to work in and then find the person who can make a hiring decision. Approach that person directly.

29    If you don't know anybody who knows anybody who knows anybody who knows the person with whom you want to work—or under—at a specific company, then you're going to have to be a little resourceful. The first tactic is obvious. Cold-call them. Pick up the phone and try to get the person on the line. Tell him truthfully how you would really love to work for his company and would love to meet with him for five minutes. Chances are you're not going to get past this person's assistant, however.

30    This is exactly what happened to Michael Landau when he called the national sales manager (he got her name from a friend) at Nicole Miller, a New York fashion-design company. The first four times he called, he got an assistant on the phone who was nice enough but wouldn't put her boss on the phone. This is what assistants are for.

31    Figuring that the assistant probably left at around 6 P.M., Landau called at 6:30, thinking the boss might still be there—and if so, would pick up her own phone. She was, and she did. She was nice to him but said there wasn't anything available. Standard stuff, but Landau was persistent, and as luck would have it, the CEO of the company walked into the sales manager's office. "Talk to this guy, he sounds good," the sales manager said to her colleague. The exec

repeated that the company wasn't hiring but that it was, however, always interested in meeting good people.

32      At that moment, Landau decided to fly to New York, a trip he told them he just happened to be taking. Landau started out in sales and is now happily employed in the public-relations department at Nicole Miller.

## Say Yes

33 This is the first thing you should know about interviewing: If someone asks you in an interview if you know a certain computer program (which you don't) or if you know how to drive a car (and you never have), just say yes. As Sheryl Vandermolen, a junior designer at Robert Metzger Interiors, says: "It's all about selling yourself and believing in yourself. Don't say you think you can, say you can—even if you don't know if you can."

## Research

34 "Please do your research," says Cheryl Nickerson, director of employment for Nike. "Be able to ask intelligent questions about the company and what's going on in the industry. [As an employer] you're making a judgment about that person's curiosity, their willingness to learn and grow." And where do you find information about the company? Start by reading the firm's annual report. Not doing this is a "cardinal sin," says David McNulty of Smith Barney. Just call up the company and ask that a report be mailed to you. You don't even have to leave your couch.

## Get Psyched

35 Employers want someone who's going to come in and kick ass. Interviews are about convincing the employer that you're that person. As Brian Johnson, co-owner of the Dogwater Cafe, a fast-growing restaurant chain in Florida, says, "When I'm interviewing, I'm looking for someone with a lot of energy who wants this job more than anything. I want them to basically beg me not to interview anybody else—that this is their job."

## Follow Up

36 When I was in Jules Young's office at the Friedman agency, a young woman who had just had an interview with someone at the William Morris Agency called to report back that it had gone well. Without pausing, Young said, "Drop a note off to her in the morning thanking her and saying you really want the job. Drop it off in person to the reception desk."

37      "I don't think people [write thank-you notes] as much as they think they should anymore," says Nike's Cheryl Nickerson. "If you're in the running,

that special touch of following up to say thank you may be the edge that you need." Sometimes, however, a thank-you letter isn't enough to push you over that edge. You need to do more. You need to . . .

## Be Persistent

38 When Tracy Grandstaff interviewed for her first job, at MTV, she was told that they would let her know quickly since they needed someone right away. "It took three months of me hounding this woman to get that job," she says. "I called her constantly. She couldn't make a decision." Finally, the woman told Grandstaff that it was between her and someone else and that she just couldn't decide. To which Grandstaff said, "Flat out: What do I have to say to you to give me the edge? What do you want to hear, and I'll say it. What do you want me to do? I'll do it." Apparently these questions were what the MTV executive wanted to hear. Grandstaff got the job.

## Be Nice to the Interviewer's Secretary

39 A survey of executives at the country's largest companies found that nearly two-thirds of the interviewers consider the opinion of their administrative assistants with regard to the interviewee who walks past them on their way in and out of their bosses' offices. So be smart and just say, "I just had some water, I'm fine, thank you," when they ask you if you would like anything to drink. Asking for a coffee, light, one sugar, isn't going to score you points.

40 There's no formula to any of this. Some applicants get really lucky and land something quickly. Most, however, collect a few horror stories to tell. And that's the reality: At best, getting a job has always been an elusive and difficult task. So whatever you do, don't get sucked into that slacker pity party presently taking place on couches and in bars everywhere, the one that goes like this: "Man, there's no jobs available. The baby boomers took them all."

41 As Greg Drebin, vice president of programming at MTV, says, "When people say, 'Well, now is a really hard time for the industry,' and all that . . . well, it's always a hard time. There's no such thing as 'Oh, it's hiring season; we've got all these jobs that just became available.' You know what? There's always jobs, and there's never jobs."

### Questions on Subject and Purpose

1. Drozdyk's opening example is drawn from a film, *The Graduate*, made in 1967. How effective is that example? Why might he use it?

2. Are there ever times in Drozdyk's essay when you disagree or feel uncomfortable with the advice that he is giving?

3. What assumptions does Drozdyk make about the reasons why people attend college? Do you agree with those assumptions?

## Questions on Strategy and Audience

1. Why might Drozdyk title the essay "Into the Loop"?
2. Drozdyk quotes from a number of people throughout the essay. Why might he do so, and how effective is the strategy?
3. To whom is Drozdyk writing? How specifically can you define that audience?

## Questions on Vocabulary and Style

1. How would you characterize the tone of Drozdyk's essay? (See the Glossary and Ready Reference for a definition of *tone*.)
2. Find examples of words or expressions that Drozdyk uses to connect with an audience of late teenagers and twentysomethings.
3. Be prepared to define the following words and phrases: *barrage* (paragraph 1), *catatonic* (1), *snivel* (12), *rescind* (18), *proven commodities* (23), *cold-call* (29), *cardinal sin* (34).

## Writing Suggestions

1. **For Your Journal or Blog.** Jot down in your journal or blog a list of possible internships or volunteer positions for which you might apply. Remember that such positions might not involve specific job skills but rather particular "people" skills that are transferable to many jobs. Visit your college's placement office for possible suggestions as well. Your major department might also be a source of information.
2. **For a Paragraph.** Using your list, the advice in Drozdyk's essay, and any advice that you can get from your college's placement office, write a paragraph in which you describe the process by which you (or anyone else) would apply for a specific internship or volunteer position.
3. **For an Essay.** Write an essay in which you offer advice on how an undergraduate at your college can locate and apply for internships and volunteer positions. With your instructor's approval, you might consider writing the essay for your school's student newspaper or as a brochure that could be handed out by the placement office.
4. **For Research.** In what ways is electronic communication changing the nature of a job search? For example, increasing numbers of individuals are mounting personal Web pages that advertise their talents and skills in ways somewhat similar to the old printed résumé. How are the new technologies influencing job search strategies? Research the problem and future directions. Remember that source information will have to be current, so look for very recent books and articles. You might want to use the Web to find examples, as well, or interview people. In a researched essay, bring Drozdyk's advice up to date for the early 2000s.

## For Further Study

**Focusing on Grammar and Writing.** Drozdyk uses a large number of quotations from interviewers. Look carefully at how he integrates these quotations into his essay. Try writing a set of guidelines for your classmates on how to integrate quotations into an essay.

**Working Together.** Working in small groups, brainstorm about how a first-year college student might find a great summer job. What do each of you plan to do this summer? How would you go about finding a great summer job? What would be "great" about that job? Where on campus or on the Web could you go for help in your job search?

**Seeing Other Modes at Work.** Locate the places in the essay in which Drozdyk uses a cause-and-effect strategy.

**Finding Connections.** The process example in the introductory section of this chapter, "Getting the Interview Edge 'Apprentice-Style,'" is a good pairing.

**Exploring the Web.** Can the Web help you find a job? What Web resources are available for job seekers? If you post your résumé on the Web, what are your chances of finding a job? Are there any dangers or risks in using the Web to search for a job or to post a résumé?

# Stripped for Parts

Jennifer Kahn

*A graduate of Princeton and the University of California, Berkeley, Jennifer Kahn is a writer and a contributing editor to magazines such as* Wired *and* National Geographic. *In 2003, she was awarded a journalism fellowship from the American Academy of Neurology; in 2004, the CASE-UCLA media fellowship in neuroscience. "Stripped for Parts" first appeared in* Wired *in 2003.*

**On Writing:** *Commenting on the essay, Kahn noted: "It was one of those stories that turn out to be dramatically different from the original assignment. Basically, I'd been sent out to find out what was new in the world of transplant surgery: the standard 'hooray for scientific progress' tale. Instead I was struck by how fragile the organ recovery process was. . . . In the end the piece was quite controversial; there were a lot of angry letters from people who accused me of discouraging donation."*

## Before Reading

**Connecting:** What do you know about organ donations? Are you an organ donor? Many states allow this designation to be placed on a driver's license.

**Anticipating:** What surprises you the most in the essay?

1   The television in the dead man's room stays on all night. Right now the program is *Shipmates*, a reality-dating drama that's barely audible over the hiss of the ventilator. It's 4 AM, and I've been here for six hours, sitting in the corner while three nurses fuss intermittently over a set of intravenous drips. They're worried about the dead man's health.

2   To me, he looks fine. His face is slack but flush, he breathes steadily, and his heart beats like a clock, despite the fact that his lungs have recently begun to leak fluid. The nurses roll the body from side to side periodically so that the liquid doesn't pool. At one point, a white plastic vest designed to clear the lungs inflates and begins to vibrate violently—as if some invisible person has seized the dead man by the shoulders and is trying to shake him awake. The rest of the time, the nurses consult monitors and watch for signs of cardiac arrest. When someone scratches the bottom of the dead man's foot, it twitches.

3   None of this is what I expected from an organ transplant. When I arrived last night at this Northern California hospital I was prepared to see a

fast-paced surgery culminating in renewal: the mortally ill patient restored to glorious health. In all my preliminary research on transplants, the dead man was rarely mentioned. Even doctors I spoke with avoided the subject, and popular accounts I came across ducked the matter of provenance altogether. In the movies, for instance, surgeons tended to say it would take time to "find" a heart—as though one had been hidden behind a tree or misplaced along with the car keys. Insofar as corpses came up, it was only in anxious reference to the would-be recipient whose time was running out.

4    In the dead man's room, a different calculus is unfolding. Here the organ is the patient, and the patient a mere container, the safest place to store body parts until surgeons are ready to use them. It can be more than a day from the time a donor dies until his organs are harvested—the surgery alone takes hours, not to mention the time needed to do blood tests, match tissue, and fly in special surgical teams for the evisceration. And yet, a heart lasts at most six hours outside the body, even after it has been kneaded, flushed with preservatives, and packed in a cooler. Organs left on ice too long tend to perform poorly in their new environment, and doctors are picky about which viscera they're willing to work with. Even an ailing cadaver is a better container than a cooler.

5    These conditions create a strange medical specialty. Rather than extracting this man's vitals right away, the hospital contacts the California Transplant Donor Network, which dispatches a procurement team to begin "donor maintenance": the process of artificially supporting a dead body until recipients are ready. When the parathyroid gland stops regulating calcium, key to keeping the heart pumping, the team sends the proper amount down an intravenous drip. When blood pressure drops, they add vasoconstrictors, which contract the blood vessels. Normally the brain would compensate for a decrease in blood pressure, but with it out of commission, the three-nurse procurement team must take over.

6    In this case, the eroding balance will have to be sustained for almost 24 hours. The goal is to fool the body into believing that it's alive and well, even as everything is falling apart. As one crew member concedes, "It's unbelievable that all this stuff is being done to a dead person."

7    Unbelievable and, to me, somehow barbaric. Sustaining a dead body until its organs can be harvested is a tricky process requiring the latest in medical technology. But it's also a distinct anachronism in an era when medicine is becoming less and less invasive. Fixing blocked coronary arteries, which not long ago required prying a patient's chest open with a saw and spreader, can now be accomplished with a tiny stent delivered to the heart on a slender wire threaded up the leg. Exploratory surgery has given way to robot cameras and high-resolution imaging. Already, we are eyeing the tantalizing summit of gene therapy, where diseases are cured even before they do damage. Compared with such microscale cures, transplants—which consist of salvaging entire organs from a heart-beating cadaver and sewing them into a different body—seem crudely mechanical, even medieval.

8    "To let an organ reach a state where the only solution is to cut it out is not progress; it's a failure of medicine," says pathologist Neil Theise of NYU.

Theise, who was the first researcher to demonstrate that stem cells can become liver cells in humans, argues that the future of transplantation lies in regeneration. Within five years, he estimates, we'll be able to instruct the body to send stem cells to the liver from the store that exists in bone marrow, hopefully countering the effects of a disease like hepatitis A or B and letting the body heal itself. And numerous researchers are forging similar paths. One outspoken surgeon, Richard Satava from the University of Washington, says that medicine is only now catching on to the fundamental lesson of modern industry, which is that when our car alternator breaks, we get a brand new one. Transplantation, he argues, is a dying art.

9      Few researchers predict that human-harvested organs will become obsolete anytime soon, however; one cardiovascular pathologist, Charles Murry, says we'll still be using them a century from now. But it's reasonable to expect— and hope for—an alternative. "I don't think anybody enjoys recovering organs," Murry says frankly. "You tell yourself it's for a good cause, which it is, a very good cause, but you're still butchering a human."

10      Intensive care is not a good place to spend the evening. Tonight, the ward has perhaps 12 patients, including a woman who moans constantly and a deathly pale man who reportedly jumped out the window of a moving Greyhound bus. The absence of clocks and the always-on lights create a casino-like timelessness. In the staff lounge, which smells of stale pizza, a lone nurse corners me and describes watching a man bleed to death ("He was conscious. He knew what was happening"), and announces, sotto voce, that she knows of South American organ brokers who charge $60,000 for a heart, then swap it for a baboon's.

11      Although I don't admit it to the procurement team, I've grown attached to the dead man. There's something vulnerable about his rumpled hair and middle-aged body, naked save a waist-high sheet. Under the hospital lights, everything is exposed: the muscular arms gone flabby above the elbow; the legs, wiry and lean, foreshortened under a powerful torso. It's the body of a man in his fifties, simultaneously bullish and elfin. One foot, the right, peeps out from the sheet, and for a brief moment I want to hold it and rub the toes that must be cold—a hopeless gesture of consolation.

12      Organ support is about staving off entropy. In the moments after death, a cascade of changes sweeps over the body. Potassium diminishes and salt accumulates, drawing fluid into cells. Sugar builds up in the blood. With the pituitary system offline, the heart fills with lactic acid like the muscles of an exhausted runner. Free radicals circulate unchecked and disrupt other cells, in effect causing the body to rust. The process quickly becomes irreversible. As cell membranes grow porous, a "death gene" is activated and damaged cells begin to self-destruct. All this happens in minutes.

13      When transplant activists talk about an organ shortage, it's usually to lament how few people are willing to donate. This is a valid worry, but it eclipses an important point, which is that the window for retrieving a viable organ is staggeringly small. Because of how fast the body degrades once the heart stops, there's no way to recover an organ from someone who dies at

home, in a car, in an ambulance, or even while on the operating table. In fact, the only situation that really lends itself to harvest is brain death, which means finding an otherwise healthy patient whose brain activity has ceased but whose heart continues to beat—right up until the moment it's taken out. In short, victims of stroke or severe head injury. These cases are so rare (approximately 0.5 percent of all deaths in the US) that even if everybody in America were to become a donor, they wouldn't clear the organ wait lists.

14    This is partly a scientific problem. Cell death remains poorly understood, and for years now, cadaveric transplants have lingered on a research plateau. While immunosuppressants have improved incrementally, transplants proceed much as they did 20 years ago. Compared with a field like psychopharmacology, the procedure has come to a near-standstill.

15    But there are cultural factors as well. Medicine has always reserved its glory for the living. Even among transplant surgeons, a hierarchy exists: Those who put organs into living patients have a higher status than those who extract them from the dead. One anesthesiologist confesses that his peers don't like to work on cadaveric organ recoveries. (Even brain-dead bodies require sedation, since spinal reflexes can make a corpse "buck" in surgery.) "You spend all this time monitoring the heartbeat, the blood pressure," the anesthesiologist explains. "To just turn everything off when you're done and walk out. It's bizarre."

16    Although the procurement team will stay up all night, I break at 4:30 AM for a two-hour nap on an empty bed in the ICU. The nurse removes a wrinkled top sheet but leaves the bottom one. Doctors sleep like this all the time, I know, catnapping on gurneys, but I can't shake the feeling of climbing onto my deathbed. The room is identical to the one I've been sitting in for the past eight hours, and I'd prefer to sleep almost anywhere else—in the nurses lounge or even on the small outside balcony. Instead, I lie down in my clothes and pull the sheet up under my arms.

17    For a while I read a magazine, then finally close my eyes, hoping I won't dream.

18    By morning, little seems to have changed, except that the commotion of chest X-rays and ultrasounds has left the dead man's hair more mussed. On both sides of his bed, vital stats scroll across screens: oxygen ratios, pulse, blood volumes.

19    All of this vigilance is good, of course: After all, transplants save lives. Every year, thousands of people who would otherwise die survive with organs from brain-dead donors; sometimes, doctors say, a patient's color will visibly change on the operating table once a newly attached liver begins to work. Still—and with the possible exception of kidneys—transplants have never quite lived up to their initial promise. In the early 1970s, few who received new organs lasted even a year, and most died within weeks. Even today, 22 percent of heart recipients die in less than four years, and 12 percent reject a new heart within the first few months. Those who survive are usually consigned to a lifetime regime of costly immunosuppressive drugs, some with debilitating side effects. Recipients of artificial hearts traditionally fare the worst, alongside those

who receive transplants from animals. Under the circumstances, it took a weird kind of perseverance for doctors operating in 1984 to suggest sewing a walnut-sized baboon heart into a human baby. And there was grief, if not surprise, when the patient died of a morbid immune reaction just 21 days later.

20     By the time we head into surgery, the patient has been dead for more than 24 hours, but he still looks pink and healthy. In the operating room, all the intravenous drips are still flowing, convincing the body that everything's fine even as it's cleaved in half.

21     Although multiorgan transfer can involve as many as five teams in the OR at once, this time there is only one: a four-man surgical unit from Southern California. They've flown in to retrieve the liver, but because teams sometimes swap favors, they'll also remove the kidneys for a group of doctors elsewhere—saving them a last-minute, late-night flight. One of the doctors has brought a footstool for me to stand on at the head of the operating table, so that I can see over the sheet that hangs between the patient's head and body. I've been warned that the room will smell bad during the "opening," like flesh and burning bone—an odor that has something in common with a dentist's drill. Behind me, the anesthesiologist checks the dead man's mask and confirms that he's sedated. The surgery will take four hours, and the doctors have arranged for the score of Game Five of the World Series to be phoned in at intervals.

22     I've heard that transplant doctors are the endurance athletes of medicine, and the longer I stand on the stool, the better I understand the comparison. Below me, the rib cage has been split, and I can see the heart, strangely yellow, beating inside a cave of red muscle. It doesn't beat forward, as I expect, but knocks anxiously back and forth like a small animal trapped in a cage. Farther down, the doctors rummage under the slough of intestines as though through a poorly organized toolbox. When I tell the anesthesiologist that the heart is beautiful, he says that livers are the transplants to watch. "Hearts are slash and burn," he shrugs, adjusting a dial. "No finesse."

23     Two hours pass, and the surgeons make progress. Despite the procurement team's best efforts, however, most of the organs have already been lost. The pancreas was deemed too old before surgery. One lung was bad at the outset, and the other turned out to be too big for the only matching recipients—a short list given the donor's rare blood type. At 7 this morning, the heart went bust after someone at the receiving hospital suggested a shot of thyroid hormone, shown in some studies to stimulate contractions—but even before then, the surgeon had had second thoughts. A 54-year-old heart can't travel far—and this one was already questionable—but the hospital may have thought this would improve its chances. Instead, the dead man's pulse shot to 140, and his blood began circulating so fast it nearly ruptured his arteries. Now the heart will go to Cryolife, a biosupply company that irradiates and freeze-dries the valves, then packages them for sale to hospitals in screw-top jars. The kidneys have remained healthy enough to be passed on—one to a man who will soon be in line for a pancreas, the other to a 42-year-old woman.

24      Both kidneys have been packed off in quart-sized plastic jars. Originally, the liver was going to a nearby hospital, but an ultrasound suggested it was hyperechoic, or probably fatty. On the second pass, it was accepted by a doctor in Southern California and ensconced in a bag of icy slurry.

25      The liver is enormous—it looks like a polished stone, flat and purplish—and with it gone, the body seems eerily empty, although the heart continues to beat. Watching this pumping vessel makes me oddly anxious. It's sped up slightly, as though sensing what will happen next. Below me, the man's face is still flushed. He's the one I wish would survive, I realize, even though there was never any chance of that. Meanwhile, the head surgeon has walked away. He's busy examining the liver and relaying a description over the phone to the doctor who will perform the attachment. Almost unnoticed, an aide clamps the arteries above and below the heart, and cuts. The patient's face doesn't move, but its pinkness drains to a waxy yellow. After 24 hours, the dead man finally looks dead.

26      Once all the organs are out, the tempo picks up in the operating room. The heart is packed in a cardboard box also loaded with the kidneys, which are traveling by Learjet to a city a few hundred miles away. Someday, I'm convinced, transporting organs in coolers will seem as strange and outdated as putting a patient in an iron lung. In the meantime, transplants will survive: a vehicle, like the dead man, to get us to a better place. As an assistant closes, sewing up the body so that it will be ready for its funeral, I get on the plane with the heart and the kidneys. They've become a strange, unhealthy orange in their little jars. But no one else seems worried. "A kidney almost always perks up," someone tells me, "once we get it in a happier environment."

## Questions on Subject and Purpose

1. What did Kahn expect to see at an organ transplant operation?
2. Why does Kahn get on the airplane with the heart and kidneys at the end of the story?
3. Having read the essay, have you changed your attitude toward organ donation? Do you think that Kahn wants to change your opinion?

## Questions on Strategy and Audience

1. Why might Kahn have titled the essay "Stripped for Parts"? What associations do you have with that phrase?
2. How effective is the opening paragraph? Does it make you want to keep reading?
3. What could Kahn assume about her audience?

## Questions on Vocabulary and Style

1. How is the story told or narrated to the reader? How else might the story have been told?

2. How would you describe the tone of the essay?

3. Be prepared to define the following words: *culminating* (paragraph 3), *provenance* (3), *evisceration* (4), *viscera* (4), *anachronism* (7), *sotto voce* (10), *elfin* (11), *entropy* (12), *debilitating* (19), *morbid* (19), *slough* (22), *hyperechoic* (24), *ensconced* (24).

## Writing Suggestions

1. **For Your Journal or Blog.** Why is this side of organ donation—that is, the harvesting—ignored? Record your impressions and feelings about the whole process in your journal or blog. You are not constructing an argument; you are just recording your emotions and reactions.

2. **For a Paragraph.** Based on your impressions recorded in your journal or blog, what would you want to happen to you if you had a fatal accident?

3. **For an Essay.** Living wills are often in the news. What is the process through which one makes a living will? What are the options? How is it worded? Consult some print or online sources to gather information. Then, in an essay aimed at an audience of your contemporaries, describe the process of making such a will.

4. **For Research.** In paragraph 8, Kahn quotes a stem-cell researcher who "argues that the future of transplantation lies in regeneration" through instructing the body to "send stem cells" from one part of the body to regenerate other organs in the body. The researcher says that "within five years" we might be able to do that. What is the state of stem-cell research right now, and how close are researchers to being able to regenerate organs rather than transplant them? Research the issue and the technology through online and print sources, and in a research essay, describe the process by which scientists think that this might be possible.

## For Further Study

**Focusing on Grammar and Writing.** Kahn makes extensive use of the dash in the essay. Identify all the occurrences in the essay and see if you can classify them according to the grammatical situations in which they occur. Can you then write a list of rules under which the dash is used in writing?

**Working Together.** Divide into groups. Each group should take a couple of paragraphs from the essay and rewrite the paragraphs so that the "I" of the narrator is replaced with an objective third person. What happens to the story when that is done? Can you see why Kahn chose to tell the story from her own point of view—as an observer who watched the whole process?

**Seeing Other Modes at Work.** The essay is a narrative; it also has elements of description and cause and effect (in the description of why and how the body breaks down so quickly).

**Finding Connections.** The essay could be linked with Wilfred Owen's "Dulce et Decorum Est" (Chapter 9).

**Exploring the Web.** Many sites on the Web are devoted to organ donation. Some of Kahn's other essays for *National Geographic* and *Mother Jones* are available on the Web.

# CAUSE AND EFFECT

## 🔑 ❓ KEY QUESTIONS

**Getting Ready to Write**

What is cause and effect?

Why do you write a cause-and-effect analysis?

How do you choose a subject?

How do you isolate and evaluate causes and effects?

**Writing**

How do you structure a cause-and-effect analysis?

**Revising**

How do you revise a cause-and-effect essay?
> *Retesting your subject*
> *Concentrating on the important*
> *Checking for logical organization*
> *Beginning and ending*

*Student Essay*
> *Cathy Ferguson, "The Influence of Televised Violence on Children"*

*Some Things to Remember about Writing Cause and Effect*

*Seeing Cause and Effect in Other Contexts*

**As a literary strategy**
> *Marge Piercy, "Barbie Doll"*

**As a critical reading strategy**
> *www.emedicinehealth.com, "What Causes Migraine Headaches?"*

**As a visual strategy**
> *Photograph of sitting woman*

*Additional Writing Suggestions for Cause and Effect*

# GETTING READY TO WRITE

## What Is Cause and Effect?

It is a rainy morning and you are late for class. Driving to campus in an automobile with faulty brakes, you have an accident. Considering the circumstances, the accident might be attributable to a variety of causes:

> You were driving too fast.
> Visibility was poor.
> Roads were slippery.
> The brakes did not work properly.

Visually, cause and effect can be displayed in what are called "fishbone" diagrams, tools used to analyze and display possible causes. If we used a fishbone diagram to analyze your accident, it might look like this:

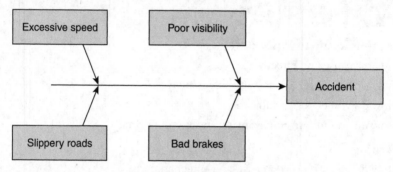

The diagram could also branch out further since the accident, in turn, could produce a series of consequences or effects:

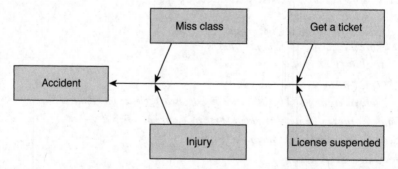

Susan Strasser, for example, uses a cause-and-effect strategy when she suggests that part of the popularity of fast-food restaurants lies in the appeal of "stylized, repetitive, stereotyped events." Notice how Strasser structures the following paragraph to show how this ritualization is one "cause" for such restaurants' popularity:

> People arrive at McDonald's—and to a lesser extent at the other chains—
> knowing what they will eat, what they will pay, what to say to the counter

person and how she or he will respond, what the restaurant will look like—in short, knowing exactly what to expect and how to behave; children learn these expectations and behaviors early in life. For some, the ritual constitutes an attraction of these restaurants; they neither wish to cook nor to chat with a waitress as she intones and delivers the daily specials. The fast-food ritual requires no responsibility other than ordering (with as few words as possible) and paying; nobody has to set or clear the table, wash the dishes, or compliment the cook on her cuisine, the traditional responsibilities at the family dinner.

Strasser turns her analysis of fast-food restaurants in the other direction—toward effects—when she discusses how fast-food eating has affected mealtime rituals at home:

> Fast foods have changed eating habits far beyond the food itself; they have invaded the mealtime ritual even at home. The chief executive officer of Kraft, Inc., maintained that eating out accustomed people to "portion control" and therefore to accepting a processor's statement that a package of macaroni and cheese serves four. "Generally speaking," one writer claimed in *Advertising Age*, "the homemaker no longer sets the table with dishes of food from which the family fills their plates—the individual plates are filled and placed before the family, no second helping." Eating out even accustoms diners at the same table to eating different food, putting home meals of different prepared foods within the realm of possibility, and altering the nature of parental discipline; freed from the "shut up—you'll eat what we're eating" rule, children experience the pleasures and also the isolation of free choice at earlier ages.*

Causes and effects can be either immediate or remote with reference to time. The lists regarding the hypothetical automobile accident suggest only immediate causes and effects, things that could be most directly linked in time to the accident. Another pair of lists of more remote causes and effects could be compiled—for example, your brakes were faulty because you did not have the money to fix them, or because of your accident, your insurance rates will go up.

Causes and effects can be either primary or secondary with reference to their significance and importance. If you had not been in a hurry and driving too fast, it might not have mattered that the visibility was poor, the roads were slippery, or your brakes were faulty. Similarly, if you or someone else had been injured, the other consequences would have seemed insignificant in comparison.

In some instances, causes and effects are linked in a causal chain: if you were driving too fast and tried to stop on slippery roads with inadequate brakes, each of those causes is interlinked in the inevitable accident. Likewise, the accident means that you will get a ticket, that ticket carries points again your license, your license could as a result be suspended, and either way your insurance rates will certainly increase.

*Susan Strasser, *Never Done: A History of American Housework* (New York: Random House, 1982), pp. 296–97.

## Why Do You Write a Cause-and-Effect Analysis?

Cause-and-effect analyses are intended to reveal the reasons why something happened or the consequences of a particular occurrence. E. M. Forster in "My Wood" examines the consequences of owning property. Joan Jacobs Brumberg in "The Origins of Anorexia Nervosa" examines some of the causes of anorexia nervosa, tracing the disease back to its origins in middle-class families in the nineteenth century. Brent Staples in "Black Men and Public Space" uses his own experiences as an urban night walker to explore the effects that he, as a young black male, has on those who share the streets with him. Veronica Chambers in "Dreadlocked" explains both why she wears her hair in dreadlocks and what those "dreads" suggest to people. Andres Martin in "On Teenagers and Tattoos" explores some of the reasons why tattoos and body piercings appeal to adolescents. Finally, Natalie Angier in "Drugs, Sports, Body Image and G.I. Joe" analyzes the possible connections between male action figures such as G.I. Joe and the use of male growth hormones and anabolic steroids among male athletes.

Cause-and-effect analyses can also be used to persuade readers to do or believe something. Andres Martin's analysis of body marking and teenagers is written for an audience of clinicians who work with adolescents. His analysis is also persuasive for he suggests that such markings provide a point of contact with patients and offer insights into their perceptions of self and reality. Brent Staples's experiences as an urban night walker challenge all of us when we realize how quickly and easily we form stereotypes—a young, large black man dressed casually on an urban street at night must be dangerous, must be someone to avoid. Natalie Angier writes more to parents than young adults, cautioning them that young women are not the only ones in our culture who have been influenced by pervasive images of extreme body types. She goes on to suggest that the effects of drug use are not only dangerous, but even counterproductive.

 **IN THE READINGS, LOOK FOR**

|  | **Possible purpose/audience interest** |
| --- | --- |
| E. M. Forster, "My Wood" | Why might this personal experience be of interest to others? |
| Joan Jacobs Brumberg, "Anorexia Nervosa" | How does the history help an audience understand the phenomenon today? |
| Andres Martin, "Teenagers and Tattoos" | Published in a journal for adolescent psychiatrists, why might this article have a broader appeal? |
| Brent Staples, "Black Men" | Why might an audience be interested in this article? (It was originally published in a magazine whose audience was women.) |
| Veronica Chambers, "Dreadlocked" | How universal might this experience be? |
| Natalie Angier, "Drugs, Sports" | How has the subject become more and more important in sports today? |

## How Do You Choose a Subject?

In picking a subject to analyze, first remember the limits of your assignment. The larger the subject, the more difficult it will be to do justice to it. Trying to analyze the causes of the Vietnam War or the effects of technology in five hundred words is an invitation to disaster. Second, make sure that the relationships you see between causes and effects are genuine. The fact that a particular event preceded another does not necessarily mean that the first caused the second. In logic this error is labeled *post hoc, ergo propter hoc* (after this, therefore because of this). If a black cat crossed the street several blocks before your automobile accident, that does not mean that the cat was a cause of the accident.

## How Do You Isolate and Evaluate Causes and Effects?

Before you begin to write take time to analyze and, if necessary, research your subject thoroughly. Remember to consider all of the major factors involved in the relationship. Relatively few things are the result of a single cause, and rarely does a cause have a single effect. Owning a piece of property—even if it is something that cannot possibly be stolen—can have a number of effects on you, as E. M. Forster discovers. He becomes far more preoccupied by his property than he ever thought possible. Veronica Chambers discovers that her dreadlocks conjure up in people's minds a whole series of different identities. She is, in the eyes of others, simultaneously a "rebel child, Rasta mama, Nubian princess, drug dealer, unemployed artist, rock star, world-famous comedienne, and nature chick."

Depending on your subject, your analysis could be based on personal experience, thoughtful reflection and examination, or research. E. M. Forster's analysis of the effects of owning property is derived completely from studying his own reactions. Brent Staples draws on his own personal experiences and those of a fellow black journalist. Veronica Chambers's analysis of her dreadlocks is based on the reactions of those around her. Andres Martin specializes in adolescent psychiatry, and his analysis depends on his experience with patients and his knowledge of published research. Joan Jacobs Brumberg's essay is built on extensive research, especially in sources in history, literature, medicine, and psychology. Natalie Angier quotes extensively from experts to establish her analysis and argument. As these selections show, sometimes causes and effects are certain and unquestionable. At other times, the relationships are only probable or even speculative.

Once you have gathered a list of possible causes and effects, the next step is to evaluate each item. Any phenomenon can have many causes or many effects, so you will have to select the explanations that seem the most relevant or most convincing. Rarely should you list every cause or every effect you can find. Generally, choose the causes and effects that are immediate and primary, although the choice is always determined by your purpose.

## IN THE READINGS, LOOK FOR

**Basis for the analysis**

E. M. Forster, "My Wood"              Personal reflection on ownership

Joan Jacobs Brumberg, "Anorexia        Historical research into the origins
Nervosa"                               of the disease

Andres Martin, "Teenagers and         Personal observation of patients and
Tattoos"                               research

Brent Staples, "Black Men"             Personal experience—Staples and a
                                       colleague

Veronica Chambers, "Dreadlocked"       Personal experience

Natalie Angier, "Drugs, Sports"        Research by experts

## PREWRITING TIPS FOR WRITING CAUSE AND EFFECT

1.  Choose a subject that can be analyzed within the amount of space that you have available.

2.  Decide whether you are exploring causes or effects. In a short paper, it is probably not possible to do both.

3.  Make a list of possible causes or effects. Test each item on your list to make sure that it is a likely cause or effect. Remember, just because something happens before or after your subject does not necessarily mean that it is a cause or effect.

4.  Rank the causes or effects in terms of their significance. Typically, you are not asked to analyze all of the possible causes or effects. Focus on the most important ones. In a short paper, you will probably not treat more than three to five causes or effects.

5.  Remember your audience. How much do they already know about your subject? Will your analysis be too complex and technical? Will it be too obvious? Either extreme presents problems.

## WRITING

### How Do You Structure a Cause-and-Effect Analysis?

By definition, causes precede effects, so a cause-and-effect analysis involves a linear or chronological order. In most cases, structure your analysis to reflect that sequence. If you are analyzing causes, typically you begin by identifying the subject you are trying to explain; then you move to analyze its causes. Natalie Angier begins by describing the excessive muscularity of the action figure G.I. Joe. If you are analyzing effects, typically you begin by identifying the subject that produced the effects; then you move to enumerate or explain what those effects were. E. M. Forster begins by describing how he came to purchase his "wood" and then goes on to describe four distinct effects that ownership has had on him.

A cause-and-effect analysis can also go in both directions. Veronica Chambers begins by remembering what it was like to have "bad" nappy hair and what that meant in the black community in the late twentieth century. She explains the causes that led to her decision to wear her hair in dreadlocks. But Chambers also moves forward, looking then at the effects that her hairstyle had on others. "My hair," she writes, "says a lot of things."

Within these patterns, you face one other choice. If you are listing multiple causes or effects, how do you decide in what order to treat them? That arrangement depends on whether the reasons or consequences are linked in a chain. If they happen in a definite sequence, arrange them in an order to reflect that sequence—normally a chronological order (this happened, then this, and finally this). This linear arrangement is similar to what you do in a process narrative except that your purpose here is to answer the question *why* rather than *how*. In "Black Men and Public Space," Brent Staples follows a chronological pattern of development. He begins with his first experience as a night walker in Chicago and ends with his most recent experiences in Brooklyn. The essay includes a brief flashback as well to his childhood days in Chester, Pennsylvania. As he is narrating his experience, Staples explores the reasons why people react as they do when they encounter him at night on a city street. At the same time, Staples analyzes the impact or effects that their reactions have had on him.

However, multiple causes and effects are not always linked in time. Brumberg's causes do not occur in any inevitable chronological order, nor do Forster's effects. If the causes or effects that you have isolated are not linked in a chain of time, you must find another way in which to order them. They could be arranged from immediate to remote, for example. When the degree of significance or importance varies, the most obvious structural choice would be to move from the primary to the secondary or from the secondary to the primary. Before you establish any sequence in your analysis, study your list of causes or effects to see whether any principle of order is evident—chronological, spatial, immediate to remote, primary to secondary. If you see some logical order, follow it.

 **IN THE READINGS, LOOK FOR**

**Organizing middles**

E. M. Forster, "My Wood"   What are the consequences or effects of owning property?

Joan Jacobs Brumberg,   Why are the historical origins or causes of the
"Anorexia Nervosa"   disease important?

*(continued)*

| | |
|---|---|
| Andres Martin, "Teenagers and Tattoos" | What is the role of the subheadings in the essay? |
| Brent Staples, "Black Men" | What organizational device ensures continuity in the essay? |
| Veronica Chambers, "Dreadlocked" | How does the essay move in two directions—back to causes and forward to effects? |
| Natalie Angier, "Drugs, Sports" | What is the shift that occurs in paragraph 18 and how is it related to cause and effect? |

 **DRAFTING TIPS FOR WRITING CAUSE AND EFFECT**

1. Plan a middle for your essay. How are you going to arrange the causes and effects? Which comes first in the body of your paper; which comes last? Are you moving from most important to least? From the chronologically first to last?

2. Place each cause or effect in a separate paragraph. Make sure the paragraph is more than one sentence long. Explain or develop each cause or effect so that the reader can clearly understand your analysis.

3. Write a purpose statement for your essay as it is developing. What are you trying to explain in the paper? Why might the reader want this knowledge? Identifying a need or interest in your prospective reader always suggests strategies by which you can begin your essay.

4. Think about the extent to which your draft is objective and factual and to what extent it is subjective and argumentative. How likely are your readers to agree with what you attribute to cause and what to effect? Have you done research to support your analysis? Cause-and-effect essays are often difficult to write simply from preexisting knowledge or from simple observation and reflection.

5. Draft an introduction and a conclusion to the essay that appeal to your reader's need for the information. Why would the reader want to have this information?

## REVISING

### How Do You Revise a Cause-and-Effect Essay?

Your success in any paper always depends on your readers. If your readers like it, if they feel that it was worth reading, if it taught them something they wanted to know or persuaded them to agree with you, then you have succeeded. Unless your readers agree, it does not matter if you think that your paper is clear and interesting. For that reason, when you are revising, always seek feedback from your readers. Perhaps in your writing class you have regular opportunities to read each other's papers, either in hard copy or online, and offer advice. Maybe your school has a writing center or writing tutors you can visit; maybe your instructor has the time to read a first draft and suggest possible revisions. If so, take advantage of those readers. Ask them specific questions; ask for their criticisms and suggestions. If such situations are not part of the formal structure of your class, ask a roommate or a friend to read your essay. Then pay attention to what he or she says.

A cause-and-effect essay is primarily explanatory and informative. It explains the reasons or causes for why something happened or the consequences or effects that come from whatever happened. The best cause-and-effect analyses are based on thoughtful analysis coupled with research. The worst cause-and-effect analyses grow only out of subjective, biased, unsubstantiated opinions. If you are sick, you want accurate, objective medical advice. What caused my illness? What are the likely side effects of this course of treatment?

When revising a cause-and-effect essay, play particular attention to the following areas: retesting your subject, concentrating on the important, checking for logical organization, and beginning and ending appropriately.

**Retesting Your Subject**    Once you have a draft of your essay, look again at your subject. Ask yourself two questions and answer each honestly. First, were you able to develop adequately your subject in the space that you had available, or were you forced to skim over the surface? Some subjects are simply too large and too complicated to be analyzed in three or four pages. Second, were you objective and accurate in what you identified as causes and effects? The world, and especially the Web, is full of bogus explanations for what caused this or what the effects of that have been. Sometimes people intentionally mislead by parading their own biases and opinions as objective facts. Readers want accurate and reliable information and analyses.

Not every subject needs research. Sometimes personal experience is adequate; sometimes we can thoughtfully and insightfully analyze a situation. Even then, though, our response is based on knowledge that has been acquired only through our own experiences. Try to check your personal knowledge against what others have experienced or written about. You always want your analysis to be based on accurate information.

**Concentrating on the Important**    You will never be given an essay assignment that says "find all of the causes or all of the effects" of something. In some instances causes and effects are many. Think about the lists of possible side effects that accompany any over-the-counter or prescription drug. Often the lists are paragraphs long. Similarly, many illnesses can result from a complex series of causes, some interacting in causal chains. In a typical writing situation, however, you need to concentrate on the major causes and effects. Once you have identified those causes or effects, number them in the order of their significance or importance. Depending on the length of your paper—is it a "regular" essay or a term or research paper?—choose to discuss only the most important.

**Checking for Logical Organization**   Look again at how you have arranged either the causes or the effects in the body of your paper. A typical organizational strategy is to put the main cause or the main effect first and then to move down the list in descending order of importance. You could move in the opposite direction, building to your strongest or most forceful cause or effect, but there would be no logical reason to place the most important cause or effect in the middle of the list. Causes and effects can also be listed in a chronological order, especially if there is a causal chain (this happens, which leads to this, which then leads to this). Other possible organizational strategies might also be appropriate, for example, from the most visible effect to the least visible. Whatever order you choose should be a conscious and thoughtful act on your part, and you should be able to defend your choice to any critic.

Another aspect of logical organization is proportion. Treat your causes or effects in paragraphs or paragraph blocks of roughly the same length. You do not want to start off with a long, detailed paragraph and then have the rest of the essay trail off into a series of ever-shorter, thinner paragraphs.

Logical organization grows out of careful, intentional arrangement of your analysis, but transitional devices can also play an important role. As you move from one cause or effect to another, make sure that you signal that move to readers. Develop each cause or effect in a separate paragraph, and start each paragraph with an explanatory statement of how this fits into what has gone before. Use parallelism and transitional phrases or markers; think of these devices as road signs for your readers to tell them what to expect ahead. For help and advice on using such devices, consult the Glossary and Ready Reference at the back of this text.

**Beginning and Ending**   Your teacher is the only reader who *has* to read your essay. Your introduction needs to catch your readers' attention and pull them into the paper. Think about why your readers would want to read an essay about this subject. What value does it hold for them? How curious might they be about the subject? What will you help them understand? Your introduction needs to be an inviting bridge between the world of your readers and the essay. Of course you will explain your thesis and your purpose for writing about this subject. Try to suggest as well, however, what is of particular interest or importance about this subject and to provoke the curiosity of readers.

Every paper needs a conclusion. Never simply stop because you have run out of time. In a short paper, a conclusion does not need to summarize the causes or effects that you have just described. They are fresh in your readers' minds. Try instead to end by stressing the significance of your analysis and how it may help readers understand the subject. Look at the conclusions that the six writers provided for their essays in this chapter. More concluding strategies for papers can be found in the Glossary and Ready Reference at the back of this text.

**IN THE READINGS, LOOK FOR**

**Introductions/conclusions**

E. M. Forster, "My Wood"
: Why is there no summary conclusion of the effects?

Joan Jacobs Brumberg, "Anorexia Nervosa"
: Why begin with the history of the first clinical descriptions of the disease?

Andres Martin, "Teenagers and Tattoos"
: How would you describe the function of the essay's conclusion?

Brent Staples, "Black Men"
: What is the effect of the strategy used in the introduction?

Veronica Chambers, "Dreadlocked"
: What is the role of the New Year's superstitions at the beginning of the essay?

Natalie Angier, "Drugs, Sports"
: What is the link between the first paragraph and the last, and why is that effective?

 **REVISING TIPS FOR WRITING CAUSE AND EFFECT**

1. Reexamine your subject. Have you been able to treat your subject adequately in the space that you have available? Do you need to narrow the subject in any way? Or is your subject too narrow to begin with?

2. Look critically at the body of your essay. Are the paragraphs substantial in length? Are they roughly proportional to one another in length? Your essay should not consist of many very short paragraphs or a couple of very long paragraphs and some very short paragraphs.

3. Evaluate your transitions. Have you provided clear transitions from one paragraph or section to another? Have you used transitional expressions or time and place markers to indicate that you are moving from one cause or effect to another?

4. Examine your conclusion. Does it just repeat the words of your opening paragraph in a slightly different way? Does it build a bridge between your subject and your reader, pointing out what is interesting or important about the subject?

5. Make a list of potential problems that you sense in your essay. These may be grammatical or mechanical, or they might be structural. Take your list and a copy of your paper to your school's writing center or to a writing tutor and ask for help. See if your instructor has the time—perhaps during office hours—to critique your draft.

## STUDENT ESSAY

For a cause-and-effect analysis, Cathy Ferguson chose to examine the effects that television's depiction of violence has on young children.

### First Draft

TV Aggression and Children

Let's face it. Television producers are out to make money. Their main concern is with what sells. What does sell? Sensationalism. People like shocking stories. In the effort to sell, the limit of the outrageous on TV has been pushed far beyond what it was, say, ten years ago. Television aggression is one aspect of sensationalism that has been exploited to please a thrill-seeking audience. Television is not showing a greater number of aggressive scenes, but the scenes portray more violent and hostile acts. Psychologists, prompted by concerned parents, have been studying the effects of children viewing increased aggression, since the average program for kids contains twenty acts of violence per hour, while the overall average is only seven acts of violence per hour. Research reveals three outstanding consequences of viewing greater TV hostility. First of all, TV aggression numbs children to real-world violence. One experiment showed that even a brief exposure to a fairly violent show made kids indifferent to the same aggression in real life. Preschoolers are especially affected by TV violence because they are usually unable to distinguish between reality and fantasy. If they see a hostile act, they are liable to believe that it is reality and accept it as the norm.

This leads to the second effect of viewing TV aggression: a distorted perception of the world. Most TV shows do not present real-world consequences of violence; thus children are getting a false picture of their world. Some kids are led to believe that acts of hostility are normal, common, expected even, and may lead a fearfully restricted life. In general, however, most children learn not how to be afraid of violence but how to be violent, which is the third and most drastic effect of viewing television aggression. Almost all studies show that kids are more aggressive after they watch an aggressive show, like "Batman" or "Power Rangers," than after watching a pro-social show like "Barney and Friends" or a neutral show. So although sensationalism, especially violent sensationalism, is making money for TV producers, it is also creating a generation that is numb to real violence, has a distorted picture of the environment, and is itself more hostile. These effects are so palpable, it is now realized that the single best predictor of how aggressive an 18-year-old will be is how much aggressive television he watched when he was 8 years old.

## Comments

After Cathy handed in her first draft, she had a conference with her instructor. The instructor commented on her effective use of examples. Because the essay contains specific evidence, the cause-and-effect analysis seems much more convincing.

Her instructor offered some specific advice about revisions in word choice, sentence structure, and paragraph division. He noted that the essay repeated the phrase "television aggression" or a related variant seven times. Since condensed forms can be confusing, he recommended that she make clear that her subject was aggression, violence, or hostility depicted on television shows. Noting that her first draft begins with five very short sentences and a single-word sentence fragment, he urged her to combine the sentences to reduce the choppy effect. Finally, he recommended that she use paragraph divisions to separate the three effects that she discusses. That division would make it easier for her reader to see the structure of the paper.

Cathy's revision addressed each of the problems that had been discussed in conference. In addition, she made a number of minor changes to tighten the prose and make it clearer.

## Revised Draft

### The Influence of Televised Violence on Children

Let's face it. Television producers are in business to make money. Their main concern is what sells, and nothing sells better than sensationalism. In an effort to gain a larger share of the audience, television producers now treat subject matter that would never have been acceptable ten years ago. The depiction of violence on television is one aspect of that sensationalism, exploited to please a thrill-seeking audience. The number of aggressive scenes shown on television has not increased, but those scenes now portray more violent and hostile acts. This is especially true on shows aimed at children.

Psychologists, prompted by concerned parents, have begun studying the effects on children of viewing this increased aggression. The average program for children contains twenty acts of violence per hour, compared to an overall average of seven acts of violence per hour. Research reveals three significant consequences of viewing violence on television.

First, aggressive acts on television numb children to real-world violence. One study showed that even a brief exposure to a fairly violent show made children indifferent to the same aggression in real life.

Preschoolers are especially affected by television because they are usually unable to distinguish between reality and fantasy. If they see an aggressive act, they are likely to believe that it is real and so accept it as normal.

This potential confusion leads to the second effect of watching violence on television: a distorted perception of the world. Some children are led to believe that acts of hostility are normal, common, and even expected. As a result, these children may lead a restricted life, afraid of the violence that they imagine lurks everywhere.

In general, however, most children learn not to be afraid of violence but how to be violent—the third and most drastic effect of viewing aggression on television. Almost all studies show that children are more aggressive after they watch a show that includes violence than after watching a show that excludes it.

All three effects are so palpable that it is now realized the single best predictor of how aggressive an 18-year-old will be is how much violence he watched on television when he was 8 years old.

## SOME THINGS TO REMEMBER WHEN WRITING CAUSE AND EFFECT

1. Choose a topic that can be analyzed thoroughly within the limits of the assignment.
2. Decide on a purpose: are you trying to explain or to persuade?
3. Determine an audience. For whom are you writing? What does your audience already know about your subject?
4. Analyze and research your subject. Remember to provide factual support wherever necessary. Not every cause-and-effect analysis can rely on unsupported opinion.
5. Be certain that the relationships you see between causes and effects are genuine.
6. Concentrate your efforts on immediate and primary causes or effects rather than on remote or secondary ones. Do not try to list every cause or every effect that you can.
7. Begin with the cause and then move to effects, or begin with an effect and then move to its causes.
8. Look for a principle of order to organize your list of causes or effects. It might be chronological or spatial, for example, or it might move from immediate to remote or from primary to secondary.
9. Remember that you are explaining why something happens or what will happen. You are not just describing how.

# SEEING CAUSE AND EFFECT IN OTHER CONTEXTS

## As a Literary Strategy

Marge Piercy's poem "Barbie Doll" uses a cause-and-effect structure in order to comment on the physical ideals that society offers to young women. As you read, think about what is the cause and what is the effect and how those two elements are arranged in the poem.

# *Barbie Doll*

Marge Piercy

*This girlchild was born as usual*
*and presented dolls that did pee-pee*
*and miniature GE stoves and irons*
*and wee lipsticks the color of cherry candy.*
*Then in the magic of puberty, a classmate said:*
*You have a great big nose and fat legs.*

*She was healthy, tested intelligent,*
*possessed strong arms and back,*
*abundant sex drive and manual dexterity.*
*She went to and fro apologizing.*
*Everyone saw a fat nose on thick legs.*

*She was advised to play coy,*
*exhorted to come on hearty,*
*exercise, diet, smile and wheedle.*
*Her good nature wore out*
*like a fan belt.*
*So she cut off her nose and her legs*
*and offered them up.*
*In the casket displayed on satin she lay*
*with the undertaker's cosmetics painted on,*
*a turned-up putty nose,*
*dressed in a pink and white nightie.*
*Doesn't she look pretty? everyone said.*
*Consummation at last.*
*To every woman a happy ending.*

## Discussion Questions

1. What happens to the "girlchild" in the story?
2. What is the cause and what is the effect in the poem?
3. What role does "Barbie" play in what happens?
4. In the final stanza, what is the significance of details describing the woman's body?
5. What reaction might Piercy be trying to evoke in her readers? How is cause and effect being used in the poem?

## Writing Suggestions

It is difficult sometimes even to be aware of the pressures generated by popular culture yet alone to be able to deal with them. How are you influenced by what you see around you—by images in magazines, in advertisements, in films, in music, in television? To what extent are those images a problem? Do they ever make you do things you shouldn't, feel bad about yourself, or feel pressured to change or conform? Explore in an essay one aspect of the influence of popular culture on your life. Possible points of departure include:

a. Your physical self—size, proportions, appearance
b. Your values or expectations in life—how do you measure success? Happiness? Fulfillment?
c. Your possessions

# AS A CRITICAL READING STRATEGY

When you are sick and visit a doctor, you want to know what has caused the problem and how it can be corrected or alleviated. Sometimes you get fairly precise answers; sometimes you get educated guesses. There might be many possible causes of a disease: often, doctors understand the symptoms and the progression of an illness or disease but cannot pin down a single cause. For example, cigarette smoking and exposure to asbestos can be causes of lung cancer, but there are many other causes as well.

Many people suffer from migraine headaches and would surely do whatever they could to prevent their reoccurrence, if only they knew what it was that caused the migraine. Read the following explanation of "What Causes Migraine Headaches" from www.emedicinehealth.com.

As you read, remember what you have learned about how to write using cause and effect and how that knowledge might help you as a reader.

- An analysis of cause explains why something happens or how it came about. An analysis of effect explains the consequences that flow from an event or situation.
- Causes and effects are related to the event by factors other than the time of their occurrence. A rainstorm right after you washed your car was not caused by your action.
- Cause-and-effect analyses tend to concentrate either on causes or on effects rather than attempting to do both.
- Causes and effects vary in importance and in timing. Some are primary and some are secondary; some are immediate and others are remote.
- Causes and effects are logically organized, typically moving from first to last, most important to least, immediate to remote.
- Cause-and-effect analyses employ transitions and parallelism to signal to the reader the structure of the analysis.

## What Causes Migraine Headaches?

Description of the physical process by which pain is produced

Medical terms defined within parentheses

Immediate cause of a migraine

No one fully understands the exact cause(s) of migraine headaches. Many experts think that a migraine begins with abnormal <u>brainstem (a part of the brain)</u> activity that leads to <u>spasms (rapid contraction)</u> of blood vessels in the <u>cerebrum (main part of the brain)</u> and <u>dura (the covering of the brain)</u>. The first wave of spasm decreases blood supply, which causes the aura that some people experience. After the first spasm, <u>the same arteries become abnormally relaxed, which increases blood flow and gives rise to migraine headache pain</u>.

Contributing cause

Certain chemicals normally found in the brain (namely, dopamine and serotonin) may be involved in causing migraines. These chemicals are called neurotransmitters because they transmit signals within the brain. <u>Neurotransmitters can cause blood vessels to act in unusual ways if they are present in abnormal amounts or if the blood vessels are particularly sensitive to them.</u>

"Triggers" set off the physical sequence that produces the pain

Triggers, however, are not the causes

Various triggers are thought to <u>bring about migraine in people who have a natural tendency for having migraine headaches.</u> Different people may have different triggers.

- Certain foods, especially chocolate, cheese, nuts, alcohol, and monosodium glutamate (MSG) can trigger migraines. (MSG is a food enhancer used in many foods, including Chinese food.)
- Missing a meal may bring on a headache.
- Stress and tension are also risk factors. People often have migraines during times of increased emotional or physical stress.

Distinguished another type of headache—not a migraine

- Birth control pills are a common trigger. Women may have migraines at the end of the pill cycle as the estrogen component of the pill is stopped. This is called an estrogen-withdrawal headache.

## As a Visual Strategy

Typically, photographs and short videos invite us to speculate on cause-and-effect relationships rather than thoroughly documenting them for us. Starting with what is pictured, we can move backward in time trying to establish what factors led to this effect, or we can move forward in time and focus on the consequences that will result. A still photograph of the flooding of New Orleans after Hurricane Katrina can trigger an analysis of the multiple causes that lead to that disaster, or it can lead to a discussion of the effects such a disaster had on the lives of those who lived there.

Consider this photograph as a static moment in time and then move either backward or forward.

## WRITING ABOUT IMAGES

1. You will never know for certain what has brought the woman in the photograph to this point or how her present circumstances will influence her future. However, you can see her as a symbol, a representative image of many people in our society who are facing similar circumstances. Using the photograph as a starting point, write an essay in response to one of the following topics.

    a. Analyze some of the major causes of homelessness in America (you might want to limit the subject by focusing, for example, on homelessness among older women).

    b. Construct a causal chain that interlinks causes to produce a result such as this.

    c. Analyze some of the major effects of homelessness on American society.

2. Advertisements, whether in print or video format, typically suggest a cause-and-effect relationship. The implication is that if you use this particular product or service, you will see these changes—in yourself, in how others see you, in your success or happiness. Find a print or video advertisement that exploits this "supposed" connection. In an essay analyze the effects that are suggested and why they might be attractive to potential customers or users. Attach a copy of the advertisement (or a description of the video) to your paper.

3. Television shows can be grouped in a variety of ways. The success of a certain type of program or a particular format is likely to breed imitators. Select one type of show that is particularly common at this time—for example, reality shows, crime dramas, game shows, adult cartoons, celebrity "watches," dramatizations of classic works of literature, cooking or home building or repair. Analyze the possible reasons for the popularity of the format or subject. Or look at the possible effects such shows have on American culture. Another option would be to look at videos on YouTube in the same ways.

## ADDITIONAL WRITING SUGGESTIONS FOR CAUSE AND EFFECT

Cause-and-effect analyses move backward or forward in time: you are either analyzing the reasons why something happened or the consequences that arise from it. Most cause-and-effect essays in writing courses focus on one direction rather than trying to explore both. Typically cause-and-effect analyses are intended to be informative, although they can also be entertaining and persuasive. Remember to keep your audience in mind. What do they already know about the subject? Do not attempt anything too simple or too obvious, but do not tackle complex and technical subjects in the space of a few pages. Always consider as well why anyone might be interested in reading your paper.

1. Why are cell phones so popular? So "essential"? What is the effect of "instant" communication in our society?

2. Why do people purchase and wear an article of clothing that advertises a product? They are, after all, walking advertisements. Why does a particular brand of anything become so desirable?

3. Why is blogging so popular? What might account for that popularity? What has been the effect of the many blogs in cyberspace?

4. Why is college so expensive? What have you come to expect from your college in terms of services, amenities, programs, and facilities?

5. Why are some people willing to risk or sacrifice their lives for the safety of others?

6. What are the causes of our culture's obsession with the "ideal" body for women or men? What are the effects of this obsession?

7. Why is YouTube so popular? What impact does it have on us and our culture?

8. What accounts for the popularity of certain sports, the growth of "extreme" sports?

9. Why are medical costs so high? What is the effect of these costs on the availability of health care options to many Americans?

10. What accounts for the popularity of electronic devices such as the iPod? The BlackBerry? What is the effect of such devices on our lives?

11. Why is oil so expensive? What will be the long-term impact of high prices on how and what Americans drive? How might high prices influence future housing patterns in the United States?

12. What has shaped your expectations of the personal "future" that you want?

13. What explains the growing interest in "organic" products? What is the impact of that interest on the agricultural industry in the United States?

14. Why are Americans so interested in self-help books and videos? What does this say about us and our culture?

15. Select a subject from another course you are taking this semester that lends itself to an analysis of causes or of effects. You could, for example, select a social problem, an historical event, an economic issue, a science concept or event, a psychological problem, or a movement in art or music.

# My Wood

E. M. Forster

*Edward Morgan Forster (1879–1970) was born in London, England, and earned two undergraduate degrees and a master's degree from King's College, Cambridge University. He is best known as a novelist, but he also wrote short stories, literary criticism, biographies, histories, and essays. His novels, many of which have been made into popular films, include* A Room with a View *(1908),* Howards End *(1910), and* A Passage to India *(1924). He published two collections of essays,* Abinger Harvest *(1936) and* Two Cheers for Democracy *(1951).*

**On Writing:** *Once, after having broken his right arm in a fall, Forster contemplated writing with his left hand: "The attempt to write with the left hand raises new hopes in the human heart. For how many years have our thoughts been transmitted by the nerves and muscles of the right hand. How much of their essence might not have been absorbed in the passage. Now when new organs are brought into play new thoughts or new parts of thoughts may find their way on to the page, how many old ones can be absent and fail to reach it. A physiological outcry may be raised at this. But at all events the thought that it may occur is new.... [T]he thoughts that have so long struggled for expression may at last find it."*

## Before Reading

**Connecting:** What would you regard as the most important "thing" that you own? Why is it most important to you?

**Anticipating:** Forster observes that owning the wood made him feel "heavy." In what sense does it make him feel "heavy"?

1   **A** few years ago I wrote a book which dealt in part with the difficulties of the English in India. Feeling that they would have had no difficulties in India themselves, the Americans read the book freely. The more they read it the better it made them feel, and a cheque to the author was the result. I bought a wood with the cheque. It is not a large wood—it contains scarcely any trees, and it is intersected, blast it, by a public footpath. Still, it is the first property that I have owned, so it is right that other people should participate in my shame, and should ask themselves, in accents that will vary in horror, this very important question: What is the effect of property upon the character? Don't let's touch economics; the effect of private ownership upon the community as a whole is another question—a more important question, perhaps, but another one. Let's keep to psychology. If you own things, what's their effect on you? What's the effect on me of my wood?

2      In the first place, it makes me feel heavy. Property does have this effect. Property produces men of weight, and it was a man of weight who failed to get into the Kingdom of Heaven. He was not wicked, that unfortunate millionaire in the parable, he was only stout; he stuck out in front, not to mention behind, and as he wedged himself this way and that in the crystalline entrance and bruised his well-fed flanks, he saw beneath him a comparatively slim camel passing through the eye of a needle and being woven into the robe of God. The Gospels all through couple stoutness and slowness. They point out what is perfectly obvious, yet seldom realized: that if you have a lot of things you cannot move about a lot, that furniture requires dusting, dusters require servants, servants require insurance stamps, and the whole tangle of them makes you think twice before you accept an invitation to dinner or go for a bathe in the Jordan. Sometimes the Gospels proceed further and say with Tolstoy that property is sinful; they approach the difficult ground of asceticism here, where I cannot follow them. But as to the immediate effects of property on people, they just show straightforward logic. It produces men of weight. Men of weight cannot, by definition, move like the lightning from the East unto the West, and the ascent of a fourteen-stone bishop into a pulpit is thus the exact antithesis of the coming of the Son of Man. My wood makes me feel heavy.

3      In the second place, it makes me feel it ought to be larger.

4      The other day I heard a twig snap in it. I was annoyed at first, for I thought that someone was blackberrying, and depreciating the value of the undergrowth. On coming nearer, I saw it was not a man who had trodden on the twig and snapped it, but a bird, and I felt pleased. My bird. The bird was not equally pleased. Ignoring the relation between us, it took fright as soon as it saw the shape of my face, and flew straight over the boundary hedge into a field, the property of Mrs. Henessy, where it sat down with a loud squawk. It had become Mrs. Henessy's bird. Something seemed grossly amiss here, something that would not have occurred had the wood been larger. I could not afford to buy Mrs. Henessy out, I dared not murder her, and limitations of this sort beset me on every side. Ahab did not want that vineyard—he only needed it to round off his property, preparatory to plotting a new curve—and all the land around my wood has become necessary to me in order to round off the wood. A boundary protects. But—poor little thing—the boundary ought in its turn to be protected. Noises on the edge of it. Children throw stones. A little more, and then a little more, until we reach the sea. Happy Canute! Happier Alexander! And after all, why should even the world be the limit of possession? A rocket containing a Union Jack, will, it is hoped, be shortly fired at the moon. Mars. Sirius. Beyond which... But these immensities ended by saddening me. I could not suppose that my wood was the destined nucleus of universal dominion—it is so very small and contains no mineral wealth beyond the blackberries. Nor was I comforted when Mrs. Henessy's bird took alarm for the second time and flew clean away from us all, under the belief that it belonged to itself.

5      In the third place, property makes its owner feel that he ought to do something to it. Yet he isn't sure what. A restlessness comes over him, a vague

sense that he has a personality to express—the same sense which, without any vagueness, leads the artist to an act of creation. Sometimes I think I will cut down such trees as remain in the wood, at other times I·want to fill up the gaps between them with new trees. But impulses are pretentious and empty. They are not honest movements towards money-making or beauty. They spring from a foolish desire to express myself and from an inability to enjoy what I have got. Creation, property, enjoyment form a sinister trinity in the human mind. Creation and enjoyment are both very, very good, yet they are often unattainable without a material basis, and at such moments property pushes itself in as a substitute, saying, "Accept me instead—I'm good enough for all three." It is not enough. It is, as Shakespeare said of lust, "the expense of spirit in a waste of shame": it is "Before, a joy proposed; behind, a dream." Yet we don't know how to shun it. It is forced on us by our economic system as the alternative to starvation. It is forced on us by an internal defect in the soul, by the feeling that in property may lie the germs of selfdevelopment and of exquisite or heroic deeds. Our life on earth is, and ought to be, material and carnal. But we have not learned to manage our materialism and carnality properly; they are still entangled with the desire for ownership, where (in the words of Dante) "Possession is one with loss."

6    And this brings us to our fourth and final point: the blackberries.

7    Blackberries are not plentiful in the meagre grove, but they are easily seen from the public footpath which traverses it, and all too easily gathered. Foxgloves, too—people will pull up the foxgloves, and ladies of an educational tendency even grub for toadstools to show them on the Monday in class. Other ladies, less educated, roll down the bracken in the arms of their gentlemen friends. There is paper, there are tins. Pray, does my wood belong to me or doesn't it? And, if it does, should I not own it best by allowing no one else to walk there? There is a wood near Lyme Regis, also cursed by a public footpath, where the owner has not hesitated on this point. He has built high stone walls on each side of the path, and has spanned it by bridges, so that the public circulate like termites while he gorges on the blackberries unseen. He really does own his wood, this able chap. Dives in Hell did pretty well, but the gulf dividing him from Lazarus could be traversed by vision, and nothing traverses it here. And perhaps I shall come to this in time. I shall wall in and fence out until I really taste the sweets of property. Enormously stout, endlessly avaricious, pseudocreative, intensely selfish, I shall weave upon my forehead the quadruple crown of possession until those nasty Bolshies come and take it off again and thrust me aside into the outer darkness.

## Questions on Subject and Purpose

1. According to Forster, what are the consequences of owning property?
2. Is there any irony in buying property from the royalties earned from a book about England's problems in India?
3. What purpose or purposes might Forster have had in writing the essay?

## Questions on Strategy and Audience

1. In what way is this a cause-and-effect essay?
2. Look at the conclusion of the essay. Why does Forster end in this way? Why not add a more conventional conclusion?
3. What expectations does Forster seem to have about his audience? How do you know?

## Questions on Vocabulary and Style

1. Characterize the tone of Forster's essay. Is it formal? Informal? How is that tone achieved?
2. Forster makes extensive use of allusion in the essay. Some of the names are easily recognizable; others are less so. Identify the following allusions (all but "c" are to biblical stories). How does each fit into the context of the essay?
   a. The wealthy man in the parable (paragraph 2)
   b. Ahab and the vineyard (4)
   c. Canute and Alexander (4)
   d. Dives and Lazarus (7)
3. Be prepared to define the following words: *asceticism* (paragraph 2), *stone* (2), *depreciating* (4), *pretentious* (5), *carnal* (5), *foxgloves* (7), *bracken* (7), *avaricious* (7), *Bolshies* (7).

## Writing Suggestions

1. **For Your Journal or Blog.** Commenting on the second effect of owning property, Forster observes: "it makes me feel it ought to be larger" (paragraph 3). To what extent does something you own make you want to own something more? Concentrate on the possession you value most highly. Does owning it ever make you want to own more? Explore the idea.
2. **For a Paragraph.** Select something you own that is important to you—a house, a car, a stereo system, a pet, something you use for recreation. In a paragraph, describe the consequences of owning it. How has it changed your life and behavior? Are there negative as well as positive consequences?
3. **For an Essay.** Extend your paragraph into an essay. Explore each of the consequences you described in a separate paragraph.
4. **For Research.** Property ownership has frequently been used throughout history as a precondition for full participation in the affairs of government (voting, for example). A number of states in this country applied such a restriction until the practice was declared unconstitutional. Using outside sources, write a research essay that explains and analyzes either the reasons for such practices or their negative consequences. Be sure to document your sources.

## For Further Study

**Focusing on Grammar and Writing.** Write a new ending for Forster's essay. Try one that follows the advice you have learned from writing the typical five-paragraph essay—that is, write a very conventional, English-class-sounding conclusion. What is the effect of adding this ending to the essay? What does this suggest about writing effective conclusions?

**Working Together.** Working with classmates in small groups, try to characterize Forster's tone in the essay. You must first define *tone* (see the Glossary and Ready Reference for help) and discuss the elements that can create or influence tone in an essay. Then isolate specific effects—things such as word choice and phrasing—that influence perceptions of tone.

**Seeing Other Modes at Work.** Although the essay does not seem to reach a conclusion about the effects of property ownership, it could easily be recast with a persuasive purpose. What would it require to make Forster's essay "argue" for or against the ownership of property? In paragraph 4, Forster uses narrative—that is, he tells a story—to illustrate the second consequence of property ownership.

**Finding Connections.** A good pairing is with Lars Eighner's "My Daily Dives in the Dumpster" (Chapter 6). To what extent do both Forster and Eighner achieve a similar insight about material possessions? Another pairing is with Peter Singer's "The Singer Solution to World Poverty" (Chapter 10).

**Exploring the Web.** A number of Websites include information about E. M. Forster and his writings, including hypertext and e-text editions of his work. You can also locate information about Merchant/Ivory Productions, the film company responsible for making, among others, film versions of Forster's novels *Howards End* and *A Room with a View*.

# The Origins of Anorexia Nervosa

Joan Jacobs Brumberg

*Born in 1944 in Mount Vernon, New York, Joan Jacobs Brumberg earned a Ph.D. in American history at the University of Virginia. She is the Stephen H. Weiss Presidential Fellow and Professor at Cornell University. She has written many articles and several books, including* Fasting Girls: The Emergence of Anorexia Nervosa *(1988), which studies the disease from historical, social, and familial perspectives. Her most recent book is* Kansas Charley: The Story of a 19th-Century Boy Murderer *(2003). The following selection is from* Fasting Girls *and was published in* Harper's *magazine.*

**On Writing:** *In her preface to* The Body Project, *Brumberg praised an editor for helping her achieve "accessibility" and "shed the girdle of academese that shapes so many historical accounts of the past."*

## Before Reading

**Connecting:** What attitudes toward food and toward mealtime do the members of your family share? Do you have "family" meals? Are there any rituals connected with mealtime?

**Anticipating:** Brumberg defines a certain environment in which anorexia nervosa emerged. What are the essential conditions of that environment?

1      Contrary to the popular assumption that anorexia nervosa is a peculiarly modern disorder, the malady first emerged in the Victorian era—long before the pervasive cultural imperative for a thin female body. The first clinical descriptions of the disorder appeared in England and France almost simultaneously in 1873. They were written by two well-known physicians: Sir William Withey Gull and Charles Lasègue. Lasègue, more than any other nineteenth-century doctor, captured the rhythm of repeated offerings and refusals that signaled the breakdown of reciprocity between parents and their anorexic daughter. By returning to its origins, we can see anorexia nervosa for what it is: a dysfunction in the bourgeois family system.

2      Family meals assumed enormous importance in the bourgeois milieu, in the United States as well as in England and France. Middle-class parents prided themselves on providing ample food for their children. The abundance of food and the care in its preparation became expressions of social status. The

ambience of the meal symbolized the values of the family. A popular domestic manual advised, "Simple, healthy food, exquisitely prepared, and served upon shining dishes and brilliant silverware . . . a gentle blessing, and cheerful conversation, embrace the sweetest communions and the happiest moments of life." Among the middle class it seems that eating correctly was emerging as a new morality, one that set its members apart from the working class.

3      At the same time, food was used to express love in the nineteenth-century bourgeois household. Offering attractive and abundant meals was the particular responsibility and pleasure of middle-class wives and mothers. In America the feeding of middle-class children, from infancy on, had become a maternal concern no longer deemed appropriate to delegate to wet nurses, domestics, or governesses. Family meals were expected to be a time of instructive and engaging conversation. Participation was expected on both a verbal and gustatory level. In this context, refusing to eat was an unabashedly antisocial act. Anorexic behavior was antithetical to the ideal of bourgeois eating. One advice book, *Common Sense for Maid, Wife, and Mother,* stated: "Heated discussion and quarrels, fretfulness and sullen taciturnity while eating, are as unwholesome as they are unchristian."

4      Why would a daughter affront her parents by refusing to eat? Lasègue's 1873 description of anorexia nervosa, along with other nineteenth-century medical reports, suggests that pressure to marry may have precipitated the illness.

5      Ambitious parents surely understood that by marrying well, at an appropriate moment, a daughter, even though she did not carry the family name, could help advance a family's social status—particularly in a burgeoning middle-class society. As a result, the issue of marriage loomed large in the life of a dutiful middle-class daughter. Although marriage did not generally occur until the girl's early twenties, it was an event for which she was continually prepared, and a desirable outcome for all depended on the ability of the parents and the child to work together—that is, to state clearly what each wanted or to read each other's heart and mind. In the context of marital expectations, a daughter's refusal to eat was a provocative rejection of both the family's social aspirations and their goodwill toward her. All of the parents' plans for her future (and their own) could be stymied by her peculiar and unpleasant alimentary nihilism.

6      Beyond the specific anxieties generated by marital pressure, the Victorian family milieu in America and in Western Europe harbored a mélange of other tensions and problems that provided the emotional preconditions for the emergence of anorexia nervosa. As love replaced authority as the cement of family relations, it began to generate its own set of emotional disorders.

7      Possessiveness, for example, became an acute problem in Victorian family life. Where love between parents and children was the prevailing ethic, there was always the risk of excess. When love became suffocating or manipulative, individuation and separation from the family could become extremely

painful, if not impossible. In the context of increased intimacy, adolescent privacy was especially problematic: For parents and their sexually maturing daughters, what constituted an appropriate degree of privacy? Middle-class girls, for example, almost always had their own rooms or shared them with sisters, but they had greater difficulty establishing autonomous psychic space. The well-known penchant of adolescent girls for novel-reading was an expression of their need for imaginative freedom. Some parents, recognizing that their daughters needed channels for expressing emotions, encouraged diary-keeping. But some of the same parents who gave lovely marbled journals as gifts also monitored their content. Since emotional freedom was not an acknowledged prerogative of the Victorian adolescent girl, it seems likely that she would have expressed unhappiness in non-verbal forms of behavior. One such behavior was refusal of food.

8      When an adolescent daughter became sullen and chronically refused to eat, her parents felt threatened and confused. The daughter was perceived as willfully manipulating her appetite the way a younger child might. Because parents did not want to encourage this behavior, they often refused at first to indulge the favorite tastes or caprices of their daughter. As emaciation became visible and the girl looked ill, many violated the contemporary canon of prudent child-rearing and put aside their moral objections to pampering the appetite. Eventually they would beg their daughter to eat whatever she liked—and eat she must, "as a sovereign proof of affection" for them. From the parents' perspective, a return to eating was a confirmation of filial love.

9      The significance of food refusal as an emotional tactic within the family depended on food's being plentiful, pleasing, and connected to love. Where food was eaten simply to assuage hunger, where it had only minimal aesthetic and symbolic messages, or where the girl had to provide her own nourishment, refusal of food was not particularly noteworthy or defiant. In contrast, the anorexic girl was surrounded by a provident, if not indulgent, family that was bound to be distressed by her rejection of its largess.

10     Anorexia nervosa was an intense form of discourse that honored the emotional guidelines that governed the middle-class Victorian family. Refusing to eat was not as confrontational as yelling, having a tantrum, or throwing things; refusing to eat expressed emotional hostility without being flamboyant. And refusing to eat had the advantage of being ambiguous. If a girl repeatedly claimed lack of appetite she might indeed be ill and therefore entitled to special treatment and favors.

11     In her own way, the anorexic was respectful of what historian Peter Gay called "the great bourgeois compromise between the need for reserve and the capacity for emotion." The rejection of food, while an emotionally charged behavior, was also discreet, quiet, and ladylike. The unhappy adolescent who was in all other ways a dutiful daughter chose food refusal from within the symptom repertoire available to her. Precisely because she was not a lunatic, she selected a behavior that she knew would have some efficacy within her own family.

## Questions on Subject and Purpose

1. According to Brumberg, when did anorexia nervosa emerge as a definable disease? Why did it emerge in that particular time period?
2. On the basis of what Brumberg writes here, who is the most likely candidate for anorexia nervosa?
3. What purpose might Brumberg have in writing about anorexia nervosa?

## Questions on Strategy and Audience

1. Why does Brumberg begin by referring to "the popular assumption that anorexia nervosa is a peculiarly modern disorder"?
2. To what extent does isolating the origins of anorexia nervosa help us understand the disorder in young people today?
3. Brumberg uses quite a few words that might be unfamiliar to many readers. What do her vocabulary choices imply about her sense of audience?

## Questions on Vocabulary and Style

1. In paragraphs 2 and 3, Brumberg quotes from two popular domestic manuals of the nineteenth century. What do the quotations contribute to her essay?
2. In paragraph 5, Brumberg uses the phrase "alimentary nihilism" with reference to anorexics. What does the phrase mean?
3. Be prepared to define the following words: *malady* (paragraph 1), *imperative* (1), *reciprocity* (1), *dysfunction* (1), *bourgeois* (1), *milieu* (2), *ambience* (2), *wet nurses* (3), *gustatory* (3), *unabashedly* (3), *antithetical* (3), *taciturnity* (3), *burgeoning* (5), *stymied* (5), *alimentary* (5), *nihilism* (5), *mélange* (6), *individuation* (7), *autonomous* (7), *penchant* (7), *prerogative* (7), *caprices* (8), *emaciation* (8), *assuage* (9), *largess* (9), *flamboyant* (10), *efficacy* (11).

## Writing Suggestions

1. **For Your Journal or Blog.** How would you characterize your mealtimes? Do you care about the circumstances in which you eat? Do you have to eat with someone else? Can you just grab something on the run? Explore your attitudes toward mealtime. Do not just accept what you are doing without thinking about it. What do you expect of meals? Why?
2. **For a Paragraph.** Define your "ideal" body. Then in a second paragraph speculate on the reasons why that body type or shape seems "ideal."
3. **For an Essay.** Cultural historians have observed that American society is "obesophobic" (excessively or irrationally fearful of fat and being fat). Certainly weight consciousness permeates American society and the weight-loss industries are multimillion dollar businesses. Why?
4. **For Research.** Anorexia nervosa is only one of a number of diseases that are common today but were previously unknown or undiagnosed. Other examples include Alzheimer's disease, osteoporosis, premenstrual syndrome, and chronic fatigue syndrome. Select a "new" disease or disorder, and research its history.

When was it first defined? What might account for its emergence during the past decade or two? If you are using information from electronic sources, such as the Web, make sure that the information is authoritative. Be sure to document all of your sources, including electronic ones, wherever appropriate.

## For Further Study

**Focusing on Grammar and Writing.** Brumberg uses quite a few words that are not part of most people's working vocabularies. Underline every unfamiliar word in the essay. Next to each word, write down what you guess it might mean. Check your guess against a dictionary definition.

**Working Together.** Working in small groups, discuss the reasons why our culture has a fear of "fatness." Brainstorm about possible reasons for this obsession with thinness. Each group should present its ideas to the class as a whole. As a class, try to construct an analysis of the causes that could be used as the framework for an essay on the topic.

**Seeing Other Modes at Work.** In tracing the origins of anorexia nervosa, Brumberg uses narration as well as cause-and-effect strategies. How is narrative used in the essay?

**Finding Connections.** A excellent pairing is with Margaret Atwood's "The Female Body" (Chapter 8) or with Natalie Angier's "Drags, Sports, Body Image and G.I. Joe" (this chapter). Another, more unusual, pairing is with Tom Haines's "Facing Famine" (Chapter 2).

**Exploring the Web.** The Web has extensive resources for dealing with anorexia nervosa and related eating disorders.

# On Teenagers and Tattoos

Andres Martin

*Andres Martin received his M.D. from the Universidad Nacional Antonoma de Mexico in 1990. He is currently a professor and medical director of the Child Psychiatric Impatient Service at Yale University. He specializes in inpatient child and adolescent psychiatry and psychopharmacology. A widely known authority, he is the author of many professional publications.* "On Teenagers and Tattoos" *was first published in the* Journal of Child and Adolescent Psychiatry *in 1997.*

## Before Reading

**Connecting:** Do you have any tattoos or piercings? How many? How old were you when you got each?

**Anticipating:** Martin suggests reasons why adolescents get tattoos and piercings. Do you recognize any of these reasons as ones that motivated you or a friend to get either a tattoo or a piercing?

> The skeleton dimensions I shall now proceed to set down are copied verbatim from my right arm, where I had them tattooed: as in my wild wanderings at that period, there was no other secure way of preserving such valuable statistics.
>
> —Melville, *Moby Dick*

1   Tattoos and piercing have become a part of our everyday landscape. They are ubiquitous, having entered the circles of glamour and the mainstream of fashion, and they have even become an increasingly common feature of our urban youth. Legislation in most states restricts professional tattooing to adults older than 18 years of age, so "high end" tattooing is rare in children and adolescents, but such tattoos are occasionally seen in older teenagers. Piercings, by comparison, as well as self-made or "jailhouse" type tattoos, are not at all rare among adolescents or even among school-age children. Like hairdo, makeup, or baggy jeans, tattoos and piercings can be subject to fad influence or peer pressure in an effort toward group affiliation. As with any other fashion statement, they can be construed as bodily aids in the inner struggle toward identity consolidation, serving as adjuncts to the defining and sculpting of the self by means of external manipulations. But unlike most other body decorations, tattoos and piercings are set apart by their irreversible and permanent nature, a quality at the core of their magnetic appeal to adolescents.

2    Adolescents and their parents are often at odds over the acquisition of bodily decorations. For the adolescent, piercing or tattoos may be seen as personal and beautifying statements, while parents may construe them as oppositional and enraging affronts to their authority. Distinguishing bodily adornment from self-mutilation may indeed prove challenging, particularly when a family is in disagreement over a teenager's motivations and a clinician is summoned as the final arbiter. At such times it may be most important to realize jointly that the skin can all too readily become but another battleground for the tensions of the age, arguments having less to do with tattoos and piercings than with core issues such as separation from the family matrix. Exploring the motivations and significance [underlying] tattoos (Grumet, 1983) and piercings can go a long way toward resolving such differences and can become a novel and additional way of getting to know teenagers. An interested and nonjudgmental appreciation of teenagers' surface presentations may become a way of making contact not only in their terms but on their turfs: quite literally on the territory of their skins.

3    The following three sections exemplify some of the complex psychological underpinnings of youth tattooing.

## Identity and the Adolescent's Body

4  Tattoos and piercing can offer a concrete and readily available solution for many of the identity crises and conflicts normative to adolescent development. In using such decorations, and by marking out their bodily territories, adolescents can support their efforts at autonomy, privacy, and insulation. Seeking individuation, tattooed adolescents can become unambiguously demarcated from others and singled out as unique. The intense and often disturbing reactions that are mobilized in viewers can help to effectively keep them at bay, becoming tantamount to the proverbial "Keep Out" sign hanging from a teenager's door.

5    Alternatively, feeling prey to a rapidly evolving body over which they have no say, self-made and openly visible decorations may restore adolescents' sense of normalcy and control, a way of turning a passive experience into an active identity. By indelibly marking their bodies, adolescents can strive to reclaim their bearings within an environment experienced as alien, estranged, or suffocating or to lay claim over their evolving and increasingly unrecognizable bodies. In either case, the net outcome can be a resolution to unwelcome impositions: external, familial, or societal in one case; internal and hormonal in the other. In the words of a 16-year-old girl with several facial piercings, and who could have been referring to her body just as well as to the position within her family: "If I don't fit in, it is because I say so."

## Incorporation and Ownership

6  Imagery of a religious, deathly, or skeletal nature, the likenesses of fierce animals or imagined creatures, and the simple inscription of names are some of the time-tested favorite contents for tattoos. In all instances, marks become

not only memorials or recipients for dearly held persons or concepts: they strive for incorporation, with images and abstract symbols gaining substance on becoming a permanent part of the individual's skin. Thickly embedded in personally meaningful representations and object relations, tattoos can become not only the ongoing memento of a relationship, but at times even the only evidence that there ever was such a bond. They can quite literally become the relationship itself. The turbulence and impulsivity of early attachments and infatuations may become grounded, effectively bridging oblivion through the visible reality to tattoos.

7      Case Vignette: "A," a 13-year-old boy, proudly showed me his tattooed deltoid. The coarsely depicted roll of the dice marked the day and month of his birth. Rather disappointed, he then uncovered an immaculate back, going on to draw for me the great "piece" he envisioned for it. A menacing figure held a hand of cards: two aces, two eights, and a card with two sets of dates. "A's" father had belonged to Dead Man's Hand, a motorcycle gang named after the set of cards (aces and eights) that the legendary Wild Bill Hickock had held in the 1890s when shot dead over a poker table in Deadwood, South Dakota. "A" had only the vaguest memory of and sketchiest information about his father, but he knew he had died in a motorcycle accident: The fifth card marked the dates of his birth and death.

8      The case vignette also serves to illustrate how tattoos are often the culmination of a long process of imagination, fantasy, and planning that can start at an early age. Limited markings, or relatively reversible ones such as piercings, can at a later time scaffold toward the more radical commitment of a permanent tattoo.

## The Quest of Permanence

9  The popularity of the anchor as a tattoo motif may historically have had to do less with guild identification among sailors than with an intense longing for rootedness and stability. In a similar vein, the recent increase in the popularity and acceptance of tattoos may be understood as an antidote or counterpoint to our urban and nomadic lifestyles. Within an increasingly mobile society, in which relationships are so often transient—as attested by the frequencies of divorce, abandonment, foster placement, and repeated moves, for example—tattoos can be a readily available source of grounding. Tattoos, unlike many relationships, can promise permanence and stability. A sense of constancy can be derived from unchanging marks that can be carried along no matter what the physical, temporal, or geographical vicissitudes at hand. Tattoos stay, while all else may change.

10      Case Vignette: A proud father at 17, "B" had had the smiling face of his 4-month-old baby girl tattooed on his chest. As we talked at a tattoo convention, he proudly introduced her to me, explaining how he would "always know how beautiful she is today" when years from then he saw her semblance etched on himself.

11      The quest for permanence may at other times prove misleading and offer premature closure to unresolved conflicts. At a time of normative uncertainties, adolescents may maladaptively and all too readily commit to a tattoo

and its indefinite presence. A wish to hold on to a current certainty may lead the adolescent to lay down in ink what is valued and cherished one day but may not necessarily be in the future. The frequency of self-made tattoos among hospitalized, incarcerated, or gang-affiliated youths suggests such motivations: A sense of stability may be a particularly dire need under temporary, turbulent, or volatile conditions. In addition, through their designs teenagers may assert a sense of bonding and allegiance to a group larger than themselves. Tattoos may attest to powerful experiences, such as adolescence itself, lived and even survived together. As with Moby Dick's protagonist, Ishmael, they may bear witness to the "valuable statistics" of one's "wild wanderings": those of adolescent exhilaration and excitement on the one hand; of growing pains, shared misfortune, or even incarceration on the other.

12    Adolescents' bodily decorations, at times radical and dramatic in their presentation, can be seen in terms of figuration rather than disfigurement, of the natural body being through them transformed into a personalized body (Brain, 1979). They can often be understood as self-constructive and adorning efforts, rather than prematurely subsumed as mutilatory and destructive acts. If we bear all of this in mind, we may not only arrive at a position to pass more reasoned clinical judgment, but become sensitized through our patients' skins to another level of their internal reality.

## References

Brain, R. (1979). *The decorated body*. New York: Harper & Row.

Grumet, G. W. (1983). Psychodynamic implications of tattoos. *American Journal of Orthopsychiatry*, 53, 482–92.

## Questions on Subject and Purpose

1. In what ways are tattoos and piercings different from hairstyles or clothing fads?
2. According to Martin, what is the typical parental reaction to such markings?
3. What purpose might Martin have in the essay? Before you answer this, define his audience (see question 3 in Strategy and Audience below).

## Questions on Strategy and Audience

1. What is the effect on the reader of subdividing the text with additional white space and providing headings for the subsections?
2. What is the effect of including the two "case vignettes" (paragraphs 7 and 10)?
3. Who does Martin imagine as his audience, and what evidence can you cite to support your answer?

## Questions on Vocabulary and Style

1. What is the significance of the quotation from Melville's *Moby Dick*, which prefaces the essay?
2. What does the presence of documented sources in the essay suggest?

**3.** Be prepared to define the following words: *ubiquitous* (paragraph 1), *affront* (2), *demarcated* (4), *tantamount* (4), *nomadic* (9), *vicissitudes* (9), *maladaptively* (11), *volatile* (11).

## Writing Suggestions

1. **For Your Journal or Blog.** How do you react to body markings (tattoos or piercings)? In your journal or blog, jot down your thoughts. If you object to such things, why? If you would never do such things, why not? If you have such markings, what motivated you to have them done?

2. **For a Paragraph.** In a paragraph, perhaps drawing on your own experiences and certainly on your own opinions, analyze two potential effects on the individual of having such permanent body markings.

3. **For an Essay.** Interview a substantial number of friends or classmates who have tattoos and/or body piercings. Ask them why they chose their bodily adornments—what were the reasons or causes? What are the effects of having tattoos and/or piercings? How do people react to them? How does body art affect their sense of self and self-image? Make sure you have a large number of interviewees. Then, in an essay, write about the causes that they reported (whether or not they agree with the causes suggested by Martin) or about the effects that they have experienced since getting tattooed or pierced.

4. **For Research.** Martin identifies some of the reasons adolescents in America choose to make such "surface presentations." An analysis can also be done in the other direction: What are the effects of such markings? Those effects would include physical, psychological, and cultural factors. Using a variety of resources, including print and online searches, analyze in a research paper the major effects that such markings have on the person who is wearing them.

## For Further Study

**Focusing on Grammar and Writing.** How does Martin use transitional devices in the essay to move from one cause or reason to another? Do his transitions depend on words and phrases? Typographical devices? Logical organization? What do such transitional devices do for the essay?

**Working Together.** Working in small groups, divide the essay into blocks of paragraphs. Each group should look for evidence that indicates Martin's sense of audience. How does what he says and how he says it reveal his understanding of his audience?

**Seeing Other Modes at Work.** Even though the essay is a cause-and-effect analysis, Martin is also trying to persuade his readers of the value of understanding why young people mark their bodies—that the knowledge is a valuable tool in their professional roles as clinicians. Where do you see persuasive elements at work in the essay?

**Finding Connections.** An interesting pairing is with Veronica Chambers's "Dreadlocked" (in this chapter).

**Exploring the Web.** The Web has many sites devoted to tattoos and piercings, including personal experience stories, pro/con debates, parental reactions, galleries of photographs, and even suggestions on how to persuade your parents to allow you to be tattooed!

# *Black Men and Public Space*

Brent Staples

*Born in Chester, Pennsylvania, Brent Staples graduated from Widener University in 1973 and earned a Ph.D. in psychology from the University of Chicago in 1982. He worked for the* Chicago Sun-Times *as a reporter before moving to* The New York Times *in 1985. In 1994 be published a memoir,* Parallel Time: Growing Up in Black and White, *which tells the story of his childhood in Chester, a mixed-race, economically declining town. The book focuses on his younger brother, a drug dealer who died of gunshot wounds at age twenty-two.*

*"Black Men and Public Space" was originally published in* Ms. *magazine under the title "Just Walk on By: A Black Man Ponders His Power to Alter Public Space." In revised and edited form, it was reprinted in* Harper's *with the current title.*

**On Writing:** *In* Parallel Time, *Staples describes how, in his early twenties, he began to explore his voice as a writer: "I was carrying a journal with me everywhere. . . . I wrote on buses and on the Jackson Park el— though only at the stops to keep the writing legible. I traveled to distant neighborhoods, sat on the curbs, and sketched what I saw in words. Thursday meant free admission at the Art Institute. All day I attributed motives to people in paintings, especially people in Rembrandts. At closing time, I went to a nightclub in The Loop and spied on the patrons, copied their conversations, and speculated about their lives. The journal was more than 'a record of my inner transactions.' It was a collection of stolen souls from which I would one day construct a book."*

## Before Reading

**Connecting:** What precautions do you take if you have to walk at night in public spaces?

**Anticipating:** Why does Staples whistle melodies from classical music when he walks at night? What effect does that particular "cowbell" have on people?

1  **M**y first victim was a woman—white, well dressed, probably in her early twenties. I came upon her late one evening on a deserted street in Hyde Park, a relatively affluent neighborhood in an otherwise mean, impoverished section of Chicago. As I swung onto the avenue behind her, there seemed to be a discreet, uninflammatory distance between us. Not so. She cast back a worried glance. To her, the youngish black man—a broad six feet two inches with a

beard and billowing hair, both hands shoved into the pockets of a bulky military jacket—seemed menacingly close. After a few more quick glimpses, she picked up her pace and was soon running in earnest. Within seconds she disappeared into a cross street.

2      That was more than a decade ago. I was twenty-two years old, a graduate student newly arrived at the University of Chicago. It was in the echo of that terrified woman's footfalls that I first began to know the unwieldy inheritance I'd come into—the ability to alter public space in ugly ways. It was clear that she thought herself the quarry of a mugger, a rapist, or worse. Suffering a bout of insomnia, however, I was stalking sleep, not defenseless wayfarers. As a softy who is scarcely able to take a knife to a raw chicken—let alone hold one to a person's throat—I was surprised, embarrassed, and dismayed all at once. Her flight made me feel like an accomplice in tyranny. It also made it clear that I was indistinguishable from the muggers who occasionally seeped into the area from the surrounding ghetto. That first encounter, and those that followed, signified that a vast, unnerving gulf lay between nighttime pedestrians—particularly women—and me. And I soon gathered that being perceived as dangerous is a hazard in itself. I only needed to turn a corner into a dicey situation, or crowd some frightened, armed person in a foyer somewhere, or make an errant move after being pulled over by a policeman. Where fear and weapons meet—and they often do in urban America—there is always the possibility of death.

3      In that first year, my first away from my hometown, I was to become thoroughly familiar with the language of fear. At dark, shadowy intersections, I could cross in front of a car stopped at a traffic light and elicit the *thunk, thunk, thunk, thunk* of the driver—black, white, male, or female—hammering down the door locks. On less traveled streets after dark, I grew accustomed to but never comfortable with people crossing to the other side of the street rather than pass me. Then there were the standard unpleasantries with policemen, doormen, bouncers, cabdrivers, and others whose business it is to screen out troublesome individuals *before* there is any nastiness.

4      I moved to New York nearly two years ago and I have remained an avid night walker. In central Manhattan, the near-constant crowd cover minimizes tense one-on-one street encounters. Elsewhere—in SoHo, for example, where sidewalks are narrow and tightly spaced buildings shut out the sky—things can get very taut indeed.

5      After dark, on the warrenlike streets of Brooklyn where I live, I often see women who fear the worst from me. They seem to have set their faces on neutral, and with their purse straps strung across their chests bandolier-style, they forge ahead as though bracing themselves against being tackled. I understand, of course, that the danger they perceive is not a hallucination. Women are particularly vulnerable to street violence, and young black males are drastically overrepresented among the perpetrators of that violence. Yet these truths are no solace against the kind of alienation that comes of being ever the suspect, a fearsome entity with whom pedestrians avoid making eye contact.

6      It is not altogether clear to me how I reached the ripe old age of twenty-two without being conscious of the lethality nighttime pedestrians attributed

to me. Perhaps it was because in Chester, Pennsylvania, the small, angry industrial town where I came of age in the 1960s, I was scarcely noticeable against a backdrop of gang warfare, street knifings, and murders. I grew up one of the good boys, had perhaps a half-dozen fistfights. In retrospect, my shyness of combat has clear sources.

7      As a boy, I saw countless tough guys locked away; I have since buried several, too. They were babies, really—a teenage cousin, a brother of twenty-two, a childhood friend in his mid-twenties—all gone down in episodes of bravado played out in the streets. I came to doubt the virtues of intimidation early on. I chose, perhaps unconsciously, to remain a shadow—timid, but a survivor.

8      The fearsomeness mistakenly attributed to me in public places often has a perilous flavor. The most frightening of these confusions occurred in the late 1970s and early 1980s, when I worked as a journalist in Chicago. One day, rushing into the office of a magazine I was writing for with a deadline story in hand, I was mistaken for a burglar. The office manager called security and, with an ad hoc posse, pursued me through the labyrinthine halls, nearly to my editor's door. I had no way of proving who I was. I could only move briskly toward the company of someone who knew me.

9      Another time I was on assignment for a local paper and killing time before an interview. I entered a jewelry store on the city's affluent Near North Side. The proprietor excused herself and returned with an enormous red Doberman pinscher straining at the end of a leash. She stood, the dog extended toward me, silent to my questions, her eyes bulging nearly out of her head. I took a cursory look around, nodded, and bade her good night.

10      Relatively speaking, however, I never fared as badly as another black male journalist. He went to nearby Waukegan, Illinois, a couple of summers ago to work on a story about a murderer who was born there. Mistaking the reporter for the killer, police officers hauled him from his car at gunpoint and but for his press credentials would probably have tried to book him. Such episodes are not uncommon. Black men trade tales like this all the time.

11      Over the years, I learned to smother the rage I felt at so often being taken for a criminal. Not to do so would surely have led to madness. I now take precautions to make myself less threatening. I move about with care, particularly late in the evening. I give a wide berth to nervous people on subway platforms during the wee hours, particularly when I have exchanged business clothes for jeans. If I happen to be entering a building behind some people who appear skittish, I may walk by, letting them clear the lobby before I return, so as not to seem to be following them. I have been calm and extremely congenial on those rare occasions when I've been pulled over by the police.

12      And on late-evening constitutionals I employ what has proved to be an excellent tension-reducing measure: I whistle melodies from Beethoven and Vivaldi and the more popular classical composers. Even steely New Yorkers hunching toward night-time destinations seem to relax, and occasionally they even join in the tune. Virtually everybody seems to sense that a mugger wouldn't be warbling bright, sunny selections from Vivaldi's *Four Seasons*. It is my equivalent of the cowbell that hikers wear when they know they are in bear country.

## Questions on Subject and Purpose

1. What does Staples mean by the phrase "public space"? In what way is he capable of altering it?
2. What types of evidence does Staples provide to illustrate his point—that black men can alter public space?
3. What purpose might Staples have had in writing the essay?

## Questions on Strategy and Audience

1. In addition to cause and effect, what other structure is at work in the essay?
2. When the essay was first published, it was entitled "Just Walk on By." When it appeared in a slightly revised form, it was retitled, "Black Men and Public Space." What is the effect of the change in title?
3. The essay first appeared in *Ms.* magazine. What assumptions could Staples have had about his initial audience?

## Questions on Vocabulary and Style

1. What is the effect of Staples's opening sentence in the essay? Why does he write "my first victim"?
2. In paragraph 5, Staples writes the phrase "on the warrenlike streets of Brooklyn." What is a *warren?* To what does the term usually refer? Can you think of another word or phrase that Staples could have used instead that might be more vivid to most readers?
3. Be prepared to define the following words: *discreet* (paragraph 1), *dicey* (2), *errant* (2), *taut* (4), *warrenlike* (5), *bandolier* (5), *solace* (5), *entity* (5), *bravado* (7), *ad hoc* (8), *cursory* (9), *skittish* (11), *congenial* (11), *constitutionals* (12).

## Writing Suggestions

1. **For Your Journal or Blog.** Have you ever been frightened in a public space? Explore your memories or your recent experiences, and jot down a few such times. Try to capture a few details about each experience.
2. **For a Paragraph.** Select one of the experiences you entered in your journal or blog for suggestion 1, and narrate that experience in a paragraph. Why did you react as you did? Was your fear justified? You can also turn the topic around and describe a time when your presence frightened someone else while in a public space.
3. **For an Essay.** Regardless of our age or sex or color, we all provoke reactions from people who do not know us. Sometimes, in fact, we go out of our way to elicit a reaction—dressing in a certain way, driving a particular type of car, engaging in an unusual activity, wearing our hair in a peculiar style. Describe your image and behavior, and analyze how people react to you and why they react as they do.
4. **For Research.** Who mugs whom? Research the problem of assault or mugging either in the country as a whole or in your own community. What

are your chances of being mugged? Who is likely to do it to you? Where is it most likely to happen? If you decide to focus on your own community or college campus, remember to interview the local police.

## For Further Study

**Focusing on Grammar and Writing.** Staples often uses vivid verbs in telling his story. Go through the essay and make a list of such verbs. What do they suggest about how to create an arresting story or description? Do you use verbs in the same way in your writing?

**Working Together.** Staples's introduction, though brilliant, seems more appropriate for a magazine targeted for women than for men. Working in small groups, recast the opening of the essay as if it might appear in a magazine aimed at a male audience. Share your new introductions with the rest of the class.

**Seeing Other Modes at Work.** Staples uses both narration and description in the essay as well.

**Finding Connections.** An interesting pairing is with Judith Ortiz Cofer's "The Myth of the Latin Woman" (Chapter 4). Both essays deal with people's reactions to skin color or ethnicity.

**Exploring the Web.** Additional information about Staples and examples of his writing can be found at a number of Websites.

# *Dreadlocked*

Veronica Chambers

*Veronica Chambers was born in Brooklyn, the daughter, she writes, of "two black Latinos from Panama." Educated at Simon's Rock College, she has worked as a journalist, editor, and photographer for magazines such as* Sassy, Seventeen, Essence, The New York Times Magazine, Newsweek, *and, most recently,* Savoy. *She is the author of children's books as well. Her most recent book is* Kickboxing Geishas: How Modern Japanese Women Are Changing Their Nation *(2007).*

   **On Writing:** *In an interview aired on National Public Radio's* Anthem *series, Chambers said of her writing, "I go to poetry a lot. . . . I found, for example, in writing* Mama's Girl *that it was hard for me to read other people's memoirs. . . . So I read almost exclusively a lot of poetry . . . to keep myself with words, but not get myself mired in other stories."*

## Before Reading

**Connecting:** What associations do you have with dreadlocks? Are those associations stereotypes?

**Anticipating:** What do Chambers's dreadlocks mean or symbolize to her?

1    I have two relationships with the outside world: One is with my hair, and the other is with the rest of me. Sure, I have concerns and points of pride with my body. I like the curve of my butt but dislike my powerhouse thighs. My breasts, once considered too small, have been proclaimed perfect so often that not only am I starting to believe the hype, but also am booking my next vacation to a topless resort in Greece. But my hair. Oh, my hair.

2    I have reddish brown dreadlocks that fall just below shoulder length. Eventually, they will cover my aforementioned breasts, at which time I will give serious thought to nude modeling at my local art school. I like my hair— a lot. But over the last eight years my dreadlocks have conferred upon me the following roles: rebel child, Rasta mama, Nubian princess, drug dealer, unemployed artist, rock star, world-famous comedienne, and nature chick. None of which is true. It has occurred to me more than once that my hair is a whole lot more interesting than I am.

3    Because I am a black woman, I have always had a complicated relationship with my hair. Here's a quick primer on the politics of hair and beauty aesthetics in the black community vis-à-vis race and class in the late 20th century: "Good" hair is straight and, preferably, long. Think Naomi

Campbell. Diana Ross. For that matter, think RuPaul. "Bad" hair is thick and coarse, aka "nappy," and, often, short. Think Buckwheat in *The Little Rascals*. Not the more recent version, but the old one in which Buckwheat looked like Don King's grandson.

4      Understand that these are stereotypes: broad and imprecise. Some will say that the idea of "good" hair and "bad" hair is outdated. And it is less prevalent than in the '70s when I was growing up. Sometimes I see little girls with their hair in braids and Senegalese twists sporting cute little T-shirts that say HAPPY TO BE NAPPY and I get teary-eyed. I was born between the black power Afros of the '60s and the blue contact lenses and weaves of the '80s; in my childhood, no one seemed happy to be nappy at all.

5      I knew from the age of 4 that I had "bad" hair because my relatives and family friends discussed it as they might discuss a rare blood disease. "Something must be done," they would click sadly. "I think I know someone," an aunt would murmur, referring to a hair-dresser as if she were a medical specialist. Some of my earliest memories are of Brooklyn apartments where women did hair for extra money. These makeshift beauty parlors were lively and loud, the air thick with the smell of lye from harsh relaxer, the smell of hair burning as the hot straightening comb did its job.

6      When did I first begin to desire hair that bounced? Was it because black Barbie wasn't, and still isn't, happy to be nappy? Was it Brenda, the redhead, my best friend in second grade? Every time she flicked her hair to the side, she seemed beyond sophistication. My hair bounced the first day back from the hairdresser's, but not much longer. "Don't sweat out that perm," my mother would call. But I found it impossible to sit still. Hairdressers despaired like cowardly lion tamers at the thought of training my kinky hair. "This is some hard hair," they would say. I knew that I was not beautiful and I blamed it on my hair.

7      The night I began to twist my hair into dreads, I was 19 and a junior in college. It was New Year's Eve and the boy I longed for had not called. A few months before, Alice Walker had appeared on the cover of *Essence*, her locks flowing with all the majesty of a Southern American Cleopatra. I was inspired. It was my family's superstition that the hours between New Year's Eve and New Year's Day were the time to cast spells. "However New Year's catches you is how you'll spend the year," my mother always reminded me.

8      I decided to use the hours that remained to transform myself into the vision I'd seen on the magazine. Unsure of how to begin, I washed my hair, carefully and lovingly. I dried it with a towel, then opened a jar of hair grease. Using a comb to part the sections, I began to twist each section into baby dreads. My hair, at the time, couldn't have been longer than an inch. I twisted for two hours, and in the end was far from smitten with what I saw: My full cheeks dominated my face now that my hair lay in flat twists around my head. My already short hair seemed shorter. I did not look like the African goddess I had imagined. I emerged from the bathroom and ran into my aunt Diana, whose luxuriously long, straight black hair always reminded me of Diahann Carroll on *Dynasty*. "Well, Vickie," she said, shaking her head. "Well, well." I

knew that night my life would begin to change. I started my dreadlocks and began the process of seeing beauty where no one had ever seen beauty before.

9      There are, of course, those who see my hair and still consider it "bad." A family friend touched my hair recently, then said, "Don't you think it's a waste? All that lovely hair twisted in those things?" I have been asked by more than one potential suitor if I had any pictures of myself before "you did that to your hair." A failure at small talk and countless other social graces, I sometimes let my hair do the talking for me. At a cocktail party, I stroll through the room, silently, and watch my hair tell white lies. In literary circles, it brands me "interesting, adventurous." In black middle-class circles, I'm "rebellious" or, more charitably, "Afro-centric." In predominantly white circles, my hair doubles my level of exotica. My hair says, "Unlike the black woman who reads you the evening news, I'm not even trying to blend in."

10      For those ignorant enough to think that they can read hair follicles like tea leaves, my hair says a lot of things it doesn't mean. Taken to the extreme, it says that I am a pot-smoking Rastafarian wannabe who in her off-hours strolls through her house in an African dashiki, lighting incense and listening to Bob Marley. I don't smoke pot. In my house, I wear Calvin Klein nightshirts, and light tuberose candles that I buy from Diptyque in Paris. I play tennis in my off-hours and, while I love Bob Marley, I mostly listen to jazz vocalists like Ella Fitzgerald and Diana Krall.

11      Once after a dinner party in Beverly Hills, a white colleague of mine lit up a joint. Everyone at the table passed and when I passed too, the man cajoled me relentlessly. "Come on," he kept saying. "Of all people, I thought you'd indulge." I shrugged and said nothing. As we left the party that night, he kissed me goodbye. "Boy, were you a disappointment," he said, as if I had been a bad lay. But I guess I had denied him a certain sort of pleasure. It must have been his dream to smoke a big, fat spliff with a real live Rastafarian.

12      As much as I hate to admit it, I've been trained to turn my head to any number of names that aren't mine. I will answer to "Whoopi." I will turn when Jamaican men call out "Hey, Rasta" on the street. I am often asked if I am a singer, and I can only hope that I might be confused with the gorgeous Cassandra Wilson, whose dreadlocks inspired me to color my hair a jazzy shade of red. Walking through the streets of Marrakesh, I got used to trails of children who would follow me, trying to guess which country I came from. "Jamaica!" they would shout. "Ghana! Nigeria!" I shook my head no to them all. They did not believe me when I said I was from America: instead, they called me "Mama Africa" all day long. It's one of my favorite memories of the trip.

13      Once, after the end of a great love affair, I watched a man cut all of his dreadlocks off and then burn them in the backyard. This, I suspect, is the reason that might tempt me to change my hair. After all, a broken heart is what started me down this path of twisting hair. Because I do not cut my hair, I carry eight years of history on my head. One day, I may tire of this history and start anew. But one thing is for sure, whatever style I wear my hair in, I will live happily—and nappily—ever after.

## Questions on Subject and Purpose

1. What are *dreadlocks?* Do you know where the term came from?
2. When does Chambers first wear "dreads"?
3. How does wearing "dreads" change the way in which others perceive her? Does it also change the way in which she perceives herself?

## Questions on Strategy and Audience

1. In what ways is this a cause-and-effect analysis?
2. In addition to cause and effect, what other organizational strategy can you find in the essay?.
3. What expectations might Chambers have of her audience? For example, what do the allusions or names mentioned in the essay suggest about Chambers's sense of her readers?

## Questions on Vocabulary and Style

1. Are the last two sentences in paragraph 1 really sentences? If not, what are they?
2. In paragraph 6, Chambers writes: "Hairdressers despaired like cowardly lion tamers at the thought of training my kinky hair." What figure of speech is she using?
3. Be prepared to define the following words: *Nubian* (2), *aka* (3), *cajoled* (11).

## Writing Suggestions

1. **For Your Journal or Blog.** Think about yourself, a sibling, or a friend. To what extent do you or that person adopt or affect an appearance? What has influenced how you or that person looks and acts? To what extent is the appearance intended to suggest or evoke something else? Think about the choices that can be made in physical appearances (for example, hairstyles, clothing styles, piercings or tattoos, body jewelry) or in behavior (for example, mannerisms, language habits, actions). In your journal or blog try to list some possible causes and effects of such decisions.
2. **For a Paragraph.** Using your journal or blog entry as a prewriting activity, expand your cause-and-effect analysis into a paragraph. Select one element in that appearance and try to explain what brought it about and what results that element has produced.
3. **For an Essay.** Expand your paragraph writing into an essay. Instead of concentrating on a single element in that appearance, expand your analysis to include all of the aspects of both appearance and behavior.
4. **For Research.** Not so long ago, one found tattoos mostly on former soldiers and sailors and on motorcyclists. Today, many young people sport tattoos. Why? What explanation can be given for the popularity of tattoos among young adults? Andres Martin's Teenagers and Tattoos (this chapter) is one possible resource. In a research essay, explore the phenomenon and analyze

why tattoos are so popular. Other possibilities for analysis might be body piercings or extreme hairstyles or colors.

## For Further Study

**Focusing on Grammar and Writing.** What is a topic sentence, and what function does it have in a paragraph? Look critically at Chambers's essay. Does she use topic sentences? If so, what role do they play in organizing the essay? What role do they play in helping you read the essay? What does this suggest about your own writing?

**Working Together.** Divide into small groups. Each group should take one of the following sections to evaluate:

Paragraphs 3 and 4

Paragraphs 5 and 6

Paragraphs 7 and 8

Paragraphs 10 and 11

Paragraph 12

What do the details in each paragraph add to the story?

**Seeing Other Modes at Work.** Chambers's essay also uses narration throughout.

**Finding Connections.** Possible pairings might include Janice Mirikitani's poem "Recipe" (Chapter 6) and Robin D. G. Kelley's "The People in Me" and Margaret Atwood's "The Female Body" (both in Chapter 8).

**Exploring the Web.** Want to know more about dreadlocks, Bob Marley, Rastafarianism, and Veronica Chambers? Check the Web. Visit Chambers's Website at www.veronicachambers.com.

# Drugs, Sports, Body Image and G.I. Joe

Natalie Angier

*Pulitzer-prize winner Natalie Angier (1958–) is currently serving as the Andrew D. White Professor-at-Large at Cornell University. A science writer for* The New York Times, *she has published hundreds of essays and a number of award-winning books, the most recent of which is* The Canon: A Whirligig Tour of Beautiful Basics of Science *(2007). She acknowledges that she has been "a reasonably serious weight lifter for most of my adult life."*

**On Writing:** *When asked if writing was easy for her, Angier replied: "No. Mostly it's a question of trying to quiet . . . all the voices that tell you you're no good, you can't do it, every kind of criticism you can come up with. You're just trying to shut them up and let yourself go. I'd say I spend 50 percent of my time trying to get them out of the way. There are times when I do enjoy writing, but they are definitely in a minority."*

## Before Reading

**Connecting:** Much has been written about how young women's perceptions of the ideal body type have been influenced by commercial forces in our society. What about young men? Is there an ideal body type for a young male? If so, what does it look like? How has it been defined?

**Anticipating:** What factors does Angier see as responsible for the prevalence of body-enhancing drugs in the lives of young male athletes?

1    **W**hich classic American doll has been a staple of childhood from the boomer babies onward, has won iconic, if politically freighted, status in our culture, and possesses a waist so small and hemispheric projections so pronounced that no real adult could approach them without the help of potentially dangerous body enhancement therapies?

2    Barbie? Well, yes. But Barbie has a male companion in the land of the outlandish physique, and his name is not Ken. Instead, we must look to a recent model of that old trooper, G.I. Joe, to see a match for Barbie's cartoon anatomy, and to find a doll that may be as insidious a role model for boys as Ms. Triple-D top, Size-2 bottom is for girls.

3    Some researchers worry that Joe and other action-hero figures may, in minor fashion, help fan the use of muscle-building drugs among young athletes, even as doctors and sports officials struggle to emphasize that such drugs are not only risky, illegal and unsporting, but, in many cases, worthless in enhancing performance.

4    Dr. Harrison G. Pope Jr., a psychiatrist at McLean Hospital in Belmont, Mass., has studied how the morphology of G.I. Joe has evolved since the doll was introduced in 1964. Just as Barbie has become gradually thinner and bustier, Dr. Pope said, so each new vintage of G.I. Joe has been more muscular and sharply defined, or "cut," than the model before.

5    The most extraordinary G.I. Joe on the market, "G.I. Joe Extreme," wears a red bandanna and an expression of rage. His biceps bulge so much that they are larger around than his waist, and, if ratcheted up to human size, they would be larger than even the arms of the grotesquely muscular Mr. Olympias of today, said Dr. Pope.

6    Hasbro Industries, maker of the G.I. Joe dolls, disagrees with Dr. Pope's contention that the body type of the standard Joe doll has changed much over the years. The company adds that it has stopped manufacturing the "Extreme" model, although a recent shopping expedition showed that the doll was still available in toy stores.

7    G.I. Joe is the only action figure that has been around long enough for Dr. Pope to be able to make comparisons between old and new models. But he said that a survey of other popular action figures, including the Power Rangers, Batman and Cyberforce Stryker showed the same excessive muscularity.

8    Dr. Pope said the dolls might be planting in boys' minds a template for a he-man's body that cannot be attained without engaging in obsessive behaviors to build muscle and strip off fat, and then augmenting those efforts through the consumption of drugs like human growth hormone and anabolic steroids, which are synthetic versions of the male hormone, testosterone. . . .

9    "Prior to 1960, and the introduction of anabolic steroids, even the most dedicated bodybuilders couldn't get larger than a certain maximum size," Dr. Pope said. "Steroids made it possible for men to look as big as supermen, and now we see that standard reflected in our toys for the very young."

10    Given the ubiquitous images of muscularity, as well as the mounting demands on young athletes to sprint faster, vault higher, lift heavier and otherwise impress cadres of easily disgruntled sports fans, experts say it is not surprising that the use of muscle-enhancing drugs has reached pandemic proportions, even among barely pubescent boys. Some 18 percent of high school athletes in the United States are thought to use anabolic steroids, about twice the figure of [1988], according to some estimates.

11    Although performance-enhancing drugs are generally banned by athletic organizations, it is considered laughably easy to cheat and escape detection in drug screens. In addition, health food stores now offer a variety of "nutritional supplements" reputed to have anabolic properties. The supplements include creatine, DHEA, beta agonists and androstenedione, a precur-

sor of testosterone . . . made famous by the baseball slugger Mark McGwire, who admitted with pride that he ate it. Such supplements are not strictly regulated, like drugs, their side effects are uncharted and their effectiveness is unproved.

12    Doctors have long emphasized the dangers of muscle-building drugs. The use of anabolic steroids lowers the levels of protective high-density lipoproteins, suppresses sperm production and raises the risk of heart attacks, strokes and liver disease.

13    The chronic use of human growth hormone in ultra-high doses has its own hazards, among them an increased risk of arthritic-type disorders, diabetes and some cancers.

14    Yet experts acknowledge that it is not enough to harangue athletes about the risks to their health. Surveys have shown that competitive athletes—who are, after all, quite young and still unconvinced of their mortality—say they would gladly trade years of their life for the chance at winning a gold medal or breaking a world record.

15    Arnold Schwarzenegger has pointed out that top-tier athletes are not in it for the sake of "fitness," and that they often go to grueling, distinctly unhealthy extremes in their training regimens; he has said that, when he was a competitive bodybuilder, he often worked out so intensively that he vomited afterward.

16    The great Alberto Salazar twice was given last rites at the end of a marathon after pushing himself so hard in the race that he nearly died at the finish line. What is the difference between overtraining and overcompeting yourself to death, and killing yourself slowly with steroids?

17    "We can be so hypocritical," said George Annas, chairman of the health law department in the Boston University School of Public Health. "We say, it's O.K. to spend 18 hours a day training, and we put our kids through all kinds of inhumane regimens that can border on child abuse, but take one drug and that's the end of it. We're really crazy about drugs."

18    According to many researchers, the paradoxical element in the seemingly unstoppable epidemic of doping, or using performance enhancing drugs, is that most of the drugs do not work nearly as well as billed.

19    Human growth hormone may increase muscle mass, but bigger does not necessarily mean stronger, said Shalender Bhasin, a professor of medicine and chief of the division of endocrinology metabolism and molecular medicine at Charles Drew University in Los Angeles. "Patients with acromegaly, who naturally overproduce growth hormone, often have muscle hypertrophy," he said. "But their muscles are weak."

20    As for the effectiveness of anabolic steroids and other types of testosterone supplements, scientists for years debated whether the drugs truly increased muscle mass and strength, or merely bloated muscle cells with water and encouraged athletes to train harder through a placebo effect.

21    [In 1996], Dr. Bhasin and his colleagues showed in a comprehensive report in the *New England Journal of Medicine* that super-high doses of testosterone given to healthy young men could increase muscle size and muscle

strength, as measured by the ability to do exercises like bench-pressing and leg-squatting.

22    But the results were far from spectacular, and high-intensity, drug-free workouts proved nearly as good at building muscle strength as did exercise and testosterone combined. For reasons that remain unclear, said Dr. Bhasin, a pound of muscle gained through exercise is stronger than a pound of muscle gained through the grace of testosterone. He also emphasized that neither his study, nor any other that he knew of had shown testosteronelike drugs capable of improving muscle performance—that is, the capacity of a muscle to do the sports maneuver an athlete wants it to do.

23    The extra muscle bulk that comes from steroid use may drag an athlete down without compensating for the added weight through better performance. For any event that requires moving against friction or gravity, Dr. Bhasin said, including sprinting, pole-vaulting or swimming, and for endurance activities like marathon running, taking testosterone may be counterproductive.

24    Some athletes know as much, and sneer at their doping friends. Whether performance drugs will ever be eliminated from sports, though, nobody can say. "I'm afraid I'm very cynical," Dr. Pope said. "From my research, I've seen that the use of steroids and other drugs has infiltrated deeper into sports than the vast majority of the public realizes. It's like asking, how can we turn back from nuclear weapons? The technology is there. The genie is out of the bottle."

25    It might help to begin by tinkering at Santa's workshop. Mattel has talked about releasing a more realistic Barbie doll with a thicker waist and smaller bust. How about a G.I. "Love Handles" Joe?

## Questions on Subject and Purpose

1.  What does Angier see as the causes behind the increased use of performance-enhancing drugs in athletes?

2.  How important are the quotations from sources to the points that Angier is trying to make? How and why does she use this evidence?

3.  What might Angier have hoped to accomplish by writing the essay?

## Questions on Strategy and Audience

1.  What is the effect that Angier creates with her opening paragraph-long sentence?

2.  Does Angier ever assert that the attraction of body-enhancing drugs to young men is caused by the role model provided by G.I. Joe?

3.  To whom is Angier writing? How do you know?

## Questions on Vocabulary and Style

1.  On the basis of the vocabulary used in the essay, what might be said about Angier's sense of her audience?

2. The essay opens with a fifty-two-word sentence, but the structure of that sentence is clear and logical. How does Angier achieve clarity despite sentence length?

3. Be prepared to define the following words: *freighted* (paragraph 1), *insidious* (2), *ratcheted* (5), *template* (8), *ubiquitous* (10), *cadres* (10), *pandemic* (10), *harangue* (14), *acromegaly* (19).

## Writing Suggestions

1. **For Your Journal or Blog.** Be honest. If you could change your body, how would you change it? More important, *why* would you make those changes?

2. **For a Paragraph.** Look at what you have written in your journal or blog. Try to explain in a paragraph why you feel that you want those changes. What has influenced you to desire a particular change?

3. **For an Essay.** Choose a single risky behavior that is commonly engaged in by you or your peers—cigarette smoking, binge drinking, purging, unprotected sex, recreational drug use, acts of vandalism. In an essay, explore through a cause-and-effect analysis why such behavior occurs. Even though they know such activities pose risks or are even life threatening, why do people in your peer group engage in them? Remember, interviewing peers might be an excellent source of information.

4. **For Research.** In a cause-and-effect research paper, explore either the positive or negative effects that a particular form of "enhancement" can have on performance or appearance. You might explore different types of drugs, blood doping, cosmetic surgery (for example, augmentation, implants, liposuction, "lifts"), injections. Concentrate on scientifically reliable evidence of the advantages and risks that such activities occasion.

## For Further Study

**Focusing on Grammar and Writing.** Angier uses rhetorical questions at the beginning and ending of her essay. What is a *rhetorical* question, and why might a writer use such a device especially in an introduction or conclusion of a paper?

**Working Together.** Divide the class into small groups. Ask students to discuss when they first remember being concerned about their body shape. What influenced their concern? Would anyone really argue that Barbie or G.I. Joe was a physical role model? If not, what other forces were at work?

**Seeing Other Modes at Work.** A part of Angier's essay is an argument based on the dangers of muscle-building drugs (paragraphs 11–13) and their possible ineffectiveness to accomplish what they seem to promise (paragraph 18–23).

**Finding Connections.** Angier's essay could be nicely paired with Marge Piercy's "Barbie Doll" (this chapter) and with Margaret Atwood's "The Female Body" (Chapter 8).

**Exploring the Web.** Angier has an extensive Website at www.natalieangier .com. In paragraph 10, Angier notes that in 1998 about 18 percent of high school athletes were thought to use anabolic steroids. Check the Web to see if you can find more recent statistics.

# 8

# DEFINITION

# GETTING READY TO WRITE

## What Is definition?

**def • i • ni • tion**  (def′ ə nish′ə n)  *n.* [ME *diffinicioun* < OR
*definition* & ML *diffinitio*, both < L *difinitio*] **1** a defining
or being defined **2** a statement of what a thing is **3** a
statement of the meaning of a word, phrase, etc.

On the midterm examination in your introductory economics class, only the essay question remains to be answered: "What is capitalism?" You are tempted to write the one-sentence definition you memorized from the glossary of your textbook and dash from the room. But it is unlikely that your professor will react positively or even charitably to such a skimpy (and rote) response. Instead, you realize your answer must be an extended definition, one that explains what factors were necessary before capitalism could emerge, what elements are most characteristic of a capitalistic economy, how capitalism differs from other economic systems, how a capitalistic economy works, how capitalism is linked to technology and politics. You need a narrative, a division, a comparison and contrast, a process, and a cause-and-effect analysis all working together to provide a full definition of what is a very complex term.

When you are asked to define a word, you generally do two things. First, you provide a dictionary-like definition, normally a single sentence. Second, if the occasion demands, you provide a longer, extended definition, analyzing the subject and giving examples or details. If you write an essay and use technical or specialized words that might be unfamiliar to your reader, you include a parenthetical definition: "Macroeconomics, the portion of economics concerned with large-scale movements such as inflation and deflation, is particularly interested in changes in the GDP, or gross domestic product."

##  IN THE READINGS, LOOK FOR

|  | **Why does this need a definition?** |
| --- | --- |
| Ellen Goodman, "Do-It-Yourself" | What does the title suggest might be the subject? |
| Judy Brady, "I Want a Wife" | Why isn't "a woman married to a man" enough of a definition of *wife*? |
| Robin D. G. Kelley, "People in Me" | How do you answer the question, "Who are you?" |
| Amy Tan, "Mother Tongue" | What does the title suggest about the subject? |
| Diane Ravitch, "You Can't Say That" | What words are "offensive" to you? |
| Margaret Atwood, "The Female Body" | What does the phrase *female body* suggest to you? |

Politicians are not the only people who know how to manipulate meaning by changing the definitions of the words.
*www.cartoonstock.com*

## What Is the Difference Between Denotation and Connotation?

Definitions can be denotative, connotative, or a mixture of the two. Dictionary definitions are denotative; that is, they offer a literal and explicit definition of a word. A dictionary, for example, defines the word *prejudice* as "a judgment or opinion formed before the facts are known; a preconceived idea." In most cases, however, a single sentence is not enough to give a reader a clear understanding of the word or concept.

Many words have more than just literal meanings; they also carry connotations, either positive or negative, and these connotations may make up part of an extended definition. For example, in 1944, when the United States was at war with both Germany and Japan, E. B. White was asked to write about the "meaning of democracy" for the Writers' War Board. White's one-paragraph response goes beyond a literal definition to explore the connotations and associations that surround the word *democracy*:

> Surely the Board knows what democracy is. It is the line that forms on the right. It is the don't in Don't Shove. It is the hole in the stuffed shirt through which the sawdust trickles; it is the dent in the high hat. Democracy is the recurrent suspicion that more than half of the people are right more than half of the time. It is the feeling of privacy in the voting booths, the feeling of communion in the libraries, the feeling of vitality everywhere. Democracy is the score at the beginning of the ninth. It is an idea which hasn't been

disproved yet, a song the words of which have not gone bad. It's the mustard on the hot dog and the cream in the rationed coffee. Democracy is a request from a War Board, in the middle of a morning in the middle of a war, wanting to know what democracy is.

Democracy was, to White, not simply a form of government, but a whole way of life.

Most writing situations, especially those you encounter in college, require extended definitions. The reading selections in this chapter define a variety of subjects, and they suggest how differently extended definitions can be handled. Ellen Goodman uses a series of examples of what she refers to as "self-service" to define what she means by a "do-it-yourself" economy. Judy Brady defines the word *wife* through the many associations people have with that word. Robin D. G. Kelley explains how a seemingly simple question, "What are you?", can be very difficult to answer. Amy Tan explores a definition of *mother tongue* based on her own mother's Chinese-inflected English. Diane Ravitch discovers that many words and phrases, as well as images, have been removed from textbooks because they are deemed offensive. Her essay explores through examples how these "offensive words" might be defined. Finally, Margaret Atwood uses multiple examples to define that "capacious" topic, the *female body*.

## How Much Do You Include in a Definition?

Every word, whether it refers to a specific physical object or to the most theoretical concept, has a dictionary definition. Whether that one-sentence definition is sufficient depends on why you are defining the word. Complex words and words with many nuances and connotations generally require a fuller definition than a single sentence can provide. Moreover, one-sentence definitions often contain other words and phrases that need to be defined.

For example, if you were asked, "What is a wife?" you could reply, "a woman married to a man." Although that definition is accurate, it does not convey any sense of what such a relationship might involve. Judy Brady's "I Want a Wife" defines the word by showing what men (or some men at least) expect in a wife. Brady divides and lists a wife's many responsibilities—things expected of her by an actual or potential husband. Brady's essay, comically overstated as it is, offers a far more meaningful definition of the term *wife* than any one-sentence dictionary entry. Her intention surely was to reveal inequality in marriage, and she makes that point by listing a stereotypical set of male expectations.

Writing a definition is a fairly common activity in college work. In your literature course, you are asked to define the romantic movement; in art history, the baroque period; in psychology, abnormal behavior. Since a single-sentence definition can never do justice to such complicated terms, an extended definition is necessary. In each case, the breadth and depth of your knowledge is being tested; your professor expects you to formulate a definition that accounts for the major subdivisions and characteristics of the subject. Your purpose is two-fold: to convince your professor that you have read and mastered the assigned materials, and to select among them and organize them, often adding some special insight of your own, into a logical and coherent response.

## IN THE READINGS, LOOK FOR

| | From where does the information come? |
|---|---|
| Ellen Goodman, "Do-It-Yourself" | How much research? How much observation? |
| Judy Brady, "I Want a Wife" | Anything other than observation? |
| Robin D. G. Kelley, "People in Me" | Reactions of others? Experience? |
| Amy Tan, "Mother Tongue" | Experience and observation? |
| Diane Ravitch, "You Can't Say That" | Research taken from where? |
| Margaret Atwood, "The Female Body" | Sources of her information? |

## PREWRITING TIPS FOR WRITING DEFINITION

1. Once you have chosen or been assigned a word, phrase, or concept to define, write a short dictionary definition of it. Concentrate on its denotative meaning.

2. Write a purpose statement for your paper: "My purpose in this essay is to . . . " Use that statement as a way of testing your developing draft.

3. Describe your intended audience. How much do they know about this term? Is it technical? Complicated? Will you need to provide parenthetical definitions of other words or phrases as you are defining?

4. Determine whether visuals—diagrams, photographs, sketches— will be helpful. Check with your instructor to see if you can include such things in your essay.

5. Remember that a definition essay involves an extended definition— that is, you must add appropriate details and examples. What types of details or examples will help fill out your definition? Will they come from observation? From research? Plan a strategy by which you can gather the necessary details for an extended definition. Make a list of those details and examples.

# WRITING

## How Do You Structure a Definition Essay?

Sentence definitions are relatively easy to write. You first place a word in a general class ("A wife is a *woman*") and then add any distinguishing features that set it apart from other members of the class ("married to a man"). However, the types of definitions you are asked to write in college are generally much more detailed than dictionary entries. How, then, do you get from a single sentence to a paragraph or an essay?

Extended definitions do not have a structure peculiar to themselves. That is, when you write a definition, you do not have a predetermined structural pattern as you do with comparison and contrast, division and classification, process, or cause and effect. Instead, when you construct definitions you use all of the various strategies in this book. Ellen Goodman's definition of a "do-it-yourself" economy and Diane Ravitch's definition of an "offensive word" both depend on a series of examples. In her definition of a wife, Judy Brady uses division to organize the many types of responsibilities demanded of a wife. Robin D. G. Kelley and Amy Tan use narration as a vital part of their definitions. Margaret Atwood gathers a wide range of examples to suggest the complexity involved in the phrase "the female body," ending with an imaginative contrast between the brain of a man and that of a woman.

Once you have chosen a subject for definition, think first about its essential characteristics, steps, or parts. What examples would best define the subject? Then plan your organization by seeing how those details can be presented most effectively to your reader. If you are breaking a subject into its parts, use definition or possibly even process. If you are defining by comparing your subject to another, use comparison and contrast. If your subject is defined as a result of some causal connection, use a cause-and-effect structure. Definitions can also involve narration, description, and even persuasion. The longer the extended definition, the greater the likelihood that your paper will involve a series of structures.

 **IN THE READINGS, LOOK FOR**

|  | **How does the definition work?** |
|---|---|
| Ellen Goodman, "Do-It-Yourself" | Examples, but how are they organized? |
| Judy Brady, "I Want a Wife" | Denotation or connotation or both? |
| Robin D. G. Kelley, "People in Me" | When does defining by a single culture become difficult or impossible? |
| Amy Tan, "Mother Tongue" | Is there an academic definition of *mother tongue*? |
| Diane Ravitch, "You Can't Say That" | How vital are the examples to the definition? |
| Margaret Atwood, "The Female Body" | Denotation or connotation? Both? Why? |

## DRAFTING TIPS FOR WRITING DEFINITION

1.  Look at the list of details and examples that you have gathered as preparation for writing. Can you sort them into structural categories as a first step in planning an organization for your essay? For example, do any involve comparison and contrast? Division or classification, cause or effect? Narration or description? Process? Remember, extended definitions make use of other structural patterns.

2.  Make sure you have considered all the connotations of the word or concept that you are defining. Readers have associations with terms that are not necessarily part of the terms' denotative definitions.

3.  Think about your audience's prior knowledge about this subject. Does your essay involve technical concepts or specialized knowledge? Use your statement of intended audience as a way of judging how much explanation you will need to provide.

4.  Remember, like every essay, your definition paper needs an introduction, a body or middle, and a conclusion. As you write, jot down an outline of the developing structure. Middles are the longest and most complicated. In a definition essay, you are likely to include in your middle structures derived from the other writing modes discussed and illustrated in this text.

5.  Plan at least two different introductions to your essay: make one a straightforward explanation of what you are defining; make the other more reader-friendly. Maybe you could begin with an example or a story, maybe with a provocative statement.

## REVISING

### How Do You Revise a Definition Essay?

You look for a definition of a word or concept in a dictionary or an encyclopedia to find out what it means—you need the information to understand the word or concept. You expect to come away with a clear understanding of the meaning. If you are confused by other terms used in the definition, or if the information presented is not clear, logical, and easily understood, then your needs have not been met. All definitions, including the extended definition essays that you write in academic courses, must meet the tests of clarity and comprehension. As you are revising your definition essay, enlist the help of other readers, especially peer readers. After they have read your paper, ask them to rephrase the definition in their own words. Have they understood what you are trying to explain? Ask them to identify any words or phrases that they do not understand or cannot define themselves. Address all potential problems as you revise your draft.

When revising a definition essay, pay particular attention to audience, organization, and the beginning and ending of your essay.

**Paying Attention to Your Audience**   Look again at your statement of intended audience and your readers' responses. Have you adequately and clearly defined your subject? Have you used words readers will understand? If your definition contains technical words and phrases, make sure they are defined in context for your readers. You can do so in two ways. First, you can insert a parenthetical definition (enclosed either within a pair of commas or within parentheses) after the word or phrase—for example, "hyperactivity (feelings of restlessness, fidgeting, or inappropriate activity when one is expected to be quiet)." Second, you can include a definition or an example in the sentence without enclosing it in commas or parentheses—for example, "Hyperactivity refers to feelings of restlessness, fidgeting, or inappropriate activity (running, wandering) when one is expected to be quiet."

**Checking Organization**   Your essay needs a clear organizational structure. Outline your draft to see if the sections of the essay fit together in a way that is easy to follow. Broadly speaking, definition essays can be organized either inductively or deductively. In an inductive organization, you could begin with a sentence definition and then expand that definition by using examples, developing contrasts, explaining cause and effect, or by any of a number of other strategies. You could also invert the pattern to a deductive structure: your examples and details come first, leading then to a sentence definition placed near the end of your essay.

   As you move from section to section, make sure you clearly signal to your reader what follows. For instance, write topic sentences that introduce the subject to be covered in the next paragraph or section. Or subdivide your text using typographical devices such as centered headings, numbered sections, or extra white space. If your extended definition makes use of any of the other strategies discussed in this text—for example, comparison, contrast, process—review the advice in that chapter as you revise what you have written.

**Beginning and Ending**   Writing the middle of any essay is generally easier than writing either the beginning or the ending, but a good definition essay needs both a strong introduction and a strong conclusion. When you consult a dictionary or a textbook for a definition, you expect it to be clear, concise, and informative. When you read an extended definition in a magazine or on a Website, you expect it to also be interesting, to reach out and pull you into the piece. In extended definitions that you write for courses, try to find a reader-friendly way to begin. Avoid opening sentences that begin like these: "According to Webster's dictionary, ADHD is defined as . . . " or "ADHD is when . . . ." Instead, can you start with an example? With an interesting fact or quotation? Can you begin with a provocative statement? In a writing class, your reader is typically reading because the subject and the approach are readable and interesting, not because he or she needs the information.

   Similarly, resist the temptation to end your essay with a simple repetition of the short definition of your subject or with a paraphrase of the opening of your essay. Do not just stop your essay either, providing no sense of closure.

Your reader needs to feel that the essay is now over—it has reached its logical and appropriate conclusion. Study some of the endings that the writers in this chapter use for their essays. You can also check the Glossary and Ready Reference at the back of this text for additional suggestions on effective conclusions.

---

 **IN THE READINGS, LOOK FOR**

| | **Beginning and ending** |
|---|---|
| Ellen Goodman, "Do-It-Yourself" | Why begin with questions? |
| Judy Brady, "I Want a Wife" | How effective is the final sentence as a conclusion to the essay? |
| Robin D. G. Kelley, "People in Me" | In what sense is the essay an answer to its first sentence? |
| Amy Tan, "Mother Tongue" | In what way is the opening example (paragraph 3) appropriate for the subject of the essay? |
| Diane Ravitch, "You Can't Say That" | How is the final sentence a key to part of the reason that Ravitch is opposed to the censorship of words? |
| Margaret Atwood, "The Female Body" | What is the effect of the quoted letter at the opening of the essay? |

---

 **REVISING TIPS FOR WRITING DEFINITION**

1.  Ask a peer or a classmate to read your essay and to comment on the clarity of your definition. Does your reader understand all of the words and concepts you have used in your definition? What might need further explanation or definition?

2.  Check the body of your essay again. Do you see a clear organizational pattern? If you have used any of the other strategies discussed in this book, check the relevant chapters for advice on how to structure and develop each one.

3.  Make sure your structure is clear. Have you clearly signaled transitions as you move from section to section in your essay? Have you written topic sentences for each section? Have you included any typographical devices—for example, subheadings, extra white space, numbered sections—to signal the structure of the paper?

4.  Evaluate your examples. Have you provided enough examples or details to support your generalizations? Are your examples and details really helpful in defining your subject? Are they all relevant?

5.  Look carefully at your essay's title. A title is a part of the appeal of an essay. "Essay #5" or "Definition Essay" are simply not titles.

# STUDENT ESSAY

Sherry Heck's essay started from a simple set of directions: "Write an extended definition of a word of your choice." Sherry's approach to the assignment, however, was very different from everyone else's in the class. In her purpose statement, Sherry wrote, "I wanted to inform a general audience in an amusing way of the connotations and associations that accrue to the word *fall*. I got the idea while thumbing through a dictionary looking for words!" Her first draft reads as follows.

## First Draft

Falling

When you were four years old, covered in scrapes and bruises, the word <u>fall</u> was probably too familiar. Perhaps you went exploring, discovering the creek in the woods, and following it to its falls. Summers would end too quickly and fall would arrive, and Mom would send you off to school.

You mastered the art of walking, yet it remained all too easy to fall over yourself in front of your peers. The popular kids would laugh, sending you to fall into the wrong crowd. As you sprayed graffiti triumphantly, you fell into agreement with your friends that this was the best way to slander the principal.

Then one day, you are sitting in school and you feel someone's glance fall on you. You fall silent and stare back. Soon you find yourself falling for that special someone, and you fall in love. Eventually, you have a huge falling out with that person. Your friends have long abandoned you, leaving you no one to fall back on. Your spirits fall, and you feel like the fall guy around your old peers.

Eventually, out of school, you fall into a good job, and you are able to fall out of your trance. Determined not to fall short of your career goals, you fall into line with society. Events seem to fall into place. The pace of the job speeds up, and several people fall out of the rat race. Their jobs fall to you, tripling your workload. It is difficult not to avoid falling from power, and your life's plans begin to fall through.

Alone, rejected, and jobless, you begin to blame your misfortunes on the root of all evil, the fall of Adam and Eve. Life continues, and you ponder this thought until your friends begin to fall off. Your face falls at the thought of your own fall. Your bones are weak, and falling means more than a scraped knee. Your blood pressure falls more easily. These physical worries all disappear when one day, after feeling a free-fall sensation, you fall asleep, peacefully, forever.

## Comments

Sherry met with her instructor, Nathan Andrews, to go over her preliminary draft. He encouraged her to watch that she not repeat phrases—for example, in the fourth paragraph, Sherry had repeated *fall out* twice. After they had brainstormed some additional *fall* phrases, he encouraged her to search for more in the dictionaries in her school's library. He also suggested that she underline each *fall* phrase so that the reader could more easily see the wordplay. In her revised essay, Sherry was able to add a number of new examples.

## Revised Draft

### Infallible

When you were four years old, covered in scrapes and bruises, the word <u>fall</u> was probably too familiar. Perhaps you went exploring, discovering the creek in the woods, and following it to its <u>falls</u>. Summers would end too quickly and <u>fall</u> would arrive, and Mom would send you off to school.

You mastered the art of walking, yet it remained all too easy to <u>fall all over yourself</u> in front of your peers. The popular kids would laugh, sending you to <u>fall in with</u> the wrong crowd. As you sprayed the graffiti triumphantly, you <u>fell in agreement</u> with your friends that this was the best way to slander the principal. Your behavior was leading you to <u>fall afoul</u> of the law.

Then one day, you are sitting in school and you feel someone's glance <u>fall on</u> you. You <u>fall silent</u> and stare back. Soon you find yourself <u>falling for</u> that special someone, and you <u>fall in love</u>. Eventually, you have a huge <u>falling out</u> with that person. The relationship <u>falls apart</u>. Your friends have long abandoned you, leaving you no one to <u>fall back on</u>. Your cries for help <u>fall on deaf ears</u>. Your <u>spirits fall</u>, and you feel like the <u>fall guy</u> around your old peers.

Eventually, out of school, you <u>fall over backwards</u> to get a good job, and you are able to <u>fall out of your trance</u>. Your love life has <u>fallen by the wayside</u>. Determined not to <u>fall short</u> of your career goals, you <u>fall into line</u> with society. Events seem to <u>fall into place</u>. The pace of the job speeds up, and several people <u>fall on their faces</u>. Their jobs <u>fall to you</u>, tripling your workload. You <u>fall behind</u> in your work. It is difficult not to avoid <u>falling from power</u>, and your life's plans begin to <u>fall through</u>.

Alone, rejected and jobless, you begin to blame your misfortunes on the root of all evil, the <u>Fall</u> of Adam and Eve. Life continues, and you ponder this thought until your friends begin to <u>fall off</u>. Your <u>face falls</u> at the thought of your own <u>fall</u>. Your bones are weak, and <u>falling</u> means more than a scraped knee. Your <u>blood pressure falls</u> more easily. These physical worries all disappear when one day, after feeling a <u>free-fall</u> sensation, you <u>fall asleep</u>, peacefully, forever.

## SOME THINGS TO REMEMBER WHEN WRITING DEFINITION

1. Choose a subject that can be reasonably and fully defined within the limits of your paper. That is, make sure it is neither too limited nor too large.
2. Determine a purpose for your definition.
3. Spend time analyzing your subject to see what its essential characteristics, steps, or parts are.
4. Write a dictionary-type definition for your subject. Do this even if you are writing an extended definition. The features that set your subject apart from others in its general class reveal what must be included in your definition.
5. Choose examples that are clear and appropriate.
6. Decide which of the organizational patterns will best convey the information you have gathered.
7. Be careful about beginning with a direct dictionary definition. There are usually more effective and interesting ways to announce your subject.

## DEFINITION IN OTHER CONTEXTS

## AS A LITERARY STRATEGY

# *Girl*

Jamaica Kincaid

Wash the white clothes on Monday and put them on the stone heap; wash the color clothes on Tuesday and put them on the clothesline to dry; don't walk barehead in the hot sun; cook pumpkin fritters in very hot sweet oil; soak your little clothes right after you take them off; when buying cotton to make yourself a nice blouse, be sure that it doesn't have gum on it, because that way it won't hold up well after a wash; soak salt fish overnight before you cook it; is it true that you sing benna in Sunday school?; always eat your food in such a way that it won't turn someone else's stomach; on Sundays try to walk like a lady and not like the slut you are so bent on becoming; don't sing benna in Sunday school; you mustn't speak to wharf-rat boys, not even to give directions; don't eat fruits on the street—flies will follow you; *but I don't sing benna on Sundays at all and never in Sunday school;* this is how to sew on a button; this is how to make a buttonhole for the button you have just sewed on; this is how to hem a dress when you see the hem coming down and so to prevent yourself from looking like the slut I know you are so bent on becoming; this is how your iron your father's khaki shirt so that it doesn't have a crease; this is how you iron your father's khaki pants so that they don't have a crease; this is how you grow okra—far from the house, because okra tree harbors red ants; when you are growing dasheen, make sure it gets plenty of water or else it makes your throat itch when you are eating it; this is how you sweep a corner; this is how you sweep a whole house; this is how you sweep a yard; this is how you smile to someone you don't like too much; this is how you smile to someone you don't like at all; this is how you smile to someone you like completely; this is how you set a table for tea; this is how you set a table for dinner; this is how you set a table for dinner with an important guest; this is how you set a table for lunch; this is how you set a table for breakfast; this is how to behave in the presence of men who don't know you very well, and this way they won't recognize immediately the slut I have warned you against becoming; be sure to wash every day, even if it is with your own spit; don't squat down to play marbles—you are not a boy, you know; don't pick people's flowers—you might catch something; don't throw stones at blackbirds, because it might not be a blackbird at all; this is how to make a bread pudding; this is how to make doukona; this is how to make pepper pot; this is how to make a good medicine for a cold; this is how to make a good medicine to throw away a child before it even becomes a child; this is how to catch a fish; this is how to throw back a fish you don't like, and that way something bad won't fall on you; this is how to bully a man; this is how a man bullies you; this is how to love a man, and if this doesn't work there are other ways, and if they don't work don't feel too bad about giving up; this is how to spit up in the air if you feel like it, and this is how to move quickly so that it doesn't fall on you; this is how to make ends meet; always squeeze bread to make sure it's fresh; *but what if the baker won't let me feel the bread?*; you mean to say that after all you are really going to be the kind of woman who the baker won't let near the bread?

## Discussion Questions

1. Why might Kincaid entitle her story "Girl"? If you were trying to write a title that reflected the content of the story, what might that title be? Is your title interesting and effective?

2. What is *benna*? You will probably need to look up the word on the Web.

3. Presumably the speaker in the story is the girl's mother. How would you characterize her tone in the story? Why might she be passing on this range of advice? How would you feel if your mother or father talked to you in this way?

4. What is the effect of stringing together these sentences of advice with semicolons? Why not subdivide or paragraph the story? What does this arrangement contribute to the story?

5. In what sense is the story an example of how definition can be used in a literary text? What is the story defining?

## Writing Suggestions

1. Kincaid's story is similar in approach to Judy Brady's "I Want a Wife" (in this chapter): both define terms through cataloging expectations or responsibilities. Suppose that your mother or father had a similar conversation with you, what would they say to you about being a daughter/woman/wife or a son/man/husband? In an essay, offer a definition based on what you sense as their expectations of you. Do not try to imitate Kincaid's structure.

2. Definitions tell us what something is. We look up a word or a phrase in a dictionary or encyclopedia so that we understand it. Definitions, though, can also suggest or offer new perspectives on the familiar; they allow us to see things in a fresh way. Write a definition in which you offer a creative way of capturing a term, a new way of seeing it. Consider the following possibilities:

   a. A part of the human body

   b. A common, useful object such as a hairbrush, a computer mouse, a pen, eyeglasses or contacts, a digital watch, a camera phone, a ceiling fan

   c. A term connected with being a student—dropping or adding a course, auditing, being a work-study student, cramming for an exam, group projects, internships, service learning

# AS A CRITICAL READING STRATEGY

What is it? That is a question you ask—consciously or unconsciously—every time you encounter something new or something you do not understand. You consult a dictionary to understand unfamiliar words you encounter; you expect that textbooks will clearly explain and define technical concepts. Definition can be pretty straightforward for simple subjects but fairly complex and extended for more complicated subjects.

Read the following definition of attention deficit hyperactivity disorder (ADHD) from the online Columbia Electronic Encyclopedia. As you read, remember what you have learned about how to write a definition and how that knowledge might help you as a reader.

- A sentence definition places a word in a general class ("a chronic, neurologically based syndrome") and then adds distinguishing features that set it apart from other members of the class ("characterized by any or all of three types of behaviors").

- A definition essay is an extended definition in which additional information or details are added to clarify or explain further the subject.

- Definitions must take into consideration the prior knowledge of readers. A technical or complicated subject is likely to require parenthetical definitions of other words and phrases. An effective definition is measured by its clarity in explaining the subject to its readers.

- The primary purpose of a definition essay is to provide its readers with information. Clarity and logical organization are essential.

- Definitions make use of a range of possible organizational strategies: they might provide examples; classify or divide the subject; use process, narration, or description; compare or contrast the essay topic with a topic that helps clarify the definition; or separate causes and effects.

Definition has no single structural pattern that is always used; it is a composite of other patterns employed together.

| | |
|---|---|
| Dictionary definition | Attention deficit hyperactivity disorder (ADHD), |
| Definition describes behaviors | formerly called hyperkinesis or minimal brain dysfunction, a chronic, neurologically based syndrome characterized by any or all of three types of behavior: hyperactivity, distractibility, and impulsivity. |
| Each behavior is then defined | Hyperactivity refers to feelings of restlessness, fidgeting, or inappropriate activity (running, wandering) when one is expected to be quiet; distractibility to heightened distraction by irrelevant sights and sounds or carelessness and inability to carry simple tasks to completion; and impulsivity to socially |

inappropriate speech (e.g., blurting out something without thinking) or striking out. Unlike similar behaviors caused by emotional problems or anxiety, ADHD does not fluctuate with emotional states. While the three typical behaviors occur in nearly everyone from time to time, in those with ADHD they are excessive, long-term, and pervasive and create difficulties in school, at home, or at work. ADHD is usually diagnosed before age seven. It is often accompanied by a learning disability.

Although the behaviors can be commonly found, in ADHD they are consistent and do not fluctuate

## AS A VISUAL STRATEGY

Larger dictionaries include illustrations as part of the definitions for many words. When the word being defined is a concrete noun, for example, a picture is often a better way of defining that word than is a sentence-long description. If you want to know what a *quoin* is, the picture that a typical

dictionary includes is far more helpful than a definition that reads "the external corner of a building, esp., any of the large squared stones by which the corner of a building is marked." On the other hand, if the word is an abstract noun, such as *economy*, or an adverb such as *slowly*, or a verb such as *seemed*, a picture is either impossible or simply not helpful.

Complex words or subjects often resist being defined by a few words. If someone asks "Who are you?" you might find that you could give a wide range of answers. If you are traveling internationally, the definition of self you must provide is your passport; if you are registering for courses, your definition of self is a Social Security number or your student ID. Consider this photograph—a collage of credit cards and identity cards.

## WRITING ABOUT IMAGES

1. What is in your wallet? How do those items define you? Sit down with your wallet, purse, or backpack and look at what it contains. If someone found it and tried to discover who you were and what you were like, what would they be able to tell about you from what you carry? Using the evidence that you carry around, write an essay of self-definition.

2. Businesses try to create a brand image, a self-definition in a sense, with which consumers would want to identify. That image might evidence itself in all of the advertisements that the company produces, the physical appearance of its stores or products, the product or service line that it markets, even the appearance of its retail employees. Think of a company—for example, a fast-food chain, a fashion company, a retail chain—and look at how it chooses to represent itself to the public. Using images from magazines or photographs, describe the self-definition or "image" that the company is projecting to consumers. Analyze why a company might choose to define itself in that particular way.

3. Consider searching for love on the Internet. How would you represent yourself online? Write a profile of yourself that defines who you are. Remember, a self-definition is not just a physical description. In fact, who you are is better defined by your interests, obsessions, favorite things, dreams, hopes, emotions.

## ADDITIONAL WRITING SUGGESTIONS FOR DEFINITION

When we come across a word or phrase that is not familiar, we consult a dictionary, either in print or online. As necessary and as helpful as dictionaries are, however, entries are typically limited to a single sentence. Often, we need an extended definition, one that provides both denotation and connotation, explains the term in great depth, and offers a series of examples. Definition essays offer just that—extended definitions that potentially draw upon all of the writing strategies examined in this text. The following suggestions invite you to write an extended definition of a complex term.

1. How would you define a *terrorist*? An *insurgent*? Can a terrorist ever be seen by another culture as a *martyr*?

2. What exactly does the Bill of Rights mean when it says, "the right to bear arms"?

3. What is the difference between an *idol* and a *hero*?

4. How would you define *adulthood*? Would it be any different than how your parents might define it?

5. What does *being disrespected* mean? What would be the necessary conditions under which one might feel "dissed"?

6. How would you define *success*?

7. What constitutes *plagiarism*? How does the law define the term? Can you plagiarize common knowledge? Does plagiarism occur only when you reproduce someone else's work word for word?

8. What did the phrase the "separation of church and state" mean when it was written into the U.S. Constitution?

9. What is *patriotism*? How is it manifested? What kinds of action might be labeled *unpatriotic*?

10. What is, or was, the "American Dream"?

11. How would you define the term *marriage*?

12. When you were younger, what did it mean "to be going out" with someone? What does it mean now?

13. Define a particular type or style of music—rock, rap, punk, heavy metal, alternative rock.

14. What does the term *free trade* mean? What are the conditions under which it operates? In what sense is it "free"?

15. Pick a word that you and your friends use frequently, a word whose meaning is not likely to be found in a dictionary. Write a definition of the term and provide examples of how and when it might be used or applied.

# *Our Do-It-Yourself Economy*

Ellen Goodman

*Ellen Goodman, a Pulitzer Prize–winning op-ed columnist, is syndicated in nearly four hundred newspapers in the United States. Many of her columns have been collected in six books, the most recent of which is* Paper Trail: Common Sense in Uncommon Times *(2004). This essay originally appeared in the* Boston Globe *in 2004.*

**On Writing:** *When asked what challenges she saw in writing columns, Goodman replied: "I think what interests me usually is two things. One is the writing process, which is always interesting, and sometimes I like playing with words. . . . I do consider that play—not play in the easy sense, but play in that my mind just goes that way and I enjoy that. The other thing I really like is thinking about ideas and what it means and where it all fits into most of American society, to people's lives."*

## Before Reading

**Connecting:** When you visit an ATM, pump your own gasoline at a self-service station, or scan and bag your own groceries at a supermarket, have you ever stopped to think that people were once paid to do these jobs and that machines (and you) have replaced them?

**Anticipating:** We hear about how the "service" sector is a large, and growing, segment of the U.S. economy. What, though, does Goodman mean when she talks about the self-service economy?

1　**H**ave you seen those economists scratching their heads trying to understand the jobless recovery? Every time they run the numbers they end up with a question mark: How is it possible that only 1,000 new jobs were created in the past month?

2　Well, maybe it's time we let them in on our little secret. The economy has created hundreds of thousands of new jobs. Only they aren't in the manufacturing sector. They aren't even in the service economy. They're in the self-service economy.

3　Companies are coming back to life without inviting employees back to work for one simple reason: They are outsourcing the jobs to us. You and I, my fellow Americans, have become the unpaid laborers of a do-it-yourself economy.

4    It all began benignly enough a generation ago when ATMs replaced bank tellers. The average American child may know that money doesn't grow on trees; it grows out of walls.

5    The ATM followed the self-service gas station. At first in the classic bait and switch, we were offered a discount for being our own gas jockey; now we have to pay a premium to have a person fill 'er up.

6    Now gradually, we are scanning our own groceries at the supermarket, getting our own boarding passes at airport kiosks and picking up movie tickets from machines that don't call in sick, go on vacation, or require a pension.

7    People who used to have secretaries now have Microsoft Word. People who used to have travel agents now have the Internet. People who used to drop off their film to be developed have been lured into buying new cameras for the joy of printing or not printing pictures ourselves.

8    We also serve (ourselves) by being required to wait longer for the incredible shrinking support system. When was the last time you called your health plan? The service consists of a hold button, a list of phone options, and the strategic corporate decision that sooner or later a percentage of us will give up.

9    Remember 411? If you actually want information from a phone company today, you have to pay someone in Omaha to give you the new number of a neighbor in Albany.

10    If the phone breaks, you may have to dial fix-it-yourself. A new chapter in the annals of the self-service economy comes from a friend who was told by Verizon to go find the gray box attached to her house and test the line herself. The e-mail instructions told her merrily: "You don't have to be a telephone technician or an electrical engineer." Next year they'll be telling her to climb the telephone pole.

11    Then of course there is the world of computers. We have all become our own techie. A Harvard Business School professor actually told a reporter recently that we fix them ourselves because: "There's a real love of technology and people want to get inside and tinker with them." My friends have as much of a desire to tinker with computer insides as to perform amateur appendectomies.

12    But tech support has become less reliable than child support checks from an ex-husband. Consumer reports show that 8 million people a year contact the tech support lines at software companies, and one-third of them don't get any help. These same companies have laid off more than 30,000 support workers and replaced them with messages telling us to fix our "infrastructure migration" by performing an "ipconfig/release" and "ipconfig/renew."

13    As for online help? If my Web server was managing 911, I would still be on the floor somewhere gasping for breath. The only part of the self-help economy that keeps us aloft is a battery of teenagers fed and housed solely because they can get the family system back up.

14    Oh, and if we finally find someone to perform a so-called service call, we end up with an alleged appointment for that convenient hour known as "when the cows come home."

15     I don't know how much labor has been transferred from the paid to the unpaid economy, but the average American now spends an extraordinary amount of time doing work that once paid someone else's mortgage. The only good news is that the corporations can't export the self-help industry to Bombay. Or maybe that's the bad news.

16     People, actual human beings who work and interact, are now a luxury item. The rest of us have been dragooned into an invisible unpaid labor force without even noticing. We scan, we surf, we fix, and we rant. To which I can only add the motto of the do-it-yourself economy: Help!

## Questions on Subject and Purpose

1. What are the connotations that we have with the phrases *do-it-yourself* and *self-service*?

2. At several points, Goodman talks about *outsourcing* jobs. The practice is much in the news, but to what does it refer?

3. What possible purpose or purposes might Goodman have in the essay? Is she arguing that these types of jobs—for example, bank tellers, gasoline station attendants, typists—ought to be restored?

## Questions on Strategy and Audience

1. How does Goodman "define" the do-it-yourself economy? What strategy does she use?

2. The term *do-it-yourself* suggests that we choose to do something, that we make an intentional decision. In fact, the situations that Goodman describes are ones in which we are increasingly unable to choose. Can you think of another title for the essay? Write one and explain why you think it is as effective or more effective than the original.

3. What could Goodman assume about her audience?

## Questions on Vocabulary and Style

1. How would you describe the tone of the essay? It is formal or informal? What factors governed your choice?

2. What is a rhetorical question (see the Glossary and Ready Reference at the back of this text), and how and why does Goodman use it in the essay?

3. Be prepared to define the following words: *benignly* (4), *dragooned* (16), *rant* (16).

## Writing Suggestions

1. **For Your Journal or Blog.** How would you describe the job or career that would appeal the most to you? Be serious, not humorous. Focus not on the specific field, but rather on the qualities, responsibilities, or benefits that would be the most appealing to you in any job.

2. **For a Paragraph.** If you work part-time or full-time now, or have had a summer job or a job while in high school, describe what you did and define the nature of the position. Did it have a title? How might it be described if you had to write an advertisement for such a position?

3. **For an Essay.** Interview a number of students, about what they are looking for in an ideal job or career. Try to conduct at least a two dozen interviews with a variety of people. Using their answers as your database, write a essay in which you define the ideal job or career.

4. **For Research.** Goodman's reservations about the self-service economy are not shared by many in the business community. Most argue that the change to self-service is what Americans want because of the time savings involved. On the Web, search for the term *self-service economy*. Drawing from Web resources, write an essay that offers an extended definition of the term as seen from the point of view opposite to Goodman's.

## For Further Study

**Focusing on Grammar and Writing.** The colon (:) is a mark of punctuation that many writers use infrequently, if at all. Goodman uses a colon in paragraphs 1, 3, 10, 11, and 16. What are the rules that govern these uses? More than one rule may apply.

**Working Together.** Goodman defines the do-it-yourself economy by providing a series of examples. How does she arrange those examples in the essay? Divide into small groups and analyze the structure of the middle of the essay. Try to find a principle of order or arrangement.

**Seeing Other Modes at Work.** Goodman's essay primarily defines what she means by a do-it-yourself economy, but there are also clear persuasive elements, even though she does not argue for a course of action.

**Finding Connections.** Goodman's essay could be paired with Claudia O'Keefe's "The Traveling Bra Salesman's Lesson" and Bruce Raynor's "Protect Workers' Rights" (both in Chapter 9).

**Exploring the Web.** Goodman has her own Website at www.ellengoodman.com. You can find, among other things, some of her columns, interviews with her, and a brief biography.

# I Want a Wife

Judy Brady

*Judy Brady was born in 1937 in San Francisco, California, and received a B.F.A. in painting from the University of Iowa. As a freelance writer, Brady has written essays on topics such as union organizing, abortion, and the role of women in society. Currently an activist focusing on issues related to cancer and the environment, she has edited several books on the subject, including* One in Three: Women with Cancer Confront an Epidemic *(1991).*

*Brady's most frequently reprinted essay is* "I Want a Wife," *which originally appeared in* Ms. *magazine in 1971. After examining the stereotypical male demands in marriage, Brady concludes,* "Who *wouldn't* want *a wife?"*

## Before Reading

**Connecting:** In a relationship, what separates reasonable needs or desires from unreasonable or selfish ones?

**Anticipating:** What is the effect of the repetition of the phrase "I want a . . ." in the essay?

1 I belong to that classification of people known as wives. I am A Wife. And, not altogether incidentally, I am a mother.

2 Not too long ago a male friend of mine appeared on the scene fresh from a recent divorce. He had one child, who is, of course, with his ex-wife. He is obviously looking for another wife. As I thought about him while I was ironing one evening, it suddenly occurred to me that I, too, would like to have a wife. Why do I want a wife?

3 I would like to go back to school so that I can become economically independent, support myself, and, if need be, support those dependent upon me. I want a wife who will work and send me to school. And while I am going to school I want a wife to take care of my children. I want a wife to keep track of the children's doctor and dentist appointments. And to keep track of mine, too. I want a wife to make sure my children eat properly and are kept clean. I want a wife who will wash the children's clothes and keep them mended. I want a wife who is a good nurturant attendant to my children, who arranges for their schooling, makes sure that they have an adequate social life with their peers, takes them to the park, the zoo, etc. I want a wife who takes care of the children when they are sick, a wife who arranges to be around when the children need special care, because, of course, I cannot miss classes at school. My

wife must arrange to lose time at work, and not lose the job. It may mean a small cut in my wife's income from time to time, but I guess I can tolerate that. Needless to say, my wife will arrange and pay for the care of the children while my wife is working.

4    I want a wife who will take care of my physical needs. I want a wife who will keep my house clean. A wife who will pick up after me. I want a wife who will keep my clothes clean, ironed, mended, replaced when need be, and who will see to it that my personal things are kept in their proper place so that I can find what I need the minute I need it. I want a wife who cooks the meals, a wife who is a good cook. I want a wife who will plan the meals, do the necessary grocery shopping, prepare the meals, serve them pleasantly, and then do the cleaning up while I do my studying. I want a wife who will care for me when I am sick and sympathize with my pain and loss of time from school. I want a wife to go along when our family takes a vacation so that someone can continue to care for me and my children when I need a rest and change of scene.

5    I want a wife who will not bother me with rambling complaints about a wife's duties. But I want a wife who will listen to me when I feel the need to explain a rather difficult point I have come across in my course of studies. And I want a wife who will type my papers for me when I have written them.

6    I want a wife who will take care of the details of my social life. When my wife and I are invited out by my friends, I want a wife who will take care of the babysitting arrangements. When I meet people at school that I like and want to entertain, I want a wife who will have the house clean, will prepare a special meal, serve it to me and my friends, and not interrupt when I talk about the things that interest me and my friends. I want a wife who will have arranged that the children are fed and ready for bed before my guests arrive so that the children do not bother us. I want a wife who takes care of the needs of my guests so that they feel comfortable, who makes sure that they have an ashtray, that they are passed the hors d'oeuvres, that they are offered a second helping of the food, that their wine glasses are replenished when necessary, that their coffee is served to them as they like it. And I want a wife who knows that sometimes I need a night out by myself.

7    I want a wife who is sensitive to my sexual needs, a wife who makes love passionately and eagerly when I feel like it, a wife who makes sure that I am satisfied. And, of course, I want a wife who will not demand sexual attention when I am not in the mood for it. I want a wife who assumes the complete responsibility for birth control, because I do not want more children. I want a wife who will remain sexually faithful to me so that I do not have to clutter up my intellectual life with jealousies. And I want a wife who understands that *my* sexual needs may entail more than strict adherence to monogamy. I must, after all, be able to relate to people as fully as possible.

8    If, by chance, I find another person more suitable as a wife than the wife I already have, I want the liberty to replace my present wife with another one. Naturally I will expect a fresh, new life; my wife will take the children and be solely responsible for them so that I am left free.

9      When I am through with school and have a job, I want my wife to quit working and remain at home so that my wife can more fully and completely take care of a wife's duties.

10     My God, who *wouldn't* want a wife?

## Questions on Subject and Purpose

1. In what way is this essay a definition of a wife? Why does Brady avoid a more conventional definition?
2. Is Brady being fair? Is there anything that she leaves out of her definition that you would have included?
3. What purpose might Brady have been trying to achieve?

## Questions on Strategy and Audience

1. How does Brady structure her essay? What is the order of the development? Could the essay have been arranged in any other way?
2. Why does Brady identify herself by her roles—wife and mother—at the beginning of the essay? Is that information relevant in any way?
3. What assumptions does Brady have about her audience (readers of *Ms.* magazine in the early 1970s)? How do you know?

## Questions on Vocabulary and Style

1. How does Brady use repetition in the essay? Why? Does it work? What effect does it create?
2. How effective is Brady's final rhetorical question? Where else in the essay does she use a rhetorical question?
3. Be prepared to define the following words: *nurturant* (paragraph 3), *hors d'oeuvres* (6), *replenished* (6), *monogamy* (7).

## Writing Suggestions

1. **For Your Journal or Blog.** What do you look for in a possible spouse or "significant other"? Make a list of what you expect or want from a relationship with another person. Once you have brainstormed the list, rank each item in order of importance—which is most important, and which is least important? If you are in a relationship right now, try evaluating that relationship in light of your own priorities.
2. **For a Paragraph.** Using the material that you generated in your journal or blog entry, write a paragraph definition of the kind of person you seek for a committed relationship. Be serious. Do not try to imitate Brady's style.
3. **For an Essay.** Define a word naming a central role in human relationships, such as *husband, lover, friend, mother, father, child, sister, brother,* or *grandparent.* Define the term indirectly by showing what such a person does or should do.

4. **For Research.** What does it mean to be a wife in another culture? Choose at least two other cultures, and research those societies' expectations of a wife. Try to find cultures that show significant differences. Remember, interviews might be a good source of information—even e-mail interviews with wives in other cultures. Using your research, write an essay offering a comparative definition of *wife*. Assume that your audience is American. Be certain to document your sources, including any interviews or e-mail conversations.

## For Further Study

**Focusing on Grammar and Writing.** The most distinctive stylistic feature of Brady's essay is the repetitive sentence opener "I want a wife who . . . ." Normally, no one would ever advise you to repeat the same sentence structure over and over, let alone to repeat the same words again and again. How effective is the strategy in Brady's essay? Why might she have consciously chosen to repeat this structure? How is this structure appropriate for what the narrator is saying?

**Working Together.** Working with classmates in small groups, brainstorm ideas for an essay titled "I Want a Husband." Each group should compile a list of duties or responsibilities to be included in such an essay. Once the planning is done, each group should share its ideas with the class as a whole.

**Seeing Other Modes at Work.** Throughout the body of the essay, Brady uses division to organize the "duties" of a wife. How is division crucial to the definition of a wife that Brady offers?

**Finding Connections.** Related essays include Anna Quindlen's "The Name Is Mine" (Chapter 1) and Margaret Atwood's "The Female Body" (this chapter).

**Exploring the Web.** Visit a group of Websites devoted to marriage and marital contracts—get a range from the most conservative to the most liberal. What do couples say when they take their wedding vows? Do women still promise to "obey" their husbands?

# The People in Me

Robin D. G. Kelley

*Robin D. G. Kelley (1962– ) was born in New York City and raised in Harlem, Seattle, and Pasadena, California. A graduate of California State University, Long Beach, Kelley earned his M.A. and Ph.D. at the University of California, Los Angeles. Currently a professor of history and ethnic studies at the University of Southern California, Kelley has been called "the preeminent historian of black popular culture writing today." The author and editor of many books, Kelley's most recent collections of essays include* Yo' Mama's DisFunktional!: Fighting the Culture Wars in Urban America *(1997) and* Freedom Dreams: The Black Radical Imagination *(2002).*

**On Writing:** *Complimented in an interview on the accessibility of his writing, Kelley replied, "That's the biggest compliment, because that's the one thing I try to achieve, only because I can't understand academic writing myself. I'm just not that smart."*

## Before Reading

**Connecting:** Who are the people in you? What do you know about your ancestors?

**Anticipating:** Kelley prefers the word *polycultural* rather than *multicultural*. Why? What is the difference?

1 **"S**o, what are you?" I don't know how many times people have asked me that. "Are you Puerto Rican? Dominican? Indian or something? You must be mixed." My stock answer has rarely changed: "My mom is from Jamaica but grew up in New York, and my father was from North Carolina but grew up in Boston. Both black."

2 My family has lived with "the question" for as long as I can remember. We're "exotics," all cursed with "good hair" and strange accents—we don't sound like we from da Souf or the Norwth, and don't have that West Coast-by-way-of-Texas Calabama thang going on. The only one with the real West Indian singsong vibe is my grandmother, who looks even more East Indian than my sisters. Whatever Jamaican patois my mom possessed was pummeled out of her by cruel preteens who never had sensitivity seminars in diversity. The result for us was a nondescript way of talking, walking, and being that made us not black enough, not white enough—just a bunch of not-quite-nappy-headed enigmas.

3 My mother never fit the "black momma" media image. A beautiful, demure, light brown woman, she didn't drink, smoke, curse, or say things like "Lawd Jesus" or "hallelujah," nor did she cook chitlins or gumbo. A vegetarian,

she played the harmonium (a foot-pumped miniature organ), spoke softly with textbook diction, meditated, followed the teachings of Paramahansa Yogananda, and had wild hair like Chaka Khan. She burned incense in our tiny Harlem apartment, sometimes walked the streets barefoot, and, when she could afford it, cooked foods from the East.

4    To this day, my big sister gets misidentified for Pakistani or Bengali or Ethiopian. (Of course, changing her name from Sheral Anne Kelley to Makani Themba has not helped.) Not long ago, an Oakland cab driver, apparently a Sikh who had immigrated from India, treated my sister like dirt until he discovered that she was not a "scoundrel from Sri Lanka," but a common black American. Talk about ironic. How often are black women spared indignities *because* they are African American?

5    "What are you?" dogged my little brother more than any of us. He came out looking just like his father, who was white. In the black communities of Los Angeles and Pasadena, my baby bro' had to fight his way into blackness, usually winning only when he invited his friends to the house. When he got tired of this, he became what people thought he was—a cool white boy. Today he lives in Tokyo, speaks fluent Japanese, and is happily married to a Japanese woman (who is actually Korean passing as Japanese!) He stands as the perfect example of our mulattoness: a black boy trapped in a white body who speaks English with a slight Japanese accent and has a son who will spend his life confronting "the question."

6    Although folk had trouble naming us, we were never blanks or aliens in a "black world." We were and are "polycultural," and I'm talking about all peoples in the Western world. It is not skin, hair, walk, or talk that renders black people so diverse. Rather, it is the fact that most of them are products of different "cultures"—living cultures, not dead ones. These cultures live in and through us every day, with almost no self-consciousness about hierarchy or meaning. "Polycultural" works better than "multicultural," which implies that cultures are fixed, discrete entities that exist side by side—a kind of zoological approach to culture. Such a view obscures power relations, but often reifies race and gender differences.

7    Black people were polycultural from the get-go. Most of our ancestors came to these shores not as Africans, but as Ibo, Yoruba, Hausa, Kongo, Bambara, Mende, Mandingo, and so on. Some of our ancestors came as Spanish, Portuguese, French, Dutch, Irish, English, Italian. And more than a few of us, in North America as well as in the Caribbean and Latin America, have Asian and Native American roots.

8    Our lines of biological descent are about as pure as O. J.'s blood sample, and our cultural lines of descent are about as mixed up as a pot of gumbo. What we know as "black culture" has always been fluid and hybrid. In Harlem in the late 1960s and 1970s, Nehru suits were as popular—and as "black"—as dashikis, and martial arts films placed Bruce Lee among a pantheon of black heroes that included Walt Frazier of the New York Knicks and Richard Rountree, who played John Shaft in blaxploitation cinema. How do we understand the zoot suit—or the conk—without the pachuco culture of Mexican American youth, or low riders in black communities without Chicanos? How can we discuss black visual artists in the interwar years without reference to the Mexican

muralists, or the radical graphics tradition dating back to the late 19th century, or the Latin American artists influenced by surrealism?

9       Vague notions of "Eastern" religion and philosophy, as well as a variety of Orientalist assumptions, were far more important to the formation of the Lost-Found Nation of Islam than anything coming out of Africa. And Rastafarians drew many of their ideas from South Asians, from vegetarianism to marijuana, which was introduced into Jamaica by Indians. Major black movements like Garveyism and the African Blood Brotherhood are also the products of global developments. We won't understand these movements until we see them as part of a dialogue with Irish nationalists from the Easter Rebellion, Russian and Jewish émigrés from the 1905 and 1917 revolutions, and Asian socialists like India's M. N. Roy and Japan's Sen Katayama.

10      Indeed, I'm not sure we can even limit ourselves to Earth. How do we make sense of musicians Sun Ra, George Clinton, and Lee "Scratch" Perry or, for that matter, the Nation of Islam, when we consider the fact that space travel and notions of intergalactic exchange constitute a key source of their ideas?

11      So-called "mixed race" children are not the only ones with a claim to multiple heritages. All of us are inheritors of European, African, Native American, and Asian pasts, even if we can't exactly trace our bloodlines to these continents.

12      To some people that's a dangerous concept. Too many Europeans don't want to acknowledge that Africans helped create so-called Western civilization, that they are both indebted to and descendants of those they enslaved. They don't want to see the world as One—a tiny little globe where people and cultures are always on the move, where nothing stays still no matter how many times we name it. To acknowledge our polycultural heritage and cultural dynamism is not to give up our black identity. It does mean expanding our definition of blackness, taking our history more seriously, and looking at the rich diversity within us with new eyes.

13      So next time you see me, don't ask where I'm from or what I am, unless you're ready to sit through a long-ass lecture. As singer/songwriter Abbey Lincoln once put it, "I've got some people in me."

## Questions on Subject and Purpose

1. Why is the question "What are you?" not a simple one?
2. The first section of the essay (through paragraph 5) deals with Kelley's family. What does their story have to do with the rest of the essay?
3. What might be Kelley's purpose in the essay?

## Questions on Strategy and Audience

1. Does Kelley's opening paragraph catch your attention? Why or why not?
2. How would you characterize the first five paragraphs in Kelley's essay? What is he doing? What organizational strategy does he use?
3. In what way is the example of his brother's child (paragraph 5) a perfect example of the polyculturalism that Kelley is talking about?

## Questions on Vocabulary and Style

1. Can you find examples in the essay of informal, even colloquial word choices?
2. Can you find examples in the essay of formal word choices?
3. Be prepared to define the following words: *patois* (paragraph 2), *pummeled* (2), *nondescript* (2), *enigmas* (2), *demure* (3), *entities* (6), *reifies* (6).

## Writing Suggestions

1. **For Your Journal or Blog.** To what extent can you see in American culture, or perhaps in the things in which you are interested, evidence of polycultural heritage? Think about food, music, clothing or hairstyles, behavior, language habits, popular idols. Think about your friends—in high school, at college. In your journal or blog make a list of things central to your life and your friends' lives that are clearly derived from cultures and heritages other than your own.
2. **For a Paragraph.** Select one example that you recorded in your journal or blog (or a series of related examples) and in a paragraph explore the appeal that such a thing has for you and/or your friends.
3. **For an Essay.** Explore the question that Kelley begins with. If someone asked you, "What are you?", how would you reply? In an essay define yourself (and/or your family).
4. **For Research.** Select a word or phrase such as *race, nationality, ethnic origin, multicultural,* or *polycultural* and research what it means. Drawing upon your research, write an extended definition of that term. Be sure to document your sources fully.

## For Further Study

**Focusing on Grammar and Writing.** Kelley encloses quite a few words and phrases within quotation marks. When do you use quotation marks in this way? What is the difference between using quotation marks and using italics? After you have examined the essay, try writing some advice to student writers about when to put words and phrases into quotation marks.

**Working Together.** Working in small groups, focus on the concluding paragraph of the essay. Each group should write a new conclusion for the essay. Perhaps it might be a more conventional "freshman English" ending. Share your new endings with the whole class. What similarities do the new endings have? What do they do that Kelley didn't? Which type of ending is more effective and why?

**Seeing Other Modes at Work.** In the first half of the essay, Kelley uses narration to discuss his own family.

**Finding Connections.** Interesting pairings include Denzy Senna's "The Color of Love" (Chapter 5) and Veronica Chambers's "Dreadlocked" (Chapter 7).

**Exploring the Web.** Interviews with Kelley and some of his other essays can be found on the Web. Search under his name and the word *interview* or *essay*.

# Mother Tongue

Amy Tan

*Born in Oakland, California, in 1952 to Chinese immigrants, Amy Tan graduated from San Jose State University with a double major in English and linguistics and an M.A. in linguistics. Tan did not write fiction until 1985, when she began the stories that would become her first and very successful novel,* The Joy Luck Club *(1989), also a popular film. Tan's children's book* The Chinese Siamese Cat *(1994) is the basis for the daily animated television series,* Sagwa, The Chinese Siamese Cat *(PBS). Her most recent novel is* Saving Fish From Drowning *(2005).*

**On Writing:** *Asked about her writing, Tan responded: "I welcome criticism when I'm writing my books. I want to become better and better as a writer. I go to a writer's group every week. We read our work aloud." In another interview she commented, "I still think of myself, in many ways, as a beginning writer. I'm still learning my craft, learning what makes for a good story, what's an honest voice."*

## Before Reading

**Connecting:** How sensitive are you to the language that you use or your family uses? Are you ever conscious of that language? Are you ever embarrassed by it? Are you proud of it?

**Anticipating:** In what ways does the language of Tan and her mother "define" them in the eyes of others?

1   I am not a scholar of English or literature. I cannot give you much more than personal opinions on the English language and its variations in this country or others.

2   I am a writer. And by that definition, I am someone who has always loved language. I am fascinated by language in daily life. I spend a great deal of my time thinking about the power of language—the way it can evoke an emotion, a visual image, a complex idea, or a simple truth. Language is the tool of my trade. And I use them all—all the Englishes I grew up with.

3   Recently, I was made keenly aware of the different Englishes I do use. I was giving a talk to a large group of people, the same talk I had already given to half a dozen other groups. The nature of the talk was about my writing, my life, and my book, *The Joy Luck Club*. The talk was going along well enough, until I remembered one major difference that made the whole talk sound wrong. My mother was in the room. And it was perhaps the first time she had heard me give a lengthy speech, using the kind of English I have never used

with her. I was saying things like, "The intersection of memory upon imagination" and "There is an aspect of my fiction that relates to thus-and-thus"— a speech filled with carefully wrought grammatical phrases, burdened, it suddenly seemed to me, with nominalized forms, past perfect tenses, conditional phrases, all the forms of standard English that I had learned in school and through books, the forms of English I did not use at home with my mother.

4      Just last week, I was walking down the street with my mother, and I again found myself conscious of the English I was using, the English I do use with her. We were talking about the price of new and used furniture and I heard myself saying this: "Not waste money that way." My husband was with us as well, and he didn't notice any switch in my English. And then I realized why. It's because over the twenty years we've been together I've often used that same kind of English with him, and sometimes he even uses it with me. It has become our language of intimacy, a different sort of English that relates to family talk, the language I grew up with.

5      So you'll have some idea of what this family talk I heard sounds like, I'll quote what my mother said during a recent conversation which I videotaped and then transcribed. During this conversation, my mother was talking about a political gangster in Shanghai who had the same last name as her family's, Du, and how the gangster in his early years wanted to be adopted by her family, which was rich by comparison. Later, the gangster became more powerful, far richer than my mother's family, and one day showed up at my mother's wedding to pay his respects. Here's what she said in part:

6      "Du Yusong having business like fruit stand. Like off the street kind. He is Du like Du Zong—but not Tsung-ming Island people. The local people call putong, the river east side, he belong to that side local people. That man want to ask Du Zong father take him in like become own family. Du Zong father wasn't look down on him, but didn't take seriously, until that man big like become a mafia. Now important person, very hard to inviting him. Chinese way, came only to show respect, don't stay for dinner. Respect for making big celebration, he shows up. Mean gives lots of respect. Chinese custom. Chinese social life that way. If too important won't have to stay too long. He come to my wedding. I didn't see, I heard it. I gone to boy's side, they have YMCA dinner. Chinese age I was nineteen."

7      You should know that my mother's expressive command of English belies how much she actually understands. She reads the *Forbes* report, listens to *Wall Street Week*, converses daily with her stockbroker, reads all of Shirley MacLaine's books with ease—all kinds of things I can't begin to understand. Yet some of my friends tell me they understand 50 percent of what my mother says. Some say they understand 80 to 90 percent. Some say they understand none of it, as if she were speaking pure Chinese. But to me, my mother's English is perfectly clear, perfectly natural. It's my mother tongue. Her language, as I hear it, is vivid, direct, full of observation and imagery. That was the language that helped shape the way I saw things, expressed things, made sense of the world.

8      Lately, I've been giving more thought to the kind of English my mother speaks. Like others, I have described it to people as "broken" or "fractured" English. But I wince when I say that. It has always bothered me that I can think of no way to describe it other than "broken," as if it were damaged and needed to be fixed, as if it lacked a certain wholeness and soundness. I've heard other terms used, "limited English," for example. But they seem just as bad, as if everything is limited, including people's perceptions of the limited English speaker.

9      I know this for a fact, because when I was growing up, my mother's "limited" English limited *my* perception of her. I was ashamed of her English. I believed that her English reflected the quality of what she had to say. That is, because she expressed them imperfectly her thoughts were imperfect. And I had plenty of empirical evidence to support me: the fact that people in department stores, at banks, and at restaurants did not take her seriously, did not give her good service, pretended not to understand her, or even acted as if they did not hear her.

10      My mother has long realized the limitations of her English as well. When I was fifteen, she used to have me call people on the phone to pretend I was she. In this guise, I was forced to ask for information or even to complain and yell at people who had been rude to her. One time it was a call to her stockbroker in New York. She had cashed out her small portfolio and it just so happened we were going to go to New York the next week, our very first trip outside California. I had to get on the phone and say in an adolescent voice that was not very convincing, "This is Mrs. Tan."

11      And my mother was standing in the back whispering loudly, "Why he don't send me check, already two weeks late. So mad he lie to me, losing me money."

12      And then I said in perfect English, "Yes, I'm getting rather concerned. You had agreed to send the check two weeks ago, but it hasn't arrived."

13      Then she began to talk more loudly. "What he want, I come to New York tell him front of his boss, you cheating me?" And I was trying to calm her down, make her be quiet, while telling the stockbroker, "I can't tolerate any more excuses. If I don't receive the check immediately, I am going to have to speak to your manager when I'm in New York next week." And sure enough, the following week there we were in front of this astonished stockbroker, and I was sitting there red-faced and quiet, and my mother, the real Mrs. Tan, was shouting at his boss in her impeccable broken English.

14      We used a similar routine just five days ago, for a situation that was far less humorous. My mother had gone to the hospital for an appointment, to find out about a benign brain tumor a CAT scan had revealed a month ago. She said she had spoken very good English, her best English, no mistakes. Still, she said, the hospital did not apologize when they said they had lost the CAT scan and she had come for nothing. She said they did not seem to have any sympathy when she told them she was anxious to know the exact diagnosis, since her husband and son had both died of brain tumors. She said they would not give her any more information until the next time and she would

have to make another appointment for that. So she said she would not leave until the doctor called her daughter. She wouldn't budge. And when the doctor finally called her daughter, me, who spoke in perfect English—lo and behind—we had assurances the CAT scan would be found, promises that a conference call on Monday would be held, and apologies for any suffering my mother had gone through for a most regrettable mistake.

15      I think my mother's English almost had an effect on limiting my possibilities in life as well. Sociologists and linguists probably will tell you that a person's developing language skills are more influenced by peers. But I do think that the language spoken in the family, especially in immigrant families which are more insular, plays a large role in shaping the language of the child. And I believe that it affected my results on achievement tests, IQ tests, and the SAT. While my English skills were never judged as poor, compared to math, English could not be considered my strong suit. In grade school I did moderately well, getting perhaps B's, sometimes B-pluses, in English and scoring perhaps in the sixtieth or seventieth percentile on achievement tests. But those scores were not good enough to override the opinion that my true abilities lay in math and science, because in those areas I achieved A's and scored in the ninetieth percentile or higher.

16      This was understandable. Math is precise; there is only one correct answer. Whereas, for me at least, the answers on English tests were always a judgment call, a matter of opinion and personal experience. Those tests were constructed around items like fill-in-the-blank sentence completion, such as, "Even though Tom was _____, Mary thought he was _____." And the correct answer always seemed to be the most bland combinations of thoughts, for example, "Even though Tom was shy, Mary thought he was charming," with the grammatical structure "even though" limiting the correct answer to some sort of semantic opposites, so you wouldn't get answers like, "Even though Tom was foolish, Mary thought he was ridiculous." Well, according to my mother, there were very few limitations as to what Tom could have been and what Mary might have thought of him. So I never did well on tests like that.

17      The same was true with word analogies, pairs of words in which you were supposed to find some sort of logical, semantic relationship—for example, "*Sunset* is to *nightfall* as _____ is to _____." And here you would be presented with a list of four possible pairs, one of which showed the same kind of relationship: *red* is to *stoplight, bus* is to *arrival, chills* is to *fever, yawn* is to *boring.* Well, I could never think that way. I knew what the tests were asking, but I could not block out of my mind the images already created by the first pair, "*sunset* is to *nightfall*"— and I would see a burst of colors against a darkening sky, the moon rising, the lowering of a curtain of stars. And all the other pairs of words—*red, bus, stoplight, boring*—just threw up a mass of confusing images, making it impossible for me to sort out something as logical as saying: "A sunset precedes nightfall" is the same as "a chill precedes a fever." The only way I would have gotten that answer right would have been to imagine an associative situation, for example, my being disobedient and staying out past sunset, catching a chill at night, which turns into feverish pneumonia as punishment, which indeed did happen to me.

18    I have been thinking about all this lately, about my mother's English, about achievement tests. Because lately I've been asked, as a writer, why there are not more Asian-Americans represented in American literature. Why are there few Asian Americans enrolled in creative writing programs? Why do so many Chinese students go into engineering? Well, these are broad sociological questions I can't begin to answer. But I have noticed in surveys—in fact, just last week—that Asian students, as a whole, always do significantly better on math achievement tests than in English. And this makes me think that there are other Asian-American students whose English spoken in the home might also be described as "broken" or "limited." And perhaps they also have teachers who are steering them away from writing and into math and science, which is what happened to me.

19    Fortunately, I happen to be rebellious in nature and enjoy the challenge of disproving assumptions made about me. I became an English major my first year in college, after being enrolled as pre-med. I started writing nonfiction as a freelancer the week after I was told by my former boss that writing was my worst skill and I should hone my talents toward account management.

20    But it wasn't until 1985 that I finally began to write fiction. And at first I wrote using what I thought to be wittily crafted sentences, sentences that would finally prove I had mastery over the English language. Here's an example from the first draft of a story that later made its way into *The Joy Luck Club*, but without this line: "That was my mental quandary in its nascent state." A terrible line, which I can barely pronounce.

21    Fortunately, for reasons I won't get into today, I later decided I should envision a reader for the stories I would write. And the reader I decided upon was my mother, because these were stories about mothers. So with this reader in mind—and in fact she did read my early drafts—I began to write stories using all the Englishes I grew up with: the English I spoke to my mother, which for lack of a better term might be described as "simple"; the English she used with me, which for lack of a better term might be described as "broken"; my translation of her Chinese, which could certainly be described as "watered down"; and what I imagined to be her translation of her Chinese if she could speak in perfect English, her internal language, and for that I sought to preserve the essence, but neither an English nor a Chinese structure. I wanted to capture what language ability tests can never reveal: her intent, her passion, her imagery, the rhythms of her speech and the nature of her thoughts.

22    Apart from what any critic had to say about my writing, I knew I had succeeded where it counted when my mother finished reading my book and gave me her verdict: "So easy to read."

## Questions on Subject and Purpose

1. What does the title "Mother Tongue" suggest?
2. How many subjects does Tan explore in the essay?
3. How does Tan feel about her mother's "tongue"?

## Questions on Strategy and Audience

1. In paragraph 6, Tan quotes part of one of her mother's conversations. Why?
2. After paragraphs 7 and 17, Tan uses additional space to indicate divisions in her essay. Why does she divide the essay into three parts?
3. Tan notes in paragraph 21 that she thinks of her mother as her audience when she writes stories. Why?

## Questions on Vocabulary and Style

1. How would you characterize Tan's tone (see the Glossary and Ready Reference for a definition) in the essay?
2. In paragraph 20, Tan quotes a "terrible line" she once wrote: "That was my mental quandary in its nascent state." What is so terrible about that line?
3. Be prepared to define the following words: *belies* (7), *empirical* (9), *benign* (14), *insular* (15), *semantic* (16), *hone* (19), *quandary* (20), *nascent* (20).

## Writing Suggestions

1. **For Your Journal or Blog.** What makes up your "mother tongue"? To what extent is your language (such things as word choice, pronunciation, dialect, and second-language skills) influenced by your parents, your education, the part of the country in which you grew up, and your peers? Make a series of notes exploring those influences.
2. **For a Paragraph.** Using the information that you gathered for your journal or blog entry, write a paragraph in which you define your "mother tongue." Try to define the influences that have shaped both how and what you say.
3. **For an Essay.** Tan suggests that a certain type or dialect of English is a language of power, that if you speak and write that English, people in authority will listen to you and respect you. How might that public, powerful English (sometimes referred to as "edited American English") be defined?
4. **For Research.** Linguists have defined a wide range of dialects in the United States. Choose one of the dialects that interests you—a reference librarian or your instructor can help you find a list. You might choose one based on the geographical area in which you live or one defined by your heritage. Using the resources of your library, write a definition of that dialect. What are its distinctive features? Where did those features come from? Where is this dialect spoken in the United States? What are some particularly colorful examples? Be sure to document your sources wherever appropriate.

## For Further Study

**Focusing on Grammar and Writing.** Tan occasionally writes an extremely long sentence. For example, look at the final sentences in paragraphs 3, 9, 13, 14, and 17, and the next to last sentence in paragraph 21. How can Tan write such a long sentence and still achieve clarity? Choose one or more of these sentences and analyze how it is constructed. What is essential in a very long sentence?

**Working Together.** Working in small groups, choose one of the following topics and examine its role in the essay as a whole.

1. The introduction, with its emphasis on language (paragraphs 1 and 2)
2. The transcription of her mother's conversation (6)
3. The example of the stockbroker (10–13)
4. The example of the CAT scan (14)
5. The examples from the verbal sections of achievement tests (16 and 17)

**Seeing Other Modes at Work.** At several points in the essay, Tan talks about the "different Englishes" that she uses. How does she use classification to help structure the essay?

**Finding Connections.** Interesting pairings are with Judith Ortiz Cofer's "The Myth of the Latin Woman" (Chapter 4), Robin D. G. Kelley's "The People in Me" (this chapter), and Richard Rodriguez's "None of This Is Fair" (Chapter 9).

**Exploring the Web.** Read online interviews with Tan, watch video clips of her talking about her books, listen to audio excerpts from her works. Her Website is www.amytan.net.

# You Can't Say That

Diane Ravitch

*Diane Ravitch, a graduate from Wellesley and Columbia University (Ph.D. in history), is a former assistant secretary of education in the administration of President George H. W. Bush. The author of many books and hundreds of articles, she is currently Research Professor of Education at New York University. Her most recent book,* The English Reader: What Every Literate Person Needs to Know *(2006), is co-edited with her son Michael. This article originally appeared in the* Wall Street Journal *in 2004.*

   **On Writing:** *In an interview, Ravitch talked about how some famous literary works might be retitled to eliminate objectionable words:* "The New York Times *suggested once that* The Old Man and the Sea *would become* The Elderly Man and the Sea, *but even that title would have to be changed, because 'elderly' is unacceptable, 'man' is unacceptable, and so is 'sea.' References to 'man' are considered unacceptable, as they exclude half the human race. The issue with 'the sea' is that it may be a form of regional bias to expect children who don't live near a sea to answer a test question that contains references to an unfamiliar terrain. So it would become* A Person Catches a Fish. *Of course, if the animal rights people get into the act, even the fish would have to go."*

## Before Reading

**Connecting:** How do you feel about censorship? Can you think of any situations in which you think it might be appropriate to remove or to prevent from publication certain words, phrases, or images?

**Anticipating:** Specifically, what is it that Ravitch finds most troubling about this "policing" of language?

1   To judge by the magazines we read, the programs we watch or the music lyrics we hear, it would seem that almost anything goes, these days, when it comes to verbal expression. But that is not quite true.

2   In my book *The Language Police*, I gathered a list of more than 500 words that are routinely deleted from textbooks and tests by "bias review committees" employed by publishing companies, state education departments and the federal government. Among the forbidden words are "landlord," "cowboy," "brother-hood," "yacht," "cult" and "primitive." Such words are deleted because they are offensive to various groups—feminists, religious conservatives, multiculturalists and ethnic activists, to name a few.

3        I invited readers of the book to send me examples of language policing, and they did, by the score. A bias review committee for the state test in New Jersey rejected a short story by Langston Hughes because he used the words "Negro" and "colored person." Michigan bans a long list of topics from its state tests, including terrorism, evolution, aliens and flying saucers (which might imply evolution).

4        A textbook writer sent me the guidelines used by the Harcourt/Steck/ Vaughn company to remove photographs that might give offense. Editors must delete, the guidelines said, pictures of women with big hair or sleeveless blouses and men with dreadlocks or medallions. Photographs must not portray the soles of shoes or anyone eating with the left hand (both in deference to Muslim culture). To avoid giving offense to those who cannot afford a home computer, no one may be shown owning a home computer. To avoid offending those with strong but differing religious views, decorations for religious holidays must never appear in the background.

5        A college professor informed me that a new textbook in human development includes the following statement: "As a folksinger once sang, how many roads must an individual walk down before you can call them an adult." The professor was stupefied that someone had made the line gender-neutral and ungrammatical by rewriting Bob Dylan's folk song "Blowin' in the Wind," which had simply asked: "How many roads must a man walk down before you call him a man?"

6        While writing *The Language Police*, I could not figure out why New York State had gone so far beyond other states in punctiliously carving out almost all references to race, gender, age and ethnicity, including even weight and height. In June 2002, the state was mightily embarrassed when reports appeared about its routine bowdlerizing on its exams of writers such as Franz Kafka and Isaac Bashevis Singer.

7        The solution to the puzzle was recently provided by Candace deRussy, a trustee of the State University of New York. Ms. DeRussy read *The Language Police* and she too wondered how the New York State Education Department had come to censor its regents exams with such zeal. She asked the department to explain how it decided which words to delete and how it trained its bias and sensitivity reviewers.

8        At one point, state officials said that since June 2002 (the time of the debacle) they have adhered to only one standard: "Test developers should strive to identify and eliminate language, symbols, words, phrases, and content that are generally regarded as offensive by members of racial, ethnic, gender, or other groups, except when judged to be necessary for adequate representation of the domain." Ms. DeRussy guessed (correctly) that the state was holding back the specific instructions that had emboldened the bowdlerizers. She decided to use the state's freedom-of-information law to find out more. Months later, a state official sent her the training materials for the bias and sensitivity reviewers, which included a list of words and phrases and a rationale for language policing.

9        So here is how New York made itself an international joke. The state's guidelines to language sensitivity, citing Rosalie Maggio's "The Bias-Free

Wordfinder," says: "We may not always understand why a certain word hurts. We don't have to. It is enough that someone says, 'That language doesn't respect me.'" That is, if any word or phrase is likely to give anyone offense, no matter how farfetched, it should be deleted.

10    Next the state asked: "Is it necessary to make reference to a person's age, ancestry, disability, ethnicity, nationality, physical appearance, race, religion, sex, sexuality?" Since the answer is frequently no, nearly all references to such characteristics are eliminated. Because these matters loom large in history and literature—and because they help us to understand character, life circumstances and motives—their silent removal is bound to weaken or obliterate the reader's understanding.

11    Like every other governmental agency concerned with testing, the New York State Education Department devised its own list of taboo words. There are the usual ones that have offended feminists for a generation, like "fireman," "authoress," "handyman" and "hostess." New York exercised its leadership by discovering bias in such words as "addict" (replace with "individual with a drug addiction"); "alumna, alumnae, alumni, alumnus" (replace with "graduate or graduates"); "American" (replace with "citizen of the United States or North America"); "cancer patient" (replace with "a patient with cancer"); "city fathers" (replace with "city leaders").

12    Meanwhile, the word "elderly" should be replaced by "older adult" or "older person," if it is absolutely necessary to mention age at all. "Gentleman's agreement" must be dropped in favor of an "informal agreement." "Ghetto" should be avoided; instead describe the social and economic circumstances of the neighborhood. "Grandfather clause" is helplessly sexist; "retroactive coverage" is preferred instead. The term "illegal alien" must be replaced by "undocumented worker."

13    Certain words are unacceptable under any circumstances. For example, it is wrong to describe anyone as "illegitimate." Another word to be avoided is "illiterate." Instead, specify whether an individual is unable to read or write, or both. Similarly, any word that contains the three offensive letters "m-a-n" as a prefix or a suffix must be rousted out of the language. Words like "manhours," "manpower," "mankind" and "manmade" are regularly deleted. Even "penmanship," where the guilty three letters are in the middle of the word, is out.

14    New York identified as biased such male-based words as "masterpiece" and "mastery." Among the other words singled out for extinction were *white collar, blue collar, pink collar, teenager, senior citizen, third world, uncivilized, underprivileged, unmarried, window or widower,* and *yes man.* The goal, naturally, is to remove words that identify people by their gender, age, race, social position or marital status.

15    Thus the great irony of bias and sensitivity reviewing. It began with the hope of encouraging diversity, ensuring that our educational materials would include people of different experiences and social backgrounds. It has evolved into a bureaucratic system that removes all evidence of diversity and reduces everyone to interchangeable beings whose differences we must *not* learn about—making nonsense of literature and history along the way.

## Questions on Subject and Purpose

1. Ravitch is writing about censorship as it occurs in what specific context?
2. Ravitch includes the examples of offensive words in a Langston Hughes short story (paragraph 3) and a line from a Bob Dylan song (5). How do these two examples fit with her argument that censoring certain words can "make nonsense of literature and history"?
3. Do you sense from the essay that Ravitch might find some forms of language censorship acceptable?

## Questions on Strategy and Audience

1. In what sense is this reading a definition essay? That is, what term does Ravitch seem to be defining even though she does not provide a single-sentence definition?
2. Think about your answer to question 1. What strategy does Ravitch use in the essay to define that term if it is not a dictionary-like definition?
3. What expectations might Ravitch have of her audience?

## Questions on Vocabulary and Style

1. How would you describe the tone of the essay and what evidence would you cite to support your conclusion?
2. What is ungrammatical about this line in paragraph 5: "As a folksinger once sang, how many roads must an individual walk down before you can call them an adult"?
3. Be prepared to define the following words: *punctiliously* (paragraph 6), *bowdlerizing* (6), *debacle* (8)

## Writing Suggestions

1. **For Your Journal or Blog.** Listen carefully to yourself and to those around you for at least a day. Jot down every name or label that you use or that you hear others use that might be offensive. What does the list reveal?
2. **For a Paragraph.** Select a common word that has a range of connotations or associations. In a paragraph, define that word by including a series of examples of how the word might be used.
3. **For an Essay.** Write an extended definition of a word that carries a range of connotations. Get your instructor's approval of your choice of a word.
4. **For Research.** Research the history of one "hate" word, especially a word that might have been used against you or a friend. Where did it originate? Why? What connotations does the word have? Have those connotations changed over the years? The many dictionaries in the reference section of your school's library will be a good place at which to start your research.

## For Further Study

**Focusing on Grammar and Writing.** Items in a series in a sentence can be separated by commas or, under special circumstances, semicolons. Compare some examples in paragraphs 2, 8, 11, and 14. What seems to govern the use of semicolons rather than commas to separate elements in a series?

**Working Together.** Divide into small groups and discuss examples of language that some or all in the group find offensive. What is it about the words that is offensive?

**Seeing Other Modes at Work.** The essay also has persuasive elements; look, for example, at the final paragraph.

**Finding Connections.** It is not just words that people find offensive, but also images. An interesting pairing would be with Margaret Atwood's "The Female Body" (this chapter).

**Exploring the Web.** More information about Ravitch and her books can be found at her Website www.dianeravitch.com. The Web contains many articles written by Ravitch and an extensive number of interviews with her. Searching for the phrase *textbook censorship* will produce an abundance of Web sources.

# The Female Body

Margaret Atwood

*Margaret Atwood was born in Ottawa, Canada, in 1939. She received a B.A. from the University of Toronto in 1961 and earned an M.A. at Radcliffe College in 1962. A poet, essayist, short story writer, and novelist, Atwood has enjoyed critical and popular acclaim throughout her writing career, winning numerous awards and honorary degrees. Her work has explored broad themes of feminism, dystopia, and the opposition of art and nature, but always through the eyes of an individual. Her best known novel is* The Handmaid's Tale *(1986), in which a totalitarian state assigns roles to women according to their reproductive abilities.*

**On Writing:** *At a meeting of the Toronto Council of Teachers of English, Atwood was asked about the importance of punctuation in good writing. She commented on her own use of punctuation: "I've recently taken up a new device, which is the set of dashes. Some people overuse this quite a lot—everything is a set of dashes—but in prose I'm tending to prefer it to parentheses. In prose fiction a lot is associative, one idea suggests another which can lead to an interposition in the middle of a sentence. The question is, how do you set that off? Sometimes you can do it with parenthesis, but sets of dashes are often quite useful."*

## Before Reading

**Connecting:** What image is suggested to you by the phrase "the female body"?

**Anticipating:** Does Atwood's essay fulfill your expectations of an essay on the "female body"? Why or why not?

. . . entirely devoted to the subject of "The Female Body." Knowing how well you have written on this topic. . . this capacious topic . . .

Letter from *Michigan Quarterly Review*

### 1

1   I agree, it's a hot topic. But only one? Look around, there's a wide range. Take my own, for instance.

2   I get up in the morning. My topic feels like hell. I sprinkle it with water, brush parts of it, rub it with towels, powder it, add lubricant. I dump in the fuel and away goes my topic, my topical topic, my controversial topic, my capacious topic, my limping topic, my nearsighted topic, my topic with back problems, my badly behaved topic, my vulgar topic, my outrageous topic, my

aging topic, my topic that is out of the question and anyway still can't spell, in its oversized coat and worn winter boots, scuttling along the sidewalk as if it were flesh and blood, hunting for what's out there, an avocado, an alderman, an adjective, hungry as ever.

## 2

3    The basic Female Body comes with the following accessories: garter belt, panti-girdle, crinoline, camisole, bustle, brassiere, stomacher, chemise, virgin zone, spike heels, nose ring, veil, kid gloves, fishnet stockings, fichu, bandeau, Merry Widow, weepers, chokers, barrettes, bangles, beads, lorgnette, feather boa, basic black, compact, Lycra stretch one-piece with modesty panel, designer peignoir, flannel nightie, lace teddy, bed, head.

## 3

4    The Female Body is made of transparent plastic and lights up when you plug it in. You press a button to illuminate the different systems. The circulatory system is red, for the heart and arteries, purple for the veins; the respiratory system is blue; the lymphatic system is yellow; the digestive system is green, with liver and kidneys in aqua. The nerves are done in orange and the brain is pink. The skeleton, as you might expect, is white.

5    The reproductive system is optional, and can be removed. It comes with or without a miniature embryo. Parental judgment can thereby be exercised. We do not wish to frighten or offend.

## 4

6    He said, I won't have one of those things in the house. It gives a young girl a false notion of beauty, not to mention anatomy. If a real woman was built like that she'd fall on her face.

7    She said, If we don't let her have one like all the other girls she'll feel singled out. It'll become an issue. She'll long for one and she'll long to turn into one. Repression breeds sublimation. You know that.

8    He said, It's not just the pointy plastic tits, it's the wardrobes. The wardrobes and that stupid male doll, what's his name, the one with the underwear glued on.

9    She said, Better to get it over with when she's young. He said, All right, but don't let me see it.

10    She came whizzing down the stairs, thrown like a dart. She was stark naked. Her hair had been chopped off, her head was turned back to front, she was missing some toes and she'd been tattooed all over her body with purple ink in a scrollwork design. She hit the potted azalea, trembled there for a moment like a botched angel, and fell.

11    He said, I guess we're safe.

## 5

12    The Female Body has many uses. It's been used as a door knocker, a bottle opener, as a clock with a ticking belly, as something to hold up lampshades, as a nutcracker, just squeeze the brass legs together and out comes your nut. It bears torches, lifts victorious wreaths, grows copper wings and raises aloft a ring of neon stars; whole buildings rest on its marble heads.

13     It sells cars, beer, shaving lotion, cigarettes, hard liquor; it sells diet plans and diamonds, and desire in tiny crystal bottles. Is this the face that launched a thousand products? You bet it is, but don't get any funny big ideas, honey, that smile is a dime a dozen.

14     It does not merely sell, it is sold. Money flows into this country or that country, flies in, practically crawls in, suitful after suitful, lured by all those hairless pre-teen legs. Listen, you want to reduce the national debt, don't you? Aren't you patriotic? That's the spirit. That's my girl.

15     She's a natural resource, a renewable one luckily, because those things wear out so quickly. They don't make 'em like they used to. Shoddy goods.

6

16     One and one equals another one. Pleasure in the female is not a requirement. Pair-bonding is stronger in geese. We're not talking about love, we're talking about biology. That's how we all got here, daughter.

17     Snails do it differently. They're hermaphrodites, and work in threes.

7

18     Each Female Body contains a female brain. Handy. Makes things work. Stick pins in it and you get amazing results. Old popular songs. Short circuits. Bad dreams.

19     Anyway: each of these brains has two halves. They're joined together by a thick cord; neural pathways flow from one to the other, sparkles of electric information washing to and fro. Like light on waves. Like a conversation. How does a woman know? She listens. She listens in.

20     The male brain, now, that's a different matter. Only a thin connection. Space over here, time over there, music and arithmetic in their own sealed compartments. The right brain doesn't know what the left brain is doing. Good for aiming though, for hitting the target when you pull the trigger. What's the target? Who's the target? Who cares? What matters is hitting it. That's the male brain for you. Objective.

21     This is why men are so sad, why they feel so cut off, why they think of themselves as orphans cast adrift, footloose and stringless in the deep void. What void? she asks. What are you talking about? The void of the universe, he says, and she says Oh and looks out the window and tries to get a handle on it, but it's no use, there's too much going on, too many rustlings in the leaves, too many voices, so she says, Would you like a cheese sandwich, a piece of cake, a cup of tea? And he grinds his teeth because she doesn't understand, and wanders off, not just alone but Alone, lost in the dark, lost in the skull, searching for the other half, the twin who could complete him.

22     Then it comes to him: he's lost the Female Body! Look, it shines in the gloom, far ahead, a vision of wholeness, ripeness, like a giant melon, like an apple, like a metaphor for "breast" in a bad sex novel; it shines like a balloon, like a foggy noon, a watery moon, shimmering in its egg of light.

23     Catch it. Put it in a pumpkin, in a high tower, in a compound, in a chamber, in a house, in a room. Quick, stick a leash on it, a lock, a chain, some pain, settle it down, so it can never get away from you again.

## Questions on Subject and Purpose

1. What appears to be the occasion for Atwood's essay?
2. In what ways might this essay be considered a definition of *female body*?
3. Is it true, as Atwood notes in section 7, that the structure of the brain varies with gender?

## Questions on Strategy and Audience

1. Why might Atwood have chosen to divide the essay as she does?
2. Why doesn't Atwood write transitions to bridge from one section of the essay to another instead of dividing it into sections?
3. The letter from the magazine refers to the topic as "capacious." What does that word mean? In what way does that word suggest the shape and nature of Atwood's response?

## Questions on Vocabulary and Style

1. How would you characterize Atwood's tone in the essay? (See the Glossary and Ready Reference for a definition of *tone*.)
2. In what context might you expect to find section 3 of the essay? What does it sound like?
3. Be prepared to define the words *alderman* (paragraph 2) and *sublimation* (7).

## Writing Suggestions

1. **For Your Journal or Blog.** Suppose you had been invited to write something (an essay, a poem, a story) about either the male or the female body. What would you say? In your journal or blog, jot down some possible ideas for your response.
2. **For a Paragraph.** Select one of the ideas that you came up with in your journal or blog writing, and expand that into a developed paragraph. Remember to use example—either a variety of different ones or a single, extended one—to develop your definition.
3. **For an Essay.** In section 5, Atwood makes numerous references to the ways in which the female body has been used to sell products. Similarly, advertisers today also use male bodies. Judging just from the images of women or of men presented in advertisements, write an essay about how the female or male body is defined in our culture.
4. **For Research.** How have society's definitions of *masculinity* and *femininity* changed over time? Choose one of the two terms and research its shifting definitions over the past two hundred years. What did society expect of a man or a women in 1800? In 1900? In the early 2000s? What is considered masculine or feminine? Remember, no single reference source will provide you with the answers. You may need to infer the definitions from the roles that society forced on men and women and the images that represented those roles. Be sure to acknowledge your sources wherever appropriate.

## For Further Study

**Focusing on Grammar and Writing.** The first three paragraphs in Atwood's essay contain quite a few sentence fragments. How many can you find? What makes each a fragment? Try adding words to each fragment to make it into a sentence. What is gained or lost in the process? Can a sentence fragment be effective? Under what circumstances?

**Working Together.** Divide into seven small groups. Each group should take one of the numbered sections of the essay and (1) determine the focus of that section, (2) speculate on why Atwood might have chosen to include that perspective, and (3) suggest how that section contributes to the effect that the entire essay creates.

**Seeing Other Modes at Work.** In section 7, Atwood contrasts the male brain with the female brain. How is that contrast important to the points that she is trying to make?

**Finding Connections.** Interesting pairings are with Janice Mirikitani's "Recipe" (Chapter 6), Marge Piercy's "Barbie Doll" (Chapter 7), and Jamaica Kincaid's "Girl" (this chapter).

**Exploring the Web.** Atwood maintains an extensive Website: www.owtoad. com. In addition, information about Atwood and her work can be found on dozens of other Websites.

# 9

# ARGUMENT AND PERSUASION

## 🔑 ❓ KEY QUESTIONS

**Getting Ready to Write**

Where do you begin when you want to argue or persuade?

What is the difference between arguing and persuading?

What do you already know about arguing and persuading?

How do you analyze your audience?

What does it take to convince a reader?

**Writing**

How do you connect your thesis and your evidence in an argument?

How do you make sure that your argument is logical?

How do you structure an argument?

**Revising**

How do you revise an argumentative or persuasive essay?

*Understanding and respecting your opposition*
*Being honest and fair*
*Ending forcefully*

*Student Essay*

*Beth Jaffe, "Lowering the Cost of a College Education"*

*Some Things to Remember About Writing Argument and Persuasion*

*Seeing Argument and Persuasion in Other Contexts*

**As a literary strategy**

*Wilfred Owen, "Dulce et Decorum Est"*

**As a critical reading strategy**

*www.teenadvice.about.com, "Top 5 Reasons Youth Should Vote"*

**As a visual strategy**

*World War I recruiting poster*

*Additional Writing Suggestions for Argument and Persuasion*

## GETTING READY TO WRITE

We live in a world of persuasive messages—billboards, advertisements in newspapers and magazines, commercials on television and radio, pop-ups and advertisements on nearly every Website, signs on storefronts, bumper stickers, T-shirts and caps with messages, and manufacturers' logos prominently displayed on clothing. Advertisements demonstrate a wide range of persuasive strategies. Sometimes they appeal to logic and reason—they ask you to compare the features and price of one car with those of any competitor and judge for yourself. More often, though, they appeal to your emotions and feelings: you will not be stylish unless you wear this particular style and brand of shoe; you are not a real man or a sophisticated woman unless you smoke this brand of cigarette; you simply must have the newest cell phone; you have not signaled your success in the world unless you drive this particular foreign-made automobile.

### Where Do You Begin When You Want to Argue or Persuade?

When you want to argue or persuade, you start with a *thesis*—something that you want to convince others of. *Thesis* is derived from a Greek word that means "placing," "position," or "proposition." In How to Write an Essay at the beginning of this text, a thesis was defined as your position on the subject. A thesis lets your reader know exactly where you stand on the subject and what to expect in the essay you have written. Joshua Ortega in "Water Wars: Bottling Up the World's Supply of $H_2O$" writes a clear thesis that covers the first half of his essay:

> Whether in America or less-developed countries, the evidence is as clear as the plastic it's sold in—bottled water, compared to good tap water, is not worth the costs, whether they be environmental, health-related or economic.

Ortega's subject is bottled water, the kind we buy in plastic bottles from vending machines or stores. He makes his position clear, bottled water is not worth the costs. The sentence then goes on, as many thesis sentences do, to specify exactly what those "costs" are—environmental (making and disposing of plastic bottles degrades the environment), health-related (bottled water is not more healthful and pure than tap water), and economic (why pay for something that is a human right?). Ortega's thesis sentence actually forecasts his argument as a whole.

Argument and persuasion always seek to convince an *audience* to do or to believe something. They never simply entertain or inform; rather, they create logical or emotional appeals to achieve an intended goal. The effectiveness of an essay of argument or persuasion lies in whether the reader agrees with the writer's position or performs some type of requested action. The cleverest, most artistic, and amusing advertisement is a failure if it does not "sell" the product. On the other hand, arguments exist because there are at least two sides to the issue. You try to persuade an audience to accept your point of view or to perform or endorse the action that you request by supplying evidence. That evidence, as we will see, can be quite varied. However, no matter how reliable and extensive your evidence, that alone may not get your audience to agree with you. Your goal, then, is to convince them of the validity and reasonableness of your position.

 ## IN THE READINGS, LOOK FOR

|  | Thesis or claim—can you locate the full statement in the text? |
| --- | --- |
| Katherine Porter, "Value of College" | College education is worth its costs. |
| Linda Lee, "Case Against College" | Not everyone needs college. |
| Claudia O'Keefe, "Traveling Salesman" | Move on and find new "synergies." |
| Bruce Raynor, "Workers' Rights" | Workers' rights everywhere must be protected. |
| Fredrik Segerfeldt, "The Private Sector" | Privatization of water resources can help. |
| Joshua Ortega, "Water Wars" | Water resources, like water, should not be for sale. |
| Martin Luther King, Jr., "I Have a Dream" | Do not give up the struggle for human equality. |
| Richard Rodriquez, "None of This" | Affirmative action programs must reach the truly disadvantaged. |

## WHAT IS THE DIFFERENCE BETWEEN ARGUING AND PERSUADING?

Sometimes a distinction is made between argument and persuasion: *argument* seeks to win over an audience by appealing to reason; *persuasion*, on the other hand, works by appealing to an audience's emotions, feelings, prejudices, and beliefs. Rarely, however, do you find one strategy without the other. As a result, the words are generally linked together, as they are in the title of this chapter.

William Junius Wilson appeals to logic when he argues that the "school-to-work transition" is problematic for many young Americans. He cites specific factual evidence to establish the magnitude of the problem:

> The problem of school-to-work transition confronts young people of all ethnic and racial backgrounds, but it is especially serious for black youths. According to a recent report by the U.S. Bureau of Labor Statistics, only 42 percent of black youths who had not enrolled in college had jobs in October after graduating from high school a few months earlier in June, compared with 69 percent of their white counterparts. The figures for black youngsters in

inner-city ghetto neighborhoods are obviously even lower. The inadequate system of school-to-work transition has also contributed significantly to the growing wage gap between those with high school diplomas and those with college training. In the 1950s and 1960s, when school-to-work transition was compatible with the mass production system, the average earnings of college graduates was only about 20 percent higher than those of high school graduates. By 1979, it had increased to 49 percent, and then rapidly grew to 83 percent by 1992.

Thus, the school-to-work transition is a major problem in the United States, and it has reached crisis proportions in the inner-city ghetto.

In the face of such evidence, few readers would dispute the need to attack this problem. Later in this chapter, in the debate about the value of a college education, Katherine Porter cites a body of statistical evidence to support her assertion that graduates of four-year colleges average substantially more income over a working lifetime than graduates of two-year programs or of high school.

As a example of an argument that appeals to readers' emotions, notice how the writer of this editorial from the magazine *The Disability Rag* persuasively argues against the substitution of the phrase "physically challenged" for "physically disabled":

> "Physically challenged" attempts to conceal a crucial fact: that the reason we can't do lots of things is not because we're lazy or because we won't accept a "challenge," but because many things are simply beyond our control—like barriers. Like discrimination. People who favor "physically challenged" are making a statement: Barriers, discrimination, are not problems for us, but challenges. We want those barriers, we almost seem to be saying—because by overcoming them we'll become better persons! Stronger. More courageous. After all, isn't that what challenges are for.
>
> Until you have made it your responsibility to get downtown, and discovered that there are no buses with lifts running on that route, you may not fully comprehend that it isn't a personal "challenge" you are up against, but a system resistant to change.

Similarly, Martin Luther King, Jr., in his famous "I Have a Dream" speech, appeals to his listeners' (and readers') emotions. Despite differences in strategy, the objective in both argument and persuasion is the same: to convince readers to believe or act in a certain way.

---

 **IN THE READINGS, LOOK FOR**

**Source of evidence or data**

| | |
|---|---|
| Katherine Porter, "Value of College" | Where did she find her statistics? |
| Linda Lee, "Case Against College" | How persuasive is her personal example? |
| Claudia O'Keefe, "Traveling Salesman" | Is her father's story relevant? Her own? |
| Bruce Raynor, "Workers' Rights" | Why begin with the Pillowtex example in an essay that uses statistics? |

| Fredrik Segerfeldt, "The Private Sector" | What is the basis of his argument? What type of evidence? |
| Joshua Ortega, "Water Wars" | How persuasive are the many statistics and facts? |
| Martin Luther King, Jr., "I Have a Dream" | On what does King base his optimism about the future? How does that influence you as a reader? |
| Richard Rodriquez, "None of This" | What does his personal experience contribute to his argument? |

People tend to associate argument with reason and factual evidence and to associate persuasion with emotional appeals. Salespeople are persuaders, as are those who use the "soapbox" approach.

## What Do You Already Know About Arguing and Persuading?

Perhaps you have not thought about your extensive experience in constructing arguments and in persuading an audience. Every time you try to convince someone to do or to believe something, you argue and persuade. Consider a hypothetical example. You are concerned about your father's health. He smokes cigarettes, avoids exercise, is overweight, and works long hours in a stressful job. Even though you are worried, he is completely unconcerned and has always resisted the family's efforts to change his ways. Your task is to persuade him to change or modify his lifestyle, and doing so involves making the dangers clear, offering convincing reasons for change, and urging specific action.

Establishing the dangers is the first step, and you have a wide range of medical evidence from which to draw. That evidence involves statistics, testimony or advice from doctors, and case histories of men who have suffered the consequences of years of abusing or ignoring their health. From that body of material, you select the items that are most likely to get through to your obstinate father. He might not be moved by cold statistics citing life-expectancy tables for smokers and nonexercisers, but he might be touched by the story of a friend his age who suffered a heart attack or stroke. The evidence you gather and use becomes a part of the convincing reasons for change that you offer in your argument. If your father persists in ignoring his health, he is likely to suffer some consequences. You might, at this point, include emotional appeals in your strategy. If he is not concerned about what will happen to him, what about his family? What will they do if he dies?

We will assume you got your father to realize and acknowledge the dangers inherent in his lifestyle and to understand the reasons why he should make changes. What remains is to urge specific action. In framing a plan for that action, consider your audience. If you urge your father to stop smoking immediately, join a daily exercise class, go on a thousand-calorie-a-day diet, and find a new job, chances are that he will think your proposal too drastic even to try. Instead, you might urge a moderate plan, one that phases in changes over a period of time and offers compromises.

## How Do You Analyze Your Audience?

An essay of argument and persuasion, unlike any other type of writing described in this text, has a special purpose—to persuade its audience. Because you want your reader to agree with your position or act as you urge, you need to analyze your audience carefully before you start to write. Try to answer each of the following questions:

- Who are my readers?
- What do they already know about this subject?
- How interested are they likely to be?
- How impartial or prejudiced are they going to be?
- Is my subject one that strongly challenges their lifestyle or their ethical or moral beliefs and values?
- What values do my readers share with me?
- What types of evidence are most likely to be effective with them?
- Is my plan for requested agreement or action reasonable?

Your argumentative strategy should always reflect an awareness of your audience. Look again at the hypothetical case of the unhealthy father.

It is obvious that some types of evidence would be more effective than others and that some solutions or plans for action would be more reasonable and therefore more acceptable than others.

Another important consideration in any argument is to anticipate your audience's objections and be ready to answer them. Debaters study both sides of an argument so that they can effectively counter any opposition. In arguing about abortion, for example, the right-to-life advocate has to be prepared to deal with subjects such as abnormal fetuses or pregnancies that resulted from rape or incest. The pro-choice advocate must face questions about when life begins and when the rights of the unborn might take precedence over the mother's rights.

 **IN THE READINGS, LOOK FOR**

| | Assumption about audience |
|---|---|
| Katherine Porter, "Value of College" | Aimed at parents? Children? Educators? |
| Linda Lee, "Case Against College" | Aimed at parents or children? |
| Claudia O'Keefe, "Traveling Salesman" | What does place of publication suggest about audience? |
| Bruce Raynor, "Workers' Rights" | Business or labor audience? |
| Fredrik Segerfeldt, "The Private Sector" | Who reads financial magazines and newspapers? |
| Joshua Ortega, "Water Wars" | Who would a union president address? |
| Martin Luther King, Jr., "I Have a Dream" | Originally a speech—where and before whom? |
| Richard Rodriquez, "None of This" | What does author's background suggest about his sense of audience? |

## What Does It Take to Convince a Reader?

In some cases, nothing will persuade your reader. For example, if you are arguing for legalized abortion, you will never convince a reader who believes that an embryo is a human being from the moment of conception. Abortion to that reader will always be murder. It is extremely difficult to argue any position that is counter to your audience's moral or ethical values. You will also find it difficult to argue a position that is counter to your audience's normal patterns of behavior. For example, you could reasonably argue that your readers ought to stop at all stop signs and obey the speed limit. However, the likelihood of persuading your audience to always do these two things—even though not doing so means breaking the law—is slim.

These cautions are not meant to imply that you should only argue "safe" subjects or that winning is everything. Choose a subject about which you feel strongly; present a fair, logical argument; express honest emotion; but avoid distorted evidence or inflammatory language. Even if no one is finally persuaded, at least you have offered a clear, intelligent explanation of your position.

In most arguments, you have two possible types of support: you can supply factual evidence, and you can appeal to your reader's values, assumptions, and beliefs. Suppose you are arguing that professional boxing should be banned because it is dangerous. Your readers may or may not accept your premise, but they would expect you to support your assertion. Your first task would be to gather evidence. The strongest evidence is factual—statistics dealing with the number of fighters each year who are fatally injured or mentally impaired. You might quote appropriate authorities—physicians, scientists, former boxers—on the risks connected with professional boxing. You might relate several instances of boxing injuries or even a single example of a particular fighter who was killed or permanently injured while boxing. You might describe in detail how blows affect the human body or brain; you might trace the process by which a series of punches can inflict permanent brain damage. You might catalog the effects that years of physical punishment can produce in the human body. In your argument, you might use some or all of this factual evidence. Your job as a writer is to gather the most accurate and most effective evidence and present it in a clear and orderly way.

You can also appeal to your reader's emotions and values. You could argue that a sport in which a participant can be killed or permanently injured is not a sport at all. You could argue that the object of a boxing match—to render one's opponent unconscious or too impaired to continue—is different in kind from any other sport and not one that we, as human beings, should condone, let alone encourage. Appeals to values can be extremely effective.

Effective argumentation generally involves appealing to both reason and emotion. It is often easier, however, to catch your reader's attention through an emotional appeal. Demonstrators against vivisection, the dissecting of animals for laboratory research, display photographs of the torments suffered by these animals. Organizations that fight famine throughout the world show photographs of starving children. Advertisers use a wide range of persuasive tactics to touch our fears, our anxieties, our desires. But the type of argumentative writing that you are asked to do in college or in your job rarely allows for only emotional evidence.

One more factor is crucially important in persuading readers. You must sound (and be) fair, reasonable, and credible to win the respect and approval of your readers. Readers distrust arguments that use unfair or inflammatory language, faulty logic, and biased or distorted evidence.

## PREWRITING TIPS FOR WRITING ARGUMENT AND PERSUASION

1. Consider your choice of subject carefully in light of the proposed length of the paper. How complex is the topic? Can you realistically do justice to it with the space available? Or should you impose some restrictions on the topic? Remember, you are taking a stand or a position on the topic; you are arguing in support of that position.

2. Analyze the audience to whom you are writing. What assumptions or ideas do they already have about this subject? Does the subject involve deeply held beliefs, either moral or ethical? For example, it is easier to persuade an audience to register to vote than it is to persuade an audience to support physician-assisted suicide.

3. Be sure to anticipate what your opponents are likely to feel and think about the subject—regardless of how "right" you think your position is. Make a list of possible objections or counters to each point you are making. The quality of an argument is always improved when you thoroughly understand both sides of the issue.

4. Remember that in college-level writing, you need specific, accurate information to argue convincingly. Facts, statistics, and quotations from authorities carry weight with your readers. Most arguments in college writing need more than unsubstantiated personal opinions.

5. Write a specific statement of the action or reaction that you want to elicit from your audience. As you write and revise, refer to that statement as a way of checking your developing argument.

## WRITING

### How Do You Connect Your Thesis and Your Evidence in an Argument?

Stephen Toulmin, a British philosopher, developed a simplified model for argument in the 1950s that is widely used in speech and communication, as well as in writing. Toulmin's model of an argument consists of three essential parts that could be visually displayed in the following way:

The **claim**
(the thesis)

The **data**
(the evidence or
support for the claim or thesis)

*connected by*

The **warrant**
(the assumptions, values, and common beliefs that connect the claim/thesis
and the data/evidence)

It is relatively easy to recognize claims or theses, because they are explicitly stated in a thesis statement. Similarly, identification of data or evidence poses no difficulty, as data are explicitly provided. The warrants, on the other hand, are more puzzling, especially because they are often not explicitly stated in the written or oral argument. In addition, any argument might have more than one unwritten or unspoken warrant, and a writer and readers might have different warrants! Essays of argument are not commonly constructed around the Toulmin model (unless a teacher asks that an essay be divided into claim, data, and warrant). Rather, the Toulmin model is used for analysis—in preparing an argument and in reading an argument.

What then is the value of warrants, if they are unspoken, unwritten, and variable? It is important for you as a writer to realize what you are basing your argument on, just as it is important for your audience to understand the link you are making between your thesis and your evidence. When you and your audience share warrants, you are more likely to be convincing to your readers. The warrants serve as a common ground for agreement. Consider an example from a presidential election:

| Claim: | Candidate A is not fit to be President because he is not patriotic. |
| Data: | Candidate A did not serve in the military. |
| | Candidate A refuses to wear a flag pin in his lapel. |
| Possible warrants: | Patriots would wear flag pins. |
| | Anyone who would not wear a flag pin is unpatriotic. |
| | Military service is the only way in which to demonstrate patriotism. |

Why is Toulmin's model important when writing and reading arguments? Because it asks you to consciously identify how the claim and evidence are connected.

## Practice: Identifying Claims and Warrants

The boxed In the Readings exercises in this chapter ask you to locate and examine the claim (thesis) and data (evidence) for each of the essays in the chapter. See if you can identify the warrants that are used or implied in each case to link the claim to the data. Remember, each essay is likely to have more than one warrant, and the warrants are not usually explicitly stated.

*Possible warrants*

Katherine Porter, "Value of College"
Linda Lee, "Case Against College"
Claudia O'Keefe, "Traveling Salesman"
Bruce Raynor, "Workers' Rights"
Fredrik Segerfeldt, "The Private Sector"

Joshua Ortega, "Water Wars"
Martin Luther King, Jr., "I Have a Dream"
Richard Rodriquez, "None of This"

## How Do You Make Sure that Your Argument Is Logical?

Logic, or reason, is crucial to an effective argument. Try to avoid logical fallacies or errors. When you construct your argument, make sure that you avoid the following common mistakes:

- **Ad hominem argument** (literally, to argue "to the person"): criticizing a person's position by criticizing his or her personal character. If an underworld figure asserts that boxing is the manly art of self-defense, you do not counter his argument by claiming that he makes money by betting on the fights.

- **Ad populum argument** (literally, to argue "to the people"): appealing to the prejudices of your audience instead of offering facts or reasons. You do not defend boxing by asserting that it is part of the American way of life and that anyone who criticizes it is a communist who seeks to undermine our society.

- **Appeal to an unqualified authority:** using testimony from someone who is unqualified to give it. In arguing against boxing, your relevant authorities would be physicians or scientists or former boxers—people who have had some direct experience. You do not quote a professional football player or your dermatologist.

- **Begging the question:** assuming the truth of whatever you are trying to prove. "Boxing is dangerous, and because it is dangerous, it ought to be outlawed." The first statement ("boxing is dangerous") is the premise you set out to prove, but the second statement uses that unproved premise as a basis for drawing a conclusion.

- **Either-or:** stating or implying that there are only two possibilities. Do not assert that the two choices are either to ban boxing or to allow this brutality to continue. Perhaps other changes might make the sport safer and hence less objectionable.

- **Faulty analogy:** using an inappropriate or superficially similar analogy as evidence. "Allowing a fighter to kill another man with his fists is like giving him a gun and permission to shoot to kill." The analogy might be vivid, but the two acts are much more different than they are similar.

- **Hasty generalization:** basing a conclusion on evidence that is atypical or unrepresentative. Do not assert that every boxer has suffered brain damage just because you can cite a few well-known cases.

- **Non sequitur** (literally, "it does not follow"): arriving at a conclusion not justified by the premises or evidence. "My father has watched many fights on television; therefore, he is an authority on the physical hazards that boxers face."

- **Oversimplification:** suggesting a simple solution to a complex problem. "If professional boxers were made aware of the risks they take, they would stop boxing."

## How Do You Structure an Argument?

If you are constructing an argument based on a formal, logical progression, you can use either *inductive* or *deductive* reasoning. An *inductive argument* begins with specific evidence and moves to a generalized conclusion that accounts for the evidence. The writer assumes the role of detective, piecing together the evidence in an investigation and only then arriving at a conclusion. An inductive structure is often effective because it can arouse the reader's interest, or even anger, by focusing on examples. If your thesis is likely to be rejected immediately by some readers, an inductive strategy can be effective, because it hides the thesis until the readers are involved in your argument. Jonathan Swift's narrator in his satire "A Modest Proposal" (Chapter 10) begins his essay by pointing to a conspicuous social problem in Ireland: the large number of poor, starving children. Swift's contemporary readers would have likely agreed with his observation: "Whoever could find a fair, cheap, and easy method of making these children, sound, useful members of the commonwealth would deserve so well of the public as to have his statue set up for a preserver of the nation."

Having established the magnitude of the problem and his own disinterested situation (he himself has no young children), Swift delays his outrageous solution until nearly halfway through the essay: a portion of the children should be sold for food! The inductive pattern allows Swift to draw his readers into the essay, winning their initial agreement to the magnitude of the problem and the reasons for it. Had he announced his proposed "solution" first, no one would have bothered to read the essay.

In contrast to an inductive argument, a *deductive argument* starts with a general truth or assumption and moves to provide evidence or support. Here the detective announces who the murderer is and then proceeds to show us how she arrived at that conclusion. Linda Lee in "The Case Against College" signals her thesis even in her title. Two paragraphs into the essay, Lee makes her argumentative, and provocative, assertion: "Not everyone needs a higher education." In the rest of her essay, Lee provides the support that leads to her conclusion, drawing from statistics and from her own experience with her son. A deductive argument immediately announces its thesis, so it runs the risk of instantly alienating a reader, especially if it is arguing for something about which many readers might disagree.

The simplest form of a deductive argument is the *syllogism*, a three-step argument involving a major premise, a minor premise, and a conclusion. Few essays—either those you write or those you read—can be reduced to a syllogism. Our thought patterns are rarely so logical; our reasoning rarely so precise. Although few essays state a syllogism explicitly, syllogisms do play a role in shaping an argument. For example, a number of essays in this textbook begin with the same syllogism, even though it is not directly stated:

| **Major premise:** | All people should have equal opportunities. |
|---|---|
| **Minor premise:** | Minorities are people. |
| **Conclusion:** | Minorities should have equal opportunities. |

Despite the fact that a syllogism is a precise structural form, do not assume that a written argument will imitate it—that the first paragraph or group of paragraphs will contain a major premise; the next, a minor premise; and the final, a conclusion. Syllogisms can be basic to an argument without being the framework on which it is constructed in the same way that arguments have warrants even though the warrants are not explicitly stated.

No matter how you structure your argument, one final consideration is important: end your paper decisively. The purpose of argument and persuasion is to get a reader to agree with your position or to act in a particular way. Effective endings or conclusions can take a variety of forms. You might end with a call to action. For example, Martin Luther King's speech "I Have a Dream" rises to an eloquent, rhythmical exhortation to his audience to continue to fight until they are "free at last."

You might end with a thought-provoking question or image. In "None of This Is Fair" Richard Rodriguez, aware of the poor and the silent who are generally bypassed by opportunity despite affirmative action programs, ends his essay with an arresting image: "They are distant, faraway figures like the boys I have seen peering down from freeway overpasses in some other part of town."

If you use personal experience as evidence in your argument or inject yourself into the argument in some way, you might end as Linda Lee does in "The Case Against College." Throughout the essay, Lee has used her son as an example of a child not ready for college. After two years in college and two years of working, her son has found a job that he loves. Now, four years later, he has had, she notes, "his own graduation day . . . and he did it, for the most part, in spite of college." Claudia O'Keefe frames her essay by beginning and ending with her experience at a flea market in West Virginia. Another option is to end your essay by asserting or repeating the thesis for which you have been arguing. The final sentences of Bruce Raynor's "Protect Workers' Rights" make explicit—for the first time—his argument in the essay: "we need rules for the global economy that protect workers' rights." Finally, Peter Singer, who in "The Singer Solution to World Poverty" (Chapter 10) has made us increasingly uncomfortable by pointing out our moral obligation to sacrifice to help the needy children of the world, reminds us one final time that we are in the same situation as the fictional Bob, who could save a child's life by sacrificing his savings.

**DRAFTING TIPS FOR WRITING ARGUMENT AND PERSUASION**

1.  Look carefully at how you have structured your essay. Did you begin with a position and then provide evidence (deductive order), or did you begin with specific examples and then draw your conclusion (inductive order)? Why did you choose the order that you did? Consider the other order.

2.  Rate the points that you are making in terms of their effectiveness or power. Within that inductive or deductive pattern, have you placed your strongest points first or last? Are the points arranged in an effective way? Consider other possible arrangements.

3.  Use a color highlighter to mark all the specific evidence you have included in the essay. Remember, details—accurate, factual, logical— are vital to making an argument effective. Have you included enough? Do the details meet the tests of accuracy? Remember that each body paragraph needs specifics, not just generalizations or unsubstantiated opinions.

4.  Use a color highlighter to mark all of the emotionally charged words and phrases in your essay. Remember, you are not selling a product or writing a negative "attack ad" for a political campaign! Think about how your audience will react to those charged words and phrases. Avoid distorted or inflammatory language.

5.  Document all information and quotations taken from sources. Not to do so is to plagiarize. Morever, the documentation allows your readers to evaluate the types of sources or informants you have used. You can find more advice on plagiarism and documentation in Chapter 11: The Research Paper.

## REVISING

### How Do You Revise an Argumentative or Persuasive Essay?

Argument and persuasion are particularly reader oriented. That is, the goal of argument and persuasion is not simply to inform or to entertain readers; rather, the goal is to convince readers to commit to a certain course of action or to agree with (or at the very least to understand) the writer's stand on the issue or subject. Argument presumes that there is at least one other side, that disagreement already exists about the subject. Persuasion suggests that readers can be brought into agreement with the writer's position.

Readers typically approach argument and persuasion with some pre-formed opinions; they are not generally completely neutral about the subject. In some cases, readers will not actively resist a point of view, even if they will not commit to the desired course of action. For example, surely few people in the United States believe that smoking tobacco is healthy. Those who smoke might not disagree with an essay meant to persuade smokers to stop, but that does not mean they will stop. Habit and addiction can be far stronger than logical argument or emotional appeal. On subjects that touch on deeply held religious or ethical beliefs, many readers will never be persuaded to accept an argument that runs counter to those beliefs. If your readers believe in intelligent design, they will never accept your argument that evolution is the only answer to the origins of human life.

Because argument and persuasion seek to engage an audience in particular ways, it is especially important to involve readers in the revising stage of your essay. Aim to enlist a minimum of several readers, ideally readers who do not agree with you or who will not agree just to please or get rid of you. Ask them to react to your argument. Do they agree with you? Why or why not? Is this a subject about which they could be open-minded? What is your strongest argument? What is your weakest? What might it take to convince them that even if you are not right, you have articulated a position that they can understand and respect?

When writing an argumentative or persuasive essay, pay particular attention to the following areas: understanding and respecting your opposition, being honest and fair, and ending forcefully.

**Understanding and Respecting your Opposition**    In planning, writing, and revising argument and persuasion, you need to be aware of the other sides that can exist to your argument. Debaters prepare by being able to argue either side of an issue; lawyers in a courtroom have to anticipate and be ready to counter arguments made by their adversaries. As you write and revise, you must decide which points you have to concede and which points can be refuted. Fredrik Segerfeldt in "The Private Sector Can Get Water Flowing to the Poor" concedes that the privatization of water resources has had problems in the past that have resulted in "strong feelings" and even "violent protests." "Many privatizations," he writes, "have been troublesome." He attributes the problems, however, to "regulatory bodies . . . that were non-existent, incompetent or too weak," "contracts [that were] badly designed," and "sloppy" bidding processes. These problems, he concludes, "do not make strong arguments against privatizations as such, but against bad privatizations." Segerfeldt acknowledges problems. He must, or his opposition will accuse him of misrepresenting the evidence. On the other hand, he uses the concession to explain where he thinks privizations have gone wrong in the past. Anytime you are arguing, remember to anticipate the objections and counterarguments of those who will disagree with you.

**Being Honest and Fair**    Everyday of your life you are surrounded by attempts at persuasion and argument. Little children throw temper tantrums because they are not getting what they want; a television political advertisement denounces the untrustworthiness and seemingly criminal behavior of the opposition; a print commercial implies that the "good" life lies in owning this particular car or watch or drinking this expensive brand of vodka; a salesperson and the manager try to close the deal by pressuring you. In much of such argument and persuasion the goal is winning—winning by any means, no matter how unscrupulous, deceitful, or biased. That is never the goal of argumentative or persuasive writing in college. As you review your draft, look again at the nature of the evidence you are presenting and the language that you have used. Is the information accurate and fair? Is your language free from inflammatory words and phrases?

**Ending Forcefully**    Conclusions to essays of argument and persuasion are especially important. Your conclusions complete the stand or position that you have been advocating, and they are what remains in your readers' mind. If you are urging readers to commit to a particular course of action (for example, to register and then vote), you need to end with a specific request or call to action. If you are trying to get readers to agree with your position, you need to remind them again of what that position is and why they should agree with you.

---

### 🔍 IN THE READINGS, LOOK FOR

|  | **Conclusion** |
|---|---|
| Katherine Porter, "Value of College" | How does Porter end and why? |
| Linda Lee, "The Case Against" | How does the essay end and why at that particular place? |
| Claudia O'Keefe, "Traveling Salesman" | Why does the essay begin and end in the West Virginia flea market? |
| Bruce Raynor, "Workers' Rights" | What strategy does Raynor use in his conclusion? |
| Fredrik Segerfeldt, "The Private Sector" | What is the call to action here? |
| Joshua Ortega, "Water Wars" | What is the call to action here? |
| Martin Luther King, Jr., "I Have a Dream" | How does King end his speech and why is this an appropriate strategy for this message and situation? |
| Richard Rodriquez, "None of This" | Why end with an image? Is it effective? |

## REVISING TIPS FOR WRITING ARGUMENT AND PERSUASION

1.  Find several classmates or peers to read your draft—this is vitally important in writing argument and persuasion. Ask your readers to evaluate honestly your position in the paper. Do they agree with you? Why or why not? If they disagree, what are their reasons? Can you address those reasons?

2.  Look back to your list of counterarguments—arguments those who disagree with you might use in reply. Have you anticipated objections? Have you conceded what cannot be disputed? Your essay must acknowledge and confront the position of your opposition.

3.  Check the list of logical fallacies or errors in this chapter. Have you avoided each of these in your essay?

4.  Have you provided a clear organizational pattern? Outline your essay. Does it make sense? Are you following an inductive or deductive order? Have you arranged your points in an effective order? Have you clearly signaled your transitions from one point to another?

5.  Remember, conclusions are especially important in argument and persuasion. Look at what you have written. What do you want your readers to do at the end of your essay? Are you urging a course of action? Are you just trying to change the way in which they understand the issue?

## STUDENT ESSAY

Beth Jaffe decided to tackle a subject on the minds of many career-minded, dollar-conscious college students: why do you have to take so many courses outside of your major? Beth's argument is sure to arouse the attention of every advocate of a liberal arts education, and you might consider exploring the subject in an argument of your own.

### First Draft

Reducing College Requirements

With the high costs of college still on the rise, it is not fair to make college students pay for courses labeled "requirements" which are not part of their major. Although many students want a well-rounded college education, many cannot afford to pay for one. By eliminating all of the requirements that do not pertain to a student's major, college costs could be cut tremendously. At the University of Delaware, for example, a student in the College of Arts and Science is required to take twelve credits of arts and humanities, twelve of culture and institutions of time, twelve of human beings and their environment, and thirteen of natural phenomena or science which include at least one lab. Although some of their major courses may fit into these categories, many others do not. Frequently students do not like and are not interested in the courses which fit into the four categories and feel they are wasting their money by paying for courses they do not enjoy, do not put much work into, and usually do not get much out of. It should be an option to the student to take these extra courses. Why should a humanities or social studies major have to take biology or chemistry? Many of these students thought their struggle with science was over after high school only to come to college and find yet more "requirements" in the sciences. Students are getting degrees in one area of concentration. They should be able to take only courses in their field of study and not have to waste their money on courses they have no desire to take.

## Comments

Beth's essay, with her permission, was duplicated and discussed in class. Not surprisingly, it provoked a lively reaction. One student asked Beth whether she was serious and exactly what it was that she was proposing. Beth admitted that she did not advocate turning a college education into career training but that she had a number of friends who were deeply in debt because of their four-year education. "Why not just cut some requirements?" Beth asked. Several other students then suggested that since she did not really advocate an extreme position, maybe she could find a compromise proposal. Her instructor added that she might find a way of rewording her remarks about science classes. Few people, after all, are sympathetic to a position that seems to say, "I don't want to do that. It's too hard. It's too boring."

When Beth revised her paper, she tried to follow the advice the class had offered. In addition, she made the problem vivid by using her roommate as an example and by pointing out what specifically might be saved by her proposal.

## Revised Draft

### Lowering the Cost of a College Education

When my roommate graduates in June, she will be $20,000 in debt. The debt did not come from spring breaks in Fort Lauderdale or a new car. It came from four years of college expenses, expenses that were not covered by the money she earned as a part-time waitress or by the small scholarship she was awarded annually. So now in June at age 21, with her first full-time job (assuming she gets one), Alison can start repaying her student loans.

Alison's case is certainly not unusual. In fact, because she attends a state-assisted university, her debt is less than it might be. We cannot expect education to get cheaper. We cannot expect government scholarship programs to get larger. We cannot ask that students go deeper and deeper into debt. We need a new way of combating this cost problem. We need the Jaffe proposal.

If colleges would eliminate some of the general education course requirements, college costs could be substantially lowered. At the University of Delaware, for example, a student at the College of Arts and Science is required to take twelve credits of arts and humanities, twelve of culture and the institutions of time, twelve of human beings and their environment, and thirteen of natural phenomena or science, including at least one laboratory course. Approximately half of these requirements are fulfilled by courses which are required for particular majors. The others are not, and these are likely to be courses that students are not interested in and so get little out of.

If some of these requirements were eliminated, a student would need approximately twenty-five fewer credits for a bachelor's degree. A student who took a heavier load or went to summer school could graduate either one or two semesters earlier. The result would cut college costs by anywhere from one-eighth to one-fourth.

The Jaffe proposal does decrease the likelihood that a college graduate will receive a well-rounded education. On the other hand, it allows students to concentrate their efforts in courses which they feel are relevant. Perhaps most important, it helps reduce the burden that escalating college costs have placed on all of us.

## SOME THINGS TO REMEMBER WHEN WRITING ARGUMENT AND PERSUASION

1. Choose a subject that allows for the possibility of persuading your reader. Avoid emotionally charged subjects that resist logical examination.
2. Analyze your audience. Who are your readers? What do they already know about your subject? How are they likely to feel about it? How impartial or prejudiced are they going to be?

3. Make a list of the evidence or reasons you will use in your argument. Analyze each piece of evidence to see how effective it might be in achieving your end.

4. Honest emotion is fair, but avoid anything that is distorted, inaccurate, or inflammatory. Argue with solid, reasonable, fair, and relevant evidence.

5. Avoid the common logical fallacies listed in this chapter.

6. Make a list of all the possible counterarguments or objections your audience might have. Think of ways in which you can respond to those objections.

7. Decide how to structure your essay. You can begin with a position and then provide evidence, or you can begin with the evidence and end with a conclusion. Which structure seems to fit your subject and evidence better?

8. End forcefully. Conclusions are what listeners and readers are most likely to remember. Repeat or restate your position. Drive home the importance of your argument.

## SEEING ARGUMENT AND PERSUASION IN OTHER CONTEXTS

### As a Literary Strategy

British poet Wilfred Owen served as a British soldier during World War I. The human death toll in World War I was over 8.5 million soldiers; on a single day, the British lost more than 57,000 soldiers. The third leading cause of death was poison gas, used by both sides during the war. Owen's title is taken from the Latin quotation from Horace, cited at the end of the poem, which translates "It is sweet and fitting to die for one's country." As you read the poem, think about whether Owen agreed with Horace.

# DULCE ET DECORUM EST

Wilfred Owen

*Bent double, like old beggars under sacks,*
*Knock-kneed, coughing like hags, we cursed through sludge,*
*Till on the haunting flares we turned our backs,*
*And towards our distant rest began to trudge.*

*Men marched asleep. Many had lost their boots,*
*But limped on, blood-shod. All went lame, all blind;*
*Drunk with fatigue; deaf even to the hoots*
*Of gas-shells dropping slowly behind.*

*Gas! GAS! Quick, boys! An ecstasy of fumbling,*
*Fitting the clumsy helmets just in time,*
*But someone still was yelling out and stumbling*
*And flound'ring like a man in fire or lime.—*
*Dim through the misty panes and thick green light,*
*As under a green sea, I saw him drowning.*

*If in some smothering dreams, you too could pace*
*Behind the wagon that we flung him in,*
*And watch the white eyes writhing in his face,*
*His hanging face, like a devil's sick of sin,*
*If you could hear, at every jolt, the blood*
*Come gargling from the froth-corrupted lungs*
*Bitter as the cud*
*Obscene as cancer,*
*Of vile, incurable sores on innocent tongues.—*
*My friend, you would not tell with such zest*
*To children ardent for some desperate glory,*
*The old lie:* Dulce et decorum est
                    Pro patria mori.

## Discussion Questions

1. How does Owen feel about war? How does he reveal his feelings in the poem?
2. Does the poem depend more on logical argument or on emotional persuasion? How is that strategy effective here?
3. Is describing the death of a single soldier an effective strategy? Why might Owen choose to focus on just one example and not on many? Would more examples make the poem more effective?
4. Do you think that Owen was being unpatriotic in writing this poem? Why or why not?

5. What purpose might Owen have had in writing the poem? Who might he have been trying to persuade? What might he have wanted his reader to see, feel, or understand?

## Writing Suggestions

Living as we do in a world full of advertisements, we are surrounded by persuasion—buy this, do this. Choose a social or moral issue about which you have strong feelings, and then using a single extended example persuade your audience to agree with you and/or to do something. Some possibilities might be:

   **a.** The plight of the homeless in the United States

   **b.** Dangers of addiction or at-risk behavior

   **c.** Cloning or genetic engineering

## AS A CRITICAL READING STRATEGY

The effectiveness of argument or persuasion can be measured by its success in convincing readers or bringing them to action. In our daily world, that success typically means did consumers buy the product or did they vote for the candidate or the issue you were promoting. In college writing, however, the goal is not always action but often understanding. Effective argument and persuasion is founded on evidence, on logic and reason, on the integrity and commitment of the writer. In effective college writing, the end does not justify the means.

Read the following selection from a larger article that appears at www.teenadvice.about.com, a Website devoted to "teen advice." The essay urges youth to register and vote in elections, offering five reasons why they should.

As you read, remember what you have learned about how to write an argumentative and persuasive essay and how that knowledge might help you as a reader:

- Essays of argument and persuasion always have a specific goal, typically to get readers to commit to a course of action (here, to register and vote) or to understand more fully (and hopefully to agree with) the writer's position.

- Because they are goal-driven, essays of argument and persuasion involve a thorough understanding of what the audience already knows and feels about the subject. If your position on the subject runs counter to the audience's deeply held beliefs (moral, religious, ethical), your argument is not likely to convince any reader. You can, however, at least make your position known.

- Argument and persuasion must take into consideration objections or counterarguments that the other side would offer. You cannot ignore the opposition. Your essay must concede certain points; it must refute others.

- Argumentative and persuasive essays in college writing require convincing reasons and evidence. Typically, you need to support your position with facts or quotations or logical reasoning. This is especially true if positions on the subject are debatable.
- Arguments are clearly and logically organized in one of two patterns: in a deductive pattern the position or stand is stated first and the reasons or evidence follows; in an inductive pattern evidence comes first and the position or stand follows.
- Argument and persuasion in college writing should not resort to inflammatory, emotional, or biased language or evidence. The goal is never to win at all costs.

Title states the position

## Top 5 Reasons Youth Should Vote

Writer can assume a teen audience given the Website

You live in a democracy and that means that you get a say in who runs your country, and by way of this privilege you also get a say about how your country is run. It is very easy to be blasé about your right to vote and take a

Concedes reasons why young people might not vote—takes some time and energy

"whatever, who cares" kind of attitude about it but you shouldn't brush this great honor off so quickly. Sure, registering can be a bit of a chore, and yes, you have to head down to a polling station on voting day to pull your lever, which takes some time out of your day and may cost

Conversational, appealing to audience

you a few bucks in gas, but whether you know it or not these are very small prices to pay for the right to vote. In some countries people are literally dying to be able to cast a ballot and

Argument consists of five reasons

make a difference. Here, we list <u>five very good reasons that every eligible young person should get out and vote</u>.

First reason

<u>The youth vote is sadly underestimated by party analysts</u>. Yes, it is true, the trend analysts who tell party spindoctors where to target their advertising dollars and public relations efforts

Statistics not provided since readers are not not likely to doubt

traditionally overlook the youth market. Why? Because the sad reality is that election year after election year the percentage of eligible youth who actually register and vote is small when compared with other demographics. This doesn't mean the youth market isn't a force, just that it isn't a main motivator in the drafting of campaign platforms and pre-election advertising. So, like any self-respecting rebellious young person, the natural thing to do is <u>go against the grain and do the unexpected</u>. Keep them on their toes, shock them into the 21st century and get out and vote!

Appeal to a motivation for teens

## AS A VISUAL STRATEGY

You are surrounded each day by hundreds of examples of visual argumentation and persuasion—advertisements. Sometimes advertisements appeal to reason, citing specific facts, figures, and statistics to buttress their claims.

Other times, advertisements issue subtle, persuasive appeals: if you wear this cologne or perfume, you would be irresistible; if you drove this automobile, you would be a hardy adventurer or an important professional. You might like to think that you see "through" these claims of advertisers, that you are not susceptible to their appeals. The truth, however, is that you do respond—we all do—to these visual appeals, otherwise, companies would stop advertising their goods and services.

Visuals are also used to persuade people to commit to a certain course of action or to believe in or support a particular cause. Bumper stickers, posters, and placards announce political and social agendas. In times of national conflict, posters and advertisements enlist support and participation. Consider this famous U.S. Army poster on the previous page created by artist James Montgomery Flagg during World War I and later revived during World War II.

## WRITING ABOUT IMAGES

1. Over four million copies of this poster were printed during World War I, and countless Americans found its appeal persuasive. Study the poster and then respond to one of the following topics:

   a. What is persuasive about this image? To what does it appeal? To what extent might its message have appealed to both young and old, women and men? In an essay, analyze the way or ways in which the image could be seen as persuasive at the time.

   b. How do the armed services promote enlistment in the twenty-first century? Is a static image, such as a poster or photograph, enough? Or must it be a video complete with sound? Look for advertisements that appeal to young men and women. Select one or more and in an essay analyze its persuasive elements and their potential effectiveness. Make a copy of the advertisement to hand in with your essay.

2. Select a magazine advertisement that is promoting a product for people of your age and gender. What strategies are used in the advertisement to "sell" the product? Buying or using this product implies what? If there are people in the advertisement, what do they look like and what are they doing? What is the implication for you as a possible customer? Analyze the image, explaining how and why it appeals to you or to those who are your age and gender. Include a copy of the advertisement when you hand in your essay.

3. Find two advertisements that represent contradictory positions on the same issue. The possibilities are likely to include "charged" issues such as legalized gambling, gun control, political campaigns, conflicts between personal freedoms and governmental (state or federal) regulation. Make copies of both advertisements for your instructor. In an essay, analyze how each side uses argument and persuasion to advance its position.

# ADDITIONAL WRITING SUGGESTIONS FOR ARGUMENT AND PERSUASION

Essays of argument and persuasion are directed to an audience; they attempt to get that audience to do something—follow a certain course of action, buy a specific object or service, agree with a particular viewpoint. Although the terms are often used interchangeably and any clear distinction between the two is often blurred, argument usually means drawing on evidence (facts, statistics, expert testimony, evidence) and persuasion means engaging or even manipulating emotions. Most issues can and are argued from more than one point of view, because the strongest, clearest evidence does not always persuade and strong emotional appeals often eclipse rational argument. The following list presents topics with suggestions about how they might be approached in an essay. Also listed are topics that could be expanded into an essay. Remember, argument does not embrace only extreme positions on an issue; often it involves acknowledging limits or facts and suggesting a compromise.

## POSSIBLE TOPICS EXPANDED

1. Youth and alcohol
   a. The legal age for drinking ought be lower in the United States as it is in many European countries.
   b. Given the problems with alcohol-related violence and crime, the legal drinking age ought to be strictly enforced in the United States/this state/this community/this campus.
   c. Companies should not be allowed to produce advertisements that portray drinking as "the thing" to do in social situations and that encourage the sale and use of alcoholic beverages among those who are underage.
2. Tobacco use
   a. Tobacco has clearly been linked to forms of cancer; therefore, the advertising and sale of tobacco products should be outlawed.
   b. Government has no right to infringe on an individual's personal choice to use tobacco.
3. Cell phone and texting
   a. It ought to be against the law that drivers talk on cell phones or text on cell phones while driving.
   b. Drivers should be able to use cell phones while driving, provided the phones are not handheld.
   c. Government has no right to infringe on an individual's personal choices about using cell phones.

4. Study abroad/internships/community service/service learning/mission trips
   a. Before graduation, every student should be required to complete a service learning, study abroad, or volunteer experience.
   b. College is already expensive and requires too many courses.
5. High school or undergraduate foreign language requirements
   a. Our ability to interact in and to understand the world is greatly increased by exposure to other languages and cultures.
   b. Statement "a" is correct, but such courses should be electives, not requirements.
   c. Everybody ought to learn English.

## OTHER POSSIBLE TOPICS THAT COULD BE EXPANDED

6. Guaranteed student loan programs
7. Required math courses
8. Reinstituting the military draft
9. Debt-relief for foreign nations
10. Stem cell research, genetically modified crops
11. Going green
12. Birth control, abstinence
13. Fuel-efficient automobiles
14. Seat belts, motorcycle helmets
15. Public prayer
16. Spring break—volunteering or partying?
17. Marriage
18. Women serving in combat
19. Handgun or automatic weapon ownership
20. Mandatory physical education classes

# Debate: Is a College Education Worth Its Cost?

College costs (tuition, room and board, fees, books) are increasing substantially every year. Low-cost loan programs have been sharply cut back. Financial realities have forced many students and parents to weigh the benefits of a two- or four-year college education. Schools that provide technical job training are flourishing as a more affordable alternative. These two essays debate the "value" of a college education. Porter's essay is objective and scholarly, citing evidence provided by a number of research studies; Lee's essay is subjective and draws on her experience with her son. Lee argues, for example, that the benefit or value of a college education depends upon the student's attitude and seriousness. Because of the difference in their approaches, their conclusions can be equally valid.

## Before Reading

**Connecting:** Was there ever a debate in your family or in your mind about whether it was worthwhile to attend a college or a university? Are you serious about your education? Or are you just having a good time?

**Anticipating:** Do you think that any of the evidence that Porter provides would have changed Lee's mind? Her son's motivation? Why or why not?

# The Value of a College Degree

Katherine Porter

This essay originally appeared in the ERIC Clearinghouse on Higher Education in 2002.

1     The escalating cost of higher education is causing many to question the value of continuing education beyond high school. Many wonder whether the high cost of tuition, the opportunity cost of choosing college over full-time employment, and the accumulation of thousands of dollars of debt is, in the long run, worth the investment. The risk is especially large for low-income families who have a difficult time making ends meet without the additional burden of college tuition and fees.

## The Economic Value of Higher Education

2     In order to determine whether higher education is worth the investment, it is useful to examine what is known about the value of higher education and the rates of return on investment to both the individual and to society.

3     There is considerable support for the notion that the rate of return on investment in higher education is high enough to warrant the financial burden associated with pursuing a college degree. Though the earnings differential between college and high school graduates varies over time, college graduates, on average, earn more than high school graduates. According to the Census Bureau, over an adult's working life, high school graduates earn an average of $1.2 million; associate's degree holders earn about $1.6 million; and bachelor's degree holders earn about $2.1 million (Day and Newburger, 2002).

4     These sizeable differences in lifetime earnings put the costs of college study in realistic perspective. Most students today—about 80 percent of all students—enroll either in public 4-year colleges or in public 2-year colleges. According to the U.S. Department of Education report, Think College Early, a full-time student at a public 4-year college pays an average of $8,655 for in-state tuition, room and board (U.S. Dept. of Education, 2000). A full-time student in a public 2-year college pays an average of $1,359 per year in tuition (U.S. Dept. of Education, 2000).

5     These statistics support the contention that, though the cost of higher education is significant, given the earnings disparity that exists between those who earn a bachelor's degree and those who do not, the individual rate of return on investment in higher education is sufficiently high to warrant the cost.

## Other Benefits of Higher Education

6 College graduates also enjoy benefits beyond increased income. A 1998 report published by the Institute for Higher Education Policy reviews the individual benefits that college graduates enjoy, including higher levels of saving, increased personal/professional mobility, improved quality of life for their offspring, better consumer decision making, and more hobbies and leisure activities (Institute for Higher Education Policy, 1998). According to a report published by the Carnegie Foundation, non-monetary individual benefits of higher education include the tendency for postsecondary students to become more open-minded, more cultured, more rational, more consistent and less authoritarian; these benefits are also passed along to succeeding generations (Rowley and Hurtado, 2002). Additionally, college attendance has been shown to "decrease prejudice, enhance knowledge of world affairs and enhance social status" while increasing economic and job security for those who earn bachelor's degrees (Ibid.)

7 Research has also consistently shown a positive correlation between completion of higher education and good health, not only for oneself, but also for one's children. In fact, "parental schooling levels (after controlling for differences in earnings) are positively correlated with the health status of their children" and "increased schooling (and higher relative income) are correlated with lower mortality rates for given age brackets" (Cohn and Geske, 1992).

## The Social Value of Higher Education

8 A number of studies have shown a high correlation between higher education and cultural and family values, and economic growth. According to Elchanan Cohn and Terry Geske (1992), there is the tendency for more highly educated women to spend more time with their children; these women tend to use this time to better prepare their children for the future. Cohn and Geske (1992) report that "college graduates appear to have a more optimistic view of their past and future personal progress."

9 Public benefits of attending college include increased tax revenues, greater workplace productivity, increased consumption, increased workforce flexibility, and decreased reliance on government financial support (Institute for Higher Education Policy, 1998).

## College Attendance Versus College Completion

10 In their report, "College for All? Is There Too Much Emphasis on Getting a 4-Year College Degree?" Boesel and Fredland estimate that around 600,000 students leave 4-year colleges annually without graduating. These noncompleters earn less than college graduates because they get fewer years of education. More surprising, they tend to earn less than or the same

amount as 2-year college students who have as much education. Furthermore, 2-year college students show about the same gains in tested cognitive skills for each year of attendance as 4-year college students. Students at 4-year colleges also pay more in tuition and are more likely to have student loan debts than 2-year students (Boesel and Fredland, 1999, p. viii). The authors conclude that high school graduates of modest ability or uncertain motivation—factors that increase their chances of leaving college before graduation—would be well-advised to consider attending 2-year, instead of 4-year, colleges. If they did, they would probably realize the same earnings and cognitive skill gains at lower cost and with less debt. In order to maximize the return on their time and monetary investment, students who do choose to enroll in 4-year colleges should do everything in their power to graduate. (Boesel and Fredland, 1999, p. ix).

## Conclusion

11   While it is clear that investment in a college degree, especially for those students in the lowest income brackets, is a financial burden, the long-term benefits to individuals as well as to society at large, appear to far outweigh the costs.

## References

Boesel, D., & Fredland, E. (1999). College for all? Is there too much emphasis on getting a 4-year college degree? Washington, DC: U.S. Department of Education, Office of Educational Research and Improvement, National Library of Education.

Cohn, E., & Geske, T. G. (1992). Private Nonmonetary Returns to Investment in Higher Education. In W. Becker & D. Lewis, *The Economics of American Higher Education*. Boston, MA: Kluwer Academic Publishers.

The College Board. (2001). *Trends in Student Aid 2001*. New York: The College Board.

Day, J. C., & Newburger, E. C. (2002). The Big Payoff: Educational Attainment and Synthetic Estimates of Work-Life Earnings. (Current Population Reports, Special Studies, P23-210). Washington, DC: Commerce Dept., Economics and Statistics Administration, Census Bureau. [On-Line]. Available: http://www.census.gov/prod/2002pubs/p23-210.pdf

Institute for Higher Education Policy (1998). *Reaping the Benefits: Defining the Public and Private Value of Going to College*. The New Millennium Project on Higher Education Costs, Pricing, and Productivity. Washington, DC: Author.

Rowley, L. L., & Hurtado, S. (2002). *The Non-Monetary Benefits of an Undergraduate Education*. University of Michigan: Center for the Study of Higher and Postsecondary Education.

Schultz, T. W. (1961). Investment in Human Capital. *American Economic Review*, 51: 1–17.

U.S. Department of Education (2001). Digest of Education Statistics 2001. [On-Line]. Available: http://nces.ed.gov/pubs2002/digest2001/tables/PDF/table170.pdf

U.S. Department of Education (2000). Think College Early: Average College Costs. [On-Line]. Available: http://www.ed.gov/offices/OPE/thinkcollege/early/parents/college_costs.htm

Wolfe, B. L. (1994). External Benefits of Education. *International Encyclopedia of Education*. Oxford; New York: Pergamon Press.

## Questions on Subject and Purpose

1. Porter does not limit her argument to the financial benefits of a four-year education. What other benefits does she cite?
2. Are you convinced by her argument? Why or why not?
3. What does the range of benefits to the family and society that Porter cites suggest about her purpose in the essay?

## Questions on Strategy and Audience

1. What typographical devices does Porter use in the essay and why?
2. What is the effect on the readers of the parenthetical citations of authorities and the list of references?
3. How might Porter have defined her audience? How can you tell?

## Questions on Vocabulary and Style

1. How would you describe the tone of the essay?
2. What difference in point of view do you notice between Porter's essay and Lee's essay?
3. Be prepared to define the following words: *warrant* (paragraph 3), *disparity* (5), *cognitive* (10).

## Writing Suggestions

1. **For Your Journal or Blog.** Why did you come to college? In your journal or blog, reflect on your own reasons—no matter what they were. To what extent were your reasons similar to your parents' reasons for sending you? Make some lists.
2. **For a Paragraph.** In a paragraph, identify and then explain what you see as the primary reason that you attend college. Be specific: develop that reason in some detail. Be honest.
3. **For an Essay.** Assume that a younger sibling, relative, or friend is uncertain about attending college. Write an essay intended for that person in which you either encourage or discourage. Be sure to have persuasive reasons for your position.

4. **For Research.** Although Porter cites much evidence to support the economic benefits of a four-year college education, she does not argue for the value of attending an expensive, prestigious college or university as opposed to a lower-cost one. Is there any evidence to suggest that attending an expensive institution produces a greater economic benefit? Research the question and write an essay arguing either position.

## For Further Study

**Focusing on Grammar and Writing.** How does Porter document her sources in the essay? How might she change her format if the essay were to appear in a popular magazine?

**Working Together.** The essay begins and ends with a thesis-driven paragraph. Given the potential audience appeal of such a topic (for example, parents of every college-age student), it could well have appeared in a wide-circulation magazine. Working in small groups, brainstorm about other strategies that could be used to open and close the essay. Each group should share its ideas with the class as a whole.

**Seeing Other Modes at Work.** In outlining the various categories under which the benefits of a four-year college education can be organized, Porter uses classification.

**Finding Connections.** The obvious pairing is with Linda Lee's "The Case Against College."

**Exploring the Web.** The essay cites a substantial amount of research to support its conclusions. Are there, though, any dissenting opinions or evidence to suggest that the case might be exaggerated here? Search the Web to see what else you might find.

# The Case Against College

Linda Lee

This essay first appeared in *Family Circle* magazine in 2001.

1   **D**o you, like me, have a child who is smart but never paid attention in class? Now it's high school graduation time. Other parents are talking Stanford this and State U. that. Your own child has gotten into a pretty good college. The question is: Is he ready? Should he go at all?

2   In this country two-thirds of high school graduates go on to college. In some middle-class suburbs, that number reaches 90 percent. So why do so many feel the need to go?

3   America is obsessed with college. It has the second-highest number of graduates worldwide, after (not Great Britain, not Japan, not Germany) Australia. Even so, only 27 percent of Americans have a bachelor's degree or higher. That leaves an awful lot who succeed without college, or at least without a degree. Many read books, think seriously about life and have well-paying jobs. Some want to start businesses. Others want to be electricians or wilderness guides or makeup artists. Not everyone needs a higher education.

4   What about the statistics showing that college graduates make more money? First, until the computer industry came along, all the highest-paying jobs *required* a college degree: doctor, lawyer, engineer. Second, on average, the brightest and hardest-working kids in school go to college. So is it a surprise that they go on to make more money? And those studies almost always pit kids with degrees against those with just high school. An awful lot have additional training, but they are not included. Ponder for a moment: Who makes more, a plumber or a philosophy major?

5   These are tough words. I certainly wouldn't have listened to them five years ago when my son was graduating from high school. He had been smart enough to get into the Bronx High School of Science in New York and did well on his SATs. But I know now that he did not belong in college, at least not straight out of high school.

6   But he went, because all his friends were going, because it sounded like fun, because he could drink beer and hang out. He did not go to study philosophy. Nor did he feel it incumbent to go to class or complete courses. Meanwhile I was paying $1,000 a week for this pleasure cruise.

7   Eventually I asked myself, "Is he getting $1,000 a week's worth of education?" Heck no. That's when I began wondering why everyone needs to go to college. (My hair colorist makes $300,000 a year without a degree.) What about the famous people who don't have one, like Bill Gates (dropped out of Harvard) and Walter Cronkite (who left the University of Texas to begin a career in journalism)?

8    So I told my son (in a kind way) that his college career was over for now, but he could reapply to the Bank of Mom in two years if he wanted to go back. Meanwhile, I said, get a job.

9    If college is so wonderful, how come so many kids "stop out"? (That's the new terminology.) One study showed only 26 percent of those who began four-year colleges had earned a degree in six years. And what about the kids who finish, then can't find work? Of course, education is worth a great deal more than just employment. But most kids today view college as a way to get a good job.

10    I know, I know. What else is there to do? Won't he miss the "college experience?" First off, there are thousands of things for kids to do. And yes, he will miss the college experience, which may include binge drinking, reckless driving and sleeping in on class days. He can have the same experience in the Marine Corps, minus the sleeping in, and be paid good money for it and learn a trade and discipline.

11    If my son had gone straight through college, he would be a graduate by now. A number of his friends are, and those who were savvy enough to go into computers at an Ivy League school walked into $50,000-a-year jobs. But that's not everyone. An awful lot became teachers making half that. And some still don't know what they want to do.

12    They may, like my son, end up taking whatever jobs they can get. Over the last two years, he's done roofing, delivered UPS packages and fixed broken toilets. His phone was turned off a few times, and he began to pay attention to details, like the price of a gallon of gasoline.

13    But a year ago he began working at a telecommunications company. He loves his work, and over the last year, he's gotten a raise and a year-end bonus. He tells me now he plans to stay there and become a manager.

14    So, just about on schedule, my son has had his own graduation day. And although I won't be able to take a picture of him in cap and gown, I couldn't be any more proud. He grew up, as most kids do. And he did it, for the most part, in spite of college.

## Questions on Subject and Purpose

1. How does Lee feel about a college education? What reservations does she have? Under what circumstances does she have reservations?
2. The essay appeared in a June issue of *Family Circle* magazine, probably on sale by late May. How is that timing reflected in the essay?
3. What purpose might Lee have had in the essay?

## Questions on Strategy and Audience

1. Judging just from the first sentence of the essay, to whom do you think Lee is writing?
2. Can you find a thesis statement in the essay? Where is it?
3. The essay originally appeared in *Family Circle* magazine. Have you ever seen *Family Circle*? Who is the audience for the magazine?

## Questions on Vocabulary and Style

1. What is the effect of opening the essay with a question and of addressing the reader as "you"?
2. How would you define the tone of Lee's essay? Is it formal or informal? Conversational?
3. Be prepared to define the following words: *incumbent* (paragraph 6) and *savvy* (11).

## Writing Suggestions

1. **For Your Journal or Blog.** Why did you come to college? Was it just expected of you? Did you just expect to do so? Did you consider other, noncollege options? Why or why not? In your journal or blog jot down your thoughts, memories, and experiences connected with the decision to go to college.
2. **For a Paragraph.** Do you agree or disagree with Lee's argument? In a paragraph, respond to that argument. Focus on your own experience; probably just one aspect of that experience will be enough.
3. **For an Essay.** Whether you agree with Lee or not, write a rebuttal to her essay— title it something like "The Case for College." Think of your essay as something that might be published in *Family Circle* as the other side of the argument.
4. **For Research.** Lee cites a study that found that only "26 percent of those who began four-year colleges had earned a degree in six years." Is that statistic widely accepted? Locate other studies on the same subject; check with your school's admissions or alumni office. Why is the "stop out" rate so high? What explanations does the research offer for this phenomenon? Using your research, write an essay aimed at the incoming freshman class at your school in which you try to persuade them to make good use of their college experiences.

## For Further Study

**Focusing on Grammar and Writing.** How effective is Lee's introduction? Remember the audience for which it was written. What are they likely to find appealing in it? Why might Lee choose to begin with a question rather than with a thesis statement? What is gained by delaying the thesis statement? What does this suggest about introductions for your essays?

**Working Together.** Divide into small groups. Each group should discuss what they expect their college education will do for them. How will they benefit? Are they taking advantage of this experience? Is a college education a "right" or a "privilege"? How would they react if their parents did what Lee did to her son?

**Seeing Other Modes at Work.** Lee also makes use of cause and effect in her essay, as well as narration in relating the experiences of her son.

**Finding Connections.** Besides its obvious pairing with Katherine Porter's "The Value of a College Degree," the essay can be linked with Richard Rodriguez's "None of This Is Fair" (this chapter).

**Exploring the Web.** Want to check out the statistics on college "stop out" rates or the reasons for these rates? College graduation rates vary widely from school to school. In general, the more selective the school in admission, the higher the graduation rate. Many factors, though, influence the rate. The Web has an abundance of information that can be sorted and analyzed in a variety of ways. Search for *college graduation rates* to start.

# DEBATE: Impact of Outsourcing Jobs

Probably every American is familiar with the word *outsourcing*, moving manufacturing or even service jobs to an outside, that is, independent contractor hired specifically to do that job. Businesses typically outsource tasks and services rather than hiring additional employees on their own payrolls. Increasingly, however, the term has come to refer to moving jobs outside of the United States in order to lower costs and maintain profits. Manufacturing jobs, for example, have steadily declined in the United States; more and more manufacturing and assembly is done outside of our country's borders. Even white-collar jobs—with banks, customer service departments, computer services, and legal work—have been moving elsewhere, because businesses are drawn by lower wages and benefits and an abundance of qualified workers. Those who have been displaced are angry; business and government emphasize the change from a national economy to a global one. These two essays respond to this complex problem. Neither offers a solution—which would be far too complicated for an essay—but each argues for a different approach to the problem.

## Before Reading

**Connecting:** Have you, anyone in your family, relatives, or people in your community or state felt the effects of outsourcing—the loss of well-paying jobs, plant closings, layoffs? Do you see yourself and your family as protected from such things?

**Anticipating:** Both writers use personal experience in their essays. What is the relationship between the nature of their experience and the nature of the argument that they are making?

# The Traveling Bra Salesman

Claudia O'Keefe

The essay was originally submitted to a competition sponsored by the *Economist* magazine and the Shell Oil Company in 2004. It won first prize.

1 It's a little after 10 A.M. at a 20-vehicle flea market in rural West Virginia. I'm getting worried. I haven't sold enough merchandise to pay for my $7 space fee and I didn't have any money to bring with me, not even to make change. I reach into a carton of vintage clothing to mark down my prices. My fingers grasp something silky and slippery, a lacy slip Elizabeth Taylor could have worn in *Cat on a Hot Tin Roof*. Instead of the thin, cheesy polyester and shoddy workmanship I'm used to seeing in contemporary lingerie from the same manufacturer, the older slip features quality fabric and lace that is not only sewn on straight, but will survive a hundred washings and remain looking near new.

2 This isn't what I notice first, however. It's the original price tag from 1966. I'm amazed because 38 years later I can still decipher the sales codes printed on it, codes which were on the thousands of tags exactly like it and part of my first paying job, given to me when I was eight years old.

## The Good Life

3 My stepfather was a salesman during the 1960s, traveling California and the American southwest in his big, hulking Buick, selling bras, slips, and girdles to small department stores and five-and-dimes. Whenever he returned from one of his two-week trips, he brought several lunch sacks full of torn price tags with him, evidence of product sold. My job was to sort and count the tags, at a nickel for every hundred I recorded.

4 We lived in a three-bedroom home in an upscale Los Angeles suburb, owned two cars, and took annual vacations. My brother, sister, and I never lacked any of the benefits of a middle-class upbringing, a new school wardrobe each year, copious Christmas presents, private lessons, even horses when we were older. In a medical emergency we worried more about how to get to a doctor quickly than we did about paying the bill. All of this was affordable on my dad's one sales job without incurring vast amounts of debt.

5 These days the same lingerie lines my dad marketed are now sold primarily in Wal-Mart. Instead of being crafted in the U.S.A. by American workers they are manufactured almost exclusively in China. Gone are the traveling salesmen who ferried clothing to small-town variety stores across the nation,

and their buyers who used to decide which lines to stock. Most of the old independent retailers no longer exist. A handful of chains have replaced them, with buying decisions made at the corporate level. Jobs which comfortably supported a family have been eliminated in favor of new ones paying so little employees are encouraged to apply for food stamps.

6      I have more in common today with the minimum-wage employees at my local supercenter, than my dad in his Buick cruising Route 66 with a trunk full of bras. Why? I'm currently stuck living in job-poor West Virginia. With the exception of the occasional social worker position advertised at $19K a year, the positions listed in my local paper pay $6 or less per hour. When I held one of the area's top professional jobs, as a 70-hour-per-week PR director for an arts organization, I earned just $1103 each month after taxes, no health insurance, no benefits. I understand too well the desire of unemployed and low-wage workers throughout the world who will make any sacrifice necessary, even to the point of moving some place where they are resented and vilified, in order to find work. I sympathize with the talented and skilled employees in India and Russia who are currently gobbling up my country's offshored tech jobs. Given these nations' past and current struggles with poverty or economic turmoil, I would do exactly as they are doing.

7      Unfortunately, few companies want to outsource quality jobs to West Virginia. Though I've spent the last two years trying to put together the $3,000 necessary to move myself and my mother, *Grapes of Wrath*—style, to another state with decent employment, I can't even manage to keep our utilities and rent current.

8      Feeling isolated here, I've looked outward for answers and become a financial news junkie. I comb each new statistic, wait just as eagerly for the U.S. monthly payroll report as I would if I owned stock. I take it all in, the arguments for and against free trade, the fears of those who feel the exportation of jobs will lead to a "race to the bottom," where America loses superpower status and becomes a third-world nation. I watch corporate spokespeople madly spinning their version of outsourcing's benefits, cheaper prices and increased jobs at home. I note Alan Greenspan's testimony suggesting that displaced workers must retrain themselves for the new jobs which will appear on the horizon to replace ones lost and unlikely to return. None who support this belief, however, can offer a list of the positions for which the jobless should school themselves. I sit in front of the TV where verbal combatants are engaged in a heated exchange over immigration reform. Should we be more compassionate, open our borders wider to financially depressed people willing to fill all those jobs Americans don't want? Or do we need a 50-foot razor-wire fence to protect native-born and naturalized citizens from the downward pressure on wages caused by tides of illegal aliens crossing into the U.S.?

9      I suck in as much information as I can take before crying uncle, the attack dog political ads about job creation, the surveys and polls and yelling and screaming from experts and average Americans alike.

10     Two realities stand out from all the rest.

## Moving On

11 Geography can no longer prevent jobs in developed regions such as North America and Europe from migrating to cheaper, emerging markets. The outsourcing jet has already left the terminal, cleared international airspace, and has enough fuel onboard to reach the far ends of the earth nonstop.

12 Meanwhile, those workers whose jobs have fled are crowding into that empty terminal, clamoring for protections against what they perceive as theft. They see a worker in China being paid pennies for a job that use to guarantee a nice middle-class life for their families and they're so frustrated they don't know which they want to do more, cry or shoot something, preferably a politician. They may cry, but thankfully they don't shoot. Instead they pour every ounce of their attention into complaining to those same politicians, charging them with an impossible task, returning things to the way they were.

13 I know firsthand the dangers of refusing to let go of the past. A decade ago I was a published writer with a promising career in fiction. Fiction publishing at that time was in the midst of a corporate sea change devastating to authors of the type of books I wrote. Not only wasn't pay increasing, fewer and fewer books were being bought. Not wanting to give up a career that was my whole life, I sought to adjust to my shrinking income by progressively relocating to areas of the country with cheaper and cheaper costs of living. I moved from pricey California to a slightly less expensive northern New Mexico to Florida, rural Virginia, and finally, with my money gone, any momentum I'd once had long expended, and all contacts evaporated, I came to a disgruntled rest four years ago in West Virginia.

14 Similar to my experience with publishing, Americans who have lost their jobs since January 2001 are having to adjust to the idea that the next one they find is likely to involve a pay cut. According to the U.S. Labor Department, 57 percent of those workers who found re-employment earned less than they did at their old jobs. One third took a cut of 20 percent or more in order to be employed.

15 What happens if, as several studies suggest, outsourcing continues to ramp up and those same workers are thrown on the street once more? Will their next job pay even less? Could scores of computer programmers, financial analysts, and paralegals end up like my West Virginia neighbors, huddled around a card table in a supercenter break room, using a Styrofoam cup for an ashtray while they grouse about their lives?

16 Back in the 1970s, my stepfather saw his career as a traveling bra salesman coming to an end. Though he adored the freedom of the open road, he didn't balk. He mourned and moved on. He studied for a real estate license and found a new life as a highly successful broker.

## A New Dream

17 The question is not whether it is good or bad to import workers or export jobs. The problem is that society has hit an emotional road block. My country is one tremendously divided, with pro-business and pro-worker stubbornly

pitted against each other. We're anxious. We're angry. Neither side wants to give and nothing can be solved until we acknowledge one crucial fact.

18    The past is dust. Those mythic decades, during which The American Dream was considered to be our natural right, are over. We need to wake from our state of denial, accept this golden era's passing, and get on with life. Once we agree that the past cannot be recaptured, we will at last open ourselves to solutions we haven't yet considered, to business and immigration models which are still waiting to be invented. Working as willing participants of change, we will devise ways to keep businesses from discarding employees like so much surplus machinery, while making certain there is profit for all. Ingenuity will be given free reign and the synergies we so badly need to solve this international crisis can finally come together.

19    Standing in that West Virginia flea market, I look at the vintage, never-worn slip in my hands. Back in my home state of California, at the Rose Bowl Flea Market, it would fetch $35 or more. Here, I'll have to price it at $1. In fact while I'm doing this, a woman approaches me.

20    "How much?" she asks.

21    I tell her, while pointing out that the slip is in mint condition and of a superior quality to comparable ones made today.

22    "Will you take a quarter?" she asks.

23    *Hurry*, I urge my country. Before it's too late. Only when we admit that the future awaits us can we embrace a more inclusive and thrilling successor to outmoded twentieth-century ideals, a goal without boundaries or limits, not The American Dream, but The Global Dream.

## Questions on Subject and Purpose

1. The topic for the essay competition was "Import Workers or Export Jobs?" Given the topic, how would you have expected the submitted essays to be structured?
2. Does O'Keefe answer the question that is posed by the announced topic?
3. What answer does she give to the question? What does O'Keefe see as the solution to the problem?

## Questions on Strategy and Audience

1. O'Keefe frames the essay with an experience she has in a West Virginia flea market. What does this have to do with the topic of importing workers or exporting jobs?
2. What role do the subheadings play in the essay?
3. The essay contest was sponsored by a magazine devoted to business issues and a large corporation. How might that initial primary audience have affected the essay?

## Questions on Vocabulary and Style

1. What rhetorical device does O'Keefe use in the second sentence of paragraph 11?

2. How would you describe O'Keefe's tone in the essay? What sense of herself does her writing project? Does she sound angry? Reasonable? Sad?

3. Be prepared to define the following words: *copious* (paragraph 4), *vilified* (6), *clamoring* (12), *disgruntled* (13), *synergies* (18).

## Writing Suggestions

1. **For Your Journal or Blog.** Think about the choices you make when you buy something in a store. What are the most significant factors in that decision? For example, how significant is price? Do you consider where the product was manufactured or produced? Think about your buying habits—perhaps with clothing, electronic goods, or things that you buy for your room or apartment. Reflect on your motivation.

2. **For a Paragraph.** What would it take for you to change your buying habits? In a paragraph explore the likelihood that you would make decisions such as these: buying from local producers, buying goods made in the United States, bypassing inexpensive goods that might not be substantial or of high quality.

3. **For an Essay.** The growth of discount stores, superstores, and dollar stores is fueled by consumers' desire and need to save money. As living-wage jobs disappear or are outsourced, many people are forced to spend less; that in turn increases the pressure on businesses to manufacture or produce goods at lower prices. The cycle and the problem are enormously complicated. In an essay, focus on what you as an individual and as a member of a peer group might be able to do. Argue for some possible and reasonable course of action that an individual might take.

4. **For Research.** Both O'Keefe and Bruce Raynor (in "Protect Workers' Rights") puzzle over what "new" skills or additional educational credentials might make workers the most immune to the economic pressures of outsourcing. Research the problem. What should be done to retrain workers whose jobs are outsourced? Using your research, write an essay in which you advocate an approach to such a problem. Remember that simply getting additional education does not necessarily qualify a person for a job that will not be outsourced.

## For Further Study

**Focusing on Grammar and Writing.** Finding an effective title for an essay is sometimes one of the most difficult writing tasks you face. O'Keefe's title is quite different from what you might expect, although it is connected with the example she develops in the essay. The title does not, for example, suggest that what follows is an argumentative or persuasive essay. Write some alternative titles for the essay.

**Working Together.** Divide into small groups and discuss whether the flea market story at the beginning and ending is effective. Why or why not? Propose another possible opening and ending for the essay.

**Seeing Other Modes at Work.** The essay includes narration at several points (especially in paragraphs 1–4 and 19–22). Comparison and contrast is used when the manufacturing and sales of goods in the 1960s is compared with present-day activities.

**Finding Connections.** The obvious pairing is with Bruce Raynor's "Protect Workers' Rights." An interesting pairing could also be made with Ellen Goodman's "Our Do-It-Yourself Economy" (Chapter 8).

**Exploring the Web.** In paragraph 14, O'Keefe cites statistics from the U.S. Labor Department about wage cuts that were taken by workers who lost jobs and then were reemployed. Using a search engine, locate more recent statistics on the Web. The Bureau of Labor Statistics provides information such as this.

# Protect Workers' Rights

Bruce Raynor

*The essay was originally published in* The Washington Post *in 2003. Raynor serves as president of a union of workers in the hospitality, gaming, apparel, textile, retail, laundry, and distribution industries.*

1    This summer Pillowtex Corp., successor to the century-old firm Fieldcrest Cannon, the largest unionized textile company in the country, closed its 16 textile plants and let go almost 6,500 employees in 10 states. In North Carolina, where the largest plants were located, it was the single biggest layoff in state history.

2    Pillowtex is only one of hundreds of textile mills that have closed in the past several years. For me, the Pillowtex shutdown was especially painful because for 20 years I was involved in efforts to organize a union there. In 1999 the workers finally succeeded. These workers overcame illegal threats, harassment and attempts to racially divide the workers. But the hardest-working, most dedicated workers in the world could not overcome a government policy that believes open markets and expanded trade, whatever the cost, are always justified. Problem is, the costs keep rising and the benefits never seem to trickle down.

3    The workers are now desperate. They received no severance payments. Their health insurance is gone. Mortgages, car payments and taxes aren't being paid. Kannapolis, N.C., where Pillowtex is located, has always been a textile town. There are no other jobs available. And while the union is still trying to find a buyer for the company, the local government's response for economic development is to buy an ad in *USA Today* or the *Wall Street Journal* asking Bill Gates, Oprah Winfrey or Warren Buffett to consider moving some of their business operations to Kannapolis.

4    What happened to Pillowtex workers is illustrative of destructive trends that threaten American prosperity and, indeed, the global economy.

5    Every manufacturing industry in the United States—apparel, textiles, metals, paper, electronics—has lost jobs in the past year. Over the past 36 months manufacturing employment has declined by 2.7 million. This is the longest decline since the Great Depression. The job crisis is not only in manufacturing. Since the economic recovery began, more than a million jobs have disappeared. Apparently the economy is doing well. Only workers are suffering.

6    The usual response of policymakers to manufacturing workers who have lost their jobs is to preach the virtues of education. Workers are told that if they would only acquire new skills, they would qualify for white-collar service jobs that are safe from the economic forces that have shifted millions of factory jobs to foreign countries. Perhaps that was once true.

7       Today white-collar jobs—telemarketing, accounting, claims adjusting, home loan processing, architectural practices, radiographers and even some state and local government jobs—are going offshore. In a survey of the world's 100 largest financial services firms, Deloitte Research found that these companies expect to shift $356 billion worth of operations and about 2 million jobs to low-wage countries over the next five years. These developments appear already to be affecting wages in some sectors. According to Sharon Marsh Roberts of the Independent Computer Consultants Association, outsourcing has forced down hourly wage rates by 10 percent to 40 percent for many U.S. computer consultants.

8       These trends also affect workers in developing countries. For example, since January 2000, 520 manufacturing plants have closed in Mexico, most of them moving to China. And in 2005, when all apparel and textile quotas are to be lifted, developing countries around the globe will be faced with a massive loss of jobs as the industry moves into China. For example, a United Nations study predicts that Bangladesh will lose 1 million apparel jobs when quotas are abolished. Many other countries in Africa, Asia, the Caribbean and Eastern Europe, where the apparel industry is the largest employer, will also suffer huge job losses when quotas are lifted.

9       As low as wages are in many developing countries, they can't compete with the pennies an hour paid in China. China scholar Anita Chan describes how different regions in China seek to maintain their attractiveness to foreign capital by lowering minimum wages and not enforcing labor regulations and health and safety laws. According to Chan, "though employment in the low-wage industries in China may be expanding, the wages of the workers in these industries are not rising, and for many of them have been falling." The benefits of globalization, Chan warns, "will not trickle down to those who make products."

10      So it turns out that workers in Kannapolis, N.C., Silicon Valley, Calif.; Juarez, Mexico, and Guangdong, China, have much in common. It is becoming increasingly clear that when wages and conditions of work are undercut in one part of the globe they will eventually be cut in others as well.

11      The downward spiral of lower wages and worsening working conditions is fueling popular skepticism over globalization. A prosperous economy requires that workers be able to buy the products that they produce. That means we need rules for the global economy that protect workers' rights—and not just in China—we also need [them] in the United States.

## Questions on Subject and Purpose

1. What does Raynor's title suggest about both the subject and the argument of his essay?

2. Although we might expect that as a labor leader Raynor would be most concerned about displaced workers here in the United States, why might he include the global examples in paragraphs 8 through 10?

3. Can you locate a sentence in the essay that could serve as the thesis or claim of Raynor's argument?

## Questions on Strategy and Audience

1.  What is the function of paragraph 4 in the essay?
2.  In paragraph 6, Raynor acknowledges the solution that many offer to displaced workers. What is his counterargument to that proposal?
3.  The essay appeared as an editorial in *The Washington Post*, a newspaper that is circulated locally (to Washington, D.C.) and nationally (in print and online editions). What is the value of publishing the essay in this newspaper?

## Questions on Vocabulary and Style

1.  How would you describe the tone of Raynor's essay in paragraph 3? Does the paragraph seem like logical argument or emotional persuasion?
2.  What is the effect of personalizing the situation at Pillowtex (paragraph 2)?
3.  Be prepared to define the following word: *severance* (paragraph 3)

## Writing Suggestions

1.  **For Your Journal or Blog.** What is your major and what do you imagine as your job or career once you graduate? On what basis have you made that choice? In your journal or blog, reflect on why you are making these choices. What has influenced you? Be honest with yourself—this is not an admission essay for college!
2.  **For a Paragraph.** Every college student feels at least some pressure from parents about grades, choice of major, future plans. Write a letter to your parents in which you explain and argue for one of the following: (1) why grades are or are not important to you; (2) why you have decided to change your major to another field or why you are happy with your current choice; (3) why you would like to take some time off from going to school, or consider another career option, or go to graduate or professional school (and will require several additional years of financial support!).
3.  **For an Essay.** Expand your paragraph into an essay. Before you do this, think about how your parents are likely to react to your argument. What argumentative or persuasive strategies are likely to work best with them?
4.  **For Research.** The U.S. Department of Labor, Bureau of Labor Statistics, produces employment projections—what types of jobs will be most in demand in the future. The "Occupations with the largest job growth, 2006—2016" (it can be found online using a search engine) lists twenty-nine job titles that will be highest in demand. Of the twenty-nine, twenty-three do not require a college degree. In a research essay drawing on such data, formulate a thesis and construct an argument on some aspect of this problem.

## For Further Study

**Focusing on Grammar and Writing.** How does Raynor make use of the dash (—) to insert information into a sentence? What are the conditions under which this is done?

**Working Together.** The journal or blog writing exercise in Writing Suggestions makes an excellent topic for discussion in small groups. First answer the question for yourself, then break into small groups to discuss your choices with others.

**Seeing Other Modes at Work.** Like O'Keefe, Raynor begins his essay with a narrative, tracing out what happened when the Pillowtext Corporation closed its plants.

**Finding Connections.** The obvious pairing is with Claudia O'Keefe's "The Traveling Bra Salesman's Lesson." An interesting pairing could also be made with Ellen Goodman's "Our Do-It-Yourself Economy" (Chapter 8).

**Exploring the Web.** The Web has extensive information about outsourcing, both from a worker and business point of view. For a business perspective, check out www.outsourcing.com.

# Debate: Water— Public or Private?

*Water shortages, particularly in the American Southwest, increasingly make the evening news. Severe droughts dry up lakes in the South and cities worry about having enough water to supply residents' needs—and forget about watering the lawn or washing your car. America's water shortages are nothing in comparison to those in other parts of the world. Fredrik Segerfeldt and Joshua Ortega tackle the issues of what is called the privatization of water. Large multinational corporations buy up water rights and build water treatment plants and distribution networks. Segerfeldt defends the practice, arguing that private businesses have the capital and expertise to do the task more efficiently than governments—although not more cheaply for the consumers. Ortega argues that water is a basic human right and should not be sold to businesses and corporations who then turn around and make a profit on their investment. Ortega adds one other issue to the debate, one with which all of us are familiar. Private companies bottle water which we as consumers then purchase, despite having adequate supplies of pure water freely available from our own taps. Ortega argues that bottled water is often not as pure as we would like to think and that the packaging of water in plastic bottles is environmentally unfriendly.*

## Before Reading

**Connecting:** Do you have a watercooler at home for which you purchase large bottles of water? Do you ever buy bottled water? Why spend money to purchase something that is freely available?

**Anticipating:** For arguments to exist, there has to be some validity to the points that each side raises. What seems reasonable about Segerfeldt's argument? About Ortega's? Which side do you favor?

# The Private Sector Can Get Water Flowing to the Poor

Fredrik Segerfeldt

*Segerfeldt is the author of* Water for Sale: How Business and the Market Can Resolve the World's Water Crisis *(2005). This article was originally published in* Financial Times *in August 2005.*

1    **W**orldwide, 1.1 billion people, mainly in poor countries, do not have access to clean, safe water. The shortage of water helps to perpetuate poverty, disease and early death. However, there is no shortage of water, at least not globally. We use a mere 8 per cent of the water available for human consumption. Instead, bad policies are the main problem. Even Cherrapunji, India, the wettest place on earth, suffers from recurrent water shortages.

2    Ninety-seven per cent of all water distribution in poor countries is managed by the public sector, which is largely responsible for more than a billion people being without water. Some governments of impoverished nations have turned to business for help, usually with good results. In poor countries with private investments in the water sector, more people have access to water than in those without such investments. Moreover, there are many examples of local businesses improving water distribution. Superior competence, better incentives and better access to capital for investment have allowed private distributors to enhance both the quality of the water and the scope of its distribution. Millions of people who lacked water mains within reach are now getting clean and safe water delivered within a convenient distance.

3    The privatization of water distribution has stirred up strong feelings and met with resistance. There have been violent protests and demonstrations against water privatization all over the world. Western anti-business non-governmental organizations and public employee unions, sometimes together with local protesters, have formed anti-privatization coalitions. However, the movement's criticisms are off base.

4    The main argument of the anti-privatization movement is that privatization increases prices, making water unaffordable for millions of poor people. In some cases, it is true that prices have gone up after privatization; in others not. But the price of water for those already connected to a mains network should not be the immediate concern. Instead, we should focus on those who lack access to mains water, usually the poorest in poor countries. It is primarily those people who die, suffer from disease and are trapped in poverty.

5    They usually purchase their lower-quality water from small-time vendors, paying on average 12 times more than for water from regular mains, and

often more than that. When the price of water for those already connected goes up, the distributor gets both the resources to enlarge the network and the incentives to reach as many new customers as possible. When prices are too low to cover the costs of laying new pipes, each new customer entails a loss rather than a profit, which makes the distributor unwilling to extend the network. Therefore, even a doubling of the price of mains water could actually give poor people access to cheaper water than before.

6    There is another, less serious, argument put forward by the anti-privatization movement. Since water is considered a human right and since we die if we do not drink, its distribution must be handled democratically; that is, remain in the hands of the government and not be handed over to private, profit-seeking interests. Here we must allow for a degree of pragmatism. Access to food is also a human right. People also die if they do not eat. And in countries where food is produced and distributed "democratically", there tends to be neither food nor democracy. No one can seriously argue that all food should be produced and distributed by governments.

7    The resistance to giving enterprise and the market a larger scope in water distribution in poor countries has had the effect desired by the protesters. The pace of privatization has slowed. It is therefore vital that we have a serious discussion based on facts and analysis, rather than on anecdotes and dogmas.

8    True, many privatizations have been troublesome. Proper supervision has been missing. Regulatory bodies charged with enforcing contracts have been non-existent, incompetent or too weak. Contracts have been badly designed and bidding processes sloppy. But these mistakes do not make strong arguments against privatizations as such, but against bad privatizations. Let us, therefore, have a discussion on how to make them work better, instead of rejecting the idea altogether. Greater scope for businesses and the market has already saved many lives in Chile and Argentina, in Cambodia and the Philippines, in Guinea and Gabon. There are millions more to be saved.

## Questions on Subject and Purpose

1.  What does Segerfeldt's title suggest about both the subject and the purpose of his essay?
2.  Segerfeldt concedes that the anti-privatization movement argues that water is "a human right" and must "not be handed over to private, profit-seeking interests." How does he counter this argument in his essay?
3.  What purpose does Segerfeldt seem to have in the essay? What is he trying to accomplish?

## Questions on Strategy and Audience

1.  What is the role of statistics in Segerfeldt's argument?
2.  Can you find examples where Segerfeldt qualifies his assertions—either about the failure of the public sector or the success of privatization?

3. Judging from the nature of Segerfeldt's argument, does he assume that his readers wholeheartedly endorse the idea of privatizing water?

## Questions on Vocabulary and Style

1. What is the argumentative implication of the statement that privatized water has "already saved many lives . . . [and] there are millions more to be saved" (paragraph 8).

2. Effective argument always involves acknowledging the validity of certain aspects of your opponent's arguments. To ignore criticisms or contradictory evidence merely weakens your own argument. Can you find any instances in which Segerfeldt acknowledges evidence that his opponents have or could use against his position?

3. Be prepared to define the following words: *coalitions* (paragraph 3), *anecdotes* (7), *dogmas* (7).

## Writing Suggestions

1. **For Your Journal or Blog.** What is objectionable about this proposal: The quickest way to get water to those who do not have an adequate or reliable supply is to allow a private corporation to develop means of distribution and then to sell the water. Respond in your journal or blog. Does that seem reasonable? Offensive? Why?

2. **For a Paragraph.** Sketch out an argument in a paragraph in which you either agree or disagree with Segerfeldt's position.

3. **For an Essay.** The larger issue that Segerfeldt raises divides American politics on a domestic level. To what extent should services be provided by the government or by private businesses? Who is more capable of doing it? Who will do a better job? Current debate include, for example, universal health care coverage and retirement benefits (Social Security or private IRAs). Like most subjects of arguments, each side has valid points. Select a current issue that involves this debate and in an essay argue for either side.

4. **For Research.** In paragraph 1, Segerfeldt writes: "There is no shortage of water, at least not globally. We use a mere 8 per cent of the water available for human consumption." That statistic might seem shocking considering what we hear and read about the southwestern part of the United States and Africa, for example. Use the Web to research this issue. Then in a research essay, agree or disagree with Segerfeldt's statement: "bad [water] policies are the main problem."

## For Further Study

**Focusing on Grammar and Writing.** Writers often use topic sentences in each paragraph to signal to the reader what the paragraph will be about. Topic sentences promote clarity in writing, making it easier for the reader to grasp the structure. Look carefully at Segerfeldt's paragraphs. How many have topic sentences? Remember, even though topic sentences are often the first sentence in a paragraph, that is not the only place in which they might be found.

**Working Together.** Divide into small groups and see if you can find any instances in Segerfeldt's essay in which he uses emotionally charged words or phrases to refer to the position held by those who oppose privatization.

**Seeing Other Modes at Work.** The debate between public control and private business depends on comparison and contrast.

**Finding Connections.** The obvious pairing is with Joshua Ortega's "Water Wars: Bottling Up the World's Supply of $H_2O$." Related is Tom Haines's "Facing Famine" (Chapter 2).

**Exploring the Web.** The Web includes an extensive number of sites that debate the privatization of water resources. Use a search engine to examine the arguments for and against.

# Water Wars: Bottling Up the World's Supply of H₂O

Joshua Ortega

*The essay originally appeared in the* Seattle Times *in March 2005.*

1 Clean, unpolluted, affordable water. There is nothing more important in the world—but it's in serious danger.

2 From health and environmental concerns to the very question of who should control the Earth's water supply, the issue can be distilled into a simple, opening proposition: tap, or bottled water?

3 As Americans, we are all fortunate enough to live in a country where clean, drinkable tap water is a reality, making bottled water a "luxury" rather than a necessity.

4 However, there is a perception among many people that bottled water is somehow more healthy or pure than water from their tap. This is simply an illusion of marketing.

5 A four-year study by the National Resources Defense Council (NRDC), released in 1999, found that one-fifth of the sampled bottled waters contained known neurotoxins and carcinogens such as styrene, toluene and xylene. Another NRDC study found that, out of 103 brands of bottled water, one-third contained traces of arsenic and E. coli. This means that out of a sample of 1,000 bottles sold in the U.S., at least 300 would have some level of chemical contamination.

6 But how can bottled water be contaminated and still be sold in the U.S.? The answer is simple.

7 Bottled water is one of the world's least-regulated industries, and is usually held to less-stringent standards than tap water. Since tap water is a public resource, extensive documentation on its quality and content must be made available to the consumer. There is no such accountability for bottled water, which is regulated more like a soft drink than a public resource.

8 Bottled water gives the pre-packaged impression of safety—if it's in a bottle, it must be safe and clean. Unfortunately, this is not always the case, as evidenced by the worldwide recall of Perrier in the early 1990s, in which the bottled water was found to have benzene, a poison that has produced cancer in lab animals.

9 When you factor in the devastating environmental costs associated with bottling a public, natural resource, the difference between bottled and tap becomes even clearer.

10    The most common plastic used in water bottle manufacturing is PET (polyethylene terephthalate), an environmentally unfriendly substance that actually requires 17.5 kilograms of water to produce only 1 kilogram of PET. In fact, more water is used to make PET bottles than is actually put into them.

11    The production of the plastic also produces numerous byproducts that are extremely harmful to the environment. The Container Recycling Institute reported that 14 billion water bottles were sold in the U.S. in 2002, yet only 10 percent of these bottles were recycled—90 percent ended up in the trash. That's an extra 12.6 billion plastic bottles for the landfills; bottles that contained water that was no more—and often less—healthy than tap water.

12    Granted, there are many places in the world where bottled water is the only source of drinkable water, and thus it becomes much more than a luxury item. However, bottled water is ultimately a Band-Aid solution. Rather than actually solving the problem—making public water clean, affordable and environmentally friendly—the citizens of these countries are forced to pay exorbitant prices for water that comes in an environmentally unfriendly delivery system.

13    Whether in America or less-developed countries, the evidence is as clear as the plastic it's sold in—bottled water, compared to good tap water, is not worth the costs, whether they be environmental, health-related or economic.

14    But bottled water is not the only danger to clean, affordable tap water— it is simply one part of a much larger issue.

15    *Fortune* magazine has touted water as the "best investment sector for the century." The European Bank for Reconstruction and Development has said that "water is the last infrastructure frontier for private investors." The *Toronto Globe & Mail* has stated that "water is fast becoming a globalized corporate industry." This news should send shivers down the spine of any concerned American.

16    Currently, the privatized water market is led by two French multinational corporations, Suez Lyonnaise des Eaux (builders of the Suez Canal) and Veolia Environnement, though many other multinationals are also now in the market, including American companies such as General Electric and Bechtel.

17    In the United States, recent laws have paved the way for a larger private-sector presence in America's water supply. Whereas small or local public-sector operators, such as city or county utility companies, used to control the market, now the big players of world business are getting involved.

18    For example, Veolia (formerly owned by Vivendi) bought U.S. Filter Corporation for $6 billion, and it also owns a large portion of Air and Water Technologies. Suez once purchased two of the largest producers of water-treatment chemicals, Calgon and Nalco, and also owns United Water Resources. So much fuss was made about France's opposition to the war in Iraq, yet there was little or no public outcry over the selling of U.S. water companies to foreign interests.

19    Many people will argue that the privatization of water will not affect U.S. consumers, but the facts unfortunately say otherwise. When the French privatized their water services, customer rates went up 150 percent within a few years. In Britain, water corporations have had a terrible track record. In an eight-year

period, from 1989 to 1997, four large corporations, including Wessex (a former subsidiary of Enron), were prosecuted 128 times for various infractions.

20      One of the main problems with water privatization is that the public no longer has the right to access information or data about water quality and standards. In 1998, the water supply of Sydney, Australia, currently controlled by Suez, was contaminated with cryptosporidium and giardia, yet the public had not been informed when the parasites were first discovered.

21      When the government of Ontario, Canada, deregulated its infrastructure and privatized water-testing labs, the results were disastrous for many communities. In the small Canadian town of Walkerton, seven people died and more than 200 were sickened from drinking E. coli-contaminated water in 2000.

22      The situation is even worse in Third World nations, where large financial institutions such as the IMF (International Monetary Fund) and the World Bank are actively promoting water privatization as a solution to the world's water problems. In many instances, the privatization of a nation's water supply is a requirement for debt relief or a loan. Out of 40 IMF loans that were granted in 2000, at least 12 were contingent upon water privatization.

23      The danger here is that when anything is privatized, it is then subject to pricing as decided by the open market. Many have argued that water is a basic human right, and if this is the case, as with all human rights, it should never be sold on the open market to the highest bidder. Otherwise, water will be subject to the same whims of business as any other commodity.

24      An energy crisis was bad enough—just imagine if the Enron scenario happened with water. In the words of a former director of Suez, "We are here to make money. Sooner or later the company that invests recoups its investment, which means the customer has to pay for it." These are not the people you want to be in control of your water.

25      Water corporations exist to make profits—not to preserve water's quality or affordability. Let's say they own all of the world's water, and then start selling it back to you in little plastic bottles. When the prices and the environmental costs of bottled water get too high, you may find yourself going to war over your water.

26      "The wars of the next century will be about water."

27      This is a quote from Ismail Serageldin, former vice president of the World Bank, in 1999. This is the same World Bank that encourages the privatization of the world's water supply. The same World Bank whose members have financial ties to multinational corporations such as General Electric and Enron.

28      These same multinational corporations also have stakes in the biggest industry of them all—defense and warfare. Indeed, it is a strange day when the same corporation that makes bombs and missiles also owns your water, an "industry" that putatively will be the major focus of this century's wars.

29      Some may argue that these companies are an essential part of national defense, and thus are protecting national interests by the strategic acquisition of the world's major water supplies. However, once a company owns a water supply, it could be in its best financial interest to make the water scarce and

hard to afford. Creating a problem, then marketing a solution, is a very profitable business practice—not to mention the additional profits to be gained from defending the supply in a war.

30      History is rife with conflicts over one party or another's control of a limited resource.

31      Most people will agree that the driving economic force behind today's wars is oil. A war over water would be a hundred times worse. Oil is vastly different. No one puts a gun to your head and forces you to drive. No one makes you fill your tank. Gas and oil are ultimately luxuries. Water, however, is a necessity. Taking away your water is the same thing as putting a gun to your head. This is an unacceptable proposition.

32      If there is one cause in the whole world that crosses all social, national, racial and economic lines, it's water. This is the most important issue we will face in our lifetime.

33      Thankfully, there are solutions to the problem. The simplest way to start making a difference is to choose tap water over bottled. If the taste of your local water is unappealing, buy a filter for your tap, or invest the money you would spend on bottled water into public infrastructure or watershed protection. Nothing speaks louder than where you spend your dollar. Bottled water will only be produced if there is a demand for it.

34      If you want to do more than that, then tell your representatives that you will not accept the selling of American water to foreign, multinational or corporate interests. Support public-sector projects and programs that encourage and create long-term, sustainable water solutions. Get involved with groups such as The Blue Planet Project (www.blueplanetproject.net), which is actively finding ways to solve the world's looming water crisis.

35      And above all else, remember that it's not too late. Clean, affordable water is still a reality in this country. It is our patriotic duty as Americans to ensure that it stays that way.

## Questions on Subject and Purpose

1. Ortega's essay focuses on two aspects of the privatization of water. What are they?
2. Where in the essay does Ortega shift from one aspect on the subject to another?
3. What does Ortega want his audience to do in response to these problems?

## Questions on Strategy and Audience

1. One of the first points Ortega discusses in his essay is the widespread perception that bottled water is more healthful or purer than tap water. To place it first suggests that it is an important argument to counter. Why?
2. Why might he end with the sentence, "It is our patriotic duty as Americans to ensure that it stays that way."?
3. What could Ortega assume about his audience?

## Questions on Vocabulary and Style

1. Ortega's title contains a pun. What is a pun and where is the one in the title?

2. Ortega makes the quotation in paragraph 26 a one-sentence paragraph. He could easily have combined that quotation with the paragraph that follows. Why isolate the sentence in this way?

3. Be prepared to define the following words: *stringent* (paragraph 7), *touted* (15), *contingent* (22), *recoup* (24), *putatively* (28).

## Writing Suggestions

1. **For Your Journal or Blog.** How often in the course of day or a week do you buy a bottle of water? Why do you do so, considering that you could save a considerable amount of money and "go green" by simply bringing a bottle of tap water from home or your dormitory? Reflect on your decisions to do one and not the other in your journal or blog.

2. **For a Paragraph.** In a paragraph, either defend your decision to buy bottled water or urge your fellow students to stop buying bottled water.

3. **For an Essay.** Expand your paragraph into an essay—you might consider submitting it to the student newspaper as well as to your instructor. Remember to address the objections that those who disagree with you might have about your choice. Your position does not need to be one extreme or the other; there might be room for a middle position.

4. **For Research.** Toward the end of the essay (paragraph 26), Ortega quotes a statement made by a former vice president of the World Bank: "The wars of the next century will be about water." Research that statement and the context to which it refers. To what was the speaker referring? How widespread is that thought? In a research essay, argue for or against that statement.

## For Further Study

**Focusing on Grammar and Writing.** Why begin the essay with a sentence fragment? What would it take to make the fragment a complete sentence? Try combining the fragment with the sentence following it in order to make a complete sentence. What is lost in the revision? Is anything gained?

**Working Together.** Divide into small groups and discuss which parts of Ortega's argument seem the strongest and which seem the weakest. What accounts for the difference?

**Seeing Other Modes at Work.** In many sections of his essay Ortega uses examples (statistics, facts) to buttress his argument.

**Finding Connections.** The obvious pairing is with Fredrik Segerfeldt's "The Private Sector Can Get Water Flowing to the Poor."

**Exploring the Web.** Ortega mentions several companies involved in the private water market. Look at the Websites of Veolia (www.veoliaenvironnement.com) and Suez (www.suez.com). The Web has many sites that oppose privatization, among them Blue Planet Project (www.blueplanetproject.net).

# I Have a Dream

Martin Luther King Jr.

*Martin Luther King Jr. (1929–1968) was born in Atlanta, the son of a Baptist minister. Ordained in his father's church in 1947, King received a doctorate in theology from Boston University in 1955. That same year he achieved national prominence by leading a boycott protesting the segregation of the Montgomery, Alabama, city bus system, based on ideas of nonviolent civil resistance derived from Thoreau and Gandhi. A central figure in the civil rights movement, King was awarded the Nobel Peace Prize in 1964. He was assassinated in Memphis in 1968. His birthday, January 15, is celebrated as a national holiday.*

*King's "I Have a Dream" speech was delivered at the Lincoln Memorial to an audience of 250,000 people who assembled in Washington, D.C., on August 28, 1963. That march, commemorating in part the hundredth anniversary of Lincoln's Emancipation Proclamation, was intended as an act of "creative lobbying" to win the support of Congress and the president for pending civil rights legislation. King's speech is one of the most memorable and moving examples of American oratory.*

## Before Reading

**Connecting:** Probably every American has heard at least a small portion of King's speech. Before you begin to read, jot down what you know about the speech or the phrases that you remember from recordings and television clips.

**Anticipating:** King's speech is marked by the extensive use of images. As you read, make a note of the most powerful and recurrent images that he uses.

1    **F**ive score years ago, a great American, in whose symbolic shadow we stand, signed the Emancipation Proclamation. This momentous decree came as a great beacon light of hope to millions of Negro slaves who had been seared in the flames of withering injustice. It came as a joyous daybreak to end the long night of captivity.

2      But one hundred years later, we must face the tragic fact that the Negro is still not free. One hundred years later, the life of the Negro is still sadly crippled by the manacles of segregation and the chains of discrimination. One hundred years later, the Negro lives on a lonely island of poverty in the midst of a vast ocean of material prosperity. One hundred years later, the Negro is

still languishing in the corners of American society and finds himself an exile in his own land. So we have come here today to dramatize an appalling condition.

3   In a sense we have come to our nation's capital to cash a check. When the architects of our republic wrote the magnificent words of the Constitution and the Declaration of Independence, they were signing a promissory note to which every American was to fall heir. This note was a promise that all men would be guaranteed the unalienable rights of life, liberty, and the pursuit of happiness.

4   It is obvious today that America has defaulted on this promissory note insofar as her citizens of color are concerned. Instead of honoring this sacred obligation, America has given the Negro people a bad check; a check which has come back marked "insufficient funds." But we refuse to believe that the bank of justice is bankrupt. We refuse to believe that there are insufficient funds in the great vaults of opportunity of this nation. So we have come to cash this check—a check that will give us upon demand the riches of freedom and the security of justice. We have also come to this hallowed spot to remind America of the fierce urgency of *now*. This is no time to engage in the luxury of cooling off or to take the tranquilizing drugs of gradualism. *Now* is the time to make real the promises of Democracy. *Now* is the time to rise from the dark and desolate valley of segregation to the sunlit path of racial justice. *Now* is the time to open the doors of opportunity to all of God's children. *Now* is the time to lift our nation from the quicksands of racial injustice to the solid rock of brotherhood.

5   It would be fatal for the nation to overlook the urgency of the moment and to underestimate the determination of the Negro. This sweltering summer of the Negro's legitimate discontent will not pass until there is an invigorating autumn of freedom and equality. 1963 is not an end, but a beginning. Those who hope that the Negro needed to blow off steam and will now be content will have a rude awakening if the nation returns to business as usual. There will be neither rest nor tranquility in America until the Negro is granted his citizenship rights. The whirlwinds of revolt will continue to shake the foundations of our nation until the bright day of justice emerges.

6   But there is something that I must say to my people who stand on the warm threshold which leads into the palace of justice. In the process of gaining our rightful place we must not be guilty of wrongful deeds. Let us not seek to satisfy our thirst for freedom by drinking from the cup of bitterness and hatred. We must forever conduct our struggle on the high plane of dignity and discipline. We must not allow our creative protest to degenerate into physical violence. Again and again we must rise to the majestic heights of meeting physical force with soul force. The marvelous new militancy which has engulfed the Negro community must not lead us to a distrust of all white people, for many of our white brothers, as evidenced by their presence here today, have come to realize that their destiny is tied up with our destiny and their freedom is inextricably bound to our freedom. We cannot walk alone.

7    And as we walk, we must make the pledge that we shall march ahead. We cannot turn back. There are those who are asking the devotees of civil rights, "When will you be satisfied?" We can never be satisfied as long as the Negro is the victim of the unspeakable horrors of police brutality. We can never be satisfied as long as our bodies, heavy with the fatigue of travel, cannot gain lodging in the motels of the highways and the hotels of the cities. We cannot be satisfied as long as the Negro's basic mobility is from a smaller ghetto to a larger one. We can never be satisfied as long as a Negro in Mississippi cannot vote and a Negro in New York believes he has nothing for which to vote. No, no, we are not satisfied, and we will not be satisfied until justice rolls down like waters and righteousness like a mighty stream.

8    I am not unmindful that some of you have come here out of great trials and tribulations. Some of you have come fresh from narrow jail cells. Some of you have come from areas where your quest for freedom left you battered by the storms of persecution and staggered by the winds of police brutality. You have been the veterans of creative suffering. Continue to work with the faith that unearned suffering is redemptive.

9    Go back to Mississippi, go back to Alabama, go back to South Carolina, go back to Georgia, go back to Louisiana, go back to the slums and ghettos of our northern cities, knowing that somehow this situation can and will be changed. Let us not wallow in the valley of despair.

10    I say to you today, my friends, that in spite of the difficulties and frustrations of the moment I still have a dream. It is a dream deeply rooted in the American dream.

11    I have a dream that one day this nation will rise up and live out the true meaning of its creed: "We hold these truths to be selfevident: that all men are created equal."

12    I have a dream that one day on the red hills of Georgia the sons of former slaves and the sons of former slave owners will be able to sit down together at the table of brotherhood.

13    I have a dream that one day even the state of Mississippi, a desert state sweltering with the heat of injustice and oppression, will be transformed into an oasis of freedom and justice.

14    I have a dream that my four little children will one day live in a nation where they will not be judged by the color of their skin but by the content of their character.

15    I have a dream today.

16    I have a dream that one day the state of Alabama, whose governor's lips are presently dripping with the words of interposition and nullification, will be transformed into a situation where little black boys and black girls will be able to join hands with little white boys and white girls and walk together as sisters and brothers.

17    I have a dream today.

18    I have a dream that one day every valley shall be exalted, every hill and mountain shall be made low, the rough places will be made plain, and the

crooked places will be made straight, and the glory of the Lord shall be revealed, and all flesh shall see it together.

19    This is our hope. This is the faith with which I return to the South. With this faith we will be able to hew out of the mountain of despair a stone of hope. With this faith we will be able to transform the jangling discords of our nation into a beautiful symphony of brotherhood. With this faith we will be able to work together, to pray together, to struggle together, to go to jail together, to stand up for freedom together, knowing that we will be free one day.

20    This will be the day when all of God's children will be able to sing with new meaning

> *My country, 'tis of thee,*
> *Sweet land of liberty,*
> *Of thee I sing:*
> *Land where my fathers died,*
> *Land of the pilgrims' pride,*
> *From every mountain-side*
> *Let freedom ring.*

21    And if America is to be a great nation this must become true. So let freedom ring from the prodigious hilltops of New Hampshire. Let freedom ring from the mighty mountains of New York. Let freedom ring from the heightening Alleghenies of Pennsylvania!

22    Let freedom ring from the snowcapped Rockies of Colorado!

23    Let freedom ring from the curvaceous peaks of California!

24    But not only that; let freedom ring from Stone Mountain of Georgia!

25    Let freedom ring from Lookout Mountain of Tennessee!

26    Let freedom ring from every hill and molehill of Mississippi. From every mountainside, let freedom ring.

27    When we let freedom ring, when we let it ring from every village and every hamlet, from every state and every city, we will be able to speed up that day when all of God's children, black men and white men, Jews and Gentiles, Protestants and Catholics, will be able to join hands and sing in the words of the old Negro spiritual, "Free at last! free at last! thank God almighty, we are free at last!"

## Questions on Subject and Purpose

1. What is King's dream?
2. King's essay was a speech delivered before thousands of marchers and millions of television viewers. How are its oral origins revealed in the written version?
3. In what way is King's speech an attempt at persuasion? Whom was he trying to persuade to do what?

## Questions on Strategy and Audience

1. Why does King begin with the words "Five score years ago"? Why does he say at the end of paragraph 6, "We cannot walk alone"? What do such words have to do with the context of King's speech?

2. How does King structure his speech? Is there an inevitable order or movement? How effective is his conclusion?

3. What expectations does King have of his audience? How do you know that?

## Questions on Vocabulary and Style

1. How many examples of figurative speech (images, metaphors, similes) can you find in the speech? What effect does such figurative language have?

2. The speech is full of parallel structures. See how many you can find. Why does King use so many?

3. Be prepared to define the following words: *seared* (paragraph 1), *manacles* (2), *languishing* (2), *promissory note* (3), *unalienable* (3), *invigorating* (5), *inextricably* (6), *tribulations* (8), *nullification* (16), *prodigious* (21).

## Writing Suggestions

1. **For Your Journal or Blog.** It is impossible for most people to read or hear King's speech without being moved. What is it about the speech that makes it so emotionally powerful? In your journal or blog, speculate on the reasons the speech has such an impact. What does it suggest about the power of language?

2. **For a Paragraph.** In a paragraph, argue for equality for a minority group of serious concern on your campus (the disabled; a sexual, racial, or religious minority; returning adults; commuters).

3. **For an Essay.** Expand the argument you explored in a paragraph to essay length.

4. **For Research.** According to the U.S. Census Bureau, 43 million Americans have some type of physical or mental disability. Like members of other minorities, the disabled regularly confront discrimination ranging from prejudice to physical barriers that deny them equal access to facilities. The federal government, with the passage of Title V of the Rehabilitation Act in 1973 and the Americans with Disabilities Act of 1990, has attempted to address these problems. Research the problem on your college campus. What has been done to eliminate discrimination against the disabled? What remains to be done? Argue for the importance of such changes. Alternatively, you might argue that the regulations are burdensome and should be abandoned. Be sure to document your sources wherever appropriate.

## For Further Study

**Focusing on Grammar and Writing.** What is a paragraph? Once you have a working definition, look at the twenty-seven paragraphs in this essay. What theoretical and grammatical principles does King seem to use in deciding when to begin a new paragraph? Do his principles change as the essay progresses? When and why? What does the essay suggest about the structure and nature of paragraphs?

**Working Together.** Working in small groups, divide King's essay into blocks of paragraphs. Locate all the instances of parallelism in your section (check the

Glossary and Ready Reference for a definition and examples of parallelism). How many examples can you find?

**Seeing Other Modes at Work.** How does King's use of narration early in his speech contribute to his persuasive purpose?

**Finding Connections.** Aspects of the same subject are explored in Richard Rodriguez's "None of This Is Fair" (this chapter) and in Brent Staples's "Black Men and Public Space" (Chapter 7).

**Exploring the Web.** Extensive online resources are available for King, including texts of his speeches, video and audio clips, texts of sermons, and photographs.

# None of This Is Fair

Richard Rodriguez

*Born in 1944 in San Francisco to Spanish-speaking Mexican-American parents, Richard Rodriguez first learned English in grade school. Educated in English literature at Stanford, Columbia, and the University of California at Berkeley, Rodriguez is best known for his conservative opinions on bilingual education and affirmative action, and in "None of This Is Fair" he uses his personal experience to argue that affirmative action programs are ineffective in reaching the seriously disadvantaged. Yet he also suggests in his two autobiographical works,* Hunger of Memory: The Education of Richard Rodriguez *(1982) and* Days of Obligation: An Argument with My Mexican Father *(1992), that he harbors deep regret at losing his own Hispanic heritage when he became assimilated into the English-speaking world. His most recent book is* Brown: The Last Discovery of America *(2002).*

> *Basically, the phrase "affirmative action" refers to policies and programs that try to redress past discrimination by increasing opportunities for underrepresented or minority groups. In the United States, the major classifications affected by affirmative action are defined by age, race, religion, national origin, and sex. The phrase was coined in 1965 in an executive order issued by President Lyndon Johnson that required any contractor dealing with the federal government to "take affirmative action to ensure that applicants are employed ... without regard to their race, creed, color, or national origin." In the decades following, affirmative action, in the form of weighted admissions policies, became a potent tool for colleges and universities seeking increased enrollments of previously underrepresented students. Controversy has always surrounded such policies, and in recent years a number of states have enacted legislation banning race-based admissions selection.*

> **On Writing:** *In an interview, Rodriguez noted: "It takes me a very long time to write. What I try to do when I write is break down the line separating the prosaic world from the poetic world. I try to write about everyday concerns—an educational issue, say, or the problems of the unemployed—but to write about them as powerfully, as richly, as well as I can."*

## Before Reading

**Connecting:** To what extent has your education—in elementary and secondary schools—provided you with opportunities that others have not had?

**Anticipating:** Why did it trouble Rodriguez to be labeled as a "minority student"?

1    **M**y plan to become a professor of English—my ambition during long years in college at Stanford, then in graduate school at Columbia and Berkeley—was complicated by feelings of embarrassment and guilt. So many times I would see other Mexican-Americans and know we were alike only in race. And yet, simply because our race was the same, I was, during the last years of my schooling, the beneficiary of their situation. Affirmative Action programs had made it all possible. The disadvantages of others permitted my promotion; the absence of many Mexican-Americans from academic life allowed my designation as a "minority student."

2    For me opportunities had been extravagant. There were fellowships, summer research grants, and teaching assistantships. After only two years in graduate school, I was offered teaching jobs by several colleges. Invitations to Washington conferences arrived and I had the chance to travel abroad as a "Mexican-American representative." The benefits were often, however, too gaudy to please. In three published essays, in conversations with teachers, in letters to politicians and at conferences, I worried the issue of Affirmative Action. Often I proposed contradictory opinions. Though consistent was the admission that—because of an early, excellent education—I was no longer a principal victim of racism or any other social oppression. I said that but still I continued to indicate on applications for financial aid that I was a Hispanic-American. It didn't really occur to me to say anything else, or to leave the question unanswered.

3    Thus I complied with and encouraged the odd bureaucratic logic of Affirmative Action. I let government officials treat the disadvantaged condition of many Mexican-Americans with my advancement. Each fall my presence was noted by Health, Education, and Welfare department statisticians. As I pursued advanced literary studies and learned the skill of reading Spenser and Wordsworth and Empson, I would hear myself numbered among the culturally disadvantaged. Still, silent, I didn't object.

4    But the irony cut deep. And guilt would not be evaded by averting my glance when I confronted a face like my own in a crowd. By late 1975, nearing the completion of my graduate studies at Berkeley, I was so wary of the benefits of Affirmative Action that I feared my inevitable success as an applicant for a teaching position. The months of fall—traditionally that time of academic job-searching—passed without my applying to a single school. When one of my professors chanced to learn this in late November, he was astonished, then furious. He yelled at me: Did I think that because I was a minority student jobs would just come looking for me? What was I thinking? Did I realize that he and several other faculty members had already written letters on my behalf? Was I going to start acting like some other minority students he had known? They struggled for success and then when it was almost within reach, grew strangely afraid and let it pass. Was that it? Was I determined to fail?

5    I did not respond to his questions. I didn't want to admit to him, and thus to myself, the reason I delayed.

6      I merely agreed to write to several schools. (In my letter I wrote: "I cannot claim to represent disadvantaged Mexican-Americans. The very fact that I am in a position to apply for this job should make that clear.") After two or three days, there were telegrams and phone calls, invitations to interviews, then airplane trips. A blur of faces and the murmur of their soft questions. And, over someone's shoulder, the sight of campus buildings shadowing pictures I had seen years before when I leafed through Ivy League catalogues with great expectations. At the end of each visit, interviewers would smile and wonder if I had any questions. A few times I quietly wondered what advantage my race had given me over other applicants. But that was an impossible question for them to answer without embarrassing me. Quickly, several persons insisted that my ethnic identity had given me no more than a "foot inside the door"; at most, I had a "slight edge" over other applicants. "We just looked at your dossier with extra care and we liked what we saw. There was never any question of having to alter our standards. You can be certain of that."

7      In the early part of January, offers arrived on stiffly elegant stationery. Most schools promised terms appropriate for any new assistant professor. A few made matters worse—and almost more tempting—by offering more: the use of university housing; an unusually large starting salary; a reduced teaching schedule. As the stack of letters mounted, my hesitation increased. I started calling department chairmen to ask for another week, then 10 more days—"more time to reach a decision"—to avoid the decision I would need to make.

8      At school, meantime, some students hadn't received a single job offer. One man, probably the best student in the department, did not even get a request for his dossier. He and I met outside a classroom one day and he asked about my opportunities. He seemed happy for me. Faculty members beamed. They said they had expected it. "After all, not many schools are going to pass up getting a Chicano with a Ph.D. in Renaissance literature," somebody said, laughing. Friends wanted to know which of the offers I was going to accept. But I couldn't make up my mind. February came and I was running out of time and excuses. (One chairman guessed my delay was a bargaining ploy and increased his offer with each of my calls.) I had to promise a decision by the 10th; the 12th at the very latest.

9      On the 18th of February, late in the afternoon, I was in the office I shared with several other teaching assistants. Another graduate student was sitting across the room at his desk. When I got up to leave, he looked over to say in an uneventful voice that he had some big news. He had finally decided to accept a position at a faraway university. It was not a job he especially wanted, he admitted. But he had to take it because there hadn't been any other offers. He felt trapped, and depressed, since his job would separate him from his young daughter.

10     I tried to encourage him by remarking that he was lucky at least to have found a job. So many others hadn't been able to get anything. But before I finished speaking I realized that I had said the wrong thing. And I anticipated his next question.

11      "What are your plans?" he wanted to know. "Is it true you've gotten an offer from Yale?"

12      I said that it was. "Only, I still haven't made up my mind."

13      He stared at me as I put on my jacket. And smiling, then unsmiling, he asked if I knew that he too had written to Yale. In his case, however, no one had bothered to acknowledge his letter with even a postcard. What did I think of that?

14      He gave me no time to answer.

15      "Damn!" he said sharply and his chair rasped the floor as he pushed himself back. Suddenly, it was to *me* that he was complaining. "It's just not right, Richard. None of this is fair. You've done some good work, but so have I. I'll bet our records are just about equal. But when we look for jobs this year, it's a different story. You get all of the breaks."

16      To evade his criticism, I wanted to side with him. I was about to admit the injustice of Affirmative Action. But he went on, his voice hard with accusation. "It's all very simple this year. You're a Chicano. And I am a Jew. That's the only real difference between us."

17      His words stung me: there was nothing he was telling me that I didn't know. I had admitted everything already. But to hear someone else say these things, and in such an accusing tone, was suddenly hard to take. In a deceptively calm voice, I responded that he had simplified the whole issue. The phrases came like bubbles to the tip of my tongue: "new blood"; "the importance of cultural diversity"; "the goal of racial integration." These were all the arguments I had proposed several years ago—and had long since abandoned. Of course the offers were unjustifiable. I knew that. All I was saying amounted to a frantic self-defense. I tried to find an end to a sentence. My voice faltered to a stop.

18      "Yeah, sure," he said. "I've heard all that before. Nothing you say really changes the fact that Affirmative Action is unfair. You see that, don't you? There isn't any way for me to compete with you. Once there were quotas to keep my parents out of certain schools; now there are quotas to get you in and the effect on me is the same as it was for them."

19      I listened to every word he spoke. But my mind was really on something else. I knew at that moment that I would reject all of the offers. I stood there silently surprised by what an easy conclusion it was. Having prepared for so many years to teach, having trained myself to do nothing else, I had hesitated out of practical fear. But now that it was made, the decision came with relief. I immediately knew I had made the right choice.

20      My colleague continued talking and I realized that he was simply right. Affirmative Action programs *are* unfair to white students. But as I listened to him assert his rights, I thought of the seriously disadvantaged. How different they were from white, middle-class students who come armed with the testimony of their grades and aptitude scores and self-confidence to complain about the unequal treatment they now receive. I listen to them. I do not want to be careless about what they say. Their rights are important to protect. But inevitably when I hear them or their lawyers, I think about the most seriously

disadvantaged, not simply Mexican-Americans, but of all those who do not ever imagine themselves going to college or becoming doctors: white, black, brown. Always poor. Silent. They are not plaintiffs before the court or against the misdirection of Affirmative Action. They lack the confidence (my confidence!) to assume their right to a good education. They lack the confidence and skills a good primary and secondary education provides and which are prerequisites for informed public life. They remain silent.

21    The debate drones on and surrounds them in stillness. They are distant, faraway figures like the boys I have seen peering down from freeway overpasses in some other part of town.

## Questions on Subject and Purpose

1. In paragraph 4, Rodriguez makes reference to the "irony" of the situation. In what ways was it ironic?
2. Why does Rodriguez decide to reject all of the offers?
3. Is Rodriguez criticizing affirmative action policies? How could such policies reach or change the lives of those who are really seriously disadvantaged?

## Questions on Strategy and Audience

1. To what extent does Rodriguez present a formal argument based on an appeal to reason? To what extent does he attempt to persuade through an appeal to emotion? Which element is stronger in the piece?
2. What is the difference between objectively stating an opinion and narrating a personal experience? Do we as readers react any differently to Rodriguez's story as a result?
3. What expectations does Rodriguez have of his audience? How do you know that?

## Questions on Vocabulary and Style

1. In paragraphs 11 through 18, Rodriguez dramatizes a scene with a fellow student. He could have just summarized what was said without using dialogue. What advantage is gained by developing the scene?
2. Be prepared to discuss the significance of the following sentences:
   a. "For me opportunities had been extravagant" (paragraph 2).
   b. "The benefits were often, however, too gaudy to please" (2).
   c. "The phrases came like bubbles to the tip of my tongue" (17).
   d. "Always poor. Silent" (20).
3. What is the effect of the simile ("like the boys I have seen . . .") Rodriguez uses in the final line?

## Writing Suggestions

1. **For Your Journal or Blog.** What made you pursue your education? What are the important motivating factors? Explore the questions in your journal or blog.

2. **For a Paragraph.** Describe a time when you encountered an obstacle because of your age, gender, race, religion, physical ability, physical appearance, or socioeconomic status. Describe the experience briefly; then argue against the unfairness of such discrimination.

3. **For an Essay.** Are minorities and women fairly represented on the faculty of your college or university? Check the proportion of white males to minority and women faculty members, looking not only at raw numbers but also at rank, tenure, and so forth. Then, in an essay, argue for or against the need to achieve a better balance.

4. **For Research.** Rodriguez feels that as a result of "an early, excellent education" (paragraph 2), he was no longer "a principal victim of racism or any other social oppression." If the key to helping the "seriously disadvantaged" lies in improving the quality of elementary and secondary education, how successful have American schools been? Has the quality of education for the disadvantaged improved in the past twenty years? Research the problem. Then write an essay in which you evaluate some existing programs and make recommendations about continuing, expanding, modifying, or dropping them. Be sure to document your sources wherever appropriate.

## For Further Study

**Focusing on Grammar and Writing.** Rewrite paragraphs 11 through 18, changing the dialogue into indirect discourse (a model would be paragraphs 4–6). What is the difference between the two strategies? What are the advantages and disadvantages of each? What happens to the essay when this change is made? What does Rodriguez gain by dramatizing the situation with the other teaching assistant? What does this activity suggest about using dialogue at appropriate times in your own essays?

**Working Together.** Rodriguez objects to affirmative action policies because they do not reach the seriously disadvantaged. How, though, might that be done? What changes might a writer argue for? Divide into small groups and brainstorm some possible solutions to the problems that Rodriguez sees.

**Seeing Other Modes at Work.** Rodriguez uses narration throughout the essay, relating his own experiences as part of his persuasive strategy.

**Finding Connections.** Interesting pairings include Judith Ortiz Cofer's "The Myth of the Latin Woman" (Chapter 4) and Amy Tan's "Mother Tongue" (Chapter 8).

**Exploring the Web.** Extensive resources for Richard Rodriguez, including biographies, interviews, and a number of his essays, can be found online. A wide range of Websites are devoted to affirmative action policies.

# 10

# COMBINATIONS AT WORK

The essays in the first nine chapters of this text are grouped according to the particular organizational patterns that they show. These organizational patterns can be labeled in a variety of ways: modes, rhetorical structures, ways of knowing, patterns for writers. Regardless of what they are called, each pattern has distinguishing features and distinctive elements and structures. Organizational patterns are the common building blocks of most writing; indeed, most are also the common ways in which we come to know and perceive. They are, in that sense, worth studying and practicing on their own.

Most of the essays in the earlier chapters of this text involve more than one mode or pattern or strategy. Except in a very short essay, it is rare to find only a single pattern at work. For example, narration rarely occurs without description; process includes narration; definition uses all of the patterns. In fact, for every essay in this book, the section Seeing Other Modes at Work identifies at least one other pattern that can be seen in the essay. Still, each essay in the earlier chapters is placed where it is because it predominantly displays one pattern.

In this chapter you will find classic essays that involve a mixture of strategies at work. The essays show how writers combine patterns into a whole; in that sense they are extensions of the other chapters in this text. As you read, notice how the patterns interact and combine to make an artistic whole.

# A Modest Proposal

## For Preventing the Children of Poor People in Ireland from Being a Burden to Their Parents or Country, and for Making Them Beneficial to the Public

Jonathan Swift

*Jonathan Swift (1667–1745) was born in Dublin of an English Tory family and entered Trinity College in 1682, studying for a career in the church. He was ordained in 1695 and was assigned to a small country parish in Kilroot, Ireland. Swift traveled to England several times hoping for advancement, and in 1713 he was made dean of St. Patrick's Cathedral in Dublin. A satirist and an active propagandist for the Tory party and the Irish cause, Swift is best known for* A Tale of a Tub *(1704),* Gulliver's Travels *(1726), and "A Modest Proposal" (1729).*

*Swift's "modest proposal" grew out of a number of factors and conditions that had reduced the Irish people to poverty. First, England had long regarded Ireland, not as a sister kingdom, but as a colony to be exploited. Toward the end of the seventeenth century, the English Parliament had passed a number of restrictive laws to control Irish agriculture and thereby protect English industries. The measures severely reduced Irish revenues and food production. Second, Irish titles, estates, and appointments were part of the English patronage system and were given to Englishmen who had no interest in Ireland's welfare and who did not reside there. Revenue generated in Ireland was spent in England. Swift himself had estimated that absentee landlords drew off as much as two-thirds of all Irish revenues. Third, for three years prior to 1729, Ireland had suffered a near famine occasioned by the failure of grain crops. Irish people were starving to death. Swift's ironic proposal was intended to dramatize Ireland's plight and to rebuke the English for their failure to help.*

**On Writing:** *In his poem "Verses on the Death of Dr. Swift," Swift noted:*

> As with a moral view designed
> To cure the vices of mankind:
> Yet malice never was his aim;
> He lashed the vice but spared the name.
> No individual could resent,
> Where thousands equally were meant.
> His satire points at no defect
> But what all mortals can correct.

## Before Reading

**Connecting:** What does the word *modest* suggest to you? In what way is this a "modest proposal"?

**Anticipating:** How do the verses quoted in On Writing apply to "A Modest Proposal"?

## Looking for Combinations

Swift's essay is primarily persuasive, but it uses other strategies as well. Fairly obvious are classification and cause and effect. Can you locate those patterns in the essay? Can you find any others at work? What role do these strategies or patterns play in the essay as a whole?

1    It is a melancholy object to those who walk through this great town,[1] or travel in the country, when they see the streets, the roads, and cabin-doors crowded with beggars of the female sex, followed by three, four, or six children all in rags, and importuning every passenger for an alms.[2] These mothers, instead of being able to work for their honest livelihood, are forced to employ all their time in strolling, to beg sustenance for their helpless infants, who, as they grow up, either turn thieves for want of work, or leave their dear native country to fight for the Pretender in Spain,[3] or sell themselves to the Barbadoes.[4]

2    I think it is agreed by all parties that this prodigious number of children, in the arms, or on the backs, or at the heels of their mothers, and frequently of their fathers, is in the present deplorable state of the kingdom a very great additional grievance; and therefore whoever could find out a fair, cheap, and easy method of making these children sound and useful members of the commonwealth would deserve so well of the public as to have his statue set up for a preserver of the nation.

3    But my intention is very far from being confined to provide only for the children of professed beggars; it is of a much greater extent, and shall take in the whole number of infants at a certain age who are born of parents in effect as little able to support them as those who demand our charity in the streets.

4    As to my own part, having turned my thoughts for many years upon this important subject, and maturely weighed the several schemes of other projectors,[5] I have always found them grossly mistaken in their computation.

---

[1]Dublin.
[2]A contemporary estimate placed the number of itinerent beggars in Ireland at 34,425.
[3]Irish Catholics had been recruited to fight for Spain and France against England. One attempt in 1719 had tried to restore the "Pretender," James Stuart, to the English throne.
[4]Large numbers of Irishmen emigrated to the British West Indies.
[5]For Swift, a "projector" was one who proposed foolish plans.

It is true a child just dropped from its dam may be supported by her milk for a solar year with little other nourishment, at most not above the value of two shillings, which the mother may certainly get, or the value in scraps, by her lawful occupation of begging, and it is exactly at one year old that I propose to provide for them, in such a manner as, instead of being a charge upon their parents, or the parish, or wanting food and raiment for the rest of their lives, they shall, on the contrary, contribute to the feeding and partly to the clothing of many thousands.

5     There is likewise another great advantage in my scheme, that it will prevent those voluntary abortions, and that horrid practice of women murdering their bastard children, alas, too frequent among us, sacrificing the poor innocent babes, I doubt, more to avoid the expense than the shame, which would move tears and pity in the most savage and inhuman breast.

6     The number of souls in Ireland being usually reckoned one million and a half, of these I calculate there may be about two hundred thousand couples whose wives are breeders from which number I subtract thirty thousand couples who are able to maintain their own children, although I apprehend there cannot be so many under the present distresses of the kingdom, but this being granted, there will remain an hundred and seventy thousand breeders. I again subtract fifty thousand for those women who miscarry, or whose children die by accident or disease within the year. There only remain an hundred and twenty thousand children of poor parents annually born: the question therefore is, how this number shall be reared, and provided for, which, as I have already said, under the present situation of affairs is utterly impossible by all the methods hitherto proposed, for we can neither employ them in handicraft or agriculture; we neither build houses (I mean in the country), nor cultivate land: they can very seldom pick up a livelihood by stealing until they arrive at six years old, except where they are of towardly[6] parts, although I confess they learn the rudiments much earlier, during which time they can however be properly looked upon only as probationers, as I have been informed by a principal gentleman in the County of Cavan, who protested to me that he never knew above one or two instances under the age of six, even in a part of the kingdom so renowned for the quickest proficiency in the art.

7     I am assured by our merchants that a boy or a girl before twelve years old, is no saleable commodity, and even when they come to this age, they will not yield above three pounds, or three pounds and half-a-crown at most on the Exchange, which cannot turn to account either to the parents or the kingdom, the charge of nutriment and rags having been at least four times that value.

8     I shall now therefore humbly propose my own thoughts, which I hope will not be liable to the least objection.

9     I have been assured by a very knowing American of my acquaintance in London, that a young healthy child well nursed is at a year old a most

[6]Promising.

delicious, nourishing and wholesome food, whether stewed, roasted, baked, or boiled, and I make no doubt that it will equally serve in a fricassee, or a ragout.

10     I do therefore humbly offer it to public consideration, that of the hundred and twenty thousand children already computed, twenty thousand may be reserved for breed, whereof only one fourth part to be males, which is more than we allow to sheep, black-cattle, or swine, and my reason is that these children are seldom the fruits of marriage, a circumstance not much regarded by our savages, therefore one male will be sufficient to serve four females. That the remaining hundred thousand may at a year old be offered in sale to the persons of quality, and fortune, through the kingdom, always advising the mother to let them suck plentifully in the last month, so as to render them plump, and fat for a good table. A child will make two dishes at an entertainment for friends, and when the family dines alone, the fore or hind quarter will make a reasonable dish, and seasoned with a little pepper or salt will be very good boiled on the fourth day, especially in winter.

11     I have reckoned upon a medium, that a child just born will weigh twelve pounds, and in a solar year if tolerably nursed increaseth to twenty-eight pounds.

12     I grant this food will be somewhat dear, and therefore very proper for landlords, who, as they have already devoured most of the parents, seem to have the best title to the children.

13     Infant's flesh will be in season throughout the year, but more plentiful in March, and a little before and after, for we are told by a grave author,[7] an eminent French physician, that fish being a prolific diet, there are more children born in Roman Catholic countries about nine months after Lent than at any other season; therefore reckoning a year after Lent, the markets will be more glutted than usual, because the number of Popish infants is at least three to one in this kingdom, and therefore it will have one other collateral advantage by lessening the number of Papists among us.

14     I have already computed the charge of nursing a beggar's child (in which list I reckon all cottagers, labourers, and four-fifths of the farmers) to be about two shillings per annum, rags included, and I believe no gentleman would repine to give ten shillings for the carcass of a good fat child, which, as I have said, will make four dishes of excellent nutritive meat, when he hath only some particular friend or his own family to dine with him. Thus the Squire will learn to be a good landlord and grow popular among his tenants, the mother will have eight shillings net profit, and be fit for work until she produces another child.

15     Those who are more thrifty (as I must confess the times require) may flay the carcass; the skin of which artificially dressed,[8] will make admirable gloves for ladies, and summer boots for fine gentlemen.

16     As to our city of Dublin, shambles[9] may be appointed for this purpose, in the most convenient parts of it, and butchers we may be assured will not be wanting, although rather recommend buying the children alive, and dressing them hot from the knife, as we do roasting pigs.

[7]François Rabelais (1494?–1553), a French satirist.
[8]With art or skill.
[9]A meat market.

17      A very worthy person, a true lover of his country, and whose virtues I highly esteem, was lately pleased, in discoursing on this matter to offer a refinement upon my scheme. He said that many gentlemen of this kingdom, having of late destroyed their deer, he conceived that the want of venison might be well supplied by the bodies of young lads and maidens, not exceeding fourteen years of age, not under twelve, so great a number of both sexes in every country being now ready to starve, for want of work and service and these to be disposed of by their parents if alive, or otherwise by their nearest relations. But with due deference to so excellent a friend, and so deserving a patriot, I cannot be altogether in his sentiments. For as to the males, my American acquaintance assured me from frequent experience that their flesh was generally tough and lean, like that of our schoolboys, by continual exercise, and their taste disagreeable, and to fatten them would not answer the charge. There as to the females, it would, I think with humble submission be a loss to the public, because they soon would become breeders themselves: and besides, it is not improbable that some scrupulous people might be apt to censure such a practice (although indeed very unjustly) as a little bordering upon cruelty, which I confess, hath always been with me the strongest objection against any project, howsoever well intended.

18      But in order to justify my friend, he confessed that this expedient was put into his head by the famous Psalmanazar,[10] a native of the island Formosa, who came from thence to London, above twenty years ago, and in conversation told my friend that in his country when any young person happened to be put to death, the executioner sold the carcass to persons of quality, as a prime dainty, and that, in his time, the body of a plump girl of fifteen, who was crucified for an attempt to poison the emperor, was sold to his Imperial Majesty's Prime Minister of State, and other great Mandarins of the Court, in joints from the gibbet, at four hundred crowns. Neither indeed can I deny that if the same use were made of several plump young girls in this town who, without one single groat to their fortunes, cannot stir abroad without a chair,[11] and appear at the playhouse and assemblies in foreign fineries, which they never will pay for, the kingdom would not be the worse.

19      Some persons of a desponding spirit are in great concern about that vast number of poor people, who are aged, diseased, or maimed, and I have been desired to employ my thoughts what course may be taken to ease the nation of so grievous an encumbrance. But I am not in the least pain upon that matter, because it is very well known that they are every day dying, and rotting, by cold, and famine, and filth, and vermin, as fast as can be reasonably expected. And as to the younger labourers they are now in almost as hopeful a condition. They cannot get work, and consequently pine away from want of nourishment, to a degree that if at any time they are accidentally hired to common labour, they have not strength to perform it; and thus the country and themselves are in a fair way of being soon delivered from the evils to come.

[10]An imposter who in 1704 published a fictitious account of Formosa.
[11]A sedan chair.

20    I have too long digressed, and therefore shall return to my subject. I think the advantages by the proposal which I have made are obvious and many, as well as of the highest importance.

21    For first, as I have already observed, it would greatly lessen the number of Papists, with whom we are yearly overrun, being the principal breeders of the nation, as well as our most dangerous enemies, and who stay at home on purpose with a design to deliver the kingdom to the Pretender, hoping to take their advantage by the absence of so many good Protestants, who have chosen rather to leave their country than stay at home and pay tithes against their conscience to an idolatrous Episcopal curate.

22    Secondly, the poorer tenants will have something valuable of their own, which by law may be made liable to distress, [12] and help to pay their landlord's rent, their corn and cattle being already seized, and money a thing unknown.

23    Thirdly, whereas the maintenance of an hundred thousand children, from two years old, and upwards, cannot be computed at less than ten shillings a piece per annum, the nation's stock will be thereby increased fifty thousand pounds per annum, besides the profit of a new dish, introduced to the tables of all gentlemen of fortune in the kingdom, who have any refinement in taste, and the money will circulate among ourselves, the goods being entirely of our own growth and manufacture.

24    Fourthly, the constant breeders, besides the gain of eight shillings sterling per annum, by the sale of their children, will be rid of the charge of maintaining them after the first year.

25    Fifthly, this food would likewise bring great custom to taverns, where the vintners will certainly be so prudent as to procure the best receipts for dressing it to perfection, and consequently have their houses frequented by all the fine gentlemen, who justly value themselves upon their knowledge in good eating; and a skilful cook, who understands how to oblige his guests, will contrive to make it as expensive as they please.

26    Sixthly, this would be a great inducement to marriage, which all wise nations have either encouraged by rewards, or enforced by laws and penalties. It would increase the care and tenderness of mothers towards their children, when they were sure of a settlement for life, to the poor babes, provided in some sort by the public to their annual profit instead of expense. We should soon see an honest emulation among the married women, which of them could bring the fattest child to the market. Men would become as fond of their wives, during the time of their pregnancy, as they are now of their mares in foal, their cows in calf, or sows when they are ready to farrow, nor offer to beat or kick them (as it is too frequent a practice) for fear of a miscarriage.

27    Many other advantages might be enumerated. For instance, the addition of some thousand carcasses in our exportation of barrelled beef; the propagation of swine's flesh, and improvement in the art of making good bacon, so much wanted among us by the great destruction of pigs, too frequent at our

[12]Subject to seizure because debts were not paid.

tables, and no way comparable in taste or magnificence to a well-grown, fat yearling child, which roasted whole will make a considerable figure at a Lord Mayor's feast, or any other public entertainment. But this and many others I omit, being studious of brevity.

28      Supposing that one thousand families in this city would be constant customers for infants' flesh, besides others who might have it at merry meetings, particularly weddings and christenings; I compute that Dublin would take off annually about twenty thousand carcasses, and the rest of the kingdom (where probably they will be sold somewhat cheaper) the remaining eighty thousand.

29      I can think of no one objection that will possibly be raised against this proposal, unless it should be urged that the number of people will be thereby much lessened in the kingdom. This I freely own, and it was indeed one principal design in offering it to the world. I desire the reader will observe, that I calculate my remedy for this one individual Kingdom of Ireland, and for no other that ever was, is, or, I think, ever can be upon earth. Therefore let no man talk to me of other expedients: Of taxing our absentees at five shillings a pound: Of using neither clothes, nor household furniture, except what is of our own growth and manufacture: Of utterly rejecting the materials and instruments that promote foreign luxury: Of curing the expensiveness of pride, vanity, idleness, and gaming in our women: Of introducing a vein of parsimony, prudence, and temperance: Of learning to love our country, wherein we differ even from Laplanders, and the inhabitants of Topinamboo: Of quitting our animosities and factions, nor act any longer like the Jews, who were murdering one another at the very moment their city was taken: Of being a little cautious not to sell our country and consciences for nothing: Of teaching landlords to have at least one degree of mercy towards their tenants. Lastly, of putting a spirit of honesty, industry, and skill into our shopkeepers, who, if a resolution could now be taken to buy only our native goods, would immediately unite to cheat and exact upon us in the price, the measure and the goodness, nor could ever yet be brought to make one fair proposal of just dealing, though often and earnestly invited to it.

30      Therefore I repeat, let no man talk to me of these and the like expedients, till he hath at least a glimpse of hope that there will ever be some hearty and sincere attempt to put them in practice.

31      But as to myself, having been wearied out for many years with offering vain, idle, visionary thoughts, and at length utterly despairing of success, I fortunately fell upon this proposal, which as it is wholly new, so it hath something solid and real, of no expense and little trouble, full in our own power, and whereby we can incur no danger in disobliging England. For this kind of commodity will not bear exportation, the flesh being of too tender a consistence to admit a long continuance in salt, although perhaps I could name a country which would be glad to eat up our whole nation without it.[13]

32      After all I am not so violently bent upon my own opinion as to reject any offer, proposed by wise men, which shall be found equally innocent, cheap,

[13]England.

easy and effectual. But before some thing of that kind shall be advanced in contradiction to my scheme, and offering a better, I desire the author, or authors, will be pleased maturely to consider two points. First, as things now stand, how they will be able to find food and raiment for a hundred thousand useless mouths and backs? And secondly, there being a round million of creatures in human figure, throughout this kingdom, whose whole subsistence put into a common stock would leave them in debt two millions of pounds sterling; adding those who are beggars by profession, to the bulk of farmers, cottagers, and labourers with their wives and children, who are beggars in effect; I desire those politicians who dislike my overture, and may perhaps be so bold to attempt an answer, that they will first ask the parents of these mortals whether they would not at this day think it a great happiness to have been sold for food at a year old, in the manner I prescribe, and thereby have avoided such a perpetual scene of misfortunes as they have since gone through, by the oppression of landlords, the impossibility of paying rent without money or trade, the want of common sustenance, with neither house nor clothes to cover them from the inclemencies of weather, and the most inevitable prospect of entailing the like, or greater miseries upon their breed for ever.

33   I profess in the sincerity of my heart that I have not the least personal interest in endeavouring to promote this necessary work, having no other motive than the public good of my country, by advancing our trade, providing for infants, relieving the poor, and giving some pleasure to the rich. I have no children by which I can propose to get a single penny; the youngest being nine years old, and my wife past child-bearing.

## Questions on Subject and Purpose

1. What is Swift's thesis? Summarize it in a sentence or two.
2. Swift explains his motive for writing in the final paragraph. Is he being serious? How much of what he says can be taken seriously?
3. What could Swift hope to accomplish by offering such an outrageous proposal?

## Questions on Strategy and Audience

1. Is Swift's essay persuasive? Be prepared to explain why you think that Swift's proposal either succeeds or fails.
2. Does Swift direct his criticism toward any specific group or groups?
3. What is the digression that Swift mentions in paragraph 20? What purpose does it serve?

## Questions on Vocabulary and Style

1. Characterize the tone of the essay. How is that tone achieved? How does it contribute to the effect of the essay?

2. Trace the following throughout the essay and be prepared to explain the function of each:
   a. animal imagery
   b. monetary, statistical terminology
   c. food imagery
   d. death imagery

3. Be able to define the following words: *importuning* (paragraph 1), *alms* (1), *sustenance* (1), *dam* (4), *raiment* (4), *rudiments* (6), *nutriment* (7), *fricassee* (9), *ragout* (9), *repine* (14), *flay* (15), *maimed* (19), *encumbrance* (19), *vintners* (25), *emulation* (26), *farrow* (26), *yearling* (27), *expedients* (29), *parsimony* (29).

## Writing Suggestions

1. **For Your Journal or Blog.** In your journal or blog, make a list of social problems in the United States that might be the subject of a "modest proposal." They might grow out of economic issues (lack of jobs in certain parts of the country, low-paying jobs, inadequate or unaffordable daycare), medical issues (no health coverage, catastrophic medical costs), or any similar topic. Brainstorm a list of possibilities.

2. **For a Paragraph.** In a paragraph, draw up a modest (and outrageous) proposal for dealing with one of the problems. Swift has already suggested selling children as food, so you cannot use that again. Be imaginative and try to develop your proposal in sufficient detail to make a substantial paragraph.

3. **For an Essay.** Expand your paragraph into an essay. Remember that in addition to your outrageous solution, you must provide a number of more realistic and workable possibilities. It is not enough to be critical; you need to make solid, reasonable suggestions as well. Although Swift's strategy is to shock, he also offers sound possible solutions as well. That is an essential part of the assignment.

4. **For Research.** The problems about which Swift writes have not disappeared from the world. Every year, thousands of children starve to death, particularly in Africa. Peter Singer's essay, "The Singer Solution to World Poverty" (this chapter), in addition to many of the world social services organizations, such as Save the Children and CARE, can provide detailed documentation of the problem. The problem is of such magnitude that many people, although they might be sympathetic and wish to help, feel it is simply too large for them to make any difference. In a serious research essay, suggest possible ways in which we as a nation might help combat this problem. First, document the magnitude of the problem, then suggest possible, serious solutions.

## For Further Study

**Focusing on Grammar and Writing.** Swift uses parallelism extensively in his essay, especially in paragraphs and in sentence structures. How many instances of parallelism can you locate in the essay? How does parallelism work to make the essay clearer and more readable?

**Working Together.** Swift creates a persona in the essay—a narrator who is not Swift but a fictional creation. Divide into groups so that each group can be assigned an equal number of paragraphs from the essay. Each group should study the assigned block of paragraphs and analyze the values, character, and voice of the persona. What does he sound like? What are his distinctive characteristics? How do you know that he is a persona and not Swift himself?

**Seeing Other Modes at Work.** In addition to persuasion, the essay makes use of classification and cause and effect.

**Finding Connections.** An interesting pairing is with Peter Singer's "The Singer Solution to World Poverty" (this chapter).

**Exploring the Web.** The Web has many sites devoted to Swift's writing and "A Modest Proposal," as well as sites that document the problem of poverty in the United States and in the world.

# *Once More to the Lake*

E. B. White

*Elwyn Brooks White (1899–1985) was born in Mount Vernon, New York, and received a B.A. from Cornell in 1921. His freshman English teacher was William Strunk, whose* Elements of Style *White revised in 1959 and made into a textbook classic. In 1925 White began writing for* The New Yorker *and was one of the mainstays of that magazine, his precise, ironic, nostalgic prose style closely associated with its own. From 1937 to 1943, he also wrote the column "One Man's Meat" for* Harper's. *His books include the children's classic* Charlotte's Web *(1952),* The Second Tree From the Corner *(1954),* The Essays of E. B. White *(1977), and* The Poems and Sketches of E. B. White *(1981).*

*White revisited the Belgrade Lakes in Maine in the summer of 1936. The essay was not written until 1941 and was published in his collection* Essays of E. B. White *that same year.*

**On Writing:** *Commenting on his writing, White observed: "Sometimes I'm asked how old I was when I started to write, and what made me want to write. I started early—as soon as I could spell. In fact, I can't remember any time in my life when I wasn't busy writing. I don't know what caused me to do it, or why I enjoyed it, but I think children often find pleasure and satisfaction in trying to set their thoughts down on paper, either in words or in pictures. I was no good at drawing, so I used words instead. As I grew older, I found that writing can be a way of earning a living."*

## Before Reading

**Connecting:** Have you ever revisited a place where you and your family vacationed some years before? Or a neighborhood or town in which you once lived? Was the experience the same as you remembered?

**Anticipating:** Why does White get so confused about who is the father and who is the son in the essay? What is he suggesting?

## Looking for Combinations

White's primary structural mode in the essay is narration—he tells us a story. However, he uses other modes as well. For example, the essay uses description extensively and comparison and contrast. Can you locate those patterns in the essay? Can you find any others at work? What roles do these strategies or modes play in the essay as a whole?

1    **O**ne summer along about 1904, my father rented a camp on a lake in Maine and took us all there for the month of August. We all got ringworm from some kittens and had to rub Pond's Extract on our arms and legs night and morning, and my father rolled over in a canoe with all his clothes on; but outside of that the vacation was a success and from then on none of us ever thought there was any place in the world like that lake in Maine. We returned summer after summer—always on August 1st for one month. I have since become a salt-water man, but sometimes in summer there are days when the restlessness of the tides and the fearful cold of the sea water and the incessant wind that blows across the afternoon and into the evening make me wish for the placidity of a lake in the woods. A few weeks ago this feeling got so strong I bought myself a couple of bass hooks and a spinner and returned to the lake where we used to go, for a week's fishing and to revisit old haunts.

2        I took along my son, who had never had any fresh water up his nose and who had seen lily pads only from train windows. On the journey over to the lake I began to wonder what it would be like. I wondered how time would have marred this unique, this holy spot—the coves and streams, the hills that the sun set behind, the camps and the paths behind the camps. I was sure that the tarred road would have found it out and I wondered in what other ways it would be desolated. It is strange how much you can remember about places like that once you allow your mind to return into the grooves that lead back. You remember one thing, and that suddenly reminds you of another thing. I guess I remembered clearest of all the early mornings, when the lake was cool and motionless, remembered how the bedroom smelled of the lumber it was made of and of the wet woods whose scent entered through the screen. The partitions in the camp were thin and did not extend clear to the top of the rooms, and as I was always the first up I would dress softly so as not to wake the others, and sneak out into the sweet outdoors and start out in the canoe, keeping close along the shore in the long shadows of the pines. I remembered being very careful never to rub my paddle against the gunwale for fear of disturbing the stillness of the cathedral.

3        The lake had never been what you would call a wild lake. There were cottages sprinkled around the shores, and it was in farming country although the shores of the lake were quite heavily wooded. Some of the cottages were owned by nearby farmers, and you would live at the shore and eat your meals at the farmhouse. That's what our family did. But although it wasn't wild, it was a fairly large and undisturbed lake and there were places in it which, to a child at least, seemed infinitely remote and primeval.

4        I was right about the tar: it led to within half a mile of the shore. But when I got back there, with my boy, and we settled into a camp near a farmhouse and into the kind of summertime I had known, I could tell that it was going to be pretty much the same as it had been before—I knew it, lying in bed the first morning, smelling the bedroom, and hearing the boy sneak quietly out and go off along the shore in a boat. I began to sustain the illusion that he was I, and therefore, by simple transposition, that I was my father. This sensation persisted,

kept cropping up all the time we were there. It was not an entirely new feeling, but in this setting it grew much stronger. I seemed to be living a dual existence. I would be in the middle of some simple act, I would be picking up a bait box or laying down a table fork, or I would be saying something, and suddenly it would be not I but my father who was saying the words or making the gesture. It gave me a creepy sensation.

5      We went fishing the first morning. I felt the same damp moss covering the worms in the bait can, and saw the dragonfly alight on the tip of my rod as it hovered a few inches from the surface of the water. It was the arrival of this fly that convinced me beyond any doubt that everything was as it always had been, that the years were a mirage and there had been no years. The small waves were the same, chucking the rowboat under the chin as we fished at anchor, and the boat was the same boat, the same color green and the ribs broken in the same places, and under the floor-boards the same fresh-water leavings and debris—the dead helgramite, the wisps of moss, the rusty discarded fishhook, the dried blood from yesterday's catch. We stared silently at the tips of our rods, at the dragonflies that came and went. I lowered the tip of mine into the water, tentatively, pensively dislodging the fly, which darted two feet away, poised, darted two feet back, and came to rest again a little farther up the rod. There had been no years between the ducking of this dragonfly and the other one—the one that was part of memory. I looked at the boy, who was silently watching his fly, and it was my hands that held his rod, my eyes watching. I felt dizzy and didn't know which rod I was at the end of.

6      We caught two bass, hauling them in briskly as though they were mackerel, pulling them over the side of the boat in a businesslike manner without any landing net, and stunning them with a blow on the back of the head. When we got back for a swim before lunch, the lake was exactly where we had left it, the same number of inches from the dock, and there was only the merest suggestion of a breeze. This seemed an utterly enchanted sea, this lake you could leave to its own devices for a few hours and come back to, and find that it had not stirred, this constant and trustworthy body of water. In the shallows, the dark, water-soaked sticks and twigs, smooth and old, were undulating in clusters on the bottom against the clean ribbed sand, and the track of the mussel was plain. A school of minnows swam by, each minnow with its small individual shadow, doubling the attendance, so clear and sharp in the sunlight. Some of the other campers were in swimming, along the shore, one of them with a cake of soap, and the water felt thin and clear and unsubstantial. Over the years there had been this person with the cake of soap, this cultist, and here he was. There had been no years.

7      Up to the farmhouse to dinner through the teeming, dusty field, the road under our sneakers was only a two-track road. The middle track was missing, the one with the marks of the hooves and splotches of dried, flaky manure. There had always been three tracks to choose from in choosing which track to walk in; now the choice was narrowed down to two. For a moment I missed terribly the middle alternative. But the way led past the tennis court, and something about the way it lay there in the sun reassured me; the tape had

loosened along the backline, the alleys were green with plantains and other weeds, and the net (installed in June and removed in September) sagged in the dry noon, and the whole place steamed with midday heat and hunger and emptiness. There was a choice of pie for dessert, and one was blueberry and one was apple, and the waitresses were the same country girls, there having been no passage of time, only the illusion of it as in a dropped curtain—the waitresses were still fifteen; their hair had been washed, that was the only difference—they had been to the movies and seen the pretty girls with the clean hair.

8    Summertime, oh summertime, pattern of life indelible, the fadeproof lake, the woods unshatterable, the pasture with the sweetfern and the juniper forever and ever, summer without end; this was the background, and the life along the shore was the design, the cottages with their innocent and tranquil design, their tiny docks with the flagpole and the American flag floating against the white clouds in the blue sky, the little paths over the roots of the trees leading from camp to camp and the paths leading back to the outhouses and the can of lime for sprinkling, and at the souvenir counters at the store the miniature birch-bark canoes and the post cards that showed things looking a little better than they looked. This was the American family at play, escaping the city heat, wondering whether the newcomers in the camp at the head of the cove were "common" or "nice," wondering whether it was true that the people who drove up for Sunday dinner at the farmhouse were turned away because there wasn't enough chicken.

9    It seemed to me, as I kept remembering all this, that those times and those summers had been infinitely precious and worth saving. There had been jollity and peace and goodness. The arriving (at the beginning of August) had been so big a business in itself, at the railway station the farm wagon drawn up, the first smell of the pine-laden air, the first glimpse of the smiling farmer, and the great importance of the trunks and your father's enormous authority in such matters, and the feel of the wagon under you for the long ten-mile haul, and at the top of the last long hill catching the first view of the lake after eleven months of not seeing this cherished body of water. The shouts and cries of the other campers when they saw you, and the trunks to be unpacked, to give up their rich burden. (Arriving was less exciting nowadays, when you sneaked up in your car and parked it under a tree near the camp and took out the bags and in five minutes it was all over, no fuss, no loud wonderful fuss about trunks.)

10    Peace and goodness and jollity. The only thing that was wrong now, really, was the sound of the place, an unfamiliar nervous sound of the outboard motors. This was the note that jarred, the one thing that would sometimes break the illusion and set the years moving. In those other summertimes all motors were inboard; and when they were at a little distance, the noise they made was a sedative, an ingredient of summer sleep. They were one-cylinder and two-cylinder engines, and some were make-and-break and some were jump-spark, but they all made a sleepy sound across the lake. The one-lungers throbbed and fluttered, and the twin-cylinder ones purred and purred, and that was a quiet sound too. But now the campers all had outboards. In the daytime, in the hot mornings, these motors made a petulant, irritable sound; at

night, in the still evening when the afterglow lit the water, they whined about one's ears like mosquitoes. My boy loved our rented outboard, and his great desire was to achieve singlehanded mastery over it, and authority, and he soon learned the trick of choking it a little (but not too much), and the adjustment of the needle valve. Watching him I would remember the things you could do with the old one-cylinder engine with the heavy flywheel, how you could have it eating out of your hand if you got really close to it spiritually. Motor boats in those days didn't have clutches, and you would make a landing by shutting off the motor at the proper time and coasting in with a dead rudder. But there was a way of reversing them, if you learned the trick, by cutting the switch and putting it on again exactly on the final dying revolution of the flywheel, so that it would kick back against compression and begin reversing. Approaching a dock in a strong following breeze, it was difficult to slow up sufficiently by the ordinary coasting method, and if a boy felt he had complete mastery over his motor, he was tempted to keep it running beyond its time and then reverse it a few feet from the dock. It took a cool nerve, because if you threw the switch a twentieth of a second too soon you would catch the flywheel when it still has speed enough to go up past center, and the boat would leap ahead, charging bull-fashion at the dock.

11      We had a good week at the camp. The bass were biting well and the sun shone endlessly, day after day. We would be tired at night and lie down in the accumulated heat of the little bedrooms after the long hot day and the breeze would stir almost imperceptibly outside and the smell of the swamp drift in through the rusty screens. Sleep would come easily and in the morning the red squirrel would be on the roof, tapping out his gay routine. I kept remembering everything, lying in bed in the mornings—the small steamboat that had a long rounded stern like the lip of a Ubangi, and how quietly she ran on the moon-light sails, when the older boys played their mandolins and the girls sang and we ate doughnuts dipped in sugar, and how sweet the music was on the water in the shining night, and what it had felt like to think about girls then. After breakfast we would go up to the store and the things were in the same place— the minnows in a bottle, the plugs and spinners disarranged and pawed over by the youngsters from the boys' camp, the fig newtons and the Beeman's gum. Outside, the road was tarred and cars stood in front of the store. Inside, all was just as it had always been, except that there was more Coca Cola and not so much Moxie and root beer and birch beer and sarsaparilla. We would walk out with a bottle of pop apiece and sometimes the pop would backfire up our noses and hurt. We explored the streams, quietly, where the turtles slid off the sunny logs and dug their way into the soft bottom; and we lay on the town wharf and fed worms to the tame bass. Everywhere we went I had trouble making out which was I, the one walking at my side, the one walking in my pants.

12      One afternoon while we were there at that lake a thunderstorm came up. It was like the revival of an old melodrama that I had seen long ago with childish awe. The second-act climax of the drama of the electrical disturbance over a lake in America had not changed in any important respect. This was the big scene, still the big scene. The whole thing was so familiar, the first feeling

of oppression and heat and a general air around camp of not wanting to go very far away. In midafternoon (it was all the same) a curious darkening of the sky, and a lull in everything that had made life tick; and then the way the boats suddenly swung the other way at their moorings with the coming of a breeze out of the new quarter, and the premonitory rumble. Then the kettle drum, then the snare, then the bass drum and cymbals, then crackling light against the dark, and the gods grinning and licking their chops in the hills. Afterward the calm, the rain steadily rustling in the calm lake, the return of light and hope and spirits, and the campers running out in joy and relief to go swimming in the rain, their bright cries perpetuating the deathless joke about how they were getting simply drenched, and the children screaming with delight at the new sensation of bathing in the rain, and the joke about getting drenched linking the generations in a strong indestructible chain. And the comedian who waded in carrying an umbrella.

13     When the others went swimming my son said he was going in too. He pulled his dripping trunks from the line where they had hung all through the shower, and wrung them out. Languidly, and with no thought of going in, I watched him, his hard little body, skinny and bare, saw him wince slightly as he pulled up around his vitals the small, soggy, icy garment. As he buckled the swollen belt suddenly my groin felt the chill of death.

## Questions on Subject and Purpose

1. Why does White go "once more" to the lake?
2. In what ways does White's son remind him of himself as a child? Make a list of the similarities he notices.
3. What is the meaning of the final sentence? Why does he feel "the chill of death"?

## Questions on Strategy and Audience

1. How does White structure his narrative? What events does he choose to highlight?
2. No narrative can record everything, and this is certainly not an hour-by-hour account of what happened. What does White ignore? Why, for example, does he end his narrative before the end of the actual experience (that is, leaving the lake)?
3. Why is White's son never described?

## Questions on Vocabulary and Style

1. At several points White has trouble distinguishing between who is the son and who is the father. Select one of those scenes and examine how White describes the moment. How does the prose capture that confusion?
2. Can you find examples of figurative language—similes and metaphors, for example—in White's essay? Make a list.
3. Be prepared to define the following words: *placidity* (paragraph 1), *gunwale* (2), *primeval* (3), *teeming* (7), *premonitory* (12), *languidly* (13).

## Writing Suggestions

1. **For Your Journal or Blog.** Choose a particular year from your elementary school experience. It would probably be easiest to choose a year like third or fourth grade. In your journal or blog, make a list of what you remember from that year. What was the school's name? Your teacher's name? What did the classroom look like? Where did you sit? What happened that year? Who were your friends? Allow a day or two at least to pass while you try to remember, and you will discover that more and more details will surface. Record as many details as you can in your journal or blog.

2. **For a Paragraph.** In a paragraph, re-create for the reader a moment out of that year in school. Narrate the experience and describe the setting. Do not try to make the moment significant or earthshaking. Remember that you can fill in or add details that are true to the time or that could have happened.

3. **For an Essay.** You do not have to be middle-aged to have the experience of returning somewhere that you have been some years before and sensing either changelessness or change. More often, things change rather than stay the same. Think about your experiences. Have you ever reexperienced something some years later—a summer vacation to the same place, an encounter with someone who was a good friend some years before, a visit to a house, apartment, or neighborhood in which your family once lived? Find an experience that you have had twice, separated by at least several years. Re-create those experiences for your reader and, like White, speculate on what you have learned or sensed from the two.

4. **For Research.** What is your earliest memory? What factors control memories? Is it possible to remember events that took place before you could talk? To what extent do memories grow out of photographs? Are memories actually stored and retrieved, or are they re-created by the mind? What kinds of memories are most easily recalled? In a research paper, try to answer some of these questions; use both online and print sources.

## For Further Study

**Focusing on Grammar and Writing.** The essay averages twenty-four words per sentence. How does White manage to structure his sentences so that they can contain so much information yet remain clear? You might want to focus on a single paragraph, looking carefully at the sentences it contains, or a single sentence, de-combining that sentence into a series of shorter, simpler sentences.

**Working Together.** Divide into small groups. Each group should choose one descriptive passage in the essay. What does White focus on? How does this description contribute to the essay? Possible passages to analyze include these:

1. Bedroom in the morning (paragraph 2)
2. Fishing scene (5)
3. Bottom of the lake (6)
4. Road to the farmhouse (7)
5. Tennis court at "dry noon" (7)
6. Arrival (9)
7. Motorboats (10)

**Seeing Other Modes at Work.** Although the basic pattern in the essay comes from narration, White uses description extensively to create the vivid scenes he experiences.

**Finding Connections.** Another essay about the identification between a father and a child is Scott Russell Sanders's "The Inheritance of Tools" (Chapter 3). One dealing with a daughter and her mother is Amy Tan's "Mother Tongue" (Chapter 8).

**Exploring the Web.** Ever wonder what the lake might have looked like? Visit Belgrade Lakes in central Maine on the Web. Check out the many Websites devoted to the life and work of E. B. White.

# *The Singer Solution to World Poverty*

Peter Singer

*Peter Singer (1946–), born in Australia, is Ira W. DeCamp Professor of Bioethics at the University Center for Human Values at Princeton. A pro-lific author on a wide range of ethical issues, Singer has been referred to as "maybe the most controversial [ethicist] alive. . . . [and] certainly among the most influential." His most recent book, cowritten with Jim Mason, is* The Way We Eat: Why Our Food Choices Matter *(2006). This essay originally appeared in* The New York Times Magazine.

**On Writing:** *In an interview, Singer had this to say about the ef-fects of argument: "I think we are (mostly) rational beings and rational argument does move people to action particularly when it gets them to see that what they are doing is inconsistent with other beliefs that they have and other values that they have that are important to them. But it is also true that we are self-interested beings to some extent. That's part of our nature and you can't get away from that. . . . If we put a rational ar-gument in front of people, some are moved by it a lot of the way, it moves others a little bit of the way, and some people just shrug it off because it is too much against what they want to do."*

## Before Reading

**Connecting:** How much money do you contribute annually to organizations seeking to care for children in need throughout the world?

**Anticipating:** As you read, think about whether Singer's essay has persuaded you to change your own behavior. Why or why not?

## Looking for Combinations

Singer's purpose is persuasive, but persuasion uses a variety of other strategies to achieve its end. In places, Singer uses narration, comparison and contrast, and classification. Can you locate those patterns in the essay? Can you find any others at work? What roles do these strategies or modes play in the essay as a whole?

1  In the Brazilian film *Central Station,* Dora is a retired schoolteacher who makes ends meet by sitting at the station writing letters for illiterate people. Suddenly she has an opportunity to pocket a thousand dollars. All she has to do is persuade

a homeless nine-year-old boy to follow her to an address she has been given. (She is told he will be adopted by wealthy foreigners.) She delivers the boy, gets the money, spends some of it on a television set, and settles down to enjoy her new acquisition. Her neighbor spoils the fun, however, by telling her that the boy was too old to be adopted—he will be killed and his organs sold for transplantation. Perhaps Dora knew this all along, but after her neighbor's plain speaking, she spends a troubled night. In the morning Dora resolves to take the boy back.

2　　Suppose Dora had told her neighbor that it is a tough world, other people have nice new TVs too, and if selling the kid is the only way she can get one, well, he was only a street kid. She would then have become, in the eyes of the audience, a monster. She redeems herself only by being prepared to bear considerable risks to save the boy.

3　　At the end of the movie, in cinemas in the affluent nations of the world, people who would have been quick to condemn Dora if she had not rescued the boy go home to places far more comfortable than her apartment. In fact, the average family in the United States spends almost one third of its income on things that are no more necessary to them than Dora's new TV was to her. Going out to nice restaurants, buying new clothes because the old ones are no longer stylish, vacationing at beach resorts—so much of our income is spent on things not essential to the preservation of our lives and health. Donated to one of a number of charitable agencies, that money could mean the difference between life and death for children in need.

4　　All of which raises a question: in the end, what is the ethical distinction between a Brazilian who sells a homeless child to organ peddlers and an American who already has a TV and upgrades to a better one, knowing that the money could be donated to an organization that would use it to save the lives of kids in need?

5　　Of course, there are several differences between the two situations that could support different moral judgments about them. For one thing, to be able to consign a child to death when he is standing right in front of you takes a chilling kind of heartlessness; it is much easier to ignore an appeal for money to help children you will never meet. Yet for a utilitarian philosopher like myself—that is, one who judges whether acts are right or wrong by their consequences—if the upshot of the American's failure to donate the money is that one more kid dies on the streets of a Brazilian city, then it is in some sense just as bad as selling the kid to the organ peddlers. But one doesn't need to embrace my utilitarian ethic to see that at the very least, there is a troubling incongruity in being so quick to condemn Dora for taking the child to the organ peddlers while at the same time not regarding the American consumer's behavior as raising a serious moral issue.

6　　In his 1996 book, *Living High and Letting Die*, the New York University philosopher Peter Unger presented an ingenious series of imaginary examples designed to probe our intuitions about whether it is wrong to live well without giving substantial amounts of money to help people who are hungry, malnourished, or dying from easily treatable illnesses like diarrhea. Here's my paraphrase of one of these examples:

7    Bob is close to retirement. He has invested most of his savings in a very rare and valuable old car, a Bugatti, which he has not been able to insure. The Bugatti is his pride and joy. In addition to the pleasure he gets from driving and caring for his car, Bob knows that its rising market value means that he will always be able to sell it and live comfortably after retirement. One day when Bob is out for a drive, he parks the Bugatti near the end of a railway siding and goes for a walk up the track. As he does so, he sees that a runaway train, with no one aboard, is running down the railway track. Looking farther down the track, he sees the small figure of a child very likely to be killed by the runaway train. He can't stop the train and the child is too far away to warn of the danger, but he can throw a switch that will divert the train down the siding where his Bugatti is parked. Then nobody will be killed—but the train will destroy his Bugatti. Thinking of his joy in owning the car and the financial security it represents, Bob decides not to throw the switch. The child is killed. For many years to come, Bob enjoys owning his Bugatti and the financial security it represents.

8    Bob's conduct, most of us will immediately respond, was gravely wrong. Unger agrees. But then he reminds us that we too have opportunities to save the lives of children. We can give to organizations like UNICEF or Oxfam America. How much would we have to give one of these organizations to have a high probability of saving the life of a child threatened by easily preventable diseases? (I do not believe that children are more worth saving than adults, but since no one can argue that children have brought their poverty on themselves, focusing on them simplifies the issues.) Unger called up some experts and used the information they provided to offer some plausible estimates that include the cost of raising money, administrative expenses, and the cost of delivering aid where it is most needed. By his calculation, $200 in donations would help a sickly two-year-old transform into a healthy six-year-old—offering safe passage through childhood's most dangerous years. To show how practical philosophical argument can be, Unger even tells his readers that they can easily donate funds by using their credit card and calling one of these toll-free numbers: (800) 367-5437 for UNICEF; (800) 693-2687 for Oxfam America.

9    Now you too have the information you need to save a child's life. How should you judge yourself if you don't do it? Think again about Bob and his Bugatti. Unlike Dora, Bob did not have to look into the eyes of the child he was sacrificing for his own material comfort. The child was a complete stranger to him and too far away to relate to in an intimate, personal way. Unlike Dora too, he did not mislead the child or initiate the chain of events imperiling him. In all these respects, Bob's situation resembles that of people able but unwilling to donate to overseas aid and differs from Dora's situation.

10    If you still think that it was very wrong of Bob not to throw the switch that would have diverted the train and saved the child's life, then it is hard to see how you could deny that it is also very wrong not to send money to one of the organizations listed above. Unless, that is, there is some morally important difference between the two situations that I have overlooked.

11    Is it the practical uncertainties about whether aid will really reach the people who need it? Nobody who knows the world of overseas aid can doubt

that such uncertainties exist. But Unger's figure of $200 to save a child's life was reached after he had made conservative assumptions about the proportion of the money donated that will actually reach its target.

12    One genuine difference between Bob and those who can afford to donate to overseas aid organizations but don't is that only Bob can save the child on the tracks, whereas there are hundreds of millions of people who can give $200 to overseas aid organizations. The problem is that most of them aren't doing it. Does this mean that it is all right for you not to do it?

13    Suppose that there were more owners of priceless vintage cars—Carol, Dave, Emma, Fred, and so on, down to Ziggy—all in exactly the same situation as Bob, with their own siding and their own switch, all sacrificing the child in order to preserve their own cherished car. Would that make it all right for Bob to do the same? To answer this question affirmatively is to endorse follow-the-crowd ethics—the kind of ethics that led many Germans to look away when the Nazi atrocities were being committed. We do not excuse them because others were behaving no better.

14    We seem to lack a sound basis for drawing a clear moral line between Bob's situation and that of any reader of this article with $200 to spare who does not donate it to an overseas aid agency. These readers seem to be acting at least as badly as Bob was acting when he chose to let the runaway train hurtle toward the unsuspecting child. In the light of this conclusion, I trust that many readers will reach for the phone and donate that $200. Perhaps you should do it before reading further.

*

15    Now that you have distinguished yourself morally from people who put their vintage cars ahead of a child's life, how about treating yourself and your partner to dinner at your favorite restaurant? But wait. The money you will spend at the restaurant could also help save the lives of children overseas! True, you weren't planning to blow $200 tonight, but if you were to give up dining out just for one month, you would easily save that amount. And what is one month's dining out compared to a child's life? There's the rub. Since there are a lot of desperately needy children in the world, there will always be another child whose life you could save for another $200. Are you therefore obliged to keep giving until you have nothing left? At what point can you stop?

16    Hypothetical examples can easily become farcical. Consider Bob. How far past losing the Bugatti should he go? Imagine that Bob had got his foot stuck in the track of the siding, and if he diverted the train, then before it rammed the car it would also amputate his big toe. Should he still throw the switch? What if it would amputate his foot? His entire leg?

17    As absurd as the Bugatti scenario gets when pushed to extremes, the point it raises is a serious one: only when the sacrifices become very significant indeed would most people be prepared to say that Bob does nothing wrong when he decides not to throw the switch. Of course, most people could be wrong; we can't decide moral issues by taking opinion polls. But consider for yourself the level of sacrifice that you would demand of Bob, and then think about how

much money you would have to give away in order to make a sacrifice that is roughly equal to that. It's almost certainly much, much more than $200. For most middle-class Americans, it could easily be more like $200,000.

18      Isn't it counterproductive to ask people to do so much? Don't we run the risk that many will shrug their shoulders and say that morality, so conceived, is fine for saints but not for them? I accept that we are unlikely to see, in the near or even medium-term future, a world in which it is normal for wealthy Americans to give the bulk of their wealth to strangers. When it comes to praising or blaming people for what they do, we tend to use a standard that is relative to some conception of normal behavior. Comfortably off Americans who give, say, 10 percent of their income to overseas aid organizations are so far ahead of most of their equally comfortable fellow citizens that I wouldn't go out of my way to chastise them for not doing more. Nevertheless, they should be doing much more, and they are in no position to criticize Bob for failing to make the much greater sacrifice of his Bugatti.

19      At this point various objections may crop up. Someone may say, "If every citizen living in the affluent nations contributed his or her share, I wouldn't have to make such a drastic sacrifice, because long before such levels were reached the resources would have been there to save the lives of all those children dying from lack of food or medical care. So why should I give more than my fair share?" Another, related objection is that the government ought to increase its overseas aid allocations, since that would spread the burden more equitably across all taxpayers.

20      Yet the question of how much we ought to give is a matter to be decided in the real world—and that, sadly, is a world in which we know that most people do not, and in the immediate future will not, give substantial amounts to overseas aid agencies. We know too that at least in the next year, the United States government is not going to meet even the very modest United Nations–recommended target of 0.7 percent of gross national product; at the moment it lags far below that, at 0.09 percent, not even half of Japan's 0.22 percent or a tenth of Denmark's 0.97 percent. Thus, we know that the money we can give beyond that theoretical "fair share" is still going to save lives that would otherwise be lost. While the idea that no one need do more than his or her fair share is a powerful one, should it prevail if we know that others are not doing their fair share and that children will die preventable deaths unless we do more than our fair share? That would be taking fairness too far.

21      Thus, this ground for limiting how much we ought to give also fails. In the world as it is now, I can see no escape from the conclusion that each one of us with wealth surplus to his or her essential needs should be giving most of it to help people suffering from poverty so dire as to be life-threatening. That's right: I'm saying that you shouldn't buy that new car, take that cruise, redecorate the house, or get that pricy new suit. After all, a thousand-dollar suit could save five children's lives.

22      So how does my philosophy break down in dollars and cents? An American household with an income of $50,000 spends around $30,000 annually on

necessities, according to the Conference Board, a nonprofit economic research organization. Therefore, for a household bringing in $50,000 a year, donations to help the world's poor should be as close as possible to $20,000. The $30,000 required for necessities holds for higher incomes as well. So a household making $100,000 could cut a yearly check for $70,000. Again, the formula is simple: whatever money you're spending on luxuries, not necessities, should be given away.

23    Now, evolutionary psychologists tell us that human nature just isn't sufficiently altruistic to make it plausible that many people will sacrifice so much for strangers. On the facts of human nature, they might be right, but they would be wrong to draw a moral conclusion from those facts. If it is the case that we ought to do things that, predictably, most of us won't do, then let's face that fact head-on. Then, if we value the life of a child more than going to fancy restaurants, the next time we dine out we will know that we could have done something better with our money. If that makes living a morally decent life extremely arduous, well, then that is the way things are. If we don't do it, then we should at least know that we are failing to live a morally decent life—not because it is good to wallow in guilt but because knowing where we should be going is the first step toward heading in that direction.

24    When Bob first grasped the dilemma that faced him as he stood by that railway switch, he must have thought how extraordinarily unlucky he was to be placed in a situation in which he must choose between the life of an innocent child and the sacrifice of most of his savings. But he was not unlucky at all. We are all in that situation.

## Questions on Subject and Purpose

1. Singer labels himself a "utilitarian" philosopher. How does he explain what that means?
2. Is there any limit for Singer to how much money one ought to give away for overseas aid?
3. What type of response do you think that Singer hopes from his audience? Expects from his audience?

## Questions on Strategy and Audience

1. Why might Singer choose to begin with the example of Dora in the Brazilian film *Central Station*?
2. The text of the essay is separated after paragraph 14 by a centered asterisk (*). What division does this indicate in the essay itself?
3. What assumptions could Singer make about his audience?

## Questions on Vocabulary and Style

1. What is an analogy? Does Singer use analogy in his argument?
2. Why is the effect of including the telephone numbers for UNICEF and Oxfam America in the essay?
3. Be prepared to define the following words: *affluent* (paragraph 3), *incongruity* (5), *ingenious* (6), *altruistic* (23), *arduous* (23).

## Writing Suggestions

1. **For Your Journal or Blog.** Over the course of a week, jot down in your journal or blog a detailed list of how you spent your money. Try to record everything. For each expenditure over fifty cents, write an explanation for where and why the money was spent. At the end of the week, make some notes about your spending habits.

2. **For a Paragraph.** What did your journal or blog reveal? In a paragraph, explore your values and either defend or criticize your behavior.

3. **For an Essay.** Singer notes (citing the research of someone else) that a two-hundred-dollar donation would "help a sickly two-year-old transform into a healthy six-year-old." That works out to about fifty-five cents per day yearly. Could you and your friends, even as college students, find a way to trim fifty-five cents a day (or less than four dollars a week) out of what you already spend? In an essay aimed at undergraduates at your school, argue for a schoolwide campaign to get everyone to contribute to such a cause.

3. **For Research.** Why is it that the richest nation in the world is one of the world's poorest contributors to overseas aid? In an essay research this situation. How much does the United States contribute? What factors have accounted for our current position? Are there good reasons why we as a nation should not contribute more? In an essay arguing either side, take a stand on the overseas aid policy of the United States.

## For Further Study

**Focusing on Grammar and Writing.** Choose one or more of Singer's longer paragraphs and look closely at how it is organized. You might want to outline it. Does the paragraph achieve unity and coherence? How? Does the paragraph have a topic sentence? Does it use transitional devices to link sentences together? What observations could you make about effective body paragraphs based on the example you studied?

**Working Together.** Singer divides his essay into four parts, each marked by the addition of extra white space between the blocks of paragraphs. Divide into small groups; each group should take one of the blocks to examine. Why is this section set off? What unifies it?

1. Paragraphs 1–5
2. Paragraphs 6–14
3. Paragraphs 15–17
4. Paragraphs 18–24

**Seeing Other Modes at Work.** Singer's essay uses comparison and contrast, especially as he makes extensive use of analogy in establishing links among the decisions facing Dora, Bob, and the reader.

**Finding Connections.** Interesting pairings are with Tom Haines's "Facing Famine" (Chapter 2) and Lars Eighner's "My Daily Dives in the Dumpster" (Chapter 6).

**Exploring the Web.** The Web offers a number of sites where you can read more of Singer's work, explore the objections that some critics have to some of his ethical stands, and make a contribution to UNICEF, Oxfam America, or the relief agency of your choice.

# 11

# THE RESEARCH PAPER

## KEY QUESTIONS

**Getting Ready to Write**

What is the freshman research paper?

How does a research paper differ from other papers?

Why are you asked to write a research paper?

How much of a research paper is direct quotation from sources?

How do you find a topic for a research paper?

*Student Writers: Selecting a Topic*

How do subject, topic, and thesis differ?

Do you start writing with a formal thesis?

**Starting Your Research**

How do you plan a search strategy?

    *Searching by author and title*
    *Searching by subject headings*
    *Searching by keywords*

How do you locate books on your subject?

    *Using reference books as a starting place*

*Caution: Using Wikipedia as a Source*

    *Finding books in the library's catalog*
    *Browsing the library's bookshelves*

How do you locate online sources about your subject and topic?

    *Choosing a search engine*

*Tips for Starting a Web Search on Google*

    *Learning how to search the Web*

## GETTING READY TO WRITE

### What Is the Freshman Research Paper?

The research paper is typically the longest and most demanding of the papers assigned in a freshman writing course. It is longer in length than a regular paper, involves gathering and using information from a variety of reliable sources, and includes formal documentation (such as parenthetical citations, endnotes, and a bibliography). Some schools offer special sessions with the library staff to show students how to locate print and online sources. Often a research paper is done in a series of stages, so that the instructor can follow the progress. For example, your instructor might ask for an initial statement of topic and thesis, a conference to check on your progress, a first draft of the paper, and a copy of all the sources that you quoted in the paper (to make sure you documented your quotations correctly). Not surprisingly, the formal research paper often is weighted more heavily than the other papers you have written because it requires so much more work.

## How Does a Research Paper Differ from Other Papers?

All effective writing involves some form of research. To write a laboratory report in chemistry, you use the information gathered from performing the experiment. To write an article for the student newspaper on your college's latest tuition increase, you include information gathered in interviews with college administrators, students, and parents. To answer a midterm examination, you marshal evidence from lecture notes and from the required readings. Even for an essay in which you recount an experience from your past, you must search your memory to re-create the events and your reaction to them.

Although all writing uses sources (printed, online, memory, observations, interviews), not all writing meets the special considerations associated with a research paper. A research paper not only formally documents its sources, but it also exhibits a particular approach to its subject. A research paper is not just a collection of information about a subject. Instead, a research paper poses a particular question or thesis about its subject, and then it sets out to answer that question or test the validity of that thesis.

Approach defining a topic for your research paper and gathering sources the same way that a scientist sets about exploring a problem. The idea behind research—all research in every field—is to isolate a particular aspect of a subject, to become an expert in that defined area, and to present a conclusion about the material. Because research papers have a thesis, they differ significantly from the informational overviews presented in encyclopedia articles. Many writers initially confuse the two forms of writing. The confusion probably goes back to grade school when a teacher assigned us a report on our favorite planet. Most of us went to an encyclopedia (either the print or online version), looked-up our choice of planet, and copied down the entry. Such a strategy will never work for a college research paper.

As you start the process of selecting a topic and defining a thesis, keep in mind that **a research paper is not an encyclopedia article**.

## Why Are You Asked to Write a Research Paper?

Of all the papers that you will write in college (and in graduate and professional school should you go on), the research paper is the type of writing you will encounter the most often. Naturally, then, research papers are required in most first-year writing courses because writing a research paper gives you the opportunity to tackle a large problem, to learn to use your library's collections and online resources, to make decisions about how reliable your sources are, to learn how to work quotations in to your text, and to become familiar with a formal system to document your research citations.

## How Much of a Research Paper Is Direct Quotation from Sources?

The research paper provides an important experience in learning how to integrate source material such as quotations and statistics into your own prose. The verb *integrate* is crucial. A research paper is not a collection of quotations stitched together with an occasional sentence of your own. A research paper is written in your own words. Quote your sources where necessary, but do not quote any more than necessary. The ideal research paper—in any college course—is probably 80 percent your own prose and no more than 20 percent direct quotation (and even that number is fairly high). Later in this chapter, you will find advice on how to reduce the amount of quoted material and how to know when to quote.

Because a research paper involves using sources, you must be careful not to plagiarize and you must quote accurately. Plagiarism and how to avoid it is explained in detail later in this chapter. Under no set of circumstances should you buy a paper or copy a paper from a friend or from the Internet. Plagiarism from the Web is increasingly easy to detect. In addition, every person has a distinctive writing style that is manifest in elements such as vocabulary choices and sentence structures. Someone else's prose does not sound like your prose. It is rather like lip-synching to a song sung by a professional artist—no one is going to believe it is you!

## How Do You Find a Topic for a Research Paper?

In every essay in this book you can identify at least one topic for a research paper. In addition, your instructor might make an assignment or suggest a certain kind of paper. A research paper is likely to require several weeks of work, so ideally you should choose something that is appealing. The two student writers we are following in this chapter chose their subjects in quite different ways. Kristen LaPorte was enrolled in a writing course that was intended for music majors; everyone in the course was to choose a topic related in some way to music. Kristen started with the idea of music therapy, a career in which she was interested, and then decided to focus on people with Alzheimer's disease. Bailey Kung's instructor assigned the type of research paper he wanted—one that presented both sides of a value conflict. Fascinated by the graffiti she has observed in New York City, Bailey decided to examine two conflicting views: graffiti is art; graffiti is vandalism. Consider what each said about her topic choice.

**STUDENT WRITERS: SELECTING A TOPIC**

**Kristen**

It took me a little time to actually get to my final topic for my research paper. Since our class was a music-oriented English class [a section intended for freshman music majors], we all had to choose some topic in the field of music, but it was fairly open. Since I am going into music education, I naturally wanted to research and write about something in the area of how music can help people. Music therapy has also always been an interest of mine. Since my passion lies with elementary students, I originally thought of writing something about music and students with exceptional needs. Since other students in the class had the same idea, I decided to stick with that general subject but concentrate instead on how music is used with the elderly. Since that was still too broad, I eventually decided to look at music and the Alzheimer's patient.

**Bailey**

I wanted to come up with a unique topic that I would enjoy writing about, not just writing about abortion or legalizing marijuana. Our instructor gave us a list of value conflicts to get us started with brainstorming. One that caught my eye was related to free speech and freedom of expression. Graffiti struck me as a perfect example. Ever since my first few visits to New York City, I have been fascinated with graffiti. To think that such amazing works of art were the products of vandalism had hardly occurred to me before. Of course, taking a few cans of paint to a wall that doesn't belong to you is illegal. But if the results were so wonderful, would the artists still be punished? And isn't freedom of expression a Constitutional right? I was predisposed to the opinion that graffiti can be a form of art, but the argument that graffiti is vandalism is reasonable too. In my paper I was able to look at both sides without having to choose one.

## How Do Subject, Topic, and Thesis Differ?

Whether you select one of the research paper topics provided in this book or one suggested by your instructor, remember how *subject*, *topic*, and *thesis* differ. As you move from one to another, you narrow the scope of your paper. Kristen's original idea for a research paper was a subject—"music therapy," which was already much more focused than simply saying "music." As she thought about that subject, however, she narrowed its scope, which made her paper more focused and, therefore, easier to research and write. Her topic became "music therapy and the Alzheimer's patient." Her thesis, the final step, had to state a definite position on that topic: "Although other forms of therapy may be beneficial, music therapy proves to be one of the most effective treatment options for Alzheimer's patients, either individually or in a group, to help in areas such as concentration, general attitude, and communication." Notice how in each step the statement gets more sharply defined:

| | |
|---|---|
| **Subject:** | Music |
| **Narrower subject:** | Music therapy |
| **Topic:** | Music therapy and the Alzheimer's patient |
| **Thesis:** | "Although other forms of therapy may be beneficial, music therapy proves to be one of the most effective treatment options for Alzheimer's patients, either individually or in a group, to help in areas such as concentration, general attitude, and communication." |

The key to planning, researching, and writing the research paper is to define progressively what it is that you are writing about. Think of the impossibility of trying to research the topic music or even music therapy. You would have thousands of potential sources. Moreover, when you try to write about a *subject*, you are much more likely to fall into the trap of thinking about your paper as an informational, encyclopedia-like article (for example, "here is a general overview of the types and methods of music therapy"). Remember, a research paper is not an informational summary.

## Do You Start Writing with a Formal Thesis?

Often you will not know what you want to write about or what you might say about a subject or topic until you start researching, and even drafting. An effective, workable thesis typically evolves and gets refined as you work on your research paper. As you look for sources, you will realize that you need to narrow your focus. Nothing is more sobering than to conduct a search for sources and turn up hundreds or even thousands of citations. Think of your initial thesis as a working thesis that will be refined and sharpened in the process of preparing the research paper.

## STARTING YOUR RESEARCH

Research takes time, but the key to getting quality sources that are truly related to your topic—and getting them in the shortest amount of time—is to plan a search strategy. Your instructor will probably tell you that you need to have a variety of sources—books, articles from magazines and journals, information from Websites or government documents, interviews with experts. No research paper should be based on one or two sources; no research paper should be based solely on Web resources. Either strategy poses problems: You will not get a range of information and opinions if you use only one or two sources. Websites can be full of erroneous information—you can post anything on the Web and make it look professional and trustworthy.

## How Do You Plan a Search Strategy?

For most college papers, your information will come from *secondary* sources—typically books, articles (print or online), Websites—that report the research done by others. Depending on your subject, you might also be able to use *primary* sources—original documents (historical records, letters, works of literature) or the results of original research (laboratory experiments, interviews, questionnaires).

Finding usable sources is not hard, no matter what your subject, but it does require knowing how and where to look. A quick tour of your college or university library, with its miles of shelves, or an hour on the Web will vividly demonstrate that you need to know what you are looking for and how to find it. The first step is to find subject headings and keywords that can be used to retrieve information.

**Searching by Title or Author**    Author and title searches are the easiest to perform, but they require prior knowledge. Who wrote the article or the book? What exactly was its title? Any mistake in spelling or in word order and your search comes to a dead end. Author or title searches work if you have a citation, perhaps from another source or from a bibliography. Always look at the sources quoted or referred to in any book or article that seems relevant to your topic. They might lead you to other valuable sources.

**Searching by Subject Headings**    The subject headings used in library catalogs and periodical indexes are part of a fixed, interlocking system that is logically organized and highly structured. The idea is not to list every possible subject heading under which a particular subject might be found, but to establish general headings under which related subjects can be grouped. Most libraries use the subject headings suggested by the Library of Congress and published in the *Library of Congress Subject Headings* (LCSH), a five-volume set of books typically found near a library's catalog or reference area. In addition, most periodical indexes use the same system or one so similar that the LCSH headings will still serve your purpose. As a result, the most efficient way to begin a subject search is to check the LCSH for appropriate subject headings under which books and articles on your subject will be listed.

For example, suppose you were surprised to read that even today, women earn less than 80 percent of what men earn doing the same job. You want to research why that disparity exists and what is being done to remedy that inequality. Exactly what keywords or subject headings would you look under in a library catalog, a database, or a periodical index to find appropriate sources: *Women? Work? Job discrimination? Salaries?* Unless you know where to begin, you might waste a considerable amount of time guessing randomly or conclude (quite wrongly) that your library has no information on the topic. If you consulted the *Library of Congress Subject Headings*, you will find cross-references that lead you to the following:

---

Equal pay for work of comparable value
   USE Pay equity
**Equal pay for equal work** (*May Subd Geog*)
   Here are entered works on equal pay for jobs that require identical skills, responsibilities, and effort. Works on comparable pay for jobs that require comparable skills, responsibilities, effort, and working conditions are entered under Pay equity.
   BT   Discrimination in employment Wages
   RT   Women—Employment
   **—Law and registration** (*May Subd Geog*)
      BT Labor laws and legislation
Equal pay for work of comparable value
   USE Pay equity

---

The LCSH uses abbreviations to indicate relationships among subjects. By following the cross-references, you can conduct a more thorough search. The relationships that are signaled include these:

**Equivalence:**    USE

**Hierarchy:**    BT (broader term)

                  NT (narrower term)

**Association:**    RT (related term)

Having checked the key to using the headings, you know from these entries not to search under "Equal pay for work of comparable value" since the heading is not in bold type; instead, you are told to use "Pay equity." The best heading under which to search for books and articles related to your topic is "**Equal pay for equal work**." The abbreviation *May Subd Geog* indicates that the heading might be subdivided geographically, for example, "Equal pay for equal work—Delaware." The LCSH also suggests other possibilities: for a broader term, use "Discrimination in employment" or "Wages"; for a related term, use "Woman—Employment." You will find relevant information under all of these possible headings. In general, no one subject heading will lead you to all of the books your library has on a particular topic.

Here are a few cautions to keep in mind when using subject headings:

1. Always check the *Library of Congress Subject Headings* first to find the best headings to use for your subject. The quickest way to short-circuit your search strategy is to begin with a heading that you think will work, find nothing, and conclude that your library has no information on that topic.

2. Remember that the headings used might not be as specific as you want. You might need to browse through a group of related materials to find the more precise information you are seeking.

Subject headings use a *controlled vocabulary*; that is, all information about a particular subject is grouped under a single heading with appropriate cross-references from other related headings. For example, if your subject is "capital punishment," you do not also need to look under the headings "death penalty," "execution," or "death row." Controlled vocabularies do, however, place some restrictions on your search strategy. Subject headings are not always, for instance, as precise as you would like them to be. Furthermore, very recent subjects might not appear in the classification scheme for several years.

**Searching by Keywords**   Online searching offers an alternative to subject heading searches—a *keyword* search. A keyword is a significant word, almost always a noun, that is used in the title (or someplace else in the computerized record) of books, reports, and articles. By combining keywords, you can conduct very precise searches. To learn how to combine keywords and what "operators" to use (such as *and*, *near*, and *or*, which indicate the relationships between those keywords), you must study the help menu of the computer search engine you are using. Keyword searches that do not specify the relationship between the keywords will produce unwieldy strings of "hits" (that is, records that contain those words). The computer just lists every record that contains those words anywhere: one word might appear in the title, one in subject heading assigned to the book, and a third in the title of the collection in which the book is housed. Keyword searches are especially valuable when you cannot find the appropriate heading (for example, "glass ceiling," referring to the limited promotion possibilities for someone within a company or organization) or when you want to combine several concepts (for example, "children" and "violence" and "television").

When you locate a relevant book by using a keyword search, check to see what subject headings were used to classify the book. This information is displayed in the full view of the book's record. Use those subject headings to search for other books classified in same way.

Keyword searches also have limitations. Often you are simply guessing what the keywords might be. Maybe you selected keywords that will work and maybe you did not. The computer will never prompt you to modify your search or to use another term or phrase. Remember, the word or phrase you are searching for must be found in some part of the record. If it is not, you will never retrieve the source.

The most effective search strategies use both subject searches and keyword searches. That is the only way to maximize your results.

## How Do You Locate Books on Your Subject?

Books are an excellent source of information for a research paper provided that your subject is not so new or so focused that it is not likely to be treated in a book. Locating books on your subject and topic involves a series of stages.

**Using Reference Books as a Starting Place**   If you do not have a fairly detailed knowledge about your subject, encyclopedias and dictionaries can be good places to begin your research. Before consulting such reference works, however, remember three important points:

1.  Encyclopedias and dictionaries are only good as *starting* points to obtain a basic overview of a subject. You will never be able to rely solely on such sources for college-level research.

2.  Encyclopedias and dictionaries range from general works that cover a wide range of subjects (such as the *Encyclopedia Britannica*, *Encyclopedia Americana*, and *Collier's Encyclopedia*) to highly specialized works focused around a single field or subject.

3.  Although some encyclopedias are available in electronic formats (for example, *Encyclopedia Britannica* has a version known as *Britannica Online*), many of the most detailed and specialized encyclopedias and dictionaries are currently only available in print form.

Because general encyclopedias provide information about a variety of subjects, they can never contain as much information about a single subject as you can find in an encyclopedia that specializes in that subject. For this reason, you might begin a search with a specialized encyclopedia. The word *specialized* here refers primarily to the more focused, in-depth subject coverage that these works offer; most of the articles are written in nontechnical language. The word *dictionary*, as it is used in the titles of such works, means essentially the same thing as *encyclopedia*—a collection of articles of varying lengths arranged alphabetically.

 **CAUTION: USING WIKIPEDIA AS A SOURCE**

Everyone at one time or another uses Wikipedia. The name is derived from a combination of two words: *wiki* (a type of collaborative Website) and *encyclopedia*. Wikipedia is what is called an open-source information Website, which means that anyone—including you or your teacher—can contribute an article or edit an existing one. The articles in Wikipedia must draw upon existing knowledge, that is, on material that has been published elsewhere. In that sense, nothing is "original"; all entries must be documented from other sources. This is why contributors do not need special qualifications. However, because articles do not initially undergo editorial checking and scrutiny, it is possible that the articles might contain inaccurate information. Articles in some fields, most of the sciences for example, are generally quite accurate, but that is not true for every field.

Wikipedia has the advantage of timeliness. On its Website, Wikipedia notes that it is "continually updated, with the creation or updating of articles on topical events within seconds, minutes or hours, rather than months or years with printed encyclopedias." You can find information in Wikipedia that cannot be found in print volumes or online encyclopedias. Read Brock Read's "Can Wikipedia Ever Make the Grade?" (Chapter 1) for more information.

**Most instructors, colleges, and universities will *not* accept information from Wikipedia as a source for a research paper because it is not regarded as a reliable scholarly resource.**

Your school is likely to have a wide range of specialized encyclopedias and dictionaries. Probably most of these will be located in the reference section of your library. To locate these reference tools, try the following steps:

1. Consult a guide to reference works. The following guides are widely available in college and university libraries. Use one or more of them to establish a list of possible works to consult.
   - Robert Balay (Ed.), *Guide to Reference Books*, 11th ed. (1996)
   - *Bowker's Best Reference Books: Arranged by Subject Heading*, 2 vols. (2005)

2. Check in the library's catalog under the headings "Encyclopedia and Dictionaries—Bibliographies," "[Your subject]—Dictionaries," and "[Your subject]—Dictionaries and Encyclopedias." You can also do a keyword search using these terms.

3. Ask a reference librarian for advice on the specialized sources likely to be relevant to your topic.

4. Check your library's electronic database to see if any dictionaries or encyclopedias are networked into it.

**Finding Books in the Library's Catalog**   Every library maintains a catalog that lists materials held in its collections. The record for each item often provides a wide range of information, but it always includes the author's name, the title of the item, and a few of the most important subject headings. Most college and university libraries are computerized. All of the information about each item is contained in one large database. Users can access holdings through a computer terminal, searching by keywords, by author, by title, by subject, and often by date or place of publication. Most online catalogs not only display call numbers but also tell you whether the item you want has been checked out or is on the shelves. Often you do not have to visit the library to search its catalog; the catalog is accessible from home or from your dorm room via modem or network cabling.

When you start a search for books in a library's catalog, remember these key points:

- Always read the help menu the first time you use an online catalog. Do not assume that you know how the search functions work. Knowing how to search makes the difference between disappointment and success.

- All catalogs—whether cards filed in drawers or computer records—list only material owned by that particular library or other libraries in the area or state. No library owns a copy of every book. Increasingly, online catalogs also provide access to *WorldCat*, which is a "union" catalog—that is, it lists other institutions that own the book. Although books that are not held by your school's library can be obtained from other schools on what is called *interlibrary loan*, the process can be slow and not easily accessible to undergraduates.

- Library catalogs list books (by author, title, and a few subject headings) and journals (only by title). Library catalogs never include the authors or titles of individual articles contained in journals or magazines. In that sense, the library's catalog provides access to only a portion of the information that is available in any library.

- Much of the information on any subject—and generally the most current information—is found in journal articles, not in books. Remember as well that certain subjects might not be treated in a book-length study. For example, if a subject is very current or too specialized, probably no book has been published about it. Because of this, a search for sources should never be limited to the references found in a library catalog. You must check the various periodical indexes (in print and online).

- In initial searches for information, you are typically looking for subjects or keywords; that is, you do not have a specific title or author to look up. Searching keywords or subjects in a library catalog is considerably more complicated than it might initially seem, because the subject headings used in a library catalog are often not what you might expect. Similarly, when you use a keyword, you only retrieve information on sources that use that keyword. That is why you need a search strategy. Review the advice in this chapter on searching by subject and keyword.

**Browsing the Library's Bookshelves**   This heading probably strikes you as silly—libraries have miles of shelves. Isn't it a waste of time to browse? Actually, it isn't. Libraries group books together based on a subject classification, often the Library of Congress system. Whenever you locate a particular book that looked promising in the library's catalog, look on the shelves immediately around it. Often you will find other books that deal with the same subject.

## How Do You Locate Online Sources About Your Subject and Topic?

The Web has expanded so fast that no one can calculate its size. In 1997, it contained 320 million Web pages; by 1999, the number was 800 million; the last realistic estimate came in 2005 and the number then was placed at 19.2 billion. Given that growth, it is not surprising that no *search engine* (the term applied to software programs that index information on the Web) can retrieve it all. In fact, search engines do not really search the Web when you type in a word or phrase. Rather, each search engine searches its own database, which has been compiled by robot programs called "spiders" that crawl over the Web locating possible sites to include.

**Choosing a Search Engine**   Typically when you search the Web, you go to your favorite search engine, probably Google, and type in a word or phrase. Immediately, a list of relevant Websites appears. Remember though, the nature of what you retrieve is related to the effectiveness of the search term (the keyword or key phrase) that you type in. For almost any subject you can type a variety of synonyms and related terms, and your results will vary somewhat each time. Before you start a Web search, think about a search strategy that will cover more than a single word or phrase. Google or Yahoo! Search are not the only search engines available. Guides to searching the Web urge you to use more than one search engine, as studies have shown that more than 80 percent of the pages retrieved by one search engine are not retrieved by another.

The University of California, Berkeley, maintains a series of tutorials on "Finding Information on the Internet" which is regularly updated. One in the series is titled "Recommended Search Engines" (available at www.lib.berkeley.edu/TeachingLib/Guides/Internet/SearchEngines.html). Although it acknowledges Google as the largest, it also recommends Yahoo! search and Ask.com. The tutorial includes a comparison of the three and indicates what you can and cannot do on each. The tutorial is an excellent place to learn how searches work and how you can control and maximize results from every search. Many Web users do not realize that each search engine has a help feature—just like your library's online catalog—where you can find out how to use it more efficiently.

 **TIPS FOR STARTING A WEB SEARCH ON GOOGLE**

The homepages of search engines offer advice on how to make Web searches more efficient. Since Google is so popular, let's use it as an example:

1. On the homepage, click first on About Google
2. At the next screen click on Help
3. At the next screen click on Web Search
4. At the next screen click on Search Tips

    The options that are then displayed include these:
    Search Basics
        Web Search glossary
        Searching made easy
        Finding people
        Use of punctuation
        Use of common words
    Advanced Search Tips
        Wildcard search
        Country or domain search
        Date search
        Searching U.S. sites

In addition to the large search engines, the Web contains many subject directories, specialized, subject-focused directories that you can search. The one used by many librarians is *Librarians' Internet Index*, which can be found at www.lii.org. It lists Websites that are reliable and accurate under a series of subject headings such as arts and humanities, health, law, science, business, and society and social sciences. A helpful tutorial on subject directories, "Recommended Subject Directories," also compiled by the University of California, Berkeley, is available (www.lib.berkeley.edu/TeachingLib/Guides/Internet/SubjDirectories.html).

**Learning How to Search the Web**    People generally assume that you search the Web simply by going to a search engine such as Google or Ask.com and typing in a word or phrase. That is one way to search, but it tends to give you many listings that are not really related to the subject you are searching. As an alternative, and one which few people use, you can search the Web by starting with a subject directory. A subject directory is a search engine that gathers together Websites under subject headings, like those mentioned in the previous paragraph. This allows you to search for your term or keyword only in databases that are related to your subject.

Simply typing in a keyword or a subject word into a search box will give you a huge number of hits, or references, that are listed together only because each one contains—somewhere—the word or phrase you typed in. An initial search for a single word might turn up thousands of sites and documents, the majority of which are irrelevant to your topic. Just as in the case of a keyword search in an online library catalog, you need to narrow your search by using precise terms and what are called *operators*.

 **USING PRECISE WORDS AND OPERATORS IN YOUR WEB SEARCH**

*Precise words* are the key to an effective search. Develop a list of synonyms or related subjects when you begin a search. If you do not enter the right keyword or the exact subject heading, vital resources might be irretrievable. A good search generally involves searching multiple terms rather than searching a single word or phrase. Remember, also, to use at least two different search engines in every Web search. Different engines will retrieve different documents.

*Operators* are words or symbols that signal the relationship between words in a search entry. You can find a list of operators on the Website of any of the search engines. Here are a few examples that are particularly effective in Web searches:

"      "    Place a phrase in quotation marks to find occurrences of that particular phrase in exactly that word order rather than any other possible arrangement of the words.

*Example*

"dark matter" (the quotation marks will guarantee that the search looks only for the phrase "dark matter" and not the two words separately)

| | |
|---|---|
| + or *and* | Attach the plus or an *and* between words to indicate that the words must appear together in a document. |

*Examples*

business and theft
computers +viruses

| | |
|---|---|
| − or *not* | Attach the minus as a prefix to a word or *not* between words to indicate that the second word cannot also appear on the page. |

*Examples*

Frankenstein −Dracula (only references to Frankenstein without references to Dracula)

| | |
|---|---|
| * or ? | Most search engines have a symbol for truncation (literally cutting off), sometimes called a wildcard. Truncation or wildcard symbols are essential when a word might have alternate spellings (theater or theatre) or alternate endings (theater, theaters, theatrical). |

*Examples*

theat?
theat*

## How Do You Evaluate Sources You Find on the Web?

Retrieving Websites that look promising is only part of the problem. Anyone can post anything (or nearly anything) on the Web. Just because it is there, just because it looks professional and scholarly, is not a guarantee that you can trust the information that it contains. How do you know what to trust? Never use information from a site without being cautious.

For comprehensive suggestions about evaluating Websites, three online resources are especially helpful:

- "Evaluating Web Pages: Techniques to Apply & Questions to Ask" prepared as part of "Finding Information on the Internet" by the Library at the University of California, Berkeley (found at www.lib. berkeley.edu/TeachingLib/Guides/Internet/Evaluate.html)

- "Evaluating Information Found on the Internet" prepared by the Library at Johns Hopkins University (found at www.library.jhu.edu/ researchhelp/general/evaluating/index.html)

- *Librarians' Internet Index* (found at www.lii.org) offers descriptions of other guides to "evaluating Web resources"—search using that heading

Look carefully at any Website that you access and think about the following:

1. Who is the author or creator of the Website? Do you have any information about that person? Is she or he a recognized authority in the field? Is the Website hosted by a provider who does "personal" pages such as AOL or GeoCities? Or does the Web address end with *gov* (government) or *edu* (educational institutions), which would suggest more editorial control over the content?

2. Is there any indication that the Website is sponsored or published by a national organization? A company or corporation? A newspaper or magazine? Is there any reason why the sponsor or publisher might want to stress information that is favorable to it? Or that supports its agenda?

3. Is there any bias immediately evident that would suggest the Website contains more propaganda or more advertisement than impartial information?

4. Is the Website up-to-date? Is the site being maintained?

5. If the Website contains facts and statistics, does it document where they came from? Are links to other sites included?

## How Do You Find Sources Published in Magazines and Journals?

The greatest amount of information on almost any topic will not be found in books or on Websites, but in magazines and journals. College and university libraries do not use the term *magazine*; they refer to *periodicals* or *serials*. These two terms indicate that the publication appears periodically or that it is an installment in a larger series. Most of the magazines sold at your local newsstand—whether issued weekly, biweekly, or monthly—will not be found in your college or university library. Correspondingly, most of the journals (periodicals and serials) found in your library's periodical room cannot be purchased at a newsstand. They are too specialized; they appeal only to a limited audience; they publish articles based on research rather than opinion; and they are aimed at a scholarly rather than a general reader. Most, if not all, of the research that you do for college papers should be done in journals that can be found in your library.

The way in which libraries provide access to journals is changing. More and more libraries are discontinuing their subscriptions to printed copies of journals and are providing instead electronic access to journals. The switch has some significant advantages. Many databases include not just a bare bibliographic citation or a short abstract or summary, but also the full text of the article. Some journals are exclusively available as electronic documents. In general, computer technologies have significantly increased access to periodical literature, although that access is often through an online document that must be read on a screen or printed off.

Increased access does not necessarily mean, however, that it is always easier to find the information you need. For example, there is no single index to all periodical literature. Similarly, many newspapers are not indexed at all. Instead, you have to consult a variety of indexes, depending on the particular subject that you are researching. Indexes to periodicals are available in two forms. Some come as printed volumes, with regular supplements, that are typically kept in the reference section of a library. Others are available in electronic formats, and you search for information in the databases using keywords or subjects. Your library's online catalog will indicate what electronic databases are available for searching periodical literature.

Printed indexes require you to search your subject through a series of separate volumes devoted to particular years. Once you have the citations, you need to find the appropriate bound volumes of the journals in your library. Admittedly, working this way is a slow process. Electronic databases, on the other hand, allow you to conduct an instant search using multiple search terms in many sources published over a multiyear period. If the database includes full-text formats, you can retrieve the text (sometimes even with illustrations) within seconds. Electronic databases make the task of retrieving articles quite simple. Not surprisingly, printed indexes are disappearing and are gradually being replaced by electronic ones.

## Where Do You Start Your Search for Periodical Sources?

When you are ready to start your research for sources in periodicals, first visit your school's library. Meet with a librarian who is a subject specialist. Explore the types of indexes that are available. Where are they located? How can you access them? Are there printed indexes available? What periodical indexes are available online? Check your library's computer network or Web page. What is available varies from school to school.

For example, at my university, the library maintains an extensive listing of indexes that are available for searching. This listing includes some indexes that are only available in print form and some that are only available in electronic form. The listing, which can be found on the library's Website, also indicates the date when indexing began and the subjects and periodicals included in the index. The listing can be accessed through subject groupings (arts and humanities, business and economics, engineering, government, law and politics, health sciences, life science, physical sciences, and social science) or through a simple alphabetical listing.

The list of indexes that follows is representative. Your library might have all or only some of these. Publishers market different packages of databases, so the names might change as well, depending on the service to which your library subscribes.

- General Indexes: *Good places to start*. These three sets of indexes are held by many libraries. Check to see if any or all are available at your school's library.

    *Academic Onefile* (covers 1980–). Provides coverage of nearly every discipline. Also indexes national news magazines and newspapers.

*LexisNexis Academic* (coverage varies depending on the section). Composed of five sections: news, business, legal research, medical, and reference. Also has a detailed "Help" on how to use the different sections.

*The New York Times Index* (covers 1851–). Indexes news and articles in the newspaper. Since many libraries subscribe to *The New York Times* and since it is a national newspaper, it can be a useful source of information. This index and a group of other specialized indexes to *The Times* are available in both print and electronic forms.

- Specialized Periodical Indexes: *The Next Step*. About two hundred indexes to the periodical literature in specialized subject areas are available. Any library is likely to have a number of these; most will not have them all. Visit your library and ask what is available. In some cases, similar coverages are provided by indexes that have different names. The following listing includes those most widely held and used.

  *Art Abstracts/Art Index* (covers 1929– for indexing; 1994– for abstracts). Indexes periodicals, yearbooks, and museum bulletins in art areas such as archaeology, architecture, art history, city planning, crafts, films, graphic arts, photography.

  *Biographical and Genealogy Master Index*. Indexes biographical dictionaries, encyclopedias, and other reference sources. The place to begin for biographical information about people living or dead. Widely available in print and also in electronic format.

  *Biological and Agricultural Index* (covers 1983–). Indexes articles on biology, agriculture, and related sciences in scholarly and popular periodicals.

  *Computer Database* (covers 1996–) and *Computer Science Index* (covers 1996–). Indexes journals devoted to computer science, electronics, telecommunications, and microcomputer applications. Full-text format is available for many journals.

  *ERIC* [U.S. Department of Education Resources Information Center] (covers 1966–). Indexes with abstracts, articles in professional journals in education and other educational documents. Most libraries will also have print guides to ERIC materials.

  *General Business File ASAP* (covers 1980–). Indexes and abstracts periodicals on a broad range of business, management, trade, technology, marketing, and advertising issues. Full-text format is provided for many of the periodicals.

  *Health Reference Center Academic* (covers 1980–). Indexes medical journals and consumer health magazines as well as health-related articles in general-interest magazines. Many essays are available in full-text format.

*MLA International Bibliography* (covers 1922– in print format; 1926– in electronic format). Indexes articles and books on modern languages, literature, linguistics, and folklore.

*PsycINFO* (covers 1887–). Indexes and abstracts journals in areas such as psychiatry, nursing, sociology, education, pharmacology, and physiology.

*Sociological Abstracts* (covers 1963–). Indexes and abstracts journals in sociology and related areas such as anthropology, economics, demography, political science, and social psychology.

*Web of Science* (covers 1900–). Indexes citations and abstracts of articles in scholarly journals in all areas of science.

## How Do You Locate Government Documents Relevant to Your Topic?

The U.S. government is the world's largest publisher of statistical information. For many research topics, government documents represent an excellent source of information. Most college libraries house collections of such documents, often in a special area. Government documents are arranged by a Superintendent of Documents call-number system that indicates the agency that released the document. Check with your reference or government documents librarian for help in locating relevant documents for your research. The following indexes are good starting points for research:

- *Marcive Web DOCS* (covers 1976–). Indexes U.S. government publications cataloged by the Government Printing Office.
- *LexisNexis Congressional* (covers 1789–). Indexes U.S. legislative information.
- *LexisNexis Statistical* (covers 1973–). Indexes and abstracts statistical publications produced by federal and state governments, by international and intergovernmental organizations, and by private publishers. Includes a searchable version of the information contained in the *Statistical Abstract of the United States*.

## How Do You Interview People for a Research Paper?

Depending on your topic, you may find that people—and not just books and articles—will be an important source of information. If you decide to interview someone in the course of your research, choose a person who has special credentials or knowledge about the subject. For example, while working on an essay about alcohol use on campus, you might decide that it would be valuable and interesting to include specific information about the prevalence of drinking at your school. To obtain such data, you could talk to the dean of students or the director of health services or campus security. You might also talk to students who acknowledge that they have had problems with alcohol.

Once you have drawn up a list of people to interview, plan your interviewing strategy. When you first contact someone to request an interview, always explain who you are, what you want to know, and how you will use the information. Whether you are doing an interview in person, on the telephone, or through e-mail, establish guidelines for the interview. For example, students who have had problems with drinking are not going to want their real names used in an essay. Once you have agreed on a time for an in-person or telephone interview, be on time. If you are using e-mail for the interview, make sure that your source knows when you will need a reply.

No matter what the circumstances of the interview, always be prepared: do some fairly thorough research about the topic ahead of time. Do not impose on your source by stating, "I've just started to research this problem, and I would like you to tell me everything you know about it." Prepare a list of questions in advance, the more specific the better. However, do not be afraid to ask your source to elaborate on a response. Take notes, but expand those notes as soon as you leave the interview, while the conversation is fresh in your mind. If you plan to use any direct quotations, make sure that your source is willing to be quoted and that your wording of the quotation is accurate. If possible, check the quotations with your source one final time.

Quotations from interviews should be integrated into your text in the same way as quotations from printed texts. Make sure quotations are essential to your paper, keep them short, use ellipses to indicate omissions, and try to position them at the ends of your sentences. When you are quoting someone who is an expert or an authority, include a reference to her or his position within your text, setting off that description or job title with commas:

> "We've inherited this notion that if it pops up on a screen and looks good, we think of it as fairly credible," said Paul Gilster, author of *Digital Literacy* (Wiley Computer Publishing, 1997).

 ## STUDENT WRITERS: LOCATING SOURCES

### Kristen
Finding sources was actually not that difficult a process at all. I found a few Websites by using a search engine, but in the end most of my sources were books. Our library had many books that were incredibly useful for researching. Since I did not have time to read a number of books, I looked at their tables of contents and indexes for things that I thought sounded useful. Then I would skim the chapters as needed.

### Bailey
I already admired the work of Banksy, a well-known stencil graffiti artist from Britain, so my research began with a section of his Website that reproduced newspaper articles about his work. One article in particular

mentioned Britain's Anti-Social Behaviour Bill, which allows authorities to remove graffiti from private property if the owner doesn't clean it up within an allotted time period. I thought this was extremely interesting, but the article on the Website had been scanned and did not contain enough information for me to do a bibliographical citation, so I had to find a copy of the bill, hence the UK Parliament document on my list of works cited.

I wanted to explore anti-graffiti laws to see what the punishment was and how the law defines graffiti, and since my instructor encouraged us to localize our topics, I had to find the graffiti laws for Delaware. Using a Google search, I came across a Website that listed graffiti laws from a number of states. This was helpful, but it was difficult to decipher the legal jargon so that I could translate it into something that my readers might understand. This process was slow.

We were required to use a variety of sources, so I also searched the library catalog for books, databases for periodicals, and the Web for the most current information and legal documents. In our library I found a small section in the stacks that contained books about graffiti. I flipped through them, looking particularly for books with text in addition to pictures. Interestingly, I found a few sources outside of the "graffiti section": one book about criminology and another about modernism. These books used graffiti as an example under a broader topic. They provided different approaches to the topic, which helped me construct a balanced paper.

## How Do You Evaluate Your Print Sources?

At this point in your research, you will have identified a number of sources that you could use in preparing your research paper. Your paper should be based on a variety of sources, not just one or two. A single source represents one point of view and necessarily contains a limited amount of information. A wide range of sources are available for any subject: encyclopedias and other reference books; books; articles in specialized journals, popular magazines, and newspapers; pamphlets; government documents; interviews; research experiments or studies; electronic mail postings or documents from Web pages. Your instructor might specify both the number and nature of the sources that you are to use, but even if the choice is up to you, select a varied set of sources.

As you gather sources, you need to pay attention to their quality. Are they accurate, up-to-date, and unbiased? Not every source will meet those criteria. Just because something is in print or posted on a Website does not mean that it is true or accurate—just think of the tabloid newspapers and celebrity magazines displayed at any supermarket checkout. In your search for information, you need to evaluate the reliability and accuracy of each potential source, because you do not want to base your paper on inaccurate, distorted, or biased information.

Of course evaluating sources is less difficult if you are already an expert on the subject you are researching. But how can you evaluate sources when you first start to gather information? The problem is not as formidable as it at first seems, for you regularly evaluate written sources when you try to answer day-to-day questions. For example, if you are interested in information about the best way to lose weight, which of the following sources would you be most likely to trust?

- An article in a supermarket tabloid newspaper ("Lose Ten Pounds This Weekend on the Amazing Prune Diet")
- An article in a popular magazine ("How to Lose a Pound a Week")
- A Website that urges the value of a particular weight loss program that it is promoting or selling (for example, electrotherapy treatments, a liquid diet plan, "sweat" wraps)
- An article in your local newspaper written by a local columnist offering advice on weight loss
- A magazine article published in 1930 dealing with popular diets
- A book written by physicians, dietitians, and fitness experts published in 2009
- A Website maintained by the American College of Sports Medicine

You would probably reject the tabloid newspaper article (not necessarily objective, accurate, or reliable), the Website urging a particular program (potentially biased and likely to exaggerate the value of that particular treatment), and the article published in 1930 (out of date). The articles in the popular magazine and the local newspaper might have some value, but given the likelihood that their authors are not authorities, the limitations of space, and the audience for whom they are written, they would probably be too general and too sketchy to be of much use. The best sources of information would be the book written in 2009 by people with credentials in the field and the Website maintained by a recognizable medical authority.

Guidelines are helpful in evaluating print sources for a research paper, just as they are in evaluating information retrieved from the Web. A good source must meet the following tests:

1. **Is the source objective?** You can access objectivity in several ways. For example, does the language in the work, and even in its title, seem sensational or biased? Is the work published by an organization that might have a special and possibly skewed interest in the subject? Does it contain documented information? Are there bibliographical references—footnotes or endnotes, lists of works consulted? How reliable are the "authorities" quoted? Are their titles and credentials cited? The more scholarly and impartial the source seems, the greater the likelihood that the information it contains can be trusted.

2. **Is the source accurate?** Reputable newspapers and magazines make serious efforts to ensure that what they publish is accurate. Similarly,

books published by university presses or by large, well-known publishing houses are probably reliable, and journals published by scholarly or professional organizations and the Websites that they maintain very likely contain information you can trust. For books, check reviews to see readers' evaluations.

3. **Is the source current?** In general, the more current the source, the greater the likelihood that new discoveries will be considered. Current information might not be crucial in writing about literary works, but it makes a great deal of difference in many other fields.

4. **Is the source authoritative?** What can you find out about the author's or sponsor's credentials? Are they cited elsewhere? What does the nature of the source tell you about the author's expertise?

## WRITING

### How Does Researching Help You Write Your Paper?

You can, of course, start writing as soon as you have a topic, or preferably a thesis. But because of the length of the research paper and because the paper involves using sources and documenting them, do not expect to complete all of your research before you begin writing. As you gather information, your paper and your thesis might change. Despite your most diligent efforts to find a specific topic within a larger subject, you might begin your research strategy with a topic that is really just a subject—too large to research effectively and write about within the limits of a freshman English research paper. If you accumulate a mountain of published sources, you need to focus your topic and your thesis more precisely. The research stage actually helps you define your thesis.

 **STUDENT WRITER: DRAFTING**

**Bailey**
The hardest parts of a paper, for me, are the introduction and conclusion. That said, it always helps to write my introduction first. I use the five-paragraph essay as a model (but not as the rule) and the process of writing the opening paragraph forces me to define my thesis and organize my body paragraphs.

What eventually became the conclusion began as informal brainstorming notes. It always helps me to get my ideas down quickly before I go into formal writing mode and have to construct complex sentences—this is a disorganized form of outlining.

## How Do You Integrate Sources Into Your Paper?

Even though much of the information in a research paper—facts, quotations, statistics, and so forth—is taken from outside sources, a research paper is not a cut-and-paste collection of quotations with a few bridge sentences written by you. A research paper is written in your own words with quotations and documentation added whenever necessary. You can control your quotations by remembering several points:

- **Ask yourself if a quotation is really necessary**. If something is common knowledge, you do not need to quote an authority for that information. Any information that is widely known or that can be found in general reference works does not need to be documented—provided that it appears in your own words.

- **Keep your quotations as short as possible.** Do not let your paper become large chunks of indented direct quotations.

- **Avoid strings of quotations.** Never pile up quotations one after one. Rather, interpret and control the material that you are using and provide transitions that tie the quotations into your text.

- **Learn to paraphrase and summarize instead of giving direct quotations.** What is important is the idea or the facts that you find in your sources, not the exact words. Paraphrasing means putting a quotation into your own words; summarizing means condensing a quotation into the fewest possible words.

- **Use ellipses to shorten quotations.** An ellipsis consists of three spaced periods (not two, not four). It is used to indicate that a word, part of a sentence, a whole sentence, or a group of sentences has been omitted from the quotation.

## How Do You Shorten a Quotation Using Ellipsis?

An ellipsis is a series of three spaced periods (...) that is inserted into a quotation to show the omission of words or phrases or even whole sentences. An ellipsis helps to shorten a quotation, to omit what is unnecessary. Under no circumstances should an ellipsis be used to change or obscure the meaning of the original quotation.

If you omit a sentence or more from a quotation, then you add a fourth period to the three. If you remove either the opening or closing part of a quotation, you do not need ellipses in either place.

**Original:** "My teacher observed that many writers in introductory writing courses find that writing becomes easier the more frequently it is done."

**Removing: words** "Many writers ... find that writing becomes easier the more ... it is done."

Style guides for writers offer extensive advice on using ellipses when quoting sources.

## Why Do You Need to Acknowledge and Document Your Sources?

Research papers require documentation. As a writer, you need to document and acknowledge all information that you have taken from sources. The documentation serves three purposes:

1. **Documentation acknowledges your use of someone else's work.** Whenever you take something from a published source—statistics, ideas, opinions, whether quoted or in your own words—you must indicate where it comes from, thereby acknowledging that it is not your original work. Otherwise, you will be guilty of academic dishonesty. Students who borrow material from sources without acknowledgment—that is, who plagiarize—are subject to some form of academic penalty. People in the real world who do so can and will be sued.

2. **Documentation gives you greater credibility as a writer.** Documentation lets your readers know that you did not create these statistics, facts, quotations to suit your paper or to strengthen your argument. Your readers can see and evaluate, if necessary, the sources that you used.

3. **Documentation helps your readers locate other sources of information on the topic.** Notes, lists of works cited, and bibliographies are vital to someone who is researching the same topic.

## How Do You Document Sources If You Are Writing for Magazines and Newspapers

Most readers of newspapers and magazines would not welcome parenthetical citations, footnotes or endnotes, or lists of works consulted or cited. Scholarly articles and books, however, always include documentation. Magazine and newspaper articles typically attribute information to a source within the text without providing an exact reference. For example, Joshua Ortega quotes a provocative statement in his article, "Water Wars: Bottling Up the World's Supply of $H_2O$" (Chapter 9), by just identifying who said the statement and when: "'The wars of the next century will be about water.' This is a quote from Ismail Serageldin, former vice president of the World Bank, in 1999." When Ortega cites a statistic, he does a similar thing: "A four-year study by the National Resources Defense Council (NRDC), released in 1999, found that one-fifth of the sampled bottled waters contained known neurotoxins and carcinogens such as styrene, toulene and xylene." Attributions are necessary in both cases, but since the article appeared in a newspaper, the writer provided no formal documentation.

The place of publication—and its expected or intended audience—has much to do with how an essay or article is documented. For example, compare how documentation is handled in Brock Read's (Chapter 1) "Can Wikipedia

Ever Make the Grade?" (published in a newspaper intended for an audience employed in higher education) and in Katherine Porter's (Chapter 9) "The Value of a College Degree" (published as an academic paper).

## What Documentation System Do You Use in Your Paper?

Different disciplines use different documentation, or citation, systems. Later in your studies, you may be asked to use a system different from the one you learn in an introductory writing course. Nearly all English courses use the MLA model; other humanities and social science courses typically use the APA form. MLA stands for the Modern Language Association, an organization of teachers of modern foreign languages and of English. A full guide to that system can be found in either the *MLA Style Manual and Guide to Scholarly Publishing* (3rd edition, 2008) or the version intended for students, the *MLA Handbook for Writers of Research Papers* (7th edition, 2009). The APA is the American Psychological Association, and its style guide, *Publication Manual of the American Psychological Association* (5th edition, 2001) is widely used in the social sciences.

Documentation systems are standardized guidelines that have been agreed on by organizations and fields. There is nothing sacred or "right" about one versus another. Standardization provides a fixed format for giving bibliographical information. Even the marks of punctuation are specified. No one expects you to memorize a particular citation system.

Style guides are intended to serve as models. Look at each of your sources, noting its particular features. What type of source are you dealing with? How many authors or editors did it have? In what format was it published? Then look for a similar example in the style guide for the citation system you are using; use that sample as a model. Citation formats for the types of sources most commonly used in a first-year research paper in a writing course are given on the next few pages. The range of possible sources for any topic is large, so you might have a source that does not match any of these common examples. For a complete guide, consult the MLA or APA manuals. Both can be found in the reference area of your school library.

## Can You Find Software Programs to Help with Documentation?

In recent years a number of software programs, referred to as individual bibliographical management products, have become available. They allow you to import data directly from an online database available through your school's library or to enter your own sources and convert the bibliographical citations into a number of different formats such as MLA, APA, Turabian, or Chicago. Programs such as RefWorks, EndNote, ProCite, and RefMan are popular and in widespread use. This type of program makes doing bibliographical citations simple and foolproof. Check with your library's reference section to see what is available. In all likelihood, there will be workshops or handouts to show you how to use these products.

## How Do You Work Quotations Into Your Text?

Both the MLA and APA systems acknowledge sources with brief parenthetical citations in the text. These refer the reader to the "List of Works Cited" (the MLA title) or "References" (the APA title) at the end of the paper for the full bibliographic reference. For in-text references in the MLA system, the author's last name is given along with the number of the page on which the information appears. For in-text references in the APA system, the author's last name is given along with the year in which the source was published and—for direct quotations—the page number. Note in the following examples that the punctuation within the parentheses varies between the two systems.

Here is how a quotation from an article, "Immuno-Logistics," written by Gary Stix, that appeared in the June 1994 issue of *Scientific American* would be cited in the two systems:

MLA:    The major vaccines—those for diphtheria, pertussis, tetanus, polio, measles, and tuberculosis—cost less to make than they do to distribute: "The United Nations Children's Fund, for example, spends a total of $1.50 on the vaccines.... A tenth of what a government then has to disburse for labor, transportation, training and refrigeration to get these vaccines to infants and young children" (Stix 102).

APA:    The major vaccines—those for diphtheria, pertussis, tetanus, polio, measles, and tuberculosis—cost less to make than they do to distribute: "The United Nations Children's Fund, for example, spends a total of $1.50 on the vaccines.... A tenth of what a government then has to disburse for labor, transportation, training and refrigeration to get these vaccines to infants and young children" (Stix, 1994, p. 102).

Note that in both cases, the parenthetical citation comes before any final punctuation.

If you include the author's name in your sentence, you omit that part of the reference within the parentheses.

MLA:    According to Gary Stix, the major vaccines—those for diphtheria, pertussis, tetanus, polio, measles, and tuberculosis—cost less to make than they do to distribute: "The United Nations Children's Fund, for example, spends a total of $1.50 on the vaccines.... A tenth of what a government then has to disburse for labor, transportation, training and refrigeration to get these vaccines to infants and young children" (102).

APA:    According to Gary Stix (1994), the major vaccines—those for diphtheria, pertussis, tetanus, polio, measles, and tuberculosis—cost less to make than they do to distribute: "The United Nations Children's Fund, for example, spends a total of $1.50 on the vaccines.... A tenth of what a government then has to disburse for labor, transportation, training and refrigeration to get these vaccines to infants and young children" (p. 102).

## What If Quotations Are Too Long to Work into a Sentence?

A quotation of more than four lines (MLA) or more than forty words (APA) should be indented or set off from your text. In such cases, the parenthetical citation comes after the indented quotation. Here is how a quotation from "A Weight That Women Carry" by Sallie Tisdale, which appeared in the March 1993 issue of *Harper's* magazine, would be cited in the two systems:

MLA:    Sallie Tisdale points out the links between weight "reduction" and the "smallness" that society presses upon women:

> Small is what feminism strives against, the smallness that women confront everywhere. All of women's spaces are smaller than those of men, often inadequate, without privacy. Furniture designers distinguish between a man's and a woman's chair, because woman don't spread out like men. (A sparawling woman means only one thing.) Even our voices are kept down. (53)

APA:    Sallie Tisdale (1993) points out the links between weight "reduction" and the "smallness" that society presses upon women:

> Small is what feminism strives against, the smallness that women confront everywhere. All of women's spaces are smaller than those of men, often inadequate, without privacy. Furniture designers distinguish between a man's and a woman's chair, because women don't spread out like men. (A sprawling woman means only one thing.) Even our voices are kept down. (p. 53)

Note in both cases that the parenthetical citation comes after the final period.

If you are quoting material that has been quoted by someone else, cite the secondary source from which you took the material. Do not cite the original if you did not consult it directly. Here is how a quotation from an original source—a nuclear strategist writing in 1967—quoted on page 357 in a 1985 book written by Paul Boyer and titled *By the Bomb's Early Light: American Thought and Culture at the Dawn of the Atomic Age* would be cited.

MLA:    Explaining how Americans' views of the atom bomb shifted during the 1950's, Albert Wohlstotter, a nuclear strategist, commented in 1967: "Bright hopes for civilian nuclear energy" proved to be "an emotional counterweight to . . . nuclear destruction" (qtd. in Boyer 357).

APA:    Explaining how Americans' views of the atom bomb shifted during the 1950's, Albert Wohlstotter, a nuclear strategist, commented in 1967: "Bright hopes for civilian nuclear energy" proved to be "an emotional counterweight to . . . nuclear destruction" (cited in Boyer, 1985, p. 357).

In certain situations, you may need to include additional or slightly different information in your parenthetical citation. For example, when two or more sources on your list of references are by the same author, your citation will need to make clear to which of these you are referring; in the MLA system you do this by including a brief version of the title along with the author and page number: (Tisdale, "Weight," 53). (Note that this is generally not a problem in the APA system because works by the same author will already be distinguished by date.) For works that do not indicate an author, mention the title fully in your text or include a brief version in the parenthetical citation.

Unless a quotation is only a few words long, try to place it at the end of a sentence. Avoid "sandwich" sentences in which a quotation comes between two parts of your own sentence. If you introduce a several-line quotation into the middle of a sentence, by the end of the sentence the reader will probably have forgotten how your sentence began.

When you place a quotation at the end of a sentence, use a colon or a comma to introduce it. The colon signals that the quotation supports, clarifies, or illustrates the point being made.

> One advice book, *Common Sense for Maid, Wife, and Mother*, stated: "Heated discussion and quarrels, fretfulness and sullen taciturnity while eating, are as unwholesome as they are unchristian."
>
> Joan Jacobs Brumberg, "The Origins of America Nervosa" (Chapter 7)

If the introductory statement is not an independent clause, always use a comma before the quotation. For example, in the following sentence, the introductory clause ("As Brian Johnson . . . says") is not a complete sentence.

> As Brian Johnson, co-owner of the Dogwater Cafe, a fast-growing restaurant chain in Florida, says, "When I'm interviewing, I'm looking for someone with a lot of energy who wants this job more than anything else."
>
> Charlie Drozdyk, "Into the Loop" (Chapter 6)

If a complete sentence follows a colon, the first word after the colon may or may not be capitalized. The choice is yours, as long as you are consistent. However, if the colon introduces a quotation, the first word following that colon is capitalized.

## PLAGIARISM, ACADEMIC DISHONESTY, AND THE MISUSE OF SOURCES

The Writing Program Administrators (WPA) Website offers the following definition of plagiarism: "In an instructional setting, plagiarism occurs when a writer deliberately uses someone else's language, ideas, or other original (not common knowledge) material without acknowledging its source" (www.wpacouncil.org). Every college and university has a policy on plagiarism and academic dishonesty. If a student is found guilty, the school assesses some form of penalty, typically ranging from a failure on the paper to suspension from school.

Plagiarizing sources occurs on a variety of levels—all of which are serious. This section offers a quick overview with some examples. Most likely, your college will have guidelines on defining and avoiding plagiarism. Your instructor can explain the types of plagiarism and show you how to avoid each.

Several forms of plagiarism are obvious: submitting a paper obtained from a paper-writing service or from another student; using chunks of someone else's writing and simply inserting it without quotation marks and documentation into your paper. Material taken from the Web is easily identifiable when certain search techniques are applied. Remember, you have a distinctive writing style—you use a certain level of vocabulary and a certain type of sentence structure. You have a written "voice." After a short time, your instructor develops a sense of when the words on the page are really yours and when they are not. Your writing style is as distinctive as your speaking style.

Plagiarism is not limited to copying a whole paper or even a group of paragraphs. It is not defined by the quantity of material that is taken from a source without acknowledgment. Other forms of plagiarism (sometimes called "misuse of sources") include the following abuses or mistakes.

Your source reads:

"A number of European studies raised concerns about the increased risk of benign ear tumors and effects on the brain function of long-term cellphone use. If such risks exits, those most likely to be affected were children, said Stewart, and the younger the child, 'the greater the danger.' Children were more vulnerable because their brains were still developing and their skulls thin, making it easier for radiowaves to penetrate."

(Kamala Hayman, "Cellphones 'A Risk to Youngsters' ")

- **Misuse of source: using exact words from source without quotation marks**

    Young children should probably not be using cell phones since they pose a possible health hazard. <u>A number of European studies</u> had <u>raised concerns about the increased risk</u> of <u>benign ear tumors and effects on the brain function of long-term cell phone</u> users. Also, the study stated that <u>children were more vulnerable because their brains were still developing and their skulls thinner, making it easier for radiowaves to penetrate</u> (Hayman, 72).

- **Misuse of source: using someone else's ideas, words, and structure of sentences and paragraphs without using quotation marks and without acknowledgment of the source**

    Adding some words or synonyms does not change the fact that the paragraph is structured in form and content around the source.

    Young children should probably not be using cell phones since they pose a possible health hazard. Some European research studies posed questions about the dangers of benign ear tumors and the effect on brain ability of long-term cell phone users. These studies also indicated that children were more susceptible because their brains were still growing and their skulls were thinner, making it easier for radiowaves to damage the brain.

# REVISING

The process of revising a research paper is no different than revising a regular-length essay. Because the research paper is longer, more detailed, and written over an extended period of time, make sure you get feedback from readers. Often your instructor will ask you to submit a complete first draft before turning in a final copy. In some cases you might be able to take your finished paper to a writing center or a writing tutor for additional help. Not everyone has problems with the same parts of a paper, but as you see in the comments from Kristen and Bailey, both had trouble with the beginning and ending.

 **STUDENT WRITERS: REVISING**

### Kristen

Writing a research paper can sometimes be a little overwhelming. Everyone has trouble with different sections. For me, it is introductions and conclusions. About 100 percent of the time, I do not write an introduction until the paper is completely finished. I have a topic and a thesis, of course, but it is hard for me to write an engaging introduction until the body of the paper is finished.

### Bailey

I did find it useful to go back and edit my introduction after the rest of the paper was written. At that point I had a better idea of what exactly I had to introduce. My first draft had a very general introduction with a definition of graffiti and the identification of the value conflicts. I realized after rereading and peer editing that this was a terribly boring way to begin a paper, but I wasn't sure how to fix it. I left myself notes to come up with something better. For my final draft, I added what are now the first three sentences to introduce the conflict as it manifests itself in real life. Graffiti is about visibility and the problem comes when people have different reactions to it. By taking the topic "back to the street," so to speak, I show where I got the idea and identify the issue.

As for the conclusion, I left it for last. Early drafts had no conclusion at all, which is not at all useful for peer editing. For the conclusion, I like to consider what the paper's argument means on both a small and large scale, so I tie it up in terms of what I've already mentioned, then briefly discuss other implications that I haven't talked about yet.

## What Should You Check in Your Final Review?

Before you hand in your research paper, check again each of the following items:

1. If your instructor specified a certain format (for example, double-spaced pages, margins of a certain size, cover sheet laid out in a certain way), make sure you followed the directions.

2. Check each quotation in your text—do not skip proofreading them! Verify that you quoted your sources accurately.

3. Make sure that you have not unintentionally misused a source (review that section in this chapter). Have you placed quotation marks around every group of words or every sentence taken word for word from a source?

4. Check to see if your parenthetical documentation is done correctly (review that section in this chapter).

5. Review your documentation. Do you have your List of Works Cited or References in proper format? Check each item, following either the MLA or APA system. Getting it right is part of the assignment.

6. Consider your title. Does it accurately reflect your essay? Every paper must have a real title—"Research Paper" is not an option.

 ## MLA DOCUMENTATION—2008 AND 2009

With the publication of the 2008 edition of the *MLA Style Manual and Guide to Scholarly Publishing* (3rd edition) and the *MLA Handbook for Writers of Research Papers* (2009, 7th edition), the Modern Language Association reworked the format for documentation of sources. The new system reflects the changes in how researchers access information through libraries and computers. Increasingly, lists of works cited include Web documents and articles and even books accessed through electronic databases rather than print sources. An abbreviated guide to the order of components in a citation follows. For more information consult either of the MLA guides.

### Article or essay in a print (as opposed to an online) periodical

1. Author's or authors' name followed by a period
2. Title of the article or essay in quotation marks followed by a period
3. Italicized title of periodical
4. Volume number or date of publication followed by a colon
5. Page numbers on which the article appears followed by a period
6. The word *Print* to indicate the form in which the article appeared

### *Examples*

Milgrom, Mordecai. "Does Dark Matter Really Exist?" *Scientific American* August 2002: 48–52. Print.

Monasterky, Richard. "Searching for Extra Dimensions and the Ultimate Theory." *Chronicle of Higher Education* 18 July 2008: 45. Print.

### Article or essay accessed in an online database

Order of information is identical to a print citation with the following additions:

1. Italicized title of the database
2. The word *Web* to indicate how the article was accessed
3. Date on which the material was accessed *(continued)*

*Examples*

Monasterky, Richard. "Searching for Extra Dimensions and the Ultimate Theory." *Chronicle of Higher Education* 18 July 2008: 45. *Expanded Academic ASAP.* Web. 16 Sept. 2008.

Lederman, Leon. "What We Will Find Inside the Atom." *Newsweek.* International edition. 15 Sept. 2008. *LexisNexis.* Web. 16 Sept. 2008.

## Printed book

1. Author's or editor's name followed by a period
2. Italicized title of the book followed by a period
3. Edition, if other than first, followed by a period
4. Place of publication, publisher, date of publication followed by a period
5. The word *Print* to indicate the form in which it was accessed

*Example*

Thomas Armstrong. *Multiple Intelligences in the Classroom.* 2nd ed. Alexandria VA: Association for Supervision and Curriculum Development, 2000. Print.

## Web document

1. Author's or editor's name followed by a period
2. Title of the document in quotation marks followed by a period
3. Italicized title of the Website
4. The word *Web* to indicate the form in which it was accessed
5. Date on which the material was accessed

*Examples*

"Cosmos." *Encyclopedia Britannica Online.* Encyclopedia Britannica Online, 2008. Web. 16 Sept. 2008.

"Dark Matter." *Imagine the Universe.* NASA Goddard Flight Center, 22 Aug. 2008. Web. 16 Sept. 2008.

## Other types of sources

MLA now adds a word at the end of a bibliographical citation to indicate exactly what medium the work was produced in—for example, Radio, Television, CD, DVD, Videocassette, Audiocassette, Film, Performance, Print, Photograph.

## URLs

MLA no longer uses URLs (uniform resource locators—or Web addresses) in documentation. The *MLA Style Manual* notes that the inclusion of URLs of Web sources in works-cited-lists has "proved to have limited value . . . for they often change, can be specific to a subscriber or a session of use, and can be so long and complex that typing them into a browser is cumbersome and prone to transcription errors." It continues, "Readers are now more likely to find resources on the Web by searching for titles and authors' names than by typing URLs. You should include a URL as supplementary information only when the reader probably cannot locate the sources without it."

## How Do You Prepare a "List of Works Cited" or "References" Page?

At the end of your essay, on a separate sheet of paper, list all of the sources that you cited in your paper. In the MLA system, this page is titled List of Works Cited (with no quotation marks around it); in the APA system, it is titled References (also without quotation marks). This list should be alphabetized by the authors' last names so that readers can easily find full information about particular sources. If a source has not indicated an author, then alphabetize it by its title. Both systems provide essentially the same information, although arranged in a slightly different order.

- **For books:** the author's or authors' names, the title, the place of publication, the publisher's name, and the year of publication
- **For articles:** the author's or authors' names, the title, the name of the journal, the volume number and/or the date of that issue, and the pages on which the article appeared
- **For electronic sources:** the author's or authors' names, the title, date of publication, information on how the source can be accessed, and the date on which you accessed the material. Dates are important in citing electronic sources because the source may change its electronic address or even disappear.

Note in the following sample entries that in MLA style, the first line of each entry is flush with the left margin and subsequent lines are indented five spaces. If you are to use the APA format, ask your instructor which of APA's two recommended formats you should use: the first line flush left and subsequent lines indented five spaces (as shown here) or the first line indented five spaces and subsequent lines flush left.

---

**Books**

*A book by a single author*

MLA: Boyer, Paul. *By the Bomb's Early Light: American Thought and Culture at the Dawn of the Atomic Age.* New York: Random House, 1985. Print.

APA: Boyer, P. (1985). *By the bomb's early light: American thought and culture at the dawn of the atomic age.* New York: Random House.

*An anthology*

MLA: Ibieta, Gabriella, ed. *Latin American Writers: Thirty Stories.* New York: St. Martin's, 1993. Print.

APA: Ibieta, G. (Ed.). (1993). *Latin American writers: Thirty stories.* New York: St. Martin's Press.

*A book by more than one author*

MLA: Burns, Ailsa, and Cath Scott. *Mother-Headed Families and Why They Have Increased.* Hillsdale, NJ: Erlbaum, 1994. Print.

APA: Burns, A., & Scott, C. (1994). *Mother-headed families and why they have increased.* Hillsdale, NJ: Erlbaum.

*A book with no author's name*

MLA: *Native American Directory.* San Carlos, AZ: National Native American Co-operative. 1982. Print.

APA: *Native American Directory.* (1982). San Carlos. AZ: National Native American Co-operative.

*An article or story in an edited anthology*

MLA: Quartermaine, Peter. "Margaret Atwood's Surfacing: Strange Familiarity." *Margaret Atwood: Writing and Subjectivity.* Ed. Colin Nicholson. New York: St. Martin's, 1994. 119–32. Print.

APA: Quartermaine, P. (1994). Margaret Atwood's Surfacing: Strange familiarity. In C. Nicholson (Ed.). *Margaret Atwood: Writing and subjectivity* (pp. 119–132). New York: St. Martin's Press.

*An article in a reference work*

MLA: "Film Noir." *Oxford Companion to Film.* Ed. Liz-Anne Bawden. New York: Oxford UP, 1976. 249. Print.

APA: Film Noir. (1976). In L.-A. Bawden (Ed.), *Oxford companion to film* (p. 249). New York: Oxford University Press.

## Articles

*An article in a journal that is continuously paginated (that is, issues after the first in a year do not start at page 1)*

MLA: Lenz, Nygel. "'Luxuries' in Prison: The Relationship Between Amenity Funding and Public Support." *Crime & Delinquency* 48 (2002): 499–525. Print.

APA: Lenz, N. (2002). "Luxuries" in prison: The relationship between amenity funding and public support. *Crime & Delinquency, 48,* 499–525.

*Note:* When each issue of a journal does begin with page 1, also indicate the issue number after the volume number. For MLA style, separate the two with a period: 9.2. For APA style, use parentheses: 9(2).

*An article in a monthly magazine*

MLA: Milgrom, Mordecai. "Does Dark Matter Really Exist?" *Scientific American* Aug. 2002: 42–52. Print.

APA: Milgrom, M. (2002, August). Does dark matter really exist? *Scientific American,* 42–52.

*An article in a weekly or biweekly magazine*

MLA: Gladwell, Malcolm. "The Moral-Hazard Myth." *New Yorker* 24 August 2005: 44–49. Print.

APA: Gladwell, M. (2006, Aug. 24). The Moral-Hazard Myth. *New Yorker,* 44–49.

*An article in a daily newspaper*

MLA:  Lacey, Marc. "Engineering Food for Africans." *New York Times* 8 Sep. 2002, Sunday National Edition, sec. 1:8. Print.

APA:  Lacey, M. (2002, September 8). Engineering food for Africans. *New York Times*, Sunday National Edition, sec. 1, p. 8.

*An editorial in a newspaper*

MLA:  "Stem Cell End Run?" Editorial. *Washington Post* 24 Aug. 2005, sec. A14. Print.

APA:  Stem cell end run? (2005, August 24). [Editorial]. *Washington Post*, sec. A, p. 14.

*A review*

MLA:  Hitchens, Christopher. "The Misfortune of Poetry." Rev. of *Byron: Life and Legend, by Fiona MacCarthy. Atlantic Monthly* Oct. 2002: 149–56. Print.

APA:  Hitchens, C. (2002, October). The misfortune of poetry. [Review of *Byron: Life and legend*, by Fiona MacCarthy]. *Atlantic Monthly*, 149–56.

## Other Sources

*An interview*

MLA:  Quintana, Alvina. Personal interview. 13 June 2002.
Worthington, Joanne. Telephone interview. 12 Dec. 2002.

*Note:*  APA style does not include personal interviews on the References list, but rather cites pertinent information parenthetically in the text.

*A film*

MLA:  *Silkwood*. Writ. Nora Ephron and Alice Arden. Dir. Mike Nichols. With Meryl Streep. ABC, 1983. Film.

APA:  Ephron, N. (Writer), & Nichols. M. (Director). (1983). *Silkwood* [Motion picture]. Hollywood: ABC.

*More than one work by the same author*

MLA:  Didion, Joan. *Miami*. New York: Simon & Schuster, 1987. Print.
_____. "Why I Write." *New York Times Book Review* 9 Dec. 1976: 22. Print.

APA:  Didion, J. (1976, December 9). Why I write. *New York Times Book Review,* p. 22.
Didion, J. (1987). *Miami*. New York: Simon & Schuster.

*Note:*  MLA style lists multiple works by the same author alphabetically by title. APA style lists such works chronologically beginning with the earliest.

**Electronic Sources**    Increasingly the sources that we use for writing research papers are electronic—full-text articles taken from electronic databases available through libraries, journals that exist only in electronic form, documents taken from Websites, e-mail from people whom we have interviewed. Even books today are available—and sometimes only available—in an electronic format. The most recent edition of the *MLA Handboook for Writers of Research Papers* (7th edition, 2008) includes a section on citing electronic publications, as does the *Publication of the American Psychological Association* (5th edition, 2001). Three of the most common types of electronic sources used in freshman English research papers are listed here. For a fuller guide, consult the *MLA Handbook*. If you want additional help, ask your instructor or the reference department in your library for assistance in locating a published style guide in your area of study.

---

*An e-mail message*

MLA:    Miller, George. "On revising." E-mail to Eric Gray. 7 March 2008.

APA:    Miller, G. (2008, March 7). On revising.

The crucial pieces of information in citing an e-mail include the name of the writer, the title of the message (taken from the subject line), the recipient, and the date on which the message was sent.

*Full-text article from a periodical available through a library database*

MLA:    Seligman, Dan. "The Grade-Inflation Swindle." *Forbes* 18 Mar. 2002: 94. *Expanded Academic ASAP*. Web. 27 Sept. 2002.

APA:    Seligman, D. (2002, March 18). The grade-inflation swindle. *Forbes* p. 94. Retrieved September 30, 2002, from Expanded Academic ASAP.

*Information from a Website*

MLA:    Barndt, Richard. "Fiscal Policy Effects on Grade Inflation." 27 Sept. 2002. Web. 5 Nov. 2002.

APA:    Barndt, R. (2002, September 27). Fiscal policy effects on grade inflation. Retrieved October 3, 2002, from http://www.newfoundations.com/Policy/Barndt.html

---

## STUDENT RESEARCH PAPERS

The two papers that follow were written to fulfill the research paper requirement using the MLA documentation style as required by the instructors. Be sure to consult your instructor to determine which documentation style you should use.

Kristen LaPorte's paper has been annotated to point out important conventions of research writing and documentation. Notice that the paper does not begin with a title page. Check with your instructor to see whether you need a title page or an outline.

Kristen LaPorte
ENGL110, Section 43
Dr. Taylor

## Music as a Healing Power: A Look into the Effect of Music Therapy on Alzheimer's Patients ①

① Title centered and not underlined

② Text is double-spaced throughout

② The major motion picture *The Notebook*, released in 2004, followed a love story between Noah and Allie Calhoun, a couple who met while they were teenagers and never truly found love anywhere else. Because of a tragic accident, Allie began to suffer from severe dementia to the point that when she looked at Noah, the love of her life, he was unrecognizable to her. However, even in her condition, she was able to sit down at a piano and play a piece by Chopin by memory that she learned as a teenager (*The Notebook*). ③

③ 'Hook' introduction to catch the reader's attention

Even though a fictional movie serves as the inspiration for this example, it could realistically be possible. Music has an intangible power that continues to be increasingly explored, and it truly works miracles where some medical treatments have fallen short. As illustrated in *The Notebook*, Allie still has the ability to remember music even though she suffers from severe dementia. Alzheimer's disease is the most common form of dementia and has no cure. However, different therapies are offered to help memory restoration. Although other forms of therapy may be beneficial, music therapy proves to be one of the most effective treatment options for Alzheimer's patients, either individually or as a

⑤ LaPorte 2

④ Thesis statement

group, to help in areas such as concentration, general attitude, and communication. ④

In order to see the impact of music on Alzheimer's patients, a general overview of the disease itself is necessary. Alzheimer's is the most common form of dementia, a disease that affects the brain. Symptoms of Alzheimer's can be as minor as losing your house keys or forgetting a hair appointment. However, more symptoms such as disorientation, impaired speech, or even forgetting family members, begin to take over as the disease progresses. There are many hypothesized causes of Alzheimer's, and they all tend to point to brain cells. Whether it be the death of brain cells due to viral infection, collection of toxins in brain cells (which leads to damage), genetic factors, or a decline in the immune system due to age, damage to brain cells takes the lead for causing Alzheimer's (Check 40–47). ⑥

⑥ Parenthetical citation with author's last name and page number. No punctuation. Information taken from source, but not a direct quotation

As mentioned previously, no cure can completely eliminate Alzheimer's from the system; however, antidepressants or tranquilizers are usually given to help with the patient's state of mind. In addition to these treatment options, music therapy continues to grow in popularity today as an alternative treatment. The use of music therapy does not rid the brain of Alzheimer's, but, in conjunction with medical treatment, music's power produces positive steps towards a better means of living and dealing with the disease.

LaPorte 3

⑦ Notice pro-
portion of au-
thor's own prose
to quotations.
Quotations kept
to a minimum,
no long indented
quotations

⑦ Many definitions of "music therapist" exist in the professional world. Dr. Donald Michel, a professor from Texas Women's University, describes a music therapist as someone who knows not only "about the behavior sciences in general, but also about the interactions of music and man" (Michel 4–5). The word "interactions" plays a key role in this definition. An Alzheimer's patient may not be the easiest person to deal with, but the creation of a trustworthy relationship needs to occur for progress to be achieved. Therefore, a music therapist must have patience and the willingness to spend time with an individual. In order to get Registered Music Therapist (RMT) certification, one must successfully complete four years at a school with an accredited music therapy program in addition to completing a six-month internship. Music therapists should also be knowledgeable about music in general if they wish to use music as a medical tool. Dr. Michel summarizes these qualities quite well by saying, "The music therapist today is a professional trained person who knows how to use his unique medium, music, to influence desirable changes in his patients" (Michel 11). Music therapists can use discretion to evaluate their environments, patients, and other similar factors to decide what activities to use in a therapy session. For example, different styles of music therapy can include exercises in singing, rhythm, movement, instrumentation, or a combination of all four. As Gary Ansdell states in his book *Music*

LaPorte 4

*for Life: Aspects of Creative Music Therapy with Adult Clients*, "music involves an irreducible alchemy between mind and body, self and other . . . . and it is the music therapist's job and skill to help anyone to the point where they can 'become music'; where music can act within and between them" (13). (8)

⑧ Author's name and title of book given in text, parenthetical citation needs only page number

The medical aspect of Alzheimer's and the world of music therapy fit together like pieces of a puzzle to create a working, intertwined relationship. To begin with, music therapy generally occurs in a scheduled session-type atmosphere instead of a casual meeting in the patient's bedroom or similar setting. There are many reasons why music therapists sometimes choose to conduct a one-on-one therapy session with an individual patient. Depending on the patient's stage in the disease and current mental capacity, among other factors, a group setting might be too overwhelming. Frustration and aggravation are common personality characteristics of Alzheimer's patients. It would be unwise to place a patient with these traits into a group setting because he or she could potentially setback the progress of the entire group. Also, Dr. Frans Schalkwijk points to "poor ego-function" (33): working in groups can either help or hinder a patient's ego. If successful, the patient can feel more confident about himself or herself. Conversely, if a patient is struggling with a certain task, such as playing the right rhythm with mal-

LaPorte 5

lets, and sees other patients successfully completing the same task, that could be the source of possible regression.

One-on-one therapy has also proven enormously helpful with keeping attention. Alzheimer's patients often struggle with keeping focus on a task at hand and often wander with no purpose. It proves much harder for the patient to get distracted and lose concentration with just the patient and a therapist in the room. Gudrun Aldridge conducted a study with a 55-year-old woman who was having a hard time with everyday activities such as cooking on her own or even finding words to speak. She had some past musical interest and ability, which made her family consider music therapy as a option. She demonstrated the ability to produce simple rhythms using two sticks and a drum. Aldridge also used improvisation in the therapy. Because the patient had the responsibility of creating an improvised rhythm to go with a certain melody, her concentration increased (G. Aldridge 146). ⑨ As Aldridge states in her study, "intentionality, attention to, concentration on and perseverance with the task in hand are important features of producing musical improvisations" (161). Her success with the rhythms caused the patient to experience a more uplifted and hopeful attitude (160–61). ⑩ Aldridge also discussed a study conducted by Fitzgerald-Cloutier in 1993. The procedure con-

⑨ Sources include two different people with last name Aldridge so first initial is given

⑩ First citation included a quotation, the second attributes information to source, but nothing is quoted

LaPorte 6

sisted of several reading sessions where the therapist simply read to the patient. The patient sat still for twice the amount of time in the music therapy sessions than in the reading sessions (G. Aldridge 144). These results further prove the positive effect that music has on a patient's attention span.

Although individualized music therapy involves only the therapist and the patient, the format actually helps the patients control their behaviors toward each other outside of the session. Because of a positive experience with music therapy, patients show increased sociability and apply what they just learned in the session. For example, Sambandham and Schirm referenced a study conducted by Pollack and Namazi that "showed that individualized music therapy resulted in increased social interaction both during and after music sessions for eight AD [Alzheimer's Disease] (11) residents" (79). Another study conducted by J. R. Wolfe concluded that patients who underwent music therapy seemed to have better participation in activities as well as better attitudes in general in contrast to other patients who were not subjected to music therapy (Sambandham and Schrim 80). Based on these two examples, one can clearly see the effect that individualized attention achieves in patients. Alzheimer's patients are not a different species; they like to feel valued and cared for like

(11) Brackets indicate that the writer provided the explanation for AD

any other human being, and individualized music therapy helps to achieve that goal.

One-on-one therapy sessions are not the only environments where Alzheimer's patients show an increase in socialization. In fact, there are many arguments for implementing group therapy sessions instead of individual ones. David Aldridge draws a conclusion based on Clair and Bernstein's research by saying, "working in groups [helps] to promote communicating, watching others, singing, interacting with an instrument, and sitting" (D. Aldridge 195). Many patients only have interactions with the other residents during a once-a-week music therapy session, so this socialization time proves to be quite important. Music therapy truly serves as one of the only therapy options that promotes unity among the patients. Other types of therapy, such as reading and exercise, are strictly individual. By creating a group atmosphere, the patients can simply enjoy making or listening to music while temporarily building relationships with one another, even though they may not remember them in the future.

Similar to individualized therapy, group music therapy factors help patients with focus and attention. Imagine the patience needed to get young children to sit still and focus in a small group, and then imagine what a difficult time a music therapist would have keeping a group of fading Alzheimer's patients on the

LaPorte 8

same track. In reality, attentiveness in group therapy sessions with Alzheimer's patients truly surpasses any previous notions. When the patients know they must work together to complete a common goal, their concentration increases. Schalkwijk discusses a case study with Miranda, a patient who struggled to pay attention and not talk when it was not her turn. The conductors of the experiment decided to put her into a new group setting to see how she would interact and fit in with new people. The group did an activity where one person created a rhythm and then the rest of the group imitated it on their instruments. Miranda was absolutely overjoyed and very proud when the others repeated her original rhythm. The exercise turned into a popular activity where different patients would create unique melodies and the others would copy them. The exercise helped to maintain the patients' attention, while giving them a sense of accomplishment (Schwalkwijk 74–75).

Music therapy directly relates to communication and speech as well. Specific songs often are used to express exactly what someone is feeling because music evokes intense emotions. Alzheimer's patients are no exception to this phenomenon, and communication, or even a lack thereof, plays a role in music therapy. Gudrun Aldridge supports the use of music therapy in relation to language. She states, "While language deterioration is a feature of cognitive deficit, musi-

LaPorte 9

cal abilities appear to be preserved. This may be because the fundamentals of language are musical and prior to semantic and lexical functions in language development" (G. Aldridge 140). Aldridge brings up a very important point. Infants often make incomprehensible musical noises before they can speak their first words. Because of the nature of language development, music never leaves us. As a result, even when the mind wanders in stages of Alzheimer's, a musical foundation can always be found and re-discovered.

As mentioned previously, there are many treatment options available for Alzheimer's. No single medicine can prevent memory loss from occurring; however, certain drugs help control certain symptoms. Antidepressants are commonly prescribed to assist with the patients' attitudes, especially if they are still aware of the deterioration of their memory. Tranquilizers such as Valium are sometimes prescribed as well. However, with these medical approaches come the normal physical side effects such as dizziness, drowsiness, and even decreased motor control (Check 64–65). Why then go through these side effects, when none of these medicines will improve the patient's condition? Although an antidepressant might help with the attitude of a patient, music therapy can produce the same result without putting any added chemicals into the body and results in nothing but positive effects.

LaPorte 10

When I began writing this research paper, I intended to conduct an interview with a music therapist in the Newark area about working with elderly Alzheimer's patients. However, I called every nursing home and assisted living center in the area, and not one had a music therapist on staff. This astounding realization speaks about the growing nature of the field of music therapy. The profession has not become a standard treatment yet, though this research indicates that more and more facilities should consider incorporating music therapy into their programs. With Alzheimer's patients, music therapy can drastically improve concentration, attitude, and communication through individual or group sessions. Overall, music can help connect people through a common medium and also helps patients re-connect with themselves despite their state of memory.

William Check reports a number of eye-opening statistics in his informative book about Alzheimer's. He observes, "Health experts predict that if no advances in treatment or prevention of the disease are made, in the year 2040 . . . (12) half the American population will suffer from dementia before they die" (16). (13) This figure is sobering. Music therapy may not be able to cure half of America in 2040, but it can make a difference. Music truly has an indescribable, intangible power to heal, and a patient suffering from Alzheimer's can benefit remarkably from music therapy treatment.

(12) Ellipsis (three spaced periods) indicates words omitted to shorten the quotation

(13) Vivid quotation provides effective closure for the essay

LaPorte 11

# List of Works Cited ⑭

⑭ 'List' is on a separate page

⑮ Sources are alphabetized by author's last time or by title if no author

⑮ Aldridge, David. *Music Therapy Research and Practice in Medicine: From Out of the Silence*. London: Jessica Kingsley Publishers, 1996. Print.

Aldridge, Gudrun. "Improvisation as an Assessment of Potential in Early Alzheimer's Disease." *Music Therapy in Dementia Care: More New Voices*. Ed. David Aldridge. London: Jessica Kingsley Publishers, 2000. 139–65. Print.

Ansdell, Gary. *Music for Life: Aspects of Creative Music Therapy with Adult Clients*. London: Jessica Kingsley Publishers, 1995. Print.

Check, William. *Alzheimer's Disease*. New York: Chelsea House, 1989. Print.

Michel, Donald E. *Music Therapy*. 2nd ed. Springfield, MA: Charles C Thomas, 1985. Print.

*The Notebook*. Dir. Nick Cassavetes. Perf. Ryan Gosling, James Garner, Rachel McAdams, and Gena Rowlands. New Line Cinema, 2004. DVD.

Sambandham, Mary and Victoria Schrim. "Music as a Nursing Intervention for Residents with Alzheimer's Disease in Long-Term Care." *Geriatric Nursing* 16.2 (1995): 79–83. *ScienceDirect*. Web. 20 April 2007. ⑯

⑯ Source accessed electronically includes date of access

LaPorte 12

Schalkwijk, F. W. *Music and People with*

*Developmental Disabilities: Music Therapy,*

*Remedial Music Making and Musical*

*Activities.* Trans. Andrews James.

London: Jessica Kingsley Publishers,

1994. Print.

Bailey Kung
ENGL 110, Section 114
Dr. Lehman

## Graffiti: Art or Vandalism

A name or image spray-painted on a wall can elicit smiles, stares, or scowls. Some believe that graffiti is art, some find it fascinating, and some see it as a nuisance. In truth, graffiti is all of these things: a form of creative expression, an intriguing part of urban (and even suburban) environments, and a product of vandalism. Graffiti ranges from crudely spray-painted words or images to stylized name tagging and complicated stencils fashioned on whatever surface is available. Generally, the more visible the canvas, the better; subway trains, freight cars, and blank walls are the most popular. There are three major types of graffiti: gang, hip-hop, and political. (Another form is popular graffiti, which generally takes the form of insulting or lewd messages written on restroom walls.) Gang and political graffiti focus primarily on communication of power and opinion, respectively. Hip-hop graffiti is more "artistic," emphasizing skill and technique. The creators of graffiti, called "writers," have a variety of motivations, all of which produce forms of self-expression. However, because of its appearance on public and private property, graffiti is vandalism. For many people, it represents gang culture and criminal activity, eliciting a sense of unease. A conflict of interest arises between individual graffiti writers and the community at large, parallel to the clash of rights and restrictions. Writers are guaranteed the right to freedom of expression, but the products of this expression both break local laws and offend the members of the community in which they are created.

By definition, graffiti is a drawing or inscription on a wall or other public surface. Originating on cave walls as a form of communication (Edgar), graffiti has evolved into what might be called an art form. According to Janice Rahn's *Painting Without Permission: Hip-Hop Graffiti Subculture*, hip-hop graffiti as we know it today existed in the form of names scrawled on subway trains and public property in the 1960s. It became more prevalent in the 1970s as a part of the hip-hop music movement in inner-city areas, particularly in New York City's South Bronx (2). By the 1980s, graffiti was accepted into the art world, with its renegade spirit and innovative forms. Artists like Jean-Michel Basquiat and Keith Haring took street art to the galleries and were able to build successful careers (Gablik 106–109). Hip-hop graffiti can be considered an art form in itself, as it is a form of self-expression and creativity.

The most elementary form in graffiti, a tag, is a sort of stylized signature usually scribbled quickly to signify the writer's presence (Edgar). Taggers generally use markers, preferring to make their own or buy those that can be modified (Rahn 10). A tagger can develop his or her style and become a "writer," moving to larger, multicolored, and more complicated works called "pieces," which are spray painted on walls or trains. "Throw-ups" are also a popular form, involving only lettering and a few colors; the aim is to "throw it up" as fast as possible. Most graffitists, especially in hip-hop culture, do not advocate the use of any tools except for specialty caps, which create better spray patterns than the nozzle that comes on a spray can. Nevertheless, some artists have expanded their repertoire to include complex stencils and mural-like paintings. No matter what the technique, a writer's goal is to create something that is highly visible.

Graffiti is meant to be seen. Hundreds of people will pass a wall while walking the streets in just one day. Thousands use the subway system, and a tag or piece painted on the side of a freight train car has the potential to reach a whole country. Like art or advertising, there is an emphasis on sharing. Unlike advertising, graffiti does not aim to please, but rather to be very public. The writer who takes the biggest risk to tag a prime location is afforded the most respect from his or her graffiti colleagues. While some writers and gangs put most of their energy into tagging every possible surface to claim territory, others focus more on perfecting technique and developing skill.

For example, hip-hop graffitists have developed what is known as "wildstyle," a complex system of lettering that is nearly impossible for a non-graffitist to read. It involves three dimensional, overlapping and intertwining letters, often enhanced by arrows and other details. Wildstyle is completely freehand and requires a high level of skill; it is used primarily for impressing fellow writers. Like some artists, graffitists sometimes keep "black books," small notebooks for sketching ideas and recording autographs: the tags of fellow writers. When creating large pieces, graffiti artists may enlarge sketches, creating a wall-sized, spray-painted work from a pen drawing without the use of grids or measurements. Such a grand scale sometimes requires the writer to work in layers, putting up rough outlines and returning later to fill in colors. The most attractive and interesting pieces are those that contain a variety of expertly blended colors, complicated forms, and three-dimensional effects. All of these effects are achieved with nothing but the writer's expert handling of a mere aerosol spray can.[1]

Each graffiti writer has his or her own unique motivation. Political graffitists deface billboards or write on walls in order to verbally attack the institutions of society that they disagree with or find offensive; ultimately, the goal is to express one's opinion. Generally, gang members write to claim "turf" or attack other gangs. Hip-hop writers aim to hone their talents and gain respect. Gang and hip-hop writers seem to be motivated by a desire to belong to a group. Gangs band together for protection and power; hip-hop writers make a creative community in which to compete and learn. Some members of this community believe strongly in the notion that they are beautifying an otherwise drab and uninviting environment. Montreal writer DSTRBO says, "People find graffiti offensive, but I find concrete gray buildings offensive, like we're living in a world where the people with the least amount of imagination make the rules" (Rahn 41). Not surprisingly, these are the same type of graffitists who may be hired to paint murals.

The underlying motivation for all graffiti, however, is self-expression, the exercise of the right to free speech. Due to its visual format, graffiti becomes a tangible manifestation of character. In 1984, a group of visiting European hotel managers took a tour of New York City and rode on a freshly cleaned subway train. *The New York Times* reported that several of the visitors were disappointed to "not have something that's part of the local color" (qtd. in Austin 3). One mentioned that his country had "graffiti on [its] monuments in Rome and we don't whitewash them when Americans come over" (qtd. in Austin 3). University of Delaware student Pamela Townsend agrees with this sentiment, calling graffiti an intriguing and perfectly acceptable feature of her environment (Townsend).

Advertisers frequently cash in on the popularity of the graffiti movement, targeting those consumers who find graffiti interesting. Some use the graffiti style for the "cool" factor, implying that a product has some sort of street credibility. Companies have also been known to hire writers to spray-paint ads. The

---

[1]The background information in this and the previous two paragraphs appears in multiple sources from the bibliography. For in depth coverage, see especially Phillips and Rahn.

British clothing line Boxfresh picked up the style of London sticker graffitist Solo One and eventually signed a deal that allowed it to print stickers that included Solo One's tag (Alvelos 187). Successful campaigns have also been executed for the advertisement of album releases, plays, films, and even Calvin Klein perfume (Alvelos 184). For example, in 1997, a stenciled silhouette appeared on the walls of London buildings. Several weeks later, the same silhouette was found on fly-posters as promotional art for a Robert Miles single. Consumers were familiarized with an image, and then made a connection to a product (Alvelos 182). Both graffiti and the posting of bills (fly-posters) are illegal activities, but law enforcement tends to ignore them while companies reap the financial rewards.

Even writers do not agree on whether graffiti is art or vandalism. The conflict here is not legal, but rather between the individual "artists" and the graffiti community. In addition to those who believe that graffiti is a sort of beautification, there are those writers, most notably Jean-Michel Basquiat and Keith Haring, who have crossed into the legitimate art world, displaying and selling canvas works in galleries. Advertisers have also cashed in on the graffiti style, using it to target an urban demographic and in some cases even hiring writers to paint advertisements. The graffiti aesthetic aims to "instill an aura of 'cool,' of 'street credibility,' on the advertised product" (Alvelos 184). While some graffitists see publicity as an opportunity for more people to see their work, purists see the legitimizing of the medium as a sort of blasphemy. They vehemently declare that graffiti *is* vandalism. The illegality of graffiti is an important concept, as it represents the original form and, more importantly, affects the outcome of a piece. When working on a wall or subway car, it is essential for writers to execute their ideas quickly and expertly. However, with a canvas made especially for painting and an unlimited amount of time to artfully engineer an image, the artist loses some credibility. These beliefs are also rooted in the notion that gallery art, in particular, consists of "pretty pictures to sell to rich people" (Rahn 176) and "has a lot of negative connotations and it alienates people" (*Banksy*).

Arguments about semantics aside, creating graffiti is vandalism: the destruction or damaging of property without the consent of the owner. In contrast to advocates, graffiti opponents (a group which includes government officials, "legitimate" artists, and members of the general public) do not believe that self-expression can transcend the law. Furthermore, some feel that graffiti robs people of a sense of safety. Because graffiti is often associated with gangs and other subversive behavior, people find its appearance on subway cars, for instance, to be very disturbing. When a gang claims territory in a certain area, its "violent lifestyle" comes along with the tag (term from Phillips 313). Additionally, the "dissing" (disrespecting usually by crossing out or writing over) of another gang's tag can be construed as a threat from which rival gang fights ensue (Phillips 313).

In comparison to more serious crimes such as robbery and homicide, graffiti is a minor offense. However, graffiti can be seen as a gateway to other criminal activities. The connection is established through what is called the Broken Windows theory, which posits that crime increases in an environment that appears to be neglected. George L. Kelling and James Q. Wilson argue, "At the community level, disorder and crime are usually inextricably linked, in a developmental sequence. Social psychologists and police officers tend to agree that if a window in a building is broken and is left unrepaired, all of the rest of the windows will soon be broken." They continue,

> Knowing this helps one understand the significance of such otherwise harmful displays as subway graffiti. As Nathan Glazer has written, the proliferation of graffiti, even when not obscene, confronts the subway rider with the inescapable knowledge that the environment he must endure for an hour or more a day is uncontrolled and uncontrollable, and that anyone can invade it to do whatever damage and mischief the mind suggests. (Kelling and Wilson)

Spearheaded by politicians, some cities have launched aggressive anti-graffiti campaigns. In the 1970s, New York City Mayor John Lindsay created an Anti-Graffiti Task Force that aimed to stamp out graffiti and included organizations that were affected by the "plague," such as the Mass Transit Authority. The Task Force lobbied for better paint removers, more easily removable ink and paint, and resistant coatings for surfaces (Austin 86–7), and by 1973 it was spending $10 million per year on removal efforts (Austin 91). Lindsay's successors followed his example, embarking on anti-graffiti crusades themselves. Mayor Rudy Giuliani made the Anti-Graffiti Task Force permanent in 1995. He saw "graffiti as a symptom of this kind of urban decay, and set about eradicat-ing it—especially in the subway system, where for years commuters had been harassed and victimized by gangs of troublemakers and criminals, and intimi-dated and demoralized by the proliferation of graffiti vandalism" (Hall). Mayor Michael R. Bloomberg has continued the campaign to eliminate graffiti vandal-ism in the city, making the Anti-Graffiti Task Force—"part of the city's larger Citywide Vandals Task Force, a group that handles everything from spray-painted shop grates to vandalized bus-stop kiosks" (Hall). The city's current anti-graffiti law, which prohibits individuals younger than twenty-one from possessing spray paint and broad-tipped markers, is being challenged by seven artists who believe it encroaches on their right to free speech (Trotta).

A similar law in Wilmington, Delaware, requires parental consent for the sale of spray paint and broad-tipped markers to minors, and a bill is currently being considered to extend the law to all of New Castle County (Basiouny). State law prohibits only the action of creating graffiti, defined as the damag-ing of "public or private real or personal property without the permission of the owner by knowingly, purposely or recklessly drawing, painting or making any significant mark or inscription thereon" ("Graffiti, Delaware"). The pun-ishment for a graffitist includes a fine payable to the state, reparations for the damages caused to the property in question, and community service hours, at least half of which must consist of graffiti clean-up ("Graffiti, Delaware").

Whether a graffitist is motivated by the desire to communicate, assert so-cial position, or simply create a form of art, he or she is practicing self-expression. Yet the proliferation of graffiti causes passersby to feel uneasy and can lead to an increase in illicit behavior. Writers may contribute to the local color of a city, but politicians create a positive image for themselves when they campaign against graffiti; people feel as if their leaders are doing something effective and working for social change. Since graffiti is clearly both an artistic form and an act of vandalism, the problem lies in deciding which interpretation will become "law" (meaning which is most commonly accepted and acted upon). When graffiti is accepted, there seems to be a double standard regarding the degree of acceptability of different types of graffiti. The more 'pictorial' incarnations of graffiti, such as murals or stencils, seem to be tolerable because they are based on image more than language; words are more threatening than pictures because the message is conveyed clearly, without hiding behind symbolism. Gang graffiti is dangerous, popular graffiti is lewd (yet marginally entertaining), political graffiti is either offensive or admirable depending on political leanings, and hip-hop graffiti is artistic. Obviously, it would be unjust and ineffective to stamp out just one form of graffiti while largely ignoring the others, not to mention the difficulty authorities would incur while trying to draw the line between subversive, neutral, and benevolent graffiti.

Contrary to the Broken Windows theory, graffiti does not always lead to criminal activity. In fact, it can lead away from it. Hip-hop graffiti can be an outlet for youth to "expand their horizons and overcome the constrictions of growing up among the urban poor" (Phillips 314). Writers make contacts, develop skills, and channel their energies to art rather than gang membership. Additionally, graffiti may also prove itself as a mechanism of social mobility, a gateway to "wind up in art school, the gallery, and other mainstream work" (Phillips 314). Keith Haring, for example, started out drawing simple chalk pictographs in subway stations and gradually moved to gallery work, which would eventually be able to sustain him financially (Gablik 106). Jean-Michel Basquiat scribbled sentences in subways and sold handmade postcards and clothing before being invited to participate in an exhibit called "New York/New Wave." From there, he was asked to join a gallery and, like Haring, became successful in the "legitimate art world" (Gablik 108–9). Without their beginnings in graffiti, Basquiat, Haring, and many others may never have found a positive way to channel their energies. Additionally, graffiti can serve as inspiration to both established and aspiring artists.

Unfortunately, when it comes to graffiti, free speech becomes a crime. If graffitists truly believe in their "art" enough to break the law to create it, they commit a sort of civil disobedience. Conveying one's point of view does not come without consequences, even when the law is not in question. Self-expression is always open to criticism, and graffiti writers must be willing to accept the repercussions of their actions.

## List of Works Cited

Alvelos, Heitor. "The Desert of Imagination in the City of Signs: Cultural Implications of Sponsored Transgression and Branded Graffiti." *Cultural Criminology Unleashed.* Ed. Jeff Ferrell. Portland, OR: Glasshouse, 2004. 181–91. Print.

Austin, Joe. *Taking the Train: How Graffiti Became an Urban Crisis in New York.* New York: Columbia UP, 2001. Print.

*Bansky.* Web. 10 April 2006. http://www.bansky.co.uk.

Basiouny, Angie. "NCCo Vote on Graffiti Bill Tabled." *The [Wilmington, DE] News Journal,* 26 April 2006. Web. 26 April 2006.

Edgar, Kathleen. "Young Gangs." *Youth, Violence, Crime, and Gangs: Children at Risk.* Detroit: Gale, 2004. Print.

Gablik, Suzi. *Has Modernism Failed?* New York: Thames and Hudson, 1984. Print.

"Graffiti, Delaware." *Institute for Intergovernmental Research.* Web. 24 April 2006.

Hall, Annette. "The Mayor's Anti-Graffiti Task Force." *The Cooperator: The Co-op and Condo Monthly.* Sept. 2005. Web. 22 April 2006.

Kelling George L. and James Q. Wilson. "Broken Windows: The Police and Neighborhood Safety." *Atlantic Monthly.com.* March 1982. n. page. Web. 22 April 2006.

Phillips, Susan A. *Wallbangin': Graffiti and Gangs in L.A.* Chicago: U of Chicago Press, 1999. Print.

Rahn, Janice. *Painting Without Permission: Hip-Hop Graffiti Subculture.* Westport, CT: Bergin & Garvey. 2002. Print.

Townsend, Pamela. Personal Interview. 20 April 2006.

Trotta, Daniel. "Artists Challenge NYC Anti-Graffiti Law." *Reuters.* 25 April 2006. Web. 26 April 2006.

# GLOSSARY AND READY REFERENCE

This Glossary and Ready Reference has two purposes. First, it is a quick and simple guide to the terms used in discussions of writing. Second, it is a quick reference guide to the most common writing and grammar problems. For a fuller analysis of grammar and the mechanics of writing, refer to a grammar handbook.

**Abstract** words refer to ideas or generalities—words such as *truth*, *beauty*, and *justice*. The opposite of an abstract word is a concrete one. Margaret Atwood in "The Female Body" (Chapter 8) explores the abstract phrase *female body*, offering a series of more concrete examples or perspectives on the topic.

**Allusion** is a reference to an actual or fictional person, object, or event. The assumption is that the reference will be understood or recognized by the reader. For that reason, allusions work best when they draw on a shared experience or heritage. Allusions to famous literary works or to historically prominent people or events are likely to have meaning for many readers for an extended period of time. Martin Luther King Jr. in "I Have a Dream" (Chapter 9) alludes to biblical verses, spirituals, and patriotic songs. If an allusion is no longer recognized by an audience, it loses its effectiveness in conjuring up a series of significant associations.

*agr* **Agreement** problems commonly come in three areas. Subjects and verbs must agree in number (both singular or both plural) and person (first, second, third).

> The paper are due. (paper is)
> The requirements on the syllabus is not clear. (requirements are)

Pronouns and their antecedents must agree in person, number, and gender.

> A student must preregister to ensure getting their courses. (his or her courses)

Verb tenses need to agree within a paper—that is, if you are writing in past tense (the action happened yesterday), you should not then switch to present tense (the action is happening).

**Analogy** is an extended comparison in which an unfamiliar or complex object or event is likened to a familiar or simple one in order to make the former more vivid and more easily understood. Inappropriate or superficially similar analogies should not be used, especially as evidence in an argument. See faulty analogy in the list of logical fallacies in Chapter 9.

**Argumentation** or persuasion seeks to move a reader, to gain support, to advocate a particular type of action. Traditionally, argumentation appeals to logic and reason, while persuasion appeals to emotion and sometimes prejudice. See the introduction to Chapter 9.

**Cause-and-effect** analyses explain why something happened or what the consequences are or will be from a particular occurrence. See the introduction to Chapter 7.

**Classification** is a form of division, but instead of starting with a single subject as a division does, classification starts with many items, then groups or sorts them into categories. See the introduction to Chapter 4.

*cliché* **Cliché** is an overused common expression. The term is derived from a French word for a stereotype
*d* printing block. Just as many identical copies can be made from such a block, so clichés are typically words and phrases used so frequently that they become stale and ineffective. Everyone uses clichés in speech: "in less than no time" they "spring to mind," but "in the last analysis," a writer ought to "avoid them like the plague," even though they always seem "to hit the nail on the head." An exercise on clichés can be found in the Focusing on Grammar and Writing activity with the essay by Read (Chapter 1).

*coh* **Coherence** is achieved when all parts of a piece of writing work together as a harmonious whole. If a paper has a well-defined thesis that controls its structure, coherence will follow. In addition, relationships between sentences, paragraphs, and ideas can be made clearer for the reader by using pronoun references, parallel structures (see **Parallelism**), and transitional words and phrases (see **Transitions**).

*coll* **Colloquial expressions** are informal words and phrases used in conversation but inappropriate
*d* for more formal writing situations. Occasionally, professional writers use colloquial expressions to create intentional informality. David Bodanis in "What's in Your Toothpaste?" (Chapter 4) mixes colloquial words (*gob, stuff, goodies, glop*) with formal words (*abrading, gustatory, intrudant*).

**Comparison** involves finding similarities between two or more things, people, or ideas. See the introduction to Chapter 5.

**Conclusions** should always leave the reader feeling that a paper has come to a logical and inevitable end, that the communication is now complete. As a result, an essay that simply stops, weakly trails off, moves into a previously unexplored area, or raises new or distracting problems lacks that necessary sense of closure. Endings often cause problems because they are written last and hence are often rushed. With proper planning, you can always write an effective and appropriate ending. Keep the following points in mind:

1. An effective conclusion grows out of a paper—it must be logically related to what has been said. It might restate the thesis, summarize the exposition or argument, apply or reflect on the subject under discussion, tell a related story, call for a course of action, or state the significance of the subject.

2. The extent to which a conclusion can repeat or summarize is determined in large part by the length of the paper. A short paper should not have a conclusion that repeats the introduction in slightly varied words. A long essay, however, often needs a conclusion that conveniently summarizes the significant facts or points discussed in the paper.

3. The appropriateness of a particular type of ending is related to a paper's purpose. An argumentative or persuasive essay—one that asks the reader to do or believe something—can always conclude with a statement of the desired action—vote for, do this, do not support. A narrative essay can end at the climactic moment in the action. An expository essay in which points are arranged according to significance can end with the major point.

4. The introduction and conclusion can be used as a related pair to frame the body of an essay. Often in a conclusion you can return to or allude to an idea, an expression, or an illustration used at the beginning of the paper and so enclose the body.

An exercise in writing conclusions can be found in the Focusing on Grammar and Writing activity with the essay by Forster (Chapter 7).

**Concrete** words describe things that exist and can be experienced through the senses. Abstractions are rendered understandable and specific through concrete examples. See **Abstract.**

**Connotation and denotation** refer to two different types of definition of words. A dictionary definition is denotative—it offers a literal and explicit definition of a word. But words often have more than just literal meanings, for they can carry positive or negative associations or connotations. The denotative definition of wife is "a woman married to a man," but as Judy Brady shows in "I Want a Wife" (Chapter 8), the word *wife* carries a series of connotative associations as well.

**Contrast** involves finding differences between two or more things, people, or ideas. See the introduction to Chapter 5.

**Deduction** is the form of argument that starts with a general truth and then moves to a specific application of that truth. See the introduction to Chapter 9.

**Definition** involves placing a word first in a general class and then adding distinguishing features that set it apart from other members of that class: "A dalmatian is a breed of dog (general class) with a white, short-haired coat and dark spots (distinguishing features)." Most college writing assignments in definition require extended definitions in which a subject is analyzed with appropriate examples and details. See the introduction to Chapter 8.

**Denotation.** See **Connotation.**

**Dependent clauses** are also called subordinate clauses. As the words *dependent* and *subordinate* imply, they are not sentences and cannot stand alone. A clause is made dependent by a subordinating word that comes at the beginning of the clause, reducing it to something that modifies another word in the sentence. Common subordinating words are either conjunctions (such as *although, because, if, since, when, where*) or relative pronouns (such as *which, that, what, who*). Dependent clauses are set off from the rest of the sentence with a comma:

> Although you have a test on Friday, your paper is due on Friday.
>
> Your paper, which must be at least ten pages in length, is due on Friday.

**Description** is the re-creation of sense impressions in words. See the introduction to Chapter 3.

**Dialect.** See **Diction.**

**Diction** is the choice of words used in speaking or writing. It is frequently divided into four levels: formal, informal, colloquial, and slang. Formal diction is found in traditional academic writing, such as books and scholarly articles; informal diction, generally characterized by words common in conversation contexts, by contractions, and by the use of the first person (I), is found in articles in popular magazines. Bernard R. Berelson's essay "The Value of Children" (Chapter 4) uses formal diction; Judy Brady's "I Want a Wife" (Chapter 8) is informal. See **Colloquial expressions** and **Slang.**      *d*

Two other commonly used labels are also applied to diction:

- **Nonstandard** words or expressions are not normally used by educated speakers. An example would be *ain't.*

- **Dialect** reflects regional or social differences with respect to word choice, grammatical usage, and pronunciation. Dialects are primarily spoken rather than written but are often reproduced or imitated in narratives. William Least Heat Moon in "Nameless, Tennessee" (Chapter 3) captures the dialect of his speakers.

**Division** breaks a subject into parts. It starts with a single subject and then subdivides that whole into smaller units. See the introduction to Chapter 4.

**Documentation** involves acknowledging the use of direct quotations and facts taken from someone else's writing. If you do not document your sources, you are guilty of plagiarism (see Chapter 11: The Research Paper). Documentation involves enclosing direct quotations within quotation marks ("), providing a parenthetical citation in your text, and listing the source on a list of sources or references at the end of your paper. Detailed advice and helpful models can be found in Chapter 11. Exercises in integrating quotations into your text can be found in the Focusing on Grammar and Writing activities for the essays by Drozdyk (Chapter 6), Kelley (Chapter 8), and Porter (Chapter 9).      *doc*

**Essay** literally means "attempt," and in writing courses the word is used to refer to brief papers, generally five hundred to one thousand words long, on tightly delimited subjects. Essays can be formal and academic, like Bernard R. Berelson's "The Value of Children" (Chapter 4), or informal and humorous, like Judy Brady's "I Want a Wife" (Chapter 8).

**Example** is a specific instance used to illustrate a general idea or statement. Effective writing requires examples to make generalizations clear and vivid to a reader. See the introduction to Chapter 1.

**Exposition** comes from a Latin word meaning "to expound or explain." It is one of the four modes into which writing is subdivided, the other three being narration, description, and argumentation. Expository writing is information-conveying; its purpose is to inform its reader. This purpose is achieved through a variety of organizational patterns, including division and classification, comparison and contrast, process analysis, cause and effect, and definition.

**Figures of speech** are deliberate departures from the ordinary and literal meanings of words in order to provide fresh, insightful perspectives or emphasis. Figures of speech are most commonly used in descriptive passages and include the following:

- **Simile** is a comparison of two dissimilar things, introduced by the word *as* or *like*. Maya Angelou in "Sister Monroe" (Chapter 2) describes Sister Monroe as standing before the altar "shaking like a freshly caught trout."
- **Metaphor** is an analogy that directly identifies one thing with another. After Scott Russell Sanders in "The Inheritance of Tools" (Chapter 3) accidentally strikes his thumb with a hammer, he describes the resulting scar using a metaphor: "A white scar in the shape of a crescent moon began to show above the cuticle, and month by month it rose across the pink sky of my thumbnail."
- **Personification** is an attribution of human qualities to an animal, idea, abstraction, or inanimate object. Gordon Grice in "Cought in the Widow's Web" (How to Revise an Essay) refers to male and female spiders as "lovers."
- **Hyperbole** is a deliberate exaggeration, often done to provide emphasis or humor. Margaret Atwood in comparing the female brain with the male brain (Chapter 8) resorts to hyperbole: "[Female brains are] joined together by a thick cord; neural pathways flow from one to the other, sparkles of electronic information washing to and fro . . . The male brain, now, that's a different matter. Only a thin connection. Space over here, time over here, music and arithmetic in their sealed compartments. The right brain doesn't know what the left brain is doing."
- **Understatement** is the opposite of hyperbole; it is a deliberate minimizing done to provide emphasis or humor. In William Least Heat Moon's "Nameless, Tennessee" (Chapter 3), Miss Ginny Watts explains how she asked her husband to call the doctor unless he wanted to be "shut of" [rid of] her. Her husband, Thurmond, humorously uses understatement in his reply: "I studied on it."
- **Rhetorical questions** are questions not meant to be answered but instead to provoke thought. Barbara Ehrenreich in "In Defense of Talk Shows" (Chapter 4) poses a series of rhetorical questions toward the end of her essay: "This is class exploitation, pure and simple. What next—'homeless people so hungry they eat their own scabs'? Or would the next step be to pay people outright to submit to public humiliation? For $50 would you confess to adultery in your wife's presence? For $500 would you reveal your thirteen-year-old's girlish secrets on Ricki Lake?"
- **Paradox** is a seeming contradiction used to catch a reader's attention. An element of truth or rightness often lurks beneath the contradiction.

An exercise in using figurative language can be found in the Focusing on Grammar and Writing activity with the essay by Angelou (Chapter 2).

*frag* **Fragment** (sentence) is anything that is not a complete sentence but is punctuated as if it were. Fragments can be intentionally written—advertisements, for example, make extensive use of fragments

("The latest discovery! Totally redesigned!"). Fragments are common in written dialogue. In most college writing situations, though, make sure that you write only complete sentences. Fragments can be either long or short—their length has nothing to do with whether they are fragments. Since every sentence must contain a subject and a verb, fragments are lacking one or the other, typically the verb. The presence of a word at the beginning of the fragment can subordinate a clause, changing what would have been a sentence into a fragment.

> Rain fell. (subject + verb) = sentence
>
> Despite the high winds and rains. (no verb) = fragment
>
> Although it was windy and rainy ("although" subordinates what follows) = fragment

Most fragments occur when a long subordinate clause comes at the end of a sentence and it is then separated and punctuated as if it were a sentence:

> Our class decided to walk to the library to see the video. Although it was very windy and raining heavily. ("although" clause is separated from the sentence to which it belongs).

Exercises in recognizing fragments can be found in the Focusing on Grammar and Writing activities with the essays by, Haines (Chapter 2), Davis (Chapter 3), Atwood (Chapter 8), and Ortega (Chapter 9).

**Generalizations** are assertions or conclusions based on some specific instances. The value of a generalization is determined by the quality and quantity of examples on which it is based. Bob Greene in "Cut" (Chapter 1) formulates a generalization—being cut from an athletic team makes men superachievers later in life—on the basis of five examples. For such a generalization to have validity, however, a proper statistical sample would be essential.

**Hyperbole.** See **Figures of speech.**

**Illustration** is providing specific examples for general words or ideas. A writer illustrates by using examples.

**Independent clauses** are complete sentences. As the word independent suggests, they are capable of standing alone.

**Induction** is the form of argument that begins with specific evidence and then moves to a generalized conclusion that accounts for the evidence. See the introduction to Chapter 9.

**Introductions** need to do two essential things: first, catch or arouse a reader's interest, and second, state the thesis of the paper. In achieving both objectives, an introduction can occupy a single paragraph or several. The length of an introduction should always be proportional to the length of the essay—short papers should not have long introductions. Because an introduction lays out what is to follow, it is always easier to write after a draft of the body of the paper has been completed. When writing an introduction, keep the following strategies in mind:

1. Look for an interesting aspect of the subject that might arouse the reader's curiosity. It could be a quotation, an unusual statistic, a narrative, or a provocative question or statement. It should be something that will make the reader want to continue reading, and it should be appropriate to the subject at hand.

2. Provide a clear statement of purpose and thesis, explaining what you are writing about and why.

3. Remember that an introduction establishes a tone or point of view for what follows, so be consistent—an informal personal essay can have a casual, anecdotal beginning, but a serious academic essay needs a serious, formal introduction.

4. Suggest to the reader the structure of the essay that follows. Knowing what to expect makes it easier for the audience to read actively.

An exercise in writing introductions can be found in the Focusing on Grammar and Writing activities with the essay by Lee (Chapter 9).

**Irony** occurs when a writer says one thing but means another. E. M. Forster ends "My Wood" (Chapter 7) ironically by imagining a time when he will "wall in and fence out until I really taste the sweets of property"—which is actually the opposite of the point he is making.

**Metaphor.** See **Figures of speech.**

*dang* **Misplaced and dangling modifiers** occur when a modifying or limiting element in a sentence
*mod* cannot be clearly connected with what it modifies. A misplaced modifier creates a sentence that is awkward and confusing for the reader:

> The instructor returned the papers to the students with grades. (Did only the students who had grades receive their papers?)
>
> The instructor returned the graded papers to the students.

A dangling modifier has no element to modify, so it "dangles" unattached to the sentence.

> Returning the papers, the students were relieved.
>
> After the instructor returned the papers, the students were relieved.

**Narration** involves telling a story, and all stories—whether they are personal-experience essays, imaginative fiction, or historical narratives—have the same essential ingredients: a series of events arranged in an order and told by a narrator for some particular purpose. See the introduction to Chapter 2.

**Nonstandard diction.** See **Diction.**

**Objective writing** takes an impersonal, factual approach to a particular subject. Bernard R. Berelson's "The Value of Children" (Chapter 4) is primarily objective in its approach. Writing frequently blends the objective and subjective together. See **Subjective.**

**Paradox.** See **Figures of speech.**

¶ **Paragraph** is both a noun and a verb. A paragraph (noun) is a block of text set off by white space and indented. To paragraph (verb) means to construct those blocks. The length of paragraphs varies considerably in printed texts. Newspaper articles, because they appear in narrow columns, often put each sentence in a separate paragraph. Articles in magazines or books generally have longer paragraphs. Paragraphing, then, does depend on the format of the printed page. Paragraphing can also achieve emphasis by setting something apart. In a composition class where papers are word-processed on full sheets of paper, you should avoid extremes—no one-page or two-page long paragraphs (allow your reader to rest!), no large clumps of tiny paragraphs (unless you are writing dialogue!).

Even though paragraphing can vary because of print format and emphasis, most paragraphs in college essays are constructed using a model such as this:

> Topic sentence (which states the controlling idea in what follows)
>
> Body sentences (which provide the details that support that idea)
>
> Concluding or transition sentence (which summarizes, extends, or provides a transition into the next paragraph)

Typical problems with paragraphs include these:

> Not enough paragraphs—not marking for the reader the structure of the paper, making it difficult to read
>
> Too many paragraphs—paragraphs not developed with enough details or skipping quickly from one idea to another, creating a choppy disconnected effect
>
> Paragraphs not logically organized—ideas out of sequence, lacking topic sentences

Exercises in paragraphing can be found in the Focusing on Grammar and Writing activities with the essays by Williams (Chapter 3), King (Chapter 9), and Singer (Chapter 10).

**Parallelism** places words, phrases, clauses, sentences, or even paragraphs of equal importance in //
equivalent grammatical form. The similar forms make it easier for the reader to see the relationships that exist among the parts; they add force to the expression. Martin Luther King, Jr.'s "I Have a Dream" speech (Chapter 9) exhibits each level of parallelism: words ("When all God's children, black and white men, Jews and Gentiles, Protestants and Catholics"), phrases ("With this faith, we will be able to work together, to pray together, to struggle together, to go to jail together, to stand up for freedom together"), clauses ("Go back to Mississippi, go back to Alabama, go back to South Carolina, go back to Georgia, go back to Louisiana, go back to the slums and ghettos of our northern cities"), sentences (the "one hundred years later" pattern in paragraph 2), and paragraphs (the "I have a dream" pattern in paragraphs 11–18). Exercises in parallalism can be found in the Focusing on Grammar and Writing activities with the essays by Perkins (Chapter 2), Sedaris (Chapter 5), and Swift (Chapter 10).

**Person** is a grammatical term used to refer to a speaker, the individual being addressed, or an individual being referred to. English has three persons: first (*I* or *we*), second (*you*), and third (*he, she, it,* or *they*).

**Personification.** See **Figures of speech.**

**Persuasion.** See **Argumentation.**

**Point of view** is the perspective the writer adopts toward a subject. In narratives, point of view is either first person (I) or third person (he, she, it). First-person narration implies a subjective approach to a subject; third-person narration promotes an objective approach. Point of view can be limited (revealing only what the narrator knows) or omniscient (revealing what anyone else in the narrative thinks or feels). Sometimes the phrase "point of view" is used simply to describe the writer's attitude toward the subject.

**Premise** in logic is a proposition—a statement of a truth—that is used to support or help support a conclusion. For an illustration, see Chapter 9 (How Do You Structure an Argument?).

**Process** analysis takes one of two forms: either a set of directions intended to allow a reader to duplicate a particular action or a description intended to tell a reader how something happens. See the introduction to Chapter 6.

**Pronouns** are words used in place of nouns. For a full discussion of the eight types of pronouns, *prn*
consult a grammar handbook. In writing, two types of problems are extremely common. First, always use *who* when you are referring to people—never *that* or *which*. Second, pronouns must agree with their antecedent (that is, the word to which it refers) in person, number, and gender. Typical pronoun problems:

> A student <u>that</u> was late missed the assignment. (who)
>
> <u>A student</u> must hand in <u>their</u> paper on Friday. (student is singular; *their* is plural)

**Proofreading** is the systematic checking of a piece of writing for grammatical and mechanical errors. Proofreading is quite different from revision; see **Revision.**

**Punctuation marks** are a set of standardized marks used in writing to separate sentences or *pn*
parts of sentences or to make the meaning of the sentence clear. Punctuation marks exist only in writing; they have no oral equivalent. Punctuation marks are used to signal the boundaries or parts of a sentence; they reveal the sentence's meaning. It is very difficult to read a passage in which the punctuation marks have been removed. The choice of when to use what mark is determined by how the sentence is structured. The most common problems with punctuation in writing come in a limited range of situations:

a. **Periods (.)** come at the end of complete sentences. Before you use a period at the end of what you think is a sentence, make sure that it is a **sentence** and not a **sentence fragment.**

b. **Colons (:)** are used in only two situations in writing: first, to introduce a quotation, a list, or a series (just as it is used in this sentence); second, to signal a link between two parts of a sentence. In this second instance, a colon works as an equals (=) sign, signaling that what comes after the colon is an example or restatement of what comes in the first half of the sentence.

> Jose had one goal this semester: to write an "A" paper.

c. **Semicolons (;)** are "half" colons and are used primarily in two writing constructions. First, they are used to link together two sentences either without a connecting word or with a certain group of connecting words:

> Your research paper is due on Friday; it cannot be late.
>
> Your research paper is due on Friday; moreover, it cannot be late.

Second, a semicolon is used to separate items (phrases, clauses) in a series that already has internal commas. The semicolon helps the reader to see what belongs with what.

> An effective research paper shows several characteristics: the use of accurate, appropriate, and varied source materials; careful and accurate documentation of those sources; and clear, effective prose.

d. **Commas (,)** have the widest range of uses of all of the punctuation marks. Commas are used to link, to separate, and to enclose. They link when they are used with a coordinating conjunction (such as *and, but, for*) to link two sentences together.

> Your research paper is due on Friday, and it cannot be late.

They separate items in a series (Bring a bluebook, a pencil, and a dictionary to class), or two or more adjectives that could be linked with *and* (Revising can be a slow, painful process), or introductory elements at the start of a sentence:

> If you are uncertain of the spelling of a word, always look it up.
>
> Finally, do not forget to bring your dictionaries to class.

They enclose elements that are interjected or inserted into a sentence—things like nonessential phrases and clauses (the meaning of the sentence is not changed if the interrupter is omitted):

> All students who miss three or more classes will fail the course. (The words "who miss three or more classes" cannot be omitted from the sentence without changing its meaning.)
>
> Mr. Rodriguez, the instructor of the course, has a very strict attendance policy. (The interrupter could be omitted without changing the meaning, and so it is set off with commas.)
>
> Your exam, unfortunately, falls just before spring break.

*poss*

e. **Apostrophes (')** are used in three situations in writing: first, to mark the omission of letters in a contraction (can't = cannot); second, to signal ownership or possession ("It was Tanya's paper"); and third, to mark plurals of letters and numbers (Tanya got all A's on her essays).

f. **Dashes (—)** are two unspaced hyphens with no spaces between the dash and the letter that precedes and follows it and no space between the two hyphens. Dashes are used either alone to add something to the end of a sentence or in pairs to surround or enclose something that is interjected into a sentence.

> The paper is due on Friday—don't forget!
>
> The paper—and it must be typed—is due on Friday.

g. **Parentheses ( )** always occur in pairs. Like commas and dashes, they are used to insert something into a sentence. Typically, parentheses minimize the importance of the insertion, while dashes emphasize it.

> The paper (it must be at least ten pages long) is due Friday.
>
> The paper—it must be at least ten pages long—is due Friday.

h. **Quotation marks (")** are used to enclose dialogue—words that characters or people speak—and to enclose direct quotations taken from print sources.

Exercises in using punctuation can be found in the following Focusing on Grammar and Writing activities: parentheses—Casares (Chapter 1), Cofer (Chapter 4), Ephron (Chapter 6); colons—Senna (Chapter 5), Eighner (Chapter 6), Goodman (Chapter 9); semicolons–Senna (Chapter 5), Eighner (Chapter 6); commas–Danticat (Chapter 1), Senna (Chapter 5), Ephron (Chapter 6); dashes—Casares (Chapter 1), Hopkins (Chapter 2), Sanders (Chapter 3), Senna (Chapter 5), Kahn (Chapter 6), Ephron (Chapter 6), Raynor (Chapter 9); quotation marks—Least Heat Moon (Chapter 3), Rodriguez (Chapter 9).

**Purpose** involves intent, the reason why a writer writes. Three purposes are fundamental: to entertain, to inform, and to persuade. These are not necessarily separate or discrete; they can be combined. An effective piece of writing has a well-defined purpose.

**Revision** means "to see again." Revision involves the careful, active scrutiny of every aspect of a paper—subject, audience, thesis, paragraph structures, sentence constructions, and word choice. Revising is more complicated and more wide-ranging than proofreading; see **Proofreading.**

**Rhetorical questions.** See **Figures of speech.**

**Run-on sentences** are also called "fused" sentences and occur when two independent clauses *run-on* (sentences) are fused or run together because a mark of punctuation or a connecting word has *f sent* been omitted. The independent clauses in such a sentence (compound) must be separated.

> Your paper is due Friday it cannot be late (run-on sentence)
>
> Your paper is due Friday, and it cannot be late.
>
> Your paper is due Friday; it cannot be late.

**Satire** pokes fun at human behavior or institutions in an attempt to correct them. Judy Brady in "I Want a Wife" (Chapter 8) satirizes the stereotypical male demands of a wife, implying that marriage should be a more understanding partnership.

**Sentence variety** is achieved by mixing up structural sentence types (simple, compound, complex, *sent* compound–complex). No essay should contain only one sentence type. Exercises in sentence con- *vary* struction and variety can be found in the Focusing on Grammar and Writing activities with the essays by Greene (Chapter 1), Momaday (Chapter 3), Bodanis (Chapter 4), Daum (Chapter 5), Brady (Chapter 8), Tan (Chapter 8), and White (Chapter 10). An exercise on simple sentences can be found in the Focusing on Grammar and Writing activity with the essay by Zinsser (Chapter 5).

**Sentences** are traditionally defined in English as groups of words that express a complete thought, beginning with a capital letter and ending with a final mark of punctuation such as a period, question mark, or exclamation mark. Grammatically, a sentence must contain a subject and a predicate (verb). Sentences are not defined by length; anything that is punctuated as if it were a sentence but does not express a complete thought and does not have both a subject and predicate is called a **sentence fragment.** Sentences can also be called **independent clauses** or main clauses. Sentences are classified in a variety of ways, but the traditional classification by structure is most helpful to the writer.

• **Simple** sentences contain one independent clause, that is, one subject and one predicate. A simple sentence is a stripped-down sentence that contains no other clauses (either independent or dependent). Typically, simple sentences are short and easy to read and understand. They are not necessarily only a few words in length since they can contain modifying words such as adjectives and adverbs. The danger of using too many simple sentences is that it makes your paper sound like something written for grade-school students.

> Your paper is due on Friday. (complete thought, one subject, one predicate)
>
> Your research paper with photocopies of your sources is due on Friday. (complete thought, one subject, one predicate, modifying words and prepositional phrases)

- **Compound** sentences contain two independent clauses (sentences) linked by a coordinating word and a mark of punctuation (typically a comma or semicolon).

> Your paper is due on Friday, and it cannot be late.
>
> Your paper is due on Friday; it cannot be late.

- **Complex** sentences contain one independent clause and one or more dependent clauses (not sentences on their own).

> Although we also have a test that day, your paper is due on Friday. ("Although . . . day" is not a sentence; it is a dependent clause)
>
> Although we also have a test that day, your paper, which must be at least ten pages in length, is due on Friday. ("which . . . length" is another dependent clause)

- **Compound-complex** sentences contain two independent clauses and at least one dependent clause

> Although we also have a test that day, your paper is due on Friday, and it cannot be late. (dependent, independent, independent)

**Simile.** See **Figures of speech.**

*d*
*ww* **Slang** is common, casual, conversational language that is inappropriate in formal speaking or writing. Slang often serves to define social groups by virtue of being a private, shared language not understood by outsiders. Slang changes constantly and is therefore always dated. For that reason alone, it is wise to avoid using slang in serious writing.

*sp*
*ww* **Spelling** errors are common—every writer misspells words occasionally. Advice on being aware of your tendency to misspell and on coping with the problem can be found in How to Revise an Essay. Many misspelled words are simply typographical errors that can be caught by carefully proofreading your paper. Always allow time to do so; always use a dictionary if you are unsure of the spelling. Automatic spell-checkers on word-processing programs will eliminate many misspellings, but they will not signal when you have written the wrong word in the context. For example, be aware of the differences among these commonly misused words:

1. affect—verb, "to influence"
   effect—typically a noun meaning the "result"; as a verb, "to bring about"
2. than—signals comparison, as in "faster than"
   then—signals time sequence, as in "and then the race began"
3. its—the possessive form (think of *hers* and *his*, which do not have apostrophes)
   it's—the contraction for "it is"
4. there—a pronoun that "points out," as in "there are the books"
   their—a plural possessive pronoun signaling belonging to, as in "their apartment"
   they're—the contraction for "they are"

Frequently, words do not mean what we think that they do. Do not use a word in a paper unless you are confident of its meaning. If you are unsure, always check a dictionary first.

**Style** is the arrangement of words that a writer uses to express meaning. The study of an author's style would include an examination of diction or word choice, figures of speech, sentence constructions, and paragraph divisions.

**Subject** is what a piece of writing is about. See also **Thesis.** Linda Lee's thesis in "The Case Against College" (Chapter 9) is "not everyone needs a higher education."

**Subjective** writing expresses an author's feelings or opinions about a particular subject. Editorials or columns in newspapers and personal essays tend to rely on subjective judgments. Writing frequently blends the subjective and the objective; see **Objective.**

**Syllogism** is a three-step deductive argument involving a major premise, a minor premise, and a conclusion. For an illustration, see Chapter 9.

**Thesis** is a particular idea or assertion about a subject. Effective writing will always have an explicit or implicit statement of thesis; it is the central and controlling idea, the thread that holds the essay together. Frequently, a thesis is stated in a thesis or topic sentence. See **Subject.** A detailed explanation of a thesis and how to write one can be found in How to Write an Essay.

**Titles** are essential to every paper, and "Essay 1" or "Paper 1" or "Cause and Effect Essay" do not qualify as titles. No company would call its product "Automobile" or "Breakfast Cereal." A title creates reader interest; it indicates what will be found in the essay. Consider some of the strategies that writers use for their essays in this *Reader:*

1. Place or personal names (typically in narrative or descriptive essays): "Nameless, Tennessee," "The Way to Rainy Mountain"
2. The promise of practical or informational value: "What's in Your Toothpaste?" "The Origins of Anorexia Nervosa," "Can Wikipedia Ever Make the Grade?"
3. An indication of subject and approach (especially in argument essays): "In Defense of Talk Shows," "The Case Against College"
4. A play on words relevant to the subject of the essay: "Virtual Love" (about Internet dating) and "Mother Tongue" (about how the writer communicates with her mother in English)
5. A provocative word or phrase used in the essay: "Salvation," "The Village Watchman," "The Inheritance of Tools," " I Want a Wife"

Writers often use a **colon** in a title, separating a title from what is called a subtitle. A colon (:) is like an equals (=) sign. It signals that what is on one side is roughly equivalent to what is on the other. Typically, the title (to the left of the colon) is a catchy or a general phrase; the subtitle (to the right of the colon) is a more specific statement of what is to be found in the essay; for example, "The Value of Children: A Taxonomical Essay," "Revision and Life: 'Take It from the Top—Again'," "Into the Loop: How to Get the Job You Want after Graduation."

**Tone** refers to a writer's or speaker's attitude toward both subject and audience. Tone reflects human emotions and so can be characterized or described in a wide variety of ways, including serious, sincere, concerned, humorous, sympathetic, ironic, indignant, and sarcastic.

**Topic sentence** is a single sentence in a paragraph that contains a statement of subject or thesis. The topic sentence is to the paragraph what the thesis statement is to an essay—the thread that holds the whole together, a device to provide clarity and unity. Because paragraphs have various purposes, not every paragraph will have a topic sentence. The topic sentence is often the first or last sentence in the paragraph. Exercises in writing and recognizing topic sentences can be found in the Focusing on Grammar and Writing activities with the essays by Britt (Chapter 5), Brooks (Chapter 6), Chambers (Chapter 7), and Segerfeldt (Chapter 9).

**Transitions** are links or connections made between sentences, paragraphs, or groups of paragraphs. By using transitions, a writer achieves coherence and unity. Transitional devices include the following:

1. Repeated words, phrases, or clauses
2. Transitional sentences or paragraphs that act as bridges from one section or idea to the next
3. Transition-making words and phrases

Transitional words and phrases can express relationships of various types:

- Addition: again, next, furthermore, last
- Time: soon, after, then, later, meanwhile
- Comparison: but, still, nonetheless, on the other hand
- Example: for instance, for example
- Conclusion: in conclusion, finally, as a result
- Concession: granted, of course

An exercise in using transitions can be found in the Focusing on Grammar and Writing activity with the essay by Martin (Chapter 7).

**Typographical devices** are used to indicate subdivisions, sections, or steps within an essay and to call the reader's attention to a particular section or even word. As the word *typographical* implies, these are devices that have to do with typesetting (or word processing) and include such things as **bold face,** *italics,* underlining, subheadings, numbers, letters, and bullets (•, +) used to mark off sections of a text, as well as extra white space to separate blocks of paragraphs or sentences. Newspapers, magazines, Web pages, and business documents all make extensive use of typographical devices. An exercise in using typographical devices can be found in the Focusing on Grammar and Writing activity with the essay by Berelson (Chapter 4).

**Understatement.** See **Figures of speech.**

**Unity** is a oneness in which all of the individual parts of a piece of writing work together to form a cohesive and complete whole. It is best achieved by having a clearly stated purpose and thesis against which every sentence and paragraph can be tested for relevance.

*ww* **Wrong word** is simply a word that is not used appropriately. Typically, the writer has chosen a word that does not mean what the writer thinks it does. Sometimes it is used to refer to a word that is too formal or too learned for the context and audience. Other inappropriate words include **clichés, slang,** and **colloquial expressions.** Exercises in word choice can be found in the Focusing on Grammar and Writing activities with the essays by Quindlen (Chapter 1), Ehrenreich (Chapter 4), and Brumberg (Chapter 7).

# CREDITS

# INDEX